THE CLUBMAKER'S ART

ANTIQUE GOLF CLUBS AND THEIR HISTORY

by Jeffery B. Ellis

ZEPHYR PRODUCTIONS, INC.

The Clubmaker's Art: Antique Golf Clubs and their History © Copyright 1997
by Zephyr Productions Inc.

Designed and produced by: Opus Productions Inc., 300 West Hastings Street,
Vancouver, British Columbia, Canada V6B 1K6

Front & Back Cover Photo: Derik Murray

This book may be ordered from the publisher.
Published by:
Zephyr Productions Inc.
P.O. Box 1964
Oak Harbor, Washington 98277
Phone (toll free): 1-888-394-9333

Library of Congress Card Catalog Number: 96-90369

ISBN 0-9653039-0-X (Hardcover Edition)
ISBN 0-9653039-1-8 (Limited Edition)

96-90369
CIP

10 9 8 7 6 5 4 3 2 1

Printed and bound in Hong Kong.

Troon Clubs, page 29

*T*here is nothing so fascinating to a golfer as his clubs. The golf ball is doubtless as indispensable to his enjoyment, but its life is too brief for it to obtain any hold on the golfer's affection. A ball that has been once or twice round the links without losing its paint and pristine rotundity is sometimes complacently exhibited, but this, be it said, is done more in token of the player's marvellous skill than as evidence of the ball's lasting qualities. . . .

But with the golfer's clubs it is very different. Every one in his bag is a cherished friend, whose worth has been proved in many a tight place. The non-golfer 'findeth all clubs much the same,' but any golfer would be able to pick out his own clubs from a hundred others without any difficulty. He knows them, as a shepherd his sheep, by "heid mark." Their shape, their colour, their grips, even their dents and bruises, are engraved on his brain by the burin of sweet and poignant memories. A man's clubs become almost members of his body, and certainly, if their capacity for conveying pleasure and pain to his senses is to measure the matter, the comparison is not overstrained.

/// ——————————— ///

(Garden G. Smith, *Golf Illustrated*, 31 July 1908: 111)

ACKNOWLEDGMENTS

Thank you to the many wonderful people who helped me with this work, and a special thank you to a few specific individuals in particular:

SAUNDRA SHEFFER Editor extraordinaire: Getting you to line edit my final manuscript was the luckiest thing to happen to me in years. You are not only talented, you are a saint! Dear reader, for every glitch that remains, a hundred have been removed.

SAUNDRA SHEFFER & MARGE DEWEY Curators of the Ralph Miller Golf Library in Industry Hills, California: Thank you for your tireless and always enthusiastic help. I'll be glad to look through the old boxes in your library anytime.

KAREN BEDNARSKI USGA museum curator 1989–1996; Director, World Golf Hall of Fame, Ponte Vedra Beach, Florida: Thank you for making the resources of the USGA museum, staff, and library available for my work. Your professionalism is impeccable and your integrity second to none. And thank you for your input, advice, suggestions, and perspective. Best.

DICK STRANAHAN Curator of the World Golf Hall of Fame in Pinehurst, South Carolina, before it closed: Thank you for going above and beyond the call of duty in my behalf. I will always be grateful for the extra day you allowed me to spend in the Probst library.

DOROTHY BROWN British Columbia Golf House and Museum curator: Thank you for the history of Scotland. Now get on the phone; I'm sitting here waiting for your call.

PATTY MORAN U.S.G.A. staff: Thank you, thank you. I hope you didn't break a copy machine or your back in my behalf. I'm surprised you could read my writing.

BOB KUNTZ Collector, club restorer, historian, and gentleman: Thank you for sharing your files with me and thank you for your kind example and the grace you've bestowed upon the golf collecting world.

KAREN KUHL Golf Collectors Society know-it-all: Thank you for your help with all the loose ends, wandering pages, and the copy machine.

JIM LEAPTROTT One "knowledgeable good collector": Everything I know I learned from Jim.

RHOD MCEWAN Scottish table tennis master: I demand a rematch!

WES HARRIS Phantom of the bus: Thanks for the edits on wheels.

VINCE HAGEL Author and teacher: Your patience, willing suggestions, and input were invaluable to me. Thank you for helping me feel free to ask. If only I knew writing like you know writing.

HERB MATTER The most generous man ever to attend a golf collectors meeting, God love him: Thank you for being so good to me. How can one person know so much about the Foulis family?

ALAN F. JACKSON Historian: I am indebted to you for sharing your research that was ultimately published as *The British Professional Golfers 1887–1930, A Registry*. Your meticulous accuracy and thorough research are surpassed only by your incredible generosity. Thank you. (Alan Jackson's research, the most complete and accurate of its type, not only lists the professionals and the years they worked at a particular location, it also provides a cross reference list of courses in the U.K. and the professionals who served them. Mr. Jackson made his research available to me in 1990 and provided me with updates as it continued.)

ROBERT SMITH One of a kind: Thank you for your help. You are missed.

VIVIAN MACMILLAN Literary type: Your review of my work proved most helpful.

CHRIS SAXMAN Architect: Thank you for helping me with more than this book. Oh yes, my rent is much too high and I want to use your fax machine.

STEVEN VAN DULKEN The British Library's Patent Documentation Officer: Thank you for your willingness to fill in a few gaps from 7,000 miles away.

ANGELA HOUSTON Research historian: Thank you for doing the dirty work. It took me less than a day at Kew to recognize that you are a trooper of the highest order!

LANCE ENHOLM Basketball junkie: Thanks for your understanding, friendship, and cooperation in helping make some of these pages a reality. Now, keep driving the lane.

PETER CRABTREE Former President of the British Golf Collectors Society 1994–1995: Your friendly discussions and genuine unbiased nature have served me well during my writing; your example serves your fellow collectors.

TOM ENNIS Music Mogul: Your encouragement and support remain deeply appreciated.

MICHAEL JAY Photographer: Thanks for your "how to" instruction and your gentlemanly kindness.

DERIK MURRAY, DAVID COUNSELL, DON BULL, JOSEPH LLAMZON, GUYLAINE RONDEAU, & SUZANNE BRYCE Opus Productions: Working with you was the best decision I've made in a long time.

SUSAN AND LEAH Wife and stepdaughter: I'm the lucky one!

LES, PENNY, STEPHEN, JOAN & MOM Family: Thank you for your unfailing belief. Words of gratitude pale in the light of your love. This book would still be a dream without your support. I'm forever in your debt.

DAD Thanks for taking me golfing.

FOREWORD

As curator of the USGA museum and library, I received dozens of inquiries each week about golf clubs. How old is this club? Who made it? What is its purpose? Is it valuable? Often the caller had a club that is common and the answers were easy. But more and more, as the hobby of collecting golf memorabilia has grown and collectors have become increasingly sophisticated, there are no ready answers to their questions. We spent hours, days, and sometimes weeks attempting to trace the origin or history of a particular club. Occasionally, we were fortunate and able to unravel the mystery. Other times our search was fruitless.

The publication of *The Clubmaker's Art: Antique Golf Clubs and their History* will be an enormously useful resource for everyone interested in the memorabilia of golf. Jeff Ellis has devoted years to meticulously researching those golf clubs that have shaped the game. His investigation, which encompasses not only the printed word but also the actual clubs found in both public and private collections throughout the world, was conducted with the diligence and passion that only a collector of these very same objects could possess.

The result is a remarkable compilation of historical information and valuable commentary about antique clubs and their collectibility. In the world of golf, no other volume which deals with the equipment of the game is comparable in scope, depth or scholarship to *The Clubmaker's Art*. Not only is *The Clubmaker's Art* the most complete and well-documented book of its genre, it will endure for years as such.

Already widely known and respected for his knowledge of antique golf clubs, Jeff Ellis has made an immense contribution to all of us in the collecting world—and to the literature of the game.

KAREN BEDNARSKI
Director, World Golf Hall of Fame
(Curator, USGA Museum 1989–1996)

PREFACE

In this book you will discover a wide spectrum of golf clubs made over four centuries, from the 1600s to the 1900s. Rather than presenting commonplace clubs—those that possess little or nothing to set them apart from the huge number of clubs that look just like them—this book concentrates on the antique clubs used during the formative years of the game and those that later shaped the game and its rules. You will also learn about the people who designed these clubs and the businesses that produced them.

Examining the vast array of shapes and styles developed, mechanisms designed, and materials employed in constructing an antique golf club, one recognizes the collective genius of the early clubmakers. These men were genuine artisans who created with their hands and gave continuous thought to their work. Their painstaking efforts, tedious labors, inventive minds, and meticulous standards are reflected in the beauty of their creations; and their art, the clubs they crafted, has generated a fascinating area of study.

The collecting of antique golf clubs is still in its infancy, but interest is growing rapidly. Yet, even in this burgeoning market, little is known about the clubs themselves. The most desirable antique clubs are rarely seen, and little specific information about them has been published during their rise to collectibility. In days past, anyone who wanted to learn about the many individual clubs that are now highly collectible had to glean whatever bits of information he or she could in discussions with other collectors or in the few books that touch on the subject. This book will change all that.

What I have put together in this book is neither perfect nor the final word. Certainly further discoveries and information will come to light. However, I have attempted to present the history and personality of every club as accurately as possible, with great respect given to documented sources and little or none given to questionable, undocumented, or unidentifiable sources. I hope that you will enjoy seeing and reading about these clubs as much as I enjoyed researching and writing about them.

J. B. E.

USEFUL INFORMATION
FOR THE READER

AUTHOR'S REFERENCES TO KNOWN EXAMPLES OF SPECIFIC CLUBS

Throughout this book, I have referred to my own experience and knowledge in order to arrive at the relative rarity of various clubs. I have personally inspected many collections, public and private, in both the United States and Great Britain. I have had countless conversations with other collectors about the rarity of various clubs. My sole occupation since 1979 has been as a dealer of collectible and antique golf clubs. I've attended virtually every major golf auction held in the United States, England, and Scotland since 1985. However, I readily acknowledge that I do not know the whereabouts of every antique golf club ever made. More rare clubs will be located, adding to the totals for individual clubs provided herein. I have personally viewed and photographed all of the clubs pictured in this book with the exception of the Troon clubs. I have viewed them on numerous occasions, but the photos used were taken by Martin McCready, with the permission of Mr. James Montgomery, secretary of the Royal Troon Golf Club, and the gracious aid of Bob Pringle and Peter Lewis.

CLUB MARKS

When documenting any writing found on a golf club, I often used slashes ("\") in order to separate one line from the next as found on the club—example: "Spalding \ Rob't T. Jones Jr. \ Kro Flite."

CLUB MEASUREMENTS

In the section on long nose clubs, I've provided the measurements of each clubhead. The face depth is measured at the deepest point of the face. The width of the head is the distance between the leading edge and the very back of the head (not the distance across the sole, which is less). The length of the head is the straight line distance between the tip of the nose and the back of the neck. This measurement is easily ascertained by placing a straightedge ruler across the face. Make sure the ruler runs parallel with the sole; tilting the ruler in any other direction can greatly increase or decrease this measurement.

BRITISH MONETARY SYSTEM

In documenting various golf clubs, this book occasionally includes the original price of the club. Prior to 1971, the British "pound sterling" was equal to 20 shillings or 240 pence (12 pence to the shilling). Prices are usually cited as originally advertised—"12s. 5d." is 12 shillings and 5 pence, as is "12/5." (In "12s. 5d.," "d." is the abreviation for "denari," a latin term).

REFERENCES CITED

I have used the "author-date system," according to the rules of the Modern Language Association, to provide the parenthetical documentation in this book. For book citations, the author-date system requires that a parenthetical reference include the author's last name; the year of publication, followed by a comma; and the page reference—example: (Park 1896, 11). Any information cited in the text is omitted from the parenthetical reference. By looking up the author and the year of publication in the "List of References Cited" on pages 566–568, the reader can find the particulars of the document cited. For periodical citations, the author-date system requires that a parenthetical reference provide the name of the periodical, followed by a comma; the date of the periodical, followed by a colon; and the page number—example: (*Golf Illustrated*, 1 Jan. 1900: 25).

*N*early every one carries a play club, an instrument consisting of many parts. It has no legs, but a shaft instead. It has, however, a toe. Its toe is at the end of its face. Although it has no body, it has a sole. It has a neck, a head, and clubs also have horns. They always have a whipping, but this has nothing to do directly with striking the ball. There is little expression in the face of a club. It is usually wooden; sometime, however, it has a leather face. Clubs, without being clothed, occasionally have lead buttons, but never any button-holes. Clubs' heads are some black, some yellow, but colour is not due to any racial difference. From this description it will be easy to understand, without a diagram, what a club is like.

/// ——————————— *///*

(Sir Walter Simpson; Simpson 1887, 21-22)

TABLE OF CONTENTS

TABLE OF CONTENTS

TABLE OF CONTENTS

TABLE OF CONTENTS

TABLE OF CONTENTS

MECHANICAL CLUBS
359

TABLE OF CONTENTS

TABLE OF CONTENTS

TABLE OF CONTENTS

Choosing a club, like taking a wife, is a terribly risky proceeding for most golfers. Some know what they want, but can't find it; others, in desperation, make a blind choice in the hope that they may draw a prize.

(*Golf Illustrated*, 21 July 1911: 90)

Overview

COLLECTING

This book deals with "antique" golf clubs—those clubs made during the wood shaft era, which ended a few years after steel shafts were legalized by the United States Golf Association in 1925 and by the Royal and Ancient Golf Club of St. Andrews in 1929. When John Fischer captured the 1936 U.S. Amateur, the last major golf championship won by a player using wood shaft clubs, the general manufacturing and marketing of wood shaft clubs had already come to a close.

Before considering the primary areas of antique club collecting, it is necessary to understand how many antique clubs were made, when they were made, and how many have survived. Answering these questions requires estimating the number of golfers existing at various times.

In the early 1800s there were far fewer golfers than there were at the end of the 1800s:

Prior to 1837 there were only fifteen golf clubs [societies] in existence in this country . . . ; to-day there are over 1193 clubs in the United Kingdom (The Golfer, 30 June 1897: 510).

If each of the fifteen golf clubs that existed in 1837 had an average membership of seventy-five golfers (a generous estimate), there were approximately 1,100 golfers in the world at that time. If each player used six or seven clubs, approximately 6,600 to 7,700 clubs were in use in 1837. This is an incredibly small amount when compared to the number of clubs in use only sixty years later.

In 1897, based on an estimated average of 200 members per club (a reasonable estimate), the 1,193 clubs in the United Kingdom had an aggregate membership of approximately 235,000 golfers. If each golfer used six or seven clubs, then 1.4 million to 1.6 million clubs were in use in the U.K. three years before the turn of the twentieth century!

The number of American golfers was reported by *Golf*, a British publication, as follows:

In 1895 there were 76 established Golf Clubs in the United States, having a membership of about 15,000. To-day there are over 750 flourishing Clubs and over 200,000 players (9 Jan. 1899: 340).

Therefore, if 15,000 players had six or seven clubs each, approximately 90,000 to 105,000 clubs were in use in the United States during 1895. By 1899 the number of golfers had jumped dramatically, and the number of clubs in use soared to between 1.2 million and 1.4 million!

In 1915 Jerome Travers (four time U.S. Amateur Champion and the 1915 U.S. Open Champion) reported the number of U.S. golfers as follows:

There are 1,300 golf clubs now in the United States. . . . These 1,300 clubs have a playing, or rather an active playing, list of 350,000 members. There is no way of telling just how many dabble at golf occasionally, but there are certainly several hundred thousand more. Some expert statisticians have figured that at least a million people are playing golf now in the United States; but this seems to be a trifle high. As an estimate 350,000 active players isn't far wrong, for each club will average 250. Many clubs run up to 800 to 1,000 members, and few fall below 200, so 250 to the club is certainly a low estimate (Travers 1915, 16-19).

Further on in his article, Travers, acknowledging that many golfers carry ten to fifteen clubs, recommends using only nine clubs. Accordingly, if 350,000 golfers used nine clubs each, over *three million* wood shaft clubs were in use in the United States in 1915. This figure does not take into consideration his estimate of the "several hundred thousand more" who "dabble at golf occasionally." If the estimate of one million U.S. golfers given in Travers's article is used, then approximately *nine million* wood shaft golf clubs were in use in 1915. Either way, by 1915, somewhere between three million and nine million wood shaft clubs were in use in the U.S. This number does not reflect the millions of clubs purchased in the U.S. between 1915 and the end of the wood shaft era nor the millions more purchased over the years in the United Kingdom. Not to be forgotten are large numbers of golfers located throughout the world. In 1911 the number of golfers belonging to golf clubs *worldwide* was estimated at 840,000 (Golfing, 11 May 1911: 12).

These estimated figures reflect the staggering number—literally millions and millions—of wood shaft clubs produced before the end of the wood shaft era. In support of these numbers, a few isolated reports document the large volume of golf clubs and club components handled by a few makers.

In 1894 Messrs. H.J. Gray & Sons, golf club and ball makers, had a substantial inventory of raw heads:

We are informed that they have about 60,000 thoroughly seasoned blocks of beech and apple for club heads (Golf, 6 Apr.: 54).

The May 13, 1898 issue of *Golf*, announces:

The Forth Rubber Company has just made a "record" in the way of "large orders," having just placed in the hands of George Nicoll, Leven, the well-known maker, a commission to supply 10,000 cleek, iron, and mashie heads, and the "gigantic deal" has been accepted by the Leven man . . . (165).

In 1900, discussing the number of machine-made clubheads shipped into the U.K., *Golf* (ny) reported:

The C. McG. & C. Co. [Crawford, McGregor & Canby] alone ship 100,000 machine-made golf heads to Great Britain every year (Jan. 1900: 25).

In the January 11, 1907 issue of *Golf Illustrated*, A.G. Spalding & Bros. advertised having a "Quarter of a Million Golf Shafts" and only accepted orders between 1,000 and 10,000 pieces (57).

Of all these numbers, the most staggering is found in the June 6, 1902 issue of *Golf Illustrated* which reports a supplier to the golf trade was holding almost two and a half *million* shafts:

One of the largest wholesale manufacturers of golf club shafts and heads are Messrs. Remer and Company, Limited, Timber Manufacturers, Liverpool. The extent of their business may be gathered from the fact that they have 200,000 dozen seasoned shafts in stock, while they also do a large trade in turning heads of persimmon, dogwood, and beech (88). [This information is corroborated in a brief report about Remer and Co. titled "2,400,000 Handles in Stock" found in Golfing (4 Sep. 1902: 30).]

Although the golf clubs made during the wood shaft era numbered well into the millions, they had a low survival rate. Like pre-1930 automobiles, toys, and duck decoys, only a small percentage of the clubs made before 1930 remain. Fragile by nature, a large number broke while in use. If they didn't break, they became outdated. Consequently, over the years, large numbers of wood shaft clubs were discarded or used as firewood, tomato stakes, children's toys, etc. Wood shaft golf clubs did not attract significant numbers of collectors or receive a meaningful level of public preservation until the early 1980s.

Most of the old wood shaft clubs ever made have been lost forever, but surviving examples still number in the millions. The remaining clubs, however, are primarily those made between 1900 and 1930, when the vast majority of all wood shaft clubs were produced.

With this elementary understanding of hickory shaft clubs and their general numbers (both the number made and surviving) established, the three basic areas of collecting—the old, the unusual, and the cleekmarks—are presented next.

The Old Clubs. Clubs made prior to 1890, when there were comparatively few golfers, are collectible for their age alone.

Prior to 1890 the number of golfers grew slowly. Before 1837 there were approximately fifteen organized golf clubs in the United Kingdom. This number grew to twenty-four golf clubs in 1851, but there were still only sixty golf clubs in the U.K. in 1870. By 1885, however, there were 161 golf clubs, and over the next five years the game of golf started to show signs of rapid expansion. Following 1889 golf began a period of phenomenal growth. The number of golf clubs in the United Kingdom grew from 290 in 1889 to 479 by 1891; 1,357 by 1900; and 2,729 by 1910 (Lewis 1994, 12-13).

The numbers are similar for the growth of golf in America. The oldest permanently established golf club in North America is Royal Montreal, founded November 4, 1873. The oldest permanent golf club in the United States is the St. Andrews Golf Club at Yonkers-on-Hudson, New York, established November 14, 1888. By 1895 America had seventy-six golf clubs with a membership of approximately 15,000. By January 1, 1899, there were over 750 flourishing clubs and over 200,000 players (*Golf*, 9 Jan. 1899: 340).

Clearly, the game of golf blossomed between 1890 and 1900. This growth was nothing short of spectacular and continued into the twentieth century. Consequently, the *typical* clubs made during that time are not rare. Not only are there plenty of remaining examples, the typical clubs all look basically the same. Furthermore, they do not look much different, in terms of style and shape, from the traditional clubs produced during the steel shaft era.

The earlier a typical golf club dates prior to 1890, the more collector interest it will generate. The clubs made before 1850, termed feather ball clubs, are eminently collectible. By 1850, the feather ball was well on its way to obsolescence due to the introduction of the gutta percha ball in 1846-1848. Woods, irons, and putters were all developed prior to 1850, though in rudimentary form. These historic relics represent the foundation from which the modern golf club evolved.

Clubs collected solely because of their antiquity are loosely termed *early clubs*.

The Unusual Clubs. Along with early clubs, distinctly unusual clubs are keenly sought after by collectors. By definition, unusual clubs occupied only a small portion of the golf club market. However, the collectibility of an unusual club is based more on design than rarity. The more a club departs from the traditional club of its time, the better.

In one sense, pre-1885 clubs are unusual. The woods made then, termed "long nose" woods, look radically different from modern woods. The standard irons made before 1885 are also distinct to a degree, but those made before 1850 are extraordinary.

The category of unusual clubs, however, consists primarily of the clearly peculiar and uniquely creative clubs made after 1885. Hoping either to aid golfers in their dedicated struggle to get the ball in the hole or to help the clubs withstand the effort, clubmakers developed a variety of implements that incorporated a fascinating array of designs and ideas.

Aiding the golfer, however, was not the clubmaker's only motivation for coming up with an unusual design. The other goal was market share. If a clubmaker or inventor designed a unique club that became widely accepted as the "better way," his or her idea could prove profitable. Consequently, unusual club designs were often patented.

A few of the early innovations in club design have proved their worth, remaining in use today. However, most of the visionary ideas and designs failed the test of time. Some "creative clubs" even gave rise to new rules which declared them illegal. The innovative clubs that endured, and those that did not, both played a part in shaping the golf club and the game as we know it today. In fact, not only are the so-called "unique, special, and innovative" features of today's clubs found in antique clubs, the world of antique clubs includes even more extreme designs.

Identifying an unusual club is easy. Forget about the *cosmetics* of the club—the writing on the back of the head and any dots, dashes, or lines on the face—and look at its *structure*. Ask yourself the following questions: Is the club different from the standard golf club of its age? Is the club visually interesting? Is there anything peculiar about the material used to construct the club? How original is the club's design?

Does it appear to have a specific out-of-the-ordinary purpose? The answers to these questions will indicate how unusual the item is.

Unusual clubs, patented or not, are commonly referred to as *patent clubs*.

The Cleekmarks. Prior to the 1890s, a mark on a golf club, if there was one, identified the club's maker or its owner. After 1890 it became common practice for golf professionals to purchase—either finished or raw—clubheads, shafts, and grips and then assemble or otherwise prepare them for sale. Irons were then marked with information relating to the maker, the seller (a professional or a retail establishment), or both. These identifying marks are "cleekmarks."

A trademark stamped on a club, registered or not, is also referred to as a cleekmark. A trademark might include the maker's name or a design such as a horse, heart, flower, knight, rope, arrow, snake, lion, gun, crown, etc. Robert Condie, for example, stamped a small rose on the back of his clubheads. Before a Condie iron sold at the retail level, it was often marked with the name and location of the seller.

Because these marks include such a variety of designs and reflect a vast array of locations and people, some cleekmarks are more interesting than others. Cleekmarks, on their own, constitute the least competitive collecting category for two reasons: (1) Cleekmarks were used during a period when the number of golf clubs in circulation numbered in the *millions*—and most of them had cleekmarks; (2) The bulk of these clubs are the standard woods, irons, and putters of their day. Between 1890 and 1925 the *standard* iron and wood head evolved very little. Stand them side by side and they appear to be quite similar.

The general availability of cleekmarks is a positive aspect of their collectibility. Because most antique clubs have cleekmarks, a person who collects cleekmarks can enjoy the hobby at reduced expense. Cleekmarks also provide a direct tie to the history of golf and the makers from long ago.

This book deals primarily with the early clubs that formed the game of golf and the distinct and unusual patent clubs that shaped the game and its rules.

VALUES

In days past, due to a lack of available information on specific antique clubs (especially the rare clubs), many collectors relied on price guides as an indicator of a club's historical importance and collectibility. In practice, this method produces inaccuracies. Not only was the history of most clubs unexplored, many highly collectible clubs were unknown at the time the guides were published.

Price guides are fine for collecting coins and baseball cards, but, except in a most superficial way, they do not work for collecting golf clubs. Existing sports cards and coins number in the billions, are well-documented, trade daily at card and coin shops all across America, and are universally categorized by condition. Existing antique golf clubs, on the other hand, do not number in the billions, are not well-documented, are difficult to locate and view for purchase, and are not universally categorized by condition.

The quantity of fine collectibles within the antique club collecting world does not begin to approach that in the sports card or numismatic worlds. Although common wood shaft clubs are consistently available and sell on the open market, thereby demonstrating a general market value, many unusual and unique clubs rarely, if ever, become available. Consequently, a large number of scarce and eminently collectible clubs have little or no track record. In fact, a high percentage of the clubs presented in this book are not listed in any price guides.

Besides giving only the most basic differences between the prices of common and good collectibles, price guides are frequently inaccurate. They often reflect only one sale when there were others to consider. They may be incomplete, lacking a clear report on wear, damage, finish, and replaced parts for both clubhead and shaft. They may even be fabricated, occasionally specifying values for clubs that have never sold or that the author of the price guide has never seen sell. Price guides may be outdated, many assigned values taken from sales made years ago. Occasionally, a collector will decide not to buy a club because it was offered at more than was listed in a guide. Later he learns he made a mistake when he does not get another chance to acquire such a club.

In order to be a successful collector, it is far more important to answer fundamental questions about a club—who made it, why was it made, when was it made, what is its place in history, what compares to it, and how rare is it—than to locate it in a price guide.

The answers to these questions combine to determine the value of a club because no single factor, with the possible exception of condition, determines the collectibility of a club. (If a club is completely ruined and unidentifiable, no other questions need be asked, even if it is an extremely rare, early, or unusual club.) Because various collectors will arrive at different answers to these questions, the more educated a collector is, the better his or her evaluation will be.

This book will address the question of value but only by educating collectors and helping them to make their own determinations. If a collector desires actual prices on which to base his or her judgments, he or she must spend some time studying the antique club market. This is easily done in a number of different ways such as consulting past and current catalogs from auction houses or dealers; joining and attending local and national Golf Collectors Society gatherings; and by talking to other collectors or dealers.

The value of a good collectible is based on the *buyer's perspective*, not a published price guide. A club that might be worth a particular amount to one person will often be worth a different amount to someone else. Consider the following experience.

In July of 1989, the author attended the Sotheby's golf auction held in Glasgow, Scotland. A brass Buchan patent adjustable iron in fine working condition, the first of its type ever offered at auction, was put up for sale as lot 416. It was estimated at $500 to $750, and the audience believed the estimate. The club sold for $500.

One year later, another Buchan adjustable iron in similar condition was offered for sale as lot 145 at the Phillips golf auction held in Edinburgh, Scotland. This time, despite its $350 to $750 estimate, the Buchan iron sold for *$9000*. While the $9000 price astounded the collecting community, which labeled it as extreme, the day of the $500 hickory shaft adjustable iron of *any* kind passed in the echo of an auctioneer's gavel. Why? Because perspectives had changed.

As perspectives in the market change, prices change. Furthermore, perspectives usually differ from one person to the next. However, it is important to understand when a club will *never* be worth the current asking price. Consider the following examples.

Spending $10,000 for a Tom Morris long nose club made in the 1920s, complete with a Tom Morris decal on the shaft, is a horrendous mistake which can never be rectified. Some 1850s-1860s examples could justify that price, but Morris long nose clubs made after 1900 were produced as *replicas*, to sell as nostalgia or tourist items. Such clubs were neither made by Morris nor do they display his craftsmanship. Old replicas aren't worth much more than new ones.

Spending $6,000 for an over-restored Tom Morris long nose wood with major cracks in the head, the name nearly obliterated, shoe polish added to the finish, and the face filed and reworked is a serious mistake. The buyer of this club will not be able to sell it to a knowledgeable collector for anywhere near the same price. Heavily damaged and reworked clubs are worth only a small fraction of the price for nice original examples.

Spending $2,000 for a Walter Hagen "Concave" sand wedge will find the buyer waiting *many* years before the consistent sale price for this item might reach that level. Hagen Concaves are quite common and not very old, relatively speaking, and currently (1997) sell in the $500 range, if nice.

Occasionally, in order to acquire a prime piece, one has to know when to pay a top price and, on rare occasion, when to overpay. Obviously overpaying should not become a habit, but the astute collector will recognize when an item is so rare and so historically valuable that paying "double" is still a good buy (to say nothing of the value of the opportunity). It takes a great deal of education and experience, not to mention a *broad* perspective, to make this judgement.

The top collections in the world, in any category, were built with more interest in the pieces acquired than in getting a good deal. Sometimes a collector makes an excellent deal and gets more than his money's worth. Other times, collectors will stretch to their financial limits in order to take advantage of what may be their only chance ever to own a particular item, an item they obviously hold in extremely high esteem.

Knowing when to go the extra mile for a golf club requires much knowledge about clubs. Accurate determinations (perceptions) of a club's importance and availability come no other way.

GOLF CLUB DATING

Determining the age of a club is important to the collector. In many instances, a club can be dated within a year or two. In some cases, it can only be assigned to a general period of time. In the toughest instances, coming within fifty years of the actual making of the club is as close as can be reasonably expected.

There are three primary reference sources which accurately document the age of a golf club: (1) clubmaker and manufacturer catalogs; (2) books, magazines, or newspapers that published reviews, descriptions, or advertisements of specific clubs; (3) U.S. and British trademarks, registered designs, and patent records. However, a large array of collectible clubs were never offered in a catalog, advertised in a magazine, nor granted legal protection.

A fourth method used to date clubs, at least in general terms, is to research biographical information about the maker, learning who he was, when he was born, when he died, and when he worked at a particular location. For example, a long nose club marked "J. Allan" was made by James Allen, the first professional at Westward Ho! Because he was born in 1848 and died in 1897, his long nose clubs date after 1866, when he started working at Westward Ho!, and before 1890, the end of the long nose era. However, early long nose woods were not often marked with the maker's name. Irons made prior to 1800 were never so marked; prior to 1850, very few were marked.

Like unmarked clubs, clubs marked with the name of a maker who made clubs across many decades (McEwan, Morris, Park, etc.) are difficult to date. Knowing whether a club produced by an enduring clubmaker is an earlier or later example of their work is essential to understanding the club's historical importance. A clubmaker's early work was different from his latter work; not only did the clubmaker's talents evolve, so did golf clubs in general.

Unmarked and otherwise ambiguous clubs can be dated by comparison. A club's shape, style, size, and other construction characteristics reflect the time period when it was created. To make accurate comparisons, however, the appraiser needs to understand the four previous methods *and* must have extensive experience handling clubs similar to the one he or she is trying to date.

Two additional sources are occasionally used to date the oldest clubs in a general way. First, a few old prints and paintings depict clubs. The dates of these pictures help date the clubs they portray. Second, a few of the well-established golfing societies in the U.K., such as the Royal and Ancient Golf Club of St. Andrews, Royal Blackheath, The Honourable Company of Edinburgh Golfers, the Glasgow Golf Club, etc., own sterling silver presentation clubs, some of which date from the 1700s. Although they were not made by clubmakers, sterling silver clubs were modeled after actual clubs. The question that remains about the early silver clubs is whether they were modeled after an old favorite, or after what was being made at the time. After all, these silver clubs were made to reflect the game of golf and its novel traditions, not to play golf with.

Currently, few people understand how to date unmarked golf clubs accurately. Consequently, many clubs end up being represented as older than they actually are. It seems to be human nature for people to think that the wood shaft golf club they own must be at least 100 years old, maybe 150 years old! Ninety-nine percent of the time it is not.

GOLF CLUB DATING TRAITS: In order to determine the approximate age of either an unmarked club or a club made by an enduring clubmaker, the interested individual must examine *all* of a club's characteristics. No single characteristic offers conclusive proof of anything. Furthermore, the individual must know the clubmaking characteristics found in clubs from different eras.

To this end, the basic elements of club construction as they relate to dating a club are presented next. Because irons have different construction characteristics from woods, they will be examined separately. Putters fall into either category, wood or iron, depending on the material of the putter head.

These golf club dating guidelines are discussed in greater detail as specific clubs are described and pictured throughout this book.

Traits To Examine On An Iron Head Club:

Writing on the club	Blade crease	Club weight
Face scoring	Hosel thickness	Shaft material
Head material	Hosel length	Shaft construction
Blade size	Hosel nicking	Shaft length
Blade shape	Head texture	Grip material

Writing on the club. Is there any writing on the head or the shaft?

This is usually the first factor considered. If an iron has a cleekmark (any type of identifying mark provided by the maker or seller of the iron), it was most likely made after 1890. Only a small percentage of pre-1890 irons exist, and few of them are marked. Given a cleekmark, the club can be further defined by noting when the maker was in business, at a particular location, or using a particular mark. Not all of the many different cleekmarks in existence can be traced to their makers, but the very nature of the mark still helps date a club.

As a rule, the more writing on a club, the more modern it is. "Warranted Hand Forged" and "Made in Scotland" indicate the club was made after the mid-1890s, when advertising became important.

The less writing on a club, the earlier it *might* date. The earliest irons almost never have writing on them. They were usually made by blacksmiths who did not care about advertising or identifying their work. Still, there are a number of later irons from the 1890s and early 1900s with no writing on them. These clubs lack any other early characteristics and are usually of little interest.

Often a patent club is marked with its patent date. Unless a club was kept in production for many years, which was unusual, a patent date is an excellent indicator of the club's approximate age.

There may also be a name stamped on the shaft, a practice which originated during the mid to late 1880s. However, shafts were occasionally replaced and marked by the clubmaker who did the work. For example, in addition to making clubs, R. Forgan & Son did a significant amount of business repairing clubs.

Face scoring. Are there any scoring lines or other types of scoring marks on the face?

Because all early irons have smooth, unscored faces, some people think a smooth face identifies a pre-1910 iron. This is not always true. Clubmakers offered smooth face irons, as one option among many, for years after 1910. Consequently, a smooth face by itself does not date an iron. However, if an iron has *original* scoring marks of some kind, the chances are extremely high that it was made after 1895.

Head material. What metal is used to construct the head?

Iron was the primary metal used throughout the entire wood shaft era, but brass and gunmetal were also used to make both putters and lofted irons. Pre-1910 lofted irons made from either brass or gunmetal, however, are few and far between. Non-rusting metal was used in the 1890s and thereafter.

Blade size. Is the blade larger than normal, larger than the iron blades made today? Is the blade small, or about the size of a silver dollar? How thin is the blade?

The earliest irons often have a head much larger and thicker than the traditional twentieth century iron. In 1906 the "giant niblick," which has the largest blade of any iron, was first produced. Because the head was so broad, the blade was extremely thin to keep the overall weight manageable.

If the head is extremely small, the blade being *only slightly larger* than a silver dollar, the club is probably a "track iron." Track irons, also termed "rut irons," were used from the early 1800s until the 1880s. If the blade is very small but *notably larger* than a silver dollar, the club is probably a rut niblick dating from the late 1880s or later.

Blade shape. Is the iron blade concave? Is it hooked? Does it have a square toe? Does it look unusual in shape or construction?

Irons from approximately 1850 and earlier usually have a distinctly concave face. Some have a curve or "hook" to the blade. A few concave face irons were made following the turn of the twentieth century, but they are usually much lighter and smaller than an early iron. A toe that appears to be "square" or chopped off is a characteristic of many irons made prior to the end of the 18th Century.

If the blade has an unusual shape or style, it is termed a "patent club." In almost all cases, such clubs date after 1889 when the first patent on an iron club was granted.

Blade crease. This term refers to the area where the topline of the blade intersects the side of the hosel. Does the angle between the top of the blade and the hosel form a sharp crease, appearing as a sharp "cut," or does it have a small, smooth, and rounded transition?

Irons made before 1885 have a sharp blade crease. They lack any type of transition between the top of the blade and the side of the hosel. The blade simply runs *straight* into the side of the hosel.

After 1885-90, as irons became more refined, clubmakers began to finish the blade crease by smoothing it out. The tiny area where the topline of the blade and the hosel intersect was blended together.

A few square toe irons do not have a blade crease. Instead, the blade appears to flow or sweep up into the hosel, making it impossible to point to one spot where the blade stops and the hosel begins. Irons with this trait are the oldest irons known.

Hosel thickness. How thick is the hosel (the neck of an iron club)?

The irons made before 1850 have the thickest hosels. Between 1850 and 1890, the hosel underwent a period of refinement and downsizing. By 1900 it approached the traditional size used throughout the twentieth century.

Hosel length. How long is the hosel?

Expect five to six inch hosels on pre-1850 irons. By 1900 the hosel length of an ordinary iron had dropped to approximately four inches. Thereafter, hosels usually measured between 3 1/2 and 4 inches in length. There were, however, a few putters with very thin hosels approximately seven inches long made during the 1920s.

Hosel nicking. Does the top of the hosel have nicking? Is it distinct or dramatic? Does it have a "sawtoothed" appearance? Is the nicking wider at the top of the hosel or does the nicking consist of thin or small nicks, perhaps not very distinct? Is the nicking uniform and even? Instead of nicking are there machine-made lines around the top of the hosel?

Early irons (pre-1850) have the most dramatic nicking or "knurling," as it is sometimes called. Their nicking often appears sawtoothed or even claw-like. Employed to help attach the head to the shaft, nicking on early irons was done by hand and is unmistakably distinct and uneven.

From the early 1800s to the late 1880s, hosel nicking underwent a period of downsizing and refinement. By 1900 the nicking at the top of the hosel no longer played a major part in attaching the head to the shaft. It existed primarily for decoration and was often minimal or nonexistent.

Head texture. Does the head show any signs of hand forging such as an uneven face, hammer marks on the blade, or a hammer weld visible on the hosel? Or does the head appear to be smooth, even, and symmetrical?

Irons made before 1850 usually show many signs of hand forging. The blade will normally be less than smooth and even. High and low spots will often be noticed. On some irons, the blacksmith's hammer marks are visible. The hosel might show clear evidence of the hammer weld, a seam running lengthwise down the hosel. The earliest irons, reflecting the tools used to make them, usually look exceptionally crude and unrefined.

As irons from the early 1800s continued to evolve, they became more refined and symmetrical. By the 1880s, the cleekmaker, working with a smaller piece of metal, had perfected his craft to a high degree. Irons became practically flawless in appearance and much more usable. They also looked very similar to the traditional iron shapes of the twentieth century.

Club weight. Is the iron extremely heavy or relatively light?

The weight of an ordinary iron from 1910 is not much different from that of a 1990 iron, but there is no mistaking the war club from 1800. The overall weight of a "heavy iron" often approximates a pound and a half or more. As heavy irons evolved between 1800 and 1850, their weight steadily declined. Furthermore, not all irons made prior to the early 1800s are extremely heavy. Prior to 1800, two basic types of irons were produced: "heavy irons" and "light irons." Light irons, however, are often just as heavy or heavier than either the cleek or the lofter made after 1850.

Shaft material. Is the shaft hickory? Are there any knots in the wood? Most antique wood shaft irons were made with hickory shafts. Prior to 1800, shafts were also made from different types of wood, such as ash, greenheart, hazel, or elm. Shafts were occasionally made from ash, greenheart, lemonwood, lancewood, etc. between 1800-1900. Although knots weaken a wood shaft, a knot is a wonderful characteristic. It is evidence of an early club, made when clubs were crude and unrefined.

Shaft construction. Is the shaft quite thick? Is it perfectly symmetrical and even across its entire length. Is the shaft thin? Are there any flat spots on the shaft? How is the end of the shaft cut?

Because early irons were used only to extricate the ball from trouble, they required shafts worthy of the battle. Consequently, early irons have thick shafts. These shafts were split and finished by hand. Because the wood was split, not sawn and lathed to shape, early shafts were true and strong. (Sawn shafts were often cut slightly across the grain, weakening the shaft; split shafts followed the grain down their length.) Hand split shafts in early clubs are usually asymmetrical. A few flat spots or an oblong area (in cross section) can often be found. Shaft asymmetry is usually not visible to the eye but is easily discovered by holding the shaft in one hand and turning it with the other. Any unevenness or flat spots can be felt.

The grip end of the earliest shafts was usually cut straight off and left with an unbeveled edge, a characteristic which normally dates to the 1700s and earlier.

Shaft length. Does the club appear to be extraordinary in length?

Some early irons measure as much as 43 inches or longer—an extremely long length for an iron. If an iron shaft is exceptionally long and the rest of the club's characteristics fit "early iron," the club was probably made in the eighteenth century or earlier.

Grip material. Is the grip made from sueded leather, listing, hard-finished leather, or bare wood?

Clubs made before 1800 may have simple listing grips (thick fabric wrapped around the shaft), crude leather grips, or no grips at all. The early listing grips evolved and were eventually covered with sueded sheepskin. Consequently, a collector should understand that removing the sheepskin on the grip of any nineteenth century club will expose an "underlisting" which is basically the same material found in a listing grip.

Older irons often have a shaft large enough to grip without adding any material. If a club was designed for use without a grip, it will not have nail holes in its shaft (small tack-like nails were normally used at the top and bottom of a grip to help fix it in place).

If an early club has a listing grip, the top and bottom of this grip will be fastened in one of two ways. The ends with be either nailed in place, the tops of the nails bent over, or it will be wrapped with whipping or fabric.

Hard-finished leather grips, tried as far back as the 1700s, are normally found on clubs from around 1900 and later. Sueded leather (sheepskin) grips, also tried early in the history of golf, were prominent throughout the entire nineteenth century. They died out in the early 1900s.

Traits To Examine On A Wooden Head Club:

Long nose – bulger	Head size	Shaft construction
Writing on the club	Head material	Shaft length
Head shape	Neck shape	Grip material
Lead shape	Scoring lines	Neck joint
Face depth	Shaft material	Long nose – bulger

Long nose – bulger. Is the wood a "long nose," identified by a long, thin head, or is it a bulger, characterized by a short, stocky head similar to today's clubs?

Besides making long nose woods, which normally date prior to 1890, and bulgers, which date after the late 1880s, clubmakers also made "transitional" woods. Dating between the 1880s and the late

1890s, transitional clubheads were not as long as a long nose and not as short as a bulger.

If a club is a bulger, it was made after 1888. Examining traits number 2 and 14 will help determine if a bulger is an earlier or later example. However, long nose woods were made over centuries.

If the club is a long nose, the following characteristics need to be examined to narrow down the date of its creation.

Writing on the club. Is there any writing on the head?

Most woods are marked only with the maker's name and, sometimes, location. Knowing when and where a maker was working helps date his clubs in general terms. A long nose wood without any marks may date to the feather ball era.

Head shape. Is the face curved? Does the head have a teardrop shape?

The faces on earlier long nose woods are normally more curved, heel to toe, than those on later examples. Reminiscent of a teardrop, the heads on earlier long nose clubs are often quite broad across the toe and less so in the heel. Still, some are distinctly slender throughout.

Lead shape. Is the lead backweight flush with the head or does it protrude? On a pre-1800 wood, the lead backweight often protrudes a little behind the head.

Face depth. Is the face depth greater than one inch?
The faces on pre-1820 woods are known to be rather deep. Pre-1800 examples sometimes measure as much as 1 1/4 inches in depth. These clubs lack the refinement which occurred between 1830 and 1850 when faces slimmed down to one inch in depth. During the 1850s, faces were made a little deeper in order to withstand the increased hardness of the gutty ball, introduced in the late 1840s. By the late 1880s many long nose clubs were once again constructed with deep faces measuring up to 1 1/4 inches in depth.

Head size. Is the head unusually long for a long nose club? Does it appear unusually small?

Early long nose clubheads, especially those made before 1800, were often quite long, measuring six inches or more between the tip of the toe and the back of the neck (see p. 8 for how to measure). Prior to 1880, short and small woods shaped like ordinary long nose woods were also made. Termed "wooden niblicks," most of these clubs date between the 1860s and 1880s. "Semi-long nose" clubs, also called "transitionals," are intermediate in head length and date from the 1880s and 1890s. Some transitional clubs are often mistaken for wooden niblicks (see p. 88).

Head material. Is the long nose club made from wood or another material such as aluminum?

Genuine long nose clubs are ordinarily made from wood: thorn, apple, pear, and beech being the most common. The main exception is the Johnston patent long nose wood produced in 1876 with a vulcanite head (see p. 82). William Mills produced many aluminum fairway clubs and putters which look like long nose clubs. Because these clubs date to the early 1900s, they are not true long nose clubs.

The term "long nose" denotes more than a clubhead shape. It identifies the era when long nose clubs were made. Simply possessing such a shape does not qualify a club to be classified with those long nose clubs actually made before 1890. Such post-1890 clubs are referred to as "long nose style" clubs.

Neck shape. Is the neck big and thick, or is it thin and delicate? During the last twenty years of the feather ball era, necks were thin and elegant. Woods made before then had necks with slightly more size and substance. Clubs made after 1850 reverted to necks of sizable proportions. The 1850-70 club will often have a thin head but a somewhat thicker neck. This was done to strengthen the club to prevent it from breaking against the hard gutta percha ball. During the 1880s and into the 1890s, clubs were often made with extremely thick necks.

Scoring lines. Does your favorite long nose club have any scoring lines like those on a modern day driver? Hopefully not.

Scoring lines on a long nose, if any at all, were usually created by turning a file on edge and dragging it across the face. These marks are very small, thin, and usually installed at an angle. When actual scoring lines are present, deep-cut lines sawn straight across the face, they were either added to the club later, or the club dates near the end of the long nose era or thereafter.

Shaft material. Is the shaft hickory, ash, or some other wood? Are there any knots in the wood?

Most long nose clubs have hickory shafts. Prior to 1800, in addition to hickory, shafts were also made of hazel, ash, lancewood, and even elm. Ash continued to be used occasionally until 1850. Thereafter it was rarely used. A number of other woods were occasionally used during the long nose era but never accepted on a large scale; greenheart being the most notable.

Knots weaken a wood shaft, but a few wood shafts do have knots. Such a shaft indicates an early club made when clubs were crude and unrefined. A knot in the shaft is a significant feature.

Shaft construction. Is the shaft quite thick or rather thin? Is it smooth and symmetrical? Is the edge at the grip end of the shaft bevelled?

Woods made prior to 1820 often have thick shafts. Between 1830 and 1850, shafts became thin and refined. Thereafter, shafts were made slightly thicker but never as thick as the earliest shafts.

Asymmetry is a common characteristic among woods made prior to 1850. The older the club, the more obvious this trait appears. In early times, shafts (being hand split and worked to shape) were not perfectly smooth and symmetrical in cross-section. However, shaft imperfections are not readily visible. By holding the shaft in one hand and rotating the head with the other, any flat spots or oval areas can be readily felt.

Many of the earliest shafts were cut off on the grip end and left unbeveled around the edge. This is an early characteristic usually found on clubs made before 1800.

Shaft length. How long is the club?

When comparing like clubs (middle spoon to middle spoon, etc.), pre-1800 clubs are often longer than post-1800 clubs.

The traditional length of a play club (driver) during the 1800s is somewhere between 43 and 44 inches. This will occasionally vary by an inch or two. Play clubs made in the 1800s rarely approach 47 inches in length, but play clubs made in the 1700s often do. Exceptionally long shafts, however, are not to be expected of all pre-1800 woods. Shaft lengths will vary according to the purpose of the long nose wood (the more lofted woods used shorter shafts) and the desire of the original owner.

Grip material. Does the club have a sueded sheepskin grip, a listing grip, or a hard-finished leather grip?

Woods made prior to the end of the 1700s usually have listing grips. Sheepskin grips were commonplace throughout the 1800s, though they were used to some extent before 1800 and in the early 1900s. Hard-finished leather grips were commonly used in the early 1900s and later.

Neck joint. How is the head attached to the shaft—splice neck or socket neck?

After 1890 clubmakers tried many ways of attaching clubheads to shafts. The most common methods were the "splice neck" and the "socket neck." To the collector, these neck joints are distinguishing factors when dating a bulger head wood.

Used in the construction of all long nose clubs, splice necks required cutting the neck and the shaft at corresponding angles. The shaft and head were then glued together and bound with whipping. Splice necks were used to assemble transitional woods and the early bulgers. Many splice neck woods were made after the turn of the twentieth century, but their production slowed to a halt between 1910 and 1920.

In 1891 Robert Anderson received a patent for a "socket neck" wood. This method of attaching the head to the shaft simply required inserting the tapered end of a shaft into a hole bored in the neck. The shaft was glued in place, and the top of the neck was covered with whipping. For years socket necks were unpopular. By 1904, however, they had supplanted the splice neck as the primary method for joining the head to the shaft. The socket neck joint is still the primary method used to assemble woods today.

THE CONDITION FACTOR

Condition is the most basic factor in determining the collectibility of a golf club. It is more important than the club's age, maker, historical importance, or rarity, because a club in poor condition is little more than a shadow of its former self.

The more original a club is, the better. Therefore, a collector needs to understand the current condition of a club in comparison with its original state. The ideal situation, of course, is to find clubs in near-perfect or mint condition.

Mint condition, meaning "to appear as new and unused," implies no damage and little, if any, use. A refinished club or a club reworked in any way can *never* accurately be called "mint." Such clubs are refinished, reworked, or restored—not mint.

Nearly all antique clubs have been used or knocked around when not in use. Consequently the vast majority of them are not in mint condition. Understanding this, collectors find normal wear to be perfectly acceptable. However, when moving into the area of damage, re-paired damage, restoration, and over-restoration, the collector must be careful. There are many different degrees and types of damage and restoration; some of it is tolerable and some of it is not.

The condition of a golf club is best considered on a case by case basis. Nevertheless, a brief general discussion about condition, as it relates to woods, irons, and putters, follows.

Condition Characteristics Important To Woods And Wood Head Putters:

Structural condition. Any cracks, chips, dents, breaks, weathering, missing pieces, or other damage should be clearly identified and examined.

Antique woods, especially long nose clubs, are often found with their heads in pieces, missing pieces, or with major cracks. They are also found with small hairline cracks, nicks, and dents. Old woods can have uncracked heads but still show significant wear, especially on the face.

The location of any damage and how it affects the overall structure and appearance of a club are primary considerations. For example, a nice original long nose wood having a short hairline crack on the back of the head is still very desirable. The damage, which is not that significant to begin with, is not in a prominent area of the head. However, a club with a similar crack which starts at the face and runs across the top of the head, the face and top of the head being the two most prominent areas, will receive less interest among collectors. Any substantial break or prominent crack—one that draws significant attention to itself—will downgrade a club. The same is true of a distressed face. Otherwise attractive clubs are heavily downgraded if their faces are worn or missing a notable amount of wood.

The significance of any damage is best understood in terms of the club's presentation—how the club looks and how well it reflects the original workmanship. If a club has a crack but still looks good, it is a good example; but if a club looks badly damaged, it is a bad example. The acceptability of a club's condition depends on personal opinion; what might bother one collector might not bother another. Keep in mind that the further a club is from good original condition, the less interest it will command. But if a duplicate club does not exist, or there are only a few known, any weaknesses in condition become less significant.

The structural condition of the shaft is also important. The occasional bow in a shaft is perfectly acceptable and is best left alone. It can usually be straightened by someone who knows how. A cracked shaft can also be repaired. However, if the shaft is dramatically deformed, either with a pronounced bow across its length or bowed in two different directions, this is undesireable. (Reshafted clubs are discussed under replacement parts.)

Occasionally shafts were cut down from their original length. If only a few inches were removed, the shaft can be restored to its original length by adding a piece of wood. Given a proper replacement grip, such a repair becomes invisible and of minimal consequence to the club. Such a repair is unquestionably better than replacing the entire shaft.

Head shape alterations. The shape of a clubhead is of paramount importance. Head shapes are what set one maker apart from another. An altered head shape is bad news—usually very bad news. For example, if the curve in a long nose clubface has been altered, either increased or decreased, the club will receive less interest than it otherwise would. The degree to which a clubhead is altered is the degree to which the original clubmaker's work is lost.

Original finish. The condition of the original finish is an important consideration. It is used to differentiate between two examples of the same club in the same structural condition—the less evidence of wear and tear, the better. For example, dark moisture stains on a blond clubhead are unattractive. If the staining is bad enough, the club will appear downright ugly. Such a club is not as desirable as an identical blond example in a rich, even, original finish. Clubs have sold for double the amount expected because their original finish was so outstanding.

Reworked finish. This is not a desirable characteristic in any club. Collectors *always* prefer nice original condition. However, old long nose woods and other woods are occasionally found refinished or re-stored, the work often having been done years ago. Such clubs are acceptable if the work is well done and mimics the original.

Distressed clubs in poor condition can sometimes be successfully restored to their original appearance. Nobody likes to look at a club painted blue or covered by grime and gunk to the point of being unrecognizable. A club which hit one too many rocks is also unappealing. However, unless a person knows exactly what he or she is doing before working on a club—knows *exactly* where he or she is going with any restoration work and how to best approximate "original"—he or she runs a high risk of damaging, if not destroying, the collectibility of the club.

Both positive and negative things can occur when restoring clubs. Some clubs are so poorly restored, so heavily sanded or improperly prepared and stained, that they are hopeless outcasts. Some clubs simply need to have their dirty finish cleaned to let the beauty of their original finish shine through. If a club in decent structural condition has any portion of its original finish remaining, it is best to leave it alone.

Replacement parts. Everything attached to a clubhead—the lead, horn, soleplate, whipping, and shaft—can be replaced. Even a leather insert, if one existed, can be redone. When a club has a replacement part installed, its collectibility is affected. The more parts replaced, the greater the downgrade. Nevertheless, although replacement parts are not as desirable as the original components, such a part, properly selected and installed in a club missing a component, can significantly improve its desirability.

Of all the replaceable parts, whipping is the least significant. Of course, original whipping is always best, but a club with replaced whipping is still considered a good example if everything else about the club is acceptable. Some of the replacement whipping currently used is amazingly close to the original in appearance.

Replaced lead and horn (the small piece of ram's horn, bone, or fiber recessed lengthwise into the leading edge of the sole) constitute significant departures from the original. Consequently, replacing the horn or the lead downgrades an otherwise nice club, but *if* well done, it will not be an overbearing distraction. If a rare club of great historic value has its horn or lead replaced, the collector will find it easy to accept if everything else is original and attractive. After all, the collector has no other choice if he or she does not expect to locate a similar example.

A replaced shaft is never as good as a decent original one. Nevertheless, a number of wonderful collectible clubs have replacement shafts. Because breaking a shaft was a normal part of the game, clubs reshafted at the time they were in use are usually quite acceptable.

It is always better to repair the original damaged shaft if possible. A clubhead should not be reshafted unless the shaft is missing, cut down to an extremely short length, or *seriously* warped. Old clubs, reshafted today, run the risk of a poor match, especially on splice neck clubs. Care must be taken when reshafting a club.

Leather inserts were installed on long nose clubs either to keep the ball from damaging the face or to repair and stop any further face damage. If a collector could choose between two clubs, identical except that one has a leather insert, the club without the insert would be the first choice. Nevertheless, a desirable antique wood with an old leather insert is quite acceptable. After all, leather inserts were a part of the game and the clubmaker's craft.

Today, clubs with damaged faces can likewise be fitted with leather inserts. However, only the highest quality of workmanship is acceptable. Good work is measured by how hard it is to distinguish the new insert from an old one.

Replacement grips influence a club's desirability in different ways. If the club is common, a replaced grip receives greater scrutiny. If the club is a prime item, however, the grip becomes a minor consideration. Truly rare and historic clubs are not seriously downgraded if they lack their original grip (provided the original grip was not the main feature of the club). Rather, because such clubs are so desirable, an original grip adds a premium.

Ordinary replacement parts affect a long nose club more than they do a patent club. Because all long nose clubs share a similar design, their components come under greater scrutiny. On the other hand, because a patent club is collected for its uniqueness, originality, distinction, etc., its *ordinary* parts are less crucial. However, if the replacement piece is the main feature of the club—the part that makes the club collectible—it will usually downgrade a club's collectibility far more than an ordinary replacement part.

For example, Mules Patent drivers are collectible because they have a spring steel face. A Mules Patent driver with a replaced metal face would be unacceptable to most collectors. If the same club is only missing one of the four screws that hold the metal plate in place, however, concern is minimal. The missing screw can be discreetly replaced in period style.

Condition Characteristics Important To Irons And Metal Head Putters:

Structural condition. Clubheads made from iron are usually very stable. They can be dented, but they hardly ever break. Clubheads made from softer metals, such as gunmetal, brass, or aluminum, are more susceptible to dents and dings. As a result, these clubs are often quite worn, and the more battered the club, the less interest it generates.

Aluminum clubs occasionally have damaged hosels because the thin top of an aluminum hosel is prone to cracking. A simple hairline crack is a minor thing, especially if it is short, located in a less prominent area, and if nothing is missing. A hosel with a missing piece, however, is of greater concern. If the missing piece is large, it will detract from the rest of the head and emphasize the damage. If the damaged aluminum club is an ordinary Mills club (or something similar), other clubs in better condition are easily located if one is patient. Such clubs were made in quantity.

Bowed shafts do not present a problem as long as they are not severely deformed. The occasional bow in a shaft is perfectly acceptable and is best left alone until it can be straightened by someone who knows how. (On some putters, a bow was installed by design; see p. 507.) Also, a cracked shaft can usually be repaired.

Altered head shape. This usually occurs from filing, grinding, or excessive polishing. Bending the neck also alters the head. Altering a head can seriously downgrade a club. To illustrate: two Brown rake irons offered at auction a few years ago reached only half of their estimated price because their heads had been altered. On one rake, its leading edge had been ground smooth, altering the location of the leading edge and consequently the club's original shape. Also, the blade had been heavily polished. Because none of the original finish or patina remained and the "vine" face scoring was faint and stretched, the head looked modern. In short, the clubhead had arrived at an irreversibly unattractive condition.

The other Brown rake iron had been rechromed and the neck was bent (the club sat flat). Rechroming evaporates value in an antique wood shaft club. And if rechroming was not enough of a detraction, the bend in the neck provided another. It is sometimes possible to straighten such bends, but the metal may wrinkle or break in the process.

The rule of thumb for club alterations: The more dramatic the alteration, the more dramatic the drop in collectibility.

Original finish. When considering the finish of an iron clubhead which has never been cleaned, the collector has little to worry about other than rust. If an iron shows rust, it is best to leave it alone unless you know how to remove it properly. An even patina of rust is of no concern. A light coat of rust shows age and character. However, if the rust has eaten below the surface, marking the head with excessive pitting, this is a condition which adversely affects collector interest.

Rust can be removed in a proper and unobtrusive way. When antique irons were in use, it was normal to clean them with an abrasive emery cloth. Today, cleaning a rusty head is easy to do, but it is easy to damage the head in the process. Only someone who knows exactly what he or she is doing and exactly how the club should look and *exactly* how the club will appear after the rust is removed—should attempt to remove rust from an old club.

Some collectors think that rust, which is iron oxidation, must be removed or it will destroy the metal. Given enough time and moisture, it will. However, irons that have survived this long can easily wait a little longer until they fall into the hands of someone who knows how to remove rust correctly. Furthermore, deterioration can be accelerated by over-frequent cleaning.

Reworked finish. The process used to remove rust or grime from an iron head is important because cleaning a club improperly can devalue it.

A shiny finish is not the goal in iron restoration. Rather, the objective is to return the head to the condition it was in when in use, not when new. Cleaned correctly, the head will show no evidence of restoration work. And, unless the head is either chromed or made from a rustless alloy, the metal should not appear bright, shiny, or reflective. If rust is removed correctly, the head will retain a dull or sometimes brown patina. Rustless heads, usually made from a special alloy such as stainless steel, do not require any significant work to clean and should not be buffed out.

Occasionally a wood shaft iron head is found rechromed or buffed to a highly polished luster. As mentioned earlier, rechromed clubs possess little of their original collectibility. Buffed-out and highly polished clubs, although not as bad as rechromed clubs, win no prizes. Time (and a little know-how) can help bring a patina back to such clubs.

Replacement parts. With irons, only the grip and shaft are replaceable. Replacement grips influence a club's desirability in various ways. If the club is consistently available, a replaced grip receives greater scrutiny. If the club is a prime item, however, the grip becomes a minor consideration. Truly rare and historic clubs are not seriously downgraded if they lack their original grip (provided the original grip was not the main feature of the club). Because such clubs are so desirable, an original grip adds a premium.

A decent original shaft is always better than a replacement shaft. Nevertheless, a number of wonderful collectible clubs have replaced shafts.

Collectors do not automatically dismiss a rare item they have been searching for just because it has been reshafted. Since breaking a shaft was a normal part of the game, reshafted clubs are usually quite acceptable as long as the work was well done and there are no additional concerns. However, if a club is of interest because of the shaft or the shaft/hosel relationship, such as in a Seely iron, a reshafted example has little remaining collectibility.

As previously noted, a patent iron will occasionally have or need a replacement part. A replacement part is a minor problem if it is a minor aspect of the club. However, replacing a primary piece—that which provides a club's collectibility—will usually downgrade a club far more than replacing an ordinary part.

For example, a Cran iron with a replaced wooden face insert will receive much less interest than a nice original Cran. However, if an otherwise good Cran cleek has a new hosel pin, used to attach the head to the shaft, this is a minor consideration. As long as the work was properly done, the club will still be a good example. Cran irons are of interest because of their face, not their hosel or their shaft/hosel relationship.

THE TROON CLUBS

The two irons and six woods which make up the "Troon clubs" are among the oldest golf clubs in existence. They also have an excellent provenance.

At the end of the nineteenth century, during the remodeling of a home in Hull, England, these eight golf clubs were found inside a boarded-up cupboard or closet along with a Yorkshire newspaper dated 1741. The clubs were eventually given to the Troon Golf Club, in Troon, Scotland, by Adam Wood. Wood received them from "Mr. W.T. Hammond, manufacturer, Skeldon, Ayrshire, to whom they were sent by Mr. J.C. Sykes, merchant, Hull" (*Golf*, 26 Aug. 1898: 454). Wood was an original and life member of the Troon club and its Captain from May 27, 1893, to May 29, 1897. These clubs, nicknamed the "Troon clubs," remained on display at the Royal Troon Golf Club for many decades. After a brief stay in a more secure home—a bank vault—they were sent on long term loan to the British Golf Museum in St. Andrews early in the 1990s.

The August 26, 1898 issue of *Golf*, reprinting an article from *The Times*, describes these clubs and explains their significance:

The golf club, like most other implements, has been constantly changing, and our latter-day clubs are the result of a marked evolution from those used in . . . the game a hundred years ago. The change of fashion is not so great nor so apparent in this case as between the century old clubs and the earlier specimens [the Troon clubs]. The design and especially the workmanship . . . warrants us in deciding that the best part of two centuries at least has elapsed since these Golf clubs were made. . . . Mr. Balfour, the Leader of the House of Commons, has seen the clubs and gives it as his opinion that they may belong to the period of the Stuart Kings (454).

When considering the age of the Troon clubs, this author shares the belief that they, both woods and irons, date from the 1600s or possibly even the 1500s.

The clubs themselves consist of six long nose woods (drivers and spoons) and two square toe irons. Each club is stamped many times with a unique mark. The woods are stamped on the top of their heads and the irons are stamped on their shafts. The mark contains five characters:

Perhaps . . . the most interesting feature of the clubs is a stamped device which every one of them bears. . . . Essentially it consists of a figure whose outline may be described as a rhombus with the obtuse angles rounded, or an ellipse with the ends run to a point, containing a series of characters. In the upper angle there is a Royal crown, in the lower a Scotch thistle, in the middle between those emblems a five-rayed star, on the left-hand side of the star the letter I (which may stand for J), *and on the right-hand side of the star the letter C. The specific characters are isolated and of the natural colour of the wood, while the ground was black so the figure must have been impressed by stamping and not by stencilling . . . . The outline of the characters is rude and irregular. In the case of the wooden clubs the figure is repeated six times so as to imitate the general shape of the original, and on the iron clubs four times with the same intent* (455-456).

Acknowledging the fact that these characters were not completely understood, the article concludes by assuming the initials belonged to the maker and the symbols:

denote a special permission on the part of one or other of the Kings of Scotland, equivalent to a monopoly of the kind that is granted to certain tradesmen of today [1898] in the use of the Royal arms (456).

The article also mentions, however, that the marks could denote ownership.

In his book *Chronicles of Golf: 1457-1857*, Alastair Johnston suggests that the marks on the Troon clubs could date prior to 1603:

No monarch since James II was deposed in 1688 had shown any propensity for golf. It is unlikely that the office of Royal Clubmaker, which we know was first established in 1602 and was still in evidence in 1669, survived until the 1740s. What is intriguing, however, is the coupling within the motif of the Crown (representative of the reigning monarch) and the Thistle, (symbol of Scotland). However, the Kingdom of Scotland as an independent preserve dissolved in 1603 with the Union of the Crowns. Dare we speculate that the date of manufacture of these clubs, portraying a stamp of royal approval or licensed under the King's prerogative, could be attributed to a period prior to 1603? (188).

In this author's opinion, the marks on the Troon clubs denote that they were all made by the same maker. Although crafting woods and forging irons were different trades during the 1800s, this was not necessarily the case in the earliest days of the game. Consider William Mayne, the oldest known club-maker: In 1603, within one week after assuming the throne of England, King James I appointed William Mayne as

Royal Clubmaker. This appointment, declared in a document dated April 4, 1603, also called Mayne to be the "bower, club-maker, and speir-maker to his Hienes" (Johnston 1993, 58). The fact that Mayne was also a bowmaker and a spearmaker gave him the necessary credentials to make golf clubs, both woods and irons.

Because the Troon clubs date prior to 1741, they give valuable perspective to the collector undertaking the difficult challenge of dating an early club. Determining the age of any club that might have been made before 1850, of which there are only a relative few, is, at best, an educated approximation. Not one of these pre-1850 clubs is documented to the exact year of its creation. Only those clubs verified as being made before a certain time, such as the Troon clubs, or made during a certain era, such as the working years of James McEwan or Simon and David Cossar, provide benchmarks that help date other clubs. (James McEwan made clubs between 1770 and 1800; Simon and David Cossar made clubs between 1785, when Simon entered the trade, and 1816, when David followed Simon, his father, in death [see page 549].)

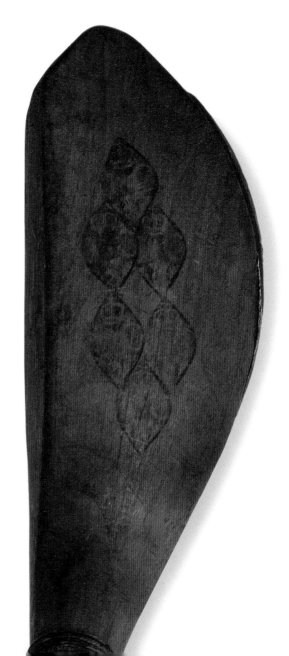

An early iron head carefully sketched by an artist, presented in the May 29, 1891 issue of *Golf* (183), also provides an interesting gauge for dating irons clubs. Together with a coin dated 1682, this iron head was found inside a cornerstone dated 1682, which was opened during alterations to the premises of Messrs. J.G. Thomson and Co., The Vaults, Leith. According to the artist's illustration, this clubhead was a "heavy iron" with a rounded toe, concave face, sawtooth nicking, and a sharp blade crease. Its weight was reported to be just over one pound.

Individually, the Troon woods possess several distinctly early characteristics. They are as follows:

Each of these woods has a splay (slanted) toe. The short edge between the end of the face and the tip of the nose is straight and flat, not rounded. This is a characteristic found primarily in the oldest of woods.

The heads are formed using parallel construction. The term parallel construction refers to a design in which the top and bottom of the head, when viewed from the face (as shown above), run nearly parallel to each other across their *entire* length. This parallel trait is easily recognized when looking directly at the face—the head maintains a uni-

form thickness across its entire length. Long nosed woods from the 18th and 19th centuries are not as rigid in their lines. Gently raised crowns, downward sloping toes, slightly deeper faces, and both thicker and thinner heels were employed together or in part.

Each head has a protruding lead backweight. The backweight, across its entire length, actually extends out of the head approximately a quarter of an inch. Pre-1800 clubs often have this characteristic, but not always and not always to the same degree.

Each head is exceptionally long and has a shallow face, a

flat lie, a thin neck, and a thick horn. Individually, these traits are not particularly illuminating. When found together in a single club, however, they are indicative of an early club.

The shafts are made from ash, and the clubheads appear to be made from hawthorn, though the wood has never been scientifically identified. These materials were often used in pre-1800 woods.

Some of the heads have knots, and accompanying cracks, in the wood. Notice the knots in the face of the middle club shown above. As clubs and clubmaking evolved, a head with a knot in the wood was considered an inferior head. Consequently, knots are more likely to be found in early woods.

The knots and cracks (the result of age, not abuse) in the heads of the Troon woods add to their beauty and desirability in a major way. These features, like the other features already mentioned, are characteristics of a very old club. Novice collectors frequently think that the newer an old club looks, the better. In actuality, because of its great antiquity and corresponding place in history, an old club should look old. A seasoned collector expects—and wants—a fine old club to show its age.

The 1898 *Golf* account describes these woods as being quite heavy and very long, the longest club measuring approximately 48 inches. The ash shafts in the woods are much thinner than the stout shafts in the irons.

The Troon irons also possess several early characteristics. The blackish-brown color and rough texture of these irons are found on only a handful of other irons. These are characteristics of a very early iron.

Both irons have identical nicking. Such large "sawtooth" nicking is not only dramatic, it is evidence of a very early club—although not all early irons have such large nicking.

The square toe on each blade sets these irons apart from round toe early irons. Both styles were made during the 1700s, but square toe irons existed prior to round toe irons. Both styles are *highly* collectible.

The way the blades on the Troon irons sweep into the hosel is a trait shared by only the earliest known irons. All round toe irons from the feather ball era and the bulk of the other known square toe irons have a sharp crease where the top of the blade and side of the hosel intersect (see p. 100).

When looking at the Troon irons, notice the massive size of their hosels. They are long and thick, two qualities that go together in irons made during the feather ball era. The previously mentioned 1898 article in *Golf* described the large iron as having a hosel 3 1/2 inches in circumference!

Another early feature of the Troon irons is that the heads are *nailed* to the shaft. Later irons have a single pin running through a hole bored through the neck.

Each Troon iron has its own distinct purpose. The smaller one is a "light iron" and the larger one is a "heavy iron." In 1790 *Hoyle's Games Improved* identifies six basic types of golf clubs, two of which were irons described as:

the Heavy Iron club, [used] when [the ball] lies deep among Stones or Mud: and the Light Iron ditto, [used] when on the surface of chingle or sandy Ground (288).

The Troon heavy iron has a distinct "spur" on the toe. According to Peter McEwan, this spur (or hollowing out of the bottom end of the toe) allowed the club to be "used hammer-wise" (*Golf*, 9 Oct. 1896: 75). By turning the club to align the entire *length* of the blade behind the ball, a ball in a rut or nestled among stones could be struck with the end of the toe. Although the spur is a characteristic of the earliest known square toe irons, not all of the earliest irons have this feature as is clearly demonstrated by the companion light iron. It was not necessary to include a spur on the light iron because the purpose of a light iron was quite different from that of a heavy iron. A spur on a light iron would be superfluous since the heavy iron had one.

The Troon heavy iron weighs 28 ounces (*Golf*, 26 Aug. 1898: 455) and served the purpose

FAR LEFT: *Light iron.*
LEFT: *Heavy iron.*

of a trouble club. It was used only when the lie of the ball was at its worst, usually among rocks or ruts. The light iron, with its sleek head and slightly longer shaft, was designed to play a ball that was easily accessible, but on the "surface of chingle or sandy ground." Clearly, the light iron, which has less loft than the heavy iron, was designed more for distance.

Out of these eight clubs, grips are found on only one wood and one iron. They are described as consisting of:

a single thickness of coarse woolen selvidge wound round the shaft and fixed thereon by its ends with horse nails bent into the form of a staple (*Golf,* 26 Aug. 1898: 455).

These grips are distinctive in their color: one is blue and the other is white with a blue edge along the greater part of its wound length. A few other very early clubs are known to have a white woolen selvidge grip, but with a red edge.

The handles on the earliest of clubs were often wrapped with woolen selvidge. Such clubs are referred to today as having a "list" or "listing" grip. Similar wrapped listing is found under the traditional sheepskin grip.

A club without a grip should be inspected to determine if it once had a grip. Finding a big nail in the grip area of the shaft, such as shown in the picture below, not only indicates the club once had a grip, it also suggests the club might be quite old. Sometimes just a nail hole is found. This also indicates the club once had a grip.

Overall, the Troon clubs have unmatched character and visual strength. They provide the standard for dating other clubs of great antiquity.

Shown here are the handles of four Troon clubs. The handle on the far left (with the blue listing) belongs to the light iron club. Note the large nails at the bottom of the grips of the neighboring shafts.

An old master, whether
of fiddles, pictures,
books, or golf clubs, will
ever command a price.

(H.S.C. Everard; Everard 1896, 18)

Long Nose

& Transitional Clubs

||| ——————————————————— |||

When first I was initiated into the mysteries of the club-making craft, the workman made the heads himself, from the very beginning—when the rough block was given him—by his own hands without the intervention of the machine; the head was first cut out of the block—firmly fixed in his vice— with what we call the breaking-out saw, and then, by means of files of various degrees of roughness, he gradually shaped and fashioned it, until it appeared as a club head . . . .

Then, like old Hugh Philip [sic], the man who fashioned a club had to be a club-maker in every sense of the word, with an artist's eye for beauty of form . . . . Each club represented the mind of the maker as to what it ought to be like . . . (Willie Auchterlonie, *Golfing*, 6 May, 1909: 33).

Based on the distinctive shape of its head, the normal wooden clubhead made before 1885-1890 and referred to above by Willie Auchterlonie is termed a "long nose." Characterized by long, thin heads with slightly concave faces (curved inward, heel to toe), long nose clubs were made in a number of distinct models, briefly described as follows:

Play Club: Also termed a "driver," a play club was used to begin play at most holes, hence the term "play" club. It was also "used throughout the green if the ball [was] lying fair, and the distance either a full drive or upwards from the hole" (Chambers 1862, 14). This club has the longest shaft and, apart from the putter, the least amount of loft.

Grassed Driver: Having the shaft length of a normal play club, grassed drivers have slightly more loft to help the golfer get the ball airborne. Along with teeing off, grassed drivers could be used on grass through the green if the ball had a good lie and maximum distance was needed.

Long Spoon, Middle Spoon, Short Spoon, and **Baffy Spoon**: These four clubs were used from normal grassy lies; which one was used depended on the length of the shot. The shaft length corresponds with the club's name, with the exception of the baffing spoon (it was at least as short as the short spoon). The faces usually increase slightly in loft as the shaft length decreases, the baffy having the most loft. The shaft of a middle spoon is often stiffer than that of a long spoon. The shaft of a baffy is usually quite firm. Baffy spoons are the least common long nose spoon. During the last thirty years of the long nose era, golfers began using iron lofters in place of baffing spoons.

In 1857 Henry B. Farnie described the functions of the various spoons:

The long and middle spoons are often pressed into doing duty for a grassed driver, from their ability to 'loft' the ball; but besides this, from their tougher build, they are admirably fitted to jerk it out of a grassy rut—or a yielding whin—or, indeed, out of the thousand and one bad lies which the best directed stroke will get into, and which would very likely shiver the more slender shaft of the grassed play-club. The short spoon, besides assisting in the rougher work of its elder brethren, is used for those beautiful and difficult half strokes on to the putting green over a hazard, when the ball lies sufficiently clear for the stroke. The Baffing Spoon . . . . is employed only for skying a ball over a hazard on to the putting ground, when the stroke is too short for any of the other spoons (1857: 18-19).

Wooden Niblick: Used to extract the ball from a difficult spot such as long grass or a cupped lie, wooden niblicks have small and well-lofted heads. They date back to the first half of the nineteenth century but were never popular because irons could serve the same purpose with greater ease and durability. In the second half of the nineteenth century, wooden niblicks were still not widely used. In spite of often having a full brass soleplate, they were still prone to breaking, and their reputation for being ineffective continued. Compared with the other clubs from their era, wooden niblicks are scarce. Consequently, when located, they are sometimes incorrectly identified as "transitionals."

Putter: The putter was generally used within thirty yards of the hole to play the ball into the hole. In their earliest days, putters had to be serviceable weapons. Sometimes, depending on the terrain and wind, they were used well outside of thirty yards.

Earlier long nose putters usually have a slight curve or hook to their face. Sometimes, usually years later, golfers would file the curve out of the face. Determining whether a flat face was originally curved can usually be done by examining the horn. The horn should be the same width across its entire length. If the toe has had its hook (curve) removed, the leading edge of the horn will be cut back closer to the wood peg holding it in place under the toe. Simply compare this peg to the other two in the horn—they should all be equidistant from the front and back edge of the horn. If the toe has been filed down, the club has been seriously damaged. Such a club will not be considered a good or true example of the maker's work.

Driving-Putter: Designed for making long putts and driving a low ball against a heavy wind, the driving putter was basically a putter head attached to a longer and stiffer shaft (a few late nineteenth century accounts assign *more* spring to its shaft). Driving putters were not as popular as spoons and putters.

Nineteenth century long nose clubs were referred to in their day by the terms just presented, but eighteenth century long nose clubs were referred to by different terms. *Hoyle's Games Improved* published in 1790 includes an article on golf which defines the clubs then in use:

There are six Sorts [of clubs] used by good Players, namely the Common Club, used when the Ball lies on good Ground; the Scraper and Half Scraper, when in long Grass; the Spoon, when in a Hollow; the Heavy Iron club, when it lies deep *amongst Stones or Mud; and the Light Iron ditto, when on the Surface of chingle or sandy Ground* (Hoyle, 288).

The men who made long nose clubs approached the business from two directions. After serving as a clubmaker's assistant or apprentice (usually for upwards of four years; see p. 349), they either continued in the trade as craftsmen by starting their own clubmaking business or they worked as professionals at a course—hiring on as the manager and/or custodian of the links (keeper of the green)—while continuing to make clubs.

Clubmaking was a tough business. Winters in Scotland were long and cold, and the number of golfers was small. To improve their financial stability, many clubmakers sought work as professionals. But, because manager/custodian wages were modest, it was the ability to craft and sell golf clubs that generated most of the professional's income.

Whether a craftsman or a professional, the makers of the attractive long nose clubs were artisans in every respect. Clubmakers had definite standards and lived by their reputations. Everything they did to a club was done with a purpose in mind—from where the wood pegs were placed in the horn, to the face depth, head width, and neck size. Clubs were well-measured and carefully crafted.

The better clubmakers shaped their clubs with just a touch more grace and style; the head was balanced in design and its profile appealed to the eye. Graceful and elegant clubs draw the most collector interest, everything else, such as age and condition, being equal.

Many long nose clubs made just before the long nose era came to a close were bulky, undistinguished, even clumsy when compared to their predecessors. There were two reasons for this. First, in trying to build a more durable club, many makers increased the thickness of their clubheads. Second, the rapidly increasing number of golfers at this time created a dramatic jump in the demand for clubs. Therefore, a number of inexperienced makers sprang into existence. Consider the words of Willie Park Jr.:

In the older days . . . the number of clubs was then limited; there was a plentiful supply of good material for their manufacture, and there were only a few makers, all of whom had a thorough knowledge of their business. It was therefore unlikely that a purchaser, however little knowledge he had of the subject, would be put in possession of worthless clubs. He had only to go to any clubmaker, state what he desired— the extent of his purchase being regulated by the length of his purse—and he was tolerably certain of getting good value for his money. Nowadays all this is entirely changed. Clubs are placed on the market by numberless makers, many of whom have but a limited knowledge of the game or of what is required to play it properly; good, well-seasoned wood is difficult to get, and is expensive, so that temptations are placed in the way of makers to manufacture clubs out of inferior material (1896, 17+).

During the 1880s, long nose woods were often made with somewhat shorter heads. Today, such clubs are referred to as "transitionals." Born because of the continual damage inflicted to the club head by the unyielding gutty ball, transitionals reflect the natural trend toward shortening the head to make it more durable and playable. Starting out as a small stylistic change, transitionals quickly evolved into the short head "bulger" of the 1890s (see p. 93-94).

True transitional clubheads, providing the transition between the end of the long nose and the acceptance of the bulger, were made in a variety of shapes and head lengths. Some are "semi-long nose" in style while others are much shorter than a long nose clubhead but still longer than the common bulger. Also, transitionals are not in proportion when compared to the overall profile of a long nose clubhead.

By 1890, the "bulger," with its short, broad head and convex face, was the new style. In 1896 Alex Patrick, the clubmaker, reported that three-fourths of all woods in use were bulgers (*The Golfer*, 12 Aug. 1896: 128).

When it was first used, the term "bulger" did not so much identify a club with a short head as it did a club with a bulge in the face. A radical idea at the time, a convex face (heel to toe) was the exact opposite of the concave or hooked face used on long nose clubs.

Although the earliest bulger clubheads were shorter than long nose clubheads, the bulger quickly evolved into a small, compact head. During this time, woods with similar compact heads were made with flat faces. Such clubs are not "bulgers" in the truest sense of the word. They were often termed "straight face" woods, such as a "straight face driver" or "straight face brassie." Because these clubs employed the small head adopted by the bulger, however, the term "bulger" was eventually used to identify any club with a compact head whether the face was bulging or straight. The short, broad head was in stark contrast to the long nose wood of the previous centuries.

The advantages of the bulger were real. The long head of the long nose inherently had a large proportion of its weight in the heel and toe, away from the point of impact. The bulger positioned most of the head weight directly behind the ball. Furthermore, a proper amount of face bulge helps reduce the amount of hook or slice in a poorly struck ball. Today's woods continue in the mold of the bulger.

Despite the bulger's widespread acceptance, a few makers continued to make long nose clubs during the 1890s and early 1900s. Such clubs were usually made in response to a customer request, the customer usually being of the "old school." In 1899 Alex Patrick of Leven and Lundin Links stated:

I make all the old-fashioned wooden clubs, and still keep a few on stock, but the orders for them are only occasional and the demand is small. A good many of my customers still use the wooden putter (*Golfing*, 12 Jan. 1899: 4).

This chapter is designed to increase the reader's understanding of long nose clubs by presenting a broad cross section of examples. It is not an exhaustive study of every clubmaker who ever made a long nose club.

The clubmakers discussed in this chapter are presented in loose chronological order, from the earliest to the latest. When more than one club from the same maker is presented, the maker's later examples will be grouped with his earliest to observe the evolution of the maker's work.

It should be noted that most early clubmakers did not mark their work, but a fair number of them are documented. In *The Chronicles of Golf: 1457-1857*, Alastair Johnston identifies the following pre-1850 clubmakers not discussed elsewhere in this book: James Pett, circa early 1600s; Andrew Bailey, circa 1735; Henry Miln, died 1755; John and David Clephane, circa 1725-1750; Thomas Comb, David Young, circa late 1700s; Mr. Donaldson, circa 1777-1815; Alexander Neilson, born 1752; Robert Neilson, born 1719 and died 1767; William Ballantyne, circa 1817-1845; David Denham, circa early 1800s; Mr Coburn, circa early 1800s; Archibald Sharpe, circa 1823-1834; Mr. Letter, circa 1830 (Johnston 1993). In *Royal Blackheath*, Henderson and Stirk list Mr. Polk and Mr. Beetson as Blackheath clubmakers in 1823 (Henderson 1981, 62).

"A.D."
ANDREW DICKSON
(1665 – 1753?)
PUTTER

Forth rush'd Castalio, and his daring foe,
Both arm'd with clubs, and eager for
the blow.
Of finest ash Castalio's shaft was made,
Pond'rous with lead, and fac'd with
horn the head.
(The work of Dickson, who in Letha dwells,
And in the art of making clubs excels)
(Mathison 1743, Canto I, lines 37-42).

"I remember," says Mr. Tytler of Woodhouselee, "in my youth to have often conversed with an old man, named Andrew Dickson, a golf club maker, who said, that, when a boy, he used to carry the Duke's golf-clubs, and to run before him and announce where the balls fell" (*Scots Magazine*, May 1792: 223 [also Cundell 1824: 24-25]).

The introductory quotations refer to "Dickson" and "Andrew Dickson" as a maker(s) of golf clubs. Earlier historians have often concluded that Mathison's Dickson was actually Andrew Dickson. And possibly he was. However, recent research has uncovered a John Dickson, born in 1710, who also was a clubmaker in Leith like his father, also named John. Therefore, he must also be considered.

Much uncertainty remains about Andrew Dickson. Accounts agree on 1665 as the year of his birth, but the year of his death has been given as both 1729 and 1753. Some historians identify him only as a ball maker while others say he was a clubmaker. This uncertainty is compounded because "Dickson" is such a common Scottish name, and numerous Dicksons were involved in making clubs and balls during the seventeenth and eighteenth centuries.

A reference to a family of Dicksons is found in the January 31, 1896 issue of *Golf*. An article titled "The Golf-Ball Makers of Leith" discusses an old minute book, "The Craft of Shoemakers in Canongate, Edinburgh," wherein Johnne Dicksonne, William Dicksonne, and Andro Dicksoun are listed as "Gowff ball" makers, in addition to being "shoe-makers," between 1639 and 1649 (440). *The Aberdeen Golfers* contains an account of a complaint filed by William Dickson and Thomas Dickson, golf ball makers in Leith, and heard by the Privey Council of Scotland in 1629 (Smith 1909, 10-11).

Given this background, there is little doubt that the Andrew Dickson referred to in the May 1792 issue of *Scots Magazine* (and possibly in Mathison's *The Goff*) was related to, or directly descended from, the Dickson family listed as golf ball and shoe makers in the 1640s. There is no doubt that he made clubs.

During this distant and unsophisticated time, a ballmaker with an established clientele no doubt received occasional requests for clubs. According to Alastair Johnston, this appears to be the case with the Dickson family:

John Dickson was a clubmaker in Leith who may have been a direct descendant of the Dickson family of ballmakers, active in Leith and Aberdeen in the 1640s. He may also have been related to Andrew Dickson, who purportedly carried the Duke of York's clubs on Leith Links back in the 1680s. The local population records list a John Dickson as a Leith clubmaker who lived from 1678 to 1729 (1993, 169).

Regarding Andrew Dickson as a clubmaker, Dr. J.G. McPherson, a golf historian and frequent contributor to *Golf Illustrated* during its early years, made the following comments (originally printed in *Land and Water*):

McEwan, the club-maker of Bruntsfield links, had shown me a club which Andrew Dickson received from the Duke of York (afterwards King James II.). Andrew was fore caddie to his Highness on the links of Leith, and a great favourite. He excelled in the art of making clubs, being considered better than William Mayne, the club-maker to James I (Golf Illustrated, 7 June 1901: 213).

A club made by Andrew Dickson was displayed at the 1911 Scottish Exhibition of National History, Art, and Industry (held in Glasgow, Scotland) and described as follows:

What is probably the oldest of the Clubs is marked "A.D.," the initials of Andrew Dickson, a club maker, of Leith, who, according to Tytler of Woodhouselee, had acted as forecaddie to the Duke of York . . . . (Scottish 1911, 901).

According to all accounts, Andrew Dickson marked his clubs with his initials. Owing to the nature of initials, however, a club stamped

"A.D." should not automatically be considered one of Dickson's. Because "A.D." could well be owner's initials, the entire club needs to be examined.

As shall be seen from the following evaluation, the putter marked "A.D." pictured on the previous page is attributed to Andrew Dickson. Stamped "A.D."—the initials of the only known clubmaker who marked his clubs with his initials—atop its head, this putter also dates to the time when Andrew Dickson was making clubs.

This club bears three other distinct marks: "James McCaul," "G.I.E. 1901 S74ae," and "J_J_." "James McCaul" is stamped above the "A.D." on the top of the head. At first glance, "James McCaul" might appear to be the maker's name and "A.D." the owner's initials. However, James McCaul was not a clubmaker. Pictured in the Reverend John Kerr's 1896 work *The Golf Book of East Lothian*, McCaul is identified as a member of the Tantallon Club in North Berwick and as one of 120 founding members of the New Luffness Club, established in 1894 (122). McCaul was also listed in the 1909 edition of *Who's Who in Golf* as:

a member of the Edinburgh Burgess Golfing Society, the Scottish Conservative Club (Edinburgh), Tantallon, North Berwick, Burgh, Archerfield, Gullane and New Luffness Golf Clubs.

A well-to-do and avid golfer, McCaul undoubtedly acquired this club, recognized it as "a keeper," and stamped his name on it. It was not uncommon for golfers in McCaul's day to mark their clubs. Also note, the "A.D." stamp has the original finish in its letters and the "James McCaul" stamp, because it was added years later, does not.

The second additional mark found on this club is located on a sticker below the grip. The sticker, handwritten in faded ink, reads, "G.I.E. 1901 S74ae." This is the identification sticker used to mark this club while it was on display at the Glasgow International Exhibition of 1901. The "S74ae" is believed to refer to the particular location within the exhibit where the club was displayed.

The Glasgow International Exhibition of 1901 was an exhibition of things Scottish. The section devoted to Fine Art, Scottish History, and Archaeology also included, for the first time, a display of what many consider to be their favorite of all things Scottish: golf.

The Reverend John Kerr, one of the game's greatest historians and author of the landmark work *The Golf Book of East Lothian*, was charged with assembling historical relics depicting the game. The exhibition catalog lists many different feather balls and early clubs such as the Troon clubs, Philp clubs, Jackson clubs, square toe irons, early irons, and a club it identifies as:

2805. Club by Dickson of Leith 1700, who as a boy carried the Duke of York's clubs on the Leith Links. Lent by D. McEwan & Son (International 1901, 252).

It is doubtful that this putter and the club "lent by D. McEwan" are one and the same. Nevertheless, it is clear that the Glasgow International Exhibition of 1901 was trying to present the earliest artifacts available.

The Dickson putter discussed on these pages was most likely part of a collection of clubs displayed at this exhibition. In the exhibition catalog, several clubs were listed using specific identification (a Philp play club); several were listed using only general identification (a long spoon); and many others were listed only as a group (six early woods).

The total number of clubs displayed, including unshafted heads, approached two hundred. Of the few remaining clubs which have a G.I.E. 1901 sticker on their shafts, most are held by the Royal and Ancient Golf Club of St. Andrews or the organization that lent them.

The third mark, the "J_ J_" stamp, is found on the thick ash shaft just above the G.I.E. sticker. This unique shaft stamp, with a short line after each "J" instead of the period usually used with initials, is unmistakable and unlike any others known . . . except one.

In one of the world's top antique club collections there is a *very* early round toe sand iron with an *identical* "J_ J_" shaft stamp, also on an extremely thick ash shaft. This stamp is significant because it connects two very early clubs: They once belonged to the same owner.

Testifying to the great antiquity of this putter, the shaft is not only extraordinarily thick and made from ash, it has two small knots located midway between the head and the grip. Knots, which actually weaken the shaft, are found primarily in the oldest shafts (see p. 25).

The size of this clubhead indicates great antiquity. This putter is shaped unlike anything made by Peter McEwan, Hugh Philp, John Jackson, Robert Davidson, or anybody else after 1800. In addition, it looks nothing like the clubs made by James McEwan or either of the Cossars (Simon or David) between 1770 and 1800. Dickson's putter is dramatically bigger and much older.

This Dickson putter possesses the broadest, most bulbous head of any known early putter. It measures approximately 5 3/4 inches in length, 2 1/2 inches in width, and 1 1/4 inches in depth. This is substantially thicker and wider than the Cossar putter

(late 1700s-early 1800s) in the James River Golf Club's golf museum in Newport News, Virginia. Their Cossar putter, finished in red keel, measures 5 7/8 inches in length, 2 1/4 inches in width, and 1 1/16 inches in face depth (see p. 549).

It has been stated that clubs made before 1800 always have a red keel finish. This is not correct. When red keel was used, it was used primarily in the second half of the 18th century. The Troon clubs, two woods belonging to the Earl of Wemyss (residing near Musselburgh, Scotland), a late 1600s wood displayed at Royal Musselburgh Golf Club, an early to mid-1700s spoon at Royal Burgess Golf Club, and

two other privately owned unmarked long nose woods from the mid 1700s are all examples of early clubs, still with their original finishes, which are not finished with red keel.

Two other woods relate to this Dickson putter; one has a similar head shape and the other is also marked "AD". The first club is a long spoon belonging to the Royal Blackheath Golf Club. (They describe this club, displayed among their small array of square toe irons, as their earliest wood). Like the Dickson putter, this long spoon has a thick ash shaft and a bulbous head (the broadest of any known long nose) that measures 2 3/4 inches in width. It appears to date from the first half of the 18th century.

The other club, a long spoon which could date prior to 1753, is the only other known long nose club stamped "A.D." Photographs of this club reveal a head shape different (thinner front to back) from the putter pictured here, and its "A.D" stamp is notable for its single dot midway up between the initials. Therefore, this long spoon and the putter marked "A.D." may have been made by different makers—perhaps there was a father/son duo of Andrew Dicksons just as there was a pair of John Dicksons working during this time. However, both clubs do share similarities and are of such great antiquity that either one could have been made by Andrew Dickson.

Quite possibly, he made *both* clubs but at different points in his career or in response to the desires of two different customers. (Just as square toe and round toe irons coexisted, so did bulbous head and thin head woods.) Too little is known to identify the maker of either club absolutely. However, given that these two clubs are the *only* known long nose clubs stamped "A.D." and that both are of such great antiquity, both clubs are duly attributed to the craftsman who marked his clubs "A.D." during the period when these clubs were made.

At this point it should be noted that C.B. Clapcott, an early twentieth century golf historian, once reported that Andrew Dickson was *not* a clubmaker. He proposed this in the December 1934 issue of *Golf Monthly* (Johnston 1985, 397-401). Referring to the "Dickson/Andrew Dickson" quotations by Mathison in *The Goff* and Mr. Tytler in Cundell's *Rules of the Thistle Club*, Clapcott challenges Tytler's reference to Andrew Dickson as a clubmaker by making an unwarranted assumption based on a single word

in *The Goff*. Because Mathison used the present tense "excels" to describe Dickson the clubmaker, Clapcott *assumes* that Dickson must have been in his prime in 1743, when *The Goff* was published. Therefore, Clapcott reasons, Tytler's account of Dickson working as a forecaddie, which would have occurred in 1681 or 1682, must be wrong.

In his account, Tytler recalled having "often conversed" with an old man named Andrew Dickson who made clubs. Dickson told him that as a boy "he used to carry the Duke's golf-clubs, and to run before him and announce where the balls fell." Clapcott surmises that it is impossible to act as a forecaddie while caddying. Therefore, Clapcott reasons, since Mr. Tytler was confused about the caddie business, he must have been confused when calling Dickson a clubmaker. To Mr. Clapcott, basing his assumption on the January 31, 1896 account in *Golf* previously referred to (3rd paragraph on p. 38), Tytler's Andrew Dickson was a ballmaker, not a clubmaker. Then Clapcott, assuming that ballmakers were

never clubmakers, also assumes that because the Duke played a match in 1681/1682 partnered with a Mr. Patersone from the Patersone family of ballmakers, a ballmaker's son would be the logical choice for a caddie . . .

Without even considering the possibility of more than one "Dickson" making clubs in 1743 (it is now known that John Dickson Jr. was doing so), Clapcott tries to discount Dickson as a clubmaker by stacking assumption after assumption on one word in Mathison's *The Golf:* "excels." This term was unfairly taken to signify middle age, as if the ability to craft a worthy club was automatically lost later in life. This author believes "excels" as used by Mathison more accurately refers to established stature, reputation, and known ability—not age. (If Andrew Dickson did not die until 1753, "excels" could easily refer to him in 1743.)

Regarding Clapcott's conclusions that Tytler was an unreliable source and that it was impossible to act as a forecaddie while caddying, this author believes Dickson did indeed carry clubs *and* act as a forecaddie during the same round of golf *exactly* as Mr. Tytler reported.

In golf's earliest days, working as a caddie and a forecaddie at the same time was entirely possible because most early golfers did not hit the ball very far. According to Willie Park Jr., in 1896, when gutta percha balls were used, 175 yards was a first class drive:

An extraordinarily long shot may be made now and again, but experience proves that 200 yards is about the average limit of really long driving; 170 or 180 yards may be considered first-class, and anything over 150 yards is fairly good (Park, 89).

Feather balls did not travel as far as gutta percha balls, nor were the clubs used with feather balls as effective as those used in Park's day. When recalling the change from feather balls to gutta percha balls, H. Thomas Peter stated:

The gutta percha balls, however, have much to do with the lower scoring, the guttas being greatly superior in flying power (1890, 20).

When discussing long nose clubs, Harold Hilton noted that the bulger, in use by 1890, hit the ball consistently farther:

The old-fashioned club was certainly an elegant construction, but it was more elegant than effective. And it was almost impossible to strike with it in the same forceful manner that the

leading players do nowadays with the newer implements (1903, 124).

Judging from the advances in the game by 1896—clubs far better suited to their purpose, a more athletic golf swing, and a superior ball—it is doubtful that the average golfer using feather balls *two hundred years earlier* could drive much beyond 160 yards. W.E. Hughes, in his book *Chronicles of Blackheath Golfers,* drew a similar conclusion:

In this last connection a bet of the 26th June, 1813, acquires additional interest. "Mr. Laing bets that in the course of the season he will drive a ball 500 feet (say 167 yards), he having the chance of ten strokes to accomplish it. Mr. Laing, in 1818, some five years afterwards certainly, won both the medal of the 'Knuckle' Club and the silver club of the Blackheath Golfers, so that he may be taken as above the average of players, and the bet looked upon as some criterion of what was considered at that time a good drive with the old feather ball" (1897, 49).

Given the reduced distance of a golf shot during the feather ball era, there was nothing to prevent a caddie from handing his player a club and then advancing 75 to 100 yards, to the nearest knoll or observation point, for a clear look at the landing area. The game three

hundred years ago was certainly relaxed enough for players to wait forty-five seconds or so for a caddie to walk briskly to a forward vantage point. Personally, if I were a young kid caddying for royalty in the early 1680s, I would have had no problem *running* the short distance necessary to establish myself as a lookout. Come to think of it, *running* is *exactly* what Dickson is described as doing! Mr. Tytler was quoted correctly and his memory was clear.

Clapcott's assumption that ballmakers were never clubmakers was not accurate. No less than Tom Morris is an example of one who primarily made balls and then switched to making clubs. And Morris was taught to make clubs by the famous *ballmaker* Allan Robertson (see p. 62). Furthermore, the Dickson family of ballmakers had two other clubmakers in John Dickson and son, previously mentioned. Surely there could have been others.

Little is known about the individuals who made implements in the earliest periods of golf's history. So, with great respect for C.B. Clapcott as a golf historian, this author disagrees with his dismissal of Tytler's account in *The Rules of the Thistle Club,* but does agree with his 1946 commentary on *The Goff.* In examining the passage describing Castalio's club as "The work of Dickson," Mr. Clapcott, having his own change of heart, states, "That the club was the work of 'Dickson who in Letha dwells' shows that it was made by the master craftsman of that time" (Johnston 1985, 443).

The Dickson putter is flanked on its left by a circa 1835 Jackson putter and on its right by a circa 1860 Wilson putter. The huge size of the Dickson putter indicates that it was made long before either of the other two clubs.

In 1790 the names given to the different types of long nose clubs were:

the Common Club, used when the Ball lies on good Ground; the Scraper and Half Scraper, when in long Grass; the Spoon, when in a Hollow (Hoyle 1790, 288).

Dating back to approximately 1750, this "scraper" is quite heavy (being loaded with lead) and has a fair amount of loft—good characteristics against high grass.

This club has other distinctive characteristics. To begin with, a semicircular, block letter stamp was used to mark a name on the top of the head, toward the toe. A small mark of triangular design was stamped above and below the name. Unfortunately, the lettering is now too faint to be completely readable, but it was undoubtedly the maker's mark or that of the owner. Knowing, however, that at least one club from the 1700s is marked with lettering in a semicircular pattern is of significant interest because no others are currently known.

The lead protruding from the back of the head, and the three lead plugs visible on the sole, are also significant characteristics. Playing on unrefined courses, early golfers often encountered long grass and needed a heavy club to swing through it, hence the large amount of lead.

Only very early woods have a protruding lead backweight, but such a backweight need not be present for a wood to date before 1800.

The head measures 6 inches long, 2 1/8 inches wide, and 1 1/16 inches in face depth. The length of the club is 43 inches, the same length as many nineteenth century play clubs.

The shaft appears to be made from white hickory. Hickory shafts dating from the 1700s are more common than was believed by early twentieth century golf historians, some of whom calculated that hickory shafts came into use toward the middle of the nineteenth century. Although hickory was not routinely used as a shaft material in the 1700s, a small but significant number of eighteenth century clubs have original hickory shafts.

Listing grips, such as this club has, are often found on *very* old clubs. However, the way this listing grip is fastened in place is highly unusual. At the bottom of the grip the listing is wrapped over twice; then it spirals up the shaft where it wraps two or three times around the top of the shaft, the final wrap being *sewed* closed. On such an old club, nails are normally used to tack the ends of a listing grip in place.

The following aspects of this club, when considered together, help set it apart from anything made in the 1800s: The head is well hooked with most of the loft towards the heel of the face. The butt of the shaft is cut straight across and its edge left unbeveled. The top of the head near the lead backweight rounds down to meet it. The lead protrudes well beyond the back of the head. The head is exceptionally long and has a graceful bend at the neck. The original whipping is thick twine. This club has a listing grip and it is *sewed* closed at the upper end. The faint lettering on the head is curved.

TOP LEFT: *The sole of this mid-1700s "scraper" (long spoon) has three circular lead plugs or "buttons." They helped weight this head for use in long grass.*

RIGHT: *This view shows the 1 1/8 inch deep face. Note the distinctly early twine whipping used on the neck.*

CENTER: *The listing grip is characteristic of clubs from the 1700s and earlier. Note that the final wrap is sewed shut. Also note that the end of the shaft is cut straight across and left unbeveled around its edge. Such traits are often found in the clubs from the 1700s and earlier.*

BOTTOM: *The top of the head has very faint lettering high on the toe. As is evident from the faint lettering, the finish on this club is not the original finish. Note that the lead backweight protrudes behind the head. This is a characteristic commonly found in pre-1800 woods. On the top of the head, knots are visible in the light area of the wood. The wood is so dense (hard) in that area that it is unable to absorb stain.*

UNKNOWN MAKER
"P.G." SHORT SPOON

The short spoon pictured has a broad, lofted clubhead and measures only 37 inches in overall length. In addition to the normal duties of a short spoon—to provide a well-lofted shot when approaching the green or immediate area of the hole—this club could also serve as an approach putter when a short chip was needed.

The distinctly bulbous head measures 2 1/4 inches in width, 5 3/4 inches in length, and 1 1/8 inches in face depth. The face is hooked and lofted. The "P.G." initials in the head are probably those of the owner.

During the 1700s, just as irons could have either a round toe or a square toe, long nose woods could be either long and sleek or big and bulbous. These differences probably coincided with the golfer's preferences for his particular course or game. This baffy spoon appears to date to the early 1800s.

These pictures show the grace and style of an early long nose short spoon. This example is in lovely original condition, the underlying golden finish still visible through the layer of grime and darkened shellac which covers the head.

It is best to let such nice old clubs keep their original patina and look like nice old clubs. Occasionally a bit of restoration work or a small amount of touching up will benefit a club. However, any restoration work should be done only by someone with previous experience or under their guidance. The grime on this clubhead can be cleaned off, but it is not doing any harm. It maintains a prized quality in any club: untouched original condition.

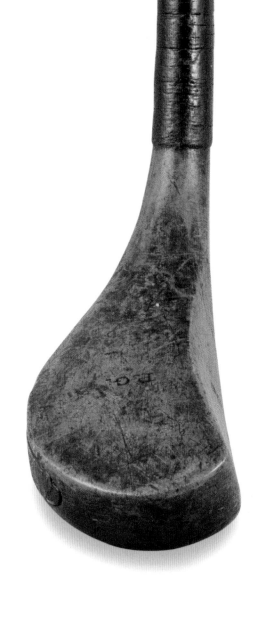

McEWAN

JAMES (1747-1800)

PETER (1781-1836)

son of James

DOUGLAS (1809-1886)

son of Peter

PETER (1834-1895)

son of Douglas

DOUGLAS (1869-1921)

son of Peter

MIDDLE SPOON

PRESENTATION PUTTER

PUTTER

BAFFING SPOON

PLAY CLUB

As Hugh Philp was to St. Andrews, so was the firm of McEwan and Son to Edinburgh and Musselburgh (Golf, 27 Sep. 1895: 51).

The name "McEwan" identifies more than a long nose club—it belongs to the most famous family of early clubmakers. Established in 1770 by James McEwan, the McEwan clubmaking business was passed down from father to son for well over a century. And they knew their craft—McEwan clubs were always well-known for their fine quality:

[In 1770] James left Stirling and settled in Edinburgh as a club maker, since that time the name "McEwan" on a club has been recognized as the hallmark of excellence (Golf Illustrated, 16 Nov. 1900: 139).

According to an article published in 1896 about the McEwan family, James McEwan stamped a thistle, the emblem of Scotland, into the top of the clubhead above "J. McEwan." When Peter McEwan took over the business following the death of James in 1800, the "J." was literally struck from the "J. McEwan" stamp (*Golf*, 9 Oct.: 74-75). Today, these statements about James McEwan and his stamps appear to be only partially true.

Currently, only three McEwan clubs bearing the "thistle" stamp are known. They were made by James McEwan, as demonstrated by the thistle stamp and pre-1800 characteristics found in each head, but they are marked "McEwan," not "J. McEwan." Furthermore, three additional McEwan clubs resemble those that are thistle-stamped. Apparently James did not stamp all his clubs with the thistle or with "J. McEwan."

Peter McEwan, a sixth generation descendant from James McEwan, once stated, "The same stamp was used for about 120 years. . . . I still have it in my possession" (*Golf Illustrated*, 4 Feb. 1960). Peter's "120 years," however, did not begin in 1770, when James began business. The vast majority of McEwan clubs are stamped identically—using only one stamp or one style of stamp—but the *earliest* known McEwan clubs (the thistle-stamped McEwans, the pictured blond McEwan, and three others), bear a slightly different stamp: the letters are closer together and the "c" is not underlined. Consequently, there are at least two, and possibly four, different types

LEFT: *This circa 1800 McEwan clubhead measures 1 1/8 inches deep, 6 inches long, and 2 5/16 inches wide. The original whipping appears to be pitched string. The shaft, which measures 42 inches long, is not symmetrical. Grasping the shaft in one hand while turning the shaft with the other hand will reveal various flat spots. The original golden blond finish shows minimal wear. This club, dating from the early 1800s or possibly the late 1700s, is an outstanding middle spoon in every regard.*

BELOW: *A prominent knot is visible in the face of the McEwan middle spoon. This knot adds to the desirability of this club because a knot is a characteristic found in early clubs. As the game of golf became more popular and the number of makers grew, so did the criteria for acceptable clubs. As the 1800s progressed, clubmakers were more inclined to use clear wood and avoid knots.*

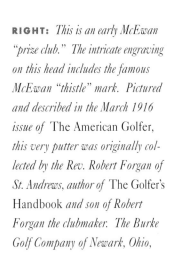

RIGHT: *This is an early McEwan "prize club." The intricate engraving on this head includes the famous McEwan "thistle" mark. Pictured and described in the March 1916 issue of* The American Golfer, *this very putter was originally collected by the Rev. Robert Forgan of St. Andrews, author of* The Golfer's Handbook *and son of Robert Forgan the clubmaker. The Burke Golf Company of Newark, Ohio,* knew of Mr. Forgan's collection and asked to borrow his display of eleven antique clubs to add to their own display at a San Francisco exhibition. Rather than lend the clubs, Rev. Forgan preferred to sell them. The purchase was made, and the clubs helped the Burke Golf Company win a blue ribbon at the exhibition. In addition, the article describes this club as the "Engraved Swan Putter, 1800" (356). This club has been repaired.*

of McEwan name stamps. The first three stamps in the following list would be the oldest:

The "J. McEwan" stamp. No example known.

The "McEwan" stamp with most of the "J." removed (just enough metal remains to provide a small dent in front of "McEwan" when stamped into the head). Possibly one example is known. (It is difficult to determine if such a small dent was caused by a maker's stamp or by normal wear.)

The "McEwan" stamp with its letters close together and a plain (not underlined) "c." This is the McEwan stamp found on the earliest known McEwan clubs. The letters on this stamp are not only closer together than those in the following stamp, they are also slightly *different*.

The "McEwan" stamp with the underlined "c." This was the stamp referred to by Peter McEwan in 1960. It was apparently used from the early 1800s onward. (No less than two slightly different stamps of this type were actually used, one having a little more space between the letters than the other.)

The McEwan presentation putter/prize club pictured and discussed on this and the facing page has an interesting past. As pictured in the March 1916 issue of *The American Golfer*, this club had a band of some type around its head, down toward the heel, and for a good reason: The head was broken. When the present owner acquired the club it had pieces missing from that area. To make the club presentable, restoration work was necessary. However, this is a small price to pay for preserving such a singular item. Of course, a perfect example of this club in original condition would be best, but it is doubtful that an identical club was ever made.

Only one other known McEwan club is so artistically carved. Engraved with crossed clubs, the word "Far," the name "McEwan," two golf balls, and additional scrolling, this club (a circa 1840 play club) does not include the McEwan thistle.

Both engraved McEwan woods were probably "prize clubs" awarded to the winners of two different competitions. Sometimes entire sets of (unengraved) woods were awarded as prizes for a competition (see Smith 1867, 11). Presentation clubs, made as perpetual awards for annual competitions, were usually crafted in sterling silver. Most of the existing ones are displayed in the clubhouses of old English and Scottish clubs.

The face repair on this McEwan putter, as shown above, is clearly evident. The horn was repaired directly below the face repair. Serious repairs are never good news. However, the great age and rich history of the club required that it be rescued. Prior to being restored, this club was broken and missing a few pieces of wood.

Prompted by the death of Peter McEwan in September of 1895, *The Golfer* printed a brief historical sketch of the McEwan family. In part, it reads as follows:

James McEwan came from Stirling to Edinburgh, and his Burgess Ticket of this city describes him as a golf-club-maker at Bruntsfield Links. He was succeeded in business by his son Peter, born 1781, who supplied clubs to all the then golfing places— Aberdeen, Montrose, Perth, and Blackheath, and had also, as agent at St. Andrews, Davie Robertson, father of the famous Allan. This certainly carries us many decades back in the history of golf. In 1802 Peter took as wife a daughter of the golf-ball maker, Douglas Gourlay, who began business at Bruntsfield Links in 1780. In 1836, on the death of Peter McEwan, his son Douglas, a noted clubmaker, took the helm, and eleven years later opened a branch at Musselburgh, which thrived so well that before many years it became the headquarters of the firm. Douglas, when age began to tell upon him, returned to the Bruntsfield place of business, and left his son, whose death has so suddenly come to pass, in charge at Musselburgh. This was in 1865, and Peter, who at that time was in his thirty-second year, had begun work as a clubmaker in 1846, so that he was within a year of completing half a century's work in the business. Some three years ago the veteran club-maker opened a branch of his establishment in connection with the Formby Club at Freshfield, Lancashire, and personally took up the superintendence, being accompanied by three of his sons, and leaving his son Douglas at the head of affairs at Musselburgh (20 Sept. 1895: 203).

The circa 1840s McEwan putter pictured above has a head 5 5/8 inches long, 1 7/8 inches wide, and 1 inch deep. The 1 inch face depth is typical of clubs made during the last twenty years of the feather ball era, as are the long head and slender neck. This putter measures 34 1/2 inches in length.

Two circular holes filled with lead are found on the sole of this club. These lead plugs naturally make the head heavier, but such plugs were sometimes used to keep the lead backweight from falling out. By drilling a hole or two into the bottom of the head, the clubmaker could pour molten lead into the back cavity and have the lead literally turn a corner (flow to the sole) inside the head. After it cooled, the lead would be secured to the head.

This little-used circa 1850 baffing spoon has many prime characteristics: fine original condition, a graceful head shape, plenty of style, and few comparables. It also has a minimal crack that begins at the back-weight cavity and extends just onto the top of the head. This sort of incidental cracking, which probably occurred when the clubmaker poured in the hot lead, is a minor blemish. Not only is it small, it attracts very little attention. The head measures 5 3/4 inches in length, 2 1/8 inches in width, and 1 1/8 inches in face depth. The overall length of the club is 37 inches.

The term "cutty" was explained as follows:

Turning to the Burns glossary in Allen Cunningham's edition, 1834, we find the following definition; —"Cutty short, used of a spoon broken in the middle." The expression "a cutty spoon," was therefore probably quite a common one in the earlier part of last century and the "baffy," or perhaps both the "baffy" and the ordinary "short spoon" quite naturally received this appellation (Golf, 1 Mar. 1901: 185).

Besides having the shortest shaft in the spoon family, baffing spoons were often just a little wider and thicker through the head to accommodate the added loft.

In 1857 Henry B. Farnie described the baffing spoon:

Why it is called by either this sobriquet, or by its other title "the cutty," we leave speculative readers to determine; although its more common appellation, "baffing," is most probably descriptive of the thump produced in making the stroke. It is employed only for skying a ball over a hazard on to the putting green, when the stroke is too short for any of the other spoons (Farnie, 19).

This circa 1860-65 McEwan play club consists of an unused head (5 3/4 inches long, 1 7/8 inches wide, and 1 inch deep) attached to a 45-inch greenheart "fishing rod" shaft. A fishing rod shaft is exceptionally long and slender, like a fishing rod, and sometimes has a thick wood grip shaped like its fishing rod counterpart.

This wood grip has a metal collar at its base and a brass end cap stamped "Anderson & Son, Princess St., Edinburgh, Patent 1892." In addition to producing and selling golf clubs, R. Anderson & Sons was primarily a "Fishing-tackle Manufacturer and General Sports Warehouse" as advertised in the back of Charles Chambers's 1887 book, *Golfing*. This club is believed to be a salesman's sample assembled by Anderson & Sons. Using a handsome long nose clubhead to display this beautiful shaft is certainly understandable.

The lower portion of the whipping is replaced. (It is best to retain as much of the original whipping as possible and apply replacement whipping where the original whipping is missing.)

Because this club has such an exquisite head and shaft combination, its value exceeds even that imparted by its impressive long nose qualities. The unused condition of this club also adds a premium to its collectibility.

Although attractive, the exceptionally thin shaft did not prove durable nor was its enhanced flexibility beneficial. Having a golfer grip a thick, round piece of bare wood proved impractical. Consequently, few fishing rod shafts remain. The author knows of only four others identical to this one, two of which are on display at the British Golf Museum in St. Andrews, Scotland.

In the early 1900s, A.G. Spalding & Bros. briefly marketed their own fishing rod drivers in Great Britain. These clubs are "three to four inches longer than ordinary drivers, but they lie flatter and are lighter in the head" (*Golfing*, 5 Nov. 1903: 38). Spalding did not promote a special grip.

UNKNOWN MAKER
PUTTER, LEFT-HANDED

Clubmakers, as a rule, are not fond of making left-hand clubs. It reverses, so to speak, their whole method of procedure in the making of clubs, and consequently entails a good deal of painstaking labour (Golf, 3 Oct. 1890: 39).

Left-handed long nose clubs *were* made, but not many. This particular example was crafted before feather ball clubs became thin and refined. Measuring 5 3/8 inches in length, 1 7/8 inches in width, and 1 1/16 inches in face depth, this head has the bulk indicative of earlier, unrefined examples. Its teardrop shape (with the head broader near the toe), the thick and wide ram's horn, the heavy twine whipping, the asymmetrical shaft, and the knots in the wood all help date this club to approximately 1825.

Some collectors, to their disadvantage, will ignore a club if it is not stamped with a name. By failing to consider the qualities of the club itself, such collectors risk missing some truly historic clubs. They do not realize that most early clubs are unmarked.

The farther back in time you look, the fewer clubmakers there were who marked their work. Understanding this, do not summarily dismiss or pass over an unmarked long nose club. Consider what the club actually is and what period of time it represents. Do not become fixated on name recognition. Any pre-1850 club, marked or unmarked, is a prime collectible if in good condition. Such clubs are very historic and difficult to acquire.

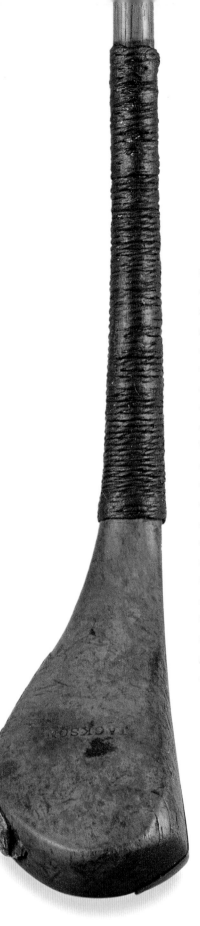

JOHN JACKSON
(1805-1878)
PUTTER &
BAFFING SPOON

To Johnny Jackson...belongs the honour of reviving golf club and feather ball making in Perth within the present [nineteenth] century. For many years previous to 1824 the trade seems to have been extinct in Perth, and clubs and balls were got from Edinburgh and St. Andrews. The formation of the Royal Perth Club was the means of Jackson setting up business. Johnny, who was a native of Perth, and a nephew to George Penny, the author of "Traditions of Perth," soon proved himself to be a workman of ability, and in a short time the apple-heads issued from Princes Street were known far and wide. The material and workmanship of the clubs turned out by Jackson were such that many of the clubs are in existence at the present day, and still doing duty with older players, notwithstanding their elongated heads (Baxter, 1899, 32).

When only twenty years old, Jackson was employed by the Perth Golfing Society:

Jackson had originally been retained as the Officer of the Club in 1825, a role which required him to attend to a myriad of its affairs. He proved himself to be a craftsman of ability, and he gravitated naturally to his function as a clubmaker. His workmanship, as well as the quality material that he insisted on using, earned his clubs the respect that heretofore had been reserved for the legendary Hugh Philp or the McEwans (Johnston 1983, 527).

John Jackson's clubs possess all the traits of a master at his craft: style, grace, and quality workmanship. Although Jackson was making clubs during the same period as Hugh Philp and Douglas McEwan, very few of his clubs remain compared to the number of known McEwan and Philp clubs.

The putter pictured on this page dates from approximately 1835-1840 and has a head 5 3/8 inches in length, 1 15/16 inches in width, and 1 inch in face depth. The original golden blond head has seen better days, as indicated by the thin cracks on the face and the wear on the toe. Also, the whipping is not original. Although this club shows evidence of its age, a graceful and present-able head remains. Considering the overall desirability and rarity of Jackson's clubs, this one is still a fine example. For a collector to settle only for a nearly unused Jackson is practically to guarantee never owning one at all.

Notice the distinct hook to the clubface. Older putters were normally made with slightly curved faces. Sometimes the owner of the club would file the face flat. This type of alteration downgrades a club's collectibility. (See page 39 for a picture of the sole of this club.)

The prime Jackson baffing spoon shown here approaches the pinnacle of elegance in a golf club. The head is long and graceful. The face is beautifully curved. All the angles and lines of the head's shape appear to flow. The original finish is untouched. There is no damage to the head anywhere. The whipping is not original, but this is easily excused. To reject such a masterpiece because it lacks its original whipping would be like refusing to play Augusta National Golf Club because a little casual water was on the course.

This circa 1830-35 baffing spoon is an early example of Jackson's work. The head measures 6 inches long, 2 1/4 inches wide, and 1 3/32 inches in face depth. The overall length of the club is 37 inches.

In addition to making clubs during the second quarter of the nineteenth century, Jackson made clubs well into the gutty ball era. According to the most expert collectors, a presentation set of nine Jackson clubs that sold at auction in 1987 were from approximately 1860. The Rev. T.D. Miller reported that Jackson was "still going strong" in 1864 when he relocated his business to "a wooden shop on Athole Street . . . and later to the top of North Methven Street" (1935, 57). Jackson continued making clubs into the 1870s.

Because Jackson made clubs in the feather ball era as well as the gutty ball era, some of his clubs command more attention than others. The ultimate Jackson clubs are the elegant, refined ones of the feather ball era. However, since examples of John Jackson's work are so rare and desirable, any Jackson club is well worth owning if the condition is at all reasonable.

HUGH PHILP

(1782-1856)
LONG SPOON
LONG SPOON
MIDDLE SPOON
"LAIDLAY" PUTTER

This genius made such beautiful and perfect wooden putters that he has come to be regarded as the Amati or Stradivarius of Golf, and a genuine "Philp" today is worth untold gold. The long narrow faces of these clubs and their perfect balance are well known to connoisseurs (Golf Illustrated, 5 Oct. 1900: 12).

It was Hugh Philp who first departed from the primitive models of the stone age and began to make golf clubs that looked as though they were intended for some gentler work than the crushing in of an enemy's skull or the manufacture of broken flint for road-building. Philp had an eye for graceful lines and curves, and his slim, elegant models remain to-day things of beauty . . . . Moreover, as any fine crusted golfer will tell you, Philp was the only man who ever knew how to make a perfectly balanced wooden putter. The few specimens that still exist are acknowledged "old masters," and are only to be exchanged against much fine gold (Harper's Weekly, 2 Oct. 1897: 986).

Ever since his death in 1856, Hugh Philp has been universally recognized as clubmaking's finest artisan. His clubs have been copied and even forged, complete with his name. Philp's clubs were collectible 100 years ago. During the 1890s, a few people actually advertised in *Golf*, a weekly periodical, offering to purchase his work at prices well above the cost of any new club. His craftsmanship was often compared to that of legendary and fabled violin maker Antonio Stradivari. Even a few aluminum head putters made in the early 1900s were modeled after Philp's designs.

Philp was more than a talented clubmaker. His reputation for being meticulous was legend:

Philp, in the olden times, was in the wont of spending half a day agreeably putting the finishing touches to a club after it had been handed over by his workmen as completed (*The Golfer*, 3 Nov. 1894: 184).

Today, Hugh Philp's legacy continues unabated. He is considered the *premier* long nose clubmaker. He set the standard by which the work of other clubmakers is measured. Decent examples of his clubs are cherished.

The 42-inch long spoon pictured on the facing page measures 5 3/4 inches in head length, 1 7/8 inches in width, and 1 inch in face depth. Formerly owned by the Arbroath Golf Club, in Arbroath, Scotland, this nearly unused example was displayed in their clubhouse for years before being sold, to raise funds, in the early 1980s.

Because Hugh Philp's clubs have been highly sought after ever since his death, many examples remain. Approximately 190 are known. The opportunity to obtain a nice Philp is, in many ways, rarer than the club itself. Many examples are held by golf organizations ranging from the R&A and the USGA to such venerable clubs as The Honorable Company of Edinburgh Golfers (Muirfield) in Scotland and the Los Angeles

Country Club. The remaining examples are primarily in the hands of serious collectors. Therefore, a Philp in nice condition rarely becomes available.

The 42-inch Philp long spoon pictured on this page is one of only five known examples marked "H. Philp" in *script*. Robert Davidson routinely stamped his clubs in script, and Tom Hood stamped a large percentage of his clubs in script, but Philp stamped only a few of his clubs that way. It is thought that Philp used his script stamp to identify either his personal clubs or the presentation clubs he made for a particular person or occasion. This particular script-stamped clubhead measures 5 1/2 inches long, 2 inches wide, and 1 inch in face depth.

A leather face insert, as found in this Philp, was usually installed to improve a club's durability or to repair damage. With the advent of the gutty ball, leather inserts were used more and more because the hardness of the gutty ball caused greater wear and tear to the clubhead. (In the feather ball era, the ball was more inclined to break or suffer damage than the club.) Even though it is not something collectors specifically seek in a club, a leather insert will not keep an otherwise nice collectible club from being desirable so long as the insert is old, attractive, and well done. The craftsmanship required to install the insert, as well as the use of the insert itself, is of historical merit.

In 1899 a letter requesting information about Hugh Philp was sent to the editor of *Golf*. The response came from the hand of none other than Robert Forgan, the successor to Philp's business and one of Philp's two former assistants. (In addition, Robert Forgan was related to Hugh Philp through Forgan's marriage to the daughter of James Berwick, Philp's brother-in-law.) Forgan's letter reads in part as follows:

Hugh Philp died April 6, 1856, in his seventy-fourth year. He served no apprenticeship to club-making, but was bred to the trade of joiner and house carpenter. He carried on that business in Argyle Street, St. Andrews; and as there were no club makers in St. Andrews at that time, the golfers began to take their clubs to him to be repaired; and after a time they got him to come down to the links where he had a shop where the Grand Hotel is now built. That would be somewhere between 1820 and 1825 [during September of 1819 Philp was appointed official clubmaker to the Society of Golfers at St. Andrews]. Some few years after that he bought the property now occupied by Tom Morris, where he died in 1856. I don't know where he was born, nor how long he made clubs, but I have heard him say that he made them for over fifty years. I was his assistant when he died—his former assistant having left him in 1852 and opened a club maker's shop on the ground where the Marine Hotel is now built. His name was James Wilson, and was twenty-three years Mr. Philp's assistant. [Andrew Strath was also an apprentice to Philp (Tulloch 1908, 22).] I was four years Mr. Philp's assistant, and I succeeded to the business which is now carried on under the name of R. Forgan and Son (Golf, 3 Feb. 1899: 412).

A few putters stamped both "Forgan" and "Philp" are known. In the past, these clubs were believed to signify the result of a business partnership during Philp's lifetime. This is not correct. These clubs were made by Robert Forgan & Son years after Philp's death, out of respect for the inheritance of Philp's business and the continued popularity of Philp's clubs, especially his putters. It was also good business for Forgan to remain linked to Philp. Philp/Forgan putters were produced briefly during the 1890s as indicated by their fork splice and awkward head shape which does not begin to resemble anything made by the master himself. Also, the "H. Philp" lettering stamped on those clubs is unlike anything found on a genuine Philp.

Although recently reshafted and rewhipped, the circa 1850 Philp clubhead on this page is a solid example. Its lines are graceful and elegant, and Philp's original finish remains untouched.

A wonderful article recalling Hugh Philp, originally cited as from "*Chambers Journal*, 1859," was reprinted in 1899. Titled "Hugh Philp The Master," it provides an illuminating glimpse into his daily life. It reads in part:

Could the past be re-lived, you might enter Hugh's shop with me; as it is, do so in fancy. It is not a very commodious habitation, being a small square box erected on the convenient brink of the course at the commencement of the links. Round the walls are ranged boxes filled with finished clubs for the golfer to choose from; piles of embryo handles and heads, and quantities of doubtful material, yet undeveloped, strew the ground; overhead are horizontal racks of clubs belonging to some of Hugh's customers, who claim a kind of prescriptive right to keep their sets in his shop; and in one corner is Hugh's own particular bench. The shop is evidently a place where golfers of all descriptions . . . congregate; caddies waiting engagements, gentlemen players smoking their pipes, chatting with Hugh, or selecting their clubs. Hugh himself is polishing and stamping his name on some clubheads. For many and many a year to come these letters which he is branding on the clubs will serve for Hugh's best epitaph, and golfers yet to be will sigh for the 'touch of that vanished hand' which fashioned so deftly and so well. He is clad in his invariable snuff-colored garb, and his silver-rimmed spectacles are pushed upward on his brow. His keen black eye is glittering with the fun of some golfing story he has been relating to a group of players. Hugh had plenty of these tales, and told them with a dry comicality which was irresistible. But you should have seen Hugh play a match. As a rule, he did not much care about leaving his shop to play regular matches with gentlemen golfers, but occasionally took a round when the chances were a little in his favour. Hugh thoroughly understood both the etiquette and saving policy of the game, and never if possible took his match before the burn hole, which left only one hole more to play. He could, therefore, with every degree of plausibility, solace his beaten opponent with the idea that it was a very, very close match—indeed, that there was no saying how the next might go. . . . (Golfing, 16 Nov.: 24).

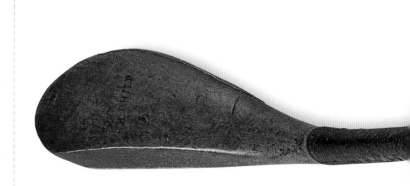

The exquisite Philp putter pictured here was once part of an unused set of nine Philp clubs presented by Sir Hew Dalrymple, Bart., of Luchie, to John E. Laidlay, a two-time British Amateur Champion and runner-up in the 1893 British Open. Recognized as a one of a kind, Laidlay's set of nine Philps was displayed, at the request of the Reverend John Kerr, at the Glasgow International Exhibition of 1901.

It was also at Reverend Kerr's suggestion that the archaeology committee of the Glasgow International Exhibition included an exhibit on golf. In return, the committee put Kerr in charge of preparing the display. The Glasgow International Exhibition of 1901 opened in May and ran for six months. To allay the fears of lenders, their golf treasures were housed in an isolated, fireproof structure, lighted throughout by electricity and guarded day and night. (Upon completion of the exhibition, the structure was to remain as a permanent art gallery and museum.) Within this grand building the "Laidlay" Philp clubs were displayed in their own special case. It was recognized, even then, that Laidlay's Philps were of greater significance than the normal relic. (For more on the G.I.E. of 1901, see p. 38-39)

In 1981 John Laidlay's set of Philp clubs was broken up—each club was sold individually at a Sotheby's golf auction in London, England. The certificate the Glasgow International Exhibition presented to Laidlay for lending his clubs was auctioned as the lot following the last of the nine Philps.

It is believed that Laidlay's Philps were crafted in the early 1850s with the aid of Philp's assistant, Robert Forgan. Such nine club sets were known to be awarded as "prize clubs" to the winner of a competition (see Smith 1867, 11 & 18). Although this putter has never been used, the lead in the back of the head has shifted slightly. This is not an unusual phenomenon and can occasionally be found in other clubs (see page 141). The head on this Philp putter measures 5 3/4 inches long, 2 1/8 inches wide, and only 15/16 of an inch in face depth.

J. JAMESON
PUTTER

Just as there are unmarked clubs made by unknown makers, there are clubs marked with the names of makers unknown to the collecting world. This Jameson putter is one such club. Given more time and research, there is a strong chance that a reference to this maker will be located. Until that time, this putter should be judged on its own merits.

The head, measuring 5 3/4 inches in length, 2 1/16 inches in width, and 15/16 of an inch in face depth, is shallow and broad. The crown is relatively flat. The lead weight wraps well around the back of the head. There is a rather large circular lead weight in the sole. The shaft, having an asymmetrical shape, was obviously split and worked down by hand. The head itself is made from an uncommon wood. These characteristics, along with the general shape of the head, combine to date this club to the second quarter of the nineteenth century.

Note, however, that during the 1880s some long nose clubs were made and marked by various obscure clubmakers. Mere rarity of a particular unfamiliar name does not make such a club more collectible. Circa 1880 long nose clubs with an unheard-of name often lack the stylish clubhead shape of those produced by earlier makers, and the period they depict—the end of the long nose era—is the one to which most remaining long nose clubs date. Because the Jameson has a graceful head shape from the feather ball era, it is highly collectible with or without a name. Also, since it is the only example known, it could become even more desirable should Jameson's place in history become known.

While Mr. Innes gave in to no man in his enthusiasm for the game of Golf, he was very fond of deer stalking. On one occasion, when he was so fascinated by the healthy Highland sport that he left the links for a time, young Tom Morris, his partner in many a struggle, could not help remarking: "I can not understand Mr. Innes, when he's playing as fine a game as any mortal man ever played, leavin' gowf to rin efter a wheen stinkin' beasts, and then coming back no able to het a ba' (Golf Illustrated, 9 Nov. 1900: 119).

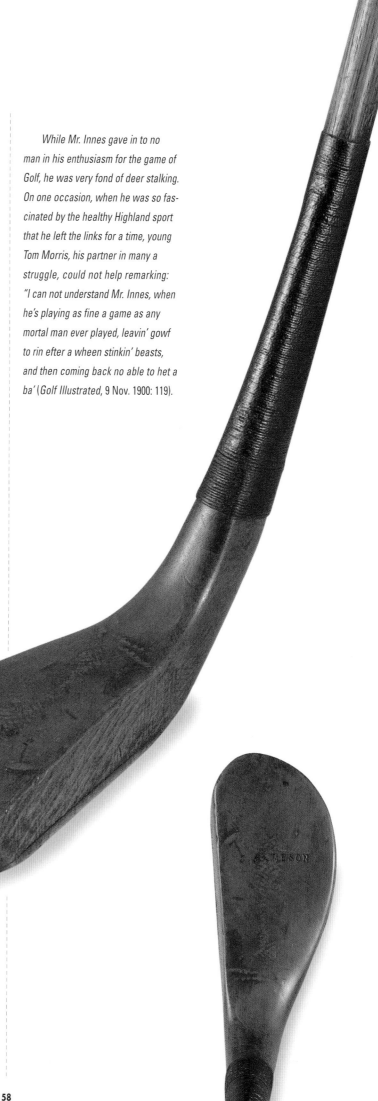

UNKNOWN MAKER

"W.S." MIDDLE SPOON

In spite of a little damage, the middle spoon pictured has character. The head, which measures 5 1/2 inches long, 1 7/8 inches wide, and 1 inch deep, is stylish. The ash shaft, measuring 40 1/2 inches, is a wonderful feature usually found on early long nose clubs, but the hard finish of the leather grip is an early characteristic rarely found on a long nose club. The one-inch face, the ash shaft, the hard-finished leather grip, the fruitwood head, the graceful head shape, and the thin neck indicate that this club was made around the 1830s-1840s.

The head, stamped "W S", is marked with the initials of a former owner. The lack of a maker's name does not identify this club as incomplete or insignificant. Rather, long nose clubs without names often date to the feather ball era when advertising the maker's name was not important.

The damage to the face of this club (a few bits of wood are missing and a small amount of fill remains) is an important factor to consider. Generally speaking, substantial face damage is a major flaw. Because this club was made during the feather ball (pre-1850) period, the most difficult era from which to collect, its flaws are easier to accept.

In the club pictured, the damage is not too prominent. Therefore, the head still provides a good representation of an early middle spoon.

FRANK BELL
PLAY CLUB

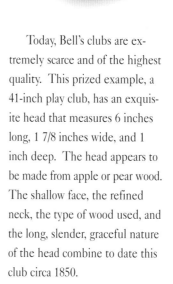

In February of 1870, towards the end of his career, Frank Bell was appointed professional and greenkeeper to the Dalhousie Golf Club in Carnoustie, Scotland, his wife taking the position of "housekeeper" at the same time:

All went well for a time, although Bell was censured for keeping a pig and allowing his dog to "run about the grounds." Bell's greenkeeping, however, was constantly criticised, and in 1874 this part of his duty was taken from him, and he was retained as clubkeeper at a reduced wage (Chapman 1968, 16).

He may not have been much of a greenkeeper, but Bell was an outstanding clubmaker:

Although ultimately sent away in disgrace after a number of domestic disagreements, [Bell] was recognised to be a craftsman of superior ability. . . . At Carnoustie he carried out his club-making in a small wooden building in front of the clubhouse . . . . Bell's place was taken in 1876 by David Mitchell, from St. Andrews (Hackney 1988, 88).

Today, Bell's clubs are extremely scarce and of the highest quality. This prized example, a 41-inch play club, has an exquisite head that measures 6 inches long, 1 7/8 inches wide, and 1 inch deep. The head appears to be made from apple or pear wood. The shallow face, the refined neck, the type of wood used, and the long, slender, graceful nature of the head combine to date this club circa 1850.

A knot in the sole, partially covered by the horn, is an excellent characteristic. It is indicative of an early club—made before a knot was considered a blemish. Also, the original golden orange finish of this head is impressive. Nice long nose woods originally finished in a color other than black or black-brown, the dominant colors used between approximately 1860 and 1890, draw an added degree of interest.

JAMES WILSON
(1803-?)
PUTTER

James Wilson learned club-making from the illustrious Hugh Philp. According to Robert Forgan, Wilson was Philp's assistant for twenty-three years (*Golf*, 3 Feb. 1899: 412; see also p. 69). Forgan, the successor to Philp's business, recalled that, in 1852, Wilson left Philp's employment "and opened a club maker's shop on the ground where the Marine Hotel is now built."

After Philp died, James Wilson and Robert Forgan, each operating his own business, became friendly rivals in the golfing mecca of St. Andrews:

They bought their wood conjointly, separated it into two lots in front of their shops and then drew lots as to which one or the other was to have (*Golf Illustrated*, 15 Mar. 1901: 239).

As his business grew, Wilson hired Andrew Strath to be his assistant (*The Golfer*, 11 Nov. 1896: 391). Today, clubs bearing Wilson's name are few and far between, but the known examples demonstrate that Wilson was a craftsman of the first order.

Wilson's clubs, dating after 1852, were made at the beginning of the gutty ball era. The stylistic changes employed to accommodate the increased hardness of the gutty ball, such as the thickening of the neck and deepening of the face, prevent gutty ball clubs from equaling the style and grace of the more attractive feather ball clubs. Nevertheless, a club by Wilson is very significant and highly desirable. In addition to working many years for Hugh Philp, Wilson himself was a brilliant clubmaker, his clubs differing only slightly from Philp's.

The James Wilson putter pictured has a face only 15/16 of an inch in depth. In addition, the head is 1 7/8 inches wide and 5 1/8 inches long. The overall length is 37 1/2 inches. This club was probably made sometime in the mid 1850s, shortly after Wilson went into business for himself. The exceptionally shallow face and refined style of this putter are still much like that of a feather ball club.

The small bit of wood missing from the toe and the small, thin crack on the face are of little consequence to the wonderful overall original condition of this club. These minor aches are little to endure since they are so unobtrusive, and Wilson clubs are so rare.

In 1862 and 1866, Westwood's St. Andrew's directory lists Wilson under "golf club and ball makers," along with George D. Brown (6 Pilmuir Links), Robert Forgan (5 Pilmuir Links), and Robert Kirk (1 Pilmuir Links) (197).

The year of 1866 is sometimes given as the year of James Wilson's death. The *Fifeshire Journal* of 5 October 1871, however, reports James Wilson placed fourth (last) in a clubmakers competition played over the links at St. Andrews (6).

TOM MORRIS
(1821-1908)
LONG SPOON
SHORT SPOON (LH)
PLAY CLUB

Every golfer who visits St. Andrews falls a victim to his sway, and carries away with him a cherished recollection of his personality. The secret of Old Tom Morris' popularity is obvious, and one look at his face is all that is required to reveal it. When a human countenance radiates forth so much worth, sense, kindliness, manliness, goodness, and truth, it commands the interest and respect of all on whom it shines, and when to that magnetic attraction of personality is added the knowledge of an upright and honourable life, lived under many difficulties and many heavy trials, our love and homage are irresistibly compelled (Golf, 23 Dec. 1898: 307).

Tom Morris is so widely known, his services in the laying out of new greens have been rendered in so many different parts of the country, his character has inspired such universal respect and affection, that any attempt to do him honour cannot properly be confined to St. Andrews. He has raised the status of the professional golfer all the world over, and has therefore a strong claim to the gratitude of every one interested in the game (Golf, 6 Sep. 1895: 502).

To the world he lived in, Tom Morris was more than a gifted clubmaker, a talented player, and a respected professional—he epitomized the game. In print he was accorded such affectionate titles as "The high priest of the hierarchy of golf," "The father of golf," "The Nestor of Golf," and "The Grand Old Man of Golf." Yet, through all the accolades and fame, he remained a kind, honest, respectful, and simple man. According to H.S.C. Everard:

To expand him into Thomas Morris would be improper, a solecism to be looked for among the profane and vulgar, an equivalent to eating peas with a knife, or any other barbarity which shocks our refined sensibilities: to the brotherhood, therefore, let him be as he is, Tom Morris, or better still, the ever-popular favorite, Old Tom (Golf, 31 Jul. 1891: 340).

Because of his personal character, Tom Morris changed the public perception of a professional golfer from that of a rogue without a *real* occupation to someone worthy of society's respect. He did this while working in the world of golf during the feather ball era, through the gutty ball era, and into the rubber core era.

Morris first played golf at his native St. Andrews when he was six or seven years old. When he was seventeen, Morris entered the golf trade. In an autobiographical article, Morris states, "I went to work at making clubs and balls, principally the latter, with Allan Robertson" (Leach 1907, 33). W.W. Tulloch, in his biography of Morris, quotes Old Tom as saying, "I learnt to mak' clubs and balls wi' Allan Robertson" (1908, 30). It is generally thought that Robertson made only balls, his father being a ballmaker. However, these firsthand references to Allan teaching Tom to be a clubmaker as well as a ballmaker cannot be denied. (The author believes that evidence of Robertson's work as a clubmaker remains to this day. Two circa 1850 long nose clubs marked "Robertson" with a stylish clubmaker's stamp, the letters forming a slight arc, are known.)

The 44-inch long spoon pictured on this and the following page is an example of Morris's early work. The head measures 5 5/8 inches long, 1 7/8 inches wide, and 1 inch deep. The 1-inch face depth is a characteristic of a feather ball club as is the well-curved face and the delicate neck. The 44 inch shaft length and the fruitwood clubhead (probably apple or pear) lend further support to dating this club in the early 1850s. Do not be put off by the grime covering the original golden finish on this head. It can be cleaned off, given the proper treatment, without damaging the original finish. The head itself is structurally sound. There is a small chip in the face, but this is a minor blemish. In fact, because this is such an early example of Morris's work, the chip has little significance. Morris's early clubs are not only extremely difficult to find, they are also his most attractive.

As a resident of St. Andrews, Morris was well acquainted with Hugh Philp. Tom's employer, Allan Robertson, not only revered and often used Philp clubs, he was known to spend time in Philp's shop simply admiring Philp's work. And since Philp was the recognized master, it is not surprising that a young and talented Tom Morris would try to emulate Philp's work. This long spoon certainly bears many distinct similarities.

In 1848 Allan Robertson, the most prolific feather ball maker in St. Andrews and Tom's employer, found Tom golfing with a gutta percha ball, such balls having just been introduced to the game. This displeased Allan greatly, and he made his displeasure known to Morris. Later that day, Tom left Allen's employ and each went his own way. Their friendship and respect for each other, however, remained untarnished throughout their lives.

Tom remained in St. Andrews until his work took him to Prestwick in 1851. Once there, he laid out the links for the Prestwick Golf Club, became custodian of the links, and "flourished as a club and ball-maker" (Tulloch 1908, 90). While at Prestwick, Morris won the respect and affection of those who knew him and, in 1861, he was made an honorary member of the Prestwick St. Nicholas Golf Club. The local population had many opportunities to see Morris display his playing skills. He won the British Open four times (1861-62-64-67) on the links of the Prestwick Golf Club, home to the first twelve British Opens.

Tom Morris was employed at Prestwick from 1851 until his resignation in the middle of 1864, when he was hired by the Royal and Ancient Golf Club of St. Andrews.

In the General Meeting of the R&A held on September 30, 1863, Alexander Herd resigned as custodian of the St. Andrews links. Major Boothby moved that a professional golfer be employed as a servant of the club, and that the entire charge of the course be entrusted to him. It was so agreed by those in attendance. At the General Meeting in May 1864, it was agreed that Tom Morris from Prestwick should be taken on for £50 per annum as payment of the custodian's salary and £20 for the upkeep of the links. Morris was formally installed in his position on January 9, 1865 (see Salmond 1956, 122-123). He remained as the acting professional and "Keeper of the Green" at the Royal and Ancient Golf Club until 1904. Old Tom then carried on in an honorary capacity until his death in 1908.

When Morris returned to St. Andrews, he established his clubmaking business in the small shop formerly occupied by Jamie Wilson. "Thereafter he shifted to Hugh Philp's shop, when G.D. [George Daniel] Brown left it; and these are still his premises" (*Golfing*, 28 May 1908: 26). Today, Morris's business remains at this very site, but in name only. Initially, his business was small—by 1871 he reportedly employed three men and one boy. His business continued to grow, however, and eventually employed many craftsman. Today many clubs remain which bear his name. Most of these examples, mirroring the growth of the game, are from the 1880s or later.

It should be noted that in 1869, Old Tom made his son, Tom Morris Jr., a partner in his club and ball making business (*East of Fife Record*, 31 Dec. 1875: 2). Young Tom, a four time British Open champion and the greatest golfer of his day, died on December 25, 1875, when only twenty-four years old. Nevertheless, Old Tom continued to advertise his business as "Tom Morris & Sons" for a few more years, as shown by the "Tom Morris & Sons" listing in *Worrell's Directory of the North Eastern Counties of Scotland 1877* (276). (J.O.F. "Jamie" Morris was Old Tom's other son.)

This early Tom Morris long spoon shows a graceful head with a slender neck and shallow face. These are characteristics of clubs from the feather ball era.

The 38 1/2-inch Tom Morris short spoon pictured on this page is unusual because it is left-handed. An 1898 commentary on left-handed clubs makes clear the rarity and disadvantages of being a left-handed golfer. It reads in part:

A left-handed professional has never been heard of, and should one suddenly arise and enter for the Open Championship, his appearance would create as great a sensation in the world of Golf as that caused by the bearded lady or the dog-face man in the outside world of normally-constituted people.

. . . In addition to being deprived of the perquisites and advantages of the left-handed cricketer, the left-handed golfer suffers many other disabilities. . .

But the chief trouble from which the left-handed learner suffers is the impossibility of getting good clubs. In the first place he has only a very limited stock to choose from. No club-maker keeps a large supply of left-handed clubs, and such as they have, are invariably made by right-handed players, so that the question of their balance and 'feel' is largely a matter of chance. Only a left-handed player can make a left-handed club with any certainty that it will be a good one.

They may comfort themselves with the reflection that left-handed-ness, per se, is no bar to excellence in Golf any more than in Cricket, and if they will apprentice themselves to Old Tom Morris or Willie Park for a season, and learn the secrets of club-making, they may yet see their names writ large in the archives of the Championship (Golf, 5 Aug. 1898: 397-398).

This left-handed club, stamped "T. Morris," was probably never used. The head measures 6 1/8 inches long, 1 7/8 inches wide, and 1 1/8 inches deep. In addition to having "SWM" stamped on the shaft in large letters, "SWM Michael, Short Spoon" is written in ink on the sole. There are a fair number of Morris clubs with such writing on their soles. Apparently, Morris did this to identify a club as made for, or sold to, a particular customer.

The whipping on the neck has been replaced. But this is only a minor shortcoming, such rare clubs in unused condition being highly sought after. Only the grip's underlisting remains on the shaft. While a replacement grip can easily be installed, it does not need to be. A club with only its underlisting remaining displays a genuine aspect of club construction not normally seen.

The Tom Morris play club pictured on this page once belonged to the Arbroath Golf Club, in Arbroath, Scotland. They sold this club, along with the Philp middle spoon pictured earlier (p. 54), in the early 1980s.

The head measures 5 1/2 inches long, 1 13/16 inches wide, and 1 1/4 inches deep. The slightly larger neck and deeper face indicate that this club was made well into the gutty ball era, circa 1875. The original golden blond finish and its lack of wear are strong features. More often than not, clubs made during this period were dark brown or black.

This club appears to be in perfect original condition except that the neck does not flow symmetrically into the shaft as is usually the case. In the lower right picture, the lack of a smooth transition between the neck and shaft is visible. The upper half of the neck slopes back toward the shaft at an angle different from the lower half of the neck.

The asymmetrical neck indicates that this club either suffered a broken shaft and was poorly reshafted or that the original lie of the club was purposely changed. Although the method of replacing a broken shaft is well understood, changing the lie on a splice neck club is not. In order to change the lie of a splice neck wood, the neck was recut at a different angle. This point is made by Thomas Carruthers when explaining his continued support for splice neck woods, as opposed to newer socket neck woods, in the early 1900s:

In the event of purchasing a new club (drilled head), after playing you find it has too flat a lie that you cannot alter; whereas the old club you can alter the lie to suit yourself (Golfing, 6 Feb. 1902: 25).

Given the pristine condition of the head and the old yet practically unused sheepskin grip, the author believes the neck on this Morris club was altered before it was sold.

Yet, even if the shaft is a replacement, this club is still a fine collectible. The major feature of a long nose golf club is its head. If the head itself is a prime example, the same head reshafted will still be deemed very desirable—though not to the extent that it would be if it had its original shaft. Much depends on how many other examples of the club exist and how well the reshaft materials and workmanship match the age of the head. Remember, a reshafted club reflects a genuine aspect of golf's history.

WILLIE DUNN
(1821-1878)
SHORT SPOON & PUTTER

Willie Dunn is one of golf's most historic figures from the nineteenth century. Hailing from Musselburgh, he and his twin brother, James, were born the same year as Tom Morris and only five years after Allan Robertson. In addition to making clubs and balls, Dunn knew how to use them. Willie participated in many challenge matches during his time. Challenge matches were the primary public medium for determining who the best golfers were in addition to providing the professional with a chance to win some money.

In two of Willie's most famous matches, both of which he lost, there is more to consider than the final score. In 1843 Dunn played a *twenty round* match over ten days against Allan Robertson, over Allan's home green, St. Andrews. Willie lost 2 down with 1 to play. In 1849 he and his brother, Jamie, played Tom Morris and Allan Robertson in a *six round* match over three courses for £400, a *very* sizable amount at the time. The Dunns lost 1 down. Not only was the length of these matches unique (two or three rounds to a match being common in those days), but so was the way in which the winner was determined.

According to Alexander Doleman, a contemporary of Dunn's, scoring for these matches was based on rounds. Victory went to whoever won the most *rounds*, not who won the most *holes* overall as was normally the case (*Golf*, 15 Jan. 1897: 332-334). Doleman points out that Dunn was leading in holes won when he was closed out in his 1843 match, losing two rounds down with one round to play. In the 1849 match, Willie and Jamie actually stood eight *holes* ahead at the conclusion of the final round, which they lost two down to lose the match by one round!

Doleman knew both Robertson and Dunn quite well. When recounting the 1843 match, Doleman revealed much about both men and their golfing skills:

The claims of Allan Robertson have been so persistently written up by his admirers . . . that Golfers in these days must think Willie Dunn was a player of a very inferior stamp to the pawky player of St. Andrews. Let me assure them they never laboured under a greater misapprehension. I remember both men well, and without for a moment wishing to depreciate the clever and pawky Allan, I must claim to say a word or two on behalf of one of the grandest players that ever lifted a club, as well as one of the most modest of men.

. . . A difference of five years separated the men in point of age, Dunn being twenty-three, while Allan was twenty-eight. Physically there was a great contrast between the two men. Allan was what we should ordinarily call a little man, of stoutish build, sharp in his movements, with . . . rather bushy whiskers, and of a cheery, kindly appearance . . . . Willie Dunn, on the other hand, was a model of a man. Standing nearly six feet in height, straight as an arrow, stout in proportion without being heavy, he had a frame that was worthy of any athlete. Allan's style was a treat to witness: the supple club with the long, beautiful swing was a fascinating sight for any golfer. Dunn's style, on the other hand, had the grand and majestic in it, and when Willie, as was his invariable custom, having struck his tee-shot, held aloft his driver waving his ball forward, as it were, in the air, you wondered when his ball was going to stop (332).

In 1851 Dunn was appointed keeper of the green at Blackheath. The 37 1/2-inch short spoon pictured on the facing page, most likely made at Blackheath, is one of the few known clubs stamped "W. Dunn." Most are stamped "Wm. Dunn" (in either large or small letters); a few are stamped "W. & J. Dunn" (made when Willie and Jamie worked together after Jamie came to Blackheath in 1854). The head, which appears to be thorn wood with a marbled brown finish, measures 5 3/8 inches long, 2 inches wide, and only 1 inch in face depth. It has a generous amount of hook and a broad, graceful appearance. All things considered, this club dates somewhere around the 1850s, either just before or just after Jamie's time at Blackheath.

The putter stamped "Wm Dunn" (small letters) pictured on this page dates circa 1865-70. The head, measuring 5 1/4 inches long, 1 7/8 inches wide, and only 1 1/32 inches in face depth, is stylish and attractive. The shaft sports a graceful St. Andrews bend (see p. 507).

Dunn remained at Blackheath until 1864. Thirteen months after the 1865 birth of his son, Willie Jr., he returned to Leith where he was clubmaker, ballmaker, and custodian to the Leith Thistle Golf Club. In 1870 Dunn moved to Musselburgh and set up his clubmaking business. Today his clubs are scarce and eminently collectible.

In recalling Willie Dunn, "An Old Blackheathen" wrote:

I have watched the play of many good golfers since, and can fully endorse every word as to Dunn being "one of the grandest players that ever lifted a club, as well as one of the most modest of men." . . . A more genial, generous hearted, and honest man than dear Willie Dunn never did, nor ever will, adorn the golfing world (Golf, 22 Jan. 1897: 348).

ROBERT FORGAN
(1824-1900)
MIDDLE SPOON
JUVENILE PLAY CLUB
DRIVING PUTTER

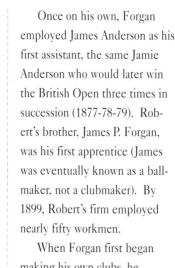

One of the best-known names in the club-making trade is that of Forgan—Forgan of St. Andrews. Wherever golf is played, and that is all the world over, Forgan's clubs have won their way. The history of the firm—formerly Robert Forgan, now Robert Forgan & Son—has been one of uniform success, and it would be strange if that were not so, for the firm has ever aimed at turning out good material (The Golfer, 11 Nov. 1896: 391).

Beginning in 1852, Robert Forgan learned clubmaking from the master clubmaker, Hugh Philp:

Forgan's first essay in the trade with which his name is now so closely identified was to saw shafts with a hand-saw out of a hickory billet five or six inches square, old Philp from time to time slackening up in the job of rasping a club-head to take a snuff and critically eye his new workman. The heads also had to be cut out of the plank with a hand breaking-out saw, which was much harder work than club-makers know anything about nowadays (The Golfer, 11 Nov. 1896: 391).

Forgan learned the art of clubmaking under Hugh Philp's guidance so well that he ran Philp's business during the last two years of Philp's life, when Hugh was very sick (*The Golfer*, 11 Nov. 1896: 391). After Philp's death in 1856, Robert Forgan continued Philp's business but under his own name. There is little doubt that kinship played a role in Forgan's taking over Philp's business. Forgan was related to Philp through Forgan's marriage to Elizabeth Berwick, the daughter of Philp's brother-in-law, James Berwick. A few historians have incorrectly surmised that a few long nose clubs bearing both the name of "Philp" and "Forgan" were made while Philp was alive, to show a partnership. Not so. Forgan made these commemorative clubs decades after Philp's death, to capitalize on Philp's legacy and Forgan's relationship to him (see p. 56).

Once on his own, Forgan employed James Anderson as his first assistant, the same Jamie Anderson who would later win the British Open three times in succession (1877-78-79). Robert's brother, James P. Forgan, was his first apprentice (James was eventually known as a ball-maker, not a clubmaker). By 1899, Robert's firm employed nearly fifty workmen.

When Forgan first began making his own clubs, he stamped them "R. Forgan" in large block letters. In 1863 Forgan began to include the Prince of Wales plume or three-feather crest on his clubheads, the result of being appointed "Golf Club Maker to H.R.H. The Prince of Wales":

The two lead buttons in the sole of the Forgan middle spoon increased the weight of this club. "A good way to increase the weight, and one which is not often practised, is to drill a hole through the exact centre of the head, and fill it with lead" (Golfing, 29 Nov. 1900: 7).

In 1863, when the Prince of Wales was elected captain of the Royal and Ancient Club, Mr. Forgan was appointed clubmaker to His Royal Highness (*Golfing*, 20 Dec. 1900: 32).

In the season 1863-1864 the Prince of Wales was elected captain of the Royal and Ancient Golf Club, and Mr. Forgan was employed to make a set of golf clubs for his Royal Highness; receiving thereafter a special appointment and diploma as golf club-maker to the Prince of Wales, which honour was also extended in 1883 to the firm of R. Forgan & Son (*The Golfer*, 11 Nov. 1896: 392).

A few years later, sometime around 1870, Forgan began marking his clubs "R. Forgan" in smaller block letters—discarding the larger letter stamp while retaining the Prince of Wales plume. Most of the remaining Forgan long nose clubs are marked with this smaller stamp.

The 41-inch middle spoon pictured on this and the facing page has a head that measures 6 inches in length, 1 7/8 inches in width, and 1 1/8 inches in face depth. The head is stamped with the large "R. Forgan" stamp and the Prince of Wales plume. Therefore, this club dates between 1863 and approximately 1870.

In 1883 Robert Forgan made his son, Thomas Berwick Forgan, a partner in his clubmaking business, restructuring it as the firm of "R. Forgan & Son" and receiving the continued endorsement of HRH the Prince of Wales" (The *Golfer*, 11 Nov. 1896, 392; see also p. 229).

Forgan clubs continued to be stamped "R. Forgan" with the Prince of Wales plume. Because Prince Edward extended his endorsement of Robert Forgan to the firm of R. Forgan & Son, Forgan did not need to change the way he marked his clubheads. But he eventually began marking "R. Forgan & Son, St. Andrews" on his shafts, when stamping shafts came into vogue a few years later.

Immediately following the death of Queen Victoria on January 22, 1901, Prince Edward succeeded to the throne of England. Sometime during the next twelve months, King Edward VII appointed the firm of R. Forgan & Son to be "Golf Club Makers to His Majesty King Edward," as advertised in the January 3, 1902 issue of *Golf Illustrated* (19). However, it was not announced until February 28, 1902, more than a year after Queen Victoria's death, that Forgan & Son were marking their clubs with the "King's Crown":

Messrs. R. Forgan and Son, St. Andrews, are now—a token of their appointment as clubmakers to his Majesty—putting a Crown on their club-heads. This takes the place of the three-feather crest which golfers have been so long accustomed to identify with Messrs. Forgan's clubs (Golf Illustrated, 28 Feb. 1902: 161).

During the interim between the Queen's death and the appointment of Forgan & Son as golf club makers to the King, and perhaps for a brief time following the appointment, Forgan & Son did not mark their clubs with either the Prince of Wales plume or the King's Crown— only "R. Forgan" in small letters (see p. 316).

Once Forgan & Son began marking their clubs with the King's Crown stamp, they continued to do so until the death of King Edward VII, in May of 1910. The use of the crown stamp in 1910 is corroborated by Forgan's Angle Shaft wood discussed on p. 506: This club is stamped with the King's Crown and the number of a British patent applied for on April 26, 1910.

In addition to making clubs, the firm of R. Forgan & Son served as one of the biggest assembly and repair shops of its day. Many shafts stamped "R. Forgan & Son" are attached to clubheads bearing somebody else's name. Some of these were clubs reshafted by Forgan, others were new clubs assembled/shafted for another seller.

The business that Hugh Philp started, Robert Forgan renamed, and Thomas Forgan helped perpetuate, was sold to the A.G. Spalding company in 1959.

It is of interest to quote Mr. Forgan's advertisement in 1859. It ran as follows:

"Original Golf Club Establishment. Established for upwards of Forty Years. Robert Forgan (Successor to the late Mr. Hugh Philp, Golf Clubmaker). Directly opposite the Golf Parlour. Has always on hand an Extensive Assortment of Clubs, First-class Full-sized Wooden Clubs, 3s. 6d each; Irons 4s 6d each; Young Gentleman's 2s 6d each. Clubs sent to all parts of the Kingdom. Old Clubs neatly repaired on the shortest notice. Links, St. Andrews, June 1859."

Philp's former foreman, James Wilson, separated from him some years before Philp's death and started in opposition; and his advertisement on the same page as Forgan's runs on the same lines as those of the latter and with the same prices. Wilson advertises that he was "23 years with the late Hugh Philp" It may be added that Forgan and Wilson, though rivals in the trade, were the best of friends . . . (St. Andrews Citizen, 22 Dec. 1900: 5).

In addition to making full-length clubs for adults, clubmakers made short clubs for children. These clubs are commonly referred to as "juvenile clubs." J.R. Gairdner once recalled being fitted for a juvenile club, in 1863, in Robert Forgan's shop:

About the age of four I was taken to Forgan's shop to be fitted with my first club. [This was approximately 1863 as Gairdner was born in 1859] Being left-handed I grasped it with my right hand above the left, and my mother suggested that I should have a left-handed club. Forgan, to my unending gratitude, replied that I must learn to play right-handed, as there were no really good left-handed golfers, and so it was settled....

With my club, minus lead or horn, I knocked corks and stones about, and balls when I could get them, until the day came when I was thought to be big enough to have a proper club (Leach 1907, 209).

This circa 1865 Forgan juvenile play club is different from most long nose clubs: It lacks a horn and lead backweight. This club was built without lead in order to lighten its overall weight so a child could swing it with ease. The length of this club is only 39 inches.

Complete without "lead or horn," the Robert Forgan juvenile club pictured matches the one described by Gairdner. This delicate long nose was made within the years immediately following 1863 (as shown by the large "R. Forgan" stamp above the Prince of Wales plume marked on the head). Only a handful of juvenile clubs date to an earlier time.

The 39 inch length of this juvenile play club is from three to six inches shorter than a normal play club. The head measures 5 1/4 inches long, 1 7/8 inches wide, and 1 inch in face depth. The shaft still retains its original sheepskin grip, with little or no listing underneath, and bears the name "Marion" (written in script with ink, now old) directly below the grip. This club apparently once belonged to an eight- to ten-year-old child named Marion.

The collector who suspects a full-length (adult) club has been altered to make it a juvenile club can examine two aspects. First, a child's spoon or play club will have a distinctly flat lie compared to an adult club. (The lie of the club also helps determine whether an adult putter was ever converted into an adult baffy or short spoon. To convert a club in this fashion is to deface it.) Second, a juvenile club will be much lighter than an adult club. This was accomplished by using little or no lead in the head and by making the head slightly smaller than normal.

There is more than meets the eye to the Forgan putter as pictured on this page. This club is an unused mid-1880s putter with the ordinary small "R. Forgan" lettering, but the entire shaft and grip is constructed from a single solid piece of wood. Made from greenheart, this particular shaft is known as a "fishing rod" shaft. Such shafts are exceptionally slender, similar to a fishing rod, and sometimes possess a grip shaped like its fishing rod counterpart. (The fishing rod grip is pictured on page 528.)

In the back pages of *Golfing*, written by Charles Chambers and published in 1887, an advertisement by "R. Anderson & Sons, Fishing-Tackle Manufacturers and General Sports Warehouse, 56 Princes Street, Edinburgh," mentions "specially prepared Greenheart shafts and new handle grip." The unmarked shaft on this putter is most likely one of Robert Anderson's shafts. Although attractive to look at, these shafts were impractical and therefore poorly received. Very few remain today. (See also pages 50 and 90.)

Like the shaft, this putter head, measuring 6 inches long, 1 7/8 inches wide, and 1 1/8 inches deep, dates to the mid-1880s. Its outstanding condition and the very rare shaft/grip make this club a top example from its time. The exceptional fishing rod shaft/grip increases the appeal of this club well beyond the same 1880 Forgan putter with a traditional shaft and grip.

The Earl of Wemyss was once playing on a Fifeshire course, accompanied by an old caddie. His Lordship got his ball at one hole so dead that to play it appeared superfluous, so he simply holed it with the toe of his boot. The caddie threw down his clubs with a horrified look, and when he found words to speak he said, "Dammit, ma Lord, gowf's gowf" (Golf Illustrated, 9 Aug. 1907: 126).

ROBERT DAVIDSON

(1801-1875)

SHORT SPOON

Robert Davidson made clubs during the feather ball era and into the gutty ball era. Few examples of his work remain. Because he was a clubmaker during the feather ball era, when there were few clubmakers, his work is eminently collectible.

Upon examining a Davidson club, the first thing a collector usually notices is the "R. Davidson" stamped in *script* on the top of the head. Only two other long nose clubmakers are known to have used a script stamp: Hugh Philp and Tom Hood. Philp stamped only a few of his clubs in script; Hood so marked a good percentage of his.

The head on this Davidson measures 5 5/8 inches in length, 2 inches in width, and 1 1/16 inches in depth. The overall length of this short spoon is 38 1/2 inches. The finish on the head has been nicely restored; the restoration work does not call any undue attention to itself. Of course, the original finish would be preferable, but because Davidson clubs are so rare and desirable, a nicely re-stored example is still very acceptable. This club appears to date circa 1860.

The recollection which many American golfers will have of the fashion of wooden clubheads which preceded the bulger stamp probably harks back to occasional glimpses of pre-historic-looking weapons with long, oblong heads, in shape much like the half of a pear, with an abnormal length of lead space at the back and with concave faces curved inward. Until about 1890 this was the general form of golf club head, and in comparison with modern-day club heads was a somewhat cumbersome and inefficient weapon for hitting a golf ball really hard.

In those days, however, the majority of players did not attempt to hit a ball really hard, not nearly so hard as the general run of players do nowadays.

This was not because they were in any sense comparatively deficient in physical strength, but for the reason that the balance of the old stamp of club head did not lend itself to hard hitting, and the man who attempted to apply the maximum of his physical powers with these clubs . . . was taking more than a great risk; he was almost courting disaster, as the mere force of the blow and the consequent quickness of the downward swing was sufficient to make the long head with the balance toward the toe of the club swing away. Mistiming was the natural result. The really long drivers in those days were invariably very wild drivers; they could hardly hope to keep straight (Hilton 1913, 56-57).

ALEXANDER GREIG
LONG SPOON

In recalling a few personalities from St. Andrews in 1850, *Golf Illustrated* identified Alexander Greig as a fine golfer:

The only scratch players in these early days were George Morris (Tom's elder brother), James Herd, William Ayton, jun., Robert Patterson and Alexander Greig (19 June 1908: 252).

In a match played on New Years Day in 1851, Greig defeated Tom Morris, winning his ball. In addition, Greig was among the Scottish professionals who competed in the 1867 "Open Tournament at Leith," held under the auspices of the Thistle Golf Club. "A well-known player in his day, but never succeeded in getting into quite the front rank," was the only comment W. Dalrymple made concerning Greig's participation in this 1867 event (*Golf Illustrated*, 9 Mar. 1900: 217).

Alexander Greig was also a clubmaker. He worked independently (listed in the Leith Post-Office Directory between 1866 and 1872 as a "golf club and ball manufacturer at 22 Duke Street"), but he eventually gave up the tribulations of private enterprise. According to T. Owen Potter, a former secretary of Royal Liverpool, Greig went to work in Jack Morris's shop. Though no date was given, Potter also reported that Greig died in Hoylake: "He was found drowned on the shore" (*Golf Illustrated*, 16 Mar. 1900: 217).

The well-made and beautifully styled circa 1860s long spoon pictured is 43 inches long. The head measures 5 3/4 inches long, 1 7/8 inches wide, and 1 1/16 inches deep. Although some of the original shellac has worn off, the head overall is in wonderful original condition. The few minor stress cracks on the face are of little consequence because they are not prominent, and this club is one of only five currently known. Interestingly, Greig used square pegs and round holes when installing the horn on this club.

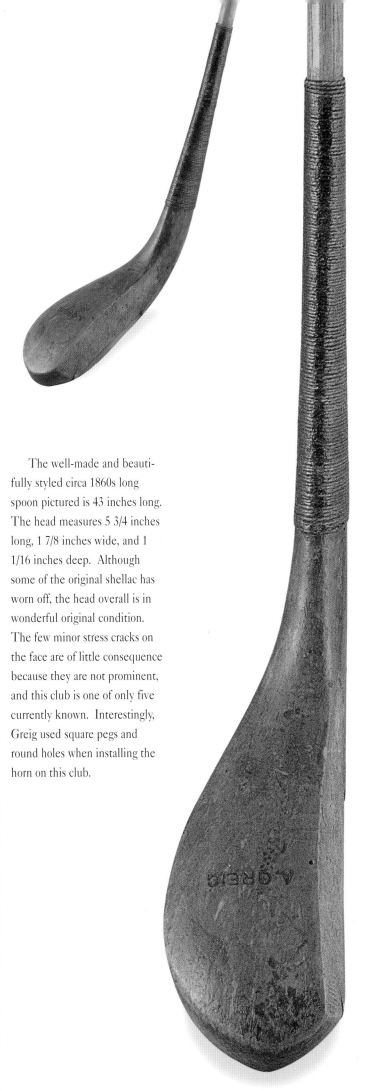

LUDOVIC G. SANDISON
(1825-1884)
PUTTER

Ludovic G. Sandison, Fishing Rod & Golf Club Maker, 118 King Street, Aberdeen. All sorts of Fishing Tackles, Golf Balls, &c. &c. Salmon and Trout Rods made to Order of the Best Materials and Workmanship (Worrell 1877, 7).

Working in Aberdeen, on the east coast of Scotland well north of St. Andrews, Sandison followed in the footsteps of Alexander Munro, Aberdeen's resident clubmaker prior to his death in 1847. As noted in the above advertisement, Sandison also made fishing equipment.

Although most early cleekmakers included their location when marking their work ("Carrick \ Musselburgh," "Anderson \ Anstruther," "Wilson \ St. Andrews," etc.), Sandison was the only long nose clubmaker to do so prior to approximately 1885.

The 36-inch putter pictured, dating around 1865-70, is stamped "L.G. Sandison \ Aberdeen." The head, measuring 5 1/2 inches long, 2 inches wide, and 1 1/4 inches deep, has a small amount of hook or curve to the face. This is as it should be, and usually was, on older putters.

Should you be advised to substitute a putting-iron for the bonâ-fide tool, shun the advice, and stick to the putter, and you will never have cause to repent (Chambers 1857, 695).

JOHN ALLAN
(1848-1897)
PLAY CLUB

John Allan, a native of Prestwick, served his apprenticeship in the club and ball making business under Tom Morris shortly after Morris returned to St. Andrews from Prestwick in 1864. A capable craftsman, Allan learned ball-making so well he "could hammer one of the old hand-hammered balls in just under three minutes, which was good work" (*Golf Illustrated*, 7 Sep. 1900: 207). While Allan was working for Morris, Morris was asked to locate someone to make clubs and teach golf at a new club in England. Old Tom recommended Allan.

In 1866 Allan became the first professional at Royal North Devon, Westward Ho! and remained there until 1886. After a short stint at Bridge-of-Weir, he returned to Prestwick St. Nicholas in 1887, taking charge of the green. He was respected for being courteous, charming, a gentleman, and a credit to the game of golf and to his homeland. Allan's contributions to the game were so positive that, after his death, he was considered to be the pioneer of all Scottish professionals who later worked at English courses, although others such as Willie Dunn Sr. preceded him. Allan also influenced many prominent golfers:

A good many of our best players, like [Horace] Hutchinson and [J.H.] Taylor, passed through his hands, and learned a good deal of their Golf from his instruction (*Golf*, 26 Feb. 1897: 425).

The eminently collectible Allan play club pictured is in perfect original condition. The original golden blond finish is still rich and strong. The overall length is 44 inches, and the gracefully hooked head measures 5 3/4 inches long, 1 3/4 inches wide, and 1 1/8 inches in face depth. John Allan marked his clubs with two different size stamps, his earlier stamp using larger letters than his latter stamp. This circa 1870 club is marked with his large letters stamp. Allan's clubs are rarely seen.

Born June 30, 1833, in Wallyford (near Musselburgh), Willie Park is a renowned figure from golf's early history. He was one of the top four professionals of his day, along with Allan Robertson, Willie Dunn, and Tom Morris. He won the first British Open, held in 1860, and went on to win three more times: 1863, '66, '75. Willie also played many a challenge match against the elite golfers of his time:

When he played a match it was never merely for people's amusement, never a matter of indifference whether he won or lost, but a serious, stern reality. In fact, if one must speak the truth, "Auld Willie" could not play a slack match, a mere friendly match. With him it was always death or glory. To his greatest friend he was the deadliest enemy while the match lasted (Golf Illustrated, 7 Aug. 1903: 105).

As a caddie, Willie learned to golf using a "large, thick stick, hooked at the end—in other words, a shinty." He was so talented using this shinty stick, he was able to beat his opponents who were using the "more orthodox weapons" (Golf, 28 Aug. 1891: 404). Gifted from the beginning, Park embarked upon his professional career at the age of twenty-one.

Willie Park's younger brothers were Mungo and David. Mungo won the British Open in 1874 and also made a few clubs of his own. Willie's son, Willie Park Jr., followed in his father's footsteps. He also became a top professional golfer (British Open champion in 1887 and 1889) and a prominent clubmaker.

Willie Park "followed the trade of a clubmaker, first at Musselburgh, then at North Berwick, and after 1875 at Musselburgh." During the last seventeen years of his life, his "weak health has been [Willie Jr.'s] chief and constant concern" (Golfing, 30 July 1903: 10). "Auld Willie," as he was affectionately called, died July 25, 1903. "For the last nine years of his life [Willie] has been stretched on a bed of sickness" (Golf Illustrated, 7 Aug. 1903: 105).

Willie Park was a fine clubmaker. His clubs are well made and highly coveted by collectors today. Unfortunately, few of them remain. The circa 1870-75 Park putter pictured on this page, stamped "Wm. Park," has a fruitwood head measuring 5 3/4 inches long, 2 inches wide, and 1 1/16 inches deep. One of Willie Park's own personal putters, on display at Musselburgh Golf Club, is very similar to this one. Like Park's own, this one does not have much hook to its face. (The face is untouched, completely original.)

Pictured on the following page is a mint Willie Park middle spoon. Beautifully styled, it is a prime example of Auld Willie's work. The head, stamped "Wm. Park," measures 1 7/8 inches in width, 1 1/16 inches in face depth, and 5 1/2 inches in length. This club, complete with Willie Park's early "large letters" stamp (the

letters are also farther apart), dates circa 1860s. Of particular interest is the full brass soleplate on this club. Full brass soleplates did not become common until the 1890s, when the clubs which had them were referred to as "brassies."

Willie Park and early brass soleplates are discussed in a biographical sketch of Gilbert Mitchell Innes written in 1900 by Dr. J.G. McPherson (*Golf Ill.*, 9 Nov.: 119). McPherson, born in St. Andrews in 1843, identifies Innes as "the best all-round amateur of the sixties," with whom he had the pleasure of playing. He credits Innes's splendid game to the lessons Innes learned while playing many matches against old Willie Park. McPherson continues by recalling how Innes used a brass sole club:

The first brassey ever I saw was Mr. Innes's. He had a brass sole to his middle spoon, which occasionally wrought wonders. . . . It was with that mid-spoon that his "steady brilliance" was best shown through the green.

Andrew Forgan recalled installing brass soles on long nose clubs during the 1860s:

I think it was Mr. Gilbert Innes who first had brass soles on a club to play off the road at Musselburgh. When I was an apprentice with my brother in St. Andrews we made mid-spoons and short spoons with brass soles for players at Blackheath. That was in 1865 (Golfing, 12 Jan. 1899: 5).

Tom Dunn recalled brass sole clubs in his article "Reminiscences of Golf Since 1855":

As the brassie is so much in evidence now, it may be interesting to know that it was first introduced at Blackheath, on account of the gravelly nature of the soil, and the number of paths and roads on the heath. Many a time have I observed, when paying a visit with my father to Scotland, during my school holidays, the uncouth remarks of the caddies, "Eh, I ken whaur he comes frae; Blackheath, naething but graivel pits there. Look at his airns" (Golf Illustrated, 18 Apr. 1902: 45).

Long nose clubs with brass soleplates were sometimes called "brassey spoons."

JOHN WALKER
PLAY CLUB

Two former British Open champions made interesting references to John "Jack" Walker. Robert Ferguson, three time Open champion (1880, '81, '82) and fine clubmaker in his own right, learned clubmaking from Jack Walker. According to Ferguson, this was after he went to Aberdeen in 1868 and, among other things, learned to make golf balls:

A year or two after this I got instruction in the art of club-making from old Jack Walker, a clever old clubmaker, who died practically in harness a year or two ago in London, where he had gone in the service of W. Park and Son (Golf Illustrated, 23 March 1906: 46).

When "only about 6 years of age" (approximately 1870), Willie Park Jr. also knew Walker. Recalling his father's clubmaking shop in approximately 1870, when Walker was employed there, Park relates:

I was too small to stand at the bench in the ordinary manner, and I used to get a chair and stand on that while I chiselled away, and suspended my operations only in time to put everything straight again before the men returned. I remember that I was very partial to the tools of one particular man named Walker, who always wondered when he came back from his dinner how it came about that the tools upon which there were such sharp edges when he had left them an hour before were now so blunt and needed a long course of the grindstone and the hone (Park 1907, 100-101).

This 44-inch play club, marked "J. Walker," has a beechwood head measuring 1 1/16 inches in face depth, 6 1/4 inches in length, and 1 7/8 inches in width. The notably long and graceful shape of the head, the relatively shallow dimension of the face, and the moderate neck date this club to the 1860s, or shortly thereafter. Despite having a reworked finish and replacement whipping, this club remains very desirable because of its lovely profile and genuine rarity.

CHARLES HUNTER

(1836-1921)

LONG SPOON

Charlie Hunter, the Grand Old Man of the West, was presented the other day by the Prestwick Golf Club with a replica of his portrait, the original of which hangs in the dining-room of the club .... There is no one, not even exccpting "Old Tom," who is more deservedly esteemed and respected, not only by his friends and neighbours at Prestwick, but by the brotherhood of golfers all the world over, than Charlie Hunter (Golf Illustrated, 21 July 1905: 61).

There is no more lovable or more highly respected man in the ranks of professional golf than Charlie Hunter, who has kept Prestwick Links for the last thirty-three years. He is to Prestwick and the West of Scotland what his old friend Tom Morris, whom he succeeded in the custodianship of Prestwick, is to St. Andrews, part and parcel of the place, and the kindly and genial natures of the two men are much alike. Charlie Hunter and his son are splendid club-makers and Jack is a first rate player, as was his father in the early days of the Championship (Golf Illustrated, 10 July 1903: 21).

Charlie Hunter did enjoy the deep affection of those who knew him. However the statement that Hunter "kept the Prestwick Links for the last thirty-three years" is inaccurate. At that time, Hunter had kept the links for *thirty-five* years. In May of 1864, Prestwick's custodian of the links, Tom Morris, was hired by St. Andrews Golf Club. Hunter succeeded Morris (for whom he had worked as an apprentice) at Prestwick, applying for the job on September 1, 1864. He remained there during the course of his life except for a brief stint, from the middle of 1865 until early 1868, when he worked at Blackheath. (Andrew Strath replaced Hunter at Prestwick. After Strath's death in 1868, Hunter returned to Prestwick.) Hunter served his club for fifty-three years until his death in 1921 (see Smail 1989, 16-18; Shaw 1938, 138-140).

The circa 1870 Hunter long spoon shown on this page is a magnificent golf club in near perfect original condition. The gracefully hooked face still shows Hunter's file marks. The head, which measures 5 5/8 inches in length, 1 1/16 inches in face depth, and 1 15/16 inches in width, is long, sleek, and stylish. Unfortunately, Hunter's later long nose clubs are not as attractive or well proportioned.

DAVID STRATH
(1850-1879)
PUTTER

Young Tom and David Strath were undoubtedly the best golfers of their too brief day. We cannot well separate them—at least we cannot speak of Davie without constant reference to Tommy, for it was in frequent single combat with the young Champion of his time that Davie proved himself a player of the finest calibre (Golf, 22 Nov. 1895: 240).

Tom Morris Jr. was the greatest golfer of his era. Born at Prestwick in 1851, "Young" Tom, or Tommy, as he was affectionately known, was the son of "Old" Tom (p. 62). In 1868, at the age of seventeen, Young Tom won his first British Open. Proving his victory was no fluke, he won the championship again in 1869 and 1870. By winning the championship three years in succession, Young Tom received the champion's belt as his *permanent* award. This belt had cost

thirty guineas (a big sum in those days) and was to be a perpetual award. It had not been anticipated that anyone would ever secure permanent possession of the prize, as the rules allowed, by winning it three times in as many years. For lack of a trophy, the Open was not held in 1871. When it was held again, in 1872, Young Tom won again. In his first three wins, all achieved at Prestwick, Young Tom averaged an extraordinarily low 76-2/3 stokes for each eighteen holes. In 1870, his score was 149 for thirty-six holes. According to A.W. Tillinghast:

It is significant that for nearly twenty years no championship winner came within eight shots of Tommy's 149. As late as 1890 the Open championship was won over the same Prestwick course by John Ball, Jr., . . . with a total of 164. Tommy was great (Golf Illustrated [ny], June 1934: 21).

Tragically, Young Tom forever remained Young Tom—he died when only 24 years old:

He married in 1873, and within a year afterwards his wife died in childbirth. This was a terrible blow to him, from which he rapidly sank, and died on 25th December, 1875, only a few months after his wife, at the early age of 24.

A beautiful monument—an admirable likeness—has been erected to his memory in the ancient burial ground of the Cathedral at St. Andrews (Golfing, 7 Dec. 1905: 14).

David Strath, Young Tom's beloved friend and golfing companion, was also young Tom's chief rival on the golf course:

In any gallery of golfing celebrities Strath must always have a place of honour, for he was the close friend of young Tom Morris and all but his equal as a golfer.

Strath's style is universally admitted to have been almost perfect, a wonderful blending of grace and power, the very "poetry of motion." He stood closer to his ball than young Tom, and he drove a very long ball which was nearly all carry . . . .

It was on the putting green that young Tom had, if anything, the advantage. Strath never had the fortune to win the Championship, but there is no question that he was fit company for the best of his time. He accomplished many wonderful feats and won many memorable matches. . . .

As a partner in a foursome Strath was unrivaled. He and young Tom were never beaten, for the simple reason that no other players had the temerity to tackle them; but he and Tom Kidd, another famous St. Andrews professional and a Championship winner, defeated the Morrises no fewer than thirteen times in succession (Golf Illustrated, 22 Sep. 1899: 423).

David Strath never won the British Open, though he finished second three times (twice to Young Tom). In 1876, he finished in a tie with Bob Martin, but refused to play off because the Championship committee had not ruled on a possible infraction incurred earlier by Strath. Martin was then declared the winner.

"Like Young Tom's, David Strath's golfing career was a short but glorious one: he died

of consumption before he was thirty years old" (Golf Illustrated, 22 Sep. 1899: 423).

David Strath was the brother of George, Willie, and Andrew Strath. George and Andrew also made clubs during the long nose era, but their work is rarely seen. The head on the circa 1870s David Strath putter shown here, marked "D. Strath," measures 5 3/8 inches long, 1 3/4 inches wide, and 1 1/16 inches deep. Strath clubs are among the most difficult to locate.

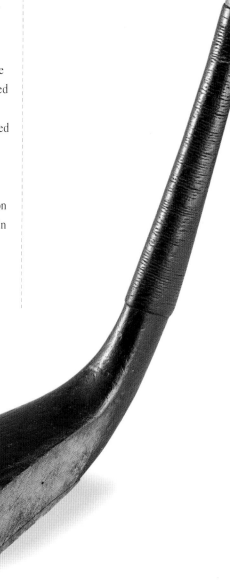

ROBERT FERGUSON
(1848-1915)
PLAY CLUB

[Robert] Ferguson had the misfortune . . . to be born a quarter of a century too early; he had passed out of the game just when the boom was beginning. In the late seventies and early eighties he was invincible, he won the Open Championship three years in succession—1880, 1881, 1882 . . . . In 1883 he tied with Willie Fernie over Musselburgh with a score of 159, but lost on the play off, so that he narrowly missed a fourth successive win. I say that Ferguson was born a quarter of a century too early, for undoubtedly he was a man of the character and temperament on a level with the great players of the present day. Golf has been his calling all his life, and although for more than twenty years now he has been but a caddie at Musselburgh, he bears no resemblance to the poor individuals who are generally connected with this precarious method of getting a living on Scottish links. . . . (Golf Monthly, Oct. 1914: 634).

Robert "Bob" Ferguson was born in 1848 at Musselburgh (Levenhall), Scotland. When eight years old, Ferguson worked as a forecaddie on the Musselburgh links. A few short years latter he was promoted to a carrying caddie, a step Ferguson took with pride (Leach 1907, 187).

In 1866 Ferguson played in and won his first tournament: the Leith tournament, promoted by the Leith Golf Club. This victory inspired Ferguson to become even better.

Backed by his supporters, Ferguson soon found himself participating in many challenge matches. The pinnacle of Ferguson's success, however, was his 1880, 1881, and 1882 British Open victories. In 1883 he almost captured the Open again, loosing by a single stroke in a 36-hole play-off. In 1884, according to Ferguson, poor health put him off his game:

Unfortunately my health broke down, and weakness following upon typhoid fever prevented me contesting for the honour the following year, and since then a younger generation of golfers has been gradually entering the field, while I have stood aside and tried to make a living as a coach (Leach 1907, 192-193).

Ferguson was also a craftsman. In 1868, during a six-week visit to Aberdeen, Scotland, he learned to make balls. By his own account, it was a year or two later before he learned to make clubs:

A year or two after [visiting Aberdeen in 1868] I got instruction in the art of club-making from old Jack Walker, a clever old clubmaker, who died practically in harness a year or two ago in London . . . This experience I gradually improved upon, and for half a dozen years in my pre-championship days I had a small club- and

ball-making business in premises at Links Place, Musselburgh (*Golf Illustrated*, 23 March 1906: 46).

Ferguson was a gifted clubmaker, but clubmaking was never his primary focus. To him, the game was the thing. With the decline of his play, Ferguson spent more of his time as a caddy and coach than he did as a club and ball maker. Consequently, few examples of his work remain. The circa 1870s Ferguson play club shown has replacement whipping and is marked "R. Ferguson" on its head, which measures 5 7/8 inches long, 1 3/4 inches wide, and 1 1/16 inches deep.

A lifelong resident of Musselburgh, Ferguson lived out his life in less than the best of circumstances, a plight shared by other professionals of his era:

The older school of professionals, . . . having fallen upon harder and harder times, notwithstanding the swelling army of golfers all over the world, eventually eked out their remaining days at a bench in the workshop repairing clubs, or, like Bob Ferguson, thrice Open Champion, the valiant opponent of Tom Morris and David Strath, being alternately prosecuted by the local justices for failure to apply for a caddie licence, or in earning a few precarious shillings in carrying clubs to opulent burgesses who were shocking bad players (Golf Illustrated, 16 Feb. 1906: 152).

Despite his fate—a three time Open Champion relegated to working as a caddie during the last twenty years of his life—Ferguson always tried, in his own simple way, to uphold the dignity that once rested on his shoulders. Throughout his life he was respected by all who knew him, including no less than J.H. Taylor:

I saw him at St. Andrews in [1895], and was struck by his appearance and quiet manner. His short, powerful frame gave me the impression of great strength, and his piercing blue eyes shone with sincerity and truth. What impressed me most of all was his soft, persuasive voice. It was so unexpected, coming from such a rugged, determined figure that it startled me. A man with such a voice could not have an enemy in the world, thought I, and further acquaintance with the speaker only confirmed this view (Golf Monthly, June 1915: 21).

THOMAS JOHNSTON
LONG SPOON,
VULCANITE HEAD

Thirteen years before Willie Park Jr. received the second patent ever issued for a golf club (see p. 239), the first such patent—a British patent (No. 2,683) dated June 29, 1876—was granted to Thomas Johnston of Edinburgh. A nearly unused example of Johnston's club is pictured. The head, marked "Johnston's Patent \ Edinburgh," is 5 1/2 inches long, 1 3/4 inches wide, and 1 inch in face depth.

According to his patent, the purpose of Johnston's invention:

consists in the employment of the well known preparation of India-rubber called vulcanite or ebonite in the construction of such club heads.

By creating a clubhead out of such material, Johnston calculated that it would not need a piece of horn and that it might not need any lead. The example pictured does not have a piece of horn, but it does have a small lead backweight fixed in place with the aid of two brass dowels.

In addition to describing a clubhead made from one uniform piece of vulcanite, Johnston's patent includes provisions for constructing a clubhead with a core:

... composed of vulcanite compound in combination with mineral powders or metal filings, or even with solid metal cores surrounded by vulcanite compound.... One advantage is that the more highly compound and denser cores can be surrounded with an outside covering of the finest or purest vulcanite which can be made, whereby a finer polish or finish can be given to such club heads than to those homogeously [sic] loaded.

All such vulcanite club heads are to be moulded to shape by the ordinary processes and means employed by and well known to rubber manufacturers.

Johnston's patent extolls the advantages of his club as follows:

The superior elasticity of the vulcanite and its comparative immunity from all climatic changes render these golf club heads much more effective ... and much more durable.

Fewer than ten Johnston clubs are known.

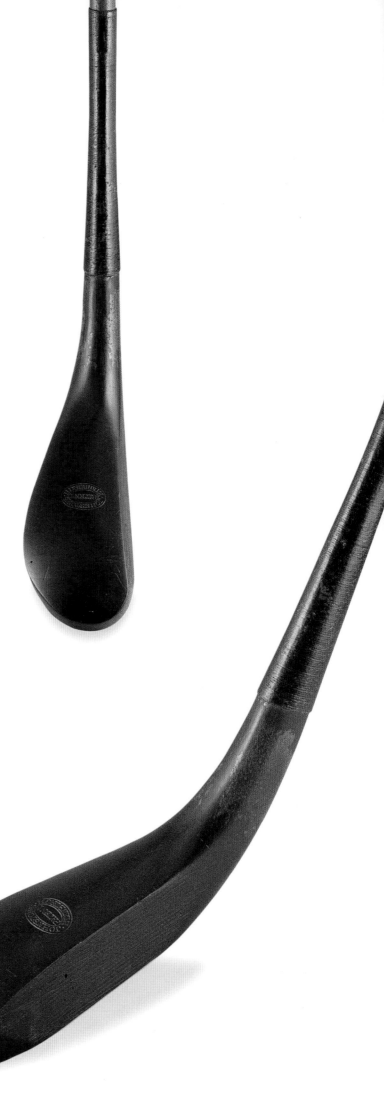

JAMES ANDERSON
(1842-1905)
DRIVING PUTTER

Jamie Anderson . . . was another beautiful player. He was short and burly, but drove a long ball, and was deadly with iron and putter. He was calm in temper and of firm nerve (Peter 1890, 40).

Jamie Anderson, the brother of David Jr. and son of "Old Da," was the first assistant Robert Forgan employed after taking over Hugh Philp's business. Anderson left Forgan to work for Tom Morris before venturing out on his own as a clubmaker. This occurred prior to 1870, as Robert Martin, the two time British Open champion born in 1853, apprenticed under Anderson a few years after becoming a caddie "at 11 or 12 years of age" (*Golf Ill.* 20 Apr. 1906: 69).

Jamie Anderson, a first class professional golfer, won the British Open three years running: 1877, '78, '79. In 1878 an incredible finish at Prestwick gave him a two-stroke victory. Anderson scored four under par over the last four holes. He holed out his approach shot on the 15th hole for an eagle three and then on the 17th hole, a par 3, he holed out his tee shot! (Miller 1935, 58)

On his hole-in-one, Anderson had originally teed up his ball "over the line." A fellow competitor looking on declared, "If that man plays that ball, he will be disqualified":

Jamie stopped and had a walk round to collect himself after the interruption. The ball was re-teed to everybody's satisfaction, and Jamie holed the stroke! "Thank ye, sir," said Jamie, turning to Mr. X., "I'm muckle obleeged to ye" (*Golf,* 23 Sept. 1898: 45).

In 1883 Anderson was hired by the Royal Perth Golfing Society. (Previously, at some point between 1864 and 1870, Perth considered hiring Anderson, who was then working for Tom Morris, to replace Watty McDonald. Perth came to terms with McDonald but only after Anderson's price was considered too high.) Later in 1883, Anderson left Perth, where he was succeeded by Robert Simpson, and moved back to St. Andrews, where he started a business next to the shop of Tom Morris.

In 1890 Jamie Anderson, listed as "an old ex-champion" working for R. Forgan & Son, finished second in the first semiannual competition of the "St. Andrews Club-makers' Golf Club" (*Golf,* 20 Dec. 1890: 208). For their 1894 springtime competition, Anderson was still listed as a Forgan employee along with his son, James Anderson Jr. By 1898, though he was then working for R.B. Wilson, Anderson's fortunes had turned for the worse. During an interview with Old Tom Morris, the interviewer alluded to Anderson's troubles:

We came on to talk about Jamie Anderson. I said I was sorry to see an old Open Champion such a "scloof," lounging at street corners for money. But Tom is a grand exception of steadiness. "Black strap" [a preparation of Dublin stout and soda water] is his only luxury. But he was sorry to hear about Jamie; only he cautiously withheld any criticism beyond mentioning some of Jamie's trials (*Golf,* 4 Nov. 1898: 175).

Before falling on hard times, Anderson crafted some impressive clubs. The nearly unused Anderson driving putter shown dates to the 1870s. The beechwood head is 5 1/2 inches long, 1 15/16 inches wide, and 1 inch deep. The 39-inch shaft length helps identify this club as a driving putter:

The driving putter is really a driver with a short stiff shaft and a deep face, more upright than an ordinary driver and flatter than an ordinary putter, and it is used for playing long putts and also for driving against a head wind; The shortness and stiffness of the shaft ensure accuracy, and the less tendency to pull or heel the ball (Park 1896, 30).

The driving putter is never now played with. It was a club with a putter head, but with a flatter angle than a putter, a shaft about the length of a middle spoon, and, though stiff, had a spring in it. It was used to play out of bents and thick grass, but as these have now disappeared, so has the club. It was convenient, too, for playing against the wind (Balfour 1887: 22).

JOHN "JACK" MORRIS
(1847-1932)
GRASSED DRIVER

Born in St. Andrews, Jack Morris was the son of George Morris, Old Tom's brother. In 1857, when George was appointed the first professional at Carnoustie, Jack assisted his father and learned a good deal about club-making. In 1869, when the Royal Liverpool Golf Club ("Hoylake") was formed, Jack Morris was hired as its first professional:

He began in a very humble way, with a shop in the stables of the Royal hotel. He was nature's gentleman, full of kindliness and humour (Farrar 1933, 103).

He held this position for sixty years, from 1869 until 1929. After fifty-six years of service, Morris was honored by Hoylake's members when they elected him a life member of Royal Liverpool.

Morris did not spend all of his time at Hoylake, however. He laid out many golf links, including "St. Annes Old Course

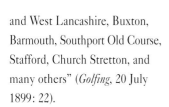

and West Lancashire, Buxton, Barmouth, Southport Old Course, Stafford, Church Stretton, and many others" (*Golfing*, 20 July 1899: 22).

Jack Morris did not make nearly as many clubs as did his uncle, Tom Morris, and stylistically they are not as shapely or graceful, either. The circa 1875 grassed driver shown represents some of Jack's better work. This club could be mistaken for a

long spoon, except that it has a 46-inch shaft. The head is 5 3/4 inches long, 1 7/8 inches wide, and 1 1/8 inches in face depth.

Along with "J. Morris," "J.W. MacFie" (probably the original owner of the club) is stamped in the top of the head. The author does not know if "J.W." was related to A.F. MacFie, the winner of the first British Amateur (held in 1885) and formerly a member of Hoylake.

One final note: Jack Morris named his eldest son, Tom, after his uncle. This Tom Morris eventually travelled to America where he worked as a golf professional, shafting and selling clubs wherever he was employed. Consequently, an occasional American-made hickory shaft club is found marked "Tom Morris."

A story of the old days is given by the famous Prestwick golfer, Charlie Hunter. One of the most remarkable games he ever took part in was at Prestwick during the midnight hours. It was a winter night—the 12th of December 1864—and the players, himself and Old Tom, Dr. Thoer and Major Crichtoe . . . . Charlie had gone to bed, but was routed out by Old Tom, who insisted that he should play in the match. They started about eleven o'clock and finished next morning about three. In those days there were only 12 holes at Prestwick. The night was dark—there was no moon—yet, marvellous to relate, only two balls were lost; and both of these were recovered next day, having only wandered a very little off the course (*St. Andrews Citizen*, 16 June 1900: 3).

Thomas Manzie was the professional at Crookham, Berkshire, from 1873 to 1875. In 1876 Manzie succeeded Robert Kirk as the professional and clubmaker to the Royal Blackheath Golf Club (Jackson 1994, 151). In 1885 Manzie was succeeded by C. Thomson, who was recommended as Manzie's successor by Tom Morris. Little more is known of Manzie other than the fact that his remaining clubs are very scarce.

The grassed driver shown is 43 1/2 inches in total length. The head, marked "T. Manzie," measures 5 1/4 inches long, 1 3/4 inches wide, and 1 1/8 inches deep. This club appears to date from somewhere in the 1870s.

The profile of the head is sleek and stylish compared to clubs produced in the 1880s.

As seen in the picture of the sole, some file marks are located at the bottom of the splice or "scair" as it is often referred to. In addition, the wood next to the tip of the shaft is much lighter because its finish has been removed. These things indicate the head was reshafted.

Although this club would be nicer if it had its original shaft, it is still a valuable example of Manzie's work. Not only are Manzie's clubs seldom seen, this clubhead is quite attractive and in nice original condition.

TOM DUNN
(1849-1902)
PLAY CLUB

Tom Dunn, son of Willie Dunn Sr. and brother of Willie Dunn Jr., learned the art of club-making from his father before starting his own business at North Berwick in 1870. Almost immediately thereafter, he accepted work as a professional:

*In the autumn of that year [1870] he accepted the appointment of professional to the London Scottish Golf Club at Wimbledon, and occupied that post for eleven years. In 1881, Tom re-entered upon the duties of custodian of the links at North Berwick, and held that position until the autumn of 1889, when he returned to London . . . as professional to the Tooting Bec Golf Club (*Golf, 8 May 1891: 130*).*

In 1894 Dunn left Tooting Bec to work as the professional and greenkeeper at the newly completed Bournemouth Corporation Golf Links.

Tom Dunn married Isabella Gourlay of the famous ballmaking family. They had two sons, John Duncan Dunn and, the youngest, Seymour Gourlay Dunn. Both sons were active in the golf business (see p 147-149).

In addition to being a club-maker, professional, greenkeeper, and true gentleman, Tom Dunn was a prolific golf course designer. Five days prior to his death, Dunn stated, "In all, I have laid out 137 golf links" (*Golf*, 25 Apr. 1902: 66). A number of these courses were located outside Great Britain.

Pictured is a prime example of Tom Dunn's work. The head on this 43 1/2-inch play club measures 5 3/8 inches long, 1 15/16 inches wide, and 1 1/16 inches in face depth. It shows little use, and the original finish is in excellent condition. Although it has a fair amount of style, this clubhead shows the evolutionary nature of the long nose. When compared with clubs from the 1850s or earlier, the head shape of this club is less graceful, the back of the head being a little broader behind the heel and into the neck. Some of this is due to the club-maker's own style, but a large part is due to the style of the day, i.e., the characteristics a club needed to be considered playable and durable in the late 1870s.

Tom Dunn also made woods that looked like feather ball clubs, complete with shallow faces and slender heads. Dunn either liked pre-1850 clubheads, and therefore made some of his clubs in that style, or he received customer requests to produce copies of "old favorites."

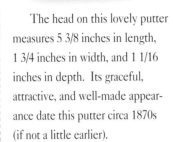

DAVID MITCHELL
(?-1883)
PUTTER

Occasionally, a long nose club marked "Mitchell" is mistakenly identified as sold by "Mitchell of Manchester," a British retail establishment that trafficked in golf goods, among other things. Marking clubs with the name of the retailer, or even "assembler," certainly occurred. However, "Mitchell" as marked on this head identifies David Mitchell, a talented, though obscure, clubmaker.

In 1876 David Mitchell replaced Frank Bell at the Dalhousie Golf Club (whose members played over the famous links at Carnoustie):

David Mitchell of St. Andrews, was appointed clubmaker and greenkeeper at an annual wage of £45. In 1881 Mitchell had to be relieved of his greenkeeping work owing to ill-health, but continued as clubmaster. . . . Mitchell died in 1883 (Chapman 1968, 16).

Prior to working at Carnoustie, Mitchell was a clubmaker at St. Andrews. At the autumn meeting of the R&A in 1871, Mitchell received second prize in the clubmakers competition, scoring 107 strokes over the old course and losing to nineteen-year-old James Beveridge (*Fifeshire Journal*, Oct. 1871: 6).

The head on this lovely putter measures 5 3/8 inches in length, 1 3/4 inches in width, and 1 1/16 inches in depth. Its graceful, attractive, and well-made appearance date this putter circa 1870s (if not a little earlier).

How delightful it was to gaze through the window of the clubmakers shop, or sidle into the shop itself, with its smell of fresh shavings, and glue, and pitched twine, and watch the various processes—to see the artist-workman remove the head every now and again from the vice, and hold it up to examine its curves, until their grace satisfied him; to observe the clean cutting of the horn-groove by hand and chisel alone, the perfect fitting of the horn, the ingenious way in which the pin-holes are pierced, first on a slant and then straight down; and to watch emerge at last, polished and varnished so that you might see yourself in it, the graceful head with all its glorious possibilities (W.L. Watson, *Golf* [ny], Feb. 1898: 25-26).

WALTER D. DAY
(1837-? EARLY 20TH CENTURY)
WOODEN NIBLICK

JAMES H. HUTCHISON
(1847-1912)
LONG SPOON

I can remember that about this day [early 1870s] I became the proud owner of a club just then coming into vogue under the name of the wooden niblick. Its head, made of wood, was very short, like that of the iron niblick, for the purpose of fitting into ruts. It was the original of the "brassey," for the idea of a rut suggested the idea of a road. There were more roads then than now, in proportion to the rest of the golfing hazards in the world . . . . And the purpose of the brass on the club's sole was to protect it from the stones, etc., of the road when used for play off such unfriendly surface. The brassey was just the wooden niblick with a sole of brass, and as all wooden niblicks began to be brazen upon the sole their very name passed into oblivion and that of brassey superseded it (Horace Hutchinson 1919, 37-38).

Wooden niblicks actually date much earlier than 1870. In 1857 wooden niblicks were described as follows:

Before leaving the subject of the spoons, we shall notice an antiquated connection of the family, now seldom met with . . . . It is called a Niblick; has a tough yet effective driving shaft; and an exceedingly small head well-spooned back. Its use is, or rather was, to drive a ball out of a rut or cap large enough to admit the "diminished" head—But it is exceedingly difficult to play with . . . . Besides, either a spoon or an iron answers the same purpose well enough (Farnie, 19).

The niblick of St. Andrews is a short, spooned wooden club; that of Musselburgh, a short, stout, iron-headed club, used for driving balls out of cart-ruts, & c. At St. Andrews, this little iron-headed club is termed a track-iron (Chambers 1857, 694).

On this and the following page, a Walter Day wooden niblick is pictured next to a James Hutchison long spoon in order to compare a wooden niblick with a long nose club, the wooden niblick being the shorter of the two heads.

Wooden niblicks made during the long nose era are hard to find. Occasionally, transitional woods from the 1880s or brassies from the early 1890s are incorrectly referred to as "wooden niblicks." A true wooden niblick comes from an earlier period of time. The misidentified clubs usually have somewhat elongated heads, certainly longer than those made in the 1900s. However, true wooden niblicks have more than just an intermediate size and a brass soleplate. They are also crafted in the same style as a long nose. The face will be curved, and the head will be shaped like a full-size long nose head, only shorter in length.

Many years after winning a competition at the age of twelve, which was in 1871, J.R. Gairdner recalled receiving a wooden niblick as his prize:

For this I gained a prize of a club to be made by Tom Morris. I declared for a wooden niblick, a club then temporarily in fashion, which with its short round head and stiffish shaft was undoubtedly a before-its-time type of our present models. By the way, I remember a few years after this being in Forgan's shop when the first brassey was brought to him for repair. His remarks ran somewhat to this effect: "The idea of taking a piece of wood, strong and elastic, binding brass on it with a lot of screw nails so as to take both strength and elasticity from it. Well, what will they do next?" (Leach 1907, 212-213).

A fine example of a wooden niblick, the Walter Day measures 5 inches in head length, 1 3/4 inches in width, and 1 1/4 inches in face depth. It dates circa 1870-75.

The head on the James Hutchison long spoon measures 5 1/2 inches long, 1 7/8 inches wide, and 1 1/8 inches in face depth. It dates circa 1875-80. Clubs that use a full brass soleplate, such as Day's wooden niblick, usually include a piece of ram's horn along the leading edge of the sole between the brass soleplate and the head. Both the brass plate and the horn helped fortify the head.

In addition to wooden niblicks, a few regular long nose clubs were made with full brass soleplates (see p. 77).

DAVID ANDERSON, JR.
(1847-1912)
PLAY CLUB

David Anderson Jr. was the son of a well-known St. Andrews personality nicknamed "Old Da," and the brother of three-time British Open champion Jamie Anderson. The known clubs marked "D. Anderson" were usually made by Junior, his father being more of a ballmaker, greenkeeper, and caddie.

The head on this unused play club, made by David Jr., measures 5 inches long, 1 7/8 inches wide, and 1 1/4 inches in face depth. This club measures 44 1/2 inches in overall length and has a greenheart fishing rod shaft, complete with an integral wood grip.

This head is proportioned such that it barely qualifies as a long nose, and the 1 1/4 inch face depth is deep by long nose standards. These things, when put together with the less than shapely outline of the beech wood head, indicate that this club was made during the middle to late 1880s when the long nose period drew to a close. Furthermore, this is when the greenheart fishing rod shaft was cast into the golf club market. (See page 50 and page 71 for descriptions of fishing rod shafts.) This Anderson play club has a shaft identical to the one on the Forgan putter previously discussed (see also page 528).

The rich golden blond color, the perfect original condition, and the rare shaft provide this club with great character and corresponding collectibility. One might speculate that the unused condition of this club can be credited to a practical golfer who quickly figured out that the wooden grip on this shaft is full of disadvantages. Not only would the sting of a poorly hit shot be *keenly* felt, but the club would be hard to hold on to, especially in wet weather.

The Play-Club is for driving, or, as it is sometimes called, swiping off the tee, and is further used throughout the green if the ball is lying fair, and the distance either a full drive or upwards from the hole to be approached (Chambers 1862, 14).

WILLIE PARK, JR.
(1864-1925)
TRANSITIONAL
SHORT SPOON

In my youngest days most boys who lived near the Musselburgh golf course played the game, and so the game came naturally to me, and so, too, did clubmaking. It seemed that the first thing one had to learn to do after discovering how to walk and the use of one's hands was how to make a golf club (Willie Park in Leach 1907, 100).

Raised on golf, Willie Park Jr. followed in his father's footsteps when he became one of the most prominent clubmakers and professionals of his day. At the early age of sixteen, young Willie was appointed greenkeeper and professional to the Ryton Golf Club (*Golf*, 12 June 1891: 228). In 1884 he returned to Musselburgh to work in his father's shop. Sometime during the next few years, as his father's health began to fail, Willie took over the business. Over the years, Willie Jr. employed many craftsmen, developed some innovative

clubs, authored a few books on golf, and designed a fair number of courses.

In 1887 and 1889 Willie demonstrated his great ability as a player by winning the Open Championship. As his fame grew, he participated in many challenge matches, the most famous of which was his loss to Harry Vardon in 1899.

The short spoon shown has a 40-inch lancewood shaft. The beech wood head measures 5 1/8 inches long, 2 inches wide, and 1 1/4 inches deep. The semi-long nose nature of this head is typical of the transitional clubs made at the end of the long nose period and dates this club around 1885-1890 as does the "Wm Park" stamp on the shaft (Willie Sr. did not stamp his shafts). The "Wm. Park" stamp used on this head belonged to Willie Jr. (To compare two different Park Sr. stamps, see pages 76-77.)

Because this club was made by such a prominent personality in the history of the game and represents his early work, it is of greater interest than similar clubs made by less prominent makers.

ALEX PATRICK
(1845-1932)
TRANSITIONAL BRASSEY

W. ANDERSON
TRANSITIONAL BRASSEY

To Golfers. J. Patrick, Clubmaker, Leven, grateful for encouragement hitherto received, and desirous to promote Golfing, is able to supply those wishing to amuse themselves at their own Clubs with best Hiccory Handles [sic] on moderate terms (Fifeshire Journal, 1 May 1856: 5).

Alex Patrick was born in 1845, two years before his father, John, set up his clubmaking business in Leven, Scotland. Alex became an apprentice to his father in 1857 and took over the family business upon his father's death in 1866. He remained as a clubmaker in Leven for most of his life. Only

between 1886 and 1891 did he take on the responsibilities of clubmaker and greenkeeper to the Royal Wimbledon Golf Club. During this time Patrick's business in Leven continued, being managed for him by one of his employees.

A fine clubmaker, Patrick was also a fine ballmaker, even making hand-hammered gutta percha balls in the 1890s:

His hand-hammered balls . . . have no superior, and are known the world over; but since the vast extension of the other great branch of the trade in recent years he has had less time to devote to this hand-hammering. . . . He sells all the leading makes, but

finds that many of his customers have still a preference for the hand-hammered (The Golfer, 12 Aug. 1896: 126).

The mahogany colored Patrick wood pictured has a full brass soleplate. This is a feature of both brassies and wooden niblicks. Although shaped like a wooden niblick, this Patrick wood is a transitional brassey as indicated by the "Patrick, Leven" shaft stamp which was not in use until the early 1890s.

Compared to the Anderson transitional also shown on this page, the Patrick has more of the long nose look of a wooden niblick. Both clubheads pictured are 4 1/2 inches long, 1 7/8 inches wide, 1 1/4 inches deep.

The W. Anderson club pictured is an attractive transitional brassey that dates from the 1890s. Note that the head is longer than the compact bulger head established in the 1890s but shorter than the traditional long nose.

The "W. Anderson" mark stamped on this head might belong to four-time U.S. Open champion Willie Anderson. But this brassey could have been made in the early 1890s by W. Anderson who once worked for Robert Forgan (see p. 316) or by Walter Anderson, the professional at Blackheath in 1889 - 1890 (Jackson 1994, 2).

Born in 1878, the son of Tom Anderson the greenkeeper at North Berwick, Willie Anderson worked as an apprentice in Alex Aitken's shop, "and for three years repaired and made clubs" (Colman 1929, 133). Willie then went to America in 1895 and worked as the pro at Misquamicut Golf Club at Watch Hill, Rhode Island. He went back to Scotland for the winter of 1896, but returned to America the following February. He left his job as professional at Watch Hill to become the professional at Baltusrol Golf Club and, by 1901, the Pittsburgh Golf Club.

CLAN GOLF CLUB COMPANY
TRANSITIONAL DRIVER

R. FORGAN & SON
BULGER BRASSEY

The wood with the original black finish pictured above and below was originally sold by the Clan Golf Club Company and is marked with their thistle trademark. The Clan Company produced the first clubs to bear a legally registered trademark, although other makers (Forgan, Carrick, etc.) had begun using logos or distinctive marks to identify their work prior to the Clan Company. The Clan Company's thistle was registered in 1891. The words "Clan" and "Regd" are included in their mark. The Clan Golf Club Company, a retail company in London that imported goods from Scotland, was in business from 1891 to 1895.

Following the demise of the Clan Golf Club Company, Spalding produced a line of "Clan" clubs which were a lower grade club according to their 1897 catalog. The early clubs sold by F.A.O. Schwartz, a retail establishment in New York City, were also marked "Clan."

The Clan transitional driver head pictured above measures 4 3/4 inches long, 2 1/4 inches wide, and 1 1/8 inches deep. Transitional clubs coexisted with early bulger woods until the late 1890s when transitionals completely gave way to the compact head of the bulger.

A piece of the horn under the leading edge of the Clan driver has broken off. However, because the missing piece only went down *into* the horn, not *through* it, the entire length of the horn is still intact. Should the club be repaired?

Replacement horn is available, and there are people today who are adept at making such a repair. However, the more original a club is, the better it is. It is far easier to accept the original horn with a bit of damage than it is a fully replaced horn. If the original horn was broken with half of it missing, some collectors would prefer to see the club restored to a more accurate likeness of its original self. It depends on how prominent and distracting the damage is. If the club is of great antiquity or unique historical value, it is best to leave it completely alone except in the most extreme circumstances.

Restoration should be approached very carefully. A club cannot be hurt by properly preserving it in an unrestored state. However, *many* a club has been ruined under the guise of "restoration."

With a head that measures 4 3/8 inches in length, 2 3/8 inches in width, and 1 1/4 inches in face depth, the nearly unused, early 1890s blond brassey pictured above and below is a true "bulger" wood. The face actually bulges out towards the target and the head is shorter and broader than a long nose. When introduced, these were radical changes. The traditional concave face inherent in the long nose wood was not only eliminated, it was *reversed*. It was thought that a "bulging" face would minimize hooking and slicing, especially for shots struck on the heel or the toe of the wood. Another reason for abandoning the length and shape of the long nose head was to locate more clubhead mass directly behind the ball.

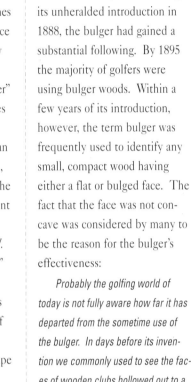

Within two years following its unheralded introduction in 1888, the bulger had gained a substantial following. By 1895 the majority of golfers were using bulger woods. Within a few years of its introduction, however, the term bulger was frequently used to identify any small, compact wood having either a flat or bulged face. The fact that the face was not concave was considered by many to be the reason for the bulger's effectiveness:

Probably the golfing world of today is not fully aware how far it has departed from the sometime use of the bulger. In days before its invention we commonly used to see the faces of wooden clubs hollowed out to a considerable concavity. . . It exaggerated the faults of heeling and toeing, slicing and hooking, which the bulger came especially to correct. It has achieved its object, for we seldom see the faces of the wooden clubs of today departing much from the plane surface. But the actual convexity of the bulger face we hardly ever see now. Some few drivers are made with the faces convex, but two or three drives hammer the convexity back to level, and this is the end of the bulge (Hutchinson 1902, 61-62).

Many golfers believed that the secret to the bulger's success was the shape of the head—compact, with the face ahead of the shaft—and not simply the outward curve of the face.

The reputation of the bulger, as a bulger, is largely due to a realization of the fact that this club owed its good qualities more to the general shape of its head than to any particular one of its face, and so the broad characteristics have survived whilst the originally predominant partner, namely the bulge, is only thrown in by the maker as an allowance for wear and tear (Golf, 17 Mar. 1897: 23).

The bulger idea brought the whole structure of the club head forward, distributing the balance more in the center of the head. To my way of thinking, this alteration in principles of balance of the wooden club has been the greatest and most lasting improvement in the make and shape of golf clubs within my recollection of the game (Hilton 1913, 56).

Today's woods continue in the mold of the bulger. The face has a distinct bulge and the head is short and compact. To whom do we give credit for this major innovation in the development of the golf club? To answer this question is to discuss Willie Park Jr. and Henry Lamb.

In October and November of 1890, Willie Park and Henry Lamb, each claiming to be the inventor of the bulger, exchanged letters through the public medium of *Golf's* "Letters to the Editor" column (*Golf*, 17 Oct. 1890: 70; 24 Oct. 1890: 86; 7 Nov. 1890: 118).

Willie Park wrote two letters wherein he claims he invented the club around 1883 and used it in 1884 and 1885, including the occasion when he "played for the championship" in 1885. After 1885 he stopped using the club for the most part. Park admits he did not conceive the name "bulger" and allows Henry Lamb credit for the term. His final comment in his last letter on the topic is, "I do not play with a bulger now."

Henry Lamb, on the other hand, states in his letter that the club he invented is unlike anything he had ever seen—he designed it, named it, began using it immediately, and in 1888 presented it to a group of professionals for their inspection. Lamb then recounts that Willie Park was among this group of professionals and that Park, upon seeing Lamb's bulger, stated, "I once made a club like that, but it was no good at all." Willie sent a second letter in response to Lamb's letter, but did not deny the remark attributed to him.

These letters show that Willie Park Jr. believed he made a club similar to a bulger as early as 1883. He used his club, but made no effort to produce or promote it. Instead, because he disliked the club, he gave up on it after a short trial.

It is not known just how much Park's club was like Lamb's bulger. But any similarities it possessed—either great or small—were of no consequence. Park's club did not influence the world of golf and remained unknown, the direct result of Park's own disapproval and rejection of whatever his club was.

Clearly, Henry Lamb should be credited with the development and introduction of the bulger. This conclusion is shared by golf historians contemporary with Willie Park Jr. In 1891, in an article about Lamb, H.S.C. Everard wrote:

Does not Mr. Lamb stand forth as the inventor of the "Bulger"? Inventor yes, but patentee, unlucky for himself, no . . . . (Golf, 9 Oct.: 57). [No one ever patented the bulger.]

Everard's article also recalls the skeptical comments Lamb initially received concerning his club, many from such prominent personalities as J.O.F. Morris and Jamie Anderson. Everard concludes his comments on the topic of Lamb and the bulger as follows:

Questioned as to the evolution of his idea, Mr. Lamb will tell you that it was merely in accordance with common sense, "If you hook, file off the toe; If you heel, file that part off." Some slight controversy has arisen as to whether Mr. Lamb is the real inventor, or Willie Park, jun. As to this, the writer is able to state that he was with Mr. Lamb at the time his idea occurred to him, that he well remembers a drawing of the proposed club on paper, that he accompanied Mr. Lamb to one of the club-makers, and heard him explain his idea, and he also remembers Mr. Lamb's first shots with his new club. At this time the writer had never heard of any similar invention by Park.

Perhaps the clearest conclusion as to who invented the bulger was given in 1902. Referring to pre-1890 golf, Horace Hutchinson states:

There was only one man in the kingdom who played with a club whose face was not intended to be a plane—and this was the late Mr. Henry Lamb, since, unhappily, deceased. He, and he alone, for he was its inventor, played with a "bulger." Now Park also appears to have once made a club with a bulging face; but . . . failed in seeing the merit of the idea. Mr. Lamb did not fail. He went on playing with the new queer thing, in the face of much derision, and with such triumphant success . . . . (61).

Henry Lamb, born in 1844, was a fine amateur golfer. He won many awards including a runner-up finish to Horace Hutchinson in the 1886 British Amateur. He was officially connected with the Royal Wimbledon Golf Club for twenty years. For thirteen of those years he carried on the arduous duties of Secretary. He died in 1893.

A bulger *iron*, produced by an unnamed source, was tried. It was found to be:

more scientific than satisfactory from a practical point of view, especially in wet weather, when the ball is apt to "skid" off the curved surface (Golf, 23 Apr. 1897: 123).

A bulger *putter* designed by Mr. E.S. Spencer, of Wimbledon, is reviewed in the February 18, 1898 issue of *Golf* (398) (see p. 258).

By 1912 the concept of "bulge and roll" or the double bulge—a face curved heel to toe *and* top to bottom—was in use:

Another club made to cheat the wind is a driver with a double bulge on the face, that is to say, the face is bulged both down and across. The idea is that the ball is hit with the center of two reverse slopes, and so a great deal of spin can be put on and the ball kept low (Ross 1912, 346).

The evolution of the wood: long nose, transitional, early bulger, bulger.

Many people declare that all they desire is exercise, and that they do not mind how badly they shape as golfers. They generally express these sentiments when they stand about six down with five to play.

(Harry Vardon; Vardon 1912: 52)

Irons

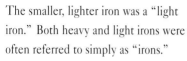

In golf's earliest days, irons were seldom used. They were called upon when the mere extraction of the ball was the objective—usually when in high grass, among rocks, or in the bottomless pit of a bunker—or when the ball found hard, sandy ground or loose pebbles which might damage a wooden head:

The old iron club was probably used nowhere but in whins, in sand, in roads, and other hazards. It was of prodigious size and weight, like a Lochaber-axe or other deadly weapon. If it was lighter, it was very concave, and had queer sharp tusks. . . . These ponderous maces of our ancestors were never used "on the green"; only in hazards (Lang 1895, 141).

The large size and heavy weight of many early irons were not the only things that precluded the general use of irons. Because of their inherent divot-taking nature, early irons were seen as destructive to the course; so much so, that it was considered "reprehensible" to use an iron "on the usual golfing ground" (*Fifeshire Journal*, 17 Feb. 1853: 3; see p. 105).

Irons were also not abundant because they were expensive, as demonstrated in the expense account books of one John MacKenzie. Between 1712 and 1715, MacKenzie incurred golf-related expenses on behalf of his three sons attending St. Andrews University. According to MacKenzie's expense account books, the price of a wood club was either 10 or 12 shillings, depending on the character of the club; the price of an iron was at least double, at 1 pound 4 shillings, 20 shillings to the pound (Hamilton 1986, 18, 25).

Because so few irons were made during golf's earliest days, few remain. Their durability, however, allowed them to be handed down from one generation to the next. Only the shaft, which could easily be replaced, was breakable.

To collectors, the term "early iron" refers to any iron club made before 1850. Such clubs, designed for use with the feather ball, were made in different shapes and styles which naturally bear the individual characteristics of their makers. However, early irons also share some common characteristics. Specifically, pre-1850 irons usually have much larger and heavier heads than their counterparts—cleeks and lofters— that followed. Early irons also have longer and thicker hosels, the tops of which bear very distinct "nicking," and thicker shafts.

Early irons were known by several different names. A large, heavy one was called a "heavy iron," "bunker iron," "sand iron," or "spade."

The smaller, lighter iron was a "light iron." Both heavy and light irons were often referred to simply as "irons."

Early irons were usually made by blacksmiths, but some of the earliest were probably made by armorers. (William Mayne, royal clubmaker to King James I in 1603, was also the King's spearmaker [see p. 30].) Unfortunately, irons made before 1850 were not marked with the maker's name. Because there were so few golfers during this time and only a meager demand for new irons, advertising for repeat business was unimportant.

Collecting early irons is a pastime for either the very rich or the very lucky. Given the great antiquity and rarity of an early iron (only 60 to 75 pre-1830 examples are known, most of them held by old Scottish or British golf clubs), whenever one becomes available it draws serious collector interest. Then again, to the unknowing, an early iron can easily be misunderstood and viewed as something of little value. The author is aware of one individual who, years back, was given a fine example of a circa 1800 early iron. The owner, at the time, thought it was too heavy and crude to be significant.

In addition to the early irons previously mentioned, "iron niblicks" or "track irons" came into prominence by 1850. These clubs were designed to dislodge a ball from the bottom of a cart track or other narrow rut during play.

The head of a track iron is very small, thick, and heavy—necessary characteristics for trying to extract a ball from the unfavorable circumstances of a cart track or other tight surroundings. Early track irons have a distinctly concave face and a hosel that measures five inches or longer. During the 1870s the faces started to flatten out. By the 1880s most clubs had flat faces. During the 1880s the blade of a track iron became slightly larger and thinner, while the hosel, or "pipe" as it was called, became smaller. By 1890, as the long hosel, tiny head, and heavy weight of the track iron were left behind, "rut niblicks," as collectors now call them, were born. The hosel nicking on a rut niblick was less prominent than it was on a track iron and was more cosmetic than functional.

After 1850 the "cleek" and "lofter" (also called a "driving iron") came into vogue. Because these clubs were downsized from earlier irons, they were more manageable and therefore more usable. Consequently, golfers began to use cleeks and lofters to approach the green. Although more refined than early irons, cleeks and lofters were still designed to complement each other, as were the old light and heavy irons.

LEFT TO RIGHT: *These six irons are arranged from the oldest to the newest. Together they provide a glimpse of the evolution of the iron. Notice how large, massive, and crude the first three irons are. The first iron on the left dates from the mid to late 1700s. Because it is so upright, the 5 1/2 inch long hosel appears much shorter than the others. Actually it is not. The second and third irons date from the late 1700s or early 1800s. Their large, concave blades are typical of irons their age. Notice the downsizing and refinement of the remaining three irons. The fourth iron, having a slightly concave and hooked face, is unmarked and dates circa 1850. The fifth iron, a Carrick lofter, dates circa 1880. The final iron, a Spalding "Rob't T. Jones" 5 iron, dates from 1931 and is a typical example, in terms of size and shape, of the vast bulk of remaining wood shaft irons.*

Between 1850 and 1890, being a cleekmaker—a clubmaker who makes only irons—became a full-time occupation. As cleekmakers became established, so did the practice of marking irons with either the maker's name or their name and location.

By 1890 golfers began supplementing their cleeks and lofters with additional iron clubs further divided as to purpose and design. The first of these spin-offs was the "mashie."

The earliest reference to a mashie is in John Forgan's 1881 work *The Golfer's Handbook* which describes a "mashy" as:

one of those fanciful clubs that have been invented in recent years, and is entirely unnecessary in the golfer's set (Forgan, 15).

In 1896 Alex Patrick declared that the mashie "has only been in use—roughly speaking—twelve years or so" (*The Golfer*; 12 Aug.: 128). Although the mashie was in use during the early 1880s, it was closer to 1890 before the mashie was in wide circulation.

Once the idea of subdividing the cleek and lofter into other irons was accepted, the flood gates of human ingenuity opened—not to mention the chance to cash in on a rapidly growing market. After the mashie came everything from the "glory iron" to the "sky iron," from the "spade niblick" to the "jigger," from the "sammy" to the "bar back cleek," ad inf.

In keeping with the growing variety of irons, the way clubs were marked also evolved during the 1890s. By 1910 the backs of iron blades were usually covered with advertising. Often an iron was marked not only with the maker's name, location, and trademark, but also with the seller's name and location. Certain clubs were even marked with their own distinctive model name. Furthermore, irons were stamped with such promotional commentary as "Warranted Hand Forged" and "Made In Scotland." Today these various marks do not identify a club

as out of the ordinary or old. Usually it is the iron *without* all the advertising that dates to an earlier period of time when fewer golfers played the game. (There were, however, some unmarked irons made in the 1890s and later. These unmarked irons should not be mistaken for earlier unmarked irons. Structurally, they are different—later unmarked irons are more refined.) Not only do marks (applied consistently to the clubs made after 1890) identify their maker and/or seller, they also play an important role in dating clubs. These marks identify the era when a club was made and can tie a club to a specific point in time if the years when a particular mark was used are known.

At the turn of the twentieth century, the iron clubs most commonly used, and all that were really necessary for the player, were the "Cleek, Mashie, Iron [such as a mid-iron], Niblick, and Putter" (Smith 1897, 11; see p. 565 for definitions). All other irons were either adaptations or modifications of these.

Complete seven to nine club sets of irons were first sold as a single item at a single price in the mid-1920s. These irons were often marked with numbers, such as "1, 2, 3, 4," etc., though irons made before then often bore single digit numbers to identify the particular model—a "2 cleek" being different from an "8 cleek," though made by the same maker. Although such clubmakers as George Lowe (p. 168) and Francis Brewster (p. 204) devised and produced matching clubs/sets in the 1890s, Irving R. Prentiss, of Philadelphia, Pennsylvania, went a step further by devising and patenting the idea of a balanced/swingweighted set of irons. Described in his U.S. patent (No. 1,516,786) applied for on April 18, 1921, and granted on November 25, 1924, Prentiss's method of measuring "swingweight" proved effective and was eventually adopted by the entire golf industry. (For more on Prentiss, see page 122; *Golf Ill.* [ny], Feb. 1930: 15, 49.)

EARLY IRONS

It is at all times a very interesting sight to see a blacksmith at work, and none the less interesting should the blacksmith happen to be a cleekmaker. Look into the shop and you see a row of grimy faced brawny armed men. As they are thrown into bold relief by the ruddy glow of the forge fires, you note with interest the play of the strong muscles beneath the skin. Some are handling the bellows and blowing up the smouldering coals into the fierce heat requisite for their purpose. As the heavy hammer comes down on that piece of iron which is destined to be the joy of some golfer, showers of fiery sparks fly in all directions. The anvil sends out a merry clang, while now and then the notes of some old Scotch song rises triumphant over the other sounds (Fifeshire Journal, 19 June 1903: 5).

In spite of their wonderfully crude and varying nature, early irons are not arbitrary creations. They are distinguished by name and purpose. According to *Hoyle's Games Improved* published in 1790, among the six basic clubs in use at that time were two different irons: the "heavy iron," used when the ball "lies deep amongst stones or mud;" and the "light iron," used when the ball lies "on the surface of chingle or sandy ground" (288).

Matching Hoyle's description of a light iron and a heavy iron, the two "Troon" irons, discussed on page 32, are of two distinct sizes—one being heavier and having a larger blade than the other. The square toe iron pictured on the previous and facing pages is nearly identical in design, shape, size, and style to the Troon light iron. They differ only in the style of their nicking.

Today, collectors distinguish the square toe iron from the round toe iron. The square toe is usually the earlier club, definitely the rarer club, and consequently the most valuable and coveted of *all* irons. Even so, early round toe irons are extremely valuable. Although the square toe iron was introduced before the round toe iron, they coexisted through the 1700s. By the early 1800s, square toe irons had faded from the game and round toe irons were the standard.

Square toe irons basically come from two generations. The earliest known square toe irons, those from the first generation, have a blade that *sweeps* up into the hosel. This characteristic is most noticeable when viewing the top-line of the blade. It simply rounds up and flows into the hosel as if the blade itself formed the hosel by wrapping around the shaft. A distinct point where the blade ends and the hosel begins cannot be found, nor is there anything remotely resembling a clear, sharp crease where the hosel meets the top-line of the blade.

Only twelve first generation irons are known: the example pictured, the two Troon irons, two irons at Royal Musselburgh, one iron at the Royal and Ancient Golf Club of St. Andrews, three irons belonging to the Earl of Wemyss (near Edinburgh, Scotland), one iron stolen from the Earl in 1992, and two additional irons (one of which is a juvenile club) privately held. These irons date to the seventeenth century and possibly even the sixteenth century. Because there are no known clubs carrying an unequivocal provenance from the 1500s (or earlier), dating a club to that century can be suggested only as a possibility.

A second generation early iron is easily recognized by the sharp crease at the point where the top of the blade intersects the side of the hosel. This area of the head is the "blade crease." A sharp and clear "cut" at the exact point of intersection is referred to as a sharp blade crease. There are approximately twenty-five square toe irons currently known that have a sharp blade crease. These irons represent the second generation of early irons, dating primarily within the 1700s. All early round toe irons have sharp blade creases. In fact, irons continued to be made with a sharp crease until the middle to late 1880s when this area of the iron head went through a period of transition, the sharp crease being filled in and smoothed over. Consequently, clubs made after approximately 1890 have a dull blade crease.

Within the realm of the square toe iron resides the "spur toe." Six known square toe irons have a "spur," or small extension of the sole out beyond the toe: the heavy iron in the Troon clubs, a privately held iron in the U.S., two irons at Royal Musselburgh, and two irons which belonged to the Earl of Wemyss until one of them was stolen in 1992 (the same club already mentioned). The October 9, 1896 issue of *Golf* [74] also pictures a spur toe iron then owned by the McEwan family. Although some collectors identify the spur as the feature which distinguishes between a first and second generation square toe iron, this is not completely accurate. Consider the Troon irons. They were obviously made by the same maker at the same point in time. Their heads are made from the same type of iron with the same surface texture. They have identical styling, and even the exceptionally large nicking is perfectly matched. Their shafts match and are marked the same. Yet only one of those irons has a spur on the toe. Does this single difference mean one of the irons was made long after the other or possibly by a different maker? Of course not. They are a perfectly matched pair!

A spur toe is the result of the *purpose* of the iron. It is not merely a "stylistic feature" reflecting structure and craftsmanship from a particular era. According to Peter McEwan, this spur, or hollowing out of the bottom of the end of the toe, allowed the club to be "used hammer-wise" (*Golf*, 9 Oct. 1896: 75). By turning the club to align the entire length of the blade directly behind the ball, the end of the toe could be used to strike a ball lying in a narrow rut or nestling among stones.

The idea, offered by some, that the spur would help an iron cut through grass makes no sense if that was the only purpose of the spur. What good does it do to cut through the grass beyond the toe? However, if the iron was also to be used "hammer-wise," to extract a ball from among stones or a rut, the idea of designing the spur to cut through grass when the club was in normal use (so as not to hinder its regular duties) makes sense.

The feature of the spur, therefore, would be needed only on one iron carried by a golfer. Given the account in *Hoyle* previously quoted, the spur would obviously be placed on the "heavy iron" because heavy irons were used when the ball "lies deep among stones or mud." Also, given the different function and purpose of a light iron (it was designed more for distance), its blade has a lower profile, less loft, and no need for a spur.

The principle to understand here is that although spur toe irons date from the first generation of square toe irons, the spur is not the only distinguishing feature. The way the top of the blade transitions into the neck is what really separates first generation from second generation irons. Such a difference speaks to the evolution in iron head construction.

The square toe light iron pictured on the previous and following pages is reshafted, the original shaft having been removed many years ago after breaking. The existing ash shaft is 43 inches long. This is the shaft length of the Troon light iron and fits within the range of club lengths for other very early irons. Ash shafts were also common in early irons. The hosel on this iron is 6 inches long.

As were all early irons, this square toe iron was made by heating and hammering a rod of iron until it was relatively flat. One end of this flattened rod was then heated and hammered around a mandrel to form the hosel. As the sides of the hosel came together, overlapping slightly, a "seam" running lengthwise down the hosel appeared. This seam was eventually blended together by much hammering. Today, this seam is also referred to as "the hammer weld." Sometimes this seam is visible on the outside of the hosel, depending on how much attention the maker gave to smoothing it. However, there will always be an overlapping seam visible *inside* the hosel. The other end of the bar of iron was pounded out flat and the blade shaped. The lie of the iron head was created by heating the iron and bending the hosel upwards. On an early club such as this, nails were used to pin the head to the shaft.

The marvelous workmanship in this early square toe iron gives additional credibility to the belief that armorers made some of the earliest known irons. This light iron is a wonderfully handsome implement, yet it is among the very oldest clubs in existence.

There are many similarities between this light iron and the Troon light iron—more similarities, in fact, than differences. The irons are alike in the overall size of the head and the shape of the blade and hosel. Even the blackish color and texture of the metal, two additional characteristics of a very early iron, are quite similar (recognizing this iron has a bit of oxidation on its surface). The only significant difference between these irons is the hosel nicking. The Troon iron has large nicking while this light iron has smaller nicking.

By crimping down around the shaft, nicking helped fasten the head to the shaft. Early irons of the same approximate age, having very similar characteristics throughout the head, shaft, and grip, often have distinctly different nicking. Because of the handmade and crude nature of early irons, nicking often reflects the style of the maker more than the age of the club. Consequently, nicking by itself is not an accurate way to date one early iron from the next, but it can be evidence of an early iron when taken into consideration with other characteristics.

One final note: The October 1994 issue of *Golf Magazine* reports that a circa 1502 square toe iron, a heavy iron with a sharp blade crease and an "R" marked on its back, sold for $1.25 million as "the oldest known club in existence" and the "only one like it in the world" (24). The seller arrived at his estimation of the date because the club was found at a castle in Scotland which King James IV may have visited, and an account from the early 1500s shows some clubs were made for the King. Because this club is marked with an "R" (the first letter of the Latin word "Rex" which means "King"), this club, so the seller's theory goes, is most likely one of the clubs made for King James IV.

In this author's opinion, that square toe iron is certainly one of the *premier* early clubs known, but it is not the oldest and does not date to 1502, nor for that matter, before approximately 1650. To begin with, this iron has the standard shape of a second generation iron, complete with a sharp blade crease, and, except for being marked with an "R", is not the only one like it in the world. No fewer than seven square toe heavy irons which also lack a spur are very much "like it" in size, construction, shape, style, and age, to say nothing of approximately fifteen other square toe irons which also have a sharp blade crease. And if this "R", which lacks an accompanying royal coat of arms, was intended to identify a king—which is debatable—which king? Gifts were given by royalty throughout history. It is entirely possible that a king in the late 1600s or 1700s gave someone a club that made its way into an old castle.

UNKNOWN MAKER
EARLY IRON

In addition to having a distinguished low profile blade shape, this mid to late eighteenth century iron possesses a number of crude and distinctly early characteristics. They are as follows:

The 5 1/2-inch hosel is extremely thick (15/16 in.), and its hammer weld is clearly evident on the back of the hosel.

The shaft is pinned through the hosel parallel with the blade, not "side to side" as is done in 99.9 percent of all the pinned irons in existence. Pinning the hosel in line with the blade inadvertently allowed the shaft to become loose inside the head. Once clubmakers understood this, shafts were pinned side to side in line with the target.

The leading edge of the blade is *ahead* of the leading edge of the hosel.

The blade is actually slightly convex. Usually an early iron has a concave face.

The blade is extremely thick, even at the top (5/16 in.). The blade is also well-lofted for an early iron and unusually shallow (1 1/2 in.).

The shaft is thick (one inch thick at the grip end) and made from greenheart. Generally speaking, the more refined the club, the thinner the shaft. The "non-hickory" shaft is significant because hickory was not the standard shaft in the earliest days of golf.

The club is very heavy (25.4 oz.) and massive in its presentation and appearance.

The club, measuring 37 inches in length, is very upright:

Golfer's generally like the lie of their heavy iron to be upright, as in a number of cases they have to stand over, or very close to, their ball—situations which would render a flat lie peculiarly inefficient (Farnie 1857, 34).

An early cleek-like iron not much different from the one pictured here, and made by the same maker, is found in a small collection of clubs at Bruntsfield Golf Club in Edinburgh, Scotland. Four similar irons are in private collections.

The iron pictured here is also the first club pictured on page 98.

UNKNOWN MAKER

EARLY SAND IRON

The fascinating early iron pictured below was formerly owned by the Royal North Devon Golf Club, Westward Ho! located on the west coast of England. In 1988 Royal North Devon sold this early iron, along with another, at auction in New York City.

In addition to the large head, concave blade, long hosel, and prominent nicking, this middle to late 1700s iron offers a few other interesting features:

The extremely uneven face, easily seen on the blade, is clear evidence of "hand hammering."

The hosel is quite small near the blade and very thick (15/16 in.) at the top.

The 5 3/8 inch long hosel is asymmetrical. On the side of the hosel, the hammer weld extends upwards and works its way around to the back of the hosel.

The leading edge of the blade is well ahead of the lower portion of the hosel.

The blade is curved or "hooked," heel to toe, in addition to being concave, top to bottom.

The common thread running through these distinct traits is their crude and primitive quality. Such crude characteristics are outstanding features to the collector. They reflect clubmaking in its infancy.

That the iron was at first mainly connected with play under abnormal conditions may be inferred both from the name of sand iron given to the heavier variety, and from the old rule which prescribed the use only of the iron after lifting out of a hazard. This restriction to the use of a club of such an unwieldy nature, as then made, was evidently a penalty equivalent to one stroke at least, for whereas nowadays the lifting out of a hazard is accompanied by the loss of two strokes, the same rule which required the use of the iron under these circumstances only added one stroke to the score (Golf, 23 April 1897: 122).

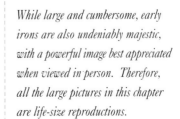

While large and cumbersome, early irons are also undeniably majestic, with a powerful image best appreciated when viewed in person. Therefore, all the large pictures in this chapter are life-size reproductions.

This early iron was once the property of his Grace the Duke of Athole, one of Scotland's pre-eminent dukes. Written in old ink on the sheepskin grip are the words "Heavy Iron." This club was most likely made expressly for the duke and therefore actually marked "Heavy Iron" to distinguish it.

The main characteristics of this late 1700s iron are as follows:

This club is very heavy. (It weighs 24.1 ozs.)

The hosel is massive, measuring 5 1/2 inches in length and 7/8 of an inch in thickness.

The blade is concave and exceptionally large, measuring 2 3/8 inches in face depth and 5/32 of an inch in thickness at the topline.

The hammer weld is visible on the side of the hosel just below the pin and at the base of the hosel next to the face.

The nicking at the top of the hosel is big, sharp, and prominently "sawtooth" in style.

The 39 1/2-inch shaft is thick and stout, measuring 11/16 of an inch at its thinnest point.

There is a sharp crease or "cut" where the top of the blade intersects the side of the hosel.

The minor crack in the shaft down by the hosel is not detrimental to this club. The head is still firmly in place and the crack is not spreading. Such discreet, small cracks do not attract undue attention and can be repaired, even to the point of disappearing, if desired. Furthermore, cracks in a shaft were a normal part of the game, especially for a club designed to handle the most difficult of lies.

This club is also pictured on page 98, second from the left.

Old-fashioned irons look like the missing link between a meat cleaver and a kitchen spoon. They all originally belonged to somebody's grandfather and are only now to be found in glass cases or in the sets of very bad players, who, according to whether they had a golfing grandfather or not, expiscate or purchase them. The player, when getting his instrument from his caddy, does not ask for an iron in the usual way. He says "Give me my heavy iron," in a tone which causes the inexperienced adversary to despair. In reality, using an old-fashioned iron is the last expedient of those who cannot loft a ball with anything else. Even this expedient often fails, but defeat is at least avenged by the destruction of the green (Simpson 1887, 24).

The heavy iron pictured here is similar to the one on the facing page. The blade is concave and quite large (2 1/4 in. deep), and the hosel is thick and long (6 in. length). The head is also very heavy (23.1 ozs.) and, at 39 inches, the shaft is nearly the same length. Even with all these similarities, this club was obviously made by a different maker. (This iron is also seen third from the left on page 98.)

The ornamental ring cut around the top of the 7/8 of an inch thick hosel adds character and charm to what is already a magnificent early iron. Because of the decorative ring, the maker of this early iron is referred to today as "the ringmaker." His actual identity, however, is unknown.

Six other early irons share this distinctive ring. One of them, formerly property of Perth Golf Club in Scotland, is nearly identical to this iron. The second iron is also quite similar, except that its hosel is pinned "heel to toe" instead of front to back like this club. (Perhaps the clubmaker pinned hosels in different directions due to indifference; perhaps the location of the hosel weld was a consideration.) The third "ringmaker" iron, property of the Royal Musselburgh Golf Club, is one of the earliest putting irons known. The fourth is a cleek-like iron similar to the iron pictured on page 102. The fifth and sixth irons, formerly owned by the Woking Golf Club, were sold in London at Sotheby's golf auction in July, 1996.

This club and the one on the preceding page are quite similar, but this club may not be quite as old. The hosel nicking found on this and the other examples of the ringmaker's clubs appears more refined. Then again, because these irons are so similar, their differences might be those of two different makers rather than a difference in period.

GOLFING is abolished on the [St. Andrews] links pro tempore on account of the snow. On Monday the golfers had recourse to the sands, as a field for their operations. . . . The tides being early and late at present, no interruption to the game takes place during the day in this new arena. 'Horses feet are somewhat detrimental to the sandy course; and the players are rather puzzled in the putting department . . . . There is one comfort, however, that there can be no objections made to the out-and-out use of clicks [cleeks, meaning irons] a practice which is considered highly reprehensible on the usual golfing ground; so much so, that a ticket was lately hung out requesting its discontinuance (Fifeshire Journal, 17 Feb. 1853: 3).

The general purpose iron pictured here (fourth from the left on page 98) dates to the end of the feather ball era. Besides having some excellent early characteristics, this iron shows elements of refinement when compared to those previously discussed. For example, the blade on this iron is not as deep (1 31/32 in. in depth) or as thick (3/32 in. at the top-line of the blade), but it is larger than that of the lofter which came into vogue during the second half of the 1800s. The blade has a definite hook to it, but is only slightly concave, top to bottom. The hosel is slightly shorter (4 7/8 in.) and thinner (25/32 in.). The nicking, while still distinctly sawtooth in style, is smaller.

An outstanding feature of this club is its exceptional provenance. This iron is one of approximately sixty clubs collected by Harry B. Wood, author of *Golfing Curios and The Like*. Published in 1910, Wood's was the first book on golf collectibles ever published.

Attached to the shaft is the small cardboard tag Harry had printed for all but three of his clubs. The tag reads:

"Lofting Iron" about 1860, used at Blackheath—makers name probably erased by continual cleaning. Note the weight when swinging.

This author, however, believes this iron dates closer to 1850 (see facing page) and that it was never marked with a maker's name.

The clubs and curios that Wood collected were given to the Manchester Golf Club, in Manchester, England, where Wood was a member. His collection remained on display there until 1986, when the Manchester Golf Club sold it in its entirety. Currently, almost all of Wood's items are found within six private collections.

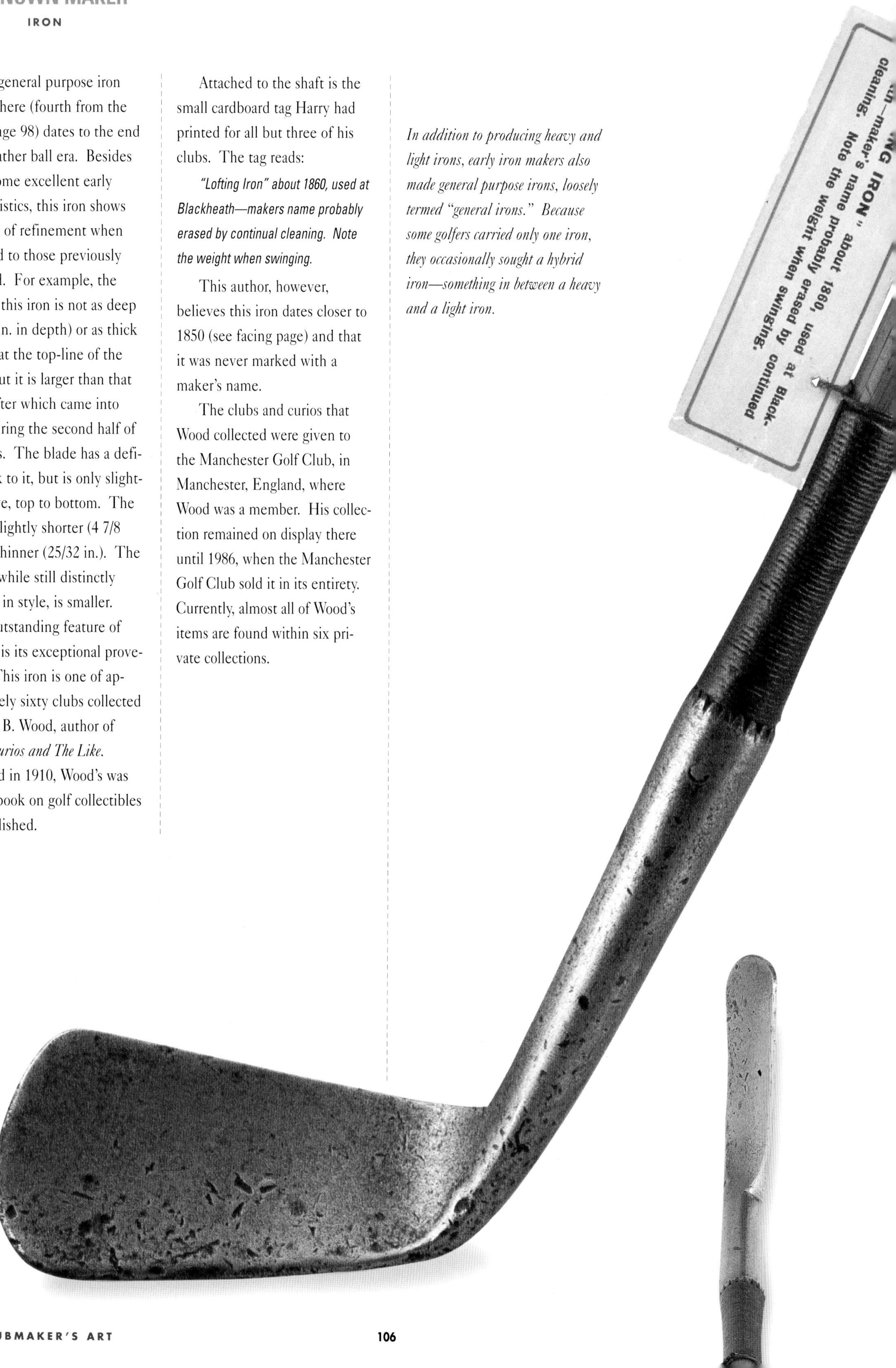

In addition to producing heavy and light irons, early iron makers also made general purpose irons, loosely termed "general irons." Because some golfers carried only one iron, they occasionally sought a hybrid iron—something in between a heavy and a light iron.

The circa 1860 iron pictured shows the early iron in transition, headed into the world of the lofter. This club has many of the features expected in a pre-1850 iron except it is more refined and not as ponderous as its earlier brothers.

The refinement becomes obvious when comparing the picture of this iron to those of the earlier heavy irons. Despite being large (two inches at its deepest point), concave, and shaped similar to a heavy iron, the blade is not as heavy. This club weighs 16 ounces. The five inch hosel length is long, but it is not quite as stout, measuring only 3/4 of an inch in thickness. The nicking is not as crude, but its substantial size and excellent character predates the typical circa 1870 iron.

The head, in keeping with its age, is not stamped with a clubmaker's name. When this head was made, most cleekmakers did not mark their work.

The shaft is stamped "R. Forgan & Son, St. Andrews," but it is highly improbable that Forgan produced the clubhead. It is much bigger than those made in 1883, when Forgan added "& Son" to his business, and it looks *nothing* like any Forgan iron known. Undoubtedly, Forgan & Son reshafted this club (clubmakers not only made clubs, they also repaired them). The head is a little loose on the shaft, as sometimes happens with a reshaft.

This iron also bears the exceptional distinction of being one of the clubs from the Harry B. Wood collection, discussed on the facing page. A portion of the tag Wood used to identify his clubs is visible in the photo. Fastened to the shaft, the tag reads:

"Iron" by R. Forgan & Son. (Stamp on shaft - that on club head being probably worn away by cleaning.) Probable date about 1850. Presented by Mr. J. H. Fulton, Broughton Park, to whose father the club belonged.

Although Harry Wood authored the first book on golf collectibles, he was not completely accurate in all his statements. For example, Robert Forgan did not go into business for himself until 1856, following the death of Hugh Philp. Forgan did not include his son as a partner in his business until 1883. Therefore, Forgan could not have made this club in 1850, the date Wood assigns to it, and the date which appears to fit. Of course, the stamp on the club head was not "worn away"; it was never there to begin with.

These five lofting irons and one mashie all date between 1870 and 1890. From the left, these clubs are marked: Anderson of Anstruther, W. Thomson (the mashie), J. Gray, W. Wilson, R. Wilson, and F.&A. Carrick. With the exception of Thomson, these names represent most of the earliest cleekmakers who marked their work. Note the sharp crease or "cut" on each iron where the top of the blade meets the hosel. This is a characteristic of the early iron that continued with the lofter. In other respects, lofters are different from early irons: they are smaller, their blades are not as broad or thick, their hosels are not as long or stout, their nicking is less prominent, and most of them have a flat face. Still, lofters are notably larger and less refined than the irons that eventually replaced them.

LOFTING IRONS

The driving [lofting]-iron nearly resembles [the bunker iron] in everything but weight; it is used amongst difficulties also, but only when the ball is intended to be, and admits of being, sent some distance. There are also finer uses to which this club is occasionally put (Henry Farnie 1857, 20).

The lofting iron is the most fascinating, the most coquettish, of all the golfer's following. Feminine, without doubt--so delightful on occasion; yet so exasperating, so untrustworthy, so full of moods and tenses (Horace G. Hutchinson 1902: 64)

The name of this club well suggests its use. It is used for what are called "short approach shots," especially when a burn, bunker, or other hazard has to be played over when in the neighborhood of one of the holes on the putting-green. This club, when properly used, gives great elevation to the ball, which seldom moves far away from the spot where it falls (W.T. Linskill 1889, 23).

As the early iron evolved, it became lighter, smaller, and more refined. Eventually, the light iron and the heavy iron gave way to the cleek and the lofter, or driving iron as it was initially termed. These two new irons continued to serve when the ball lay in high grass or among rocks or sand. Unlike early irons, however, cleeks and lofters were also used when the ball had a good lie. The cleek was designed more for distance while the lofter was designed to elevate the ball, especially on "short approach shots."

Because they had different purposes, cleeks and lofters each had their own shape. The cleek has a shallow, low profile blade, the top of which runs nearly parallel with the sole—the heel of the blade being nearly as deep as the toe. The lofter has a noticeably larger, more lofted blade, and the toe is clearly taller than the heel.

JOHN GRAY
LOFTER

F. & A. CARRICK
CLEEK

I have two excellent examples, a cleek and iron, by "Jn. Gray." These clubs were much sought after from the early 60s to 1890, and are now regarded by collectors, in conjunction with "Carrick" clubs, as the best examples of hand-forged work. Gray was a well-known and much esteemed character in the west of Scotland, a Freeman of Prestwick, a keen curler and bowler, and a member of the St. Nicholas Golf Club. He retired from business about 1890, and died at a ripe age in 1903, universally respected and regretted (Harry B. Wood 1910, 24).

Based in Prestwick, Scotland, John Gray (1824-1903) was one of the first iron makers, or cleekmakers as they came to be called, to mark his work. It is believed that Gray initially marked his clubs "J. Gray," as seen in his earliest clubs. Gray eventually began using "Jn. Gray," the mark found on most of his irons. Shown directly above (and third from the left on p. 108) is a circa 1880 John Gray lofter marked "J. Gray," though a portion of the lettering is faint. Older irons often have faint lettering because they were usually cleaned with emery cloth which gradually wore away the surface.

The blade on this club is slightly dished and measures 13/16 of an inch in depth. The 39-inch shaft, which is normal for a lofter, is stamped "A. Simpson" and is also crudely marked "G. A.," the owner's initials. Simpson's name is stamped on the shaft because he probably reshafted the head. The 16.9 ounce weight of the entire club is reasonable for a lofter, as is the 4 3/4 inch hosel length.

Stamped "A. Gray" in script, a few irons made by Andrew Gray, of Carnoustie, are known. According to Stewart Hackney, "the blacksmith Andrew Gray made some irons and cleeks from 1865 until his bankruptcy was discovered" (1988, 88). Judging from the small number of A. Gray clubs remaining, Andrew was apparently a cleekmaker for a very short time. (For more on J. Gray, see page 118.)

Francis and Archibald Carrick were first listed as "edge tool manufacturers, 1 New Street, Fisherrow," in the Musselburgh Directory for 1848-1849 (282). Prior to that time, the Musselburgh Directory listed "Alex Carrick and Sons, edge tool manufacturers," at the same location from 1840 through 1845.

Sometime in the late 1850s or 1860s, following the deaths of Francis and Archibald, their sons Alex and Archibald Jr. took over the business and continued to operate as F.&A. Carrick. For F.&A. Carrick, forging irons was a sideline to their primary business of making tools. The known Carrick irons usually date from the 1880s or earlier.

Early on, the Carricks' almost certainly made clubs that were not marked, but over time they marked their clubs with various stamps. "Carrick" is difficult to find while "F.&A. Carrick \ Musselburgh" is more common. Carrick irons were the first to include a trademark, albeit unregistered. This mark, a simple "X," is found both with and without Carrick's name stamped on the head. The Carrick clubs simply marked "Carrick" (with no "X") are believed to be the oldest marked examples.

Shown directly above (and on the far right on page 108) is a Carrick lofter marked "F.&A. Carrick \ Musselburgh" along with Carrick's "X" trademark. This lofter is very similar to the Gray lofter pictured above left. Their necks are both 4 3/4 inches in length and 3/4 of an inch in thickness. At 1 3/4 inches deep, the blade on the Carrick is only 1/16 of an inch shallower than the Gray. The Carrick shaft is 39 1/2 inches long. Even the 17 ounce overall weight of the Carrick iron differs from the Gray iron by only one-tenth of an ounce.

Not only do Carrick and Gray clubs resemble each other, they are similar to the irons made by their contemporaries. During the 1860s and thereafter, irons continued to undergo a refining process that produced a high degree of consistency among makers.

ROBERT WILSON
LOFTER

JAMES ANDERSON
LOFTER

Willie Auchterlonie, the 1893 British Open champion and famous clubmaker, provides an insight into the world of Robert Wilson (? -1906). Reflecting on his childhood, Auchterlonie recalls:

As for iron clubs of any kind, they were very difficult indeed for us to get at that time, and practically the only way in which we could ever manage to get possession of one was by going, two or three of us together, to old Bob Wilson's smithy, which stood a little way along North Street . . . and there lend him a hand by working round his turning lathe for him because, as he did not have steam power for this purpose, it all had to be done by the hand; and then occasionally for our services in this way we would get some old or spoiled head from him, and very proud indeed we were whenever this happened. Of course I need scarcely say who this old Bob Wilson was as almost every golfer knows and has heard of him. He was the first man to make iron club-heads here in St. Andrews, and these heads of his make are valuable yet, both for playing with and as curiosities, especially those with the famous horse-shoe nail in them at the back of the blade (Golf Illustrated, 9 Mar. 1906: 205).

The "horse-shoe nail" referred to by Auchterlonie is believed to be laid into the back of the blade where it turns into the hosel. In addition, Wilson's trademark was made by impressing the point of a nail into the back of the blade, behind the heel.

The circa 1880 Wilson lofter shown directly above (second from the right on page 108) is marked "R. Wilson, Maker, St. Andrews." It weighs 16.1 ounces. The hosel is 4 3/4 inches long and 3/4 inch thick; the blade is 1 7/8 inches deep. Despite wear, Wilson's mark is still easily identified. Also, note the clubhead's flat lie. This causes the area where the top of the blade intersects the hosel to appear higher than it actually is when viewed among the clubs pictured on page 108.

The year of 1845 is often given as the year of the Wilson's birth. However, the *St. Andrews Citizen* of 18 August 1906, reprinting the early minutes of the St. Andrews Mechanic Golf Club, reports:

At the annual meeting of the Club (30th September 1844) it was proposed . . . that Robert Wilson, blacksmith (a famous cleekmaker in South Street) should be the Captain of the Club, which was agreed to, upon which he begged leave to decline the offer (5).

Westwood's 1862 and 1866 directories list "R. Wilson" as a blacksmith at 199 South Street in St. Andrews.

Over thirty years ago Mr. [James] Anderson entered on business as a smith and farrier, in a quaint roadside cottage at the outskirts of the burgh, and chiefly with his own hands forged the horseshoe and shod the horse . . . occasionally turning his hand to the making of Golf-cleeks and irons, a job not unlike the forging of a horse-shoe; but for many years this was a small affair. In the best of times, when he had turned out 500 cleeks in a year he had done a big stroke of business; but the finely-made cleek led to continued increase of trade. To meet this demand Mr. Anderson introduced machinery into the polishing of the work, but all the forging is done by hand. . . . Mr. Anderson, in his blue flannel shirt, with his bushy black locks and buirdly frame, is constantly in the work, nothing escaping his eye, which largely accounts for his success (Golf, 15 July 1892: 293).

The above account, from 1892, goes on to report that James Anderson's business had grown to employ fourteen forges and more than double that number in "men and lads." In addition to stamping his clubs with just his mark, Anderson made large quantities of clubs marked with the names of his wholesale customers. Prior to his death in 1895, Anderson enjoyed the reputation of being not only one of the largest and oldest makers of iron clubs but also one the best.

The fine Anderson lofter pictured directly above (and on the far left on page 108) dates from the 1880s. Its shaft is stamped "McEwan," probably to identify who sold or reshafted this club.

In 1908 Alex Anderson, who took over his father's business in 1895, advertised, "Established over 50 years" (*Golfing*, 20 Aug.: 21). This apparently refers to the time when James or his father entered the blacksmith trade, not when James started making clubs:

It was considerably over thirty years ago that the late Mr. Anderson turned his attention to golf. At that time he had succeeded to his father's business as a country blacksmith (Golfing, 20 Apr. 1899: 4).

WILLIAM WILSON
LOFTERS

William Wilson entered the cleekmaking trade during the 1860s. According to an 1895 advertisement, Wilson had been a "cleek and iron maker for over a quarter of a century" (*Golfing*, 23 June: 25).

A Willie Wilson lofter made from gunmetal is shown directly above. Marked "W. Wilson, Maker, St. Andrews," this iron dates to the late 1880s/early 1890s. Gunmetal was used because it did not rust, it offered an attractive look, and it provided a slightly different feel. Although gunmetal blade putters became popular during the 1890s, gunmetal irons did not. It was not until the mid-1920s to early 1930s that a few makers produced brass or bronze irons in quantity, most notably the Ampco Golf Co., of Milwaukee, Wisconsin.

A lofter bearing four different stamps is shown above right. The first stamp, "W. Wilson, Maker, St. Andrews," identifies Wilson as the maker of the clubhead.

The second mark is "Peter Paxton, Eastbourne." Paxton was a professional who made clubs and balls:

Like most professionals, club and ball making was his primary actual occupation. He served his apprenticeship with Tom Hood of Musselburgh, who was at that time famous as a ball maker (*Golf*, 18 Sept. 1891: 8).

Tom Hood was also a fine clubmaker, and examples of his long nose clubs remain.

Paxton, born at Musselburgh, worked mostly in England:

When Mr. Paxton came over the Border it was to succeed his brother [John] as professional and clubmaker to the Worchester Club at Malvern [1880].... Thence he went to Eastbourne, and afterwards to Tooting Bec, one of the most influencial clubs in the country (*Golfing*, 12 Jan. 1899).

The significant number of irons marked by both Wilson and Paxton suggests that Wilson supplied Paxton with the iron heads that Paxton shafted and sold, including this one.

Paxton's mark on the head dates this club between 1888 and 1893 when Paxton was at Royal Eastbourne. This iron has a concave blade similar to "Park's Patent Lofter" patented in 1889.

The third stamp on this head is "THOM." The individually struck nature of the letters indicates that "THOM" once owned this club.

The fourth mark on this club is exceptionally historic. Stamped high on the shaft is "W.F. Davis, Montreal." This mark identifies the Montreal Golf Club which is the oldest existing golf club in North America. Established on December 4, 1873, Montreal Golf Club (elevated to "Royal" Montreal Golf Club on July 26, 1884) employed the first Scottish professional to work in North America, W.F. "Willie" Davis:

[In] 1881, the club obtained the services of W.F. Davis, of Hoylake, Cheshire, who was the first professional to come to America.... His wages were £1 a week and he agreed: "I am to get all that I can earn for making and repairing clubs and balls" (Dixie 1923, 14).

Davis learned clubmaking at Hoylake under the watchful eye of Jack Morris. But clubmaking was not Davis's only skill. In Montreal, he was "employed by the Royal Montreal Golf Club in the summer and by a bank during the winter" (*Golf Illustrated*, 31 Jan. 1902: 84). Davis did not remain in Canada:

In 1891 Davis came to the United States and laid out the first course of the Shinnecock Hills Golf Club. He took up his abode permanently in this country in 1893 as professional of the Newport Club, which position he retained until 1899, when he resigned and attached himself to the Apawamis Club, near New York (*Golf* [ny], Feb. 1902: 129).

Davis died in January of 1902, at the age of 39.

A scenario explaining all the marks on this club goes like this: Wilson made the head for Paxton, who sold it to Davis, who shafted it and sold it to his customer THOM. It is also possible that Davis simply shafted/reshafted this club for his customer or himself.

R. FORGAN & SON
LOFTER

W. THOMSON
MASHIE

In 1883 Robert Forgan made his son, Thomas, a partner in his business (p. 229). This event helps date this Forgan lofter, marked "R. Forgan & Son \ St. Andrews" on the back of the blade, as being made no earlier than 1883. It was probably made closer to 1890.

Forgan & Son did not forge iron heads until early in 1924, when they acquired the cleek-making operation of James Spence. Prior to that time, Forgan & Son purchased iron heads which they shafted and sold under their own name.

The Forgan lofter pictured directly above, with a long, narrow blade that gets deeper as it approaches the toe, is representative of all lofters. However, it is not an early example. Forgan's lofter, as demonstrated by its slightly shorter and thinner hosel, is more refined than earlier examples. The lancewood shaft is a nice feature.

A lofted iron was traditionally used to negotiate the "stymie." Although it no longer exists, the stymie was once very much a part of the game. "A stymie occurs when your opponent's ball lies directly in a line between the hole and your own ball that you cannot hole by putting" (Chambers 1862, 17; see also p. 424).

The Mashy, which is a sort of compromise between a lofting-iron and a niblick, . . . was originally intended to assist the player in getting out of bushes, rushes, and rough ground, [and] ought not properly to be classed among approach-clubs at all. It is however, a useful little weapon, and, for some reason or other, is, I think, rather easier to play than the lofting-iron (Norris 1892, 607).

A mashie has a shorter and deeper blade than a lofter. By the early 1890s, mashies were a mainstay in the golfer's arsenal. The club marked "W. Thomson," pictured above right, is larger and heavier than a typical 1890s mashie. The hosel is long and stout, there is a sharp blade crease or "cut" where the top of the blade meets the hosel, and the hosel weld is faintly visible in a few places. Judging from the shape of the blade and the characteristics of the head, this iron is an early mashie, circa early 1880s.

The head is marked "W. Thomson," but it is unclear who this identifies. This iron head might have been made by the "W. Thomson" who was a blacksmith in Abbotshall, Fifeshire, near St. Andrews (Westwood 1862, 4). Or, this iron could have been made by Willie Thomson the professional at Tynside Golf Club between 1887 and 1890 (Jackson, 1994, 93). William Thomson the lithographer from Edinburgh who received two British golf patents in 1891 probably had nothing to do with this iron. (Thompson's patent [No. 5,133] dated March 24 covered an iron with a bulge on the back of its blade. His patent [No. 21,871] dated December 15 called for constructing a wood with a metal face designed to move the weight of the head forward.) William Thomson, who participated in four British Opens during the 1880s, is quite possibly the Thomson behind this club.

In 1881, the earliest known description of a "mashy" was printed:

The "Mashy" is used for the same purposes as the Niblick proper [track iron], and only differs from it in its sole and face being straight instead of rounded. It thus looks exactly like a Sand Iron with its head cut short. The

Mashy, however, is one of those fanciful clubs that have been invented in recent years, and is entirely unnecessary in the Golfer's set (Forgan, 17).

In 1890, it was reported that George Forrester's " 'mashie' of eight years ago is now found on every green" (*East Fife Record*, 12 Sep.: 3). In 1896, Alex Patrick recalled that the mashie "has only been in use—roughly speaking—twelve years or so" (*The Golfer*, 12 Aug.: 128). These remarks indicate that the mashie began to be accepted around 1884. Understandably, the earliest mashies maintained the basic traits of the lofter, such as hosel size, while the blade was made shorter and deeper.

CLEEKS

The cleek or cleik, deriving its name either from an old Scotch word signifying "hook," or from the sharp clicking sound produced in making the stroke, is also an iron club, but lighter than either of the others. It is used chiefly for driving the ball out of rough ground when elevation is not so much an object, and when no impediments surround and obstruct the lie which would demand an heavier club (Farnie 1857, 20).

The Cleek   The introduction of the iron-headed club [as an approach club] by Allan Robertson was probably intended to supply the long-felt want of a lofting or approaching implement which would not wear out so quickly as the baffy spoon and other wooden clubs, and apart from this consideration, it would commend itself for the negotiation of awkward lies (Golf, 9 Apr. 1897: 79).

It was Allan Robertson who introduced the deadly approach game with the cleek in 1848, displacing thereby the baffing spoon (Golfing, 17 Feb. 1897: 7).

In general terms, "cleek" refers to any club made from iron. The term "cleekmaker" simply meant ironmaker.

In 1893 the derivation of the term "cleek," as applied to a golf club, was explained in a letter to the editor of *Golf*. The writer, ridiculing the idea that the term "cleek" might derive from the "sound emitted when a golf ball is struck by it," goes on to state:

In Scotch, a "cleik" means an iron hook, and the verb to "cleik" or "cleek" means to "catch up" or "snatch away" with a hook. This name, therefore, is peculiarly appropriate to a club which is specially intended to sweep away a ball out of a rather uneven or bad lie (Golf, 13 Feb. 1893: 342).

In specific terms, "cleek" refers to an iron made with little loft; a long, shallow blade; and a topline that runs nearly parallel to the sole (the toe of the blade is not noticeably deeper than the heel). The cleek, a companion iron of the lofter and track iron, is very similar to the lofter but quite different from the track iron. True examples date prior to 1890. The purpose of the cleek was defined as follows:

The cleek will loft the ball, at no great height from the ground, over the rough ground, and allow it to run on over the smoother surface up to the hole. It is a particularly useful mode of approach in the teeth of a wind (Hutchison 1902, 63).

As the golf club evolved, it became nearly impossible to define the cleek, or any other type of club, in absolute terms:

But if the modern golfer has reduced the complexity of his manifold spoons almost to the simplicity of a single brassy, he has so fully made up for this in the number and variety of his iron clubs that the modern golfing stock-in-trade bears a striking resemblance to a set of elephantine dentist's tools. There are long cleeks and short cleeks, driving cleeks, lofting cleeks, and putting cleeks; there are heavy irons and light irons, driving irons, lofting irons, and sand irons. There are 'mashies' and there are niblicks. In this multitude of golf clubs there is perhaps wisdom—somewhere— but it can scarcely be that all of them are necessary (Hutchison 1902, 62).

JOHN GRAY
CLEEK

The circa 1880 cleek shown above, stamped "Jn Gray," is a fine example of John Gray's work. The dark brown patina of the metal is not a detraction to collectors. It is smooth, shows no signs of pitting, and evenly covers the head. Furthermore, it can be lightened, given the proper treatment.

John Gray is considered to be one of the premier early cleek-makers. His clubs are collectible in any form—lofter, cleek, or track iron. (See pages 109 and 118 for Gray.)

UNKNOWN MAKER
CLEEK

Because the circa 1875 cleek below is earlier than most, it has an unusually large, thick hosel. The shaft, which is an old reshaft, is not quite thick enough to fill the top of the hosel. The head lacks a maker's mark; this is typical of many clubs its age.

F. & A. CARRICK
LOFTER

WILLIAM WILSON
CLEEK

ROBERT WHITE
CLEEK

A circa 1880 Carrick cleek, marked "F.&A. Carrick" just below "Musselburgh," is shown below. The Carrick "X" cleek-mark is visible, but the "F.&A. Carrick" mark is very difficult to see as pictured. For more on Francis and Archibald Carrick, see page 109.

A circa 1880 Willie Wilson cleek, marked "W. Wilson, Maker, St. Andrews," is shown above. Wilson continued his cleekmaking to the end of the nineteenth century. "From genuine testimonials, it would seem that Mr. Wilson's goods still bear the golden opinion they did a quarter of a century ago" (*Golfing*, 16 Mar. 1899: 6).

An early maker of such traditional irons as the cleek, lofter, and track iron, Wilson was also quite inventive. In 1893 "Mr. Wilson...constructed a machine for testing the comparative driving-powers of various players so far, at least, as initial speed is concerned" (*Golf*, 29 Sep.: 35). This machine involved the use of a ball at the end of a leather thong attached to an indicator. Wilson also devised an early "ball-marking machine" that cut lines in gutta percha golf balls (*Golfing*, 16 Mar. 1899: 6). For more on Wilson, see page 111.

In 1895 Robert White, a well-known St. Andrews cleek-maker reportedly born in 1857, promoted himself as "the oldest established Golf Cleek Manufacturer in St. Andrews" (*Golf*, 30 Aug.: 500). However, Robert Wilson and Willie Wilson (relationship unknown), both of whom were still working in 1895 as cleekmakers in St. Andrews, had made clubs there before White did. White surely knew this, therefore he may have referred to himself in such terms because, according to James Robertson, "he was the first blacksmith to go over entirely to cleek-making" (1967, 54).

The early 1880s lofter pictured directly above is stamped "R. White, Maker, St. Andrews," on the back of the blade which also bears the initials "EMS." Clubs bearing initials are not uncommon. Initials do not detract from a nice item. Rather, they provide the collector with an opportunity to identify the owner. In this case, the club was owned by E. Maxwell Stuart.

The shaft is marked "John Wisden & Co. 21 Cranbourne St., London" and "E. Maxwell Stuart." According to John Wisden, the prominent sporting goods dealer in London who sold this club, he was the first dealer to sell golf clubs in London, beginning in 1874. His firm came to be known as "London's greatest golf depot" (*Golfing*, 23 Nov. 1899: 10).

In 1899 the writer of an article titled "Wisden's" was duly impressed with Wisden's inventory:

Cases upon cases, and racks from the floor to the ceiling filled with picked clubs presented a splendid collection of choice specimens of such makes as those of Cann and Taylor, Peter Paxton, R. Forgan, Auchterlonie, J. and D. Clark, Anderson, Simpson, Ben Sayers, Tom Morris, Patrick, Braddell, Dickson, Forrester, Carruthers, Harry Vardon, and Andrew Scott (*Golfing*, 23 Nov.: 11).

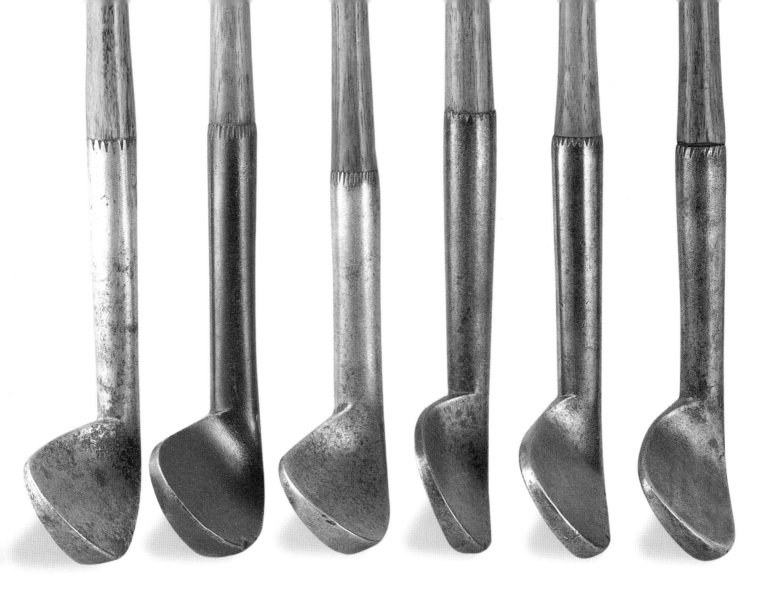

These six track irons, dating from approximately 1840 to 1880, are made by various makers. Beginning at the left, the first two are unmarked and date circa 1840 and 1850. The third was made by John Gray, circa 1860. The fourth was made by Willie Wilson, circa 1870. The fifth was made by F. & A. Carrick, circa 1875. The sixth was made by James Anderson, circa 1880. As pictured, these irons show the evolution from the cupped blade of the early track irons to the flat blade of the late track irons.

TRACK IRONS

The niblick of St. Andrews is a short, spooned wooden club; that of Musselburgh, a short, stout, iron-headed club, used for driving balls out of cart-ruts, & c. At St. Andrews, this little iron-headed club is termed a track-iron (Chambers 1857, 694).

The NIBLICK, or TRACK-IRON, is of very important service when the ball lies in a narrow cart-rut, horseshoe, or other print in sand, thick and stiff whins, or in any round deep hollow not altogether beyond the player's reach. The head, which is of iron, is very small and heavy, about one-half the size of that of the sand-iron, and is shaped into a hollow, with the iron sloping slightly backward. This peculiarity of shape enables the player to raise his ball out of difficulties from which no other club could extricate it, and ought invariably, where the above-named hazards occur, to form one of every golfer's set (Chambers 1862, 18-19).

In their day, track irons were also referred to as "niblicks" or "iron niblicks." Today collectors usually use the term "niblick" to identify the most lofted irons made after 1890, regardless of head size. They refer to the early niblicks as either "track irons" or "rut irons."

Track irons were developed before 1850. An account of golf originally printed in *The Illustrated London Almanac* in 1845 refers to track irons:

Another [club], formed of iron instead of wood, is used for making a hit at a ball when very unfavourably placed; as in a rut, where the common club would be in danger of breaking (Golf Illustrated, 21 Sep. 1900: 251).

Royal Blackheath has *two* square-toe irons with very short blades. These clubs are essentially crude track irons which date to approximately 1800 or earlier.

Track irons died out prior to 1890. They were replaced by a somewhat lighter, more refined iron/niblick (having a slightly larger head, smaller hosel, and flat face) which collectors today refer to as a "rut niblick."

Track irons date from a distant period in golf's history, when the game had but few players. Rut niblicks are much later. All too often in today's collecting world, a rut niblick is categorized as a track or rut iron. This is wrong. The difference in value between a rut niblick and a true rut iron is *very* substantial.

Not only does the club shown (also seen on p. 115) have all the characteristics expected in a track iron, its characteristics are strong. When considered together, they indicate this track iron is early—circa 1840. Consider:

The hosel is long and massive.

The blade is unmistakably thick. Not only is the sole thick, the top of the blade is much thicker than the top of a lofter or cleek blade.

The blade is deeply "cupped" or concave. Generally speaking, the more cupped the face, the older the club. This particular iron has the most distinctly cupped face of any track iron known to the author.

The blade is exceptionally compact. Early track irons usually have very short blades. The face on this iron is so small, only *slightly* larger than the ball, that one wonders how track irons were ever used effectively. Such compact heads appear born to shank!

The nicking is substantial although some of it has been lost to accommodate a reshaft.

There is a sharp crease where the top of the blade meets the hosel. All early track irons were made this way (see p. 100).

This club is remarkably heavy. When held, a track iron feels more like a *weapon* than a golf club. (A possible exception to this weight trait is found in early juvenile or ladies' track irons. They are not as thick; therefore, they weigh less. Their shafts are also shorter.)

The workmanship is crude and unrefined. Early track irons show evidence of hand hammering, such as visible traces of the hosel weld, an asymmetrical hosel, or an uneven face. The more crudely a club is fashioned, the older it is likely to be.

In the lower right picture, the dramatic curve of the blade is evident. Note that the top-line of the blade starts at the front portion of the hosel, curves well back into the center of the blade, then curves forward to meet the leading edge at the toe.

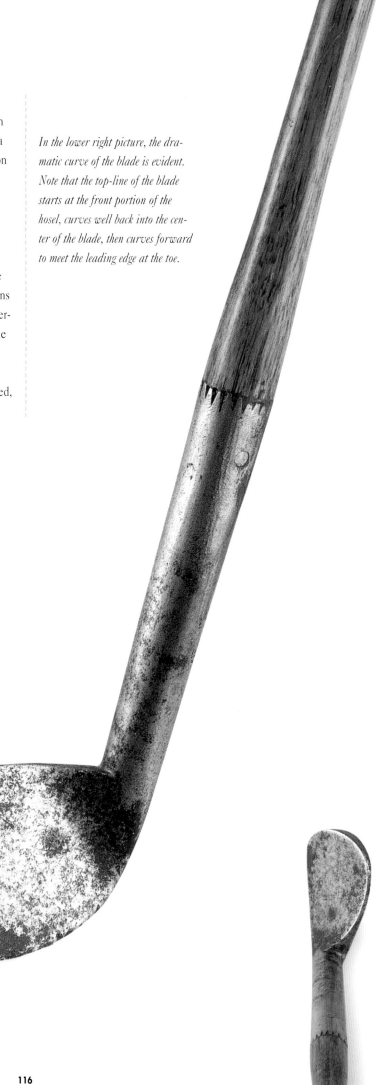

This circa 1850s early track iron is *everything* that it should be. The blade is thick, gracefully dished, incredibly small, and nearly round in profile. In addition, the hosel is thick, 5 1/2 inches long, and uneven—it is slightly tapered between the top of the hosel and the leading edge of the blade. All these characteristics are evidence of an early, well-made track iron.

With track irons, the size and style of the clubhead are of paramount importance. When evaluating a track iron, the collector should not simply consider the maker. The collector must decide how well the track iron reflects the characteristics that set a track iron apart as an unusual club.

For example, just *how* small is the head? Just *how* thick is the blade? Just *how* cupped is the face? Just *how* big is the hosel? Just *how* heavy is the club? The answers to these questions help determine the desirability of any track iron.

Also pictured on this page is a machine cut gutta percha golf ball. Dating between the 1870s and the 1890s, such balls were made by first molding the ball to shape and then cutting scoring lines into its surface. A special golf ball cutting lathe was used to cut the lines, but the earlier lathes were not as refined as later lathes. Consequently, the scoring on earlier machine cut balls lacks the symmetry of later balls. The ball pictured is an early machine cut example. Notice how unrefined and crooked the scoring lines are. (For more on golf balls, see pages 556-563.)

(This track iron is also pictured second from the left on page 115.)

Such a small head at the end of a shaft over three feet from the player's hands looks even smaller to the player holding it. And to a player using this club when two holes down with two holes to play, this clubhead could only appear microscopic!

JOHN GRAY
TRACK IRON

With a pronounced concave face, this John Gray track iron, marked "J. Gray" on the back of its blade, has a classically shaped, small, and thick head. The element of style permeates the artistic workmanship of this circa 1860 club (also pictured on page 115, third from the left.)

In 1851, when Tom Morris went to Prestwick, both Morris and Gray, a local blacksmith, became founding members of the Prestwick Golf Club and the Prestwick Mechanics Golf Club (renamed the Prestwick St. Nicholas Golf Club in 1858). The creation of these two organizations prompted Gray to include cleekmaking in his business:

Along with "Old" Tom, another founder of the new club was a local blacksmith, then apprenticed to his father at a horseshoe forge in Prestwick. John Gray was a keen golfer who was actually elected Captain of the Mechanics Club in 1852-1853. After the two new Golf Clubs were established in Prestwick, Gray added the work of forging iron golf club heads to the family business. At this time Gray was the only iron head maker in the west of Scotland and eventually no self-respecting golfer would assemble a set without a cleek or iron "hand forged by John Gray of Prestwick" (Johnston 1993, 586).

John Gray continued to make irons until he retired from business in approximately 1890 (see p. 109).

Steel can be hand forged equally as well as iron, but no golfer would use a steel head if he has first played with an iron one. The ball leaves the club better and keeps in a much better line when played off an iron head (William Wilson, *Golf*, 14 Jan. 1898: 324).

WILLIAM WILSON
TRACK IRON

I can remember the time when an iron made by Wilson, of St. Andrews, was considered a "pearl beyond price" (Harold Hilton 1903, 124).

Pictured is one of the earliest Willie Wilson clubs known. The back of this clubhead is stamped with Wilson's earliest mark: "W. Wilson \ St. Andrews." His next mark was "W. Wilson \ Maker \ St. Andrews," also in straight lines. This mark was followed by his circular mark, the most common of the three. Wilson's marks span a number of years. He began making irons in the 1860s and remained in business to the end of the century.

Dating from around 1870, the club pictured has exceptional qualities for a track iron. The blade is very small, its profile quite round; the hosel is 5 1/2 inches long and 13/16 of an inch thick, both healthy measurements for a track iron. In addition, the hosel shows the craftsmanship of a thinking man.

When viewing the life-size picture, note how the back of the hosel comes down and rounds under the blade. This gives the sole an exceptionally small "footprint" (in addition to providing evidence of true hand forging). Because this blade has less loft than most track irons, the face is closer to the leading side of the hosel. In practice,

this helped the golfer strike the ball without shanking (or "socketing," as it was once called).

This Wilson track iron is an exceptional club in another historic vein: It is one of the fifty-six clubs collected by Harry B. Wood, author of *Golfing Curios and The Like*, the first book on golf collectibles ever published. This particular club is featured in his book as club number 7 in plate VI.

The golfing curios Harry Wood collected during his life were given to the Manchester Golf Club, in Manchester, England, where Wood was a member. His collection was displayed there until 1986, when the Manchester Golf Club sold it in its entirety to two collectors. The head shown here bears a white inventory sticker from that sale.

Formerly owned by Harry B. Wood, this club carries Wood's tag which reads:

Track Iron by W. Wilson, St. Andrews, derives its name from the fact of being used to get the ball out of cart tracks, such as are frequently found on the public links of Scotland, where the townspeople have the right to cart seaweed, stones, etc. across the links, at Musselburgh and St. Andrews for example.

This Willie Wilson track iron is also pictured, fourth club from the left, on page 115.

F. & A. CARRICK
TRACK IRON

JAMES ANDERSON
TRACK IRON

J.C. SMITH & SON
RUT NIBLICK

Pictured below and above left is an 1870s Carrick track iron. "F.&A. Carrick" and Carrick's "X" trademark are stamped on the back of the head. Carrick track irons are popular among collectors because the Carricks were among the earliest iron makers to mark their work, and their clubs are well made (see p. 109). Track irons are also harder to locate than either cleeks or lofters. This club is also pictured second from the right on page 115.

Pictured above center is a typical James Anderson track iron. It has a stout hosel and a small, thick head. The blade is flat and not very circular in outline. The "Anderson - Anstruther" cleekmark on the back of the head, although somewhat faint, is still clearly identifiable. This club, also pictured on the far right on page 115, dates circa 1880. (See Anderson, p. 110)

Anderson's death, at age fifty, was believed to be:

in some measure due to the over-taxing [of] his strength as a young man when he worked all day and night at the forge, endeavoring to keep pace with the orders he received for clubs (*Golfing*, 20 Apr. 1899: 14).

By the late 1880s track irons were being replaced by a lighter, more refined iron having a slightly larger head and a smaller, shorter hosel. Such clubs are termed "rut niblicks" because they are not true rut irons. A rut niblick made from gunmetal is shown above right. At first glance this club might look like a rut iron. A second look, however, reveals a few significant differences. Compared to a true track iron, the head is not as small, the neck and blade are not as thick, and the hosel is shorter. (As pictured, the hosel of this iron looks a little longer than it is, because the lie is so flat.)

Although it is a worthy collectible, a rut niblick is not valued as highly as a rut iron. Rut niblicks come from a more modern time and vastly outnumber their progenitors. Furthermore, their larger size prevents them from being as striking as a true rut iron. Understandably, the closer a rut niblick resembles a rut iron, the more desirable it becomes.

This rut niblick, dating to the late 1880s or 1890s, is marked "J.C. Smith & Son, Montifieth" on the shaft. A 1908 advertisement by Smith & Son states, "Established 1870" (*Golfing*, 9 Apr.: 25).

IRON SETS

The concept of selling a full set of matching irons took hold during the 1920s. Prior to this, even though sets of irons consisting of four or five clubs were available, the golfer usually assembled a set of irons by choosing individual clubs, often from various makers. If the golfer found one particular iron difficult to use, he or she simply purchased a single replacement iron more to his or her liking.

During the early 1920s, irons continued to be offered individually, but a significant number of manufacturers began offering six or seven irons that "matched." From these six or seven irons the buyer could select the ones he or she wanted. As the decade progressed, so did the idea of selling a full set of matching irons. In 1926 Spalding, to name one large manufacturer, first offered a set of irons for a single price. During the mid to late 1920s, manufacturers continued to sell irons individually while increasing their promotion of matched sets, often including the putter.

TOM STEWART
R.T.J. IRON SET

The *twelve club* matched set of irons pictured above was made by Tom Stewart, the famous St. Andrews cleekmaker. This set consists of a "Driving Mashie, 1 Iron, 2 Iron, 3 Iron, 4 Iron, Mashie Iron, Mashie, Spade Mashie, Mashie Niblick, Niblick, Cleek, and Putter." In addition to Stewart's "clay pipe" trademark, each iron bears three other interesting marks on the toe: a foreman's mark, Stewart's personal mark, and the "RTJ" mark.

Stewart's foremen used various marks, such as a crow's foot, a fish, a triangle, etc., to identify who inspected and/or worked on the head. Stewart's own personal inspection stamp was a round dot punched into the back of the blade:

When old Tom [Stewart] himself personally inspected a club head and finishes it off there's a round dot punched in it. Bobby Jones had a lot of copies made of his favorite clubs and they all bore the little round dot (Rice 1953, 174).

The initials "R.T.J.," also stamped on each iron, are those of the only person ever to win the "Grand Slam" of golf: Robert Tyre Jones Jr.

Bobby Jones, as he was known, is still considered by many the greatest player the game has ever known. His record is certainly without parallel. In eight years, between 1923 and 1930, he won thirteen major championships, including the Grand Slam in 1930, while retaining his amateur status. As a player, Jones was well acquainted with Stewart's work. In fact, most of the irons Jones used were made by Stewart. According to Jones:

All of my 1930 set had been "handmade." Most of the irons bore the famous "pipe" trademark of Tom Stewart of St. Andrews. Some had been picked up as completed clubs in golf shops in this country. Others had been assembled from heads made especially for me in Stewart's forge. Whenever I had visited St. Andrews, I had gone to Stewart's to look over his shop and occasionally would stand with the finisher to be certain that he completed the head according to my taste. In those days "club-making" was part of a club professional's job. Having got my heads from Stewart, I brought them home for shafting by whatever pro we had at East Lake (1960, 182).

In 1929 Bobby Jones's personal set of clubs was stolen from the trunk of his car, but returned to him shortly afterwards. Following this experience and using his personal specifications, Jones ordered a "backup" set of irons from Stewart. Jones, the consummate amateur, authorized Stewart to produce only a single set of irons. However, Tom Stewart, the opportunistic businessman, did not stop production after fulfilling Jones's request. Clearly aware that Jones was at the top of the golf world, Stewart began to reproduce the clubs he made for Jones. These clubs were marked with Jones's initials "RTJ" in block letters on the toe or with "FO\RTJ" in script on the toe. The initials "FO" identify another famous amateur: Francis Ouimet.

These "personal" models were made in 1930, and possibly briefly during 1931. Stewart's catalog for 1930 offers, "Sets of Iron Heads made as used by Mr. Robert T. Jones" (Matthew 1987, 16). The only advertisement for these clubs the author is aware of is found in the 1931 *Fraser's International Golf Year Book* which reads, "R.T.J. Model, Pipe Brand (Tom Stewart), with Shock Absorber Shaft." Such an advertisement would have been submitted before the close of 1930, only months after Jones had won the Grand Slam. There was, however, one problem: Stewart did not have Jones's authorization to produce clubs bearing Jones's initials.

In response to a 1970 letter from John Kolehmain, who had found an iron bearing the "RTJ" stamp, Jones acknowledged Stewart's unauthorized use of his initials:

I doubt very much that the club you mention was ever in my bag. I had Tom Stewart forge some heads under my supervision and he took advantage of the situation by offering clubs for sale with RTJ stamped on them. I can account for all the clubs of the set I last used (Jones 1970).

In producing these clubs for sale, Stewart, never intending to hurt Jones, was only trying to capitalize on Bob's fame. Stewart had promoted the golf clubs of other famous players prior to Jones. According to a Stewart advertisement years earlier, he offered:

Sets of Iron Heads made simliar [sic] to those used by the late Tom Morris and the late F.G. Tait (Golfers Magazine, Sep. 1915: 95).

Tom Stewart stopped producing his RTJ copies at the request of Jones, the preeminent golfer who was also a prominent *attorney*.

Despite being *offered* as sets, Stewart "RTJ" irons were not always *sold* as sets. Rumor has it that Stewart was a shrewd businessman and, for the short period of time he was offering the RTJ irons, Stewart would send only a few to a good distributor or retailer whose account was paid up, and then only in conjunction with another healthy order. Judging from the few remaining sets of RTJ or RTJ/FO irons, this seems quite possible. The set pictured is one of only two complete twelve-club sets known. Furthermore, there are only a handful of eight- or nine-club sets known besides these.

When considering the idea of a twelve-club set of irons, remember that the USGA did not limit the number of clubs a player could carry until January 1, 1938. Lawson Little at one time carried twenty-three or twenty-four clubs, including eight different types of niblicks. The USGA initially decided on a sixteen-club limit, but they changed the limit to fourteen clubs before the rule became effective. The R&A followed with an identical rule on May 1, 1939.

Besides offering approximately eight matching clubs as a full set of irons, manufacturers also offered the same matching irons in reduced numbers, such as sets of six or four. Because it is not always possible to tell a *short* set (a set sold with a reduced number of clubs) from a *broken* full set (a set sold as eight clubs but missing one or more), and because a full set left nothing out, *and* because full sets of matching irons are difficult to find intact, collectors prefer full sets to short or broken sets.

A full set—all originally sold together—is valued higher than the total price of the individual clubs. A set is more than a certain number of clubs; it is an entity in itself. A broken set, on the other hand, is worth only the total value of the individual clubs. Among the most collectible complete sets are the Stewart RTJ and RTJ/FO sets, and the Spalding Robert T. Jones Jr. sets described next.

As clubmakers became more interested in constructing complete sets of clubs, Irving R. Prentiss of Philadelphia, Pennsylvania, devised a method of balancing clubs—of properly proportioning them from one to the next—within a set. This method, known as swingweighting, was covered under Prentiss's U.S. patent (No. 1,516,786) dated November 24, 1924. According to the patent, Prentiss, knowing that the clubs in a set vary in length, established a "uniform relationship . . . between length and weight and also between length and balance," which he expressed using two algebraic equations. The first equation was used to determine how much each individual club in a set should weigh in order to *comparatively* match the weight of the golfer's favorite club. With the respective weight of each club determined, the second equation was used to determine where the weight of each individual club should be distributed—where along the shaft the club should balance when placed horizontally across a knife edge—in order to *comparatively* match the balance point of the golfer's favorite club. Like the weight of each club, the balance point varied from one club to the next because club lengths varied from one club to the next. Prentiss's method proved effective and is still the standard for measuring clubs, though today a club needs merely to be placed on a swingweight scale.

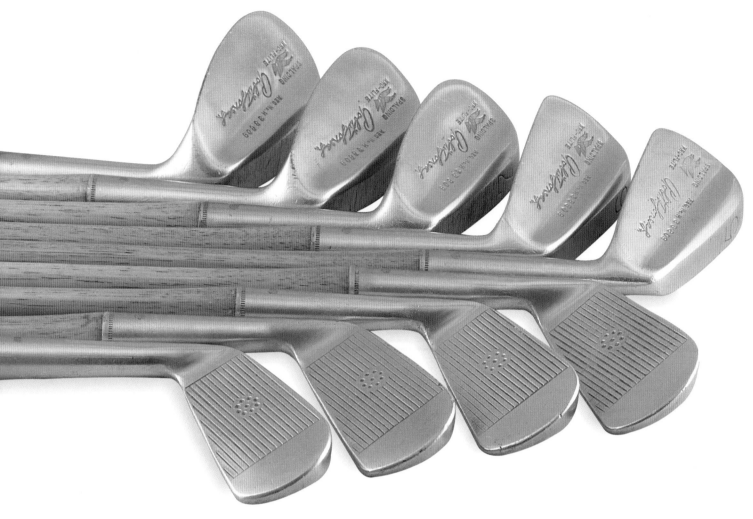

A.G. SPALDING & BROS.

ROBERT T. JONES JR.
IRON SET

Throughout his competitive career, and in keeping with his amateur status, Bobby Jones never endorsed a single golf club nor did he authorize a manufacturer to sell clubs bearing his name. However, following his retirement from competitive golf in 1930, after winning the Grand Slam, Jones entered into a promotional relationship with A.G. Spalding & Bros.

Spalding's 1932 Spring and Summer catalog, the first to list "Robert T. Jones" signature clubs, offered two different models of Jones signature iron sets, but both were available only with steel shafts. The same was true for all of Spalding's most expensive clubs in the same catalog. Steel shafts, legalized for play by both the USGA and R&A in the 1920s,

dominated the new club market by 1932. The option of custom ordering a set of "Indexed Kro-Flite Irons" (not endorsed with the Jones name) with wood shafts, instead of steel, was mentioned in only one paragraph at the end of Spalding's 1932 catalog.

Most of the steel shafts Spalding used in their irons during the 1930s were covered with "pyratone sheathing." A pyratone sheath is a thin, flexible tube of pyroxylin used to cover shafts. It is usually yellow, brown, or black, and was intended to make the metal shaft look more like wood (see p. 523). From the late 1920s through the early 1940s, pyratone was in wide use. Spalding's Rob't T. Jones Jr. clubs (also marked "Kro-Flite") with pyratone-coated metal

shafts are still very common and of little interest to most collectors. Not only were they marketed as one of Spalding's top irons and produced by the tens of thousands all through the 1930s, but Bobby Jones himself never used metal shafts in competition. By contrast, there are currently only a handful of *complete* "Spalding, Rob't T. Jones Jr." *wood*-shafted iron sets known, one of which is pictured above (this set consists of nine irons, number 1 through 9).

Spalding's wood-shafted Robert T. Jones Jr. irons were offered only in 1933. Spalding's Spring and Summer catalog for that year offered Robert T. Jones Jr. "Custom Built Registered Irons—Hickory Shaft" (48). These irons came with a registration number on the back of

each head, as shown in the set pictured. However, *steel shaft* sets of Robert T. Jones "Custom Built Registered Irons" were offered in Spalding's 1933 catalog as the top model, followed by two additional models of steel-shafted Robert T. Jones Jr. iron sets. Given the heavy promotion of steel shaft Jones clubs and the essentially complete transition of the golf market from wood to steel shafts, the Jones *wood shaft* iron sets were poorly received and never offered again. Today, the few remaining sets stand as prime collectibles along with Tom Stewart's RTJ model.

The putter on the far left is a Calamity Jane marketed by Spalding in the early 1930s. In the mid-1930s, Calamity Janes were no longer made with wood shafts, only steel.

The putter on the near left is one of 250 Calamity Jane putters reproduced in 1976 at the request of Jack Nicklaus. These replicas were given as gifts to all the pro-am participants in his inaugural Memorial tournament.

A single wood shaft Spalding iron marked "Rob't T. Jones Jr." or a wood shaft Stewart iron marked "RTJ" or "FO/RTJ" has significant collector interest. But the most famous of all the individual clubs that bear the Jones name is his putter, "Calamity Jane."

In 1932, when Spalding's hickory shaft Calamity Jane putter first appeared in their catalog, it was promoted as "an exact duplicate of the famous 'Calamity Jane'" used by Jones himself. Most were made with a dull chrome finish on the head. Only a small percentage had a "stainless" finish and were so marked.

Produced with a wood shaft for at least three years, Spalding's Calamity Jane putters were well accepted. Consequently, they become available today with some regularity. They are collectible primarily because they bear the Jones name, and they were the earliest copy of his putter available commercially. There is nothing special about the shape or structure of the putter. Prior to the early 1930s, offset blade putters with hickory shafts were made by the tens of thousands.

During the 1930s Spalding made Calamity Jane putters with pyratone covered metal shafts. Although the head was nearly the same as it was on the wood shaft version, steel shaft Calamity Janes, produced in large numbers, finish a distant second in collector interest when compared to early wood shaft examples.

In the 1960s Spalding produced another Calamity Jane putter. This version, stamped a little differently and given a shiny chrome finish, is of interest primarily to collectors who want to have one of each model.

The first thing to know about the Calamity Jane putter used by Jones in winning his major championships is—there were two! A letter Jones wrote to Gene Hitt on February 20, 1969, provides some history on both clubs:

The original Calamity Jane was given to me by Jimmy Maiden in 1920 when he was pro at Nassau, Long Island. The head bore the rose mark of a Condie iron and was probably forged sometime around the turn of the century. The head also bore the mark of W. Winton, who was probably the man who completed the club with shaft and grip.

In 1926, Spalding made a half dozen copies of this club, but these were for my personal use. I gave a few to friends, but substituted one of the copies for the original in my bag because it had become too light from continued polishing.

Spalding, with my permission, first made Calamity Janes for the market in 1931 (Matthew 1987, 13).

In 1962 *Golf Digest* published an article titled "Bobby Jones and His Calamity Jane" (May: 54-58). This article was written by J. Victor East, the person who, in 1926, duplicated Jones's original Calamity Jane putter.

East gives the original Calamity Jane's specifications as:

face loft: 8°, blade length 4-7/8", head lie 66°, head weight 9 3/4 oz., shaft length: 33 1/2" overall wt.: 15 1/2 oz.

According to East, Jones had a new putter made because:

His caddies' constant twisting of the emery cloth to indicate the putter

This putter is an early Spalding prototype. It is not marked "Spalding," its Kro-Flite "crow" cleekmark did not go into major production, and it is not marked "Jr." after Jones.

Steel shaft Calamity Janes have a thinner hosel to accommodate the thinner metal shaft. A metal shaft hosel unscrupulously reshafted with a wood shaft is easily spotted. Measuring 11/16 of an inch in diameter at the top, the hosel on a wood shaft Calamity Jane putter is thicker than it is on a steel shaft Calamity Jane putter. On Spalding-made Jones irons, the wood shaft hosels measure 21/32 of an inch in diameter while steel shaft hosels measure 17/32 of an inch.

face's "sweet spot" eventually caused a tiny depression there. Jones was enough of a technician to realize that any irregularity in the striking surface of a putter would surely cause putts to go off-line.

This is further corroborated in a letter Jones sent to the USGA when he presented them with one of the six duplicate Calamity Jane putters made in 1926—*his own*. Referring to his first Calamity Jane putter, Jones wrote:

Constant buffing and polishing finally caused the face to be so irregular that I had a copy made, and from then on used the copy. The copy is the one I am sending you (Doust 1976, 38).

J. Victor East also referred to the whipping on Calamity Jane's shaft:

Being the explosive type, Jones gave his putter some bad moments despite his generally wonderful success

with the club between 1920 and 1926. The hickory shaft almost split several times, and finally Bobby applied three whippings around the wood to firm it up.

In 1976 Jack Nicklaus had 250 exact replicas of Jones's original Calamity Jane putter made—to give as souvenirs to the participants in his inaugural Memorial tournament's pro-am event:

Nicklaus went to great lengths to get the things right. His associate, Ken Bowden, who cooked up the idea, traveled last year to Georgia, where he was allowed to take a hallowed Calamity Jane from its trophy case at the Augusta National Golf Club …Bowden had the club measured and photographed from all angles. A mould of it was made by a local dentist. The reference material was sent to Swilken of St. Andrews, the club-makers, who sub-contracted the components: the call for castings went to East

Kilbride, the sheepskin grips to Bridge of Weir, the shafts to an importer in Manchester who knows a bit about timber and golf . . . . Once assembled in Scotland last winter, Calamity Jane needed only an authentic coating of rust. The clubs were left to lie out in the raw, salty air that blows over St. Andrews. Hey presto! an antique club. . . (Doust 1976, 37).

The putter that Nicklaus copied, complete with "Rob't T. Jones Jr." stamped on the shaft, was the first Calamity Jane putter used by Jones. Jones used his first Calamity Jane for his first three major championship victories. One of Nicklaus's replicas, complete with the "authentic coating of rust" they all came with, is pictured on the facing page.

The putter Jones used in winning his last ten major championships was one of the six copies produced in 1926. This putter, now referred to as "Calamity Jane II," is simply stamped "Rob't T. Jones Jr." in script on the back of the blade. In 1938 Jones donated this putter to the USGA, where it remains on display in their museum, "Golf House." An examination of this club shows it is 33 1/2 inches in length and just as East describes. Like Calamity Jane I, the shaft has a definite crack running along its length. Three sections of whipping along the shaft still remain. The fate of the other five 1926 copies, which Jones gave to a few of his close friends, is not known.

The players of this game have always been a very studious, deeply investigating set of people. New ideas are to them as elements of life and happiness; they feed the fire of hope which burns in their minds incessantly.

(*Golfing*, 27 Mar. 1912: 24)

Patent Clubs

The collectibility of the long nose woods and early irons is embodied in their age. These relics are from a distant time when there were few golfers and the game was still in its formative years. The collectibility of patent clubs, on the other hand, is based on their ingenuity and creativity. These clubs reflect the ongoing challenge of finding a better way to advance the ball to the hole.

Patent clubs bridge the gap between the old and the new. Through their intriguing variety, ingenious creations, and dynamic innovations, they have shaped the game, its rules, and its equipment. Both early clubs and patent clubs are rewarding to collect and of great value in preserving the history, tradition, and evolution of the sport.

Broadly speaking, a "patent" is a legal right, granted by the government of a country, to the exclusive use of an invention. In effect, it gives the holder of the patent a monopoly on the use and production of their idea. A patent remains in effect for a certain period of time, usually many years, the exact number varying from country to country.

Although many golf clubs were patented, *the term "patent club" as used by collectors today has a broader meaning. It includes any weird, unusual, bizarre, odd, outlandish, strange, unique, or otherwise different golf club (compared to an ordinary golf club) whether it was patented or not.* These differences are not limited to shape and style; they also extend into methods and materials of construction.

The vast bulk of all remaining antique golf clubs are quite ordinary. There is nothing about their purpose, construction, or structural design to distinguish them from the masses of other wood shaft clubs that look the same. Other than having a coat of rust and grime and a shaft made from wood, most wood shaft clubs look a lot like the traditional clubs of the steel shaft era. When marketed, many otherwise common clubs were given distinctive *names* to try to set them apart from the masses, but they received only an insignificant tweak in *design*.

Patent clubs, on the other hand, are distinctly different in appearance and/or construction. The more they vary in appearance from an ordinary golf club, or the further their construction/structure departs from a standard golf club, the better. However, mere *cosmetic* design differences, such as dots instead of dashes on the face or dots and dashes on a face instead of line scoring, do not categorize a golf club as a patent club.

Patent clubs originated in five basic ways:

They were patented.

They began the process of obtaining a patent but did not complete it.

They were protected under "design registration" laws in Great Britain and "design patent" laws in the U.S., a registered design and a design patent being easier to obtain than patent protection. (A registered design applies to the outward appearance of an article—its look—whereas a patent [formally termed a "utility patent" in the U.S.] is concerned with an article's function, operation, manufacture, or material of construction.)

They began the process of obtaining a registered design or design patent but did not complete it.

They were produced without any effort to receive governmental protection of any kind.

Individual patent clubs fall into one of the following six production categories:

Few patent clubs, relatively speaking, were produced for many years. Only a few models enjoyed enough market acceptance to keep them in production over a long period of time.

Some patent clubs were produced in limited numbers for only a few years.

Many patent clubs were produced in very limited numbers for a short period of time.

Some patent clubs were produced only as working examples or prototypes. Such clubs never went to market. Oftentimes, only a handful of clubs (or just one club) was constructed. It is important to be careful in this area. "Homemade" clubs or clubs altered after they were originally sold are occasionally offered for sale as "prototypes," which they are not. They are usually just garbage. A prototype, almost without exception, was well made and properly finished.

Some patent clubs were made but no examples are known. We know about them because they were described in early golf publications. As golf club collecting gets more exposure, however, a few of these hidden clubs will certainly come to light.

Many patents were granted for clubs that were never produced. The patent records of these unmade clubs are their only remaining evidence. It is impossible to determine which patents were actually produced and which were not. There is always the chance that a previously unknown club will be located.

Patent clubs in general have an interesting history. The first patent for a golf club was a British patent granted in 1876 to Thomas Johnston (see p. 82). Johnston had the idea of making long nose clubs from a preparation of India rubber called "vulcanite" or "ebonite." He patented his idea and produced a few clubs. It wasn't until 1889 before Willie Park Jr., covering his design for a concave face lofter, received the second patent for a golf club (the first patent for an iron; see p. 239).

After Park received his patent, the idea of patenting golf clubs came into focus. Other inventors followed with patents covering clubs of all types, styles, shapes, and materials. Through the years, ideas on how to improve alignment, weighting, balance, shaft torque, head torque, durability, feel, materials, construction, etc., all in an effort to make the club more effective (durable, powerful, or accurate), were proposed by a diverse spectrum of inventors.

The game of golf virtually exploded around the world during the 1890s. As the number of golfers and courses grew, so did the number of clubmakers and the number of ideas and patents on how to make a better golf club. Each year after 1890 saw more new ideas to aid the golfer in his or her quest for the "perfect" club.

Between 1889 and 1900, there were 125 patents issued in Great Britain covering golf clubs: 2 in 1889, 6 in 1890, 13 in 1891, 9 in 1892, 10 in 1893, 29 in 1894, 11 in 1895, 17 in 1896, 10 in 1897, 6 in 1898, 2 in 1899, and 10 in 1900.

In the United States, the first golf club was patented in 1894. After that, there was 1 in 1895, 6 in 1896, 3 in 1897, 5 in 1899, and 7 in 1900. These figures for both the United States and Great Britain identify only the number of patents granted, not the number applied for.

In Great Britain, during the days of the wood shaft golf club, the patent process allowed the applicant to turn in a "provisional application," which provided provisional protection for his or her invention. This provisional application consisted of a brief written description of the proposed invention. (Prior to 1916, a patent number was assigned when such an application was filed. After 1916, a second number was assigned if the patent was issued.) The applicant then waited for a period of time, usually a number of months, while the patent office studied the application to determine if it described a valid invention. During that time the applicant could make additions and clarifications if needed. Also, the applicant could market his or her product, or enter into an agreement with someone else to produce and/or market it. Prior to letting the provisional patent application lapse and after its acceptance by the patent office, the applicant was required to file a final application ("complete specification") for their patent. When the final application was accepted, the applicant/inventor was granted a patent.

In the United States, the inventor's patent application, if approved, became the complete specification for their patent. Nothing else needed to be filed.

Obtaining a patent was costly and time consuming. The inventor had to go through the expense and trouble of dealing with a licensed patent agent in order to get his or her papers correctly prepared and filed. The respective governments also charged fees for filing provisional and final applications. Fees were also charged for renewing a patent, to keep it in effect.

What this means to the golf club collector today is, many golf club patents were applied for but never issued. Consequently, the patent number originally assigned to these clubs lapsed, as did any legal protection for the inventor's idea. Nevertheless, in many instances the club was produced and often had its patent number, provisional patent number, or patent date marked prominently on its head. Some of these clubs were also marked "patent applied for" or "patent pending."

Provisional golf club patent applications lapsed for one of two reasons: (1) The application was not accepted as an invention by the patent office. This rarely occurred in the early part of the twentieth century because so few golf club patents existed. (2) The application was abandoned by the applicant—the applicant did not complete his part of the patent process in due time. In Great Britain prior to 1905, this was almost always the reason for a lapsed patent, because the patent office did not begin researching applications to see if they were new until 1905.

Therefore, if a patent was not granted, it was usually because the applicant abandoned his application. Remember, during the months between the provisional and the final application, the inventor could market his club and witness how well it sold before incurring the accompanying expenses of filing a final application. If the club did not sell well or portend a promising future, the inventor could decide against spending any money on the final application. Unfortunately for historians, U.S. and British patent offices did not keep copies of abandoned applications.

A great variety of clubs were produced under their respective patents. However, a large number of patents were granted for clubs that were never marketed. Many patents were sought and received only for the idea they embodied. Actual production did not proceed if the club's patented feature(s) proved unpopular, impractical, or ineffective.

In retrospect, the patent club is a testimony to the ingenuity and creativity of yesterday's golfers and to the lengths they would go in an attempt to improve their golf game. For those who hit the ball so crooked that they risked being arrested, for those who had no time to practice and thought it was cheating for others to do so, and for those who viewed their clubs as the devil's own personal agents, what more noble quest could there have been than that which is still the never ending quest of many frustrated golfers today: to obtain a club that will make them better golfers than they are! However, not everyone took kindly to such a quest—nor to patent clubs.

In the 1890s, as patent clubs entered the world, many golfers felt that such "abhorrent monstrosities" went against the true spirit of the game. The rules of golf, however, did not define the golf club nor limit what could be created and/or used as a golf club. Furthermore, there were no rules to define *how* the golfer could use a club. Using a club shuffle-board style, croquet style, or even billiard style was not specifically outlawed. Consequently, a variety of radical clubs began to appear. As this happened, the stalwarts of the tried and true denounced any attempts to change the traditional clubs of the game they knew and loved.

In 1892 a golfer using the pseudonym "St. Andreian" wrote:

As a golfer of the old school, and one saturated with its best traditions for nearly thirty years back, I am perplexed and distressed at the continual innovations being introduced into the game. . . . If the object of the game were merely to get the ball round the course in the fewest number of strokes, irrespective of the weapons used, then no doubt many ways could be devised which would produce better results than the ordinary Golf Club. Might not one have drivers with catgut faces, or dynamite cartridges, and as for putting (as a "beginner" aptly queried in the papers the other day), is there anything to prevent one using a billiard cue on the putting green? No doubt one would be surer at short putts with a billiard cue (applied as one gracefully lay on one's stomach) than with a putter. What is the reply to that beginner's query? None, I fancy except that though the rules do not forbid it, it is not golf (Golf, 9 Dec.: 204).

In 1894 a person using the pen name of "Juvenis" wrote:

Were the shape of clubs once defined, and "regulation" measurements adopted, limiting the extremes of length, width, and depth of wooden, and iron club-heads; also prohibiting the attachment, or insertion, of the shaft in any other way than to, or into, the neck (i.e., the lateral prolongation of the head) we should not alone get rid of the numerous and unsightly abominations masquerading as golf clubs, but . . . we should hear no more discussion as to what position a player should, or should not, adopt. . . .

We shall soon have the "Hockey-knockers"—to give the wielders of these ghastly shaped clubs a name—clamouring for a square hole on the putting green!! (Golf, 9 Mar.: 411).

In 1896 "E.W.M." wrote:

I crave permission to raise my feeble voice against any such innovation as the spring-faced driver described in a recent number. And coming from a Scot, too! Where is his reverence for the noble game? What is to prevent it being reduced to a mere "penny-in-the-slot" exhibition, by the introduction of mechanical aids such as electric drivers, pneumatic gauged putters, and pendulum niblicks supported on clockwork frames? (Golf, 15 May: 211).

A column in the November 11, 1898 issue of *Golf* reads:

A golf clubs looks, and ought to be a simple thing; two pieces of wood, some string, and there you are. Nothing shows the astounding spread of the game more surely than the amazing variety of woods which are employed by the club maker. . . . They all drive 15 yards further than any two of the others . . . . And yet some old-fashioned players cling to the belief that the art of driving must be mastered by the man, not by the club (191).

In 1900 a person identified as "Light Iron" wrote:

By all means let our clever friends invent a ball, or a club, that will do its work well and last well. But let the honour of achievement be with the man, not with the implement. Otherwise let us have electric shocks concealed within our clubheads, and let us press, not in the good old-fashioned honest way, but press buttons to do the rest (Golf Illustrated, 26 Oct.: 77).

In 1894 a person using the pseudonym of "Tee-Shot" wrote:

I was playing a few days ago against a scratch player and a member of several clubs, and had brought to the ground with me a couple of new patent drivers. You may imagine my astonishment when he remarked that if he had known I was going to use them he would not have played; which remark was reiterated after halving the first hole! (Golf, 20 Apr.: 94).

As the debate over the place of patent clubs within the game of golf continued, if there was to be any place at all, the individual clubs themselves usually fell upon hard times. Most were either ignored to begin with or rejected shortly after they were tried and found to be less than what was advertised or hoped for. This fact was noted in print on many occasions:

Perhaps the two most striking features of this developing process have been the number of patents "for the improvement of golf clubs" which were taken out, and the fact that hardly any of these patents ever met with any permanent success. If we except Park's patent putter and Fairlie's curious iron clubs, we will hardly find a patent club in the pack of any first-class player (Golf, 30 Dec. 1898: 329).

Many have the inventions been; some were patented, but all have gone into obscurity (Golfing, 5 Oct. 1899: 4).

Within the past few years the market has been deluged with patent clubs, each professing to be the epitome of mechanical exactness, but scarcely one of them has made the least impression on the golfing world. The scrap heap, not the golfer's bag, has been the market they have found (Golf Illustrated, 3 Nov. 1905: 112).

The great majority of golf patents . . . have but a transient existence (Golf Illustrated, 26 Mar. 1909: 6).

In spite of the strong opinions against patent clubs, new models continued to appear. A few models had genuine potential, but most were perceived as gimmicky, ineffective, and a waste of the golfer's time:

Some golfers can never resist the temptation to produce a special club, ball, boot-stud, spat or what not for the medal or bogey round. The ordinary driver, cleek, iron and putter are not considered good enough for a competition, so the patent bell-metal bulger, the adjustable brassey, the paper-faced cleek, the convex mashie, and the parallellopipedon putter are ostentatiously put into the bag, much to the amusement of the cynic, and greatly to the disgust of the overburdened caddie. Ten years ago "patent" clubs swarmed; nowadays, in spite of the enormous increase in the manufacture and sale of golfing material, you seldom see one. By "patent" of course we mean not every harmless necessary driver or iron which embodies some useful feature worth registering, but those "cranky," "faddy," weird-looking abortions (Golf, 29 Dec, 1899: 317).

A patent club was designed not only to be more effective than other clubs but also, as witnessed by the very nature of the patent, to make money. Patent clubs were conceived within full view of a vast marketplace. The dramatic growth in the popularity of golf during the 1890s and thereafter provided a booming market with great business potential. All the inventor had to do was devise a golf club that would either last longer or help the golfer put the ball in the hole. If the idea was good enough, if many golfers felt they needed that particular club, the inventor stood to be handsomely rewarded through direct sales and/or royalties.

In reality, few inventors received financial gain for their ideas because relatively few patent clubs were ever accepted by the marketplace:

Golf club-makers do not all make fortunes. One came into the Bankruptcy Court of Glasgow last week, and from his examination he appears to have been a "patent" victim. He was now, he said, earning £3 a week in a situation with a firm of club-makers. Better this than manufacturing on one's own account with risky royalties on patents (Golf, 14 June 1895: 271).

To collectors, patent clubs span the spectrum when it comes to importance and distinction. Some patent clubs show very little ingenuity, eye appeal, or original thought. On the other hand, some patent clubs show great ingenuity, provide a strong visual image, occupy a distinct place in golf's history, and/or command great attention. These are the ingredients of the better collectibles.

Wood-shafted patent clubs established practically every innovative principle incorporated into today's golf clubs. Everything from mechanical clubheads to metalwoods were developed during the wood shaft era. And much more was developed that is now illegal under the rules of golf. In fact, the more one studies the old patents and remaining patent clubs, the more one begins to realize that there is little new in golf clubs today, only new materials with which to carry out old ideas.

In regard to the numbering of patents, it is important to understand that before 1916 the British patent system repeated the same patent numbers from one year to the next. Each year the first patent number was "1" and the following patents were numbered consecutively, never extending much beyond 30,000. Consequently, if a club is marked with a British patent number of five digits or less, the number itself indicates only that the club was patented some time before 1916. In 1916 the system for numbering British patents changed. It started with 100,001 and continued upward in numerical order, never repeating throughout the ensuing years. U.S. patent numbers have always continued in numerical order, never repeating or breaking sequence (see p. 564).

In America the design patent numbers and in Great Britain the *design registration* numbers are different from the actual *patent* numbers within each respective country. In Great Britain the design registration numbers started with the number "1" on Jan 1, 1884, and continue today in numerical sequence. U.S. design patents were also numbered in sequence through the years.

When the date of a U.S. patent is given in this book (such as a U.S. patent dated January 2, 1900), this date identifies the day the patent was *issued*. This is according to general U.S. patent office practice. However, prior to 1916, the British patent office issued patent numbers at the time of *application* and listed the patents granted for each year according to the application date of the patent. Consequently, British patents are not issued and dated in the same way as U.S. patents:

From 1892 to the present day, whenever a [British] patent was listed as "accepted" in the Journal, the publication date given at the top of the entry is a few weeks in the future.

There really is no date for early British patents. Some prefer the first filing date in Britain, others the date of acceptance. Incidentally, a problem with mentioning dates in connection with pre 1916 British patents is that they were numbered within the year of filing. Hence if GB 1000 was filed in 1910 and accepted in 1911 it belongs to the 1910 and not the 1911 series of numbers. So I would suggest using the date of filing for reference purposes. . . (Van Dulken 1994, 3).

Therefore, when a general British patent date is given in this book, it indicates the filing (application) date of the patent or the initial date when British patent laws covered an invention. The filing date is usually the initial date coverage takes effect, but not always. Foreign inventors applying for British patents were allowed to indicate whether they had applied for a patent to cover the same invention in their home country and, if they had, the application date of that patent. If a patent was later granted in Great Britain, its theoretical date of novelty for examination purposes under British patent laws could be "pushed back" seven months (1884-1901) to twelve months (1902 to present date) prior to its British filing date. This adjusted date is referred to as the "convention date."

In the remaining portion of this book, chapter headings are based on the characteristics of the different patent clubs. When a club has more than one unusual characteristic, the decision was usually made to focus on the primary or most obvious aspect of the club when placing it in a particular chapter.

*O*ne remarkable feature of the past year has been the large number of new patents in golf clubs, some of which have raised hostile criticism from many authorities. However, I myself would like to introduce to your notice a few of my own patent clubs suitable for the ensuing year, which I may justifiably claim are unique, and moreover may be used without exciting the slightest adverse comment:—

No. 1.—The screw-headed, rubber-shafted, ratchet-faced "Bunkum" driver, for preventing pulling, and slicing, and topping, or incorrect marking of card. A golfer writes: "Since using the above I have used no other. I have given up the game." Price £8.

No. 2.—The centre-balanced, 3 cylinder duplex baffy, weighted alternatively with layers of sand, cinders, and sawdust to prevent dry-rot. New method of sparking; Dreadnought head with shelves. Can be used as a portmanteau. A player writes: "Since using, all my matches have finished on the 10th green. I lost." Price, £9 10s.

No. 3.—The "Eldorado" brassie, with Thermos handle, in all sizes to hold 1/2 pint or pint. Head fitted as cigar-case. A leading amateur writes: "I love it—head and handle." Price, £7 ozs. 11 3/4 d.; charged £8.

No. 4.—The "Mustaffit," or mallet headed putter (club, not player), with telescopic gangway; can be adapted to any green. Useful in tight matches. An 18 handicap man Marconis: "The Open Championship is now within reach. Any fool can use it." Price, £18 10s.

III ——————————— *III*

All who have been making clubs for the past thirty years have still got their fortunes to make.

(William Gibson; *Golf Monthly*, Mar. 1919: 30)

Neck & Hosel Joints

Today both woods and irons are fastened to their shafts using socket necks, but this was not always the case. Over the years clubmakers showed considerable interest in the method used to attach the shaft to the head. Playability, durability, and ease of assembly were all considerations.

It is believed that the earliest clubs were made entirely from a single piece of wood, possibly hawthorn, grown from the side of a steeply sloped hill. As the wood grew and turned upward towards the sun, a natural bend between the head and the shaft was created.

The earliest known irons were constructed by simply inserting a shaft inside the hosel and fixing it in place. Irons continue to be made this way although clubmakers have tried to find a better method.

The earliest known wooden clubheads were spliced to their shafts. On these clubs, the bottom three to five inches of the shaft and the top three to five inches of the neck are cut at a corresponding angle, glued together, and wrapped with twine or "whipping." This "splice neck" method was the traditional way of attaching a wood head to a shaft throughout the entire long nose period and into the early 1900s. During their day, splice neck clubs were occasionally referred to as having a "scare" (also spelled "scair") or "scared neck." The term "scare," according to *The English Dialect Dictionary* published in 1905, meant "to fasten two pieces of wood together; to splice" (Wright, vol. 5, 243).

Splice necks were eventually replaced by "socket necks" beginning with Robert Anderson's socket joint woods covered under his British patent (No. 3,794) dated March 3, 1891. Anderson's patent describes his socket neck as follows:

The improvement consists in the glueing [sic] and fitting of the shaft into a hole bored down through the length of neck of wood head, part of the neck and shaft being bound and end of shaft wedged; instead of the head and shaft being spliced and bound as in the present method.

For a few years after Anderson received his patent, the idea of making socket neck woods languished. Apart from Robert Brand's celluloid driver, only metalwoods and combination woods with metal necks used socket joints, and only then because their necks were metal, like an iron.

For example, William Currie Jr.'s British patent (No. 5,741) dated April 3, 1891, calls for attaching a metalwood head to its shaft via a hosel socket formed just like an iron's. Claude Johnson's British patent (No. 8,954) dated May 4, 1893, calls for a metal socket in a wooden head. Charles Ashford's British patent (No. 21,383) dated November 10, 1893, covered a wood-style club, made from both wood and metal in a variety of possible combinations, having a metal socket. Dated November 20, 1893, Ralph H.C. Nevile's British patent (No. 22,157) calls for an aluminum or alloy socket head wood. The metalwoods that followed during the 1890s almost always included the socket head design.

In 1895 two different solid wood clubheads with socket necks were introduced. The first belonged to Charles Spinks and included a wide brass ring/band around its neck (see p. 135). The other socket neck wood club, George Forresters' "Drilled Neck Club," received a British design registration (No. 269,117; see p. 135). After Spinks and Forrester introduced their clubs, socket neck woods began to take hold.

By 1904 the socket head had replaced the splice neck as the primary method used to construct new woods:

The new and almost universal socket type of head for wooden clubs has undoubtedly the advantage of being neater and more durable than the old-fashioned model where the head is spliced on to the shaft, but I have long doubted whether it gives such accurate results. It has always seemed to me that the torsion of the shaft in striking must be greatly increased in view of the shortening of the connection between the shaft and the head, and the consequent alteration of the spring of the shaft (Golf Illustrated, 29 July 1904: 83).

The splice neck did not disappear immediately. A small percentage of players continued to prefer the splice neck for its perceived reduction in head torque. Consequently, clubmakers continued to make splice neck woods available well into the 1900s, when their waning demand eventually died out.

Clubmakers also experimented with combining socket and splice necks. A few clubs were constructed without a joint of any kind! These and many other types of neck joints are covered in this chapter.

ROBERT ANDERSON
SOCKET NECK,
HORN FACE, FIBER FACE

Robert Anderson's socket head wood is the father of the modern day wood in one major respect: It was the first wood patented and commercially produced with a socket neck. Patented by Anderson, a fishing tackle manufacturer from Edinburgh, Scotland, who sold golf clubs in his business "Anderson & Sons," the socket neck and its advantages are described in Anderson's British patent (No. 3,794) dated March 3, 1891:

The improvement consists in the glueing [sic] and fitting of the shaft into a hole bored down through the length of neck of wood head, part of neck and shaft being bound . . . . The advantage of this method of attachment is that the neck instead of being the weakest part as in present golf clubs [splice necks] is greatly strengthened and made practically unbreakable, and the shaft being fitted through the length of neck to sole of head the balance is thereby greatly improved.

Both Anderson socket head drivers shown are marked "Anderson & Sons \ Patent \ Edinburgh" on the top of each head. Each shaft extends through the neck and is visible on the sole, but Anderson's patent notes the shaft could socket to a limited depth within the neck.

Another interesting feature of these woods is the material on their faces. The example pictured at the far left has a large piece of horn covering the entire face. Held by two screws, one at the toe and the other at the heel, this horn forms a bulger face. The standard piece of horn remains in place across the sole, directly behind the bottom of the face horn. This horn facing represents an early attempt by Anderson to protect the face of his wood. Anderson eventually settled on something a little different.

The example pictured at the near left has what appears to be a cream colored, vulcanized fiber insert set across the center and toe portion of the face. This insert, held in place by eleven nails around its perimeter, not only protected the head; it supposedly made the ball go farther:

Messrs. Anderson and Sons, Edinburgh, have introduced an improved facing for their clubs, which is likely to supersede leather. In appearance it is like ordinary bone, but it makes the ball go much farther, and is used also in place of the bone itself [the insert extends to the sole which lacks a horn]. Some who have tried it pronounce strongly in its favour (Golf, 2 Mar. 1894: 391).

Fiber faces were tried by various makers, but a full "horn face" is seldom seen. R. Forgan & Son offered steel or horn faced drivers, but Forgan's use of horn was probably for insert material, i.e. set into a portion of the face (*Golf*, 29 Jan. 1904: 91).

In addition to making socket neck drivers and brassies under his first patent, Anderson also produced socket neck mallet putters. His second British patent, (No. 6,385) dated April 2, 1892, covered an unusually shaped, center-shafted wooden club—its striking face in line with the shaft—that could be constructed with or without a neck. His third patent, dated May 28, 1892, covered the crescent head iron pictured and discussed on page 155.

CHARLES SPINKS
SOCKET NECK

An interesting example of the development of club-making by machinery is to be found at Spinks' Works, 124, Duke Street, Leith, already well known to manufacturers for the supply of shafts. Drivers and Brassies resembling in style the famous Anderson's patent, with the variations that instead of the whipping a brass rivet binds together head and shaft, while the latter does not go right through the sole, but stops a little short, are being turned out by the dozen to any pattern, the head being made to any pattern as desired (Golf, 14 June 1895: 270).

Mr. Spinks has . . . adopted a new method of attaching a driver or brassy head to a shaft. The shaft is socketed deeply into the head, and the junction is bound by a brass ring, through which a rivet is hammered. The whipping is thus entirely dispensed with, and the appearance of the club greatly improved (Golf, 6 Sep. 1895: 503).

Pictured is a Charles Spinks driver, complete with the brass ring riveted to the neck. The head is stamped "C. Spinks \ Leith \ Patent." Other than having a brass band, the socket joint in Spinks's head is similar to Anderson's. The only difference is that the tip of the shaft is not exposed on Spinks's sole as it usually is on Anderson's.

Shortly after Spinks introduced his socket head wood, advertised as "the most reliable and farthest driving club in the world" (*Golf*, 13 Sep. 1895: 19), George Forrester followed with a socket head wood of his own. Termed "Forrester's Drilled-Neck Club," it received the following review:

G. Forrester and Sons . . . are making a great hit with an improved driving club which they have registered under the title of Forresters' Drilled-Neck Club. . . . Forrester claims for this method that it strengthens the neck of the club to such an extent as to render it unbreakable . . . ; also the spring of the shaft is brought lower down, giving increased driving power and better balance. . . . So popular have these clubs become, not only in this country but also in America, that Forrester has practically given over making any others (Golf Illustrated, 3 Nov. 1899: 99).

An early advocate of mechanized club production, Charles Spinks supplied components to the golf club trade for years before offering his own finished clubs for sale:

With the extension in the popularity of the game, the facilities for producing the necessary tools are increasing. Mr. Charles Spinks, wood turner, Pirie Street, Leith, is the latest to introduce machinery by which fully completed clubs can be produced in a very short space of time. For the last eight years he has "blocked" out golf heads, and was the inventor of a method for turning shafts, supplying the material to the trade in the rough. Owing to the changed conditions he is now producing finished clubs, and for that purpose has invented several machines, which ensure accuracy and finish. Passing through the works, where some thirty persons are employed, one sees the rough wood head "blocked out" by the "band saw." It is then transferred to a turning machine, and in a minute a neatly-shaped driver or bulger head, as it may happen to be, appears. The wood is then taken to another machine, where the cavity for the lead is hollowed out, and thence to a machine where the groove is made for the bone. After that the head is in the hands of the finishers, who soon have it attached to the shaft and ready for the market (Golf, 6 Sep. 1894: 503).

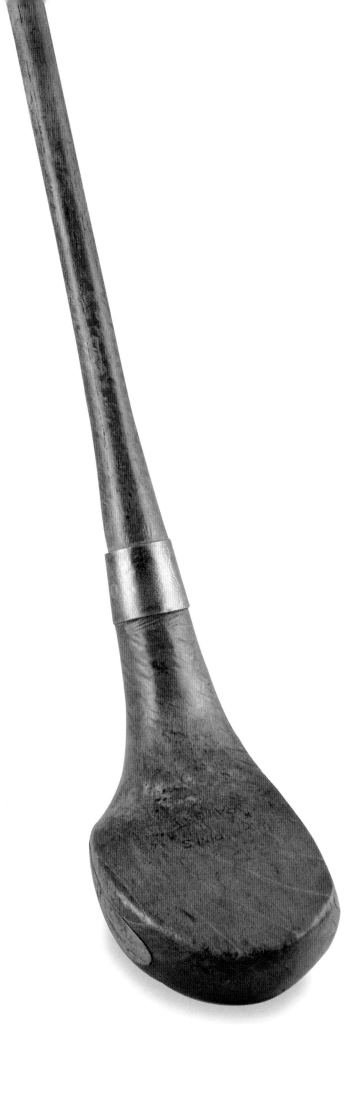

WILLIAM E. BUSSEY & JOSEPH S. PINDER

FORK SPLICE

William Eaton Bussey, a manufacturer residing in London, and Joseph Samuel Pinder, an artisan also from London, received a British patent (No. 16,953) dated October 23, 1890, that covered the wood pictured. Theirs was the first patent to deal with the neck joint of a wood. This patent also covered a sewn grip and a two-piece iron head.

Instead of the traditional splice neck, Bussey and Pinder's woods have a shaft that forks at the bottom and fits over the neck. The neck is tapered on its leading and following sides to fit the shaft. Glue and whipping secure the splice. The neck whipping has been removed from the club pictured in order to display the fork splice. Whether the shaft fits over the head or the head fits over the shaft, the neck joint is referred to as a "fork splice" whenever a "v" cut is used.

The club shown is marked "Bussey Driver" in tiny letters stamped into the lower portion of the face, towards the heel. The original "GGB, Bussey, London" decal, identifying George G. Bussey & Co., the manufacturing firm that marketed this club, is located on the top of the head.

The club pictured also has a sewn leather grip—a piece of leather placed over the handle and sewn shut with its seam running in a straight line up the back of the grip. Bussey sewn grips were made from either smooth or ribbed leather, the ribs running lengthwise up the grip. The sewn grip on this club is marked "Bussey's 'Grip' Handle."

As mentioned, Bussey and Pinder's patent also covered a two-piece iron head. Such irons and putters were produced (see p. 351). The fork splice wood, however, is the rarest of the three. Sewn grips are usually found on all of these clubs.

In 1892 Bussey and Pinder received a patent for an adjustable iron (see p. 362). In 1895 William Bussey received a British patent, (No. 11,777) dated June 17, that covered his famous club carrier made mostly from wood. Attached to the top of the carrier are two legs that support the top of the carrier when its bottom is placed on the ground. The legs fold back next to the side of the carrier when it is picked up off the ground.

ANDREW H. SCOTT

"UNBREAKABLE NECK"

FORK SPLICE

A new golf club has been brought out by Mr. Andrew H. Scott. . . . The club head is that of an ordinary bulger, but the improvement follows the uniform tendency in these modern days of Golf to shorten the neck as well as to strengthen it. The neck is short, and the shaft is attached to it by means of a splice, the strip of wood in front scarcely reaching the top of the face, and the long splice at the back coming down the curve at the heel, and running along the sole as far as the horn. [It reaches the point where the horn begins] By this method of attachment . . . additional strength is imparted to the club . . . . The club is beautifully made, and is in every respect satisfactory as a driver (Golf, 17 Aug. 1894: 539).

Andrew Herd Scott was born at Earlsferry in 1876. He is a nephew of George Forrester, the well-known clubmaker, and with him served the usual apprenticeship, working alongside of the late Jack Simpson, who was practically his tutor. . . . It was when young Scott left his native place to work with genial Charlie Hunter at Prestwick that he really came to be known as a player of outstanding merit. He returned to Earlsferry . . . and began business on his own account; and . . . has been thoroughly successful. Most golfers know either practically or by repute the unbreakable-neck club . . . for which he has secured such an unprecedented sale. . . . The celebrated amateur, Mr. H.H. Hilton, has a high opinion of Scott's patent clubs and, as a matter of fact, he is at the present time playing with one of Scott's unbreakable neck clubs . . . . (The Golfer, 22 July 1896: 73).

More than a year after he originally introduced his Unbreakable Neck club and two years after starting his own business, Scott applied for and received a British patent, (No. 21,444) dated November 12, 1895, that covered his club's fork splice neck joint. In his patent, Scott describes the joint and its qualities:

The shaft, which tapers towards one end, is formed square or rectangular in cross section at that part and enters a correspondingly shaped recess in the neck and head of the club, the said shaft passing right through same to the sole. . . . By this means a joint is made that is practically unbreakable, while it also gives more spring to the head and consequently greater power to the stroke, thereby enabling a ball to be driven further than with an ordinary club . . . .

The 42-inch Unbreakable Neck brassie pictured on this page, complete with a full brass soleplate, is stamped "A.H. Scott \ Patent No 21444" on the head and shaft.

According to Horace Hutchinson, another quality of Scott's fork splice was visual:

Perhaps its chief merit is that it enables one to see . . . if the club gets loose in the glue, and further the club head thus fastened is much less apt to get loose (1902, 67).

Scott was a fine clubmaker and his Unbreakable Neck woods were well received:

As a clubmaker [Scott] is renowned, and his clubs have a neatness of finish and a delicacy of balance which endear them to the heart of the golfer. A "Scott" club is not a hurried piece of work, but is a careful bit of workmanship. . . . There are over 7,500 [Unbreakable Neck] clubs in use in various parts of the world, and such well-known golfers as Mr. Hilton and Mr. Outhwait speak in the very highest terms of them (Golfing, 6 Apr. 1899: 5).

Scott exported his fork splice club:

A.H. Scott is also shipping golf clubs to India, and also to Egypt. All his clubs for the Orient, where the breezes are hot as well as spicy, are fitted with his patent neck, which is specially designed to prevent trouble from the heat (Golfer's Magazine, Feb. 1899: 528).

Scott used a machine to help make his fork splice clubs:

As some of our readers may be curious to know how the shaft is so neatly fitted into the head, it may be explained that the neck is cut out by a machine designed by the patentee himself. It is a circular saw or cutter, driven by a powerful gas engine, and is an ingenious machine. It works very satisfactorily. Scott has also all the latest machinery required for the manufacture of golf clubs (Golfer's Magazine, April 1898: 49-50).

A.H. Scott was also a fine player. He finished seventh in the 1896 British Open and sixth in 1903. His unbreakable neck clubs, still selling in 1906, continue to turn up today.

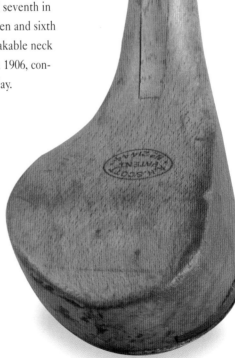

WARREN R. BRIGGS
FORK SPLICE

The latest novelty in golf clubs is a fork spliced driver made by the Bridgeport Gun Implement Company, of Bridgeport, Conn. This club was patented on March 10, 1896, by Mr. Warren R. Briggs, of Bridgeport. Mr. Briggs was one of the first in this country to start a factory for making golf clubs. His venture was known as the Outing Goods Manfg. Co. The advantages of a fork spliced club are that you get the spring right down to the point of impact—the neck is almost unbreakable with play, and it is practically impossible for it to come loose in the glue. The result is a long driving, durable club (Golf [ny], Jan 1900: 13).

Warren R. Briggs received two U.S. patents dated March 10, 1896, (No. 556,042 and No. 556, 043). These were the third and fourth U.S. patents granted for golf clubs. In his first patent, Briggs included a fork splice neck, but was more concerned with building a wooden head from a number of sectional pieces—so that a weight could be placed inside the center of the head. Briggs's second patent covered a fork splice neck on a solid (single-piece) head. It also included the possibility of building the wood head from sections.

The fork splice wood pictured was marketed by the Bridgeport Gun Implement Company under the second patent issued to Briggs. The stamp on the crown reads, "BGI Co. – Pat'd Mch 10, '96."

Concerning his fork splice, Briggs's second patent states:

The neck is cut down on a taper from top to bottom so as to leave two tapering forks . . . . Within this opening the handle of the driver is inserted, having previously been properly shaped to conform to said opening. Glue is of course used in making the joint between the handle, neck, and head, and this joint or splice is preferably wound in the usual manner. It will be observed that I obtain a splice which is exceedingly simple and strong and which does not in the slightest tend to weaken the handle, neck, or head.

Another interesting aspect of the club shown is the fact that the head was formed using steam to bend the neck. According to Briggs's second patent:

In constructing my improved driver I preferably bend a piece of wood, by the usual process of steaming and clamping, so that the head and neck are integral with the grain, running in parallel lines lengthwise of the neck and then following the bend and running lengthwise of the head.

Steaming a head to shape was thought to make it stronger (see page 298).

Briggs's second patent also refers to using an "ordinary strip of vulcanized fiber or leather which is fixed within the driving face of the club." The club shown has the leather insert.

B.G.I.'s catalog for 1900 advertised Briggs's wood as follows:

The B.G.I. Company in submitting the Patent Fork-spliced Clubs are introducing a radical change in the manner of splicing wooden clubs. The fork-spliced has all the advantages of the socket club, and in addition the strength of the club is doubled by having twice the gluing surface. These clubs resemble the one-piece clubs originated by John D. Dunn, and they drive a long ball.

B.G.I. Fork-spliced Clubs are made from the best selected bent-hickory heads, with hickory shafts. Fork-Spliced clubs can not come loose in the glue and are unbreakable at the neck.

The Bridgeport Gun Implement Company offered their "Fork-spliced Drivers" for $2.50 and their brasseys for $2.75, but only briefly. B.G.I.'s catalogs for 1901-1902 and thereafter do not offer the fork splice driver.

The author is not aware of a wood produced under Briggs's first patent. Apparently Briggs believed his second U.S. patent was the one to pursue and actually produce. His second U.S. patent was the only one also granted in Great Britain (No. 5,425 also dated March 10, 1896).

At least three left-handed fork splice woods produced by Briggs's "Outing Goods Manufacturing Company" still exist. They are marked "Brooklawn \ Pat. March 10th 1896 \Trademark \ Special" on the crown and "The Outing Goods Mfg. Co. \ Bridgeport Conn" on the shaft. These marks are extremely unusual— red ink was stamped onto, not into, the wood.

Harry C. Lee and Gardiner F. Underhill, from the firm of Lee and Underhill on Chambers Street in New York City, also produced a fork splice wood called "The Split Socket" (Golf [ny], Mar. 1910: 179). This club employed William Kilgour's U.S. patent (No. 947,882) dated February 2, 1910.

SLAZENGER & SONS
FORK SPLICE, CERAMIC GRIP

The Slazenger wood shown here is different from other fork splice clubs because its neck forks over the *front* and *back* of the shaft. Almost without exception, fork splice necks are structured side to side—extending up the leading and following sides of the shaft. Compared to a front-to-back splice, a side-to-side splice gives the neck greater strength at impact, and it helps the joint stay together.

Another highly unconventional feature of this club is its fragile *ceramic* grip. Some of the pieces broken off the base of the grip have been reset by someone trained in the craft of ceramic restoration; however, the ends of four large grooves located equidistant around the shaft under the grip remain exposed. The damage suffered by this grip is evidence of the grip's impracticality

The front-to-back fork splice and ceramic grip prevented this club from being accepted in the market.

The principle of the fork splice was explored in the 1890s. The club pictured probably dates circa 1898. A Slazenger & Sons advertisement in February of 1898 displays an artist's illustration of a club with lengthwise lines,

similar to those on this ceramic grip, running the entire length of its grip (*Golf* [ny], Feb.: 4).

Along with the three fork splice patents discussed earlier in this chapter, two additional patents covered fork splices: William Cowan and James Watson Jones's British patent (No. 16,872) dated October 5, 1891, and Thomas Gourlay's British patent (No. 12,093) dated June 29, 1892. Neither patent matches this Slazenger club.

A standard fork splice wood briefly produced by George Forrester was described, complete with an artist's illustration, in the July 4, 1901 issue of *Golfing*:

A saw cut of 1/8 inch, down the centre of the neck of [this] club is made, the two sides are then pressed out by means best known to the patentees themselves, so as to allow the shaft to be fitted securely into its position. The construction admits of the straight grain running directly up the side of the shaft where fitted into the neck of [the] club.... For the last five years Forrester and Son have been making a similar club known as the "Slip Nick," [sic] the shaft of which runs right through the heel of club to the sole. Due notice taken of their weak points has led to the manufacture of the new club under discussion (30).

The description of Forrester's "Slip Neck" club appears to identify their drilled socket wood (see p. 135).

Slazenger's, a sporting goods store originally based in London, usually sold clubs made by other makers, although they did carry their own line for a brief period. Moving beyond London, Frank Slazenger opened an outlet in New York City around 1889:

Attention is called to the fact that Frank L. Slazenger will shortly remove from 6 East 15th Street (where he has been for the past sixteen years) to his new premises at No. 8 East 28th Street. Mr. Slazenger's rapidly increasing business has necessitated the change .... Slazenger's is the oldest established house in the country for golf goods, the quality of which needing no recommendation from GOLF (Golf [ny], Aug. 1905: 296).

ARMY & NAVY
THREE-PIECE FORK SPLICE

The Army & Navy driver shown uses a third piece of wood, spliced to both the head and shaft, to provide a highly unusual fork splice. This third piece, made from what appears to be cane, is visible running down the top of the neck.

As with other innovative neck joints, this joint was designed to increase the strength of the neck and/or to alter the whip of the shaft. Locating the flex area closer to the head was a topic of conjecture during the 1890s, when this club was made. Many players thought certain neck joints could add "kick" to the shaft and therefore distance to the shot.

A fair amount of the original whipping is missing from the neck, which, for sake of illustration, is helpful. The missing whipping allows inspection of the joint.

The top of this head is marked "Army & Navy \ C.S.L. \ London." The head itself is a fine example of an early 1890s bulger—the face having a large amount of bulge. The full brass soleplate on the bottom of the head is squared off under the heel. The shaft is stamped "Army and Navy C.S.L." in a straight line.

The Army & Navy Co-Operative Society, originally sold clubs made by other makers before offering those of their own make:

Army & Navy Stores, Ltd., Victoria Street, London SW1. This was an early form of co-operative society for the Army and Navy. It issued a mail-order catalogue as early as the 1870s which went out to Service depots all over the Empire. . . . By 1890 they were carrying Forgan's range of clubs, but so great was the demand that they decided to manufacture themselves using "experienced Scottish workmen." This is how James Braid came to work there from Elie in 1893, having been persuaded to join him by Ralph Smith, another club-maker from Elie (Henderson 1979, 117).

Occasionally an 1880s iron marked "Anderson \ Anstruther" will bear the initials "A.&N.C.S.L." Such clubs were made by James Anderson and sold by the Army & Navy Co-Operative Society, Ltd.

The course consists either of eighteen or nine holes,—it is a question of available space . . . . At Westward Ho!, to take the first typical example that comes to hand, the longest hole is 462 yards, the shortest hole is 205, and the average length is 320, or thereabouts (Norris 1892, 604).

J.W. WALLIS & HARRY FULFORD

"DOVETAILED SOCKET"

J.W. "Willie" Wallis and Harry Fulford created a wood with an intricate neck joint. The shaft and head interlock in dovetail fashion, with four areas of the shaft fitting into four corresponding areas of the neck.

A Wallis and Fulford driver is shown here, although only two of the dovetails are visible in the picture. The top of the head is stamped "Fulford & Wallis, Bradford & Brough" and "Patent," though no patent record remains. Fulford probably abandoned his patent application because, in spite of its impressive appearance, the dovetailed socket did not improve the strength of the neck or the joint. Furthermore, the amount of work required to make this joint was considerable.

An advertisement for "Lillywhites, The Great Sports Outfitters" identifies Lillywhite's as the "sole London Agents for Fulford & Wallis' Patent Dovetail Socket Drivers and Brassies." The club is described as follows: "Great rigidity of neck, durability of joint, maximum length of drive, a perfect club, each 8/6" (*The World of Golf*, 21 June 1906: 223).

A 1906 advertisement for the Dovetail Socket Driver states, "The invention of 1906. New method of splicing wooden clubs. Wallis & Fulford's Patent." The qualities of the club were described as follows:

This is an entirely new style of splicing for drivers and brassies. Rigid at the neck and practically unbreakable at the point where most breakages occur. The total absence of "twist" conduces to longer and straighter driving (*Golf Illustrated*, 20 April 1906: 79).

The inventors of this club were listed in this same advertisement as "W. Wallis, the Golf Club, Brough, Yorks, and H. Fulford, Bradford Golf Club, Hawksworth, Guiseley, Yorks."

Harry Fulford learned club-making as an apprentice to the firm of Cann & Taylor, rising to the position of foreman at both Wimbledon and Mid-Surrey. Fulford, whose father was also a golf professional, was the professional at Bradford Golf Club between 1904 and 1918. He was well respected by those who knew him. When Fulford went off to fight in World War I, the members at his club kept his job open for him in anticipation of his return:

During [this] time he gave great satisfaction as a professional, helped on the course and in 1909 was also appointed assistant secretary. He enlisted in the army in 1915, the same year as his two assistants, the brothers Cotterill, were killed on the same day. Harry Fulford was paid an allowance of 15/- a week (75p) during the war, with an assurance that his job would be kept open for him. He was wounded in action in 1916 and resigned in 1918. He had been very highly regarded during his 14 years with the Club and left with the best wishes of all the members (Richardson 1991, 41).

Willie Wallis was the professional at Brough from 1904 to 1914. He then moved to Hallamshire where he worked from 1915 into the 1930s (Jackson 1994, 98).

Of minimal concern to the collector, the original lead backweight on this Fulford Patent wood is a little loose. It does not detract from the club and should be left alone.

In addition to coming loose or shifting, lead backweights were occasionally filed down. This was usually done by the owner to make the club lighter, but occasionally it was done to correct the balance of the club:

We offered in a recent issue a special golf club . . . for the best answer to the following question: "Why do some players file away some of the lead from their club heads?"

. . . . Great minds have thought alike, and quite a number of "wags" have forwarded the answer, "To make them lighter". . . . But our award was for the best answer.

[The best answer was,] "Because in many cases, after little use, the lead shifts its position, thus altering the balance of the club, hence the filing" (*Golfing*, 1 Aug 1901: 30).

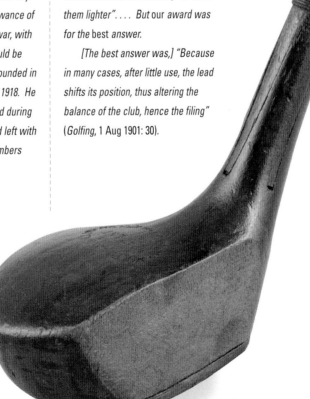

REGINALD F. WATERS
"WATERS SPRING NECK"

Reginald Fletcher Waters received a British patent (No. 21,237) dated September 25, 1906, that covered the Spring Neck driver pictured right. According to his patent, the object of his invention was to produce a club that could drive the golf ball a greater distance. Waters therefore designed the neck of his club to provide "the required spring action whilst the remainder of the shaft has the rigidity essential for consistently accurate driving of the ball." To accomplish this he calls for inlaying strips of cane or other flexible material, such as whalebone or flat steel strips, over the area where the head and shaft join.

Golf can be traced in Scottish history up to 1457. . . . In 1457, football and golf were prohibited in Scotland by act of parliament; and the cause of this was, that the youths of the north might concentrate their strength on archery, it being found by bitter experience, that when the English and Scotch encountered each other in hostile conflict, the superiority of the English bowman more than once turned the tide of battle (Fraser's Magazine for Town and Country, Aug. 1854: 206).

The Waters driver shown has four alternating strips, two of cane and two of wood, inlaid lengthwise around the lower end of the shaft and top of the neck. Only two strips are visible in the picture because the other two strips cover the back of the neck. These strips, measuring 5 3/4 inches in length, are secured "by fish glue" according to his patent. The three sections of whipping are original.

The head is stamped "Waters Spring Neck \ Pat Apld For \ Made By Percy Hills \ Crumpshall Manchester" inside an oval on the top of the head. Percy Hills was born in 1880 at Ashford, Kent, England. When he was eighteen, Hills had already worked seven years in the clubmaking trade. Hills recalls these early years in the May 3, 1906 issue of *Golfing*:

I was apprenticed at the age of 11 as clubmaker to Ramsay Hunter at Sandwich, with whom I served five years, leaving when I was just 16 to go as clubmaker to Jack White at Seaford. . . . I next went to Wembly club as clubmaker to R. Nichols, and on his leaving, I was appointed professional, at the age of 18 (20).

After leaving Wembly in 1903, Hills worked at North Manchester Golf Club in Crumpshall, a suburb of Manchester, until late 1906. He then left North Manchester to become the professional at Harrogate, where he worked until 1917. He then went on to work at Sleaford, Eastham Hall, Holme Pierrepont (Radcliffe on Trent) and United Services Gosport (Jackson 1994, 43). Throughout his career, Hills was known as a splendid clubmaker.

HARRY CAWSEY

"SPLI-SOK,"
SPLICE-SOCKET JOINT

The Spli-Sok driver combines a fork splice with a socket neck. As illustrated, the fork splice, where the upper portion of the neck forks onto the shaft, is visible on the right side of the shaft above the whipping. The upper portion of the neck, which is slightly darker than the lower portion of the shaft, is squared off at its top. The neck also extends up the left side of the shaft in mirror fashion.

The shaft, visible between the upper portions of the neck, sockets into the head under lengths of black fiber located on the front and back of the neck. Two rust-colored fiber dowels pin the fiber pieces in place. The author has also seen two Spli-Sok drivers with a side-to-side fork splice, the black fiber installed on the leading and following sides of the neck.

This pristine head is marked "Torpedo" inside the outline of a torpedo and "H. Cawsey \ Spli-Sok \ Reg'd No 346549 Brassie." The registration number dates to late 1898, when Spli-Sok clubs, without the fiber neck inlays, were first introduced. The Spli-Sock wood pictured is an improved model introduced years later and dates to around 1914, judging from the May 1914 issue of *Golf Monthly* which lists Harry Cawsey as a professional whose specialties were "Spli-Sok Drivers, Brassies, Baffies, and Cawsey Grips" (237).

Harry Cawsey was born in 1875, at Westward Ho!, England. He was the younger brother of George Henry Cawsey. Both brothers became golf professionals and were respectable players. Harry was the professional at Ashford Manor from 1902 to 1910. He then moved to Seacroft Golf Club, Skegness, where he worked into the late 1930s (Jackson 1994, 16).

The day is rather cold, and one feels chilled with hanging about [the course]. I think when we see a really good pair of players strike off, we had better go round with them. I observe . . . that the noses of some of the fair spectators are positively assuming a bluish tinge. Still the vista is not widened a yard; quite the contrary. It is really a wonder that no one has been hit.—Ah, there at last! A whack, a shriek, a sharp cry, a fall, a rushing to and fro of the crowd; someone has been hit. It is only a little boy who has been hit on the shoulder, one of the players through nervousness having struck his ball askew. Now all is right again; the boy's ears having been boxed for being in the way by a loving but sternly just parent (H.M., *Once a Week*, 12 Dec. 1863: 696).

WILLIAM P. SMITH
"THE EVOLUTION"
NECK JOINT

Three clubheads *without necks*, the products of William Percy Smith's British patent (No. 161,423) dated March 12, 1920, are pictured. A personal inspection reveals that the back of each shaft remains visible from the point where the shaft enters the head to the point where it comes out of the sole.

Smith did not like either socket or splice necks, so he sought to improve them. Smith states in his patent:

I dispense with the aforesaid socket like or wedge shaped extension and attach the head directly to the shaft . . . . Suitable means such as a screw may be provided to pass through the head of the club and the end of the shaft so as to clamp the portions of the head formed by the said recess securely to the end of the said shaft. . . .

According to my invention I form the head of the club at the heel portion

thereof with an open recess or groove of rectangular shape extending from the upper face to the sole thereof and the end of the shaft is correspondingly shaped to fit said recess.

The rectangular socket described is visible in the driver shown above left. In this club, marked "The W P Smith Sports Co Ltd \ Patent Applied For \ London," a wooden dowel, which originates in the heel portion of the face, pins the shaft to the neck. This wooden pin is by design, but Smith's patent also permits the use of metal screws as found in the other two clubs illustrated: "In some cases the said wooden pin may be substituted by a metal screw."

Although Smith's patent specifies a rectangular recess in the heel and a corresponding shaft tip, the clubs produced after his patent was granted were made

with a round recess and matching shaft tip. The clubs in the middle and on the right were made with the round recess and shaft tip. The putter (center) is stamped "The Evolution \ Reg'd" on the crown and "Pat No 161423 \ London" on the shaft. The driver (right) is stamped "The Evolution \ Reg'd" on the crown.

The fact that the head on the "patent applied for" model is loose, while the heads on the patented clubs are secure, suggests that the round recess, which wraps farther around the sides of the shaft, kept the head from coming loose and pivoting on the metal screw.

According to Smith's patent, eliminating the neck and using his unusual joint wasted less wood when making a head and strengthened the connection between the head and shaft:

By this construction I am able to save much loss in the wood during manufacture as a larger number of complete heads can be produced from a certain sized piece of wood than would be the case if they had to be made with a socket like or wedge shaped extension and furthermore greater strength is obtained than heretofore as the shaft is free from any joint above the head of the club, and a great deal of time is saved if it becomes necessary to fit a new head or shaft as the parts can be easily separated.

A W.P. Smith (Sports) Company ad in the May 1921 *Golf Monthly* offers " 'The Evolution' Drivers, Brassies, and Baffies." Three advantages are listed in their promotion:

1. Strength where the head and shaft are joined. 2. Spring in the shaft where the spring should be. 3. Longer distance combined with greater accuracy.

Isaac S. Mackie sought to overcome the perceived weaknesses of both socket and splice neck woods by combining a socket and splice neck into a two-piece shaft.

As designed by Mackie, the woods pictured below are each made from three separate pieces of wood: the head and a two-piece shaft. The two-piece shaft consists of a full-length piece and an intermediate piece. The full-length piece splices onto the back of both the neck and the upper part of the intermediate piece. The lower part of the intermediate piece sockets into the neck.

The blond driver pictured, marked "J.B. Mackie" on its head (Jack Mackie was Issac's brother), lacks the original whipping that once covered the neck joint.

Consequently, the entire splice between the intermediate piece and the shaft is visible, as is the area where the intermediate piece sockets into the head. While it cannot be seen in the photograph, the tip of the intermediate piece is visible on the sole.

Both clubs were produced under Isaac S. Mackie's U.S. patent (No. 1,098,630) dated June 2, 1914. Mackie was a Scottish golf professional who came to America in 1901. In 1898, not yet in his twenties, Mackie was known as a fine player and as a clubmaker employed by George Forrester (*Golfer's Magazine*, June: 146).

According to his patent, Mackie believed that to drive a ball with distance and accuracy:

the shaft thereof should be resilient close to the head, and the head should be firmly and rigidly united to the shaft in such a manner as to prevent it from twisting.

Mackie also believed that splice necks and socket necks performed in different ways. To him, the stability provided by a splice neck compromised the distance supplied by a socket neck, and a socket neck allowed too much torque between the head and the shaft. Therefore, in his patent Mackie sought to achieve the best of both worlds:

The principal object of my invention is to provide a club having a shaft composed of two pieces which is resilient at the portion adjacent to the head and having the head firmly and rigidly united to the shaft so as to enable the player to combine "distance" with "accuracy" of drive.

Originally, Mackie's club, complete with its two-piece shaft, was offered as "Mackie's Fishing Rod Splice" made by I.S. Mackie of Stapleton, New York (*The American Golfer*, Sep. 1914: 1063). Years later, Spalding offered these clubs, available as drivers

and brassies, in their catalogs for 1922, 1923, and 1924. They were listed as "model number RNM" in 1922 and as "model number EM" in 1923 and 1924.

As made by Spalding, Mackie's woods were wrapped with whipping around four areas of the splice. The Spalding driver below, with the black fiber sole-plate, lacks the segment of whipping that originally covered the top of the neck where the intermediate shaft piece sockets into the head. This is why the wood around the driver's socket joint is much lighter in color. This club is stamped "A.G. Spalding & Bros. \ Special" on the head and "A.G. Spalding & Bros. \ Chicopee, Mass \ EM \ Pat'd June 2, 1914" on the shaft.

Spalding-made fishing rod splice clubs are found with some degree of regularity; Mackie-made fishing rod splice clubs, on the other hand, are not.

JOHN D. DUNN
A.G. SPALDING & BROS.
B.G.I. COMPANY
WILLIAM M. RANSOM
ONE-PIECE WOODS

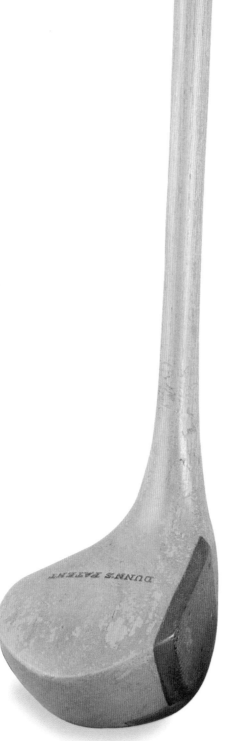

A few clubmakers dealt with neck joints by eliminating them, forming the head and shaft from one integral piece of material, either wood or iron. Their joint-less creations, known as one-piece clubs, came into prominence during the mid to late 1890s. Pictured are two prime, unused one-piece woods.

One-piece woods were tried in the mid-1800s:

The one-piece club was certainly tried over Musselburgh links fifty years ago. And, if one reflects, the probabilities are that the earliest golf-clubs were in one piece . . . (Golf, 31 Dec. 1897: 288).

In 1891 the idea of making a club out of a single piece of wood was reintroduced:

Mr. Andrew Morison, a member of the Troon Golf Club, has just taken out a patent in connection with the manufacture of drivers and brasseys. . . . The leading idea in the patent under consideration is the getting rid of the crossing of the grain and the consequent weakness; and this is accomplished by making the grain of the wood run with the bend. The curve, which is ordinarily obtained by cutting, is here imparted by pressure while the wood is being acted upon by steam. . . . It is obvious that the club may be made of one entire piece. . . . The patentee has

added another new feature to the club, also in the direction of durability. It is a well-known characteristic of the best club that the face with constant use pares off. This defect has been, to some extent, met by the insertion into the face of the club of a block of hard wood, the grain of which runs perpendicular to the face of the club, or towards the back of the club. . . . The patentee has in the meantime entrusted Willie Fernie with the manufacture of the new club (Golf, 11 Sep. 1891: 432).

Morison's British patent (No.12,207) dated July 18, 1891,

covered a wooden golf club made from a single piece of wood, as it states:

Under this invention the shaft and head of the club are both fashioned from the same piece of wood.

Morison's patent refers to either sawing out the piece of wood or steaming and bending the wood to shape. The possibility of incorporating a wood block into the face, so that its "grain is presented endwise to the ball," is also described. Therefore, Andrew

Morison is credited with being the first to present the idea of a one-piece golf club in a patent.

The next patent to include the concept of eliminating the joint between the head and shaft was applied for by Gustav A. Ruemmler, of Yonkers, New York, on February 10, 1893:

The object of my invention is to provide a strong, durable golf-stick, made out of one continuous piece of wood, thereby doing away with the joint between the handle and the head, and thus increasing its strength.

Like Morison, Ruemmler included more than one distinctive feature in his club. According to his patent, Ruemmler felt that adding a few layers of wood across the top and bottom of his clubhead would increase its durability:

In constructing the top and bottom surfaces of the head out of layers preferably alternately of stroke-wood and cross grain, thus obtain[s] a hard hitting surface and also preventing the fraying of its edges.

These layers of wood do not prevent Ruemmler's club from being considered a true one-piece. The principle behind a one-piece club is the *elimination of the joint between the head and the shaft*, not the creation of the entire head and shaft from a single piece of wood.

On January 30, 1894, Ruemmler received a U.S. patent (No. 513,733) for his one-piece wood. This patent was the first U.S. patent granted for a golf club.

Ruemmler assigned two-thirds of his patent to Walter E. Hodgman and William D. Baldwin, also from Yonkers. Hodgman then sought and received a British patent for Ruemmler's club. Hodgman's patent bears the same date as Ruemmler's U.S. patent (British patents date from their application while American patents date from their approval, see p. 130). The author is not aware of any existing examples of either Morison's or Ruemmler's one-piece club.

The next person to receive a patent for a one-piece wood was John Duncan Dunn. Born in 1872, John came from a famous family of club-makers. His father was Tom Dunn, his grandfather was Willie Dunn Sr., his uncle was Willie Jr., and his brother was Seymour. Dunn's British patent (No. 14,309) applied for on July 25, 1894, while he was working as a golf club and ball maker at "The Golf Pavilion" in Bournemouth, England, states:

My invention relates to the manufacture of wooden golf clubs, and consists in forming the head and shaft of the club in one piece, the head being bent by steaming in the ordinary manner.

Although John Dunn did not invent one-piece clubs, he *did* bring them to prominence. Dunn's one-piece wood received its first published review in May of 1895:

Tom Dunn & Son, Bournemouth, have just brought out two fine clubs. One is a patent driver, with the head and shaft all in one piece of wood, for which it is claimed that about twenty yards will be added to the drive. Both the head and the shaft are of hickory, and the head is bent to the shaft on the same principle as a hockey stick. The result is that the spring is brought down low to the head, as in short-socket clubs already in the market. The club is beautifully finished and is practically unbreakable. [The other club was a mashie with a short head] (Golf, 3 May: 131).

When Dunn's one-piece club was reviewed again seven months later, it received less flattering comments. Not only was the club identified as being "cold and collarless" because it lacked whipping, the neck was also criticized as being:

soft and pliable, without being particularly elastic, so much so, indeed, that it is quite easy to alter the lie of the head by the application of gentle pressure to the neck (Golf, 27 Dec. 1895: 338).

This review also noted that the one-piece wood was tried by Fernie some six years earlier, but "it has remained for Dunn to bring it to perfection." (The reference to Fernie identifies Morison's one-piece club, which Fernie produced.)

In response to this negative review, Tom Dunn & Son immediately sent a letter to the editor of *Golf*. The letter, published in *Golf's* next issue, reads in part:

It is mentioned that the defect in our "all-one-piece" drivers is that they are "soft and pliable." This we beg to differ with. When we first sent them out we acknowledge that they were a little soft at the neck as the wood was rather green. We had thought that the steaming of the wood would have hastened the seasoning of it. We did ourselves an incalculable amount of harm through sending these clubs out too soon. With experience we can now turn the clubs out perfect.

Then again it is mentioned that the "absence of whipping gives the clubs a curiously cold and collarless appearance." This is easily remedied. We paint them black to resemble whipping when requested to do so. It is worthy of note that although we have turned out over 600 of the all-one-piece clubs we have not had one per cent returned to us smashed, and then only through an internal flaw or the face has gone through using too high tees. Even this would have been remedied had a leather face been put on in good time.

Again, it is said that the idea originated from Fernie some six years ago. In justice to ourselves, we must say that before patenting our invention we were unaware of this.... We are also getting infinitely superior wood now (split hickory) and, as we have to pay more for it, we are compelled to raise the price.... At present we are completely sold out of all one-piece drivers, and will have none seasoned for at least a month or six weeks (3 Jan. 1896: 362).

Golf's next mention of Dunn's one-piece wood was favorable:

The "one-piece" clubs of T. Dunn and Son, Bournemouth, are being greatly improved. The wood is better, and the clubs are thoroughly seasoned. These clubs are admirably suited to tropical countries, as there is no glue to come loose. Between 800 and 900 of these clubs have been turned out, yet not one per cent has been broken (19 June 1896: 326).

By early 1897, the golf club market started to show some interest in Dunn's club, and not just in Great Britain:

Dunn's one-piece driver is said to be growing greatly in favour. Large consignments, it appears, have been sent to the Cape, America, New Zealand, The Straights Settlements, Holland, Teneriffe, and Belgium.... The shaft is of second growth split hickory, and the grain can be followed from the top of the shaft to the nose of the club without a break. There is an absence of whipping, and the spring is about six inches nearer the point of impact. The club is faced with waterproof compressed leather (The Golfer, 24 Mar. 1897: 223).

The golden blond Dunn's Patent driver on page 146 is one of the clubs patented by John D. Dunn and marketed by him and his father. The "waterproof compressed leather" insert in the face is original. Few one-piece woods made by Dunn and marked with his name remain today. The pristine condition and rich color add to the desirability of this club.

John Dunn eventually became a prominent figure among clubmakers. After leaving Bournemouth in the spring of the year, to "assist his Uncle, Willie Dunn Jr., at the new course of the Ardsley Casino Club" (*The Golfer*, 21 Oct. 1896: 325), Dunn was hired as the professional to the Buffalo Country Club, in Buffalo, New York. Shortly thereafter he was "appointed club-maker and professional to the Millionaire Club in America, that of Ardsley Casino, Dobbs Ferry, New York" (*Golf*, 19 Mar. 1897: 27).

While at the Ardsley-on-Hudson Golf Club, Dunn applied for a U.S. patent on his one-piece club (*Golf*, 30 July 1897: 401). Awaiting this patent, Dunn continued to market one-piece woods and promote himself as the "Inventor of One-Piece Clubs," but, in actuality, he was only the first to advertise and market such clubs on a sizable scale (*Golf* [ny], Sep. 1897: 61).

By the end of 1897, the Bridgeport Gun Implement Company had hired John Dunn and was offering one-piece woods produced under Dunn's "personal supervision" (Wigham 1897).

In early 1898, Dunn was put in charge of B.G.I.'s expanding golf department. During his tenure at B.G.I., Dunn promoted one-piece woods and saw them featured as the lead item in many B.G.I. advertisements.

The one-piece wood was B.G.I.'s most expensive club. Their 1898 catalog lists "Single-Piece" woods at $3.50 each while splice neck woods were $2.00. B.G.I.'s 1899 and 1900-01 catalog retained their one-piece clubs at $3.50 while introducing "Fork-spliced" and "Socket" drivers at $2.50 each. B.G.I.'s 1901-1902 and 1903 catalogs also advertised their one-piece woods.

Offering four different one-piece clubs (straight-faced driver, bulger driver, straight-faced brassie, and bulger brassie), B.G.I. advertised that Dunn's one-piece drivers and brasseys were not "turned out" but were carefully made and critically inspected in addition to being handmade.

In the marketplace, B.G.I.'s one-piece wood found acceptance; but in the U.S. Patent Office, Dunn's patent application for a one-piece wood did not:

One piece clubs have come to stay. . . . The club is the invention of Mr. J.D. Dunn . . . . Mr. Dunn's firm, the B.G.I. Co., Bridgeport, Conn., U.S.A., sold in the first year of their existence over 2,000 one piece clubs. Although fully patented in Great Britain, the United States would not grant Mr. Dunn a patent (Golf Illustrated, 3 Nov. 1899: 100).

The perceived qualities of the one-piece wood were enumerated as follows:

Golfers who have not used one piece clubs will naturally ask what their advantages are? In the first place the absence of string brings the spring about four inches nearer the point of impact, while in the two piece club the spring *is deadened by string. Another feature in one piece clubs is that the shaft tapers right down to the head. The advantage of this over a clumsy splice is obvious. The durability of all clubs steamed and bent at the neck is proverbial. The absence of any cross grain makes it impossible for them to break at the neck. To sum up, theoretically and practically we have a longer driving and a longer lasting wooden club than any other made* (Golf Illustrated, 3 Nov. 1899: 100).

However, not everyone accepted the concept of a one-piece wood:

It is said that the one-piece clubs are making way in the States. One house reports great sales of them. I am pretty well convinced that the one-piece club will never become very popular. It has its demerits, chiefest of which is, that once broken, it is practically useless (Golfer's Magazine, Jan. 1899: 485).

The B.G.I. one-piece driver pictured on the facing page, complete with a leather face insert, is a fine original example. The top of the head is marked "B.G.I. Co. \ Trademark" along with the "rampant lion" makers mark. The shaft is also stamped "B.G.I. Co." The "B.G.I." stamp bordered by the two arrows was used since February 1, 1898. The "rampant lion" U.S. trademark, used since January 1, 1897, was registered to John D. Dunn in 1900 (Kennedy 1984: 23, 33).

By the end of 1901, Dunn had left B.G.I. and was managing Crawford, McGregor & Canby's New York City store, reported to be "the largest golf store in the world" (*Golfing*, 2 Jan. 1902: 12).

When 1902 came to a close, Dunn was working in London for Messrs. Spalding & Bros., on Fetter Lane, as manager of their golf department (*Golf Illustrated*, 28 Nov. 1902: 163). Two years later, Dunn was made the managing director of the British Golf Company (*Golfing*, 7 Jan. 1904: 26). In 1906 Dunn was appointed Director of Sports to the newly formed Societe d'Hardelot (*Golfing*, 24 May 1906: 8).

On page 146, next to Dunn's patent one-piece, is another stunning one-piece driver in its original finish with original leather face insert. Marked "The Spalding" on both its head and shaft, this club is an outstanding collectible worthy of an added premium for its unused original condition. Spalding listed one-piece clubs only in their 1898 catalog.

Also produced by a few other makers such as MacGregor and Slazenger, one-piece woods were on their way out by 1904, just prior to B.G.I.'s exit from the golf market. The initial enthusiasm for the one-piece wood had been tempered by reality.

When golfers began to realize that a one-piece wood did not drive the ball any farther and that, once broken, it could not be repaired, they rethought the virtues of the club. The price of replacing a broken shaft or head on a traditional club was far less than the high price of purchasing a new one-piece club.

Three other inventors included a one-piece neck joint in their patents for a wood shaft club: William McClenahan Ransom, Riddell Gordon Carrington Smythe, and Harry Ivory Jordan.

Ransom's U.S. patent (No. 690,996) date January 14, 1902, calls for making the shaft and the entire center section of the head in line with the shaft from one piece of wood. To the center portion of the head Ransom added two blocks of wood: one to form the face and the other to form the back of the head. Ransom also received a British patent (No. 3,065) dated February 6, 1902, that covered his club (see p. 354).

Smythe's British patent (No. 20,792) dated September 11, 1908, calls for making a wood shaft that extends to the end of either a wood or *iron* head. The end of the shaft was bent in order to extend through the length of the head. The clubheads illustrated in Smythe's patent did not use a neck. It is not known whether Smythe, from Worthing, Sussex, England, ever produced any clubs.

Jordan's patent, while proposing to make shafts and heads from many strips of laminated wood, includes the possibility of making the entire club—head and shaft—from a single piece of laminated wood (see p. 356).

A word of caution: Because a one-piece wood does not use whipping, a socket head wood without whipping is often mistaken for a one-piece wood (see p. 551).

This Ransom driver does not have a neck joint. Therefore, because the shaft is integral with the head, this club is clearly a one-piece wood. The principle of the one-piece club is the elimination of the neck joint, not the elimination of inserts, horns, backweights, or added pieces to a head. The head of this Ransom driver is a multipiece head (see p. 319).

UNKNOWN MAKER
ONE-PIECE PUTTER

The one-piece putter on this page is older than the one-piece clubs already described (see p. 146-149). One-piece clubs were tried in the mid-1800s. The author has seen a broken one-piece long nose club, circa 1880, made by James Anderson.

The club pictured right and below appears to be handcrafted by a professional who was also a clubmaker, as all professionals were in the early days of golf.

The workmanship in this club shows evidence of a craftsman at his trade. Because considerable attention was given to the grain in this piece of wood, the shaft remains perfectly straight. The shaft is also symmetrical, and the head is well formed. The use of a brass faceplate stabilized the wood head against the impact of the ball. Three circular lead backweights are installed in the back of the head to bring it up to a normal weight. Finally, a solid lead soleplate is fixed in place by at least twenty-two small nails. (For similar lead plates, see pages 421 and 457).

ROBERT COWDERY
THE "WHISTLER"
ONE-PIECE IRON

Because of our company's success with solid steel fishing rods, our overly hopeful engineers tried to forge a combination club head and four sided spline shaft into what was to be, except for the grip, practically a complete club. Unfortunately, this contraption weighed far too much. It lacked flexibility. When swung at a ball it whistled like a Stanley Steamer. We still cherish a relic of this inglorious experiment. But we cherish even more the results of our second try at a golf shaft manufacture [the True Temper Stepdown Shaft] (Gurdon Leslie 1968, 27).

The one-piece iron pictured on the facing page is True Temper's first effort at producing a metal shaft. Referred to above by Gurdon Leslie, a former True Temper vice president, this club was covered under Robert Cowdery's U.S. patent (No. 1,591,363) applied for on March 22, 1922, and granted on July 6, 1926. During the 1920s, Cowdery, from Geneva, Ohio, worked for American Fork and Hoe, which grew to become the True Temper Corporation. His family had an ownership interest in the company.

In his patent, Cowdery's stated objective was to construct a shaft and head made from "one integral piece of metal, preferably steel." He observes that the metal shafts made previously were either tubular or shaped with:

holes or slots punched therein which not only gather dirt and rust but also produce a whistling noise very unpleasant to golfers.

Cowdery then states that his shaft:

is of solid cross-section, the necessary rigidity and strength being secured by fashioning the same with integral ribs of such form and disposition as to require a minimum amount of metal in order to provide the necessary strength.

Cowdery's shaft, formed with four ribs at right angles to each other, was made by subjecting the metal to:

successive rolling operations . . . whereby the body is lengthened and at the same time given the cross-sectional shape in its various parts.

Describing his shaft as "practically unbreakable," Cowdery's patent also notes that the head, being integral with the shaft, could not come loose and there was "little or no danger of the head being twisted relatively to the shaft."

The construction of Cowdery's grip is quite remarkable. The metal shaft is solid, square, and thin underneath the grip. Two lengthwise pieces of wood enclose this portion of the shaft and provide a round core over which the outer portion of the grip is applied. The outer portion of the grip consists of a number of circular leather "washers" stacked over the wooden core. When the washers were in place, a metal shoulder installed at the top of the grip pressed the washers against a metal shoulder forming the bottom of the grip. Once the grip was assembled, the leather washers were polished to the proper degree of smoothness.

Only one other patent was granted for a club similar to Cowdery's one-piece iron. Frank P. Connolly's U.S. patent (No.1,564,208) dated December 28, 1925, covered an iron head integral with the metal core of the shaft. The metal core in Connolly's shaft, which was enclosed with either wood or fiber, tapered inward as it extended upward from the head. Connolly was trying to create the effect of a weight at the end of a string. It is not known if Connolly's club was ever produced.

Other than the club pictured, the only Cowdery one-piece iron known to the author is shown in a photograph accompanying Leslie's 1968 article referred to at the beginning of this description. The caption accompanying that photograph reads in part:

The "Whistler," an early attempt to employ the rolling technique used in manufacturing fishing rods and pitch fork tines, made the shaft and head an integral unit. This one was so-called because it made a whistling noise when swung; [it] was never put into production.

Spalding's Lard shaft was also known as the "Whistler" (see page 520).

FRANK SLAZENGER
"SCREW DRIVER,"
THREADED SOCKET & SHAFT

On September 17, 1901, Frank Legh Slazenger, a British citizen residing in New York, N.Y., received a U.S. patent (No. 682,960) that covered the threaded socket driver with a screw-in shaft pictured above and below. According to his patent, the purpose of his invention was to improve the means for connecting wooden heads to their shafts so that:

there shall be a perfect continuity of contact between the wood of the shaft and the head without the application of glue or cord winding or metallic parts.

Slazenger's patent claimed the glue used in an ordinary socket or splice neck wood hindered the club's overall effectiveness:

Since the glue breaks the proper contact between the wood of the shaft and the wood of the head . . . as a consequence the life and elasticity of the wood are greatly interfered with. Moreover, the tapering socket affords an inadequate surface contact between the head and the shaft, and this weakens the club, detracts from its power, and when the glue becomes dried out and broken the head will fly off . . . .

Slazenger also received a British patent, (No. 1,675) dated January 24, 1901, that covered his threaded socket and screw-in shaft. This British patent was actually granted to Albert Egerton Legh Slazenger despite stating that it was received as "a communication from abroad by Frank Slazenger, of New York, United States of America." This patent mentions the direction of the screw threads:

The direction of the thread i.e. whether right or left handed, is formed according to the direction of play, so that the tendency of each blow or stroke is to more firmly wedge the head to the shaft.

Even though his U.S. patent (No. 682,960) opposed both gluing the neck joint and applying exterior support around the neck, Slazenger's British patent, applied for after receiving his U.S. patent, recommended "cord binding" (whipping) to strengthen the socket and included the possibility of putting a metal ferrule or other type of "shell" over the socket, after the shaft was in place, to prevent the socket from splitting.

When produced, Slazenger's threaded socket joints were glued.

On June 30, 1925, Frank Slazenger was granted a U.S. patent (No. 1,544,489) for the same idea of screwing the shaft into a threaded socket, only this time using a metal shaft. From the 1920s onward, additional patents dealing with threaded steel shafts were granted to other inventors.

The threaded socket Slazenger driver pictured, which Slazenger termed a "Screw Driver," has "Patent 682960 \ Slazenger \ New York" stamped on the crown. The shaft is stamped "Slazenger \ New York."

Slazenger's Screw Driver is the type of club that, when located in its original assembled state, is easily overlooked. There is a patent number on the head, but there is nothing visible to catch the casual eye. These clubs appear from time to time and, given care and the right amount of heat, can occasionally be disassembled for display.

A few other wood shaft clubs have screw-in shafts. Between 1893 and 1896, Spalding and Wright & Ditson included screw-in shafts in some of their irons. The provisional specification in Reginald Brougham's 1894 metalwood patent specifies screwing the handle into the socket. Horace Hutchinson, in his book *Golf* (1902), reports that Simpson of Carnoustie made an iron with a screw-in shaft. A brass blade putter selling at auction a few years ago also had a screw-in shaft, as does the club on the facing page.

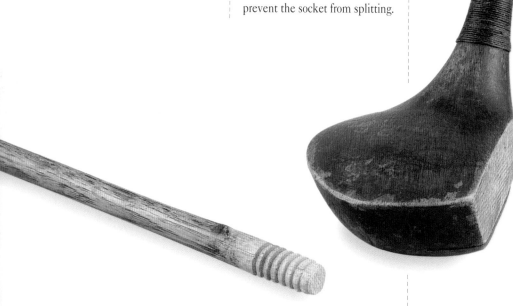

HARDMAN & WRIGHT
"HARDRIGHT DRIVER,"
THREADED SOCKET & SHAFT,
CONDENSITE HEAD

Much depends upon your drive. Players using the "Hardright" Driver Head report that it drives further by 10 to 15 per cent than any wooden club.

"Hardright" Driver Heads and Brassies are made of Condensite, one of the latest inventions of Mr. J.W. Aylsworth, who is now and for twenty-five years has been chief chemist to Mr. Thos. A. Edison.

Condensite has greater resiliency than ivory. It is absolutely non-absorbent, will not chip or crack, and wears like iron (The Golfers Magazine, May 1914: 94).

The club pictured, marked "Hardright Driver" on its neck, was originally offered by Hardman & Wright (later renamed "The Hardright Company") of Belleville, New Jersey. The head is made from "condensite" and the neck socket from aluminum. A Hardright Company advertisement defines condensite as:

a black hardened gum of peculiar properties, which maintains a brilliant polish, is absolutely non-absorbent, and will not chip or crack (The American Golfer, June 1916: 153).

A later advertisement for Hardright clubs notes, "there's no rubber in 'Hardright' heads" (*Golf Illustrated* [ny], April 1917: 45).

Hardright woods were offered two ways. Golfers could either order the finished club for $5.50 or, if they wanted a more custom club, they could order the threaded socket head for $3.50 and have their own professional fit it with a screw-in shaft:

The professional . . . can supply the shaft that exactly suits the player and can attach the "Hardright" head to it. . . . A special aluminum reinforcement tube is moulded and anchored into the body of the head itself. The shaft is shrunk, screwed in and glued . . . (Golfer's Magazine, 14 Sep. 1914: 87).

Most Hardright drivers were sold with the shaft installed. The metal neck on these "complete" models is thinner and longer than it is on the "head only" models. Also, the complete models came with the shaft pinned through a brass neck. The threaded socket head only models had an aluminum neck and no pin.

In the head only model shown above, either the shaft was never glued in place, which is possible given the unused condition of the head, or the glue used to secure the shaft failed. Either way, the ability to disassemble a club of this nature, to display its unique characteristics, adds a premium to this prime collectible.

Hardright drivers and brassies, offered in 1914 and for approximately the next five years, were available only by mail order with discounts given to professionals. Since there are so few Hardright clubs remaining, they probably sold in small numbers.

One final point: Although condensite was advertised as being extremely durable, Hardright clubs are often found in rough condition. They *can* crack, chip, and loose their rich original luster. The two examples in this book are in superb condition. (See page 306 where this club is pictured fully assembled along with a fixed shaft model.)

Beautifully formed with no evidence of a seam, the metal band located around the top of this unmarked 1875-85 cleek's hosel is made from the same metal as the head itself. So, why the metal band?

To answer this question, reference is made to three other irons, which the author has seen, which also have a metal band around the top of the hosel. On the first iron, a circa 1780-1800 early iron in the collection of the British Columbia Golf House, the metal band dates to the era of the club and appears to help hold the head to the shaft. On the second iron, a circa 1870 track iron in the USGA's antique club collection, the metal band appears nearly identical to the example pictured here, except that the hosel pin extends through it. On the third club, a circa 1900 smooth face iron, the metal band is a thin metal collar, neither well made nor finished, added in the course of a reshaft.

There are two possible reasons why the cleek pictured has an iron band around its neck. The first is to add weight to the club, which it obviously does even if that was not its express purpose.

The second reason is to aid in connecting the shaft to the head—either during the original construction or as a repair to a cracked hosel.

In 1896 a letter sent to the editor of *Golf* asked how to add weight to an existing iron. The only idea occurring to the writer was "to put a band of lead or some other metal round the socket just above the blade" (*Golf*, 20 Nov.: 196). One week later, three different readers responded with additional ideas on how to add weight to an iron:

Bore a hole in the centre of the face of the club, slightly rime out the hole on the face side, insert from the back a flat-headed bolt and rivet it to the club from the face side, then file away face level (214).

Have some lead solder put evenly over the back of the blade. A band of lead round the socket ... would not do at all, as the balance of the club would be spoilt (214).

[I] had an iron made heavier by plating the back with another metal ... It was done by William Wilson, maker of metal club-heads (214).

These answers indicate that the weight of an iron was not intentionally increased by adding material to the top of the hosel. Therefore, an iron band atop a hosel was installed to help secure the head to the shaft.

Evidence of this practice is found in a U.S. patent (No. 1,652,594) granted to Robert James Walker, of Glasgow, Scotland, on December 13, 1927. His patent covered an iron band, very similar in size and shape to the one pictured here:

My invention ... has for its object to so construct the club as to effect a better and more secure fit of the socket with the shaft of the club, thus strengthening the club at that part. ...

In carrying out this invention, I provide a metal or other band which is suitably fitted round the lower part of the shaft immediately above the head of the socket and also round the head of the socket, or the band may form an integral part of the head of the socket.

Given that metal bands existed atop a few hosels for *many* years before Walker received his patent and the fact that Walker's proposed metal band is very similar in shape and size to the one on the cleek pictured, it is clear that Walker did not invent his "invention." Rather, Walker sought a patent in order to capitalize on an old idea, a practice not unheard of in the world of golf club patents.

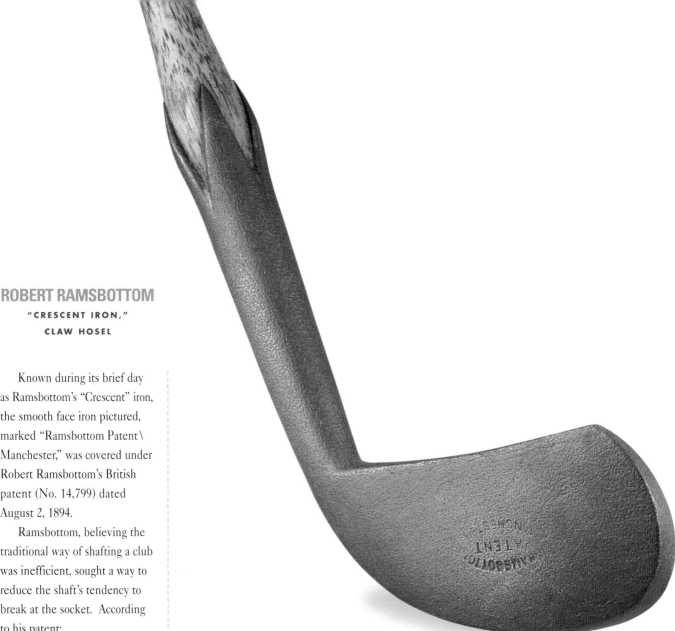

ROBERT RAMSBOTTOM
"CRESCENT IRON,"
CLAW HOSEL

Known during its brief day as Ramsbottom's "Crescent" iron, the smooth face iron pictured, marked "Ramsbottom Patent \ Manchester," was covered under Robert Ramsbottom's British patent (No. 14,799) dated August 2, 1894.

Ramsbottom, believing the traditional way of shafting a club was inefficient, sought a way to reduce the shaft's tendency to break at the socket. According to his patent:

It is obvious however that the sticks work loose in the sockets and become indented by the rim of the socket and finally break. The string binding would not tend to better secure them in the sockets, but would simply prevent the sticks (shafts) from splitting near the sockets.

Now according to my invention I make the socket itself flexible and after fitting the stick or shaft therein . . . bind both together, the peculiar construction of the socket permitting it to adjust itself to, and clip the stick.

Ramsbottom redesigned the top of the hosel to include claw-like extensions that fit up and over a large bulge near the bottom of the shaft. According to his patent:

The socket is formed with a flexible part or with flexible parts or fingers . . . formed to be as flexible as possible.

Ramsbottom's patent includes the possibility of using cord or string to help bind the top of the hosel to the shaft. Of the four Ramsbottom irons the author has seen, however, none of them had, nor did they appear to have ever had, any whipping. Nevertheless, when Ramsbottom first produced his iron, he included a copper wire around the top of the socket:

We have received from Mr. R. Ramsbottom, the Sportsman's Depot, Manchester, a specimen of his new "Crescent" iron. In this iron the sole is rounded from nose to heel, so as to admit of a ball being taken well out of a heavy grass lie or a bad cup. . . . Where, however, his club departs most materially from those now in play is in the fixing of the shaft to the socket.

The idea has been to prevent and minimise as much as possible the breaking of the club near the iron socket. . . . He has made an extra deep and wide fore-socket, into which the shaft is carefully fitted. A shoulder is turned on the socket outside, and four V's are cut from the end downwards, thus leaving four fangs projecting from the shoulder. The extreme points of the fangs are turned inwards, and are pressed into the shaft to dispense with the necessity of a pin, which is not infrequently a source of weakness. The binding is by means of copper wire, which holds all the points firmly in place and constitutes a really strong and more or less flexible joint (*Golf*, 9 Nov. 1894: 156).

Although many clubs can be reshafted and, if done properly, retain much of their collector interest, Ramsbottom's Crescent iron is the type of club that *must* have its original shaft to be considered a good specimen. A Ramsbottom iron is collectible because of its head / shaft attachment—the original shaft shaped at the hosel to correspond with the claws holding the shaft in place. If it has been reshafted, a Ramsbottom iron has lost a primary element integral to its collectibility.

Ramsbottom, a self-described "sportsman's outfitter" from Manchester, England, also produced a metalwood with a claw hosel (see. p. 281).

FRANK MURRAY

SPLICE NECK IRON & BLADE PUTTER

For centuries the "scaired" or splice neck was the primary method used to attach wood heads to their shafts. However, the concept of splicing an *iron* head to its shaft has been found only in irons designed and patented by Frank Murray of Edinburgh, Scotland.

A William Gibson & Co. advertisement for "The F. Murray Cleek" describes Murray's iron as a combination of an iron and a wooden club:

A veritable revolution in the Driving Cleek "Spliced" Irons. The F. Murray Cleek is ready. A combination of iron and wooden club. From its novel construction it combines the rigidity of the iron, with the steeliness of the wooden club—result, longer distance—supersession of the brassie—besides rendering cleek play, now so difficult to many, easy and pleasurable to all (Golf Illustrated, 3 Mar. 1911: 180).

Following its introduction, Murray's splice neck iron received positive reviews. Under the heading "A Revolution In Golf Clubs," the first review described the "Murray" club in generalities:

The "Murray" club, as it is called, is novel in construction, distinctive in appearance, beautifully finished, and from all accounts most effective. . . .

"Murrays" will be made in cleeks, driving irons, driving mashies, mashie cleeks and putters, and to any model. (Golf Illustrated, 10 Mar. 1911: 203).

The next review described the club in more detail:

Not content to be outdone by Yankee genius, a well known Scotch amateur is said to have invented a new form of iron.

. . . The heads are constructed in the ordinary way and part of the socket is then ground away to permit of an insertion of a piece of wood. This, when rendered flush, enables the shaft to be added by splicing, a unique and ingenious method of uniting an iron head to a shaft. After gluing and binding with whipping the result is a perfect combination of iron and wooden club. The construction is said to lead to an entire absence of "dirl." For the benefit of American golfers who have suffered from this annoyance without knowing it, let it be known that "dirl" is the Scottish equivalent for wrist jar.

It is claimed the splice greatly improves the "feel" of the club, be it a cleek, mid-iron, or putter, and that distance is obtainable with far less effort than with the former make of clubs. . . (Golfers Magazine, April 1911: 290).

Murray received a British patent (No. 9,439) dated April 19, 1910, that covered his splice neck irons. According to his patent, friction was necessary to make his splice effective:

This [joint] is effected by forming the lower end of the shaft with a diagonal or angled splice, and forming a corresponding splice on the adjacent part of the metal head . . . , and in the latter part also forming a groove or grooves into which is inserted a strip of wood, india rubber, or equivalent material which will form a frictional grip when the spliced part of wooden shaft is placed over same, and then secured with cord . . . .

Murray's patent also includes an alternative method for providing friction in his splice:

By a modified arrangement the metal surface of the splice would or may be formed with a series of serrations or indentations at short spaced distances apart so as to give the frictional gripping action to the adjacent spliced wooden surface.

A Murray putter and driving iron are pictured on the facing page. The putter (shown above left) is marked "The F. Murray \ Regd. No. 576946 \ Patent Applied For \ Warranted Hand Forged \ Harrods Ltd \ Special \ London S.W." Harrod's, London's world famous department store, sold this particular putter. The "star" trademark stamped on the back of the blade identifies William Gibson as the maker of this clubhead. Murray received a design registration (No. 576,946) for his club while awaiting his patent.

The iron (shown lower left on the facing page) is stamped "Wm Gibson & Co \ Kinghorn Scotland \ The F. Murray Patent No. 9439" etc., on the back of the blade. "Driving Mashie" is marked on the sole. Just what, exactly, is a driving mashie? This simple question once received more than a simple answer from Horace Hutchinson:

A club of recent invention, named the driving mashie is taking the place of the driving cleek in general use. It is practically a cleek with a very short head, or a mashie with a longer and more supple shaft than the lofting mashie, and a less laid-back face. The advantage that the short-headed mashie has over the longer-face cleek is chiefly that it can fit into a cuppy lie or heavy lie which the cleek could scarcely deal with. Also, it has the pull of massing the weight behind the point of impact (1902, 66).

Since their introduction in the mid-1890s, aluminum clubs were nearly always made with socket necks. Shown below is the exception: an aluminum putter head made with a splice neck. Although the tip of the shaft extending below the bottom of the whipping is not visible here, the splice neck is easily recognized by the long oval neck which is covered with four inches of original whipping.

The top of this putter is marked "D. Stephenson." David Stephenson was the professional at Dumfries and Galloway from 1900 to 1902, at Huntercombe from 1902 to 1906, and at Prince's, Sandwich, from 1906 until at least 1917 (Jackson 1994, 89). This long nose style putter was probably made early in Stephenson's career.

Splicing a metalwood clubhead to its shaft is unheard of, but one pair of inventors working together in the earliest days of the metalwood considered the idea. James McHardy and Frank Bryan's British patent (No. 18,555) dated October 4, 1893, covered a metalwood clubhead made from a metal shell (preferably steel) filled with gutta percha or wood (which could be exposed at the face). McHardy and Bryan's patent included the idea of splicing the neck to the shaft. The author has never seen a McHardy/Bryan club and suspects they were never made.

Armed only with a putter, Denholm, the young professional, recently went round the course of the Brighton and Hove Club in 83. An amateur who took up the match to play against him with his full set was beaten by 7 up and 6 to play (Golf, 28 Jan. 1898: 357).

Dickson's Patent "Simplex" was another method of taking weight from the socket to put into the head; in it the "hose" is replaced by a claw-hammer grip, which gives greater length to the shaft, and at the same time does away with the exposure of the end of the latter, with the open end of the grain, to the wet, which is apt to destroy the shafts of Carruthers' patent clubs inside their sockets (*Golf*, 9 Apr. 1897: 79).

In November of 1892, John and Andrew Dickson, clubmakers at 8 Braid Road, Morningside, Edinburgh, applied for a British patent (No. 20,261) on their Simplex iron. Their patent application, however, was abandoned shortly thereafter.

Instead of a normal hosel, the hosel on Dickson's Simplex consists of two iron tangs that extend up from the heel and attach to the shaft, one on each side. These two metal tangs, affixed to the shaft by two pins running through the neck, appear as a split or forked hosel. This is the same basic design Charles Seely patented in the U.S. approximately twenty years later.

The Simplex iron shown on this page is marked "Dickson's Pt 'Simplex' \ Edinburgh" and "J. Herriot \ Glasgow" on the back of the blade. When it was purchased at auction in 1985, old whipping covered the entire length of the neck, hiding the metal tangs. The whipping was very fine and contained red and blue threads inside the black outer layer. It is not known if this whipping was original to the club, but it appeared old. Of the handful of other Dickson Simplex clubs known, none of them has whipping. Dickson's Simplex irons were made for only a short time.

Prior to 1930, the term "Simplex" was used as a name for many clubs and golf related items. For example, in addition to "Dickson's Simplex" pictured here, John Ross applied for a British patent at the end of 1892 on a club titled the "Simplex." Francis Brewster produced "Brewster's Simplex" clubs and organized the "Simplex Golfing Society" (see p. 204). Robert Simpson produced a "Simplex" wood with a small brass back-weight integrally attached to the soleplate on an otherwise ordinary wood. The "Simplex Marker Company" in Philadelphia made the "Simplex Marker" which

marked golf balls. A golf glove titled "The Simplex" was produced in 1895. In 1897, the "Simplex Company" advertised "Golfine for Golf Greens" to be applied to greens to ensure against "worm casts" (*Golf*, 18 June: 308). And there were other "Simplex" products.

A few years ago golf-clubs were carried in a loose bundle and secured by a strap round the shafts when not in use, but nowadays most golfers carry them in a bag for the purpose. Such a bag is a useful requisite, and in wet weather it helps to keep the clubs dry. 'Caddie bags,' as they are called, are made in different styles to suit individual tastes (Park 1896, 53).

CHARLES H. SEELY
FORKED HOSEL

On May 14, 1912, Charles Hanford Seely of Noroton, Connecticut, received a U.S. patent (No. 1,026,181) for an iron head that uses two "steel tangs," as termed in his patent, in place of a hosel. According to Seely's patent, the reasons for constructing an iron head this way were:

to improve the balance of the club, to throw a relatively larger portion of the weight of the head nearer the medial line of the striking face thereof, to lighten the shank of the head, and to so secure the shaft to such shank as to insure a resiliency at a location near the head itself.

Seely's patent includes the possibility of attaching wood blocks to the front and back of the blade in order to transform an iron into a driver or brassie. (It is not believed that such a club was ever made.) Whipping could be applied to the neck of the iron if desired.

A.G. Spalding & Bros. produced "Seely Patent" irons from 1912 to 1919 and in the following models: driving iron, mid iron, cleek, mashie, jigger, and pitching mashie. The jigger and mashie, however, were available only from 1916 to 1919. Most of these irons were originally sold without whipping.

The principle behind the Seely iron was that of relocating weight from the hosel to the blade:

The substitution of the steel prongs for the round hosel actually reduces the weight of that part of the head one and one-half ounces, enabling us to place that additional weight in the blade, increasing the driving power and producing a club lighter in weight, more effective for distance and of better balance (The American Golfer, May 1914: inside cover).

The mashie pictured is marked "Spalding Gold Medal \ Seely Patent \ Pat'd May 14, 1912" on the back of its blade. The shaft is stamped "A.G. Spalding & Bros. Gold Medal."

The shaft stamp is a particularly welcome characteristic on this club. A shaft stamp matching the makers name almost always indicates that the head has its original shaft. However, A.G. Spalding & Bros., as well as many other makers who marked their shafts, did not always stamp their shafts. A club can, therefore, have an original shaft that does not have a shaft stamp.

Because most clubs do *not* bear shaft stamps, a mark on the shaft is only one piece of evidence used to determine the originality of a shaft—not the verdict. The neck joint itself must also be inspected. It will carry its own evidence of originality or alteration. The area where the neck is pinned should receive considerable scrutiny. Are

there any file marks around or on the pin? Is the pin a notably lighter color or made from a different material? Is the area of the hosel around the pin buffed out? The more of these questions answered "yes," the greater the likelihood the club has been reshafted.

Because the shaft is such an integral part of the Seely iron's collectibility and because Seelys were produced by a large clubmaking company for several years, a reshafted Seely has little collector interest.

Seely also received a British patent, (No. 10,910) dated May 8, 1913, that covered his forked hosel iron.

UNKNOWN MAKER

FORKED HOSEL, SWAN NECK

The maker of this club is unknown. Based on its own merits, however, this brass head putter is an outstanding collectible. The forked hosel is an exceptional feature otherwise seen only on Dickson's Simplex and Spalding's Seely irons discussed on the previous two pages. The dramatic swan neck hosel, aligning the shaft with the center of the blade, is also a splendid trait. P.A. Vaile and J.R. Brown produced clubs with similar necks (see p. 176 and 177). The way the neck extends to the ground and attaches to the bottom of the blade adds much to the stylish character of this club.

The blade itself is also singular in design. It is flat across the face, across the sole, on the end of the toe, and across the top of the blade. It is also flat across the back of the head except for an area behind the heel where the brass is hollowed out, to improve the balance of the head. Hollowing out the backside of the heel allows the toe half of this head to counterbalance the weight of such a long hosel more effectively.

A collector should not shy away from a club just because it is not stamped with a maker's name or cleekmark. Even unmarked, this club is an exceptional collectible. It combines many wonderful features in one club: the forked hosel, the swan neck, the location of the neck/blade attachment, the quasi-rectangular blade, and the weighting design. Furthermore, this putter strikes a dramatic pose and is the only one of its type known.

Knowing the maker of a club is certainly important, but it is not the reason people collect patent clubs. Collectors are usually much more interested in the nature of the club itself and the distinguishing characteristics it bears. Only after determining what a club is—a long nose, a patent club, or a common—does the maker's name begin to become important. On long nose clubs, an unmarked head can even be a *desirable* characteristic—evidence of an early club. On patent clubs, an unmarked head, such as the one pictured, usually indicates genuine rarity. When only a few clubs were made to try out an idea, the maker often did not bother to mark them. However, on common clubs, the *only* characteristic of any importance (because it is the only distinguishing characteristic between one common club and the next) is the maker's name or cleekmark.

A member of the Northwood Club some years ago possessed a driver, the head of which was composed of the following: wood, lead, fibre, leather, three 1-inch sprigs. When in use it rattled like marbles in a tin can, but the presence of the faithful friend in his bag was necessary for his confidence. Call it what you will—his fad, or fancy, or even an idolatrous worship—we who golf can understand and sympathise (Fulford 1919, 79).

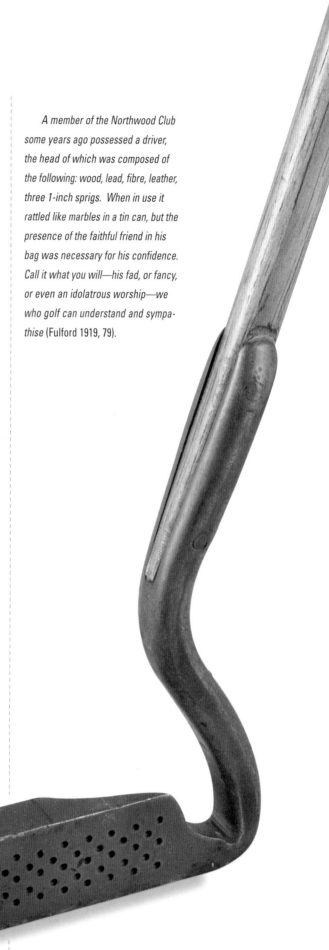

THOMAS HARROWER
"HARROWER'S PUTTER,"
STEEL CORE JOINT

An American doctor has given a strong opinion against the bicycle. He declares that the idea that cycling is a wholesome exercise is a mistake, and says that it doesn't make girls healthy and pretty; on the contrary, it makes them ugly. "The lady cyclist," he says, "may be identified by her squeaky voice, large, broad and flat hands, coarse skin, wrinkled face, and small, piercing blood-shot eyes." He has nothing to say against the lady golfer (Golf, 17 Feb. 1899: 443).

Thomas Harrower of Carnoustie— a well-known cleek maker—has invented something which is applied to all the irons. In place of the shaft fitting into the socket, and held there with an iron rivet, he has introduced a screw in the middle of the hose, into which the shaft is put, then screwed up with a left hand turn, so that when the club meets the ball, the shaft cannot unscrew. This screw is longer than the socket of the head; but he contends that the shaft is not weak- ened as is done when the rivet is driven through the ordinary socket. Thus we have a club which gives the firm, solid blow of the old Carruthers cleek, with all the advantages of the shaft being strong at the head, and with a thin steel-like socket enabling the weight to be put into the blade (Golf Monthly, Dec.1912: 786).

Thomas Henderson Harrower, a joiner living in Glasgow, Scotland, received a British patent (No. 4,326) dated February 21, 1911, that covered the putter described above and pictured below. According to his patent, the object of his invention was to:

so construct the metal club as to give a better balanced head, greater strength at the joint, simplify the fixing of the shaft to the head thereby making the socket much lighter so that more weight can actually be put in the head, and with regard to the wooden club to so construct it as to strengthen the neck at junction with the shaft.

Harrower's putter has a threaded, three-inch "steel core," three-quarters of which screws into the base of the shaft while the other one-quarter (3/4 inch as pictured) screws into the base of the socket inside the hosel. Overall, half of the threaded rod (1 1/2 inches) ex- tends above the top of the hosel when the shaft is installed.

By using a three-inch steel core, Harrower could make a short hosel. The hosel on this putter measures only 1 3/4 inches to the sole. The weight saved by short- ening the hosel was added to the head, directly behind the ball.

In addition to putters, Harrower's patent covered irons and woods. The steel core could be screwed into the hosel or formed integrally with the head. Harrower proposed covering the neck joints of his woods (which, in his patent illustrations, look like ordinary socket head woods) with either a nontraditional metal band or traditional whipping.

The putter pictured is marked "Harrower's \ No. 4326/11 \ Patent \ Putter \ Warranted Hand Forged" on the top of its head, along with Harrower's "heart" trademark. Harrower produced a significant number of putters. Various other makers produced a large number of putters similar in shape to Harrower's. Early in 1913 the clubmaking business of Thomas Harrower was absorbed by J.P. Cochrane & Company.

During the 1920s, while exploring the rapidly increasing potential for steel shafts, clubmakers encountered difficulties when installing a metal shaft in a clubhead made for a wood shaft. Because the tip diameter of a steel shaft is much smaller than it is on a wood shaft, a steel shaft would not fit properly into the neck.

The first patent to deal with the problem was a U.S. patent (No. 1,550,647) dated August 15, 1925, and granted to Herbert C. Lagerblade of Bristol, Connecticut, who assigned it to the Horton Manufacturing Company, also of Bristol. Lagerblade devised an adapter, formed from either wood or fiber, to fit on the end of a metal shaft. The adapter, with a shoulder that abuts the top of the hosel, tapers down in both directions from the shoulder. This shape allowed the adaptor to fit inside the hosel and to transition to the circumference of the steel shaft above the hosel. A Tom Stewart iron sold by Alex Campbell, a golf professional working in Brookline, Massachusetts, is pictured above and has such a fiber adapter. In order to display the entire adapter, the middle picture shows the shaft separated from the clubhead.

The Horton Manufacturing Company, to whom Lagerblade assigned his patent, made the Bristol Steel Golf Shaft. To help market their steel shafts, the Horton Manufacturing Company published directions for attaching their steel shafts to clubheads that were originally designed for

wood shafts. For irons, Horton recommended using their steel shafts fitted with wooden adapters. For woods, Horton recommended plugging the original socket with a piece of the wood shaft and then redrilling the neck to match the size of the steel shaft.

The rustless, deep-faced mashie in the bottom picture is marked "Watson's Patent \ Prov. No. 32339/29," etc. Instead of a wood or fiber adapter, it employs a metal one. Watson's British provisional patent number is 32339/29. The "/29" means 1929. This patent never received a final approval.

Shaft adapters were used not only on a few metal shafts but also on many bamboo shafts (see p. 512). A British patent (No. 217,126) dated November 1, 1923, was granted to Dutee Wilcox Flint for this very purpose. Flint's patent covered a wood ferrule similar in design to Lagerblade's.

As the years wore on, shaft adapters took various forms. They were even tried in heads designed for metal shafts. These later adapters sought to dampen shock, reduce torque, improve the strength of the joint, increase the feel transmitted to the golfer, etc.

Because ferrules are used on most steel shaft irons, wood shaft iron heads fitted with steel shafts, via adapters, are not always recognized. Easing the transition from wood shafts to metal shafts, shaft adapters for metal shafts were of brief significance.

Golf is a game played only by people accustomed to Scottish sports and Scottish scenes....Up to this time golf has made no advance whatever in the United States....

At the beginning of play each player places his ball at the edge of a hole which has been designated as a starting point. When the word has been given to start he bats his ball as accurately as possible towards the next hole, which may be either one hundred or five hundred yards distant. As soon as it is started in the air he runs forward in the direction which the ball has taken, and his servant, who is called a "caddy," runs after him with all the other nine tools in his arms. If the player is expert or lucky he bats this ball so that it falls within a few feet or inches even, of the next hole in the circle. His purpose is to put the ball in that next hole, spoon it out and drive it forward to the next further one before his opponent can accomplish the same end. The province of the "caddy" in the game is to follow his master as closely as possible, generally at a dead run, and be ready to hand him whichever implement of the game the master calls for ....

....As a general custom the players make the entire circuit of the circle and the one who gets his ball in the hole at which they began first, wins the game. Nevertheless it is sometimes agreed that the game shall be won by him who makes the largest number of holes within a given number of minutes, say twenty or thirty .

III ————————— *III*

(*Golfing Annual 1889*, 148-152. This article was originally published "in the large Sunday edition of the Philadelphia Times of February 24, [1889].")

Nerve, enthusiasm, and practice are the three essentials to success in golf, but to be great requires the gift.

(Robert Ferguson; Leach 1907, 193)

Neck & Hosel Shapes

Many a golfer has taken advantage of an unforeseen moment (a particularly bad shot coming at a particularly bad time) to teach his or her club a thing or two (physical instruction being the primary method) as witnessed by the dramatic after-market alterations (new and unusual shapes previously unknown) imparted to their club (usually when it slams into the ground, a tree, or their golf bag)! The net result is often a broken shaft or a neck bent into some weird contortion.

Years ago a few clubs were constructed with outlandish bends at the neck (not to mention other places) created by design, not unbridled frustration.

Frank Fairlie was the first to receive a patent for a club with an unusual hosel shape. His British patent (No. 6,682) dated April 18, 1891, covered an iron with the bottom of the hosel bent forward to position the blade in front of the hosel. His club, designed to eliminate "shanking," remained on the market for many years and was made by many clubmakers (see p. 166).

Willie Park Jr. received the second patent for a club with an unusual hosel shape. His British patent (No. 20,914) dated November 1, 1894, covered a putter with the lower part of the hosel bent backward to offset the blade. His putter was exceptionally popular and made for many years (see p. 170).

The third patent to cover a club with an unusual hosel shape went to Ramsey Hunter. His British patent (No. 4,810) dated March 3, 1896, covered another putter with a neck bent in order to offset the blade, though the patent called the bent portion of the neck "part of the blade." This club was a variation on Willie Park Jr.'s putter (see p. 172).

George Low was awarded the fourth patent to cover a club with an unusual hosel shape. His British patent (No. 16,560) dated March 3, 1896, covered an iron similar to Fairlie's anti-shank iron (see p. 168).

After the turn of the century, clubs with other neck shapes were built. Square hosels, such as the one patented in 1900 by Alexander Simpson (see p. 173), were tried. So, too, were swan necks, such as those patented in 1904 by James R. Brown (see p. 176) and by Percy Vaile/Frederick Ayres (see p. 176). Some putters even used inordinately long hosels, like the one patented in 1921 by William Oke (see p. 184). Of all these different neck shapes, the forked hosels, such as the one patented in 1901 by Isaac Palmer, are the most visually striking (see p. 502 and 179).

These neck shapes and others, some patented and some not, are presented in this chapter.

The Golfer's Alphabet.

A was an Ass who went to play Golf,

B was the Ball he couldn't drive off.

C was the Caddie so ready to jeer,

D was the Drive promptly bunkered, no fear!

E was the Earth in which the ball lay,

F was the Flag so far, far away.

G was the Green where the Ass fain would be,

H was the Hazard that stopped him, you see,

I was the Iron he swung quickly back,

J was the Jerk which proved quite imprac.

"**K**'s coming on," sneered a Golfer ahead,

L was the Language the Ass used instead.

M was the Mashie at last he did take,

N was the Neck which he straightway did break.

O was the Odd which now he did play,

P was the Putt that ran far astray.

Q was the Queerest of strokes ever seen,

R was the Rub called a Rub of the Green.

S was the Stimy his opponent did lay,

T was the Trouble that stimy to play.

U was the Usual stimy not talked,

V was the Villain whose stimy was baulked.

W waged War in the columns of Golf

X said " 'Xcuse me, the stimy is off"!

Y was the Youth who stimied the same,

Z was his Zeal for the grand, Grand Old Game.

(T.C.O., *Golf*, 24 July 1891: 319)

FRANCIS A. FAIRLIE
ANTI-SHANK IRON &
"THE ACE"
ANTI-SHANK PUTTER

We all know how a thing like piping an approach shot gets on one's nerves. (Harry Fulford—*Golfing*, 23 Dec. 1909: 10)

Hoping to eliminate shanking from the golfer's repertoire, Francis Archibald Fairlie devised and patented an anti-shank iron. In his British patent (No. 6,682) dated April 18, 1891, Fairlie states:

To obviate this difficulty [shanking] . . . I propose to set the socket or shank of the lofting iron or other metal headed club entirely behind the face of the driving portion or blade.

Initially, the peculiar look of Fairlie's iron kept it from being accepted. Given a little time and exposure, however, his club started to gain approval:

For about a year a new form of iron club, brought out by Mr. F. A. Fairlie, the well-known player at St. Andrews, Sandwich, Prestwick, and Wimbledon, has been steadily winning its way into public favour. When the improvement was first brought out all the cherished susceptibilities of players accustomed to the orthodox form of iron clubs were roused against it; but when it was seen that Mr. Fairlie himself made very effective use of the club while playing in important scoring competitions the new form of iron was taken up by a pretty wide circle of golfers, and made use of with admittedly surprising results (*Golf*, 14 Oct. 1892: 67).

Fairlie irons eventually became well accepted:

These patent irons are to be seen in the caddie-bags of many fine players, amateur and professional, and are almost as useful as a niblick for extricating a ball from a "cup" or other bad lie (*Golfing*, 20 Aug. 1903).

When first produced, Fairlie's anti-shank irons were made exclusively by R. Forgan & Son.

It was not long, however, before other makers started producing anti-shank irons. Surprisingly, increased backspin was also attributed to Fairlie's iron:

Perhaps the most useful invention is the Fairlie Patent Niblick . . . . You can get this club from nearly any maker, and it will get you out of many a horrid mess. You will also find it a useful club with which to play those chippy little approaches, when the ball has to be stopped as quickly as possible. It is an easy club to play with, and seems to impart a good deal of back-spin to the ball (*Golf Illustrated*, 6 July 1906: 30).

The Fairlie anti-shank neck was also produced in putters. In 1894 it was reported that J.H. Taylor, who had just won the British Open Championship at Sandwich, used an anti-shank putter:

In putting out he uses a patent cleek, with a curve at the neck backwards instead of towards the ball, as in Willie Park's cleek. With this club he holes incredibly long putts (*Golf*, 15 June 1894: 301).

According to another reference printed three years later, Taylor apparently continued to use an anti-shank putter:

There is also the putter which Taylor uses, with the twist in the neck the reverse of Park's (*Golf*, 9 July 1897: 351).

Pictured is a Fairlie anti-shank niblick and a Fairlie anti-shank putter. The back of the smooth face niblick is marked "Fairlies Model Niblick \ E.C. Warren \ Belgium" etc. next to William Gibson's "star" trademark. Gibson made the club and Earnest Charles Warren, the New Zealand born (1879) Belgium Open champion

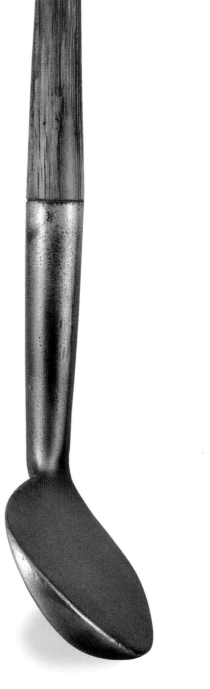

in 1906, 1907, 1908, and 1923, sold and possibly shafted the club. Warren was the professional at Knocke, Bruges, Belgium, from 1903 to 1937 (Jackson 1994, 98). The back of the Fairlie anti-shank putter pictured is marked "D. Anderson & Sons \ St. Andrews" inside a circle and "The Ace \ Special \ Warranted Hand Forged." Fairlie putters are more difficult to find than Fairlie irons—the latter being consistently available.

Born in 1854, the son of Col. J.O. Fairlie, Francis "Frank" Fairlie was "the youngest but one of six brothers" (*Golf*, 8 July 1892: 280). Fairlie was a fine amateur golfer, as demonstrated

by his tie for nineteenth in the 1892 British Open.

In addition to basic Fairlie anti-shank irons, a few uncommon Fairlie clubs were made. For example, two extremely unusual Fairlie anti-shank niblick-type clubs are known. One has a very small, almost square blade apparently designed to allow for striking a ball lying against a rock or a wall. The other, also designed for a special situation, has an incredibly lofted, oval-shaped head only slightly larger than a golf ball. Basic Fairlie irons are popular entry level collectibles, but specialty clubs with anti-shank necks draw much stronger collector interest.

GEORGE F. SMITH
ANTI-SHANK
IRONS & PUTTER

A few years after Frank Fairlie patented his anti-shank iron, George Frederick Smith, a well-known Lancashire amateur, devised his own anti-shank iron. Instead of placing the entire hosel behind the blade as Fairlie did, Smith bent back the lower half of the hosel and attached it to the top of the blade while keeping the top half of the hosel aligned with the blade's leading edge. In addition, he placed extra weight behind the toe and heel in order to better balance the club and to "counteract any inaccuracy in striking with either of these portions of the club" (*Golf* [ny], Apr. 1903: 250).

Smith's anti-shank clubs are often marked "Smith's Model"; some even include the word "Patent." However, Smith abandoned his British patent application (No. 24,849) dated Oct. 27, 1897, in which he proposed "improvements in metal headed golf clubs." This was the only golf club patent Smith applied for during the 1890s.

Three different Smith neck anti-shank clubs are pictured. The first, a niblick with an attractive crosshatched face, is marked "Peter McEwan\Southport\ Smith's Niblick \ Warranted Hand Forged" on the blade back. Born in 1873, Peter McEwan was a direct descendant from the famous family of long nose clubmakers. He served as the professional at Southport Old Links, England, from 1893 to 1902. Peter McEwan was well acquainted with George F. Smith. They were both good players and jointly held the course record of 74 at Southport until Peter's 72 in November of 1895 (*Golfing*, 15 Nov. 1895: 14).

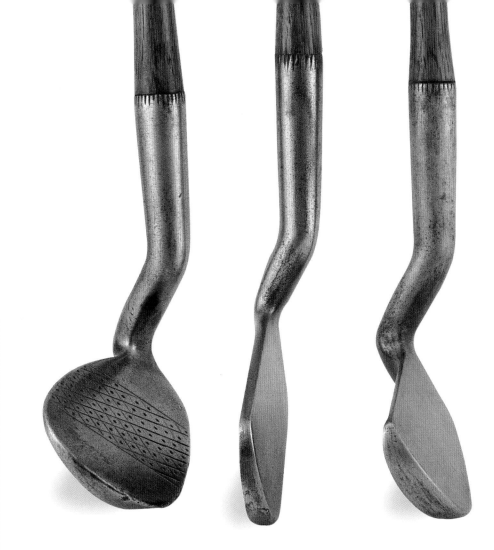

The McEwan example does not have the extra weight behind the toe, though the neck is clearly a Smith neck and the club is so marked. Smith neck irons were produced with or without heel and toe weighting.

The putter in the middle is marked "Tom Stewart \ Maker \ St. Andrews" inside an oval on the back of the blade. Underneath this mark is Stewart's famous "pipe" cleekmark, used by Tom Stewart, when he began business in the early 1890s, and, before him, by his father (see p. 446).

Stewart's putter is marked "W.H. Webb \ Frinton on Sea" on the shaft. Webb was a reputable maker of iron clubs and "no less successful as a maker of wooden clubs" (*Golf Illustrated*, 28 Mar. 1902: 251). Webb, who spent

seven years working for Tom Dunn, probably installed the shaft in this head.

The iron on the right is marked "A. Dimon \ Woking \ Hand Forged \ Special" on the back of the blade along with the "diamond" trademark used by William Winton and Company, the maker of this club. Dimon was the professional at Woking from approximately 1902 until 1938 (Jackson 1994, 25). Dimon's club has added weight behind the toe and heel; the weight behind the toe is visible in the picture.

Many different makers made Smith neck anti-shank irons. Today, they are found with regularity.

Smith and Fairlie irons aside, there were other clubs designed with the sole purpose of preventing the golfer from shanking, such as George Lowe's "all hitting face" irons (see p. 168), Hugh Logan's

Genii irons, and others. Covered under a 1905 British patent (No. 22,170), Logan's "Genii" iron is a refined example of a Smith neck. It has less bend to the hosel and therefore receives less collector interest than a Fairlie or Smith neck iron.

A few other irons reduced or eliminated the possibility of the shanked shot even though that was not their primary purpose. Robert Anderson's crescent head iron, P.A. Vaile's swan neck, J.R. Brown's swan neck, and Dwight's directional iron are a few such examples covered elsewhere in this book.

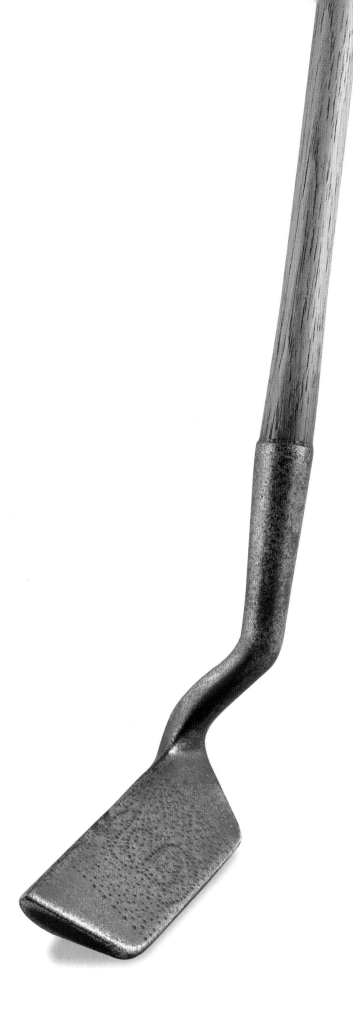

UNKNOWN MAKER
SMITH-STYLE
ANTI-SHANK IRON

Little is known about the club pictured other than it looks more like a gardening tool than a golf club! Besides an anti-shank neck, this club has a singular head shape. The leading edge is not nearly as long as the top line. The sides of the blade slope out as they extend upward from the leading edge. The blade itself has a low profile and a high degree of loft. Because the base of the blade is so thin, there is no sole to speak of.

The dot pattern on the center of the face forms the letters "SC," the only writing on the head. The owner might have marked the face, but in view of the unique head, it would not be surprising if the maker (or inventor) imprinted such a distinctive mark.

The back of the blade has a symmetrical, peculiar shape. It gradually thickens as it moves away from the sole then rapidly thins back down at the top of the blade.

Distantly related, an unusual anti-shank niblick made by Ayres was auctioned by Christie's in July of 1987. The neck on the Ayres iron was highly unusual. Its lower half curved away from and then back towards the target, forming something of a half-circle, as it approached the top of the blade. The blade was not unusual.

Visually captivating and rare clubs, like the anti-shank iron pictured, add depth and distinction to any collection. One might even say that the more a club looks like a gardening tool, the more desirable it is!

GEORGE LOWE
ANTI-SHANK
UNIFORM IRONS

George Lowe, the well-known clubmaker at Lytham and St. Anne's has recently brought out an adaptation of the Fairlie cleek, iron, and lofter. As is already pretty well known, the club-head is all striking-face, that is to say, there is no danger of heeling a ball when playing with this club. Lowe's adaptation is a very neat one, and his clubs are exceedingly well balanced and compact. Every player who uses this form of club finds that his approach play is considerably improved in distance, straightness, and certainty; and some players do not hesitate to say that their game all through has been improved a third since using these clubs. Mr. Hilton is one of the leading players who speaks in cordial praise of the club (Golf, 26 Feb. 1897: 425).

George Lowe received a British patent (No. 16,560) dated July 27, 1896, and a U.S. patent (No. 622,699) dated April 11, 1899, that covered an anti-shank iron similar to Francis Fairlie's. In both patents, Lowe also covered the production of his irons as matched sets—four different irons sharing a uniform head size:

All club heads to be made of the same size and measurements but the variations of the angles as aforesaid will adapt them so as to be used as cleeks, ordinary irons, lofting irons, and mashies. The size for all the clubs for whatever purpose used is to be 3 inches in length measuring in the middle of the face from one end to the other—1 3/8 inches in breadth across the middle of the face 5/8 inches in width at the sole or bottom of the club and the length of the hose to be 3 inches.

In addition to the four irons just mentioned, Low also produced a matching niblick, shown near right, and a putter. When compared to the other two clubs pictured here, the face of the niblick appears to break from the uniform size of "1 3/8 inches in breadth across the face." However, when placed behind the ball, the top of the niblick's face, like the top of each of the other clubfaces, is only 1 3/8 inches above the ground. Because of its considerable loft, the niblick's blade needed more surface area in order to reach the same elevation.

Lowe believed that locating the hosel at the top of the blade, away from the heel of the face, was the most valuable feature of his iron:

If . . . I were to offer a driver or brassie for sale with a heel [hosel] on the face, no golfer would buy them, so why should the iron clubs have so much of the face worse than useless? (Golfing and Cycling Illustrated, 12 Mar. 1897: 6)

Lowe's irons, often referred to in their day as Lowe's "all hitting face" clubs, were produced for several years.

The irons pictured were originally purchased together as a set. They are each marked "George Lowe \ St. Anne's-on-Sea" on the blade back and also "Hawkins's \ Never Rust \ JHI-\ Walsall" and "A.B.," the owner's initials. Each sole is marked as follows: The club on the right is stamped "Cleek," the club in the center is stamped "Iron," the club on the left is stamped "Niblick." Each of these irons has a "Hold-fast" grip installed over a sheepskin grip (see p. 529).

These irons were among the earliest to be finished in a non-rusting metal alloy. Non-rusting clubs took many forms through the years. "Nokorode," "Radite," "Stainless," "Non-rustable," "Never Rust," "Rustless," etc., were all names given to various non-rusting irons. Such clubs occasionally have a chromed look, depending on the alloy used.

Three years prior to Lowe's British patent, Slazenger & Sons adopted a process of plating irons to prevent them from rusting. A description of this process, printed in 1893, appears to describe the "Hawkin's Never Rust" finish on the club pictured:

Messrs. Slazenger and Sons . . . have adapted the "Arcas" process of plating to cleek and iron heads of golf clubs. . . . With the use of this new process, however, club cleaning is entirely obviated, as, no matter how much the club may be exposed to the elements, it never tarnishes, and all that is needed is to rub with a wet cloth, and wipe with a piece of dry leather, or use the nail brush and some soap. The "Arcas" silver alloy is composed of the metals cadmium, zinc, and silver in certain proportions. It gives the head the appearance of being made of silver; the deposit is hard, and will not crack or peel off by striking the ball; it always preserves its bright appearance (Golf, 10 Mar. : 411).

George Lowe was born at Carmyle, near Carnoustie, in 1856. In 1871 Lowe began working as an apprentice to Frank Bell, a clubmaker at Carnoustie. He later apprenticed to Tom Morris. Lowe next worked twelve years as an assistant to Jack Morris at Royal Liverpool (Hoylake). He left his job with Jack Morris for Royal

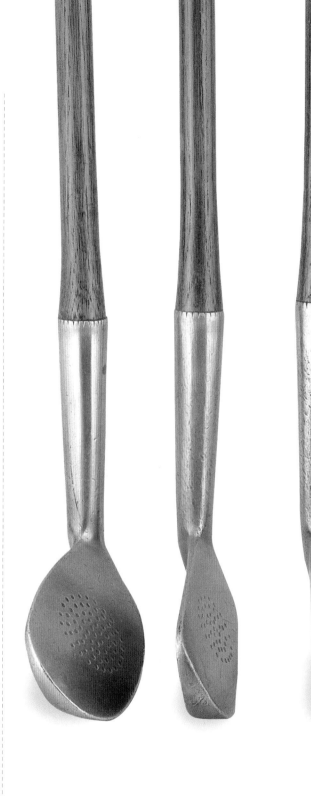

Lytham and St. Anne's-on-the-Sea where he was the professional from 1888 to 1905. After leaving Royal Lytham and being employed by St. Annes' Old Links Golf Club until 1911, he left the Old Links Club and set up a work-shop in St. Anne's. In 1920 he left St. Anne's with his wife and four sons and became a justice of the peace in Australia, at Queenscliff, Victoria (see *Golf,* 20 Mar. 1891: 5; Nickson 1985, 99-100). During his life, Lowe also "became well known as a golf architect and designed over 120 courses" (Nickson 1985, 101).

WILLIE PARK, JR.
"PATENT PUTTING CLEEK,"
OFFSET BLADE

As an instance of the gradual and complete triumph of sterling merit over prejudice and bigoted conservatism there is nothing more remarkable than Park's Patent Putter. . . . And if a man cannot putt well with it he had better give up Golf and try to invent something better (Golf Illustrated, 16 March 1900: 245).

In 1892 Willie Park Jr. produced and marketed what has generally been acknowledged to be the first offset blade putter. A radical idea when introduced, the offset blade quickly garnered its share of believers and eventually became one of the most popular developments in the evolution of the putter.

When first produced, Park's putter was reviewed in *Golf* under the title of "Willie Park's Patent Putting Cleek":

Willie Park, jun., has recently invented a new putting cleek. It is a fearful and wonderful-looking implement, and the deadliness with which he putts with it is calculated to strike terror into the hearts of any would-be opponent. During the two days' play at Musselburgh Tournament, as well as at the Bridge of Weir Tournament, he putted with nothing else, and with its aid he came in at the first-named competition five strokes before all other competitors, after being ten strokes behind the leading man, and at the last mentioned meeting no fewer than

twelve strokes before every other player, and he gives his putting cleek credit for this. All the local cracks at Musselburgh played with these clubs during the Tournament, and their form shows that their play was considerably above average. In these days of patents, golfers are apt to be dubious about new clubs, but it is hardly to be believed that any invention of so noted a player as young Willie Park is not based upon principle, and prompted by an experience which cannot but make it of service to golfers generally. The idea first occurred to Willie when he was putting with an ordinary cleek, the shaft of which had got slightly bent. He found he putted better with this than with a cleek with a straight shaft. It seemed,

so to speak, to rake the ball into the hole. This idea, worked out, produced the cleek now under review. The patent is an ordinary putting cleek, but just above the blade the socket is bent back. This bend back in the socket allows the player to get the ball into a straight line with the shaft, and as a result, he sees the whole of the ball and the face of the cleek much better than in the ordinary case. The writer has tried the cleek several times with the best results. . . . Park is already besieged with orders. We understand that it was not intended to put the cleek into the market till after the Championship competition, but Willie has found it impossible to refuse the pressing demands which have been made for these clubs (30 Sep. 1892: 37).

Park's patent putting cleek (cleek meaning "iron") was also known as Park's "wry-neck" putter (wry meaning "twisted"). A little over two years passed before Park finally applied for a patent on his club, which he received. Park's British patent (No. 20,914) dated November 1, 1894, is very brief and only specifies constructing the neck of a cleek "with a double bend or curve" at the lower portion of the hosel. Later, however, in his own writings, Park commented on how his idea originated and why it was effective:

The idea occurred during practice for a tournament, when I happened to be playing with a cleek that had a shaft slightly bent over. I observed that in putting with this cleek the balls seemed to run with more accuracy than usual, and, following up the idea, the patent putter was produced. It is difficult to explain the principle of this club. With an ordinary putter the stroke is of the nature of a push, while with this patent it is more a pull than a push. It has also the advantage of allowing the player to see the blade of the cleek while addressing the ball as the line of the shaft is in front of the blade (1896, 29).

In spite of Park's explanation, there may be more to the story of where he got the idea for an offset blade putter. In January of 1891, well over a year *before* Park introduced his wry-neck putter, A.M. Ross applied for a patent on a negative loft blade putter—a putter he entrusted *Willie Park* to produce. After a brief trial, Ross's putter was quickly abandoned. However, as produced, its blade is clearly offset. The top-line of Ross's blade lines up with the back of the hosel (see page 253).

Park's putter played a prominent role when Harry Vardon won the 1898 British Open, defeating Park himself by a single stroke and Harold Hilton by two. According to Hilton's comments originally published in the July 19, 1898 *Sporting Chronicle*, all three players were using Park's patent putter:

If Willie Park, jun. did not succeed in winning the Open Championship, he at least had the satisfaction of knowing that the man who did succeed in beating him accomplished the feat with one of the Musselburgh man's patent putters; and the extraordinary run of success attained in the series of open tournaments was probably more due to his deadly execution with this club than to any other department of this game. It is needless to go farther than to say that the winner used one of Park's patent putters, as, in truth, the first three to finish all used what I have heard termed "that wry-neck abortion of Park's." Wry-neck or not, there can be no shadow of doubt as to the popularity of this very putter (Golfer's Magazine, March 1899: 581).

In 1899 another in-depth review of Park's wry-neck putter describes the great popularity of his club:

"That wry-necked abortion of Park's" as it has been called, is no fad. On the contrary it is a very practical tool, devised and manufactured by a very practical man. The annals of Golf can show few better putters than Willie Park, jun.; and Willie has solved the mystery not only of good putting, but of bad putting as well. The putter with the "kink aft" . . . is specially devised to correct bad putting and to improve good putting. A poor player invariably does better work with this club than with one of the ordinary shape, and all the cracks who use it swear by it. . . .

The putter has had an enormous sale both here and in America. The slight prejudice which is sometimes excited by its unorthodox appearance vanishes after a few waggles, as the club has a most workmanlike feel in the hand. Of our personal knowledge we can testify to more than one case where from having been jeered at as a "wry-necked abortion" it has grown to be the most valued club in the bag. It has received perhaps more attention from first-class players, professional and amateur, than any other modern club, and a far more convincing proof of its popularity and its genuine merit than anything which we can say is the fact that it is in constant use by the following champions:—Open champions, Mr. John Ball, jun., Mr. H.H. Hilton, Harry Vardon, Willie Park, jun., and Willie Fernie; amateur champions, Mr. John Ball, jun., Mr. L. Balfour Melville, and Mr. F.G. Tait. The following well-known players:— Mr. C.E.S. Gilles (Champion of New Zealand), Mr. A.J. Balfour, M.P., Mr. Charles Hutchings, Mr. Robert Maxwell, Mr. T.T. Gray, Mr. D.M. Jackson, Mr. Josiah Livingston, Mr. Ballingall, Mr. J. Oliver, Miss Pascoe (ex-Lady champion), A. Herd, James Kinnell, Ben Sayers, Jack White (Golf Illustrated, 27 Oct.: 70).

Willie Park Jr. was not only a famous clubmaker during his day; he was also a highly respected and exceptionally talented golfer. Born in 1864, Park was only seventeen years old when he finished fifth in the 1881 British Open. He eventually won the British Open in 1887 and again in 1889. He finished in the top 6 four times between 1890 and 1900.

It is fitting that the most famous of all Park's clubs is his patent putter; young Willie often received credit for being the best there was at putting. Amazingly, Park developed his talent for putting by practicing on a brick floor! According to Park:

My father's shop was floored with bricks, and I and my boy friends putted at the saucer-like hollows that were worn in the bricks. They were the hardest holes to putt into that I have ever encountered from that day to this, and I don't think I have ever undergone such tortures on a real putting green as when seeing my well-hit balls (gutties this time), right in both strength and direction, go through the hole and out at the other side, leaving what was in circumstances still a very difficult putt to do. Everything that is exasperating in golf attracts one all the more, as I found even in those days, for, dissatisfied with our performances in the daytime, a friend and I would "borrow" the key of my father's shop at night and would spend hours there putting on the bricks by candlelight. You see, I took these putting matches very seriously. Putting has always been a strong part of my game since those days, and I often think that perhaps the training of my eye and the extreme delicacy of touch that came to me through this continual putting with marbles on bricks—I did it for years—helped me greatly when I came to do the comparatively easy putts on real greens (Leach 1907, 101).

Park was also an author and a golf course architect. His 1896 book *The Game of Golf* was the first book written by a professional. As a golf course architect his services were in demand. He laid out many courses in Europe, America, and Great Britain; Sunningdale, perhaps, being his most famous.

Two Willie Park patent putting cleeks are pictured on the facing page. One example, as shown, is marked "W. Park's \ Special" in an oval and "Patent" on the back of the blade. The other putter, with a lancewood shaft, is not marked on the back of the blade. Both shafts are stamped "W. Park." Willie Park Jr. consistently stamped his name on the shafts of his clubs.

The "W. Park's Special Patent" mark shown is the earliest mark Park used on the back of his wry-neck putters. Even so, of the two putters shown, the one with the unmarked head is older.

The hosel on the unmarked head measures 4 3/4 inches in length; the hosel on the marked example measures 4 1/4 inches. Both the hosel and the blade on the unmarked head are thicker than they are on the marked example. In general, the unmarked head is less refined than its counterpart. These differences indicate that the unmarked head was made before the marked example. There is the possibility that constant cleaning wore Park's mark off the unmarked head. (During the wood shaft era, caddies used emery cloth to clean iron heads and remove rust.) However, recognizing the early nature of this head and remembering the two years that passed before Park sought to patent his club, one can reasonably conclude that this unmarked head was probably made by Park before he applied for his patent.

One other sidelight. The blade on a Park patent putter has a notable amount of loft. In his book *The Game of Golf*, Park reminds the reader that "putting-cleeks are to be preferred with the faces slightly lofted to prevent the ball from springing" (1896, 43). Turn-of-the-century greens were less than "carpet-like," so the ability to get the ball rolling, but not bouncing, was a desirable trait in a putter.

Park's wry-neck putter ranks as one of the most popular innovations ever made in putter design. The principle of placing the golfer's hands ahead of the blade by offsetting the latter has stood the test of time. The wry-neck putter remains in widespread use, being produced in various forms by every major golf club manufacturer.

For reference, the putters marked "Willie Park's Original Bent Neck Putter" were made in the twentieth century by the George Nicoll Company.

RAMSAY HUNTER
OFFSET BLADE PUTTER

JAMES GOVAN
OFFSET BLADE PUTTER

Less than eighteen months after Willie Park Jr. received a patent for his wry-neck putter, Ramsay Hunter received a patent for the offset blade putter pictured near right. Hunter's putter, covered under a British patent (No. 4,810) dated March 3, 1896, was one of the first to provide an offset blade without copying the neck on Willie Park's wry-neck putter.

According to Hunter's patent, he created an offset blade by:

bending the head slightly to one side, while the socket or hozzel [sic] instead of running down to the lower edge or sole terminates and enters the head of the club at the upper edge of the striking surface.

In his patent application, Hunter calls the bent portion of the hosel a "portion of the head," probably in an attempt to distance his patent application from Willie Park's patent. In actuality, however, the hosel on Hunter's putter joins the top of the blade.

The Hunter putter pictured is marked "Anderson - Anstruther" inside a circle on the back of the blade, "Patent No. 4810," and "Ry Hunter, Sandwich." Hunter was the professional at Royal St. Georges Golf Club, in Sandwich, England, from about 1888 to 1900 (Jackson 1994, 46). Some of the letters in Hunter's mark are worn away, the result of using emery cloth to clean the head, as was once the custom. Nevertheless, enough of the letters remain to make a positive identification. When dealing with maker's marks, the primary consideration is accu-

rate identification—knowing for certain who made the club. Faint lettering in and of itself is not a major problem. Clubs with lettering lost from rough treatment or significant deterioration, however, are seriously downgraded because of their overall condition, not the loss of lettering.

Like Hunter, James Govan (originally a clubmaker in Hampstead, London, during the mid-1890s) designed his own offset blade putter. Covered under a U.S. patent (No. 873,423) dated December 10, 1907, Govan's putter offsets the blade by attaching the base of the hosel to the heel of the face, not the top of the blade. A left-handed, gunmetal example of Govan's putter, marked "J. Govan \ St. David,

PA \ A1 Putter \ Pat. Dec. 07" on the back of its blade, is pictured right. (Govan's patent also discusses a drilled face; see p. 172.)

One of the more popular offset blade putters was "Taylor's Bent Blade Putter," produced by Cann & Taylor. This club offsets the blade by extending it straight back, away from the target, then out behind the ball.

A few woods with distinctly offset heads were also made. Alex N. Weir produced a curved neck wood that positioned the face in line with the shaft. Upon his death, it was noted that Weir, the professional attached to Turnberry golf links, "was a first-class clubmaker, and did a large trade in his special non-slicing drivers and brassies" (*Golf Illustrated*, 6 Jan.

1911: 48). An offset wood stamped "S.B. Wallace" is also known to exist. Between 1911 and 1914, Wallace worked at Turnberry as a clubmaker under Tom Fernie. Between 1914 and 1956, he served as the professional at Cardross (Jackson 1994, 98). Perhaps the most dramatic club to incorporate the principle of an offset head is Charles Brand's wooden putter found on page 174.

Ramsey Hunter, born around 1865, in Edinburgh, learned the trade of carpenter and cabinetmaker in his father's workshop. "His training as a carpenter naturally assisted him greatly in his essays in the art of club-making" (Dalrymple 1895, 35). When Ramsay Hunter died in the spring of 1909, he left behind little money but many friends:

We are informed by Mr. A.W. Woodburn, the secretary of the Mid-Kent Golf Club, Gravesend, that the late Ramsay Hunter, who was employed at this club at the time of his death, has left his widow and family without any means. During his long engagement at Sandwich, Hunter did a very great deal for the course and for the enjoyment of golfers who play there, and as we happen to know, he did not have the best of luck in his club-making business. There must be many golfers who have a very kindly and grateful remembrance of Hunter, and who would gladly do something to assist those he has left behind in destitute circumstances. . . (*Golf Illustrated*, 23 Apr. 1909: 137).

A committee was set up at Hunter's former club to send donations to his family.

ALEX R. SIMPSON
"MAIDENHEAD" PUTTER

WILLIAM G. SMALLDON
"ALL SQUARE" PUTTER

A. Simpson, the professional of the Maidenhead Golf Club, has brought out an ingenious putter, which appears to combine many advantages which are desirable. In the first place the blade is set back well behind the line of the shaft, so that in addressing the ball a very clear sight of the head can be obtained, and the head consequently held at the true right angle to the line of putt. By an ingenious arrangement of head and socket, Simpson secures this advantageous position of the blade without any twisting of the neck. Another novel point is the shortness of the socket. It is considerably shorter than the socket of the ordinary putter, and the weight so saved is added to the striking portion of the blade. The ball appears to us to leave the putter-head with a very businesslike click and to travel in a very accurate line when properly struck. The price of the putter is 7s., and it can be obtained from A. Simpson, Maidenhead Golf Club, Maidenhead, Berks; postage extra (Golf Illustrated, 11 May 1900: 121).

Advertised as the "Shortest Socket Club now made" (*Golf Illustrated*, 11 May, 1900: 127), Simpson's "Maidenhead" putter included a short, square socket (hosel) open at the bottom and an offset blade. The Maidenhead putter shown is marked "Alex Simpson \ Maidenhead Putter \ Patent No. 4573 \ Warranted Hand Forged" on the back of the blade.

Alexander Simpson's British patent (No. 4573) dated March 10, 1900, covered his Maidenhead putter, named after the Maidenhead Golf Club where Simpson's professional duties included club

and ball making. According to his patent, Simpson left a hole in the end of his square socket so the shaft could pass through it, and he designed a short socket so extra weight could be incorporated into the blade "behind the ball giving greater power and precision of stroke." The socket is located in front of the blade, and the socket and the blade are "of course formed in one piece." Simpson also received a U.S. patent, (No. 669,864) dated March 12, 1901, that covered his putter.

At the age of fifteen, Alex Simpson joined the Monifieth club in Monifieth, Scotland, where he learned the game and became a first class player. Before entering the world of professional golf, Simpson left Scotland and worked overseas for six years:

A marine engineer by trade, Simpson went to Australia in the end of October, '85, and followed his profession on the coast there for six years.

Returning home, Simpson rejoined the Monifieth Club, and again took a leading place. Then he made golf a profession, starting with the Forfar Club (*Golfing.* 13 Sep. 1900: 24).

Simpson worked at the Forfar club from 1894 to 1896. In 1896 he became the professional at the Maidenhead club where he worked until 1909, when he moved to Stonehaven. In 1912 Simpson was hired as the professional at Old Manchester (Jackson 1994, 86).

Simpson carried a fine reputation as a clubmaker:

Simpson is a born clubmaker. He played with his "own make" in his boyhood at Monifieth, and now his "Maidenhead Putter" is about as popular a "stick" as there is on the market (Golfing, 13 Sep. 1900: 24).

Despite being "popular," Maidenhead putters were made for only a short time. Today they are seldom seen.

Also pictured is a rarely seen All Square putter, circa late 1920s. The grip, shaft, and hosel are square, and the bend in the neck is nearly 90 degrees. The shaft is stamped "Danga Wood," and a rubber wrapped grip marked "E.R. Whitcombe" etc. (see p. 531) is placed over the original leather wrap grip. The back of the head is marked "All Square" inside a square, "G" inside a star, and "W.G. Smalldon \ Rustless \ Made in Great Britain \ Hand Forged." Smalldon was the professional at Morriston, Wales, by 1921. In 1928 he left Morriston for Cardiff, Wales, where he worked for at least ten more years (Jackson 1994, 86).

Reginald Hincks of British Columbia, Canada, received a U.S. patent (No. 1,705,250) dated March 12, 1929, that covered a right angle neck nearly identical to the one on this putter.

CHARLES BRAND

OFFSET HEAD, LONG NOSE STYLE PUTTER

Born in 1849, Charles Brand was a well-established club and ball maker at Carnoustie by 1888 (*Golfing*, 30 Apr. 1908: 32). Brand made long nose and transitional clubs for a few years, but the most distinguished club he ever crafted is the putter pictured.

This handcrafted implement is one of a kind. It is the only wooden long nose style club ever made with a wry-neck! Because the neck is so dominant, so dramatically offset, the long nose nature of the head is easily overlooked; however, it is readily seen in the above picture. Viewed from the back of the head, Brand's putter has the length, shape, and look of a typical long nose putter —as would the top and front of the head if the neck were not offset.

The Brand putter pictured appears unused and in like-new condition. It was probably too odd to be popular, and it is likely that few (if any more) were ever made. This putter probably dates shortly after 1892, when Willie Park introduced his wry-neck blade putter.

In 1908 Ernest Bales received a British design registration (No. 534,443) for his "Stoneded" putter. This club is a long head mallet with a slight, but distinct, offset to its splice neck.

In 1909 Joe Anderson, a clubmaker located on St. John street in Perth, produced a putter similar to Brand's. Cast from aluminum, Anderson's long nose style "patent bent hose aluminum putter" received exposure through limited advertising in the periodicals of its day.

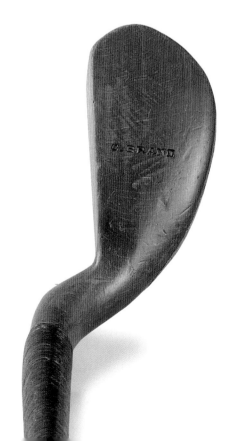

UNKNOWN MAKER
UPSIDE-DOWN HEAD, SWAN NECK PUTTER

The aluminum swan neck putter pictured below has an upside-down head (thin at the bottom, wide and flat at the top). This design raises the head's center of gravity—theoretically to impart topspin, so the ball would dive into the hole given the least opportunity—while providing the club with the thinnest of footprints, thinner than even a blade putter! A small footprint allowed this putter to negotiate "cupped" or other difficult lies found on the green.

The chance that a ball might settle into a low spot on the green was a genuine possibility when this club was used. Greens in the early 1900s did not approach the quality of today's greens. Furthermore, golfers sometimes encountered cattle on the course. *Cattle?* A 1906 advertisement by F.H. Ayres reads in part:

Every golf green should be provided with The New Patent Golf Hole and Flagstaff. It prevents holes being spoilt by sheep and cattle (*Golf Illustrated*, 1 June: 202).

SLAZENGER & SONS
THE 'EMPEROR' SWAN NECK PUTTER

Pictured above is a wooden mallet putter with a swan neck— a bent hosel that lines the shaft up with the center of the head. Marketed by Slazenger & Sons, this club is stamped "Slazenger" on the shaft and "Slazenger \ New York" on the flat portion of the toe. In addition to the stylish neck and head design, this putter has a gunmetal faceplate backed with what appears to be leather. This little-known club, believed to date shortly after 1900, is often referred to as the "Emperor" putter or the "Chinese Mallet."

JAMES R. BROWN
THE "SWAN,"
SWAN NECK PUTTER

Messrs. James Brown and Son, of Montrose, have introduced to the golfing public a putter known as the "Swan," which is commending itself to scientific players from its extreme accuracy and beautiful balance (Golfing, 21 Nov. 1905: 26).

James Ross Brown's British patent (No. 14,608) dated June 29, 1904, was the first patent granted for a "swan neck"—a bent hosel that lines the shaft up with the center of the head. However, the swan neck idea did not originate with Brown. During the 1890s, Tom Hood produced at least one putter with a swan neck. It consisted of a wooden mallet head, stamped with Hood's name in script, and an iron hosel with an integral iron sole. (This club sold at Christie's 1995 golf auction at Pebble Beach, California.) In 1895 George Nicoll, the cleek

manufacturer from Leven, introduced a blade-style putter having such a neck. Accompanied by a drawing of Nicoll's club, the December 13, 1895 issue of *The Golfer* reads in part:

The old-fashioned style of bending the shaft will be rendered unnecessary with the turn which Mr. Nicoll has given the hose (13 Dec.: 402).

The "old-fashioned style of bending" refers to the occasional practice of bowing a putter shaft in order to align the grip with the middle of the head (see p. 507).

The club pictured above was made by J.&W. Craigie and is marked "Brown's Swan Patent No. 14608" on the top of the head and "Craigie \ Montrose" on the shaft. Although it dealt mainly with putters, Brown's swan neck patent includes the possibility of producing other swan neck clubs.

No such woods or irons produced under Brown's name are known to the author.

For reference, Brown's swan neck patent also allows for attaching a small "sighting bar" (a pointer similar to a toothpick in size) to the front of the hosel, directly at the bend. The pointer could swivel into position and aim at the target. The author does not know if this sighting bar was ever produced.

Only a handful of Brown's swan neck putters remain.

Golfing Man is for the most part content to choose his golf clubs very much after the same fashion as he chooses his wife, more by luck than good guiding, and a great deal by first appearances (Golfing, 21 Oct. 1909: 14).

PEMBROKE A. VAILE & FREDERICK H. AYRES
SWAN NECK CLUBS

Less than two months after James Ross Brown applied for his patent, Pembroke Adolphus "Percy" Vaile, of Whitehall Court, in the city of Westminster, Barrister at Law of the Supreme Court of New Zealand, and Frederick Henry Ayres, a manufacturer in London, applied for a British patent that also covered a swan neck. Vale and Ayres received a patent (No. 18,161) dated August 22, 1904. Fortunately for Vaile and Ayres, the British patent office did not begin researching patent applications to check if they were unique until 1905.

The clubs described in the Vaile/Ayres patent are nearly identical to the clubs in Brown's swan neck patent. The only difference is that an imaginary line running through the shaft and top half of the hosel on Vaile's club intersects the top of the head directly over the center of the face. On Brown's club, the imaginary line intersects the center of the face.

Aware of the similarities between his and Brown's clubs, Vaile uses what sounds more like double-talk than a definition when describing the purpose of his clubs in his patent:

By means of this formation of the socket portion relatively to the head we are enabled to obtain a limited extent of spring connection.

The driver, iron, and putter pictured on the facing page are each marked "P.A. Vaile \ Patent" along with other marks. The wood is marked "F.H. Ayres Ld" on the crown, the iron is marked "John Wanamaker" in large block letters across the back of the blade, and the putter is marked

"F.H. Ayres, Ld \ Special" on the back of the blade. John Wanamaker was a retail chain that, among other things, produced and sold golf clubs in America. In 1921 *Golfing* reported "Wanamaker's Stores in Philadelphia and New York are the largest in the world and employ some 16,000 people" (Feb.: ii). Ayres was a British sporting goods manufacturer that specialized in wholesale and export trade.

Vaile and Ayres worked together on this patent, but the reason why is unknown. One can reasonably conjecture that Vaile made Ayres a partner in order to get his clubs produced and gain quick access to the British market.

By 1906, Ayres was taking out half-page advertisements that promoted "The 'Vaile' Patent Golf Clubs" as able to improve the golfer's accuracy:

The margin of error in side play renders these clubs of the utmost value to a player intent upon obtaining better direction (Golf Illustrated, 1 June, 1906: 202).

Vaile's patent clubs are of varying interest to collectors. The driver and iron are rarely seen, and the neck design is highly unusual for woods and irons. The putter is quite nice, but other clubmakers produced similar swan neck blade putters. Crawford, McGregor & Canby, for example, offered a refined example of a blade putter very similar to the Vaile (see MacGregor's 1913 and 1917 catalogs).

In addition to designing golf clubs, Percy Vaile wrote thirteen books on golf, most of them instructional. Vaile also contributed articles to various golf magazines, but he was *not* the most popular writer of his time. According to J.A.F. Moncrieff, in a letter sent to the editor of a British magazine and reprinted in America, Vaile was popular only with himself!

To the editor of Golf Illustrated: Sir,—I should be much obliged if you, or one of the readers of your estimable paper, would kindly inform me as to when and where Mr. P.A. Vaile won the all around athletic championship of the world.

I have for some time past read with absorbing interest, if not with great profit to myself, Mr. Vaile's articles on various branches of sport. These are written with such marvelous self-confidence and belief in his own wisdom that I really cannot imagine anyone, except an undisputed champion, daring to voice such opinions.

In most of these articles, Mr. Vaile proves to his own, if not to other peoples', satisfaction the utter futility of the methods of the great masters of the various games with which he deals…

He points out that James Braid's ideas as to how to pull or slice intentionally are absolutely childish. And…he makes the very interesting announcement that he is going to demonstrate to an eagerly expectant world that he knows how to play the "Push Shot" better than Harry Vardon, and that the latter's methods are absolutely wrong (The American Golfer, Dec. 1912: 125).

The understanding editor of *The American Golfer* responded:

All Honor to Mr. Moncrieff. It is indeed high time that some one should rise up and protest against the silly vapourings of such a pronounced egotist. It has always been a marvel to us how Mr. Vaile managed to find

anyone to publish his diatribes—unless on the ground that they contribute so largely to the gaiety of golfers generally. Certainly they have served no other useful purpose.

Vaile persisted with his egotistical writing style. Referring to Vaile's writing in *Puck* magazine, an editorial in the October 1914 issue of *Golf* reads:

Puck's Golf Idiot, P.A. Vaile, the only author of every kind of a golf book ever published, still continues his hammer tactics, greatly to the detriment of the grand old game…

The Golf Idiot claims to be apparently the Poo-Bah on golf; he tells us how we ought to drive, slice, pull, upward and downward swing, besides everything else a golfer should know. He styles the greatest living golfer as "poor old Vardon" when many think this grand-master could say, if he wished, that he had forgotten more than Vaile ever knew! (264-265)

EDWARD M. FITZJOHN & ELMER A. STANTON
CURVED NECK

Marked "Pat'd Dec. 18, 1917" twice on the blade back, the putter pictured was covered under a U.S. patent (No. 1,250,296) issued to Ed Fitzjohn and Elmer Stanton. This club, according to the patent, was designed with the intention of locating as much weight as possible below and behind the center of the blade while keeping the shaft and hosel in line with the center of the blade:

The main object is to establish such relation between the head and the handle that when the club is held in striking position, the head will automatically balance or adjust itself into proper position for striking the ball squarely, as distinguished from those clubs in which the shank or socket of the handle is attached to one end of the head . . . .

In other words, we have sought to bring the striking surface of the head as nearly as possible in the center of gravity of the club as a whole when suspended from the extreme upper end of the handle.

This Fitzjohn putter is wonderfully stylish, the hosel transforming with natural ease into the sole and then the blade itself. It is also in outstanding original condition, the original nickel plate finish still covering almost all of the head, which is brass underneath. The only other fixed blade Fitzjohn putter known to the author belongs to the United States Golf Association and is kept in their museum, Golf House. An adjustable Fitzjohn putter is presented on page 378.

R. FORGAN & SON
FORKED HOSEL

The forked hosel putter pictured, usable either right- or left-handed and designed to reduce clubhead torque on a mis-hit putt, dates to the 1890s. Complete with a sheepskin grip, this magnificent club is marked "R. Forgan & Son \ St. Andrews" on its shaft.

The forked hosel is obviously untraditional, but so is its attachment to the shaft. Instead of enclosing the tip of the shaft, the top of the hosel covers only the front and back of the shaft, leaving the tip exposed on both its leading and following sides.

This club was entirely hand forged and would have been difficult and time consuming to produce. It may be the only one of its kind. There was, however, a similar forked hosel iron that sold at Sotheby's 1991 golf auction in London, England.

Years after this putter was made, Otto Hackbarth produced a somewhat similar putter—the only forked hosel club produced in significant numbers—which is discussed on the following page.

OTTO G.A. HACKBARTH
FORKED HOSEL

Otto G. Hackbarth, professional at the Westwood Country Club, St. Louis, has invented a new putter of peculiar design with which he has been doing remarkably accurate work on the greens. It is modelled after the center shafted idea and he claims this prevents the club from turning when the ball is struck, with the result that the ball rolls with an overspin, hugging the ground and going perfectly straight for the hole (Golfers Magazine, August 1910: 188).

Otto Hackbarth originally sold his "peculiar" putters by mail for three dollars each. His advertisements in *The Golfers Magazine* in 1910, 1911, and 1912 claim that various golfers had used his putter successfully in competition. The best endorsement for Hackbarth's putter occurred when Chick Evans started using it, Evans being one of the foremost amateur golfers of all time (see next page).

In Hackbarth putters, the forked hosel is obviously the club's main feature. The sole is also interesting because either brass or lead is inlaid down the center of its entire length. (The putter above is inlaid with brass.) In February of 1912, Hackbarth advertised a "new improved model ready for prompt delivery" (*Golfers Magazine:* 204). It is not known if changing the material inlaid on the sole had anything to do with this new model. (The putter illustrated in Hackbarth's ads before and after February 1912 do not appear any different.)

A few Hackbarth putters are marked on the back of the head, but most, including the one pictured, are marked "Otto Hackbarth \ Pat 687539" across the sole. This is especially interesting because U.S. patent No. 687,539 was issued to Isaac E. Palmer, not to Hackbarth! Palmer's patent, issued on November 26, 1901, covered a wood shaft or metal hosel divided into two branches (see p. 502).

On December 5, 1913, Hackbarth, residing in Clarendon Hills, Illinois, applied for his own U.S. patent. Granted on November 10, 1914, Hackbarth's patent (No. 1,116,417) retained the same basic shape of his original putter but eliminated the forked hosel. The entire clubhead as designed consists of a solid, thin metal plate placed between two brass or other heavy metal blocks. The blocks, which run lengthwise across the lower half of the plate, form the body of the clubhead. Above the blocks, the sides of the metal plate angle to the shaft. The top of the plate fits inside a slit in the end of the shaft, and the plate is riveted in place.

Hackbarth's patent describes his putter as having seven objectives: balance, flexibility, torque, usability either right- or left-handed, a unique connection to the head, alignment strengths, and adjustability. The adjustability feature is the most interesting. Hackbarth allowed for changing the metal blocks of the clubhead, so the golfer could alter the loft of the club depending on how smooth or hard the putting greens were. The author has never heard of, seen, or read about a putter produced under Hackbarth's 1914 patent.

Hackbarth's earlier putter continued into the late 1920s, being offered in the Wilson-Western catalogs during that time.

The Hackbarth putter shown on this page is a popular collectible. Because of wide collector interest, the Hackbarth has been remade in recent years, but the remakes are not marked with Hackbarth's original stamping. The rarest of Hackbarth putters, and possibly the earliest one known, is found in the USGA's antique club collection. On this model, which does not have a socket atop the forked hosel, the shaft runs between the forks and into the top (center) of the clubhead.

On Hackbarth putters, the forks are sometimes cracked. Such damage can be discreetly welded solid, but repaired examples are obviously not as desirable as clean original examples.

Of German descent, Otto Hackbarth was a golf professional known for his powerful driving. He learned golf as a caddie at Oconomowoc, Wisconsin, where he worked early in his professional career. In 1905 Hackbarth applied for reinstatement as an amateur, but the USGA "first granted and afterward denied" his application (*Golf* [ny], June 1905: 374). Hackbarth eventually became the professional at Westwood Country Club in St. Louis, Missouri, and, by April of 1911, the professional at Hinsdale Golf Club in Hinsdale, Illinois. He later became the professional at Cincinnati Country Club, where he worked until 1930.

CHARLES EVANS, JR.
FORKED HOSEL

Born in 1890 in Indianapolis, Indiana, Charles "Chick" Evans Jr. was one of the greatest amateur golfers of all time. Besides winning the Western Amateur eight times (1909, '12, '14, '15, '20, '21, '22, and '23), he won the 1910 Western Open, the 1911 French Amateur Open, the 1916 and 1920 U.S. Amateurs, and the 1916 U.S. Open. He also finished second three times in the U.S. Amateur and once in the U.S. Open.

Evans was the first man to win the U.S. Open and the U.S. Amateur in the same year, a feat termed "The Double Crown." Only Bobby Jones duplicated that accomplishment, doing so while completing the "Grand Slam" in 1930. Incredibly, Chick Evans played in *fifty* U.S. Amateur Championships—a record that will likely stand forever.

Known as an excellent ball striker (he used only seven clubs— a brassie, spoon, jigger, mid-iron, lofter, niblick, and putter—to win the 1916 U.S. Open), Evans was not always thought of as a good putter. Once, when he played

Bill Fownes in the semifinals of the 1910 U.S. Amateur, Evans even resorted to putting with a midiron. When recalling this incident, Francis Ouimet stated:

It struck me as quite odd that Chick selected a midiron to putt with. I had seen many a fine golfer use this club to play their approach putt, to be sure, but from that day to this Chick is the sole player I ever noted who chose a lofted iron when near the hole (Golfing, Mar. 1923: 31).

In his match against Fownes, Evans lost the last three holes to lose 1 down. Fownes went on to win the championship.

Hoping to become a better putter, Evans tried the Hackbarth putter (see facing page). He found it helpful and used it for many years. But the Hackbarth putter, because it was so unconventional, often received exaggerated credit for Evans's success. Eventually, it became closely associated with Evans.

Evans was a lifelong amateur, so clubs bearing his name were never marketed. Nevertheless, Evans did have a unique relationship with Thomas E. Wilson & Company (one of America's larger manufacturers of sporting goods and golf clubs) that

allowed him to remain an amateur. For example, in 1921 Evans wrote *Chick Evans' Golf Book*, but it was copyrighted and published by Thomas E. Wilson & Company. Any funds Evans "earned" in the golf world were put into a trust fund which eventually established the Evans Scholars Foundation, a scholarship fund to help caddies attend college.

The putter pictured, the only such club known, is distinctive in many respects. First, it is the only forked hosel *mallet* putter known. Second, the head, which is much longer than it is wide, has been illegal under the rules of golf since 1910. Third, it came from a small club collection held by a former Wilson employee who knew Evans. Fourth, it bears the name of Chick Evans.

The unusual characteristics of this club serve a purpose. The long, narrow profile of the head provides a visual aid to help the golfer's alignment. The back of the sole angles up to keep the back of the head from catching on the ground during the takeaway and follow-through.

The angled portion of the sole is marked "Chick Evans \ Putter." "Wilson" is stamped on the back of the aluminum head.

Even though Wilson made this putter, possibly the result of Evans's own ideas on how to improve the Hackbarth putter, they did not produce it for sale. Given Wilson's obvious promotional interest in Evans, their production of a putter bearing both names, even if it was made only for Evans, is not surprising.

The October 24, 1920 issue of the *Seattle Post-Intelligencer* newspaper carried an illustration of another forked hosel putter along with an accompanying article, originating from New York, titled "And Now Chick's Famous Putter Is Kicking Up a Fuss Among the Critics." As illustrated by an artist's drawing, the putter is similar to the Hackbarth. However, the two hosel "branches" form a half-circle above the head—the shaft going into a socket directly above the center of the half-circle. The illustration, calling this putter Chick's "own invention," points to this half-circle and describes it as being made from heavy wire while the head is made of aluminum. (Perhaps the artist's illustration was merely a *conceptual* drawing of the Hackbarth putter used by Evans. Another reference in the article describes this putter as "having the ends of the blade connected with the shaft with rods of equal length." This description sounds more like a Hackbarth putter.) The article points out that Chick's putter is center-shafted in principle although the shaft does not enter the center of the head. And therein lies the reason for "kicking up a fuss among the critics."

It seems Evans and Francis Ouimet were preparing to tour England during the coming year

WILLIAM LOWE
HOSEL-BLADE PUTTER

and participate in the British Amateur at Hoylake. The Schenectady putter, long a favorite with American golfers, was not legal for play under R&A rules (see p. 193). The British felt the center-shafted design of the Schenectady offered an unfair advantage and "permits a player to 'get away with' putts hit on the heel or toe better than any other club."

Given a critical look, Evans putter was considered to operate on the same principle as the Schenectady, so the article took a stand against its use:

If the British permit Evans to inflict his freak club upon them they will show themselves wholly unworthy to be considered the defenders and upholders of the tradition of the game.

The *Seattle Post-Intelligencer* article concludes that because the center-shafted principle found in Evans's putter makes putting easier, perhaps the hole should be enlarged because that would make putting easier as well!

Born in Carnoustie, Scotland, in 1862, William Lowe was the professional at Buxton and High Peak Golf Club from 1890 until 1915, the year he died (Jackson 1994, 57). In addition to being a fine clubmaker and player, Lowe also laid out golf courses, such as the Ashbourne (Derbyshire) Golf Club.

The Lowe putter pictured above, marked "Wm Lowe \ Buxton \ Patent \ Warranted Hand Forged," has a distinctive hosel/blade relationship. Before reaching the ground, the hosel turns parallel with the ground and then extends out to the blade, which is positioned well away from the neck. Furthermore, the hosel does not end when it reaches the blade. Rather, a continuation of the hosel extends across the back of the blade. Extending the hosel out to the end of an iron head is seen in only a few patents that

deal with mechanical clubheads designed to rotate around a horizontal continuation of the hosel.

Although marked "Patent," Lowe's putter was never actually patented. However, on September 8, 1894, W. Low and T. Eddleston, of Buxton, applied for a British patent (No. 14,102) to cover "improvements in golf putters and cleeks." The putter pictured dates to that time. Note the sharp nicking, the smooth face, and the minimal amount and style of writing on the back of the blade. The author has also seen a Lowe hosel-blade putter with an offset blade similar to Willie Park's wry-neck putter. Lowe's putters have a clean, simple, and visually strong design.

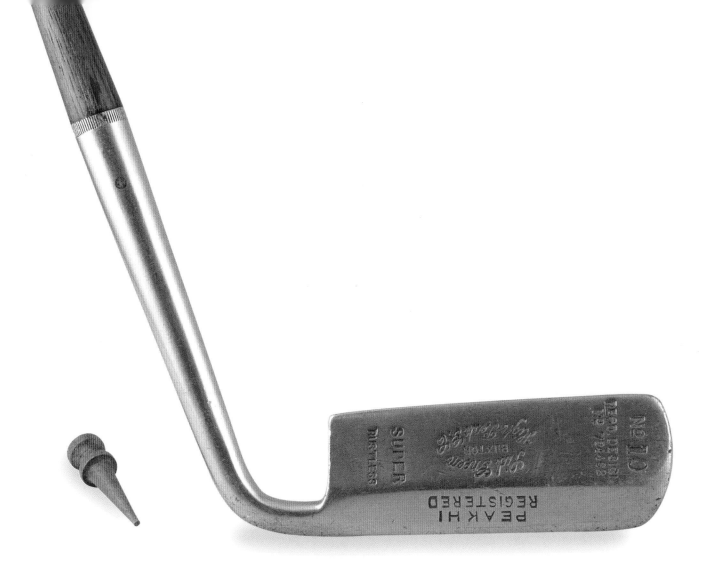

SIDNEY W. GREEN
"PEAKHI"
HOSEL-BLADE PUTTER

Covered under a British design registration (No. 784,462) granted to Sidney Warren Green on July 4, 1933, the Peakhi putter is not only slightly oversized, it has a one-inch gap between the side of the hosel and the beginning of the blade. Although Green's design registration dates to 1933, the end of the wood shaft era, his club is highly collectible because of its rarity and strong visual design.

The Peakhi putter shown is marked "Peakhi \ Registered \ Sid Green \ Buxton \ High Peak G.C." and "No. 10 \ Regd. Design \ 784,462 \ Super \ Rustless" all on the back of the blade. The face is dot punched.

Tom Stewart made a few putters similar to the Peakhi. Produced years earlier, Stewart's putter, with its smaller blade much closer to the hosel, is not as dramatic. Following Stewart's lead, J. Gourlay of Carnoustie produced a few irons and putters with an ordinary hosel attached only to the lower portion of the blade. These are usually marked "Reg. 10,745" and date around 1910. Cochrane's, Ltd. also made a few irons with a traditional hosel attached only to the base of the blade.

Two summers ago I was a witness of a strange effort at golf in which two golfers played their balls from a spot just outside the town of Mold, in Flintshire, to the top of the favourite local mountain, Moel Fammau, which is nearly 2,000 feet high, with very rough sides covered with gorse and ferns, and about three miles distant from the starting point. A ball was "holed out" on the tower on the top of the mountain in 136 strokes, four hours after the start.—Mr. Henry Leach in the Evening News (*Golfing, 7 Mar. 1912: 24*).

WILLIAM G. OKE
"NO. 2 OKE PUTTER,"
LONG HOSEL

ALBERT WHITING
"HIS OWN" PUTTER,
LONG HOSEL

Pictured are a pair of blade putters with exceptionally thin hosels that are also much longer than normal.

The putter on the far left, the "No. 2 Oke Putter," is stamped "W.G. Oke \ Reg. No 680298 \ U.S.A. Patent Applied For \ W.G. Oke \ Fulwell GC \ Special \ Warranted Hand Forged \ 2 \ Putter \ Made In England" and "Oke Brand" under a small "oak tree" trademark on the back of its blade. Born in 1892, Oke was the professional at Fulwell, England, from 1921 into the late 1930s (Jackson 1994, 71).

William George Oke received a British patent (No. 176,999) dated February 4, 1921, that covered this putter and its spindly hosel, which is 7 1/2 inches long and only 1/2-inch wide at its top. Oke's patent states that in order to perform well during the "delicate operation" of putting, the golfer must not be distracted. Consequently, Oke's putter was designed to be unobtrusive.

To begin with, the area where the hosel joins the blade is the same thickness as the top of the blade. According to Oke's patent, "this avoids distraction of the player's eye in the act of putting." Next, the exceptionally long hosel places the top of the neck joint well away from the putter blade. This places the lower end of the shaft outside of the player's "fairly limited field of vision" and, therefore, would not "serve to distract the player's eye or his attention." Oke carried the idea of thinning down his putter one

step further. He called for tapering the wood shaft without any "swell," swell being the increasing thickness of the shaft as it approaches the hosel.

Oke's patent identifies further improvements in his putter when compared to an ordinary putter. The blade on an ordinary putter head measures 4 to 4 1/4 inches long, weighs 8 1/2 ounces, and is attached to a 4-inch hosel weighing 3 1/2 ounces. The blade on Oke's putter measures 4 1/2 to 4 3/4 inches long, weighs 9 3/4 ounces, and is attached to a 6 3/4 inch hosel (as produced, it was often longer—up to 7 1/2 inches) weighing 2 1/4 ounces. Given these specifications, Oke's putter head weighed the same as an ordinary one, but postioned more weight in the blade. Furthermore, the slightly longer blade was supposedly easier to line up.

In addition to receiving a British patent, Oke received a British design registration (No. 680,289) for his putter. Oke applied for a U.S. patent on his putter, but did not complete the patent process.

Pictured near left is a rustless model of Albert Whiting's His Own putter as made by James Gourlay of Carnoustie. (A non-rustless model of Whiting's His Own putter was made by William Gibson). A variation on Oke's putter, Whiting's putter has a *square* hosel and a square shaft. Compared to Oke's hosel, Whiting's hosel is nearly as long (7 inches) and even thinner at the top (13/32 inch). Albert Whiting, brother of Fred Whiting, was the

ROBERT BLACK WILSON
"A1" DRIVING CLEEK, NO HOSEL

professional at Folkestone Golf Club in Kent, England, from 1913 to at least the late 1930s (Jackson 1994, 101).

During the 1920s, a number of blade putters were made with long, thin hosels similar to Oke's. There were, to name a few, Hendry & Bishop's "Sniper," Cochrane's "Nigger," Condie's "Triumph," Winton's "Shiva," and Vulcan's "Burma," all British-made. The Great Lakes "Whip-pet" and a "Gene Sarazen" model offered by both Wilson and Burke were American-made. MacGregor's "Craftsman" putter (with a bronze head, a long square neck, and a hickory shaft) was offered in their 1938 professional catalog.

William Gibson made two different putter models called "The Princeps." One of them had a long square hosel and square shaft similar to Whiting's. Jack White's "All Square Putter" is another putter that has a long square hosel and square shaft.

Long hosel putters, both round and square, are occasionally found. Whiting's "His Own," however, is one of the least common. It also has the thinnest hosel *and* the thinnest head of any putter. (For more on square shafts, see page 504.)

*Mr. R.B. Wilson of St. Andrews has put yet another patent club on the market, which he calls his A 1 driving cleek. A 1 because it is much after the same idea as his A 1 putting cleek, which was noticed in these columns some time ago, in that it has no hose. The shaft passes through the end of the blade, which is thickened to allow of this, to the sole of the club, resembling in this the "Carruthers" cleek, which, however, unlike Mr. Wilson's idea, has a hose (*Golf Illustrated*, 21 Feb. 1902: 144).*

Wilson's A1 driving cleek pictured is stamped "R.B. Wilson O.K. Special St. Andrews" on the back of the blade along with "A1 Cleek \ Made In Scotland" and the initials "MQ." The shaft is stamped "J.H. Norton."

Just prior to producing his A1 driving cleek, Wilson devised his A1 putter. A brief notice printed shortly after the introduction of Wilson's A1 putter acknowledged that its shaft was fastened to a hoseless head:

*It has got no hose of iron at all, the shaft instead passes through the heel of the blade, which is thickened just at that part to allow of this; in fact, it is fastened much after the style of an ordinary hammer (*Golf Illustrated*, 10 Jan. 1902: 27).*

Eliminating the hosel lowered the shaft's flex point and allowed more weight to be concentrated in the blade. Very few examples of Wilson's A1 driving cleek or his A1 putter remain.

R.B. Wilson, affectionately known as "Buff," was more than a clubmaker:

[Wilson] began his career as a golfer, but in St. Andrews he is best remembered as a newsagent. . . .

Born in East Anstruther in 1868 he arrived in St. Andrews with his family as a small boy . . . .

He served his apprenticeship as a club maker with old Tom Morris. He added to his accomplishments by producing machine made golf balls. . . .

He held several . . . appointments in England before he emigrated to the United States of America where he held several professional posts. He helped to pioneer the game of golf in Germany, but he contracted neuritis in the legs and this put an end to his golfing career.

Buff returned to St. Andrews and set up business as a newsagent and stationer, and he also retailed golf clubs.

*There was always a rack of second-hand clubs in front of the window of his shop and these could be purchased for as little as half a crown (*St. Andrews Citizen*, 23 Apr. 1977: 5; also *Golf Monthly*, Oct. 1919: 34-35).*

R.B. Wilson was not the early cleekmaker Robert Wilson. (For more on R.B. Wilson, see page 234.)

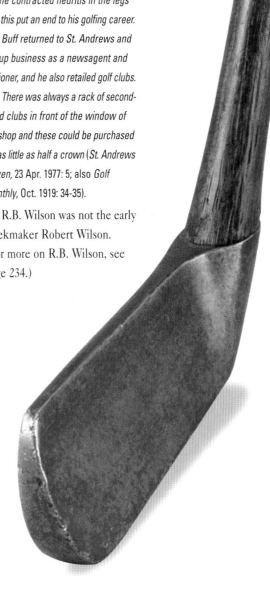

To the player who is in the throes of incapacity with a certain club, a new implement is ethereal; it holds out unbounded promise.... In times of blackest despair, he sees salvation through an avenue of shafts and heads.

Center-Shafted Clubs

On ordinary clubs, the hosel is located on the heel end of the club-head, which is the end of the head nearest the golfer. On center-shafted clubs, the hosel (or shaft, if there is no hosel) is located above, or somewhere directly behind, the center of the face. Some center-shafted clubs were made for traditional use while others were made for croquet-style use, with the golfer straddling the ball or standing directly behind it.

In addition to covering traditional center-shafted clubs and croquet-style clubs, this chapter also examines backwards-style putters. With backwards-style putters the golfer addresses the ball in normal fashion but the hosel is on the far end of the blade.

The first two patents ever granted for a center-shafted club were issued to Robert Anderson of Edinburgh, Scotland. His British patent (No. 6,385) dated April 2, 1892, described a wood with a striking face centered in line with the shaft. His British patent (No. 10,187) dated May 28, 1892, covered a crescent-shaped iron with a shaft centrally attached to the back of the head (see p. 188). In September of 1892, Sir Walter Dalrymple patented his center-shafted "hammerhead" clubs (see p. 412). One month later, George Grant patented a center-shafted driver, two irons, and putter (see p. 190).

The earliest croquet-style putter to receive any type of governmental protection was Captain Hamilton's putter covered under a British design registration issued in late 1890. His club was literally modeled after a croquet mallet (see p. 476). Hamilton's club, however, was not the oldest croquet style putter. In 1887, Sir Walter Simpson wrote:

> *There are putters made like croquet mallets, and there are perfectly upright ones. The latter are of no use to corpulent persons, as they cannot see the ball. Even the emaciated hole-out better without them (23-24).*

Only two patents covered backwards putters during the wood shaft era: Charles Dayton's U.S. patent dated November 21, 1922, and Charles Redman's U.S. patent dated June 7, 1927. These patents are discussed on page 215.

Going one step further, Ronald Evans devised a center-shafted multiface club that could be used billiard style. His club is presented on page 424.

It should be noted that a number of center-shafted clubs are discussed elsewhere in this book, primarily in the chapters titled "Mechanical Clubs," "Fixed Blade Multipurpose Clubs," and "Oversize & Undersize Clubs."

In this chapter, the description of the Schenectady putter, the most famous center-shafted club, is of particular interest. Beginning on page 193, this account covers the first official rules adopted concerning the form and make of golf clubs.

ROBERT ANDERSON
CRESCENT HEAD IRONS & OVAL HEAD PUTTER

One of the most, if not the most, powerful driving cleeks is Anderson's Patent. This cleek has the central socket at the back of the head, and the shaft is also made longer in proportion by reason of the shortness of the socket, the centralisation of the weight of the head being further emphasized by the upcurving of the ends of the sole, which gives the club the general appearance and want of beauty of a gardener's tool (Golf, 9 Apr. 1897: 80).

Robert Anderson's British patent (No. 6,385) dated April 2, 1892, covered a center-shafted wood. This was the first patent issued for a center-shafted golf club. In his patent, Anderson calculated that his center-shafted club would "prevent heeling of the ball and thereby . . . drive longer and straighter balls than by the present shape of wood clubs."

Anderson, of Princess Street, Edinburgh, next received a British patent, (No. 10,187) dated May 28, 1892, that covered a center-shafted iron. According to this patent, a center-shafted iron would:

bring the striking surface nearer to the line of the shaft so as to reduce the leverage when for example the toe of the cleek is struck against the ball whereby the club is liable to turn and thus drive the ball badly.

Accordingly, Anderson designed a crescent shaped iron head and attached the shaft to the back of the blade, directly behind the center of the face. Believing his club to be more accurate, Anderson also asserted that:

concentrating the weight of the club head nearer to the end and to the line of the shaft . . . obtain[s] a more powerful driving club.

The April 7, 1893 issue of *Golf* reports that Anderson introduced this iron to the marketplace during the preceding week (58). It received a good review which included praise for its ability to deal with a "cupped" ball. However, the club was not widely accepted.

Pictured above are two Anderson crescent head irons and an Anderson oval head putter. The irons were made in both iron and gunmetal; the gunmetal version is exceptionally difficult to obtain. The putter is much rarer than the crescent head made of iron.

The iron crescent head and the oval putter are both marked "Anderson & Son \ Princess St. \ Edinburgh" on the back of their blades. The unmarked gunmetal crescent head, which is formed just like the iron version, is in lovely original condition. Fewer than a half-dozen gunmetal crescent head irons are known.

The original shafts in Anderson's crescent irons were painted black next to the socket, as seen on the shaft of both the putter and the non-brass iron. Because crescent irons do not have hosels, the black paint made them *look* more complete.

Part of what makes Anderson's center-shafted clubs such popular collectibles today made them unattractive to golfers years ago. Horace Hutchinson, the 1886 and 1887 British Amateur champion and prominent author, once tried Anderson's oval head putter. Despite liking its performance, Hutchinson could not accept its unorthodox shape:

Hutchinson had been trying one of Anderson's putters, and then returned it with distinct approval: "It is certainly the best putter I have ever played with; but I cannot afford to use a club of that appearance!" (The Golfer, 23 June 1897: 491).

JOHN H. DWIGHT
"DWIGHT'S DIRECTIONAL IRON"

There is one man who will not accept the decision of the U.S.G.A. regarding the form and make of golf clubs, but will go on playing with his own clubs. This man is Dr. J.H. Dwight, of Des Moines [Iowa] . . . .

At the present time Dr. Dwight is having three new clubs made, a mid-iron, mashie and putter. They will be of the same build except for the slant of the face. The feature of the new club will be that the shaft will be directly back of the place where the ball is supposed to be hit and if the reasoning of the doctor is correct, all the force in the club will be centered in a straight line behind the ball, thus making it impossible to pull or slice. The principle of the . . . club is about the same as a hammer, but while the blade is only about an inch and a half at the point where it rests on the ground it is almost four inches wide at the top. . . .

Dr. Dwight is a firm believer that the present make of clubs is an architectural monstrosity. He thinks that it would be the same principle if the horse were hitched to the side of the carriage instead of in front of it and that the only possible solution of the golf club problem is a center-shafted straight-lined club, where the ball, the shaft and the weight will all be in the same line (The Golfers Magazine, 11 Feb. 1911: 185-186).

Dr. Dwight's iron puts the horse directly in front of the carriage by centering the blade in front of the hosel. Dwight's unique clubs were available as putters, mid-irons, and lofters (*The Golfers Magazine*, 11 Apr. 1911: 305). (The "mashie" mentioned in the review cited was actually a lofter.) In addition, Dwight offered a corresponding driver. It was center-shafted in principle, but not in appearance due to the unique design of its head. This wood is discussed on page 459.

Few examples of Dwight's Directional clubs remain. Not only did their unconventional design and ineffectiveness keep them from being accepted, but Dwight's clubs had the disadvantage of being produced and sold by mail order from Des Moines, Iowa—not exactly a hotbed of golf activity. The iron pictured is marked "Dwight's Directional Club \ Des Moines, IA \ Pat -" on the shaft.

In addition to Anderson's crescent iron and Dwight's directional iron, the firm of Auchterlonie and Crosthwaite produced a center-shafted iron as did John C.L. Henry. Henry's "Centro" iron, patented in 1904, has a distinctly round sole, heel to toe, and the hosel is located at the top of the blade, towards the middle. Henry also developed a center-shafted putter and wood (see Henry's Centro p. 200).

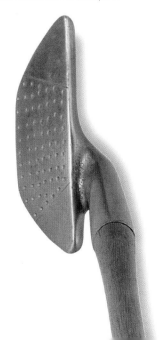

GEORGE GRANT
CENTER-SHAFTED PUTTER
& APPROACH CLUB

George Grant, of Sunnydale, Orpington, in the County of Kent, England, received a British patent (No. 17,929) dated October 7, 1892, that covered four different center-shafted clubs—a driver, mashie, approach club, and putter—constructed from various materials. According to his patent, each clubhead was to:

be made of wood, metal, or other suitable material, or of a combination of suitable materials . . . so arranged that the shaft shall run in a straight line from the hand to directly behind the point of impact of the ball.

As specified in Grant's patent, the unmarked putter head pictured consists of an oval piece of wood sandwiched between two oval gunmetal plates. A gunmetal "holder, to receive the shaft," is bolted to the head. (The nuts and bolts used with the "holder" are entirely original, identical to the patent illustrations.) A short metal rod wedged into the bottom of the shaft extends up inside the shaft to just above the head. This rod expands the tip of the shaft in order to "more securely fix it in the holder."

As illustrated and referred to in Grant's patent, the unmarked and extremely lofted gunmetal iron pictured is "an approach club." It appears designed to "more easily strike balls out of difficult places," the purpose of Grant's mashie as described in his patent. Like the putter pictured, Grant's approach club has a short steel rod, albeit a square one, that extends up into the bottom of the shaft, to help secure the head in place.

 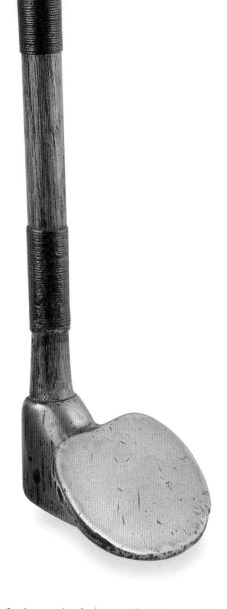

As on Anderson's center-shafted clubs, the original black paint low on Grant's putter shaft mimics the visual effect of a hosel. John D. Dunn also used black paint to achieve the look of whipping on some of his one-piece woods (see p. 147).

In addition to its obvious features, this putter has two interesting aspects that are not visible. First, a lead weight is located inside the head "between the end of the shaft and the point of impact of the ball." According to the patent, before the gunmetal plates were affixed in place, the oval wood block was hollowed out directly in its center and filled with lead. Second, this putter was covered under the first patent to ever mention *steel* shafts!

Grant's patent discusses the idea of using a metal shaft in his clubs: "The shaft when made of steel or other elastic metal, hollow or solid, or partly hollow and partly solid" was to be made from "solid metal covered with rubber" in the area of the grip, "solid or hollow steel or other pliable metal" over the length of the shaft between the grip and the head, and "solid" metal where it fits into the "holder" (the gunmetal bracket) on the back of the head. Grant also provided the option of using wood shafts by declaring, "I however fully reserve the right to use the ordinary shaft, with the new head."

Grant's suggestion to *use* a steel shaft, together with his *design* for a steel shaft, are the first such ideas ever included in a patent. Grant's patent, however, did not specifically claim these ideas. Issued in 1892, Grant's patent precedes Thomas Horsburgh's

1894 British patent (No. 8,603) for a steel shaft by more than a year and a half. According to Horsburgh's patent, its primary purpose "relates to the employment of a steel shaft for golf clubs." After stating "the shaft may be square, round, or other shape," Horsburgh spends the rest of his patent discussing how to affix his steel shaft to a clubhead (see page 498).

It is not known whether Grant ever produced any clubs with steel shafts. Grant's wood putter and approach club pictured are the only such examples known. Thomas Horsburgh, however, did make a few examples of his fascinating steel shaft club. They are on display at Baberton Golf Club, on the outskirts of Edinburgh, Scotland.

JOHN GOUICK
"PERFECT" PUTTER

Our illustration shows the latest pattern of putter, the creation of Mr. J. Gouick.... The implement is known as the "Perfect" putter, and sells at 5s. 6d. Already many well-known athletic goods dealers are selling it. The patentee sets forth the following claims for the "Perfect" putter:

The "Perfect" putter iron is of rectangular shape, looking on its face. The thickest part of the iron is along the bottom, which is half inch, and is gradually rounded up the back to three-sixteenths of an inch. The weight at centre of bottom is increased by the socket handle being carried down the back to the bottom edge. By this formation—when the club is drawn back—it has of itself a forward inclination and a truer pendulum-like stroke than any other golf putter not thus formed.

The bottom edge is rounded and curved at the ends, so that it cannot engage with the turf, which all flat-edged clubs do. The head and handle socket are one solid piece, the whole being made of cast malleable iron or cast brass. The handle is inclined either to one side or the other, so as to throw the club clear of the player's feet, and to suit right or left-handed players. The advantages of this mode of construction are that the centre of effort and the centre of gravity are made to coincide, and the stroke is true and uninterrupted (Golfing, 30 Mar. 1905: 22).

John Gouick, an ironmonger and shop fitter from Dundee, Scotland, received a British patent (No. 20,623) dated September 24, 1904, that covered the putter just reviewed and shown above. The stated objective of Gouick's invention was to provide "handles which are non-slipping and putting irons which are in correct balance and are of proper shape." To create the non-slipping grip, Gouick specified using a corrugated grip made either by cutting grooves, spiral or lengthwise, in the handle of the shaft and then wrapping the handle with leather, or by wrapping a "spaced spiral of cord around the handle and then covering it with soft leather." Gouick's patent proposes making his club from either cast malleable iron or cast brass. The author has seen only the iron version.

The Gouick putter pictured is marked "J. Gouick \ Dundee" inside an oval on the back of the blade, behind the toe. "Ptd No 20623 \ Perfect" is stamped behind the heel. The back of the head as well as the heel of the face shows evidence of tinning—a thin coating of tin or solder. Tinning an iron head was an early attempt to protect the head from rust and improve its appearance. Most of the coating, however, usually wore off over time.

ALEX ANDERSON
OVAL BLADE PUTTER

The "Anderson \ Anstruther" mark on the back of this stylish center-shafted blade putter belongs to Alex Anderson of Anstruther, Scotland. The son of James Anderson, Alex took over his father's business in the late 1800s (see Anderson, page 110). James also marked his irons "Anderson" and "Anstruther" inside a small circle, but the mark Alex used between approximately 1895 and 1910 was larger and had a circle inside as well as outside of the words. After approximately 1910, Alex used a larger (5/8 inch) replica of his father's mark.

In addition to bearing the maker's mark, the back of the blade is stamped "Warranted Hand Forged." This relatively small amount of writing is indicative of a club made around the turn of the twentieth century.

WILLIAM GIBSON
"THE DEADLY"

*Never was a putter more aptly named. The ball seems to leave the face of the club with absolute precision, and shows no inclination to turn aside in that mysterious little way it has when certain old-fashioned putters are in use. This precision engenders a feeling of confidence in the mind of a golfer using a "Deadly" putter (*Golfing, *29 Mar. 1906: 18).*

The Deadly center-shafted blade putter features a crescent-shaped blade set well ahead of the hosel. The back of the blade behind the heel is marked "The Deadly" next to Gibson's "star" trademark. The back of the blade behind the toe is marked "Benetfink \ London E.C. \ Special \ Sherardized \ Warranted Hand Forged." Judging from the minor chipping to the blade's finish, most noticeable across the top line, "Sherardized" was a process used to finish the head. William Gibson made this club, and Benetfink, a sporting goods retailer in London, sold it.

The filing on the hosel near the shaft pin indicates that the shaft was probably replaced or reset and repinned. When a new pin was used after replacing a shaft, it needed to be filed flush with the hosel. If the worker was careless, sizeable file or grinding wheel marks will remain on the hosel. Although not a perfect example, this club is acceptable because few remain.

ARTHUR A. KRAEUTER
"PENDULUM PUTTER"

On May 24, 1921, Arthur August Kraeuter, of Newark, New Jersey, received a U.S. design patent (No. 57,980) for the "Pendulum Putter" pictured above right, marked "Pendulum Putter" high on the toe of the face and "Briarcliffe" on the back of the blade. In calling this club the Pendulum Putter, Kraeuter showed little originality. No fewer than three other putters, all with the same name, were produced before his (see p. 208, 222, and 476).

In order to postion the blade's sweet-spot directly under the hosel, the blade becomes progressively thinner towards the toe.

Arthur August Kraeuter was affiliated with the Kroydon Company. Kroydon produced golf clubs during the 1920s and thereafter.

ARTHUR F. KNIGHT

"SCHENECTADY PUTTER" & "SCHENECTADY PUTTER #2"

On June 4, 1904, Walter Travis became not only the first American citizen to win the British Amateur but also the first person from outside the United Kingdom ever to win the British Amateur. In defeating Edward "Ted" Blackwell in the finals of this venerable championship, Travis used a Schenectady putter. Ever since then, the Schenectady has been associated with Travis and his victory. It has been loved, despised, copied, rejected, ruled illegal, protected, and legalized. Through it all, the Schenectady has become one of the most historic of all clubs.

According to an article titled "The Origin of the Schenectady Putter" (*The American Golfer*, Mar. 1911: 371-372), the Schenectady's story begins in the summer of 1902. Arthur F. "Bill" Knight, of Schenectady, New York, in an effort to improve his own putting, "hit upon the idea of the flat head with the shaft inserted in the center." Wasting no time, Knight made a wooden model "in the head of which he poured sufficient lead to give it the proper weight and balance." He tried this clumsy-looking club for only a week or two, receiving a fair bit of "good natured chaff from fellow players." Undaunted, he made an aluminum model:

The first one was ruined in the making and went to the scrap heap, but the second one was a success, and was substantially the same as the putter of to-day.

The article continues by recalling Mr. Devereux Emmet's visit to the Mohawk Golf Club where Knight was a member. Emmet tried the club and liked it. Knight left the putter with Emmet who happened to be a member of the Garden Golf Club where Walter Travis was also a member. A day or two after Emmet returned home:

Mr. Knight received a telegram from Mr. W.J. Travis ordering a putter like Mr. Emmet's, and one was hurriedly made and forwarded. A little later on Mr. Knight made for Mr. Travis a second putter, with slightly more loft than the first one, and this second one Mr. Travis pronounced "the best putter I have ever used."

It became obvious to other golfers that Travis liked his new putter when he used it to finish second at the 1902 U.S. Open. Prompted by Travis's outstanding finish, "Mr. Knight received over one hundred letters from prominent golfers asking for a putter like Mr. Travis's." Seeing the strong demand for his putter,

Knight wanted to call it the "Travis" putter and "to that end sought an introduction to Mr. Travis, through Mr. Emmet." Knight met with Travis, but Walter did not want the club to be named after him:

While Travis did not definitely decline the use of his name, he made it clear to Mr. Knight that he regarded "Schenectady" (the name given to the club by Mr. Emmet) as a more suitable and lasting name for the putter than his own, in which view Mr. Knight reluctantly concurred....

Without wasting time, Arthur Knight sought and received a patent for his putter in both the U.S. and the U.K. His U.S. patent (No. 723,534) applied for on August 26, 1902, was granted on March 24, 1903, the date marked on many Schenectady putters. His British patent (No. 7,507) was dated March 31, 1903, the

date of its application.

According to Knight's U.S. patent, his putter would reduce the golfer's chance for error when putting. To accomplish this, Knight designed his club "on scientific principles with a view to the symmetrical distribution of the mass with which the impact blow is delivered." Knight reasoned that placing the shaft in the center of the head provided less torque at impact, and that would give better results. Furthermore, Knight believed that the shape of his clubhead helped align and stabilize his club when putting:

This arrangement contributes not only to accurate alignment by the eye, but prevents tilting of the club head while delivering the blow, as the point of application in the forward part of the head prevents any tendency toward unstable equilibrium while the blow is being made.

Knight's center-shafted mallet putter quickly became popular. In the U.S., both Spalding and the Bridgeport Gun Implement Company offered the "Schenectady putter" in their 1903 catalogs. At the same time, Spalding also offered the Schenectady in the U.K. where it was met with immediate derision, being called "a most ugly thing to look at." It was dubbed "the 'Freak Putter'" (*Golfing*, 7 May 1903: 24). But when Walter Travis, the short-hitting Australian born golfer, used a Schenectady putter to win the 1904 British Amateur, the Schenectady bolted to the forefront of the entire golfing world.

In the 36-hole final of the 1904 British Amateur, played over the Royal St. George's course, at Sandwich, England, Travis defeated a player well known for the exceptional length of his shots. The London *Daily Express* reported that Travis "drives fully twenty to thirty yards shorter than Blackwell." However, the London *Daily News*, *Daily Express*, and

Daily Mail reported that, while Travis's game deserved praise, it was his *putting* that won the tournament for him.

Because Travis did, in fact, put on a remarkable display of putting, an influential segment of British golfers, sensitive to seeing their championship won for the first time by a foreigner, lined up against the Schenectady. They believed that the Schenectady gave the golfer an unfair advantage and Travis was their evidence, regardless of the fact that Travis had previously won the 1900, 1901, and 1903 U.S. Amateur:

> We remember the consternation that Mr. Walter J. Travis threw into the ranks of the Britishers when he won their amateur championship, the winning of which, upon analysis, they concluded was due largely to his use of a club of unorthodox construction—the famous Schenectady putter (Faust 1930, 2).

On the other side of the issue, many British golfers were duly impressed with Travis and his putter. In the six days following

Travis's victory, Spalding's London operation received orders for almost *3,000* Schenectady's (*Golfing*, 9 June 1904: 32), and Spalding was not the only clubmaker swamped with orders:

> The putting of Travis with his centre-shaft club left a tremendous impression on the golfing world. So much so that the St. Andrews cleek-makers were inundated with orders for the new type of putter. They went into full-scale production and had thousands made when [in 1910] it was announced that the R. and A. were not disposed to accept them as legal. The heads were dumped on the scrapheap a few months later in their thousands, amid the mutterings of many about the "reactionary" ruling body (Robertson 1967, 81).

While generating considerable discussion, both pro and con, the Schenectady debate escalated into the greatest controversy known to the game up to that time when, in 1910, the Royal and Ancient Golf Club of St. Andrews, to the surprise of the United States Golf Association, ruled the Schenectady illegal.

To understand how this came to pass, it is important to examine the earliest regulations, issued in 1907 and 1909, governing the construction of golf clubs:

> The design and manufacture of golf clubs developed untrammeled by official interference until the beginning of the present century, and ... the restriction incorporated in the new code of rules introduced in 1907 (Cousins 1959, 53).

This restriction (submitted by the rules committee before the end of 1907 and adopted at the September 28, 1908, General Meeting of the R&A, in consultation with the USGA) reads:

> The Rules of Golf Committee intimates that it will not sanction any substantial departure from the traditional and accepted form and make of golf clubs which, in its opinion, consists of a plain shaft and a head which does not contain any mechanical contrivance, such as springs (MacDonald 1928, 154).

In 1909 the R&A received the following question (from the Nga Motu Golf Club, in New Zealand) which dealt with the legality of a golf club: "With regard to form and make of golf clubs, is it permissible to use a small croquet mallet to putt with?" The R&A responded with their decision (No. 47) to the contrary: "A small croquet mallet is not a golf club and is inadmissible."

As a result of a further inquiry from Pickeridge Golf Club, the R&A's Rules of Golf Committee, in issuing Decision No. 71, felt the time had come to determine officially "whether the various mallet-headed implements at present in use are to be permitted or not"; the Rules of Golf Committee being "of the opinion that it is not allowable to use the vertical croquet stroke as a method of putting." It was decided to bring the whole discussion of mallet head clubs to the next general meeting of the R&A (*The American Golfer*, Dec. 1910: 154-155).

On May 10, 1910, the General Meeting of the R&A adopted the following clause, which was added to their initial restrictions on clubs (approved in 1908):

[I]t also regards as illegal the use of such clubs as those of the mallet-headed type, or such clubs as have the neck so bent as to produce a similar effect (The American Golfer, Nov. 1910: 33).

To the R&A, this new rule applied to the Schenectady putter and effectively made it illegal. However, it was left until the September 1910 meeting of the R&A for the Rules of Golf Committee to interpret this ruling via a *Note*—a Note that *clearly* outlawed the Schenectady. This Note reads:

The Rules of Golf Committee intimates that the following general considerations will guide it in interpreting this rule: (1) The head of a club shall be so constructed that the length of the head from the back of the heel to the toe shall be greater than the breadth from the face to the back of the head. (2) The shaft shall be fixed to the heel, or to a neck, socket, or hose which terminates at the heel. (3) The lower part of the shaft shall, if produced, meet the heel of the club, or (as, for example, in the case of the Park and Fairlie clubs) a point opposite the heel, either to the right or left, when the club is soled in the ordinary position for play (The American Golfer, Nov. 1910: 33).

This "Note" (ruling) not only received a very negative reaction in the United States, it was also widely criticized in Great Britain:

There are several points of interest in connection with the illegalizing of the Schenectady putter, and the mallet headed clubs generally, by St. Andrews. Not the least surprising thing is the widespread opposition to the rule on the other side. Outside of the Royal and Ancient itself it never did meet with more than negative support, and now that it has been finally adopted the consensus of opinion clearly points to the fact that a most egregious blunder has been made (The American Golfer, Nov. 1910: 32).

While golfers playing under R&A rules had to live with this decision, golfers in America did not. At the seventeenth annual meeting of the USGA, held in Chicago, Illinois, on January 14, 1911, the Schenectady was ruled legal:

The much-discussed Schenectady putter, placed under the ban by the Royal and Ancient Golf Club of St. Andrews, was saved to the golfers of the United States .... It was the sense of the delegates in this big golf convention that there was a

material difference between a mallet-headed type of golf putter and the so-called Schenectady putter.... But not in anger or a spirit of enmity and spleen did the U.S.G.A. seek to either criticise the Royal and Ancient or refuse to follow the code of rules that comes from the old-world fountain of all that is fundamental in the game of golf. Rather did the delegates emphasize, as retiring President Herbert Jaques tersely put it, that the U.S.G.A accepted the St. Andrews clause, but rejected its note of interpretation (The American Golfer, Feb. 1911: 314).

The USGA chose to adopt the same rules alterations approved by the R&A on May 10, 1910, but did not adopt the same interpretation of the rules provided by the R&A Rules Committee concerning "the form and make of golf clubs." The USGA added their own note of interpretation, which reads:

The shaft of a putter may be fixed at the heel or at any other point in the head. The term mallet-headed as above and when applied to putters, does not embrace putters of the so-called Schenectady type (The American Golfer, Feb. 1911: 315-316).

The USGA believed that because the Schenectady and other thick head putters had been accepted and used for so many years, they were, in fact, clubs of an accepted form and make. Furthermore, the term "mallet" was instinctively thought of by some members of the USGA as an implement originally designed for purposes other than golf—that it referred to:

a kind of a mallet a carpenter uses, a croquet mallet, etc., that is to say where there is a right angle centered shaft with two heads to strike with (The American Golfer, Dec. 1910: 154).

Therefore, it was resolved that the Schenectady putter would remain legal for play when the competition was under the immediate direction of the USGA.

When the USGA preserved the legal use of the Schenectady and other mallet head putters after the R&A declared them illegal, golfers in general perceived this as threatening not only the good relationship between the USGA and the R&A but also the very foundation of the game: the rules. There was great concern that the two governing bodies of the sport might end up breaking away from each other and that such a split would allow the game of golf to evolve in two dramatically different directions. Gone would be the worldwide conformity of not only the equipment but also the game itself. Fortunately, the governing bodies did not let their differences over the Schenectady diminish their desire to work together.

After the R&A modified the rule on "the form and make of golf clubs" in their May 10, 1910, General Meeting, Charles B. Macdonald wrote a letter, dated June 10, 1910, to the R&A Rules of Golf Committee (*The American Golfer*, Dec. 1910: 154-156). Macdonald, the USGA representative to the R&A rules committee, conveyed his belief that banning the Schenectady was a great mistake due to its popularity with American golfers. Furthermore, he expressed his opinion that the Schenectady was not a mallet. Macdonald had not attended the general meeting in May nor had he communicated anything prior to it because he never imagined the Schenectady would be targeted for extinction, the questions and rulings leading up to the ban having made no specific reference to the Schenectady itself.

In response to Macdonald's letter, Captain W. Burn, chairman of the R&A Rules Committee, wrote to Macdonald and expressed regret, confessing the committee had no idea that the Schenectady putter was so widely used in America. Burn also stated that, in September, the Rules of Golf Committee sought to interpret the rule in order to allow the USGA its own interpretation:

The wording is not what the Committee would have selected had it not been for the views expressed in your letter of June 10th to the Committee, who have endeavored by inserting in the Note, to leave to the United States Golf Association an opportunity of interpreting the clause to its own satisfaction without nominally refusing to adopt the Rules of Golf as passed by the R. & A. Club (The American Golfer, Dec. 1910: 155).

By allowing the USGA to adopt the same rules as the R&A but permitting them a different interpretation if they so chose, the R&A averted a breakdown between them and the USGA. Consequently, the Schenectady remained legal under USGA rules while it was illegal under R&A rules. In 1951 the R&A finally lifted their ban against the Schenectady and other center-shafted putters.

Many Schenectady putters remain today. The fact that "fully seventy-five per cent of the players in the [1916] Amateur championship at Merion used putters of the Schenectady type" is an illustration of the Schenectady's former popularity in the U.S. (*The American Golfer*, Oct. 1916: 465). Schenectady putters were still being offered in Harry C. Lee's catalog as late as 1928 (53).

Harry C. Lee & Company, of New York, sold the vast majority

of the putters marked "Schenectady Putter \ March 24, 1903." Early on, Lee became the sole licensee and manufacturer of the genuine article. Therefore, many other makers made Schenectady-style putters that were not marked "Schenectady." The aluminum Schenectady putter pictured on page 194 is one of only a few known stamped "The Schenectady Putter \ Patent Applied For." Marked "B.G.I.Co." on the sole, this Schenectady, with its original sheepskin grip, original protruding ends of the neck pin, and graceful St. Andrew's bend to the shaft, was produced before Lee became the sole licensee. Unlike most of the "patented" Schenectadys, this "Patent Applied For" model does not have an alignment line across its crown.

In addition to aluminum head models, basic Schenectady-style putters, such as the J. MacGregor "Cimetric" putter sold in the mid-1910s, were eventually made with wood heads faced with brass or steel. All are good entry level collectibles.

So, what about the magic of the Schenectady putter? Walter Travis reported that during the 1904 British Amateur he changed every club in his bag except for his putter and mashie, but his putter was never as effective thereafter:

The singular thing about the Schenectady which I used throughout the championship is that I have never been able to do anything with it since. I have tried it repeatedly but it seems to have lost all its virtue (The American Golfer, Mar. 1910: 371-372).

Arthur F. Knight, father of the Schenectady putter, also received the first U.S. patent that covered a metal golf shaft (see page 498).

W.R. POPE
"POPE'S PUTTER"

Following the introduction of the Schenectady, a few clubmakers produced center-shafted mallet putters of their own design. The more unusual ones are wonderful collectibles.

The Pope putter pictured, marked "Pope's Putter \ Rd. No. 437299" inside an oval on the back of the head, is very creative. Not only is the head rectangular but the hosel runs flush with the face and is centered between the heel and toe atop the head:

The particular feature of this club is the position of the shaft, which is set in a socket running flush with the face in the very centre of the head. At first glance it would appear as if the shaft would obscure a view of the ball, but this is not the case. The fact of the shaft being so placed enables the player to more easily play the ball from the very centre of the club face and in a direct line to the hole. A good "follow through" is all that is necessary to obtain satisfactory results with this putter (Golfing, 23 Feb. 1905: 20).

Pope also produced "Pope's Concave-Face Putter, a center shafted mallet with a concave face curved heel to toe. For more on W.R. Pope, see page 257.

D. MURRAY
OBLONG HEAD PUTTERS

SLAZENGER & COMPANY
TRIANGLE HEAD PUTTER

Made in Great Britain, the center-shafted putters pictured above left and center are both stamped "D. Murray \ Brechin" inside an oval. The wooden model is stamped twice atop its head and once on its shaft; the gunmetal model is stamped twice on its sole and once on its shaft. Fashioned on the same center-shafted principle as the Schenectady putter, Murray's putters dates prior to 1910, when the R&A ruled that center-shafted mallet putters were illegal.

The wooden model, one of two known, has a brass soleplate and faceplate. The gunmetal model, the only one known, is inlaid with wood across the crown.

This pair of Murray putters are unique in that their head shapes are exact opposites: The gunmetal head is an upside-down model of the wooden head. Even the sides and face of the gunmetal model are inverted, the face having a negative loft.

We have recently received and played with three new clubs by Messrs. F.L. Slazenger and Co., of New York . . . . They consist of a driver, brassie, and putter. . . . Regarding the putter, which has an aluminum head, the illustration on this page will convey its appearance. It is considered in America a most effective and deadly weapon of golfing warfare, and has created sensation all over the States. It is apparent from a prima facie glance at its construction, and more so when playing with it, that a slightly different movement is required for an effective putt than is necessary with the usual forms of putter. The angle farthest away from the face may be apt to catch on the ground if the usual form of action is indulged in, thus a stiffer motion is unconsciously given with it, when certainly a true putt can, with a little practice, be easily and satisfactorily played. Messrs. Benetfink and Co. [London] . . . are the sole agents for Messrs. F.L. Slazenger's clubs over here (Golfing, 23 April 1903: 26).

The aluminum head putter pictured is marked "Slazenger \ New York." In addition, it has "E.P." (owner's initials) stamped on the top of its head. Not only is the hoselless head triangular in shape, it is uniform in thickness, top to bottom. Two other club-makers made triangular head putters (see pages 382 and 422), but only Slazenger's has a single usable face. Judging from the two examples the author has seen, Slazenger's triangular putter was not nearly as popular as the cited review intimates.

JOHN S. CAIRD
HALF-CIRCLE HEAD PUTTER

The putter pictured directly above was made by John Caird. The head resembles a half-circle, and the shaft is stamped "J.S. Caird." This club predates the Schenectady and was covered under Caird's British patent (No. 19,688) dated September 5, 1896. This patent does not deal specifically with the unusual head shape of Caird's club, though the head shape was designed to help the patent achieve its objectives. Instead, it deals with the way his club is weighted.

Two large circular lead weights and one small lead weight are visible on the sole. The large weights are at opposite ends of the head, one at the toe and the other at the heel. The small lead weight is centrally located midway between the other two weights and behind the tip of the shaft. According to Caird's patent, the center lead weight could be attached to the larger lead weights by a small channel, also filled with lead. This weighting design, usable on both woods and putters, provided four advantages:

> 1st. An immovable head.
> 2nd. Perfect centre balance of the club.
> 3rd. Low flight of the ball and straight.
> 4th. Long run of the ball.

When he received his patent, Caird was working as a golf club maker at Dunbar, Scotland. In 1898 he became the professional at the City of Newcastle Golf Club. Caird worked there until 1920 (Jackson 1994, 14).

When it comes to Schenectady-style putters, those that depart the furthest from the Schenectady generate the most collector interest. The Inglis putter pictured on the facing page is a good departure because of the rectangular nature of the head; the heel and toe are "cut off" or square. The Pope, Caird, Slazenger, and Murray putters on this and the previous pages have even better collectibility. They represent more radical departures (they look nothing like the Schenectady) and have an exceptionally strong and captivating personality of their own. The Adams putter above is also quite nice. It has a compact head and reflects a complete overhaul of the traditional Schenectady.

Marked "Jeff Adams \ Coordination Putter" on the back half of the sole, this peculiar putter head has some interesting characteristics not readily apparent in the picture. The sole has two levels with the back half sloping upwards towards the top of the head. In addition, the club has a bore-through hosel. Because this head is short (heel to toe) and center-shafted, the tip of the shaft is visible underneath the toe. The Adams Coordination putter was also produced with a metal shaft.

J.R. INGLIS
RECTANGULAR HEAD PUTTER

Many wooden head putters were modeled after the basic shape and style of the Schenectady putter. These wooden mallets, usually made by such large American manufacturers as Spalding, MacGregor, Burke, etc., were often given their own distinctive look. The putter pictured above, crafted by J.R. Inglis and so stamped, is one of the more stylish examples.

A 1912 advertisement for Inglis-made clubs simply promotes "Inglis' Perfect Balanced clubs" (*Golf* [ny], Dec.: 379). Inglis, however, excelled not only at making golf clubs but also at making golf professionals.

According to an article about Inglis published in 1949 (at which time he had been the professional at Fairview Country Club in Elmsford, New York, for forty-two years), Inglis was often referred to in the eastern U.S. as "the daddy of pro golfers" because so many of his caddies and assistants went on to become golf professionals:

Among his redoubtable caddies can be numbered not only two United States Open Champions, Johnny Farrell (1928) and Tony Manero (1936), [but also] Willie Turnesa, the youngest and only amateur of the seven famous Turnesa golfers, winner of the United States Amateur Championship in 1938 and 1948 and the British Amateur Championship in 1947... (Golfing, Mar. 1949: 25).

The article listed twenty-nine other prominent professionals by name and referred to "many others."

JAQUES & SON
"FIFE" DRIVER

The rare center-shafted driver pictured above has a bore-through socket neck that exposes the tip of the shaft near the toe of the sole. The top of the head is marked "Jaques \ Maker \ London." Opened for business in 1795, Jaques & Son, of Hatton Garden, London, is the oldest sports and games manufacturer in the world. Famous for their croquet equipment ever since the middle 1800s, Jaques did not become very involved in the golf market.

In 1894 *Golf* printed a positive review of a "captive golf ball" (a practice ball with a parachute attached) which Jaques produced. In addition, the review mentions that Jaques & Son were :

also the makers of wooden and iron clubs called the "Fife Golf Clubs," each club being fitted with the "corkie" grip (Golf, 13 Apr. 1894: 72).

This driver includes the cork grip mentioned. As originally constructed, the cork covers the butt of the shaft, and a seam runs up the side of the grip. This grip is included in a picture on page 528. Cork grips were an alternative to leather grips, which became slippery when wet. However, cork was not as durable as leather.

On February 19, 1894, Jaques applied for a British patent (No. 3,494) that related to the "handles of golf clubs and irons." This patent application, which probably dealt with the "corkie" grip, either lapsed or was not granted. The only golf club or ball patent granted to J. Jaques was a British patent (No. 2,729) dated February 8, 1894, that covered his parachute ball.

JOHN C.L. HENRY
"CENTRO"
CENTER-SHAFTED DRIVER

John Chave Luxmoore Henry, of Glasgow, Scotland, received a British patent (No. 15,597) dated July 13, 1904, that covered a wood, iron, and putter designed not only to reduce the torque on a miss-hit shot but also to hit straighter shots and handle tough lies. According to his patent, his invention:

has for its object to provide an improved formation of club-head which when used in play shall ensure truer direction of drive and not tend to apply a turning or twisting strain on the user's hands while also permitting of a freer stroke at cupped balls and being less liable to cut or damage the turf.

Therefore, Henry designed center-shafted clubs:

By this construction if the ball be struck either by the toe part or heel part of the club a minimum of twisting or turning stress is applied through the shaft on the player's hand, and a truer ball is driven.

Pictured is a scarce "Centro" driver covered under Henry's 1904 patent. In addition to being marked "Henry \ Centro" on the crown, the head also bears small, unreadable lettering (the letters are filled with the original finish and darkened varnish).

The sole of this wood is cambered and the top line of the face mirrors the sole. This design maintains a consistent depth across the face and helps the club strike a ball in a cupped lie:

According to my invention . . . a wooden driver or brassie or an iron, cleek, or like club is made with the bottom or lower edge of the face of convex formation preferably in the form of an arc of a circle whose centre is directly over the middle of the club head, the upper side of the club being either flat or concave . . . so as to form a head of approximately uniform depth . . . .

The curve formation of the under part of the club head enables the player to reach well down to a ball lying in a hollow without cutting into the turf to the usual extent.

Another interesting characteristic of Henry's Centro driver is that, when viewed from directly above, the head is shaped like a half-circle. Although Henry's Centro woods and irons have a curved top line to match their sole, his putters have a straight top line and curved sole.

Henry's Centro putter is rarely seen; his wood and iron are even more rare. The author has seen only the Centro wood pictured and three Centro irons.

If the shaft is warped or crooked, which may be due to green wood, or to the habit of digging under the ball and cutting out divots at each shot, heat it in front of the fire, and then rub it liberally with oil, straightening the shaft by gradual pressure of the heated hand. It is better not to put oil on the head of wooden clubs, especially the face. If the face of the club is cracked, get the clubmaker to put in a leather face (Golf, 3 Mar. 1893: 395).

WILLIAM AUCHTERLONIE
CENTER-SHAFTED BRASSIE

I have played golf all my life, practically from my earliest recollection, still I must say that I have always done so entirely from devotion to and love of the game, and that I have never looked upon golf, in itself, as a means of livelihood; but rather I preferred to turn my attention in this matter towards the making of clubs, in which I have always taken the greatest interest and pleasure (Willie Auchterlonie, *Golf*, 9 Mar. 1906: 206).

Born in St. Andrews in 1873, William "Willie" Auchterlonie was a champion golfer and highly regarded clubmaker. Winner of the 1893 British Open, Auchterlonie nevertheless limited his golfing exploits in order to pursue his primary interest: clubmaking.

In 1887 Auchterlonie began working as an apprentice clubmaker (*Golf*, 23 Feb. 1894: 376). Before long, Auchterlonie became known "as one of the best clubmakers whom Messrs. Forgan and Son had in their service" (*Golf*, 27 Oct. 1893: 101). In October of 1893, it was reported that Auchterlonie was no longer working for Forgan but was working for himself in "the firm of Auchterlonie and Crosthwaite, 9, Union-street, St. Andrews" (*Golf*, 27 Oct.: 101).

Business was good, and less than two years after opening, Auchterlonie was exporting his clubs to America:

Auchterlonie and Crosthwaite . . . have been successful in opening up a large connection with American golfers, and they have recently appointed Mr. C.C. Bartley, of 58, Warren Street, New York, as their wholesale agent for the States (*Golf*, 13 Sep. 1895: 9).

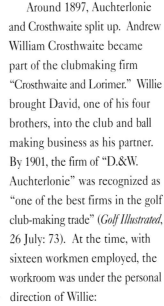

Around 1897, Auchterlonie and Crosthwaite split up. Andrew William Crosthwaite became part of the clubmaking firm "Crosthwaite and Lorimer." Willie brought David, one of his four brothers, into the club and ball making business as his partner. By 1901, the firm of "D.&W. Auchterlonie" was recognized as "one of the best firms in the golf club-making trade" (*Golf Illustrated*, 26 July: 73). At the time, with sixteen workmen employed, the workroom was under the personal direction of Willie:

The Brothers Auchterlonie personally supervise all their work . . . . Their wooden clubs are entirely handmade from beginning to end, and their iron clubs hand forged. . . . In selecting the wood for their drivers and other wooden clubs the greatest care is taken, and every piece is subjected to a close scrutiny before it is allowed to pass into the hands of the workmen at all . . . more pieces often being rejected than passed. This process of examination is repeated at various stages in the transition of the rough wood into the finished club (*Golf Illustrated*, 26 July 1901: 73).

Following in the footsteps of Old Tom Morris and Andrew Kirkaldy, Willie Auchterlonie was appointed honorary professional to the Royal and Ancient Golf Club of St. Andrews in 1935. Shortly after Willie's death at the age of 92, his son, Laurie, was appointed to the same position.

Made by Willie Auchterlonie, the center-shafted wood pictured is stamped "Auchterlonie" on the crown and "Auchterlonie, St. Andrews" on the shaft. The 41 1/2-inch shaft, the fair amount of loft, and the full brass soleplate identify this club as a brassie. An Auchterlonie putter that matches this brassie is displayed at the British Golf Museum in St. Andrews. No other examples of either club are known to the author.

Auchterlonie made a few long nose style clubs. However, he made them in 1893 or later, which was after the close of the long nose era. Consequently, his long nose style clubs are not valued like a true long nose made during the long nose era.

C.H. MERRILL

CENTER-SHAFTED WOOD

C.H. Merrill's center-shafted wood is not documented in any earlier writing, but it possesses a wide variety of significant characteristics, including a radical head shape.

The shaft is made from ash. An extremely high percentage of all wood-shafted clubs have hickory shafts, ash being more common in early clubs. Another early characteristic is that the shaft is hewn by hand. Flat spots on this shaft can be felt when turning it in one hand.

The head is bored all the way through to receive the shaft, but the shaft does not extend all the way through the head. Furthermore, it has a setscrew located on the sole to help fasten the head to the shaft.

A slip made from brass is used in place of the traditional horn. It is fastened in place by five small screws (screws being a natural choice for a metal slip).

"C.H. Merrill" is stamped on the head three times: once on the top of the head near the tip of the toe and parallel to the face, and twice on the brass slip.

The lead backweight, which has long since fallen out, was designed to protrude out of the head.

The blond finish on this head has a depth similar to the circa 1800 blond McEwan shown on page 45.

The rearward slope to the top of the head is perfectly formed; it does not cut across the grain at any point.

The wood used to make the head does not appear to be any of the woods normally used (apple, pear, beech, persimmon, etc.).

The face profile and head shape are unlike any other.

Given the brass horn, the set screw affixing the shaft in place, the use of Merrill's first two initials instead of one, and the fact that such unusual looking clubs were introduced around 1890, this club would appear to date from the 1890s. However, some of the other characteristics, such as the hand hewn ash shaft, the protruding lead weight, the deep finish, the unusual wood used in the head, and the cut of the wood, *could* date this club to a time much earlier than 1890. A key to determining when this club was made is finding out who C.H. Merrill was. Perhaps, future research will identify this individual.

Given such a spectrum of anomalies, this club is an intriguing and impressive collectible. It is well made and stands apart from all other clubs. Such creative clubs reflect the clubmaker's efforts to improve upon the traditional clubs of his time. Making a club in order to test an idea, hoping to find a "better way," was part of the game.

The author has seen one other club like this one. The other club, however, was not stamped with a name and the back of the head was flatter (possibly altered), so the backweight was flush.

HENRY R. SWENY
CROSSHEAD DRIVER

Henry Roy Sweny, of Albany, New York, devised two very unusual golf clubs—a center-shafted wood and, as pictured, a crosshead-like wood. Sweny received a U.S. patent (No. 566,101) dated August 18, 1896, that covered his center-shafted wood. As patented and produced, the splice neck on Sweny's club (the sixth club patented in the U.S.) is in line with the center of the face. The head itself comes to a distinct point at the toe, the back of the head getting progressively closer to the face as it approaches the toe. Three lead plugs are set in the back of the head. Sweny believed his center-shafted wood was more durable and easier to use:

My driver is so constructed that the grain of the wood runs from the nose of the club directly up the shaft, thus bringing the line of force in one line with the point of contact with the ball. This construction makes it almost an impossibility to break a club made this way. It was the frequent breaking of clubs last fall that suggested the idea to me, and, while circumventing this error, I found that I also made a big step in advance by getting the point of contact in line with the force, which is really the meritorious feature over all other drivers, which I accordingly have had patented. I claim that with more ease and certainty one can drive a ball as far as with the old club, that is from 175 to 190 yards, when in an expert's hands. When in the hands of only a fair player a much straighter ball results than by the use of the old club.

The wood used for the heads is persimmon. It is cut in North Carolina eighteen months previous to its use in the factory, so as to allow the most thorough seasoning. . . (The Golfer, 24 June 1896: 478).

This same article mentions another unusual club, which Sweny designed for lady golfers, but it does not describe this club:

Mr. Sweeny [sic] makes a different style for ladies, altering slightly the construction, with springy short shafts and large striking surface for the ball . . . All the heads vary by ounces and fractions in weight to suit players, and he makes seven sizes. . . .

The Sweny crosshead-like driver pictured, stamped "H.R. Sweny \ SPT'G Goods Co." on its shaft, is believed to be this club. It has a 42 1/2-inch shaft and eleven degrees of loft, typical characteristics of a lady's driver. The back of the head has four small lead plugs. The base of the sole is covered with a small brass plate. The only other known example of this club measures 38 inches and has 25 degrees of loft. The shaft in both Sweny's crosshead and center-shafted wood intersects an imaginary line extending straight back from the center of the face.

Henry Sweny was "a prominent player [and] a champion of several tournaments." While living in Albany, New York, he was "a member of several golf clubs, among them the St. Andrew's, the oldest in the country, and the Albany Country Club" (*The Golfer*, 24 June 1896: 478). The golf clubs he made were sold through his "Sweny Sporting Goods Company," as stamped on the shaft of this driver. In 1899, he stopped making golf clubs:

Harry Sweney [sic] has sold out his Golf Goods Mfg. Co. to the Golf Goods Mfg. Co., of Binghampton, N.Y. (Golf [ny], April 1899: 238).

FRANCIS BREWSTER
"SIMPLEX"
CROSSHEAD WOODS

The patent which completely protects the "Simplex" golf clubs, and which will be enforced whenever necessary, was drawn under, perhaps, the best advice obtainable; and in it I was careful to steer clear of my own or anyone else's great-grandmother's cousin's under gardener who may have driven a peg or chopped up a daisy or even struck a golf ball with some kindred instrument. (Francis Brewster, Golf Illustrated, 12 Feb. 1904: 131).

Francis Wentworth Brewster's Simplex clubs have a radical head shape, but they were also designed to provide the golfer with a complete set of clubs, from driver to putter. Pictured above is a Simplex play club and a niblick (or pitcher) as described and illustrated in Francis Brewster's British patent (No. 9,514) dated April 14, 1897. The play club, on the left, is marked "Simplex \ Patent No. 9514, 1897" on the top of its head. The heavily lofted niblick is not marked.

According to his patent, Brewster's main objective was to build a club that, because it had less "torsional movement," could hit the ball farther and straighter. To this end, Brewster's clubs are center-shafted and have a unique head shape. He described his clubs as "boat-like," referring not only to the outline of the head, which has obvious similarities, but also to the shape of the sole. Brewster felt that a sole slightly cambered from heel to toe as well as from front to back made his club more effective:

When the rockered bottom of the "Simplex" club comes in contact with the ground . . . it glances off or ricochets, thereby automatically imparting to the face of the club an upward tendency at the precise moment it strikes the ball. . . (Golf Illustrated, 29 Jan. 1904: 86).

Brewster's patent calls for installing, on the front of each head, a metal faceplate integral with a "horseshoe-shaped soleplate." As produced, the faceplates were made from brass. And the more lofted the club, the larger the faceplate. Brewster,

however, produced his putters without a faceplate—only the edge of the soleplate is visible across the bottom of the face. While including the possibility of making his clubheads from vulcanite, which did not need a metal faceplate/soleplate, Brewster's patent calls for making the clubheads from yarrah, oak, briarwood or "other suitable hard wood preferably with the grain running in the direction of its length."

A specially designed joint was used to attach the shaft to the middle of the head. The head was "bored diagonally and its upper part . . . morticed in the direction of the length of the club-head, and shouldered." Such an attachment served to seat the shaft in the head and prevent it from turning and coming loose.

Brewster's patent also mentions forming an oval (in cross-section) grip with the direction of the oval on the upper half of the

grip being different from that on the lower half. This grip would supposedly "prevent the club from twisting in the hands," which was also a main purpose of his center-shafted design. Brewster received a second British patent (No. 9,515) dated April 14, 1897, to cover the grips mentioned in his first patent. Brewster's oblong grip was not always included on his Simplex clubs.

In 1897 Francis Brewster produced a booklet titled *Golf on a New Principle: Iron Clubs Superseded*. Authored by "An Old Golfer," this booklet promotes Brewster's Simplex clubs and "the Crosshead system":

Nine out of every ten unprejudiced persons will wish to test the new system, and many who came to curse will remain to bless (Everage, preface).

At the time, Brewster's Crosshead clubs were available from "Messrs. The Crosshead Golf Club Co., Bournemouth, Hants," on the south coast of England (Everage 1897, 63).

Golf on a New Principle, along with the clubs it promotes, is reviewed in the June 25, 1897 issue of *Golf*. The review identifies the booklet's author, "An Old Golfer," as the same Mr. L. Everage who discussed "crosshead" clubs in a letter to the editor published in *Golf* only two weeks earlier. After noting the center-shafted "hammer" quality of the clubs, the review, quoting from the booklet, identifies the objectives of the Crosshead system:

The objects of the Crosshead system are to generally simplify the game, and render fewer clubs necessary; to do away with all tendency of the club-head to twist during the stroke; and to dispense with all iron clubs, thus creating a greater similarity among many strokes which are now widely different (313).

In doing away with iron clubs, the Crosshead system provided the golfer with a set of six clubs: play club, long spoon, mid-spoon, short spoon, pitcher, putter. The review also notes that J.H. Taylor had experimented with these clubs with good results in three matches. The review pointed out, however, that "unfortunately all golfers have not Taylor's adaptability." The review concludes:

We are disposed to think, not only that prejudice will be aroused against their shape, but to agree with the inventor when he says that he is considerable way ahead of present-day golfing progress in the realization of an ideal.

Despite this less than enthusiastic review, Brewster remained convinced of the validity of his design.

In 1898 a singles match and a foursome match were played in which one side used crosshead clubs, and the other used traditional clubs. The crosshead clubs were victorious in both matches, the inventor taking part in the foursome match. Describing this event and the success of those using the Simplex clubs, a reporter acknowledged the possibility that Simplex clubs might come into prominence in the near future (*Golf*, 1 Apr. 1898: 54).

If the success of the Simplex clubs in these two golf matches was supposed to establish their validity, a setback was reported a few months later in *Golfer's Magazine*. In a match between two professionals from Bournemouth, "Dunlop and Churchill," Dunlop used ordinary clubs to defeat Churchill and his Simplex clubs, 6 up with 5 to play. Their scores were 79 and 93. Using the one-sided match results as evidence, a reporter called into question the merits of crosshead clubs when he observed, "The greater power of the ordinary clubs through the green was very noticeable" (July 1898: 196).

Still, Brewster perservered and promoted his clubs as well as he could. He even used them when participating in the 1899 British Open:

A notable competitor in the Open Championship was "Mr. Crosshead," who played with the clubs of his own invention . . . . "Mr. Crosshead's" score was not a very good one, but it is open to him to retort that it would have been worse had he played with clubs of the ordinary pattern (Golf Illustrated, 16 June 1899: 8).

Brewster's clubs received welcome exposure in an article titled "The Golf-Club in Evolution" that appeared in the July 1900 issue of *Golf* published in New York (26-30). This article, which reprints a portion of the booklet *Golf on a New Principle*, explains a number of aspects about Brewster's clubs:

1. "Crosshead," as a term, relates to having the:

center of the face of the club in the same plane of action as the shaft; the face itself is well in advance of the shaft . . . and the length of the head is in the wake of the ball—in the direction of the stroke.

2. The carefully designed "rockered" sole of the crosshead clubs, whose greatest length is always with the stroke, keeps the head from digging into the ground. This sole would produce a glancing blow whereas an iron digs into the ground by operating on "the hoe principle."

3. The six clubs in the system were all that any golfer needed.

4. First time users were given specific instructions:

In addressing the ball, always stand one and one-half inches farther back than in playing with ordinary clubs.

Don't use sand or other artificial tees, but take the ball off the grass.

Always play to brush the sole of the clubs along the surface of the ground at the moment of striking.

Play your approach with confidence, high, and full at the hole, and not short, expecting to run on.

Play all bad-lying balls very firmly, and bring the nose of the club down more or less perpendicularly, striking ball and ground simultaneously, not sparing the latter.

Learn to use the six different clubs in the inverse order of their numbers giving a day to each club.

By 1904, not satisfied with his original six clubs and their poor acceptance, Brewster expanded his six clubs to eight—driver, brassie, cleek, baffie, mashie, pitcher, niblick, and putter—and formed the " 'Simplex' Golf Association," which included a "School of Golf," at Hayling Island, England. In 1904 Simplex golf clubs were still largely unknown to the general golfing public. Although many golfers had read about them, Brewster's clubs were not readily available. An article extolling the virtues of Simplex clubs, authored by "The Secretary, 'Simplex' Golf Association" and published in 1904, begins by mentioning that the Simplex club had made its debut and would have to be "reckoned with among the great variety of other implements used by those who play golf" (*Golf Illustrated*, 8 Jan.: 27). The article concludes by stating that Simplex clubs were not, nor would they be in the immediate future, available anywhere except the Simplex Golf Association's School of Golf:

In order to prevent misunderstanding, may I be permitted to state that the "Simplex" clubs will not be on the market in the ordinary meaning of the term for some time to come, and that the only way in which they will be in the meanwhile obtainable is by direct application to me at our School of Golf, Hayling Island.

The Simplex Golf Association was short-lived due to lack of interest. Undaunted, Brewster continued his steadfast belief in his clubs (see *Golf Illustrated*, 26 Apr. 1907: 94 and 21 June 1907: 253).

From the beginning, Brewster's crosshead clubs met with general disapproval. Even his patent was criticized. When confronted with the idea that his patent was not a patent at all, Brewster remarked:

From a business point of view, it is an extremely damaging attitude to have taken, and one likely to result in much injury to the interests of the "Simplex Golf Association," and involve us in needless litigation (Golf Illustrated, 12 Feb. 1904: 131).

Pictured above is a "Simplex #5" made with a head of aluminum, gunmetal, and wood. The wood visible on both sides of the head is actually the ends of two wood blocks that extend through the inside of the head. "A.W. Powell" is stamped on the side of one of the blocks and on the shaft. "Prov Protected" is marked atop the head and "5" is stamped on the back tip of the sole. This club is covered by Brewster's 1907 patent—a prompt refinement of his *1906* patent.

In 1906 Brewster received a British patent, (No. 20,614) dated September 17, in which he sought an easier way to make his clubs. Referring to his 1897 patent (No. 9,514) and acknowledging the extensive amount of hand work that went into his Simplex clubs, as well as the great quantities of time and craftsmanship necessary to produce them, Brewster states the objective of his 1906 patent as follows:

This invention . . . has for its objects to avoid the separate shaping manipulation of each such club-head, which, when made, as hitherto, of wood or wood shod with a metal sole-plate having a faceplate . . . necessitates considerable factory room and highly skilled labour and involves costliness of production, a slow output and liability of inexactitude of formation fitting and weight, and to dispense with said metal mountings, and so to reduce the labor and cost of manufacture . . . .

To remedy the earlier manufacturing problems, Brewster proposed making his clubheads in the same shape but from a metal alloy that incorporated blocks of wood within the head. This allowed him to cast the head in aluminum and still fasten the shaft in wood. Given more ease in manufacturing, Brewster expanded his original six clubs to nine ("driver, brassie, cleek, baffie, mashie, pitcher, mashie-niblic, niblic, and putter"). Even with these changes, Brewster was not satisfied. He felt he could improve his club and make it more acceptable to the market place.

In 1907 Brewster received yet another British patent, (No. 2,991) dated February 6. In this patent, which covered the club shown, he again kept the same clubhead shape, but sought to incorporate a:

protecting nosing of suitable metal of a harder nature than said alloy body part, so as the better to protect the clubhead from injury.

Brewster specified forming the "nose" or entire face of the head from gunmetal or mild steel.

During the course of producing his crosshead clubs, Brewster also received two U.S. patents. His U.S. patent (No. 581,331) dated April 27, 1897, is basically the same as his 1897 British patent. His second U.S. patent, (No. 894,809) dated August 4, 1908, covered his idea of incorporating wood blocks into heads made from an aluminium alloy, "preferably aluminium-copper, or aluminium-zinc."

Brewster's Simplex clubs, whether metal or wooden heads, are not readily available. Because they were never accepted or produced in quantity *and* because they are loaded with character, Simplex clubs are considered prize collectibles.

Brewster's only other patent was a British patent (No. 24,834) dated November 14, 1903, that covered irons made with a large flange on the sole. The flange, according to the patent, could be turned up at the very back to avoid catching on the ground during the golfer's backswing. Brewster produced his "Sole-plate irons," as they were termed, at the end of 1904 and into 1905. They were available from the Simplex Golf Association in the following models: cleek, driving mashie, mashie iron, mashie, mashie niblick, and putter. Few examples are known.

The passing of Francis Brewster was reported in the October 2, 1908 issue of *Golf Illustrated*:

Mr. Brewster was a well-known figure on many links, and was an enthusiastic golfer all his life. He was the founder of the Royal Jersey Golf Club, and one of the originators of the Meyrick Park Golf Club at Bournemouth, and an old member of Royal Wimbledon and other clubs. . . . Personally, Mr. Brewster was of a genial and kindly disposition, and always ready to promote and encourage the best interests of sport. One of the old school of golfers, playing the game in the spirit of its best traditions, Mr. Brewster will be greatly missed (26).

After Brewster's death, his Simplex clubs found one dedicated golfer who liked to play with them and did so effectively— only to have them ruled illegal!

Mr. R.H.M. Singer, who won the September Medal of the St. Andrews Thistle Golf Club, has been disqualified by the Club Committee on account of his having used, during the competition, a set of Simplex clubs—the committee holding that such clubs are "barred," in accordance with the recent decision of the Rules of Golf Committee, in regard to the form and make of golf clubs (Golf Illustrated, 28 Oct. 1910: 106).

UNKNOWN MAKER
CROSSHEAD PUTTER

Brewster's crosshead clubs are found in only a few collections. Crosshead clubs made by any *other* maker, however, are very rare indeed! The putter shown is the only one of its type currently known.

The previous description of Brewster's Simplex clubs briefly discussed the principle of crosshead clubs. For purposes of clarity, the basic characteristics of a crosshead club are: (1) The greatest length of the head extends back, directly behind the ball. (2) The shaft enters the top of the head where it intersects an imaginary line extending straight back behind the ball. (3) The golfer, when using the club, will address the ball in the traditional fashion (both feet on the same side of the ball).

If the first condition is not met but the other two are, the club is simply center-shafted. If the second condition is not met but the other two are, the club is an end-shafted mallet head, such as Dwight's directional wood. If the third condition is not met but the first two are, the club is a croquet-style or pendulum-type putter.

The crosshead putter pictured is unmarked, which is not uncommon. When making something out of the ordinary or trying out a new idea, clubmakers often did not bother to mark their work.

The lack of a maker's mark on this club does not identify it as "homemade," though homemade clubs do exist and usually carry little value (also, they are easily "invented" today).

An examination of this club reveals evidence of a talented clubmaker. The lines of the head are clean, and the workmanship is of the highest quality. Two large screws in the back of the thick brass backweight extend completely through the head and are fastened to a metal face. The metal face consists of two pieces of steel. The full-length piece sits at a right angle to the ground; the outer piece, fastened to the full length piece, provides a small degree of loft. Loft is a common trait in older putters.

JAMES MUNRO
"PENDULUM PUTTER," CROQUET STYLE

James Iverach Munro, of Edinburgh, Scotland, received a British patent (No. 14,812) dated July 4, 1896, that covered the croquet-style putter illustrated. The first croquet-style club to be patented, Munro's putter was made by the Scottish Golf Club Manufacturing Company in Edinburgh. The back of the brass head is marked "Patent Pendulum Putter" inside an oval along with "Pat. No 14812" and "S.G.C.M. Coy, Ltd \ Edinburgh." The face has crisscross scoring.

According to Munro's patent, the traditional method of putting (standing next to the ball) offered only two styles and both were bad:

In one style the clubhead leaves the line of the putt whenever it is drawn back to make the stroke, thus making it uncertain that it will return to the exact line and not be "pulled" or "heeled".... In the other style an endeavour is made to keep the club head in the line of [the] putt as the head is drawn back to make the stoke; but this endeavour involves an excessively complex motion of the wrists, elbows and shoulders which ... again introduces an element of uncertainty into the stroke.

Munro calculated that his putter would simplify the stroke and keep the blade on line, square to the target at all times, without any complex wrist motion:

The motion of the putter, when properly played is consequently as near as possible like that of an ordinary pendulum and is effected by an easy wrist movement.

To accomplish this, "the putter is swung like a pendulum between the legs." Also, Munro's putter has a slightly curved sole, so it can be used on:

rough greens or on slopes where the roughness or inclination of the ground might catch the end of the putter and spoil the stoke.

Munro's patent also asserts that his croquet-style putter would negotiate "stymies" more effectively than would an ordinary putter:

It is better adapted for playing "stymies" than an ordinary putter as a spin can be put upon the ball with equal ease from either side by striking slightly across instead of on the line of putt thus causing the ball to travel in a curved path to avoid the obstruction.

Munro's patent also includes the possibility of making his putter from wood with the shaft passing directly through the head.

Although Munro was the first to patent a croquet-style putter, he was not the first to create such a putter. In 1890 Captain Hamilton, a member of the Royal Isle of Wight Golf Club, developed a croquet-style mallet putter also called "The Pendulum Putter" (see p. 476; see also p. 211 for other earlier croquet-style putters).

Munro's pendulum putter is a fine collectible due to its historical position as the first croquet-style club to receive a patent. Furthermore, it has excellent character.

Many clubmaking firms contemporary with the Scottish Golf Club Manufacturing Company had been using machinery along with skilled craftsman for some time, but the S.G.C.M.Co. was a pioneer in "making clubs of all kinds entirely by machinery" (*Golf*, 7 June 1895: 241). They went beyond using machines merely to make rough "blocked out" clubheads and shafts like those produced by such firms as Charles Spinks, of Leith, who first sold to the trade in 1887 (*Golfing*, 12 July 1895: 28; see Spinks p. 135).

Registered in early March of 1894 as a joint-stock company, the S.G.C.M.Co. initially purchased "two machines for the manufacture of golf club heads, & c." (*Golf*, 9 Mar. 1894: 407). The only hand work in their clubs was setting the shaft flex:

The only skilled labor required in all the operations is in the tapering of the shaft to bring out the correct balances and spring of each club (The Golfer, 3 Nov. 1894: 184).

Clubs created entirely by mechanized means were controversial. Many golfers felt that a mechanically made club lacked the quality and feel inherent in handmade clubs. Other golfers believed that the precision offered by machinery could not be duplicated by hand nor could any difference be noted in the finished product except for the price—machine made clubs were less expensive.

"Machine made" refers to drop forging instead of hand forging irons and to lathing woods to shape instead of working a piece of wood to completion by hand.

William Gibson, the famous cleek maker from Kinghorn, Scotland, explains the process of hand forging:

[In hand forging, the smith begins with a bar of iron and] inserts it in his fire, heating it about 3 inches to a nice soft white heat. The socket part is then beaten out thin as ever practicable to admit of welding with safety. It is then turned round and welded on a mandrel and cress, and I may here say this welding is the most difficult and delicate in the whole operation, as if not properly done it seals the doom of the head . . . . The least flaw will show up when polished bright, with the result that the head has to be cast aside . . . . After the socket is welded up as sound as a bell, it is beaten round to the angle; the bar is again heated and the head shaped out with repeated blows of the hand hammer. The maker when fashioning a head . . . mashie, niblick, putter, or whatnot, has nothing to guide him but his eye. Hence he must be trained in the art before he can with success make a perfect model of a head. After being roughly fashioned on the bar, it is then cut off, grasped with a pair of tongs, then the loft, proper shape, lie, are accomplished; but be it noted that all these several operations are done with repeated blows, running well into 400, of the hand hammer . . . . After the head leaves the smithy it is taken to the grinding and polishing shops and there ground, buffed, stamped, and finally polished up . . . (Golfing, 13 May 1909, 14-15).

After noting that hand forging required a great deal of time and work, Gibson continues by explaining the relative simplicity of drop forging:

First a suitable model is obtained, then the shape of the model is cut out on a die or huge steel block. The socket part is then fashioned solid, then the iron to make the head is put into the die, and with heavy pressure pressed into shape; the fins or superfluous metal is then cut off . . . . The socket is then bored or drilled out for the shaft, and then ground, buffed, and finished in the usual way.

A myriad of irons are marked "Warranted Hand Forged." This phrase sounds good, but it came to mean exactly the opposite of what it said. The stamp "Warranted Hand Forged" quickly found its way onto large numbers of drop-forged clubs. As advertising became more important, so did producing the greatest number of clubs in the least amount of time. Therefore, by the early 1900s most cleekmakers were drop forging their iron heads. Only the head's final shape and weight were finished by hand. Marking an iron "Warranted Hand Forged" gave the impression of quality.

What the Warranted Hand Forged designation usually identifies is an iron head that is not *entirely* machine made. The *truly* hand forged clubs were not usually marked Warranted Hand Forged. For the most part, hand forged irons did not include any advertising on their heads beyond the maker's name and perhaps a trademark and/or the name of the seller.

To the collector, the distinction between hand forged and drop forged irons is not a big one, in and of itself. Certainly the early irons from the feather ball era are highly collectible, and they were obviously hand forged. However, a standard smooth face iron hand forged in the early 1890s by Gibson, Nicoll, Stewart, or some other maker does not attract wide attention. It's just one of the countless remaining clubs that were made in the same manner, in the same style, and at the same time. On the other hand, to assume that a Pearson slot face iron is worth very little because it, too, is hand forged is to ignore its superb creativity and inherent rarity—and be wrong by thousands of dollars.

In the making of machine made woods, a wood cutting lathe could quickly turn out large numbers of duplicate heads. What a craftsman used to spend hours fashioning by hand could be created in a matter of minutes by machinery. Despite the introduction of wood lathes, many clubmakers continued to produce wood heads by hand, some until the late 1920s (Sayers 1994: 129). The last of these traditional clubmakers used machines only to generate roughed-out heads which they then finished by hand.

Despite initial consumer resistance, mechanization brought with it some advantages—the speed with which a club could be made being the most obvious. Another benefit, perhaps not as well understood or appreciated, was that drop forging required better quality metal than did hand forging:

In former years the makers were obliged to form the sockets by welding the material, and used iron because it was easier to weld and work than steel. . . . In hand-forging poor material could be used, but the nature of the drop-forging process forbids anything but good material (Golf Illustrated, 30 Mar. 1900: 280).

Some golfers believed that making a wooden clubhead on a lathe produced a better product. The head could be accurately formed with the grain running in the proper direction, and the "severe test of machining" would break any poor quality heads, which could otherwise be "worked up by hand labour" (The Golfer, 24 Nov. 1894: 236).

Amidst their optimism about mechanization, the Scottish Golf Club Manufacturing Company was offered for sale in mid-1898 (Golf, 15 July 1898: 359). Unable to locate a buyer, they were forced to sell off their assets by year's end. The main reason offered for the failure of this limited liability company was "that most Golf club-makers have a personnel, while the Company has not." Another possibility was that the S.G.C.M.Co. "never succeeded in establishing a connection in the trade" (Golf, 23 Dec. 1898: 312).

A putter very similar to Munro's Pendulum putter, in both name and style, was devised by Robert Brand:

The "pendulum putter" just patented by Mr. Brand, of the North British Rubber Company, is a revolution in form, and necessitates a revolution in practice. The golfer must hold the new tool between his legs and putt with the ball in line with his eye and the hole (Golfing, 5 Aug. 1896: 5).

Because no golf club patent was issued in 1896 to anyone named Brand, and this review was printed one month after Munro sought his patent for a croquet-style putter with the identical name, it may be that Brand was somehow involved with Munro. (For more on Brand, see page 300.)

WILLIAM SEAR
"TORPEDO"
CROQUET-STYLE PUTTER

UNKNOWN MAKERS
CROQUET-STYLE PUTTERS

The unmarked putter pictured above left is eye-catching and well made. The wooden head is fashioned in two levels, the back of the head being lower than the front. It has a full brass soleplate. Acquired in Scotland, this putter was apparently made in the U.K.

The unmarked club pictured above center has a slight variation in its otherwise straight forward croquet design: The underside of its heel is gently rounded so that the club can be used right-handed if desired.

This feature allowed the golfer to address the ball in standard fashion on long putts and croquet style on short putts.

Despite its unconventional design, this club is well made. A long lead backweight is inlaid in the head. The sole, inlaid with a horn slip along the leading edge, is covered with a brass soleplate.

William Sear, of Harlesden Gardens, Harlesden (near London), received a British design registration (No. 510,706) dated August 31, 1907, that covered the putter pictured directly above. This putter is marked "Torpedo Putter \ Rd No. 510706" on the top of its aluminum head and "9.12" on its sole. The "9.12" refers to the clubhead weight: 9 ounces, 12 drams.

As presented in Sear's registered design, an alignment groove runs across the entire top of this head, and the back of the sole angles up to clear the ground on the golfer's takeaway and follow-through.

Croquet-style clubs usually date before 1910. In 1909 the R&A Rules Committee issued Decision No. 47 which mandated, "A small croquet mallet is not a golf club and is inadmissible." This was followed by Decision No. 71 which stated that "it is not allowable to use the vertical croquet stroke as a method of putting" (see p. 194-195).

UNKNOWN MAKER
CROQUET-STYLE PUTTER

The croquet-style putter pictured directly above appears older than the 1896 example made by James Munro and discussed on page 208. The rectangular iron head is made without any attempt to be fashionable. There are no beveled edges or rounded corners and, instead of a traditional hosel, a thin piece of iron attached to the back of the blade on both sides of the shaft wraps over the shaft to hold it in place. Compare the crude characteristics of this putter with the refined stylistic traits of both Munro's putter and Harrison's putter, on pages 208 and 212, respectively.

In spite of its primitive design, this putter reflects fine craftsmanship. A thin piece of wood is wedged into the tip of the shaft to tighten the fit between the shaft and head. This club, which may date to the 1880s, also sports a beautiful sheepskin grip.

UNKNOWN MAKER
CROQUET-STYLE PUTTER

The circa 1890s croquet-style putter pictured above right is also handmade. The edges of the sole and sides of the face are bevelled, as is the very top of the head, but the edges along both curved sections of the head are not. Furthermore, marks left when cutting each curved section to shape remain, possibly the evidence of a clubmaker simply trying out an idea without completely finishing the club. This club is masterfully shafted and pinned through the top of the face.

Both of these unmarked iron putters are *well made* despite appearing somewhat crude. Consequently, they each project the aura of a fine piece of folk art. Very few of these clubs, if any more, were made.

G.H. HARRISON
CROQUET-STYLE PUTTER

The gunmetal blade croquet-style putter pictured, one of two known to the author, was developed by G.H. Harrison, C.E., of the Royal Isle of Wight Golf Club. Loaded with character, this turn-of-the-century putter is stylish and visually dynamic in two respects.

First, the solid gunmetal head is designed with strong lines and definitive, symmetrical angles. Both sides of the blade are usable. Second, the shaft and the extraordinary eight-sided grip are made from the same solid piece of wood.

Harrison also invented another gunmetal blade putter and called it the "Harrison Patent Putter." It was end-shafted, usable either right- or left-handed, and had an identical shaft and eight-sided wood grip.

A brief review published in 1899 observed that the grip on the Harrison Patent Putter was more secure than leather for the golfer to hold on to:

In the first place it has no leather grip, the shaft being tapered to the requisite thickness in an octahedral form suggestive of a lawn tennis racquet. Sentiment and tradition apart, this strikes us as giving a surer grip of the club than the ordinary circular leather-covered handle (Golf Illustrated, 13 Oct. 1899: 18).

This review of "Harrison's Patent Putter" also told of a grooved black line cut into the top of the blade to reduce "disconcerting glitter" and a toe rounded off to reduce the possibility of "fouling" when "drawing it back or in bringing it forward." F.H. Ayres was the sole manufacturer of Harrison's Patent Putter.

Harrison's Patent Putter never received its final patent approval. It is seldom seen, and its head, which is basically conventional in shape, is not as striking as the croquet-style putter shown.

From 1896 to the end of 1908 eleven croquet-style golf clubs received either British or American patents. A few other croquet-style clubs lacking patents were also made during that time. After the R&A rulings against croquet-style putters in 1909 and 1910, only one more patent for a croquet-style putter was granted during the wood shaft era: Walter Righter's U.S. patent (No. 1,140,399) dated May 25, 1915.

It is helpful to know a little about the history of croquet in order to understand the inspiration for croquet-style golf clubs. By 1852 croquet had reached England from Ireland where it had been played for twenty years. Croquet is a descendent of "Paille Maille" (also known as "Pell Mell" or "Pall Mall"), a French game that dates back to the fourteenth century (Charlton 1988, 13-18).

Another reference to using a club and a ball croquet style is found in Steven van Hengel's book *Early Golf*. A few 17th century Delft tiles show a person playing Colf, a Dutch game similar to golf. The palyer is shown making a stroke in croquet fashion (1982, 41).

UNKNOWN MAKER
CROQUET-STYLE PUTTER

Marked "putter" on its flat sole, the club pictured appears to be either an overly upright left-handed putter or a backwards putter (the hosel is on the *far* end of the head and the blade extends toward the golfer). However, this club is neither. It is an ingenious croquet-style putter designed for use with the golfer straddling the line of the putt.

Located at the far end of the blade, the hosel extends upwards while angling back over the blade. Because the angle of the hosel is so slight, the top of the shaft is positioned directly above the opposite end of the blade, with the top of the shaft barely intersecting an imaginary line extending straight up from the toe. This intentional relationship between the toe and the shaft is easily demonstrated by placing the toe of this putter square against a wall: the top of the shaft will just touch the wall.

Bending the hosel on a left-handed putter, to make it into an unusual croquet-style putter similar to this one, would not be difficult to do. However, many of this club's features make it clear that it was originally made croquet style.

First, note the lines running up each side of the scoring dots on the face. These lines, running parallel to the hosel/shaft, are tilted slightly towards the toe. Lines running in this direction on a traditional putter are unheard of.

Second, this kind of square toe does not occur on ordinary blade putters. A standard putter has a rounded toe just like any regular iron. The original finish on the toe verifies that this blade was not cut or altered.

Third, the fact that the toe was squared so that an imaginary line continuing up from the toe would intersect the top of the shaft demonstrates that this club received thought and planning beyond that given to an ordinary putter.

Fourth, this club is perfectly balanced. When the flat sole of this putter is set on a hard, level surface, the club will stand in an upright position without any other support!

An interesting study in engineering, this putter is designed to function croquet style but without the center-shafted design found in all other croquet-style putters. This design was probably tried in an unsuccessful effort to circumvent the R&A rules that outlawed center-shafted putters beginning in 1910 (see p. 195).

The pro.'s shop is worked on these lines. You buy an iron head for 1s. 4d., a shaft for 8d., you expend four hour's labor on them, add a 3d. grip, throw in the twine, tingle-tacks, glue and wax, and sell it for 4s. 6d., after you have had it in stock for six months, if you are very lucky.—E.N.D. in the Sporting Life (Golfing, 8 July 1914: 31).

CENTER-SHAFTED CLUBS

MONEL METAL PRODUCTS
"RECONY"
BACKWARDS PUTTER

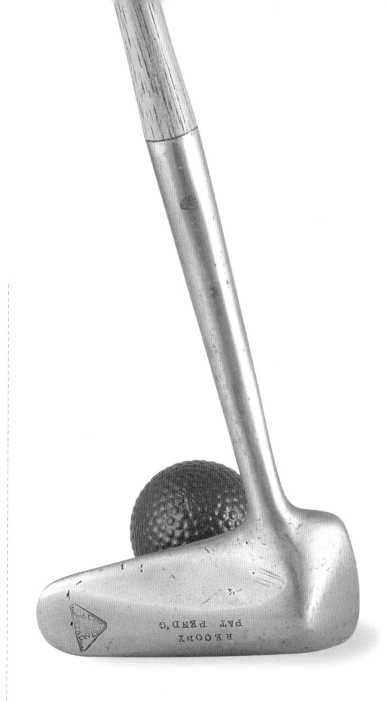

This smooth face putter is one of only a few known wood shaft "backwards" putters, so termed because the entire head, instead of extending out from the hosel and away from the golfer, extends back underneath the hosel and *towards* the golfer. To help balance this putter, the thickest part of the blade is halfway up its backside directly in line with the hosel. This area appears as a mound of sorts.

The back of this blade is stamped "Recony \ Pat Pend'g" along with the Monel Metal trademark "INCO" within a small triangle. "INCO" identifies The International Nickel Company, of Bayonne, New Jersey, the company that made the actual metal.

The Bayonne Casting Company introduced Monel Metal to the golf club market in 1912. Before then, Monel Metal was used in constructing military vessels:

The Bayonne Castings Co. of Bayonne, N.J., has introduced a golf club of an entirely new metal for golf clubs, called "Monel Metal," which is of decided advantage to the player. It is much lighter than steel, but just as hard . . . . Monel Metal is by no means a new article, for the Bayonne Castings Co. has for some time been using it for the U.S. Navy for the Florida and North Dakota; the torpedo boats Walker, Sterrett, Perkins, Roe, Terry, and Fanning (Golf [ny], Mar. 1912: 184).

This same notice reports the Bayonne Company's intention to wholesale their heads to club professionals:

The Bayonne Castings Co. at the present time proposes to sell these clubs exclusively to club professionals, furnishing them the heads of monel metal and have them make the clubs.

Spalding's catalogs for 1912, 1913, and 1914 offer irons made of Monel Metal. During the ensuing years, Monel Metal clubs were available directly from the Monel Metal Products Corporation, of Bayonne, New Jersey, (the "INCO" triangle trademark present on each club). Golfers could send for a complete catalog from the Monel Metal Products golf department as advertised in the October 1919 issue of *Golfers Magazine* (4).

By 1921 the Burke Golf Company was promoting themselves as the sole distributor of Monel Metal golf clubs made by the International Nickel Company, Bayonne, New Jersey. By 1927, Burke no longer offered Monel Metal clubs. At that time they were offering stainless steel irons. Monel Metal itself is a noncorrosive mixture of metals consisting of 67% nickel, 28% copper, 5% other metals (Burke 1922, 28). It does not rust, is easily cleaned, and will always remain bright though not highly reflective. Spalding's advertisements likened the finish of Monel Metal to that of the ordinary "five-cent piece" then in use. Most Monel Metal clubs will not hold a magnet.

Above, an original 1911 "Why Not" bramble pattern ball, made by Henley's Telegraph Works Company, London, demonstrates the correct position of the putter head when addressing the ball. Although some red balls were painted by their owners, this particular ball (which also came in white) was originally produced in this color. Red golf balls were used when light snow, frost, or daisies covered the ground.

CHARLES REDMAN
"FOLLOW THRU"
BACKWARDS PUTTER

TOM STEWART
BACKWARDS PUTTER

On July 7, 1924, Charles H. Redman, of East Orange, New Jersey, applied for a U.S. patent to cover the backwards putter pictured below. He waited almost three years, until June 7, 1927, before his patent (No. 1,631,504) was granted.

According to his patent, Redman calculated that attaching the shaft to the far end of the head would automatically line up the face with the line of play:

The center of gravity of the head and shaft is so arranged that when held horizontally or in an inclined position, the head will automatically assume a playing position in which the striking face is substantially squared or in perpendicular relationship with the line of play.

Redman also felt that the shaft, which runs parallel with the face, would act as an alignment aid:

[The head] is provided with a striking face extending substantially the entire length of the head in a vertical plane substantially parallel with the axis of said shaft, so that in playing the staff extends between the eyes of the player and said head, and may be utilized as an elongated sighting element.

Despite his technically impressive patent language, Redman's backwards putter was not accepted by the market.

Redman's backwards putter pictured is marked "W.N. Malcolm \ Special" across the center of the sole and "Capt. Pringle" towards the toe of the sole. Malcolm was probably the professional who sold this club to Pringle, the owner. The back of the head reads "Pat. Apl'd For," and the face is stamped "Follow Thru" inside an oval.

Besides Redman's, the only other patent for a backwards putter was the first one ever granted for such: Charles W. Dayton's U.S. patent (No. 1,436,579) dated November 21, 1922. By providing a face on both the front and back of a mallet head along with a comparatively small face on the end of the head, at the base of the hosel, Dayton's putter was usable left-handed, right-handed, and croquet style. It is not known if Dayton ever produced his club.

Tom Stewart, the famous St. Andrews cleekmaker, also made at least two wood shaft backwards putters: the example pictured above and an identical example that belongs to the USGA. The back of both Stewart backwards putters is marked "Special \ Hand Forged \ Made In Scotland \ Willie Kidd \ Putter" along with "T.S. St A. Reg.

Trademark" and Stewart's "pipe" cleekmark.

Dating from the late 1920s or early 1930s, Stewart's backwards putter was apparently made expressly for William "Willie" Kidd Sr. and modeled after a prototype created by Kidd, the professional at the Interlachen Country Club, in Edina, Minnesota, from 1920 to 1957. When discussing and providing the author with the above information, William "Bill" Kidd Jr. noted that his father would travel to Scotland every two or three years, purchase whatever clubheads he desired from Stewart, and then shaft and sell these clubs to the members at Interlachen upon his return.

A golf club in the West, which includes a bishop and a dozen ministers in its membership, is said to possess a larger amount of profane silence than any other club in America.

(*Golfing*, 31 Oct. 1931: 10)

Face Treatments

This chapter examines those clubs whose faces are not solid, level, or flat. Although the structural treatment given to the face often affected the head's profile, this chapter does not deal with entire head shapes as such. Also, it does not deal with inserts or cosmetic face designs.

The standard face was solid, level, and flat. Usually it was either left smooth or marked with thin lines, small dots, or a combination of both. These traditional lines and dots, known as "scoring," took many forms: straight horizontal lines, crisscross lines, randomly punched dots, dots and lines, dashes (very short lines), and dashes and dots, etc. Most scoring designs are primarily cosmetic features and do not deal with the functional aspects of a golf club, despite some advertising claims of an ability to give greater grip or spin to the ball.

Backspin irons, on the other hand, usually had deep grooves or wide slots that *did* affect the flight of the ball. This chapter includes backspin irons, but it does not depict any common examples—where the deep grooves or wide slots go straight across the face. (A common backspin iron head is shown on page 522.) Such straight line backspin irons were mass produced in the United States and Great Britain for many years after 1913 (see p. 236). Similar from one to the next, straight line backspin irons make nice entry level collectibles.

Backspin irons aside, the question of *when* irons were first marked with scoring is important.

In 1892, referring to Charles Barter's British patent (No. 6,993) dated April 23, 1891, *Golf* discussed a new patent that covered scoring lines on an iron:

The Blockley Electric Lighting and Manufacturing Company, Limited, Worcestershire, have brought out a new patent in the shape of a lofting iron. The improvement consists in grooving with horizontal lines the blade of the iron, so as to give "grip" to the ball when played. The idea, of course, is not an absolutely new one, for we remember to have seen many years ago, at North Berwick, the veteran, Mr. J.R. Whitecross, with a similar iron, though in his case the iron was notched with horizontal lines as well as with perpendicular lines, after the model of the nicking of the golf ball itself (8 Jan.: 263).

Two weeks later, *Golf* printed a letter to the editor that continued the discussion about scoring lines. The writer states that it was he who grooved the face of Mr. Whitecross's iron and that there was nothing new about the grooved lofting iron described two weeks earlier:

I observe in your issue of the 8th inst. a patent has been taken out for a new lofting-iron. I can assure you, however, that there is nothing new about it, as it is now more than twenty years ago since I grooved the face of Mr. Whitcross's [sic] iron, and others in addition to it. The only difference is this—that while the new one is cut in rectilinear lines, mine were cut diagonally and inversely, the lines being a little rougher in the pitch than a bastard-cut file. Still the idea is the same, and therefore not new. I found it of little use, and as the dirt adhered to the grooves and discoloured the balls quickly, the irons never were popular. The ball being deeply grooved, there is no need for lines on the iron also (302).

According to James K. Robertson, Tom Kidd was "the first man to 'rib' an iron club to impart stop and it won him the 1873 'Open' " (1967, 77).

In 1893 it was reported that Professor Tait had undertaken a study of grooved clubs as they affect the flight and carry of the ball:

[P.G. Tait] writes to us from St. Andrews to say that he has added more than 30 per cent. to the carry of a cleek by merely grooving the face. The grooves are ruled parallel to the lower side of the club, and the teeth thus formed are such as to bite downwards.... This idea can be applied practically to any driver by screwing on its face a thin, properly-grooved steel plate (Golf, 11 Aug. 1893: 371).

Additional comments on Professor Tait's grooved clubs indicate that grooves provide more accuracy than distance:

Golfers are a somewhat sceptical race, but probably more than one has tried Professor Tait's "grooved" clubs in some form or other. In our experience the result as regards extreme length of carry has been somewhat disappointing, though there seems to be a gain in average length of carry, and straightness of drive...Grooved clubs may be more useful for straight than for long driving. Those who have the interests of the game sufficiently at heart to make patiently the necessary trials will no doubt soon tell us further about this. Others will probably be content with the report of a golfer who borrowed a grooved cleek the other day, but soon brought it back to the club-house with the remark that "he couldn't see that the ball made any loop in the air!" (Golf, 3 Nov. 1893: 116).

These references demonstrate that a few isolated irons with scored faces were tried as far back as the 1870s before being introduced commercially in the early 1890s. The idea of putting scoring lines on irons did not blossom during the 1890s, but clearly the seed was planted. It was not long before scoring on irons—lines, dots, or dashes—became commonplace.

In an interview published in 1900, Harry Vardon, then a three time British Open champion, reports that his own set of clubs contained "one lofter and a niblick [which have] corrugated faces." Vardon speaks of these clubs as follows:

"I use the lofter when I have to, and then I think the roughened face helps to hold the ball. That's why, too, that I have a corrugated face on the niblick" (Golf Illustrated, 2 Mar.: 196).

The "corrugated faces" used by Vardon were simple lined or grooved faces, not deep-groove backspin irons. Deep-groove irons did not exist until the mid-1910s.

When the twentieth century began, scoring on iron faces (both dots and lines) had a good foothold in the market. As face scoring became a widely accepted feature, various makers continued to offer smooth face irons along with scored irons.

W.G. ROY
"PRESIDENT" WATER IRON

The 'President' is a niblick with a hole in it, which might be a very good niblick if it were not a president. It is called a president because the hole makes it clear-headed (Simpson 1887, 23).

The "President" iron, pictured on this and the facing page, was the first club ever designed to help a golfer deal with the quandary of a ball in water, floating or otherwise. Playing from water is hardly ever considered by golfers today, but it was once a very real part of the game.

In 1875, just prior to the introduction of the President iron, twenty rules governed "The Game of Golf As It Is Played By The Royal & Ancient Golf Club of St. Andrews" (Clark 1875, 274-279). According to these rules, only four exceptions allowed the golfer to move his or her ball without being penalized: mud, stymies, split balls, and laundry!

[1] A ball stuck fast in wet ground or sand may be taken out and replaced loosely in the hole it has made (275).

[2] [When two] balls lie within six inches of each other, the ball nearest the hole must be lifted till the other is played, and then placed as nearly as possible in its original position (276).

[3] If a ball shall split into two or more pieces, a fresh ball shall be put down where the largest portion of the ball lies. And if a ball is cracked the player may change it on intimating his intention of doing so to his opponent (279).

[4] When a ball lies within a club length of a washing-tub, the tub may be removed, and when on clothes the ball may be lifted and dropped behind them (275).

These rules do not contain any "free drop" provisions for *casual water*. To the early golfer trying to avoid penalty strokes, playing from water, casual or otherwise, was part of life. Consequently, ballmakers advertised and sold gutta percha golf balls that would *float*.

A series of three photographs in the June 16, 1899 issue of *Golf Illustrated* provide a fascinating pictorial account of Freddie Tait playing his floating golf ball from the middle of a green-side bunker full of casual water during the final match of the 1899 British Amateur (won on the 37th hole by Tait's opponent, John Ball Jr.). The account accompanying these photos reads in part:

The scene is the bunker at the Alps hole, the 17th. The bunker was full of water and both Mr. Ball and Mr. Tait found it with their second shots—Mr. Tait's ball lying in the middle of the water and Mr. Ball's on sand just on the edge. With great heroism Mr. Tait waded in over his boots and successfully played the floating ball on to the putting green. Mr. Ball followed suit with an equally brilliant shot, he also having to stand in the water to play it (8).

The President iron pictured is more than a water iron. It represents one of the earliest original ideas in the world of golf clubs, an idea born of a mind thinking beyond the realms of tradition and simple evolution. The bold design of this club—a gaping hole through the middle of the face—gives it a dramatic and stunning appearance. Nevertheless, it was an ineffective and unpopular club.

The President iron, or "ring mashie" as it is sometimes called, was introduced in 1879:

A New Golfing Implement . . . —A new club, or rather an important improvement on an old one, has been produced by a zealous member of the Royal Musselburgh Golf Club, Mr. W.G. Roy. The well-known iron "niblick" has always presented difficulties, especially in the hands of others than the most experienced players, and . . . frequently fails in removing a ball from the hazard. Mr. Roy's object has been to render it a sure and easy instrument even in the hands of the uninitiated, and he has submitted his improvement to . . . Tom Morris, who reports that it is quite a success—that it . . . allow(s) sand, mud, or water to pass through the opening in the head. The first club of its kind has just been made by Tom Morris, and has been presented to the Lord Justice-General, ex-Captain of the Royal and Ancient Golf Club . . . . The new weapon will be distinguished by the name of the "President." . . . The "President" . . . resembles the "niblick" in having an iron head, the

main improvement being that the iron is bored in such a way as to allow sand or mud to pass through a hole at the back, instead of being caught as formerly along with the ball (*Fifeshire Journal*, 31 July 1879: 6).

According to Garden Smith, the President iron disappeared shortly after its introduction:

How many golfers have seen a "President," or even know what it is? If we remember rightly the "President" appeared about twenty-three years ago. . . . It came, we think, from Musselburgh, and it was called after Lord President Inglis, a member of the Honorable Company, and an ardent golfer of the old school. The actual inventor, if we remember rightly was Mr. J.H.A. MacDonald, now Lord Kinsburgh [Smith's recollection was incorrect]. The club was simply an iron niblick with all the centre bored out so that only a thick ring of metal was left. It was supposed to be of great efficacy in water or sand, as it allowed the obstructing element to pass through it, and the ball received the full force of the blow. As a matter of fact it was no good. It hadn't the necessary balance or weight, and as there were practically four hitting surfaces, it was impossible to be sure that the ball had not been hit more than once, or "pushed, scraped, or spooned," within the meaning of the act. The "President" soon disappeared (*Golf* [ny], Apr. 1902: 242).

W.T. Linskill also ascribed the rejection of this club to its dreaded ability to hit the ball more than once during a stroke:

The President iron pictured was forged by James Anderson of Anstruther, Scotland (see p. 110). As shown on the previous page, "Anderson - Anstruther" inside a small circle is stamped low on the back of the blade, towards the toe. The stamp was placed at this location to accommodate the large hole through the face. The middle of the blade back is the traditional location of the maker's mark.

The author has seen seven genuine President irons. Anderson's cleekmark is clearly identifiable on four of the seven. A single example is marked with Gibson's "star" cleekmark. This club, also marked "T. Aitken \ Yarmouth," was made in the late 1890s (most likely at the request of a customer) and copied Anderson's iron in most respects. The hole is shaped the same; the hosel is quite substantial; and the blade is much thicker than an ordinary late 1870s iron. Unlike the Anderson examples, the Gibson example has a dull blade crease.

Today, the President iron stands as one of the most desirable clubs in the club collecting world. As a direct result of its strong visual characteristics and singular nature, the President

iron was reproduced on various occasions in modern times, often complete with a rustic finish. But not all of them were sold as replicas. Unfortunately, a few fake President irons were made with the intention of committing fraud—fooling unknowing collectors. Even replicas, after changing hands a few times, are occasionally represented as the real thing (see p. 552).

The President iron was one of the first irons ever developed that was not embraced by the marketplace. Prior to 1879, the square toe iron, the round toe iron, the light iron, the heavy iron, the track iron, the lofter, and the cleek were accepted as worthwhile clubs in their day. Each one endured for many years. The President iron, on the other hand, was rejected and disappeared soon after its introduction, a fact which explains its rarity.

Although the President was quickly impeached, the water iron resurfaced in the early 1890s when Peter Paxton devised such a club:

Paxton's club was not described, but what the author believes to be an example of his water iron sold at Christie's July 1992 golf auction. It was made and marked on the *hosel* by Willie Wilson, a well-known supplier of iron heads to Paxton. The blade consisted only of its outline and two evenly spaced horizontal "braces" extending heel to toe (the area above and below each brace was an open slot through the head). Before it closed in 1993, the P.G.A. World Golf Hall of Fame, in Pinehurst, North Carolina, had an example on display.

In 1899 the R&A began allowing free drops for balls lying in casual water through the green. In 1900 the USGA followed suit. Consequently, the need for a water iron after 1900 was reduced but not entirely removed. There was still no relief from casual water in a bunker or other hazard, and golfers still found their way into ditches, streams, lakes, etc.

ROBERT P. HIGGS

"DELIVERER" RAKE IRON

In addition to dealing with water, a few irons were developed to function in sand and high grass. Like water irons, these "rake" irons are extremely collectible. The Higgs Deliverer pictured is a prime example.

Designed by Robert Percival Higgs and marketed by the same Willie Aveston who had the honor of giving H.R.H. Princess Victoria several golf lessons, the Deliverer was reviewed in *Golf Illustrated*:

Willie Aveston, the well-known professional at Cromer, has brought out a special form of niblick, or mashie, which bears the excellent name of "Higgs' Deliverer." The club is made in all respects like an ordinary heavy niblick or mashie, except that half way up its face it is cut into the shape of a very wide toothed comb with the teeth downward. The advantage of the club is that sand, long grass, water, or other obstructions will to some extent pass through the face of the club when a stroke is made, thus increasing the force and accuracy of the blow.

We have tried the "Deliverer" and find that it fulfils its purpose admirably, and the teeth are so wide and flat that there is no danger of the ball being struck askew. The club is beautifully balanced and finished, and is certainly one that golfers will find of the greatest use on courses where there is a "rough." The "Deliverer," which has already met with the approval of Harry Vardon and Braid, can be had either in the niblick or mashie shape (27 Jan. 1905: 95).

Harry Vardon, J.H. Taylor, James Braid, and Aveston commented on the Higgs Deliverer as follows:

James Braid's opinion of Higg's [sic] "Deliverer" is as follows: "I have been trying the niblick. There is no doubt the idea is a good one, as it is much easier to cut through the sand with than the solid blade. I also find it a very good club for getting out of heather."

Harry Vardon says, "I have given the club a trial, and I think it is a fair good club for long grass and sand, as it takes the ball quite easily out of that sort of lie...."

J.H. Taylor writes that "the idea is most certainly a good one."

Willie Aveston, in his claims for the clubs, says: "Remember, holes are never lost or scores ruined through getting into difficulties, but almost always through inability to get out. How often a good score has been spoilt or a medal lost by the ball falling into long grass or into a bunker. We have often heard a player remark 'I should have won that match if I had not lost 3 in getting out of that bunker.' These difficulties are now overcome by the use of Higg's 'Deliverer,' sand and rough grass being good lies for this club" (Golfing, 19 Jan. 1905: 20).

The Higgs Deliverer pictured, a niblick, is marked "Reg. No. 19995 \ Higgs Deliverer \ Willie Aveston, Cromer" on the back of the head. "No. 19995" identifies the provisional patent issued to Robert Percival Higgs on September 16, 1904. Higgs later abandoned his patent application. The head was forged by Tom Stewart, as it bears Stewart's "pipe" cleekmark. The solid areas of the face are unscored.

Notice how all the writing is placed at the top of the blade back. Rake and water irons were marked *away* from their openings. The marks on an iron head, whether scoring lines or maker's marks, were added last. When applying such marks, efforts were always made to avoid the open areas. Homemade rake irons, made by someone simply cutting slots into an iron head, are seen occasionally. Such irons are exposed when the slots interrupt the writing on the back of the blade or interrupt ordinary scoring lines. Such after-market alterations ruin any value a club might have otherwise had.

Despite the initial positive review, the Higgs Deliverer with its downward teeth was of little practical value. The downward prongs could easily catch on the ground and cause the clubhead to twist off line—not to mention the possibility of injuring the golfer's wrists should the prongs catch on the ground during the swing. Consequently, it comes as no surprise that rake irons with downward teeth are extremely rare. The author has seen only four Higgs Deliverers, two of which are on display at the British Golf Museum, in St. Andrews, Scotland.

Shaped similarly to the Higgs Deliverer, a rake iron termed a "Grassie" and described as a "clumsy rake" was made in America:

The latest thing in Golf clubs comes from America. It is called a "Grassie." The head is shaped like a mashie, made very heavy, and the lower part of the head cut into thick teeth, like a clumsy rake. There are six of these big teeth, and the object of the club is to rake through the long grass and get to the ball without wasting as much strength as an ordinary club requires in a like place. When the ball is hidden from sight in a heavy clump of grass, the whole clump has to be cut away with the iron before the club touches the ball, and then not enough force remains to send the ball more than a short distance (Golf, 6 Jan. 1899: 338).

Oliver's April 1990 golf auction offered a Wright and Ditson rake iron that matched the above description in every respect. Even with a cracked shaft, this club was still the object of heavy bidding. This iron, unmarked on its head, was stamped "Wright & Ditson, Selected" on the shaft with a mark used between 1898 and 1903.

James Henry Roger, of Glasgow, Scotland, received a British patent (No. 10,736) dated May 10, 1904, that covered a rake iron similar to the Higgs Deliverer. It is doubtful that any clubs were made as illustrated in Roger's patent inasmuch as the long downward teeth of Roger's club were incorporated, in shortened form, into the Roger Brown rake iron (see p. 226).

Willie Aveston, the promoter behind the Higgs Deliverer, was born in July of 1873, at Holyhead, England. While in his youth, Aveston worked to become a baker and confectioner. This line of work, however, did not agree with him:

He had to abandon the attempt... in consequence of failing health. The great extremes of head and cold were too much for him, and he was twice attacked with rheumatic fever (Golfing 25 Oct. 1895: 28).

When baking did not pan out, Aveston turned to golf:

It was in 1889, on recovering from his third attack of rheumatic fever that Aveston first turned his attention to golf.... His aptitude for the game was noticed, and he was sent first to Oxford links and then to Yarmouth, where he learned clubmaking under George Fernie (Golfing, 31 May 1906: 34).

Aveston was the professional at Cromer (just north of London) between 1891, when he was hired at age 17, and November of 1906, when poor health forced his resignation:

Handicapped, as he is, by the crippling effects of repeated attacks of rheumatic fever, his pluck and perseverance in the face of such heavy odds have for long been the theme of admiring comment (Golfing, 8 Nov. 1906: 12).

According to J.H. Taylor, Aveston had a true friend in the Marquis of Northampton. After Aveston resigned from Cromer, the Marquis employed Aveston as his private professional for the remaining years of Aveston's life:

Among the visitors to Cromer was the late Marquis of Northampton, who was drawn towards Willie by those bonds of intimacy that radiate from such natures as Aveston possessed....

The Marquis took Aveston as his private professional to the Castle Ashby, where he enjoyed many years of quiet happiness that such a relationship between employer and employee could offer. And now I learn of his death. Willie's soul has gone to meet his Maker and give an account of his stewardship. He can present a record to his Creator of a beautiful life spent in the service of an honest and high-minded endeavor to live a life according to His precepts, and making the world a better place for having lived in it (Golfing, 1 Feb. 1918: 10).

THOMAS TAYLOR, JR.
RAKE IRON

All golf clubs have a head, face, nose, neck, back, heel, toe, and sole, but Taylor's iron also has "feet." And *serious* feet at that! According to Thomas Taylor Jr.'s. U.S. patent (No. 1,089,881) dated March 10, 1914, which covered the iron pictured:

> [Taylor's club] is not made with "rake teeth," but rather has a series of feet like miniature flat-irons so that it will crush massively and yet with great speed through the ground just below the ball.

The Taylor iron pictured is marked "Anderson - Anstruther \ The Chicago Golf Shop \ Made in Scotland \ Warranted Hand Forged \ Mashie \ 118" on the back of the blade and "Patented" on the back of the feet.

It is not surprising to find "The Chicago Golf Shop" stamped on this head. Besides promoting its operation as "the largest exclusive Golf Shop in the United States," the Chicago Golf Shop advertised "clubs made to order" (*Golfers' Magazine*, Sept. 1909: 255). Since Taylor was from Hubbard Woods, a suburb of Chicago, using the Chicago Golf Shop to produce his club made sense. The Chicago Golf Shop, in turn, employed Alex Anderson of Anstruther, Scotland, to forge the head which was probably shafted back in Chicago (the completed clubs being either delivered to Taylor or offered for sale).

Optimistic about the future of his club, Taylor received not only the U.S. patent mentioned above for his rake iron but also a U.S. design patent (No. 44,457) dated August 5, 1913, and a British patent (No. 5,340) dated March 2, 1914. However, the market did not share Taylor's optimism.

The Taylor rake pictured is one of only two known. The other example, a mid-iron marked "119" (the model number) along with all the same writing found on the mashie pictured, has five slightly smaller feet. According to Taylor's patent, his club offered many advantages:

> This invention relates to [a] novel form of head . . . constructed so as to offer less resistance to the air and to the earth, and at the same time to maintain the weight of the head back of the center of percussion or impact.
>
> Further the invention aims to provide a golf club which is so formed as to reduce the possibility of "slicing" and "pulling" and "topping" of the ball to a minimum.

Given the obvious use of Taylor's club in water, sand, and other bad lies, Taylor's patent states that the "miniature flat-iron" design of the feet allowed his club to play as a regular iron while James Roger's rake iron (p. 224) was "absolutely useless":

> Each foot extends beyond the rear or back face of the club; each foot is a least twice as deep from its front face to its rear face as the conventional clubhead. The weight of the heel is at the minimum equal to the weight of metal which it would take to fill the cavity between any two feet. This is essential in order to keep the center of weight of the head and the center of percussion exactly in the middle or center of the face of the clubhead. Without this arrangement of weight the ball when struck is "foundered" or driven along the ground and only for a short distance. If the feet were only slightly thicker "at the lower back parts" as stated in British Patent No. 10,736 of 1904 to Rogers, of which patent I am aware, the center of weight and the center of percussion would be high up toward the top of the club head and upon impact it would be like hitting a ball with the prongs of a fork or rake and such a club is absolutely useless in the game of golf.

Taylor's patent elaborates on the features of his design:

> These great heels therefore provide necessary weights which greatly increase the driving force of the club; they maintain the necessary center of weight or the center of percussion at

ARTHUR C. HAM
"HAMSOLE"
RAKE IRON & PUTTER

the exact point where it is required in a successful form of golf head, that is the center of the face; they, these great heels, reduce the possibility of "slicing" or "pulling" or "topping" of the ball to a minimum, as the weight tends to draw down the head of the club to the bottom of the ball and insure striking the ball in the proper place, that is the center of weight and the center of percussion.

Consideration of "the center of weight and the center of percussion" was important to Taylor. His patent listed it among the virtues of his sole design:

It is essential in a successful golf club head that the center of percussion and weight shall be the center of the driving face of the head, which is attained in the present invention by extending the heels of the feet so that the weight of the extension shall be at least equal to the weight of the metal it would take to fill the space or cavity between any two of the large feet.

Concerned that his club would be seen as one-dimensional or of value only when in trouble, Taylor concludes his patent by summarizing the effectiveness and overall value of his club (in theory, anyway):

One of the great virtues of this invention is, the elongated trapezoidal feet of the club-head are in weight so massive, and yet occupy so much less space than a solid base, that the club-head meets so little resistance from the ground, if the club-head gets well down under the ball its speed is hardly checked and the golf ball as a result flies farther and the desired result is more easily accomplished. It is designed especially for all the great variety of golf strokes, and is not specially applicable for acting on the ball in sand bunkers, long grass, water ditches and the like as stated in the said British Patent No. 10,736, to Rogers. . . . It gives the player greater scope, greater accuracy, greater confidence and a much higher average in quality of play.

The Hamsole iron and putter shown above have teeth not nearly as long as those on Higgs's Deliverer or as thick as those on Taylor's rake, but they do have more of them. Developed by Arthur C. Ham, the Hamsole iron is a refined rake iron with downward teeth. Ham thought that a greater number of smaller teeth would make his rake a more practical and therefore more popular golf club. Unfortunately for Ham, his rakes did not find an admiring audience.

The back of the iron head shown atop this page is marked "Arthur Ham \ N.S.G.C. \ Skegness" inside an oval along with "Special Cardinal Niblick Reg. \ Warranted Hand Forged" and the Hendry and Bishop "mitre" cleekmark. In addition, on the back of each of the teeth is a letter. Put together the letters spell out "Hamsole."

The back of the putter is marked "Arthur Ham \ N.S.G.C.

\ Skegness" inside an oval along with Hendry and Bishop's cleekmark (they forged this club for Ham) and "Rd No 641489," a British design registration number that dates to 1914.

The combination of "N.S.G.C." and "Skegness" on the back of a single iron is unusual because irons are seldom marked with two locations. "N.S.G.C." is the abbreviation for the North Shore Golf Club in Blackpool, on the west coast of England, where Ham was the professional between 1916 and 1921. Skegness is a town on England's east coast.

Arthur Ham was born in 1891. After working as a professional at Blackwell from 1910 to 1916, Ham went to the North Shore Golf Club. Between 1921 and 1924, Ham worked in Wellington, New Zealand. He then came to America and worked at Plum Hollow in Michigan (Jackson 1994, 39).

JAMES R. BROWN
"THISTLE, GENERAL, MAJOR, & PERFORATED" RAKE IRONS

JAMES H. ROGER
"ROGER BROWN" RAKE IRON

Brown's rake irons, or water irons as they are sometimes called, are among the most famous of all golf collectibles. The term "water iron" identifies a club specifically designed to play a ball from water; the term "rake iron" identifies a "garden rake-like" club designed for use in high grass or sand. These terms, water iron and rake iron, have become interchangeable because the same club often addressed all three problems: water, high grass, and sand.

The four Brown rake irons pictured above, starting at the left, are as follows:

The first example is the "Thistle." It is stamped "Browns Patent" in a small oval quite low on the back of the head along with "Montrose, N.B. [North Britain]." "Made in Britain" is

stamped on the sole. Thistles were made without cosmetic marks on their face.

The second example is the "General." It is stamped "Browns Patent" in a small oval low on the blade back and has the standard ornamental "vine" scoring included on all Majors and Generals.

The third example is the "Major." It is marked both "Browns Patent" in a straight line and "The Major" low on the back of the blade back next to the sole. "W.T.B.," the initials of a former owner, is marked on the sole. The filigree on the face is an original cosmetic touch.

The fourth example, with its shaft laying underneath the first three irons, is the "Perforated Cleek." It is marked "Browns Patent" inside an oval on the

"ball" centrally located on the back of the head. The outline of a flower enclosed inside an oval is stamped in the center of the face. The shaft, marked "A.H. Scott \ Elie," has a hairline crack repaired with whipping. Brown's perforated cleeks and mashies came with either five or six slots. Initially, they were promoted as reducing "the wind pressure on the club and adding distance to the stroke" (*Golfing*, 28 Apr. 1904: 26).

In relating the story of Brown's famous rake irons, an article in the March 1906 issue of *Fry's Magazine* titled "The Romance of a Patent Golf club" goes into great detail:

Mr. James Brown, a Montrose blacksmith . . . is not a golfer, and before he blossomed into a full-blown patentee his chief interest in the game was in taking, on Sunday mornings, sand out of the eyes of golfers who had the previous evening been exploring the sand-dunes. In the performance of this by no means simple task he had a considerable reputation. And, being of an inventive turn of mind, he set about devising a tool which would do the work of the mashie more cleanly, and thus enable the golfer—and the duffer especially—to play the game with more comfort. One night he beheld an implement in his dreams which he calculated would stagger humanity. With a plan of the club still in his mind's eye he rose from his bed . . . hurriedly dressed, and in the silent hours set to work in his smithy, on this mental pattern. Far into the night he worked, and the cocks were crowing before he returned to the blankets. Next day he was never away from his bench . . . (496).

The next day, Brown gave his "discovery" a trial performance:

To test the efficacy of his "discovery" he caused artificial bunkers to be formed on the floor of his forge, mixing the sand with considerable quantities of "slag." Sticking the shaft of an old umbrella into the model which he had just finished, he buried a ball almost out of sight, and tried to extricate it. The initial trials were very satisfactory. No sand rose to obscure his vision, but there was a certain "uncanniness" about the club which he did not like, and he determined to improve upon it before he experimented further (496-497).

During the next months, two more experimental models were tried before Brown made his breakthrough:

One Saturday evening he set to work upon an idea which had been suggested to him that afternoon while he was racking his brain and raking his garden. "Why not shape the club after the manner of an inverted rake?" he asked himself. And enamoured of the idea, he set to work, and it was nearing the "wee short oor ayont the twal" on Sunday morning ere he finished the pattern . . . . It emerged very successfully from its preliminary trials in the bunkers on the smithy floor, the ball being got out comparatively easily from an obviously almost impossible hazard. It remained for him now only to perfect the idea which had given such satisfactory results, and in a few days' time the patent office was in possession of the "Major" (497).

The "Major," an iron with long slots cut into the head from the top of the blade, was well received. Many golfers appreciated its perceived abilities:

In extricating the ball from whins or long grass the "Major" is also a powerful implement. Hitherto the grass or whin matter, forming a sort of padding, prevented clean contact with the ball, reducing very considerably the effect of the stroke; but with the "Major" the grass or sand is forced between the teeth, thus ensuring a cleanly hit ball (497).

With an upbeat conclusion, this article illustrates the popularity of Brown's rake iron by observing that some of them had been taken out of the country:

Mr. Brown's club is used in India, New Zealand, Australia, Canada, South Africa—everywhere, in fact, where natural hazards abound (497).

The initial popularity of Brown's rake irons, however, was limited. Over the course of the two years following 1904, a few advertisements for Brown's rake irons ran in *Golf Illustrated*. The ads then disappeared, never to return.

In his British patent (No. 20,343) dated September 22, 1903, James Ross Brown, identifying himself as a shipsmith from Montrose, presents four different irons. These irons are also covered in Brown's U.S. patent (No. 780,776) dated January 24, 1905. As illustrated in both patents, the four styles are as follows:

The first iron has vertical slots in the face, open at the top. Two models in this style were produced: the Major and the Major Niblick.

The second iron has vertical slots in the face, but the face is solid around its edges. This iron was produced as the General.

The third iron has lengthwise perforations across the face, not vertical slots. This style was to accommodate various irons such as the cleek, mid iron, driving mashie, mashie, bent neck putter, and straight neck putter.

The fourth and final iron has a solid border around its face and eight horizontal openings—four on each side of a thin vertical brace in the center of the head. This model was not offered for sale.

The first three styles of Brown's rake irons, as outlined in his 1903 patent, were manufactured and advertised by J. Winton of The Links, Montrose (*Golf Illustrated*, 14 Oct. 1904: 53). Established in 1890, James Winton was a well-respected clubmaker:

J. Winton, of Montrose, makes a first-rate club. The experience of years has brought this well-known club-maker's work to a high state of perfection, and as his business is both wholesale and retail, shippers would do well to write for a price list (*Golfing*, 7 Sept. 1899: 18).

In a September 1, 1905 *Golf Illustrated* advertisement for "Brown's Perforated & Center Balance Golf Irons," only the Major Mashie, a perforated face mashie, a perforated face swan neck putter, and an aluminum swan neck putter (no holes of any type in its head) were offered for sale (204). These four clubs were offered "from The Makers: J.&W. Craigie, Golf Club Manufacturers, Montrose, N.B.," Messrs. Craigie having built their reputation on handmade clubs.

Less than a year later only three types of Brown's rake irons —"the Heroes of the Hazards"—were offered in a *Golf Illustrated* advertisement: "The 'Major' Mashie the Popular All-round Iron, the 'Thistle' and 'Roger Brown' " (8 June 1906: 230). The Roger Brown and the Thistle were entirely new models. Perforated face clubs and the General were not included. In this advertisement, Brown's clubs were offered by "Brown & Son, Montrose, N.B."

The Thistle was a late entry into Brown's realm of rakes. Shortly after its introduction, it was reviewed in *Golf* (ny):

All queer looking clubs are not necessarily to be classed under the opprobrious term of freak, and the "Thistle" niblick is really a most useful addition to every golfers armory. The specific purpose of a niblick is, of course, to get a ball out of difficulty, but the old style clubs were very little better in long grass or sand than the mashie. . . . The "Thistle" has its blade divided into six teeth, giving it somewhat the appearance of a rake reversed. In grass or sand the club works with astonishing ease, as it were, combing the ball off its difficulty. In water it is equally efficacious, and it will be remembered that in the championship meeting at Englewood Mr. J.D. Foot, of Apawamis, used the 'Thistle' in getting his ball out of the water in going to the second hole. The ball was floating and he waded in knee deep to play it, making a clean shot to the fair green. F.S. [sic] Slazenger, 8 West 28th Street, keeps the "Thistle" in stock (Oct. 1906: 244).

The "Roger Brown" rake iron, pictured right, is formed with two sets of slots in its head: a short set of slots open at the bottom of the head and a long set of slots open at the top of the head. This exceptionally visual iron was covered under a British patent (No. 10,736) dated May 10, 1904, and issued to James Henry Roger, a wine merchant from Glasgow.

In his patent, Roger states his club is designed "for acting on the ball in sand bunkers, long grass, water ditches, and the like." Roger acknowledges Brown's 1903 patent in the design of his rake iron. Even the patent illustrations of his club include the same ornamental "vine" scoring found on Brown's Major and General clubs. (The Roger Brown pictured still has its ornamental vine scoring on its face, though the writing on the back of the blade is faint.) Roger's club was produced in conjunction with J.R. Brown's rake irons; hence, it was named after James Roger and James Brown.

Roger's patent presents a rake iron with downward teeth similar to the Higgs Deliverer. Furthermore, it suggests the possibility of using the idea in Robert Urquhart's 1902 patent (No. 22,590) to make the loft of the rake iron adjustable! It is not believed such a club was ever produced. It was common for a patentee to cover many options or possibilities in his patent "just in case." However, an adjustable loft Roger Brown, if one was made, would be an incredible collectible!

Because of their strong visual presence, Brown's rake irons command attention and attract collectors. They have become extremely collectible and even the Major, the least rare of all of Brown's rake irons, draws a premium price.

In terms of rarity, Brown's Major is the most common rake/water iron not only as made by Brown but also as made by all other makers. The number of Majors in existence probably outnumbers the combined total of all other rake/water irons known. Among other Brown rakes, however, the perforated face irons are seldom seen and the Thistle is even more elusive. The Roger Brown is the rarest of Brown's rakes; only four are currently known.

A thoroughly efficient cleekmaker is expected to turn out an average of 18 tools per day, but this number varies according to the nature of the implement. The forgers usually become specialists in the manufacture of certain tools, some being expert cleek or iron makers, while the forte of others lie in the turning out of mashies or putters. A good all-round man, however, is able to turn his hand to almost any description of cleek. It may be interesting to state that the majority of these cleekmakers are recruited from the ranks of country blacksmiths, as they have been found to acquire the art more readily than their town taught brethren in trade (Fifeshire Journal, 19 June 1903: 5).

BEN KNIGHT
RAKE IRON

ATLAS COMPANY
"THE RAKE," RAKE IRON

Ben Knight produced a rake iron that is very similar to Brown's Major. The primary difference between these clubs is their prongs. On Knight's rake iron, shown above right, the prongs are formed at an angle to the sole. On Brown's Major rake iron, shown on page 224, the prongs are perpendicular to the sole. Another difference is that Knight's iron does not include ornamental scoring on the prongs.

On Knight's rake iron, as on any genuine rake or water iron, all the marks are located *away* from the slots in the head. "Hand Forged" is printed sideways on the back of the heel; "Special" is sideways on the back of the toe; "Ben Knight" is in script low across the back of the blade; and "Mashie" is on the sole.

In 1921 Knight advertised himself and his abilities as follows:

Ben Knight. Courses laid out and reconstructed. Open for Winter Position. Winona Country Club, Winona, Minn. (Golfers Magazine, Sep. 1921: 47).

Knight laid out the course for the Winona Country Club and worked there as the pro from 1920 until 1951.

Knight's rake iron is a premier collectible, only two of which are currently known. It is not likely that many more examples of Knight's club will be found. After all, Ben Knight was a golf pro in a small town in Minnesota trying to market a nonessential specialty club. Knight's rake iron appears to date around the early 1920s if not earlier.

In 1927 Knight was granted his only patent for a golf club—a U.S. patent (No. 1,616,377) dated February 1. His patent covered a double-jointed grip used on a putter—the lower portion of the club could pivot in the direction of the target while the upper portion of the grip bent back toward the golfer.

Also pictured on this page, above left, is the only Atlas Company rake iron known. Marked "Atlas Co \ The Rake" along with some faint writing which is undecipherable, this iron is reminiscent of the Roger Brown rake, except the slots in its leading edge do not extend all the way back through the sole.

The non-rusting Atlas head is nonmagnetic because of a low or nonexistent iron content. Much heavier than aluminum, this head appears to use nickel as its primary metal. (Monel Metal irons, many of which are nonmagnetic, are also high in nickel content. See page 214.) Like other clubheads originally sold without a shaft, the Atlas neck lacks nicking. The non-magnetic head and the Atlas name suggests a relationship with The Atlas Works, of Sunderland, England, well-known for the production of aluminum metalwoods.

JOHN S. PEARSON
BACKSPIN/WATER IRONS

It fits into the rake/water iron category, but the slotted face of a Pearson iron was designed for an additional purpose: backspin!

As pictured above, Pearson irons were made as mashies and niblicks. The niblick has five slots in the face and the mashie has four. "J.S. Pearson" is stamped sideways on the back of each club behind the toe. In addition, each club has owner's initials. The niblick is marked "JC" on the toe of the face; the mashie is initialed "C.C." under the Pearson mark on the back of its toe.

Produced only briefly by Mac & Mac, of Oak Park, Illinois, Pearson irons were made from "Granger Steel," also known as "German Silver":

[Each head] is hand forged from Granger Steel, an extremely tough close grained white metal . . . . This metal takes a very beautiful white polish (Golfers Magazine, July 1923: 41).

Under the heading of "Your Ultimate Golf Clubs," these slotted irons were advertised as being able to provide all possible backspin as long as the golfer did not swing too hard and break the head!

The Mac & Mac granger steel back spin mashie was designed for shots within seventy-five yards of the green. It is not guaranteed for the full mashie shot, as it is impossible to produce solid German Silver tough enough to withstand the impact necessary for the blow which would send the ball eighty yards or over. The wonderful efficiency of this club comes into play on the short approach shots. The sharp edges of the slots, which are cut clear through the metal, impart all possible back spin, which heretofore could not be accomplished with any other ribbed face design on the shorter and more delicate shots (Golfers Magazine, July 1923: 41).

The "ultimate" backspin iron, according to Mac & Mac, was their dimple face mashie niblick (see p. 238).

Pearson slotted irons were available with either "flat, medium, or upright lie, in right or left hand" (Golfers Magazine, Jan. 1923: 40).

John S. Pearson was originally from Great Britain. Early in his career, Pearson was employed by James Braid to work at his benches making clubs. Then, while working as the professional and greenkeeper at West Middlesex Club in Southall, Pearson introduced his "Excelsior" putter (see p. 253), advertised as "manufactured by J.S. Pearson, golf club and ball maker, Southall" (Golf, 7 Oct. 1898: 98). Early in the twentieth century, Pearson went to America and continued in the golf business. Years later, the May 1919 issue of Golfers Magazine listed Pearson as a

"Professional and Golf Course Architect [at] The Kirkwood, Camden, S.C."

Although advertised as an effective backspin iron, Mac and Mac's Pearson iron is valued far beyond any ordinary deep groove club. Pearson irons, also advertised as "all purpose," rank at the upper end of the rake/water iron category. They have a bold visual presence, a design that allowed water and/or sand to filter through their head, and they could "impart all possible back spin" to the ball, if their advertising is to be believed. Furthermore, very few Pearson irons are known. They not only became illegal shortly after their introduction (see p. 236) but also were undesirable to begin with. Who would want to buy a mashie that could not be used outside of seventy-five yards because it might break?

R. FORGAN & SON
WATER MASHIE

Following in the fashion of Brown's perforated face cleek, this Forgan water mashie has three openings across the toe and two across the heel of its slightly concave face. To avoid losing any of the writing to the slots, all the marks on this club are stacked in a column in the center of the back of the blade. The marks are as follows: "R. Forgan & Son \ St. Andrews" inside an oval with the "King's crown" trademark. "Warranted Hand Forged \ - - - \ Mashie" is located above Forgan's oval stamp. The name of the mashie is not completely discernible because the bottom half of the letters have worn away. Still, the writing is clear enough to establish that this club has its own unique name.

The "King's crown" trademark indicates that Forgan produced this iron between 1902 and 1910 (see p. 69). Forgan's water mashie was probably produced in response to Brown's rake irons.

An undisclosed fake Forgan water mashie, easily recognized by the inexact and amateurish holes cut in the flat face of what was once an ordinary smooth face iron, sold at auction in England in January of 1994 as genuine (see p. 552). Another undisclosed fake was auctioned in Scotland in July of 1995. Despite looking more authentic, the holes in the latter imposter were incorrect, and the face was flat—not concave like the original. Furthermore, neither club was marked in any way like the original.

This Forgan water mashie was made either just before or just after the death of Thomas B. Forgan, the son of Robert Forgan. Thomas, born in 1853:

. . . received his education at the Madras College [in St. Andrews], and then went to assist his father in the business. He first set to learn the practical work of clubmaking, and thus got a thorough grasp of what constitutes a perfect club. When he rose to take fuller charge of the business every club that left the workshop was subjected to the severest scrutiny by him, and if his expert eye detected the slightest flaw the club was cast aside (St. Andrews Citizen, 5 Jan. 1907: 5).

According to the February 17, 1906 issue of the *St. Andrews Citizen*, Thomas Forgan began working for his father in 1879, and when he "entered the business 37 years ago there were six workman in the place" (17 Feb. 1906: 4).

Thomas had become a partner in his father's business by June 9, 1883, as that is the date of the first *St. Andrews Citizen* to advertise "Robert Forgan & Son, Golf Club Maker to H.R.H. The Prince of Wales" (5). During the years leading up to 1883, Robert Forgan advertised his business as "Robert Forgan, Golf Club Maker to H.R.H. The Prince of Wales" (30 Sep. 1882: 5 [and other 1882 and earlier issues]).

After the death of Thomas Forgan on December 30, 1906, one of his sons, Peter Lawrence Forgan, took charge of the firm.

WILLIAM FERNIE
"WIMP" WATER IRON

DAVID STEPHENSON
WATER IRON

The holes drilled directly through the face of the irons pictured allowed the golfer to use these club either in water or sand and possibly to add backspin to a shot from a good lie. Because any iron originally made with holes running completely through its head is highly valued by collectors, the question arises as to *when* the holes on these particular heads were drilled. Were these holes installed when each club was originally made, or were they added after each club was originally sold? The answer to this question means the difference between night and day to a collector, clubs with after-market alterations being valued at the cost of borrowing a drill. Given no early literature about either of these clubs, nor other examples, the collector is left to determine their authenticity by careful examination.

Concerning the club pictured above right: A second look at the head reveals that the holes are drilled in a pattern. They are laid out in alternating columns of two and three. These holes are also countersunk from both sides of the blade. You would not expect somebody to bother finishing these holes in such a refined fashion if this club were just a homemade experiment. Also note that the unusually deep heel of the blade allows a column of three holes directly next to the hosel.

An examination of the writing on this head reveals "Wimp" stamped on the sole. This is key information because a club given its own name will usually have a peculiar characteristic. In the case of this particular iron, the holes in the head would be the obvious reason for its unique name. The *English Dialect Dictionary, Vol. VI,* published in 1905 (contemporary with this club), defines "Wimp"

as "Of a dog: to whine" as well as "fretful, complaining" (Wright, 500). It is not known why this club was termed a "Wimp," but the author suspects it was due to the *sound* the club made when swung—a sound similar to the high-pitched whine of a dog. The author has swung this club. The holes in the face cause a subtle yet distinct whine or whistling sound as the head speeds through the air. (Spalding's Lard shaft, an early metal shaft drilled full of holes, was termed "the Whistler" because of the sound it made when swung.)

The back of this clubhead is stamped "Warranted Hand Forged \Wm. Fernie \ - - - \Special" and has Alex Anderson's "arrow" trademark stamped on the toe. The lettering is positioned to minimize loss within the holes. However, the letters identifying Fernie's location were lost to a single hole. Unlike Jack White's drilled clubheads discussed

next, this clubhead does not have any large undrilled areas, so a little loss of lettering was unavoidable.

At the beginning of the twentieth century, Alex Anderson, the maker of this club, was operating a business believed to be the largest of its kind in the British Isles:

Every one who knows anything of golf matters is aware that the establishment of "Anderson of Anstruther" is the largest of its kind in the British Isles. Founded by the late James Anderson, and now ably carried on by his son, Alexander, this large cleek and iron factory is the first feature of Anstruther which presents itself upon reaching the railway station. . . . The forges and buildings . . . are devoted to making the thousands of iron heads which are daily sent away to all parts from this little Scottish fishing village (Golfing, 14 Mar. 1901: 24).

It is generally accepted that Anderson was using his "arrow" trademark by 1905. If so, this club was made sometime thereafter, which fits in well with other water irons. However, the thickness and length of the Wimp's hosel, which measures just under five inches long, is more in keeping with an iron from the 1880s. Clearly, this club was given such a substantial hosel and deep blade, reminiscent of clubs made twenty or so years earlier, to provide the clubhead with a heavy overall weight despite having fifteen large holes.

Cleekmakers understood clubhead weight and knew how much a finished head needed to weigh in order to have good balance, feel, and utility. Therefore, the clubheads of water and rake irons were made a little thicker and otherwise "beefed up" to make up for the weight removed by the slots. Even with all its holes, this particular iron is on the heavy side, which is understandable given its purpose of getting the golfer out of trouble. In contrast, irons with holes added to their faces after they were originally sold will usually have a much lighter than normal swingweight.

Because this clubhead has such a dark patina, the lettering on the back and sole is hard to make out in a photograph of the entire head. If the patina were removed, the lettering would show up better but the head overall would look worse. It is best to leave the original patina alone, especially when the lettering is identifiable.

This iron is marked "W. Fernie." When this iron was made, two W. Fernies were working as professionals in the world of British golf: William Fernie and Willie Fernie. William was born at St. Andrews in 1863. He worked at Headingly in the 1890s and then at Glamorganshire between 1902 and 1928. Willie Fernie was born at St. Andrews in 1858. After working at Dumfries & Galloway between 1880 and 1884, he was the professional at Felixstowe from 1884 until 1887. After that, he worked as the professional at Royal Troon from 1887 until 1924, when he died (Jackson 1994, 31).

In the first half of 1891, Willie applied for a British patent (No. 4,727) on a golf club. He later abandoned this application, which dealt with "the substitution of a brass plate for the time-honoured buffalo horn on the sole of the club" (*Golf*, 3 Apr. 1891: 38).

On July 20, 1896, "W. Fernie" applied for a patent (No. 16,028) to cover "improvements in or connected with golf clubs" (*Golfing*, 2 Sep. 1896: 17). This application was also abandoned, and nothing else about the proposed improvement is known.

The club pictured below and to the left on the facing page has thirteen holes concentrated in the center of its large face—the hole in the center of the blade is surrounded by four holes which are circled by eight more. In order to understand this iron, one must remember that the *last step* in producing an antique iron was to stamp it. After describing the process of forging and finishing an iron, an article titled *How Golf Cleeks Are Made*, published in 1903, identifies this last step:

The [club] now goes through its last process, namely stamping, before being packed and sent off (*East Fife Record*, 19 June: 5).

Because this water iron was originally made with thirteen holes running though its blade, all the marks on the back of the head are, unlike an ordinary iron, located

well away from the center of the blade—the marks being added *after* the holes. "D. Stephenson \ Prince's Golf Club \ Sandwich" is stamped inside an oval behind the toe; "Hand Forged" is stamped behind the sole; "Special" is marked behind the top line; and "Niblick" along with Spalding's "anvil" trademark is stamped behind the heel (see picture below). David Stephenson was at Prince's Golf Club, in Sandwich, England, from 1906 until at least 1917 (see p. 157).

Aside from Jack White's clubs discussed next, the author is aware of two other irons originally made with circular face holes. These irons, which are a matching pair, each have a brass head with three horizontal rows of five countersunk holes drilled through the face. Each sole is marked "Pat. Pend." although a patent was never granted. Judging from their 44-inch shafts, front to back (not leading side to following side) hosel pins, and extensive evidence of hand workmanship, both of these circa 1910 brass irons were made as working models, not for retail sale.

JAMES BRADBEER

DRILLED FACE PUTTER

JACK WHITE

"CIVIC" PUTTER
& "THE DEADUN"
BACKSPIN WATER IRON

The James Bradbeer putter pictured above has forty holes drilled through a deep, offset blade. The back of the blade is marked "James Bradbeer \ Finchley" on the toe. Bradbeer was at Finchley, in Greater London, between 1900 and 1905, so his putter predates the Jack White Civic putter shown below by no less than nine years.

White's Civic putter, complete with a drilled out face which would supposedly reduce the distance the ball would roll, was introduced in 1914:

At Harrod's Jack White had a new putter on show. It has a metal head with a number of holes punched in it from back to front. It is claimed for this club that a ball struck with it will not travel so far as a ball struck with equal force with an ordinary putter (Golf Monthly, May 1914: 224).

Accompanied by an illustration of White's unusual putter, a Gibson advertisement also recalled the Civic's introduction at Harrod's, London's world famous department store:

Jack White's "Civic" putter—an instantaneous success—stock at Harrod's Exhibition sold out first day— orders booked for grosses. Jack White holed in one with the "Civic" six times in succession as dared by an American—later calls the Putter "Holey Terror." This American took four to the States. . . (Golf Illustrated, 10 Apr. 1914: 148).

The Civic putter pictured is marked "Jack White \ Warranted Hand Forged \ Horton" and "Wm Gibson & Co Ltd \ Kinghorn, Scotland" (inside an oval) behind the toe; "Civic \

Special" and Gibson's "star" trademark are stamped behind the heel.

As already noted, White designed his Civic putter with rows of holes in the face in order to, theoretically, deaden the ball upon impact and thereby reduce the distance the ball would roll. White also devised a drilled face iron—The Deadun—that shared the same objective, which it fulfilled by adding backspin. Like the perforated face water irons of the early 1900s, the drilled face Deadun was the club of choice in certain water situations.

The back of the toe on the Deadun iron pictured below is marked "Warranted \ Hand Forged \ Wm Gibson & Co Ltd. (inside an oval) \ Kinghorn \ Scotland \ Jack White." The back of the heel is stamped " 'The Deadun' \ Made In Scotland" along with Gibson's "star" trademark. All the stamps were installed sideways in order to locate as much writing as possible away from the holes running through the blade.

In addition to devising the Civic and Deadun clubs, Jack White, the 1904 British Open champion, was a very interesting character. According to his own account, he was born in 1873 at Pefferside, between North Berwick and Dunbar. At the suggestion of his uncles, Davie Grant and Ben Sayers, he learned the game as a caddie when he was eleven years old. He quickly took to the game and caddied for such notables as Tom Dunn, Jack Simpson, Bob Ferguson—a former three-time British Open champion—and J.E. Laidlay—a former two-time

British Amateur champion (Leach 1907, 141-153). White learned the art of clubmaking from Tom Dunn, since, according to White:

The life of the professional was such a very uncertain thing at that time, when he seldom got a retainer and had little winter work, that it seemed a very wise thing to do (142).

White eventually became respected not only as a player but also as a clubmaker and golf course architect:

As a clubmaker and course architect, White's skill is on a par with his ability as a player. His clubs, both of wood and iron, are famous, while his services are in constant demand for the laying out and improvement of courses (*Golfing,* 16 May 1907: 20).

White was the professional at York, Worlington, Mitcham, and Seaford before settling at Sunningdale where he was a great favorite (*Golf Illustrated,*

1 Jan. 1909: 21). White stayed at Sunningdale from 1901 until 1926, when he retired.

White's Civic putters are much easier to find than his Deadun irons. Both were made by William Gibson, but two or three Civic putters become available every year compared to the almost impossible to locate Deadun irons. The James Bradbeer putter shown on the facing page is the only such example known.

Prior to 1930, two patents which relate to drilled face clubs were granted. The first was James Govan's U.S. patent (No. 873,423) dated December 10, 1907. Besides covering an offset neck for cleeks and putters (see p. 172), Govan's patent included the idea of drilling six or seven holes through the blade at the toe as well as the heel in order to locate most of the clubhead weight in the center of the blade. Govan recommended filling these holes with lighter material, such as wood or rubber,

in order to provide a smooth face and "to prevent the apertures [from] filling with dirt." However, the holes could also be left open.

The other patent was Daniel S. Griffin's U.S. patent (No. 1,414,124) dated April 25, 1922, which covered an iron with many small holes through the blade. As designed, these holes are located across the entire blade: high and low, heel to toe. According to Griffin's patent, these holes would make the club lighter and:

less resistant to the air than the golf heads now in use, so that it may be swung with a great deal of speed.

The author has not seen a drilled face Govan or Griffin club; it is possible neither one was produced.

FACE TREATMENTS

We have received from R.B. Wilson, of St. Andrews, a putter which differs from others from the fact that on the face of it are two square holes—one at the heel and the other at the toe, punched right through. The idea is evidently to get all the possible weight in the centre of the face (Golfing, 9 Jan. 1902: 26).

R.B. "Buff" Wilson developed his model 1000 putter by the end of 1901. Having an offset blade, the 1000 putter came in two styles: a square hole (window) was located in *either* the heel of the blade or in *both* the heel and the toe.

Wilson mentions his new putter in a small advertisement found in the January 3, 1902 issue of *Golf Illustrated* (19). Later that month the same periodical printed a brief but positive review of Wilson's club:

One of Mr. R. B. Wilson's patent clubs, which were noticed the other week, viz., the (1000) putter, with the holes cut in the blade, has already met with approval from two important sources. Mr. Hilton says regarding it: "In the short trial I have given it, it seems 'very good' "; and Mr. F.S. Douglas, the American ex-Champion, considers it the best putter he has ever used, and has taken a number back to America with him (Jan. 31: 83).

The window blade putter pictured is stamped "R.B. Wilson, St. Andrews, NB" in an oval on the back of the blade and on the shaft.

Born in 1869, Robert Black Wilson learned clubmaking as an apprentice in the shop of Tom Morris. He also developed a fine golf game and eventually traveled to the United States where, in 1896, he became the professional at Shinnecock Hills Golf Club, on Long Island, New York. Spending time in both Great Britain and the United States during the following years, he made many acquaintances and proved himself to be somewhat of a character.

Wilson developed a few unusual clubs which were usually marked "patent" on the back of their heads. However, none of his clubs ever completed the patent process. Because Wilson's "patent" clubs did not stay on the market for long, they are rarely seen today.

A few of Wilson's more interesting clubs are the A1 putting cleek, which does not employ a hosel; the A1 driving cleek (p. 185), which followed on the heels of the A1 putting cleek; a spring-face iron (p. 340); and a combination driver head made from aluminum and wood (p. 295).

Wilson's window blade model 1000 putter is one of his best collectibles. Both the single and the double window blade are desirable, but the double window blade is even more so because it presents a stronger image. Interestingly, Wilson's double window blade design resurfaced in the late 1920s as a steel shaft putter. The author once viewed a picture of such a putter complete with the thinner hosel of a steel shaft club. Because of the steel shaft, the 1920s window blade putter does not approach the value of the wood shaft club. Collectors distinguish between wood shaft and steel shaft models.

WILLIAM F. REACH

**DOUBLE WATERFALL &
SINGLE WATERFALL
BACKSPIN IRONS**

Today, irons with big, deep grooves, such as the two irons pictured, are commonly referred to as "deep groove" or "backspin" irons. Designed to impart backspin to the ball, these irons were given such model names as Dead Stop, Dedstop, Stopum, Bakspin, and Baxspin by their manufacturers.

Besides having deep grooves, backspin irons were also produced with other face designs such as wide circular holes in the face, holes extending through the face, slots cut through the face, faces curved top to bottom, "waffle" scoring, "brick" scoring, "waterfall" grooves, etc. Most backspin irons, however, have deep grooves running straight across the face.

Standard deep groove irons came in two styles: "slotted" or "corrugated." With slotted grooves, the sides of the grooves are cut straight down, at a 90 degree angle, into a flat face. With corrugated grooves, the sides of the grooves round inward towards the bottom and, therefore, do not have sharp 90 degree angles. Furthermore, the surface of a corrugated face has rounded "ribs" between each groove. Both irons above have corrugated grooves while the backspin iron on page 522 has slotted grooves. Standard deep groove backspin irons were produced in great quantity and are always available to collectors.

Moving beyond the standard examples, the backspin irons pictured are more than entry level collectibles because their grooves do not run in a straight line. Nicknamed after the twice-curved scoring on its face, the double waterfall iron (above left) rarely becomes available. This example is marked "Dedstop \ Reg. U.S. Pat. Off. \ Mashie Niblick \ F-6" on the sole and "E.B. Traube\ San Francisco\ Pat. Applied For\ Spalding\ Kro-Flite" on the blade back. This club was covered under the April 20, 1920, U.S. patent (No. 1,337,958) applied for on August 23, 1919, by William F. Reach.

According to his patent, Reach designed his double waterfall iron with deep grooves surrounded by a solid border. The grooves were of "wave line form" so they would impart "a backward spin to the ball whether struck by the direct or cut shot…stroke." Reach defined the cut shot as "when the club is drawn across the ball at an angle to the line of play." Providing a solid border around the face (visible on both irons) would:

eliminate sharp corners [on the deep grooves which tend] to mar or injure the shafts and grips of other clubs carried in the same bag.

The double waterfall iron was offered only in Spalding's October 5, 1919 catalog. It was replaced by a backspin iron with a *single* waterfall face pattern (above right) in Spalding's next catalog, dated January 5, 1920. A Spalding ad in the February 1921 issue of *Golfers Magazine* (37), shows the double waterfall iron. This might have been an advertising oversight because Spalding's 1921 catalogs dated January 5, 1921 and March 5, 1921 offer only single waterfall irons.

The single waterfall iron shown is marked "Dedstop \ Reg. U.S. Pat. Off. \ F-7" on the sole along with "H.C.H.," the initials of a former owner. The back of the blade is marked "I.S. Mackie \ Lynchburg \ VA." along with "Pat'd 4.20.20 \ Spalding \ Kro-Flite \ Reg U.S. Pat. Off."

The single waterfall backspin iron was covered under William Reach's patent mentioned earlier and under his U.S. design patent (No. 55,644) applied for on March 27, 1920, and issued on July 6, 1920, which he assigned to A.G. Spalding & Brothers just as he did his double waterfall patent. The

FACE TREATMENTS

single waterfall scoring is a refinement of his double waterfall idea—the more pronounced arc of the ribs on the single waterfall made controlling a cut shot easier.

Spalding's double waterfall and single waterfall irons were available either as "pitchers" or "mashie niblicks." The single waterfall was offered throughout 1920 and 1921.

Backspin irons in general have an interesting history. Grooving an iron was first tried as far back as 1873:

Tom Kidd . . . was the first man to "rib" an iron club to impart stop and it won him the 1873 "Open," on bone hard and lightning-fast St. Andrews greens (Robertson 1967, 77).

Dated September 2, 1902, Edgar Burr's British patent (No. 19,988) covered scoring an iron or wood to provide "underspin." In Burr's patent the upper surfaces of the grooves are "perpendicular to the striking face while the lower surfaces . . . are inclined thereto." This design created a serrated face when viewed in cross-section. It is not known whether this club was ever produced.

According to Francis Ouimet, Ben Sayers invented the backspin club in 1913 (*Golfers Magazine*, Aug. 1921: 27). Covered under a British design registration (No. 625,276) issued in early 1913, Ben's "Stopum" and "Jerko" backspin irons have straight deep grooves set at an angle across the face. A few other backspin irons, such as the Maxwell "Baxpin" Mashie, were also advertised in early 1913.

In the United States, Spalding first offered straight groove backspin irons in their 1916 catalog. Acknowledged as being able to stop the ball quicker than any other type of mashie or niblick, backspin irons of similar shape and design were produced by many different makers. Before long, backspin irons became commonplace. Every class of golfer used them, even professionals. In 1921 Jock Hutchison used a backspin iron while winning the British Open.

But all was not well with these clubs. In 1921, Francis Ouimet wrote an article that, among other things, clearly expressed his uncompromising and critical attitude towards backspin clubs:

Next in order—and of great concern in golf—is to prohibit the use of the so-called backspin clubs, those that have corrugated faces, which make the approaches behave automatically even when the player is unskilled in this splendid bit of golf. These clubs have become extremely popular. Hardly a golfer but has one or more of them in his bag. A friend fondly refers to his own as his "self-player." And that's just what it is.

Such clubs got their hold during the war when no one cared to think of golf, least of all to agitate changes in the rules. Ben Sayers invented the first one in Scotland in 1913, a mashie with a scored face. It was supposed to impart a cut or draw to a ball whenever it was hit.

Some wise golfer named it the "Jerko," probably because the ball was so suddenly checked when striking the greens as to have all the appearance of being jerked. Next thing we had hold of it, and leave it to our ingenuity to improve. Now

our golfers no longer have to strive for years to perfect a check shot; all they have to do is to use a self-player. Everybody is proficient in the deadly pitch, thanks to the corrugated faces of these new clubs.

The trick of back-spinning a chip or pitch is a simple one today. Professionals still buy their mashies and mashie-niblicks with perfectly smooth faces. But all they have to do is to find a man with a die to cut steel and then have him groove the faces of these clubs as per directions. Often the cuts are an eighth of an inch deep. Their sharp edges tenaciously hold the ball at the moment of impact, imparting to it a great spin, and, at the same time, removing quite a bit of its surface. It's fine for the manufacturers of golf balls, because a ball used in this way a few times cannot help but show the marks of the scoring. . . .

The more rapidly golf is rid of such contrivances the more certain it is that matches will fall to the more proficient. Furthermore, the beauty of the game consists in playing without the use of outside agencies just as one's greatest satisfaction comes from developing skill to a high point and mastering all the shots. Doctored and doped golf have no part in the game. They are not fair. I know because I own one deep-grooved club (*Golfers Magazine*, Aug. 1921: 27).

Ouimet was not the only person against deep-groove clubs:

President Howard F. Whitney of the United States Golf Association has intimated that some action might be taken toward barring the ribbed mashie in this country (*Golfers Magazine*, Apr. 1921: 42).

The Royal and Ancient rules committee has decided to debar ribbed and slotted clubs now in use by American Golfers. The decision will not become effective until after the British Open Championship event, which will be played June 20-24 at St. Andrews (*Golfers Magazine*, June 1921: 42).

Given this pending decision, Hutchison's effective use of a backspin iron while winning the 1921 British Open created no small stir. Shortly thereafter, the R&A banned such clubs while the USGA postponed taking any action:

A rule was passed barring ribbed clubs. Probably it is a good rule, but the rule as framed was so poorly done that the United States Golf Association officials did not care to adopt it as it stood (*Golfers Magazine*, Dec. 1921: 21; see *Golfing*, Aug. 1921: 37 for official R&A rule.)

The USGA finally ruled against backspin irons. Effective January 1, 1924, slotted or punched clubs with lines more than 1/16 inch in width and less than 3/32 inch apart were barred from competition. Consequently, the companies still making deep groove clubs quit doing so. The backspin iron itself then drew back and disappeared:

The U.S.G.A. ruling prohibiting the use of rib and punch face clubs [was] strictly enforced. . . . In the 1924 Southern California championship every bag was inspected at the first tee and more than 200 clubs were ruled out (*The American Golfer*, 17 May 1924: 48).

BURKE GOLF COMPANY

"ROTARY" COMBO FACE
BACKSPIN IRON

GEORGE F. DAGNALL

" 'HANDY ANDY' KUTSPIN IRON"

The Burke Golf Company, of Newark, Ohio, was a successful golf club manufacturing company during the first half of the twentieth century. Entering the golf business in 1903 as a manufacturer of hickory shafts, Burke began making entire clubs a few years later:

The Burke Golf Company…began to make completed golf clubs in 1910. In these early days, Burke imported heads from the George Nicoll Company of Leven in Fife to complement their domestic head production. Sales grew steadily until they signed Harry Vardon, J.H. Taylor and James Braid for promotional purposes in 1917. As a result of promoting golf equipment used by players of this magnitude, business began to boom after World War I. Soon after, Walter Hagen was added to the Burke Promotional Staff, which further spurred an increase in sales (Wishon 1985, 8-1).

Above left is a "combination face" Rotary iron marked "Burke Rotary \ Monel Metal \ Special \ Mashie" on the blade back. Having both a waffle pattern and deep grooves, this clubface is quite different from the standard backspin irons of its day.

Burke also sold a "checkered face" Rotary iron. Produced in the early 1920s, this backspin club is known today as a "waffle face" iron because a waffle pattern covers the entire face. Burke's 1922 catalog describes the checkered face Rotary iron as follows:

Burke Rotary Clubs are designed with a checkered face which tends to catch in the depressions in the ball marking when used in playing cut shots. With the ordinary corrugated iron clubs, cut shots often show a tendency to bound away from the line of direction due to the way in which the spin is imparted to the ball. Burke Rotary clubs

eliminate this danger from cut shots. The surest and safest back spin clubs on the market (35).

Neither of these Rotary irons should be confused with the "brick face" backspin iron. The brick face iron was covered under a U.S. design patent (No. 55,278) granted to Arthur August Kraeuter on May 25, 1920. The scoring on a brick face iron forms small rectangles which look like a brick wall. Brick face irons are similar to waffle face irons in collector interest, and both are seen with some degree of regularity. Burke's combo face Rotary iron, however, is the rarest of the three.

Pictured above right is "Dagnall's 'Handy Andy' Special Kutspin Mashie Niblick" as stamped on the back of its head along with "WM \ Preston \ England." This wonderfully creative face pattern consists of horizontal deep grooves, vertical scoring lines, and offsetting circles placed over the entire face.

Devised by George F. Dagnall, the Handy Andy became illegal under British rules in 1921, five years before George Dagnall went from serving as an assistant professional to Alfred Miles at Merton Park, in London, to becoming a head professional (Jackson 1994, 22). Dagnall apparently designed this club before entering the world of professional golf. This was the case in 1908, when Dagnall patented a golf club while working as a self-described "art decorator" in Glasgow, Scotland. (His British patent [No. 4,784] dated March 3, covered placing a tube of mercury, liquid, or powder in a wood head.) The author has seen one other Handy Andy iron. It was offered for sale at the 1993 Sporting Antiquities golf auction held in Massachusetts.

MAC & MAC
"DEEP DIMPLE FACE"
BACKSPIN IRON

Mac & Mac, of Oak Park, Illinois, introduced the "Deep Dimple Face" backspin iron, shown above, in 1923. Designed to replace the deep groove backspin clubs declared illegal by the R&A in 1921, Deep Dimple Face irons used large round holes cut into the face in order to create backspin and eliminate side spin:

[A new type of back spin club] is being brought out this year by the Mac & Mac organization . . . . In place of the back spin ribbed face, now illegal in England, they have machined or drilled a series of accurately spaced one-quarter inch round deep depressions which . . . create the greatest possible amount of back spin which a golf club can impart to a ball. The manufacturer also claims these deep dimple markings have the faculty of actually preventing side spin, explaining that at the impact, the first cup touching the ball immediately starts this under spin motion, which is increased or multiplied as the ball is driven up the face of the club (Golfers Magazine, Mar. 1923: 58).

According to Mac & Mac's advertisements, the Deep Dimple Face backspin irons were well made:

The most deadly "stoppum" clubs ever designed. . . . The deep sharp cups grip the ball at impact and stop any tendency to side spin, changing every motion instantly to straight flying back spin.

. . . Strictly hand made throughout by master club makers. Head is hand forged from Granger steel, extremely tough grained white metal, which was necessary to permanently retain the sharp cup markings. Takes a very beautiful white polish (Golfers Magazine, Mar. 1923: 56).

This club was not successful in circumventing the R&A ban:

In [preparing for] the Northern Championship at St. Annes, American competitors were using iron clubs the faces of which had been punched with holes in such a manner that the ragged edges of the metal gripped the cover of the ball, and made it easy to impart back-spin to the shot. [Therefore, at the meeting of the Committee held on the Saturday night before the Northern Championship began, these clubs were ruled illegal.] The Americans must be dull indeed if they thought that a change from filed-edged grooves to ragged-edged holes constituted any vital difference in principle (Golfing, July 1923: 72).

The example pictured above is marked "Granger Steel \Warranted Hand Forged \ Dimple Face \ Back Spin Mashie" on the blade back with "M & M" inside a clover leaf (Mac and Mac's trademark). Available as a mashie, mashie niblick, and mid-iron, the Deep Dimple Face iron had a very short life—it became illegal under USGA rules on January 1, 1924.

The Kroydon Company, of Maplewood, New Jersey, produced Banner clubs as a separate line of golf clubs. Most Banner irons have horizontal scoring; however, a very small percentage, made for only a short time in the 1920s, have vertical scoring. No other company promoted an iron with only vertical scoring. This is not surprising given the counterproductive nature—a tendency to accentuate a hook or slice—of vertical grooves.

The iron pictured below is marked "Banner" on the blade back and "50° Niblick" on the face. Labeling the face high on the toe is unique to Banner clubs. Many were produced this way, including Banner's center-shafted "Pendulum Putter."

WILLIE PARK, Jr.

"PARK'S PATENT LOFTER"

Willie Park Jr.'s concave face lofter, covered under a British patent (No. 5,042) dated March 23, 1889, was the first iron ever patented. The only club patented and produced prior to Park's was Thomas Johnston's vulcanite wood in 1876 (p. 82).

Only two patents between Johnston's patent and Park's first patent mention golf clubs. The first was James Davidson's British patent (No. 14,349) dated November 23, 1885, which covered "improvements in handles for lawn tennis, racquet, and cricket bats, and for golf clubs and other articles." The illustrations in Davidson's patent show only the handles of tennis racquets. The other interim patent was Walter H. Cook's British patent (No. 363) dated January 7, 1889, which covered "a novel application of pulped paper stock." Cook listed his invention as applying to:

frames of rackets, "crosses" or bats used in the game of la crosse, . . . cricket bats, stumps and bales, golf clubs, croquet mallets and handles, shinty or hockey clubs, billiard and bagatelle cues and rests and for fishing rods and rests.

Cook's patent did not include an illustration, but it is unlikely that a golf club was ever produced under either Cook's or Davidson's patent, or that the patentees specifically intended to do so. Consequently, Park

produced his patent lofter under the second patent granted specifically for a golf club.

Park's patent lofter pictured on this and the following page is stamped "Park's Patent Lofter \ No. 5042" on the back of the blade. The main feature of this club, the concave face, did not originate with Park. He simply copied the concave face found on pre-1850 irons. The businessman in Park saw the concave face as profitable while the golfer in Park saw the concave face as beneficial.

According to Park's patent, the concave blade increased the amount of backspin imparted to the ball:

The construction of the head or blade . . . has for its object the striking of the lower part of the ball under its centre thereby causing the ball to revolve or spin in a backward direction while being propelled forward by the stroke of the club which has the effect of stopping the ball more suddenly when it falls on the ground . . . .

In 1889 W.T. Linskill wrote a brief but positive review of Park's first patent club:

Willie Park, jun., . . . has just brought out what will in future be called "Park's Patent Lofter." It professes to have considerable advantages over the lofting iron and mashie for the approach stroke. Its shape brings the upper part of the blade nearer the ball, so that while taking less turf it gives more "loft" and is easier to use. The blade being concave, a back spin is

given to the ball, which produces the effect which I have described above, viz. it stops the ball dead when it falls. It also raises a half-topped ball with more effect, as is confirmed by eminent golfers who have tried it. Among those who might be mentioned is Mr. A.M. Ross, who says, "It is a most decided improvement on the old form of 'pitcher' " (23).

However, not everybody praised Park's lofter. According to the two time British Amateur champion Horace G. Hutchinson, Park's club was more trouble than it was worth:

There is Park's Patent Lofter. It is claimed for it that it will pitch the ball very dead; and so it will if the ball be hit in the right place. But it is in the experience of all who golf that it does not always happen, and a little tapping with a Park's Patent is a dangerous thing. For the face is scooped spoonwise, and if you do not hit in the true

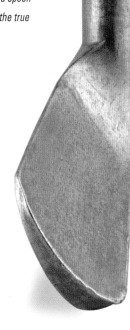

concavity of the spoon, nothing happens but the unexpected. Therefore, it is a very good weapon if you play very well with it, but a very bad one if you play badly. It is really a useful club for about one hit in ten rounds; for all the others you are better without it (Golf, 14 Nov. 1890: 136).

In 1895 a Wm. Park & Son advertisement declared "Park's Patent Lofter over 17,000 sold" and "Park's Patent Driving Cleek over 8,000 sold" (Golf, 6 Sep. 1895: 521). This is amazing information because there are very few Park Patent Lofters known to collectors at present. Worldwide, only four have sold at auction between 1985 and 1994. If the old claims are accurate, the fact that so few Park Patent Lofters remain is evidence that many clubs did not survive.

Today, collectors hold Park's Patent Lofter in high esteem primarily because of its place in history as the first iron ever to receive a patent. If not for its unique status, Park's Patent Lofter would not enjoy such strong interest even though the concave face is a good collectible feature.

Park's Patent Driving Cleek was a companion iron for his patent lofter. This low profile cleek has a flat face but a convex blade back—thin across the upper and lower edges and somewhat thicker in between. According to Hutchinson, the convex shape given to the back of the blade concentrated the weight of the head to "just opposite the spot which the ball should be hit" (Golf, 14 Nov. 1890: 136). Park did not receive a patent for his driving cleek, a fair number of which remain, but the author suspects he applied for one on July, 8, 1890. At that time, he applied for a British patent (No. 10,575) to cover "metal golf clubs"; he later abandoned his application.

Park once used his patent cleek in losing a very unusual "cleek driving competition":

A Cleek Driving Competition at Musselburgh.—On Wednesday evening, the 28th ult., a somewhat novel driving competition took place on Musselburgh Links. The competitors were Willie Park, jun., and Alexander Geir, both of them Musselburgh professionals; and the conditions of the match, which was for a stake of £5 a side, were that Park should use his own patent cleek, and that Geir should handle the cleek patented by Messrs Anderson, Princess Street, Edinburgh, some time ago. . . . [This

was probably Anderson's crescent head cleek patented in 1892, see page 188.] The Match was one of driving alone, and the actual distance with the "carry" and "run" was the test. . . . A large crowd of several hundred spectators turned out to witness the display of cleek driving . . . . Each player drove twelve balls, and the best two on each side decided the match. . . . After five or six balls had been played on both sides . . . Geir got away two particularly long and low balls, with plenty of "run" on them, and, though Park still continued to drive in fine form, although rather high, he was unable to get quite the distance reached by the other man. When a dozen balls had been played on each side, the referee had the distances of the best balls measured, when it was found that Geir's longest stroke was a distance of 184 yards, and that Park's best drive was shorter by eight feet. Geir, who was the challenger, accordingly won the stakes. The course, on account of the recent spell of fine weather, was hard and dry (Golf, 6 Apr. 1894: 53).

Willie Park Jr. also devised a few other interesting irons. Park's "Stock Exchange Mashie," described as a "mashie iron for long grass," came with a blade:

two and one-eighth inches across the deepest part of the face, and this narrows down to one and a-half inches at the heel (Golf Illustrated, 22 Dec. 1899: 292).

Park's "Spade" was a cleek-type iron:

Park's "Spade" was a weird form of cleek introduced some years since; in it the sole was straight, and the upper edge curved down at the ends, aiming, no doubt, at center balance (Golf, 9 Apr. 1897: 80).

Park also produced a patent niblick and a patent mashie. The patent mashie has a convex back like his patent driving iron. Park's patent putting cleek, compressed wood, step face iron, and Pikup woods are discussed elsewhere in this book. (Also see Willie Park Jr., page 91.)

A few irons similar to Park's Patent Lofter were produced by other makers. John and Gourlay Dunn (Tom Dunn's sons), entering a partnership as club and ball makers while at Mitcham in 1892, promoted an iron with a concave face:

The features of their approaching-iron are, that it has a rounded sole, short socket, concave face, and weight on the sole of the club. This enables one to approach the hole from any sort of lie, and the ball, when it lands, stops dead (Golf, 20 Jan. 1893: 305).

In 1896 Peter Paxton brought out a concave face mashie with a thick sole (Golf, 3 Apr. 1896: 72). Willie Wilson also made an iron similar to Park's Patent Lofter (see page 111). And there were a few other concave face irons made in the 1890s as well. Concave face irons from the 1900s, such as those patented by James and David Foulis, also turn up from time to time. (Foulis irons, covered under a U.S. patent [No. 807,736] dated December 19, 1905, have a mildly concave face.)

TOM MORRIS
PATENT NIBLICK

In addition to making and selling his share of woods, Tom Morris also sold a few irons. But, because Morris did not operate a forge, the iron clubs marked with his name were usually forged by Tom Stewart, the prolific St. Andrews cleekmaker.

Most of the irons Morris sold were traditional in nature. However, he devised three different metal head patent clubs: the dish face niblick pictured, an oval face cleek (p. 446), and a cylinder head putter (p. 247). Because Tom Morris has no superiors in the history of golf, any patent club bearing his name is an *excellent* collectible—such clubs are very difficult to find.

Morris received a British patent (No. 17,753) dated September 21, 1893, that covered his concave face niblick. According to the patent, the sole is:

. . . cut away so that the niblick can get under a ball quickly . . . . [This is] useful in driving a ball out of a "bunker," or from a bad "lie."

The dish face was borrowed from the early track iron, but the idea of forming the bottom of the club without a sole, which is the net effect of "cutting away" the sole, was original. As seen above, the back of the blade is very symmetrical. Beginning at the leading edge, the back gently rounds up to the top of the blade.

The club shown is marked "Patent 17753" with "T. Morris \ St. Andrews" inside an oval on the back of the blade, and "T. Morris\ St. Andrews" on the shaft. Although termed a niblick, Morris's iron is classified today as a rut niblick because the head is smaller than the traditional niblick. It is not, however, a rut iron (track iron) because the hosel is not as big and the blade is not as small as those found on true track irons. Furthermore, by 1893, track irons were no longer being made (see pages 115 and 120).

The shaft pictured has a fair bit of whipping around its lower end because it was cracked in the course of courageous and dedicated duty. Such damage demonstrates that being a golf club was not always easy! If the tough competitor pictured on this page could talk, he might say something like this:

Being a niblick was not an easy job in the early 1890s. You had to take on the worst situations, sometimes even hopeless situations, and make the best of it. Unfortunately, you continually risked your health for the greater good and glory of your player. You see, the idea of escaping trouble was unheard of by the egotistical play club—play clubs just wanted to hit first all the time and were only interested in how far the ball would go. The spoon family had so many conditions they wanted met before they would ever tackle a tough lie— heck, they didn't know what real trouble was. And the mashie, lofter, and cleek were all prima donnas. Sure they could handle rocky territory, but they only wanted to hit onto the green and take a bow. Therefore, it was left to a real warrior to go in and do the work, to go in and correct the mistakes of others. Now you know that to be a niblick is to be prepared for battle. And sometimes, when the battle is joined, perfect health is lost. So, don't be too critical of my shaft. I'm a seasoned veteran who did his job (Author).

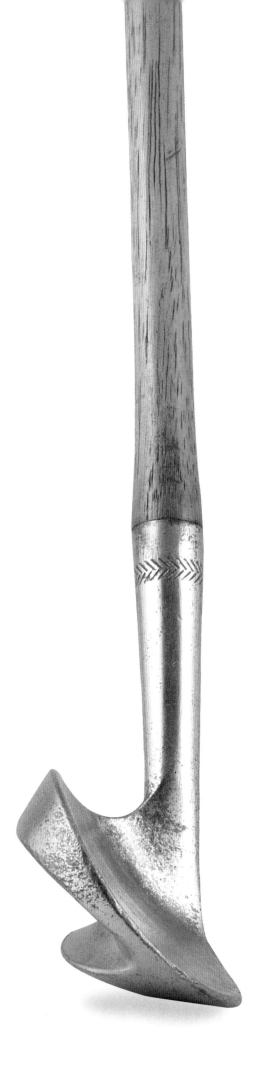

EDWIN K. MacCLAIN
"SAND WEDGE,"
CONCAVE FACE, FLANGED SOLE

On December 18, 1928, Edwin Kerr MacClain, of Houston, Texas, received a U.S. patent that covered the iron pictured. According to MacClain's patent, his iron has a large sole, referred to as a "wing" or "guide," designed to help golfers escape sand and other trouble:

It is the object of my invention to provide a club equipped with a wing or guide so shaped as to impart an upward flight to the ball when struck [and] to prevent the club head from sinking too deeply into the material below the ball, thus deflecting the blade of the club upwardly and increasing the ease and accuracy with which the ball may be moved from the sand or any other given spot.

In making a case for his flanged sole, MacClain's patent acknowledges the inherent difficulties of using a standard niblick in sand:

Where the ball is in a sand trap it is difficult to keep the ordinary niblick blade from penetrating too deeply into the sand thereby failing to knock the ball out, defeating the purpose of the stroke. When the "niblick" penetrates the sand too deeply if it is not deflected in its course by a quick turn of the wrists, a difficult and delicate operation, the ball will fall short of its intended objective and a second or third shot may be necessary to remove the ball from the difficult position where it lies.

The flanged sole is the main feature in MacClain's patent. The concave face, the club's most prominent trait, is supplemental to the sole. Another feature of this club is the cleft between the flange and the back of the head. According to the patent, the cleft could be filled in if the player wanted to increase the weight of the clubhead. Under ordinary circumstances it would be left open.

In his article "Enter the Sand Wedge," George Trevor describes MacClain's club shortly after its introduction:

The sand wedge is a deep-faced niblick weighing 25 ounces. Its identifying feature is a thick steel fin or flange, projecting outward and downward from the upper edge of the rear surface of the blade. This keeps the weight low and directly behind the point of contact.... Indeed this weapon flies at its enemy, sand, as viciously as a bantam rooster claws at its rival of the sawdust pit. The abnormally wide striking surface is concave, forming a scoop which digs deep under the ball, literally shoveling it onto the green (Trevor 1930, 63).

Trevor also recalls how Bobby Jones used MacClain's concave sand wedge in the final round of the 1930 British Open held at Hoylake. Laying two in a green side sand trap at the par five, 532 yard, sixteenth hole, Jones needed a birdie to "offset previous lapses":

"My sand wedge please," says Bobby, turning toward his Scottish caddie, adding, by way of explanation, "That extra heavy niblick with the steel fin." English eyes bulge as Mr. Jones grasps the weirdest golfing implement ever seen at time-scarred old Hoylake, a formidable weapon with a rhinocerous-hornlike projection jutting obliquely downward from the hind side of the blade....

Thus armed, Mr. Jones settles his feet firmly in the deep sand. That grotesque niblick flashes as it catches the sun .... Out pops the ball garlanded in sand; it plumps on the green so close to the cup that the gallery squeals as the rubber core rolls around the rim, finally sitting down contentedly three inches from the lip!

That recovery clinched the British Open title for Mr. Jones; that ugly duckling of a club delivered the coup de grace. The gallery, scrupulously well-behaved heretofore…now hummed with whispered inquiry. Everyone wanted to know what manner of weapon had extricated Bobby from chancery.

Trevor continues by recounting how Horton Smith became involved with MacClain's club and how Smith introduced it to Jones:

Well, there's quite a story behind the sand wedge. "Cut back" to the Savannah Open last March [1930], when Horton Smith nosed out Mr. Jones by a single stroke. Those two great golfers . . . roomed together during the Savannah tournament. It was there that Smith showed Mr. Jones the novel niblick that was later to strike the telling blow at Hoylake.

"I've bought the rights to this club from a Texas rancher who, as a hobby, dabbles with golf inventions," explains Horton. "I call it a sand wedge. It's the niftiest antidote for bunkers you ever saw."

Mr. Jones tested the new-fangled contraption, found it just what the doctor ordered, and added a sand wedge to a kit already brimming over with fifteen clubs of assorted varieties.

The club that MacClain designed and patented, Horton Smith purchased the rights to and named, and Bobby Jones used in winning the 1930 British Open, is the same club the L.A. Young Company produced under Walter Hagen's name. The example pictured on the facing page is marked "Walter Hagen" on the sole along with L.A. Young's triangle trademark. In addition, the top of the blade back is marked "Sand Wedge \ Pat'd 1695598."

Formed in 1925, the Walter Hagen Golf Company was initially located in Longwood, Florida. However, club construction problems caused by Florida's heat and humidity (when Hagen clubs were shipped to drier climates, the glue joint between the head and shaft would often dry out and cause the clubs to fall apart) prompted the relocation of Hagen's company to Detroit, Michigan, in 1927 (Wishon 1985, 17-1). The L.A. Young trademark appears on all Hagen concave wedges because the L.A. Young Company controlled the Walter Hagen Golf Company by 1927.

The L.A. Young Company advertised the Hagen concave sand wedge—"It's chief purpose is in playing from sand traps"—but not for long. The USGA declared the Hagen concave wedge illegal at their January 9, 1931, annual meeting, held in New York. In the eyes of the USGA, the problem was the concave face:

Repeated tests proved conclusively that from grass a ball could strike the club face at two different points in the same stroke. In March the following regulation was adopted:—"Clubfaces shall not embody any degree of concavity or more than one angle of loft" (USGA 1932, 193).

The real merit of the Hagen concave wedge, however, was its large, cambered, broad sole and the bounce it provides—merits that were quickly discovered:

New sand blasters, legal in their construction, are making their appearance on the market. Club designers have found that a concave face is not necessary to simplify the task of hitting the ball clear of sand traps. More necessary to the mechanics of the club is the rocker back that enables it to slide through the sand. Golfers will find the straight faced, rocker-backed club quite as effective as the spoon-like weapon that was barred by the United States Golf Association (Golfers Magazine, May 1931: 24).

Reflecting how swiftly the market moved to create "new sand blasters," The Kroydon Company's 1931 golf catalog includes a full page presentation of "The Kroydon Blaster." As illustrated in the catalog, the Blaster appears as nothing more than a steel shaft copy of the Hagen Concave Sand Wedge. As described in the catalog, however, the Blaster was sold only with a straight face:

To conform with the new ruling of the U.S. Golf Association the Kroydon Blaster will be furnished as illustrated, but with a Straight face—not concaved (3).

Between 1890 and 1930, other mashie niblick and niblick-type clubs with concave faces were made. Marketed with the idea of providing backspin and/or adding loft, these dish face irons usually have an ordinary sole. These clubs are occasionally found and usually offer the collector an interesting collectible at a modest price.

Robert Condie made an iron with a partially concave face, the lower third of the face being moderately hollowed out. (These irons were sold by James H. Hutchison, of North Berwick.) Condie, located in St. Andrews, was a well-respected cleekmaker during his day. In 1908 Condie advertised, "established over 20 years" (*Golfing*, 27 Feb. 1908: 17). Prior to entering business on his own:

Ten years with "Anderson of Anstruther" . . . taught Mr. Condie the how, when, where and wherefore of cleek making" (Golfing, 30 Mar. 1899: 14).

Gene Sarazen, occasionally credited with inventing the sand wedge, was simply one of many who sought to refine MacClain's sand wedge after it was outlawed. Sarazen, however, designed what is arguably the single most *popular* sand iron ever produced—The Wilson R-90 Sand Iron, first offered by the Wilson Sporting Goods Company in 1933. (It was listed as model R-99 in Wilson's 1933 catalog.) During the next *sixty* years, it remained in use at the highest levels of the game—including the PGA Tour—and was copied by numerous clubmakers.

As the sand wedge continues to evolve, the cambered, broad sole, the key to the sand wedge's success and the primary focus of MacClain's patent, remains in use. (For flanged irons made before MacClain's, see pages 271-272.)

Today, because they were declared illegal so quickly, Hagen concave wedges are often found in like-new condition.

ASHLEY DAVEY
DUAL FACE IRON

Early twentieth century irons made from gunmetal are uncommon, but even more rare is the gunmetal head "dual face" iron pictured, the only such club currently known. Truly extraordinary, the face of this iron not only has two different lofts (hence its dual face categorization), but it also has a large extension that rises above an otherwise normal blade.

The primary mark on the back of the head is "A. Davey \ Margate." The other mark, which is missing some of its letters, is "F. Hopper \ Westgate."

Ashley Davey, born in 1876 at Caister on Sea, became the professional at the Thanet Golf Club, in Margate, England, in 1901. Davey remained at Margate as the professional and clubmaker until 1914, when he left to fight in the First World War (Jackson 1994, 23).

F. Hopper was the professional at Westgate on Sea (Westgate & Birchington), only a few miles down the road from Margate, between 1901 and 1908 (Jackson 1994, 44).

To understand the purpose of Davey's iron, reference is made to the June 19, 1928, U.S. patent (No. 1,673,994) granted

to J.W. Quynn, of Parkersburg, West Virginia. The illustration accompanying Quynn's patent shows a club with the same basic design as Davey's: a large blade extension located above an otherwise normal blade. Quynn's blade extension, which is semi-circular, has less loft than the blade below it.

According to Quynn's patent, his objective was "to provide a club which will greatly increase distance when used in the rough or in a sand trap." Therefore, Quynn combined "the features of a lofting club and straight face of a driving club" which he visualized would perform as follows:

The inclined blade will pass under the ball giving the ball the necessary loft to lift it out of the rough, while the [upper] section which is substantially straight will contact with the ball on the follow through, giving the ball distance which is not possible with the usual lofting club.

It is not known whether Quynn ever produced his club.

THOMAS SHARPE
"DUAL FACE" MASHIE

WILLIE PARK, JR.
STEP FACE IRON

Thomas George Sharpe's British patent (No. 266) dated January 6, 1906, covered the iron pictured directly above and described it as a backspin iron:

The object of this invention is to give increased accuracy in approaching the hole by causing the ball to roll as short a distance as possible after it touches the ground. To ensure this the face of the club . . . is made at two different angles, the upper part being perpendicular or nearly so, as an ordinary club, the lower part projecting forward at an angle to the upper part.

The iron pictured is stamped "Spalding \ Gold Medal \ Hammer Forged \ Reg U.S. Pat. Off. \ DF [Dual Face]." The shaft is stamped "A.G. Spalding & Bros Gold Medal."

In 1906 a review of "Sharpe's Patent Mashie," which includes a picture of a golfer using Sharpe's iron to play a stymie shot on a putting green, describes the qualities of this dual face iron as follows:

For lofting shots over trees, hedges, or gorse-bushes, this club is invaluable, as also for playing out of bunkers, when the ball does not lie too heavily and the green is within reach. It is particularly useful for those little, slack-wristed well followed-through shots of 10 to 15 yards from rough grass up to the hole, which lift the ball almost the whole way and fall very dead. As a stymie lofter alone this mashie deserves a place in every player's bag (Golf Illustrated, 9 Nov. 1906: 125).

Offered only in Spalding's 1913 catalog, Sharpe's Dual Face mashies are few and far between.

Willie Park Jr.'s British patent (No. 9884) dated April 13, 1913, covered the iron pictured directly above. According to this patent, his "stepped or serrated face" iron has three "step like formations" which, beginning at the leading edge, "recede towards and terminate at the top line." Park calculated that the steps on his clubface would impart backspin to the ball:

The object of arranging the striking surface in the manner described is to ensure that when the ball is fairly struck by the club the point of impact will be below the centre of the ball, with the result that whilst the ball is propelled in a forward direction a rotary motion will at the same time be imparted to it. . . . [So] when the ball falls, it comes to rest at approximately the point where it landed.

Park's step face iron pictured is marked "Willie Park \ Mashie Niblick \ Pat. Applied For" on the back of the blade along with "Spalding Gold Medal" inside an oval. The number "8" is above the oval, and the Spalding "hammer" trademark is also present. The shaft is stamped "Willie Park."

In 1914 Park applied for a U.S. patent to cover his step face iron. He received a patent (No. 1,188,479) dated June 27, 1916. This was the only U.S. patent Park received for a golf club.

Spalding marketed Park's club on a small scale, never listing it in any of their catalogs. The impractical nature of Park's step face iron helps make it a great collectible.

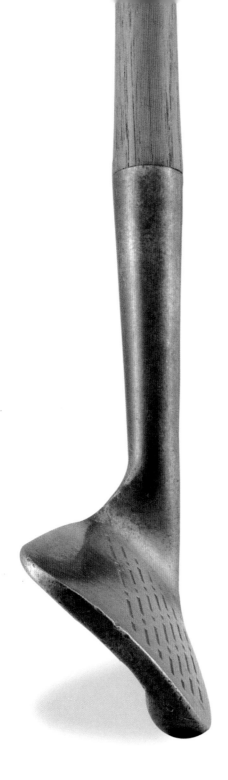

WALTER B. PEDERSON
CONVEX FACE IRON

The agricultural labourer is said by an authority to use 1,500 words in his vocabulary, and knows or can guess the meaning of 1,500 more. Intelligent farm hands and artisans command 4,000 words, while educated people have at call from 8,000 to 10,000. Journalists are credited with 12,000. Golfers, especially when in bunkers, display a larger vocabulary than any of these (Golf, 13 Apr. 1894: 72).

Unlike Willie Park's lofter with its concave face, Walter Pederson's mashie niblick, pictured, has a *convex* face. Pederson received a U.S. patent (No. 1,532,545) applied for on December 1, 1923, and issued on April 7, 1925, that covered his iron.

Pederson applied for this patent only one month before the USGA ruling against ribbed and punch face backspin irons took effect (p. 236). Hoping to fill the coming void, Pederson theorized that the convex face on his iron would allow the ball a "continued engagement" with the face at impact and therefore, as the ball rolled up the face, impart additional backspin to the ball:

The purpose of my invention is to provide a club which may, in the hands of an ordinary golfer, be successfully employed for the back spin shot without resorting to any unnatural stroke or difficult manipulation of the club while the shot is being performed. I accomplish this result by forming the striking face of the club of the mashie type with a convex surface...

. . . It has been found that this convex surface imparts to the ball a rearward rotation of back spin which will greatly curtail the forward rolling of the ball after it strikes the ground at the end of the shot.

The iron pictured is marked "Pederson \ Mfgs. \ Mount Vernon, N.Y. \ Mashie Niblick 2 \ Pat. Pend." The face is scored with intermittent short and long dashes but only on its lower half. Pederson's convex face iron met with little acceptance. Few examples remain.

Cylinder head putters, also called "drain pipe" putters, were made at different times following their introduction in the 1890s. However, the most distinguished of all was produced by Tom Morris.

The back of the Morris drain pipe putter shown is marked "Tom Morris \ St. Andrews" inside an oval above Tom Stewart's "pipe" trademark. The shaft is stamped "John Wisden & Co. \ 21 Cranbourne St. London" next to "T. Morris, St. Andrews, N.B." inside an oval. ("N.B." is the abbreviation for "North Britain," a term once used to identify Scotland.)

Morris had Tom Stewart, a respected cleekmaker in St. Andrews, forge his irons. In the words of O.B. Keeler:

Hereafter when you see on the back of a blade, the mark of T. Stewart, St. Andrews, and the old clay pipe, you will know that this club be it yours or another's was forged on order in a little old shop innocent of efficiency or quantity of production. But there undeniably was quality to the Stewart irons . . . (Rice 1953, 174).

"John Wisden \ Cranbourne St., London," as stamped on the shaft, was the sporting goods store that sold this club:

[John Wisden & Co. are] the sole London agents for Forgan, Tom Morris, and Auchterlonie, besides several other well known clubmakers. The special golf showrooms in Cranbourne-street and Great Newport-street well repays a visit (Golf Illustrated, 10 Jan. 1902: 86).

According to Wisden's claims, Wisden was the first dealer to sell golf clubs in London, beginning in 1874. During the 1890s, Wisden's became known as "London's greatest golf depot" (*Golfing*, 23 Nov. 1899: 11). After viewing Wisden's vast inventory, a reporter once stated, "the golfer who fails to make a satisfactory purchase will be hard to please" (*Golf Illustrated*, 29 Dec. 1899: 316).

It is believed that Morris developed his drain pipe putter in the early 1890s when he briefly produced his two other patent clubs—an elliptical face cleek and a dish face niblick (see p. 446 and 241). The mark on Morris's cylinder head putter is the same mark he used on the other clubs, and the sheepskin grip on this club is pre-1900.

A tip to Greenkeepers. If troubled by rabbits, a simple plan for catching them is to dig a tunnel in the ground, get into it, and make a noise like a turnip. This never fails (Golf Illustrated, 5 Apr. 1901: 3).

Oval blade putters were introduced in the 1890s. James Anderson of Anstruther, Scotland, registered a model called the "Kurtos":

[It] is called the "Kurtos," from the Greek word signifying convex. In shape it somewhat resembles an ordinary cleek, only it presents a round or convex face to the ball, and shows no edges to disturb the eye of the player. It is claimed for the new club that it will ensure a perfect run for the ball, as its formation ensures that it will neither top the ball nor cause it to jump, as is often done by an ordinary flat-faced putter (Golf, 27 May 1892: 175).

Kurtos putters have a mildly convex face, gently rounded from top to bottom, and a mildly convex blade back. Their appearance is not as dramatic as the round shape of Morris's putter.

An oval blade putter made by R.B. Wilson and pictured in the April 1903 issue of *Golf* (ny) is described in terms similar to those used to describe the Kurtos putter:

R.B. Wilson's O.K. putter . . . is convex on both sides of the blade. It is claimed for these convex faces that the ball is struck very cleanly, and that topping makes but little difference to the success of the stroke (248-249).

Wilson's putter is more oval than round—a happy medium between the Kurtos and the Morris cylinder head. (Note, Wilson marked "O.K." on various other blade putters.)

Roger Lyons Cowper-Coles, of London, received a British patent (No. 14,169) dated June 27, 1898, that covered a putter head similar in shape to the Morris cylinder putter except that it does not have a hosel, and the shaft enters directly into the top of the head.

According to his patent, Cowper-Coles formed his putter head from different materials:

as a hollow metal cylinder filled with a core . . . of wood or other light material . . . . or heavier material, such as lead.

The type of material used depended on the desired weight of the putter.

Expressing a belief shared by all developers of drain pipe putters, Cowper-Coles states that the round head will make his putter more consistent by reducing the number of mis-hit putts:

The ball will always be struck at a point which is the same distance from the ground, providing that the putter is held at the proper height whilst striking, and further, that the curved shape . . . of the head prevents it from cutting into the ground in case a stroke is made too low, and allows it to slip along the ground and avoid the missing of the stroke.

The author has never seen or heard of an example of Cowper-Coles's putter, but homemade cylinder putters with a hickory shaft inserted into the top of the head are known. Homemade clubs, however, are of little interest to collectors.

Wood-shafted cylinder putters are very collectible. The Kurtos and the other oval blade putters are rarely seen and also make nice collectibles. They are not as desirable as the cylinder putters, however, because an oval blade does not depart from the standard blade to the degree that the uniform cylinder head does.

THE COLUMBUS BRASS COMPANY

"THE ARLINGTON PUTTER," CYLINDER HEAD

The Arlington putter differs from the ordinary putter in that its cross section is a cylinder. Golfers know that with a flat-faced putter the sole is apt to catch in the ground and stick, thereby ruining the stroke. With the Arlington the sole cannot catch nor can it get under the ball so as to lift it. The striking surface must meet the ball fairly on the median line, so that the latter runs true without either back or over spin. Golfers who are in the habit of chopping their putts will do well to give the Arlington a trial. It will be furnished in two angles of lie— ordinary or upright—and either brass or nickel plated (Golf [ny], Nov. 1906: 306).

Advertised briefly in 1906, the Arlington putter came in two models:

No. 63—Regular pattern, shaft at 63° angle

No. 67—Upright pattern, shaft at 67° angle

Either style, in polished Brass or Nickel plated with selected shaft, $3.50 (Golf, [ny], Sept. 1906: 192).

The unmarked Arlington putter shown above, the only one known to the author, is a brass upright model with a 67° lie. Produced by The Columbus Brass Company, of Columbus, Ohio, the Arlington putter was unpopular and short-lived.

The Pambo Golf Clubs. Simplicity is the keynote of their excellence.... Both clubs being made of aluminum, cleaning reduced to a minimum. Being cylindrical in shape, they are suitable for left or right handed players. At whatever angle held, face of club remains always true to the ball (Golf Illustrated, 3 Sep. 1920: 702).

J.B. Fulford of Bulwell Forest, Nottingham, England, produced a pair of aluminum cylinder head clubs: the "Pambo Putter" and "Pambo the 2nd." The Pambo putter has a perfectly cylindrical aluminum head. Pambo the 2nd—designed for shots from the tee or through the green!—has a cylindrical metal head that, like a wood, is slightly bulged across its center. An advertisement for the Pambo clubs (which illustrates but mislabels the clubs) promotes their capabilities as follows:

Aluminium is a metal which has lately appeared somewhat prominently in the form of driver heads .... The metal was first placed in the hands of man by the chemist Wohler, in 1828 .... In the Paris Exhibition of 1855 it was labelled "silver from clay" .... In 1867 large ingots appeared. Pure aluminum is too soft for ordinary purposes, and like pure iron, it is little else than a curiosity, but in the form of alloys the metal has a wide field before it (Golf, 4 Jan. 1895: 294).

The "Pambo" Putter, being cylindrical in form, has no bottom edge to catch the ground. It gives a good view of the ball and occupies so little ground that it accommodates itself to undulations more readily than any other known club. All mental effort saved is clear gain to the golfer—he need concentrate only on direction and strength. The present standard is a 10 oz. aluminium head (weighted) of medium lie.

Owing to the heavy demand for the "Pambo" Putter, we now embody its essential principles in "Pambo the 2nd." This is also cylindrical in shape and can be used with excellent effect for shots from the tee or through the green. The length of shot is only limited by the driving skill of the owner — 250 yards often being obtained. Rough, grassy lies are readily negotiated. The club cuts neither turf nor ball and its peculiar shape allows a small margin of error.... Both clubs being made of aluminum (Golf Illustrated, 3 Sep. 1920: 702).

A Pambo the 2nd, marked "Pambo \ Regd 676460," is pictured. Marketed as able to play shots from tee to green, this club has a flat lie and a 39 inch overall length. Pambo putters are only 34 inches long and have an upright lie. They are also marked "Pambo \ Regd 676460." The Pambo's British design registration number dates around 1920 (see p. 564).

ANDREW H. SCOTT
CYLINDER HEAD PUTTER

Pictured is a cylinder putter made with a *wooden* head. Crafted by Andrew Scott, this putter bears the stamps of "A.H. Scott \ Elie \ Scotland" and the King's crown (a lion above a crown) as used by Scott. Scott, a fine clubmaker of high repute, was named clubmaker to King George V following the death of King Edward VII in 1910.

The alignment mark on the top of Scott's putter pictured is original. It is located directly above the sweet-spot and is covered with the same original varnish as the rest of the head. The back of the head has two round lead weights, one behind the toe and one behind the heel, located equidistant from the alignment mark. The sole, which is curved like the rest of the head, is covered with a copper plate.

A wood head cylinder putter filled with lead in its center was auctioned by Sporting Antiquities, in Andover, Massachusetts, on April 25, 1990. This particular club was stamped "A.H. Billet, Bridport." After leaving East Somerset in 1924, Billet became the professional at Bridport, England, and remained there well into the 1930s.

Like the Scott cylinder putter pictured, Billet's putter shows excellent workmanship. Though not the earliest of their type, both Scott's and Billet's putters are exceptional because they are made of wood. (For more on Andrew H. Scott, see page 136.)

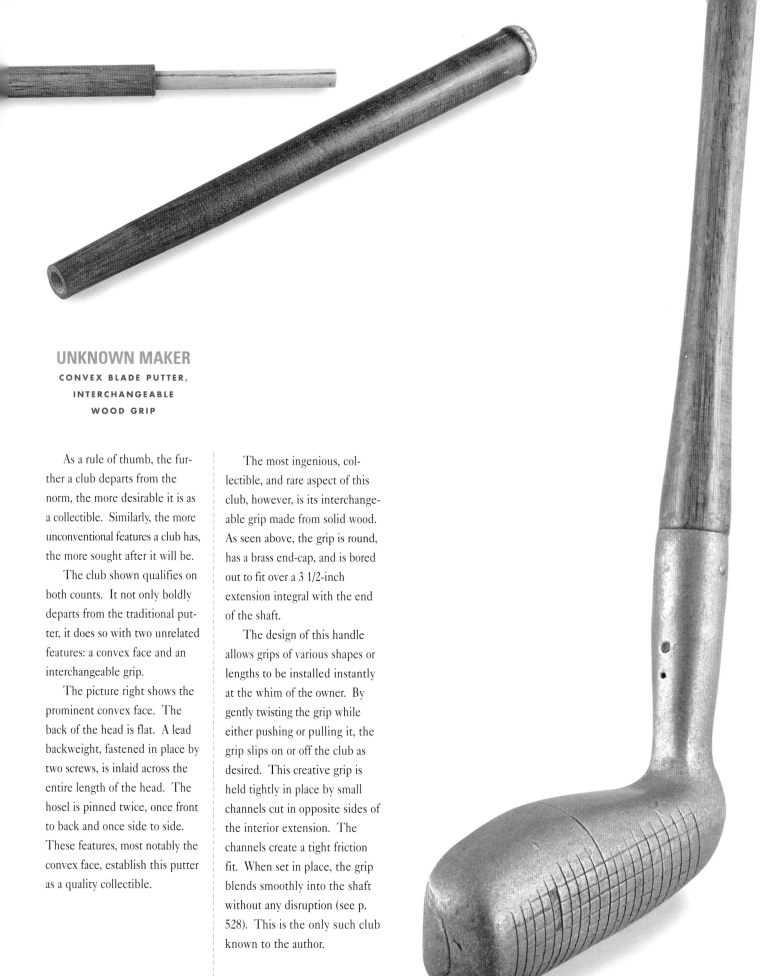

UNKNOWN MAKER

CONVEX BLADE PUTTER, INTERCHANGEABLE WOOD GRIP

As a rule of thumb, the further a club departs from the norm, the more desirable it is as a collectible. Similarly, the more unconventional features a club has, the more sought after it will be.

The club shown qualifies on both counts. It not only boldly departs from the traditional putter, it does so with two unrelated features: a convex face and an interchangeable grip.

The picture right shows the prominent convex face. The back of the head is flat. A lead backweight, fastened in place by two screws, is inlaid across the entire length of the head. The hosel is pinned twice, once front to back and once side to side. These features, most notably the convex face, establish this putter as a quality collectible.

The most ingenious, collectible, and rare aspect of this club, however, is its interchangeable grip made from solid wood. As seen above, the grip is round, has a brass end-cap, and is bored out to fit over a 3 1/2-inch extension integral with the end of the shaft.

The design of this handle allows grips of various shapes or lengths to be installed instantly at the whim of the owner. By gently twisting the grip while either pushing or pulling it, the grip slips on or off the club as desired. This creative grip is held tightly in place by small channels cut in opposite sides of the interior extension. The channels create a tight friction fit. When set in place, the grip blends smoothly into the shaft without any disruption (see p. 528). This is the only such club known to the author.

CHARLES L. LAWTON
"DEADLY OVERSPIN PUTTER,"
CONVEX BLADE

ALBERT PERCIVAL &
ERNEST WHITCOMBE
"PERWHIT PUTTER,"
CONVEX BLADE

Charles Lawton of Hancock, Michigan, received a U.S. patent (No. 1,525,137) applied for on March 20, 1922, and issued on February 3, 1925, that covered the gunmetal putter pictured, marked "Frank Brady \ The Deadly Overspin Putter" on the back of the blade and "Patents Pending" on its sole. According to Lawton's patent, the Deadly Overspin Putter will "roll the ball along close to the ground and in a straight line" because the convex face imparts overspin to the ball without "crowding it toward the ground."

The convex face of Lawton's putter was designed to strike the ball above its center:

The contact point between the club and the ball is above the center of the ball. The result is that the ball turns forward faster than when struck with an ordinary straight or flat-faced putter, and should it strike a horizontal twig, a pebble, or small clod, it climbs over such obstruction instead of being deflected aside thereby.

The flat base of the Deadly's hosel was designed with a dual purpose:

The shank or hosel is flattened at [its base] so as to make it more flexible and is widened to overcome any tendency toward torsion. The overspin of the ball is increased by this flexibility of the hosel. The player can easily reduce the thickness of this flattened portion by filing it to suit the club to his individual taste.

Because of its convex blade, the Deadly Overspin Putter appears to have a large flange. Actually, the "flange" is the sole.

Albert Frederick John Percival, of Highcliffe, England, and Ernest Robert Whitcombe, of Bournemouth, England, received a British patent (No. 247,116) dated February 11, 1926, that covered the iron putter pictured. According to their patent, the blade of their putter was to be:

approximately crescent shaped [in] cross section . . . with the convex surface thereof forming the operative face of the club.

The convex face was designed to help the golfer strike the ball with the same face angle even when the player's stroke might vary the position of the blade:

This meniscus [crescent] shape tends to ensure that the ball is struck centrally within considerable limits of variation in the position of the club, and also the configuration of the rounded bottom of the blade tends to prevent the blade from dragging or clinging to the turf either on the downward or upward swing.

The Percival and Whitcombe iron putter pictured is stamped "The PerWhit Putter \ Pat No 247116 \ Made in Scotland \ Warranted Hand Forged" along with Hendry and Bishop's "bishop's mitre" trademark in the recess across the blade back.

ALEXANDER M. ROSS
NEGATIVE LOFT
PUTTING CLEEK

JAMES ANDERSON
NEGATIVE LOFT
DUPLEX PUTTER

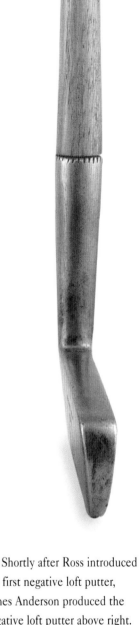

Prior to receiving their patent, Percival and Whitcombe produced their putter with a flat back. Marked "Patent Applied For," the blade resembled a short, solid rod cut in half lengthwise.

In 1898 J.S. Pearson, of West Middlesex Club at Southall, England, produced a putter with a slightly convex face. Called the "Excelsior," it "possesses a decided advantage to the ordinary pattern in that the ball flies cleaner off the convex face" (*Golfing*, 17 Nov. 1898: 23). Around the same time, George Nicoll produced a slightly convex blade putter (complete with a square toe and a blade set slightly ahead of the hosel) called the "Par Putter." Years later, a convex face putter titled May's Bulger Face Putter was produced. Unlike a true bulger wood but like the other putters just mentioned, the face on May's putter was convex top to bottom, not heel to toe. The Excelsior, the Par Putter, and May's Bulger Face Putter are more rare than the PerWhit, but, because their faces are only slightly convex, they are not as dramatic in appearance.

The latest improver of putting-cleeks is Mr. A. M. Ross, the well-known crack of the Edinburgh Burgess Club. . . . Instead of merely making the face perpendicular he has reversed the usual loft, or, in other words, when the cleek is placed beside the ball in position to play, the top edge of the face is nearer the ball than the bottom edge. In fact if a right-handed player takes a left-handed cleek and putts with it as he would with his own, he will have no difficulty in seeing what the idea of Mr. Ross is.

It is claimed for Mr. Ross's cleek that it holds the ball to the ground better than the ordinary cleek does, and that . . .the ball runs "truer." The cleek is designed for use on . . . putting-greens only, especially the short putts. . . . It would also seem that the risk of running over the hole, should the putt be played too strong, is . . . diminished.

At the same time, no club can be without its disadvantages . . . . In the first place, the cleek is not suited for putting on rough greens. . . . Again, should the ball happen to lie in a "cup" on the putting-green, if Mr. Ross's putter were used, there would be some danger of hitting twice . . . . The only other objection we see is that it is not very suitable for playing a stimy by screwing the ball past the globe blocking up the way to the hole. . . .

The manufacturer of the cleek has been entrusted to WIllie Park, jun., Musselburgh (Golf, 20 Feb. 1891: 356).

Ross's negative loft putter, the first to include an offset blade albeit incidentally, is pictured above left. The left-hand side of the blade is stamped "A.M. Ross Patent" in an oval, Willie Park style.

The review just cited notes that Willie Park was entrusted with making Ross's club "which is patented." However, in January of 1891, Ross only *applied* for a British patent (No. 1,458) to cover his club. Ross abandoned his application as golfers quickly rejected his club.

An accomplished golfer, Alexander MacKenzie Ross was also a well-known Edinburgh businessman. During the late 1890s, in addition to being managing director of the Royal Hotel in Edinburgh and other public companies, Ross was also Chairman of the Forth Rubber Company, Edinburgh, which supplied golfing requisites of all kinds (*Golfing*, 30 Nov. 1899: 13).

Shortly after Ross introduced the first negative loft putter, James Anderson produced the negative loft putter above right. The left-hand side of its blade bears Anderson's early (pre-1895) "Anderson \ Anstruther" (inside a small circle) cleekmark along with "Warranted Hand Forged." Notice that the thin sole is directly under the center of a thick topline. Because of this, Anderson's putter has the same amount of negative loft when used either right- or left-handed.

WILLIAM DUNN, JR.

**"ROTARY" &
MALLET PUTTERS,
NEGATIVE LOFT,
CONVEX FACE**

Willie Dunn, winner of the first open American championship, has opened a golf school in New York. In addition to the usual line of standard makes of clubs, Willie Dunn has a putter on sale designed especially for the "Haskell" ball. This putter has an overhang, the idea being to give a ball forward spin, like the follow shot in billiards, thus causing it to roll over irregularities on the putting green instead of being deflected from the line by them, as happens more with the Haskell than any other ball when putted with the slightest back-spin (Golfing, 27 Feb. 1902: 4).

Willie Dunn Jr. received a U.S. patent (No. 656,099) dated August 14, 1900, that covered the negative loft convex face putter described above and pictured left, marked "Willie Dunn's Rotary Putter \ Pat. Apl'd For." Dunn applied for this patent on January 5, 1900. According to Dunn's patent:

The object is to produce a putter which will make the ball cling close to the green and run more accurately than any putter which has been heretofore devised.

With this object in view the . . . face is so formed that it will strike a ball above its center, and thus deliver a blow which will give to the ball that kind of a roll which in billiards is known as a "follow."

In conjunction with the negative loft used to strike the ball above its center, Dunn's Rotary putter includes a convex face:

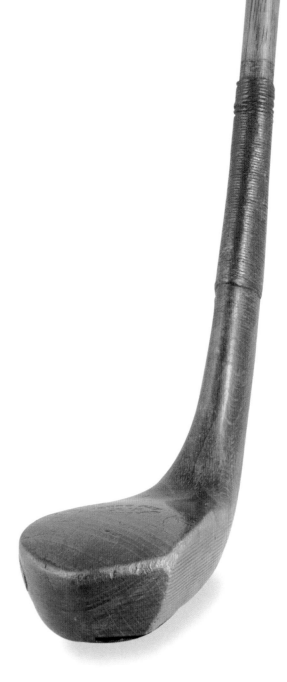

This face preferably is slightly convex from the sole to the top of the head . . . . The object in giving the face this convex form is that if the ball should be in a cuppy-lie the club will, by reason of the curved face, roll the ball out of the cup without giving it a jump.

Dunn used a wooden mallet putter to illustrate his design, but the patent also states, "The head might also be made of any metal or composition desired."

The bottom of Dunn's Rotary putter pictured *appears* to have a flange, but it does not. The face, scored with thin *vertical* lines, curves under so much that what looks like a flange is actu-

ally a very small sole with a "footprint" no wider than that of many blade putters. The flange on Dunn's putter is located on the *top* of the head.

The splice neck mallet putter pictured above is marked "Slazenger and Sons \ NY" on the crown and "Slazenger" on the shaft. The dramatic negative loft and convex face on this fine collectible are the same as are found on the mallet putter illustrated and described in Willie Dunn's patent.

An aluminum head negative loft mallet head putter shaped similar to this one and marked "Willie Dunn" was sold at the

May 1994 Sporting Antiquities golf auction held near Boston, Massachusetts.

William Winton made a blade putter with a slightly concave face, the top of which extends out over the ball. Titled the "Dead or Down" putter, Winton's club was designed to contact the ball above its center, so the ball would "gather pace somewhat in the way a billiard ball does" (*Golf Illustrated*, 14 Sep. 1900: 238). Winton's putter is also similar to Forrester's "Acme" putter produced in 1896 and shown on page 256.

The "Shaw Stewart Patent Putter," made by James Paxton, the professional at Royal Guernsey, is another topspin putter. Because the upper part of the face projects forward more than the lower part, "the ball is struck slightly above the center thereby imparting top spin" (*Golf Illustrated*, 23 Aug. 1901: 158).

The negative loft of Cann & Taylor's "Billiard Cushion" putter, covered under George William Beldam's December 11, 1911, British patent (No. 27,807), creates "follow" or topspin by providing a slight ridge high across the face. The ridge is designed to contact the ball at, or just above, its middle.

Harry E. Doerr, of St. Louis, Missouri, received a U.S. patent (No. 1,467,714) dated September 11, 1923, that covered both negative loft putters pictured right. Doerr believed, like earlier inventors of negative loft putters, that a putter could impart overspin to the ball:

It has been found that when the ball is given a rotation in the line of flight, that is an overspin or follow as corresponding rotation is called when given to the billiard ball, this overspin will tend to cause a ball to hug the ground and not lose its direction by bouncing and will also aid in causing it to drop as it passes over the lip of the cup. This overspin may be imparted to the ball by causing the striking surface of the club to engage the ball at a point above its center when hitting the ball in making the stroke.

However, unlike the developers of earlier negative loft clubs, Doerr was also interested in achieving greater consistency on *long* putts. According to his patent, by giving the concave face a radius much greater than "that of a golf ball," the shaft could be tilted back, away from the target, and the ball struck at its center instead of above it, thereby eliminating the overspin naturally imparted when using his putter in a normal fashion:

The ball may be struck approximately upon a point at the middle of its vertical height. . . . when the club shaft is tilted slightly to the rear or away from the ball. In this manner, long running up or approach putts

may be made without bouncing the ball by striking it down against the turf. The concave face permits this to be done by much smaller tilting of the club shaft than would be required were the striking face of the club formed on a plane intersecting the upper and lower edges of the striking surface.

Doerr's line-scored duplex blade putter shown is marked "Putter" on the sole. The left-handed face reads "Laclede Brass Works \ St. Louis, Mo. \ Doerr Topem \ Patent Applied For \ Pat Sep 11-23." The right-handed face reads "Warranted Hand Forged \ Firth-Stirling \ S-less [in a rectangle] \ Stainless." The smooth face gunmetal model shown is unmarked. According to an advertisement mentioned below, the gunmetal model was available for three dollars but only as a right-handed head. The buyer would have to get it shafted.

In 1922 an advertisement for "The Doerr Topem Putter, A par on your card beats a birdie in your dreams," shows only the

flanged model, made from "polished bronze," and states "the face is so constructed that the face of the putter always tops the ball" (*Golfers Magazine*, May: 53). In May of 1923, an advertisement for the "Doerr Topem Putter of Firth-Stirling" shows only the duplex blade (*Golfers Magazine*: 61). Consequently, it appears that the flanged putter was the initial design, and the blade putter was developed to allow for tilting the shaft back when playing long approach putts (the flange made tilting the shaft more difficult). The patent included an illustration of both models because it was not applied for until October 20, 1922, five months after the brass putter was advertised for sale.

The blade putter pictured, originally offered either complete with a shaft or as a head only, has a grooved Huntly-style solid wood grip (see p. 534).

GEORGE FORRESTER
"ACME" PUTTER,
FLANGE FACE

Mr. George Forrester, club and ball maker, Earlsferry, Elie, sends us a new patent metal putter, called the "Acme." The features of this club are a bent neck (which is not altogether new), and a flange on the upper edge of the head. In play, this flange quite conceals the sole edge, thus reducing the number of objects in sight of the player, and obviating consequent distraction and confusion of mind. The flange is broader at the nose than at the neck, thus presenting a level surface to the eye, and ensuring a square stroke. We have given the putter a fair trial, and are very well pleased with it. It is well made, and perfectly balanced (Golfing, 11 Mar. 1896: 13).

The ingenuity of Mr. George Forrester has evolved a new idea in the formation of an iron for putting. It is so constructed that unless with a sketch before you it is difficult to explain. However, it has a neck bent or crooked backwards, and a flange on the upper edge which, projecting over the line of the bottom edge by about three-eighths of an inch, makes it, when in the hands of a player, present apparently a solid front to the ball. Missers of short puts who have often good reason to suspect that the angles of their old favourite have played them false will find this a trusty weapon; the ball gets a straight blow, and is thus more under the mastery of the player. The putters are only newly out, and as yet have not had a severe test on the green . . . . Samples, either with a straight or bent neck, can be obtained. They are made at Anderson's cleek factory, Anstruther, a guarantee of their finish and quality (East Fife Record, 21 Feb. 1896: 4).

Forrester's Acme putter pictured is marked "G. Forrester \ Elie \ Earlsferry" on the back of the head along with "Rd No 2694--" (the last two numbers of this 1896 British design registration number are too faint to read).

In order to provide a flange that extends out over the ball, the Acme putter has a deep face. Produced only briefly, few Acme putters remain. (For more on George Forrester, see p. 450.)

Prior to 1930, the only patented putter with a flange overhanging the face was devised by Donald Swan, of Grosse Ile, Michigan. According to his U.S. patent (No. 1,678,750) dated July 31, 1928, Swan designed a large triangular flange integral with the top of the blade, the leading point of the flange centered over the ball to serve as an alignment aid. (See p. 455.)

JOHN CARRUTHERS
"VARDON PUTTER,"
CURVED FACE

NORMAN MAIN
"MAXMO"
CURVED FACE PUTTER

Two different patents from the wood shaft era incorporated the idea of curving the face inward, heel to toe. The first was a British patent (No. 14,313) dated June 25, 1904, granted to John Carruthers, a stockbroker's clerk from London. Trying to make a more accurate putter, Carruthers designed a mallet putter with a dramatically curved face, heel to toe. An aluminum head example of Carruthers club, bearing his patent number and stamped "Vardon Putter" atop its head, is shown below right. The shaft of this club is stamped "H. Vardon" in small block letters and "Mitchell \

Manchester" in large block letters. Harry Vardon was a six-time British Open Champion, and Mitchell of Manchester was the retail outlet that sold this club.

The other patent to cover a face curved heel to toe was granted to Norman Stewart Main, a solicitor from Linlithgow, Scotland. His putter is the wooden putter pictured below left. Applying for a British patent on December 30, 1927, Main received his patent (No. 304,008) on January 17, 1929. Main also received a U.S. patent, (No. 1,901,562) applied for on December 16, 1928, and issued on March 14, 1933, that covered this club.

Besides a curved face, Main's putter, called the Maxmo, has two heavy brass soleplates, one under the toe and one under the heel. Underneath these plates are large weights.

According to Main's patent, his putter would redirect, and thereby correct, the errant shot accidentally struck on either the toe or the heel. Main calculated that the added weight and curved face would compensate for the lost distance and wrong direction usually imparted to such mis-hit shots. By heavily weighting the toe and heel, Main believed the curve given to the face would not need to be exaggerated.

The Main putter shown here is marked "Maxmo\ Reg." on the crown and "Made in Scotland \ R. Forgan \ St. Andrews \ Pat. Apd. For \ Medium Lie" on the sole. Forgan produced the Maxmo putter in 1928 and promoted it as follows:

It has a new club head with the maximum moment of inertia, and a calculated curvature of face designed to minimize errors arising from inaccurate centering of club at impact (The American Golfer, May 1928: 76).

Main's patent also covered the idea of correcting shots hit on the heel or toe of wood clubs. His woods used the idea of heel and toe weighting; however, their faces curved outwards similar to the early bulgers.

The Vardon putter and the Maxmo putter were the only heel to toe curved face clubs covered under patents granted prior to 1930, but similar curved face clubs were produced independent of the patent process. Early in the twentieth century, W.R. Pope produced a concave face aluminum mallet head putter titled "Pope's Concave-face Putter." The leading side of the hosel, located midway between the heel and the toe, runs flush with a face once described as "crescent shaped" when viewed from above (*Golfing*, 23 Feb. 1905: 20). Dating somewhere around 1900, an unmarked iron with a nicely curved blade sold at Christie's July 1991 golf auction. Two other curved blade putters sold at auction between 1985 and 1993. One was marked "W.H. Hill" and may have dated from 1915 to 1925; the other was unmarked.

HARRY L. SUTTON
BULGER FACE PUTTER, MULTIPIECE HEAD

The face of the multipiece putter pictured here curves outward, heel to toe, similar to an early bulger wood. While quite distinctive and dating from 1925 or shortly thereafter, this putter, stamped "Sutton of Sutton" on its crown, was not the first to have a bulger face.

In 1891, as the bulger was establishing itself as the new standard for woods, a letter to the editor of *Golf*, signed "A.M.R." (A.M. Ross?), refers to a bulger putter:

To the Editor of GOLF. Sir,–A golfer may well say, what next? We have bulger drivers, bulger brassies, bulger short and long spoons, and now we have bulger putters. On looking into the workshop at Eastbourne last Saturday, I found that Mr. Peter Paxton (an old Musselburgh player) had his men busy making this form of club. He maintains that it putts much truer than any other description of club, either wood or iron. Before passing a definite opinion about its capabilities I would like to have a more extended trial than I had time for; but I may say, from the few strokes I made with it, that it answers its purposes much better than one would be inclined to think from the name and form of the club (11 Sept. 1891: 434).

The bulger putter was not an effective club even though it was designed to be more accurate. The bulge would supposedly compensate for a pulled or pushed stroke and redirect the ball straight to the target:

Mr. E.S. Spencer, of Wimbledon, after trials with putters of various shapes and designs, has come to the conclusion that a putter having a slightly bulged face, and well balanced, is more productive of accuracy than the straight-faced one now generally in use. The great difficulty to be mastered, is to hold the face of the putter parallel to the hole, or to the desired direction to be taken, and to maintain it in that position whilst striking the ball; any slight deviation from that position will cause a wide ball. Experience has proved that the bulger putter does not require time and nerve wasted in obtaining such a precise adjustment. It is only necessary to address the ball, and play at the hole, striking the ball with the club at the apex of the bulge, or the point of the bulge nearest the hole, which, even if the club is not quite parallel to the hole, readily catches the eye, giving a definite point to strike with (*Golf*, 18 Feb. 1898: 398).

Complete with a slight bulge across its face, Spencer's putter was available from Messrs. Cann & Taylor by the end of 1898.

The bulger putter pictured, produced by Harry L. Sutton while working as the professional at Sutton Coldfield, in Streetley, England, has a large, flat lead weight located on the sole between two pieces of aluminum, one under the toe and the other under the heel. Held in place by two screws each, these aluminum pieces are removable should the golfer desire to replace the lead weight with *rollers*! The author knows of three Sutton putters that include three rollers across the sole (see p. 387). One example is marked "Prov. Patent No. 27,230", which is a post-1916 British provisional patent application number. (The patent was not issued.) While the particular club pictured is certainly of interest to collectors, the model with the roller sole is much more so.

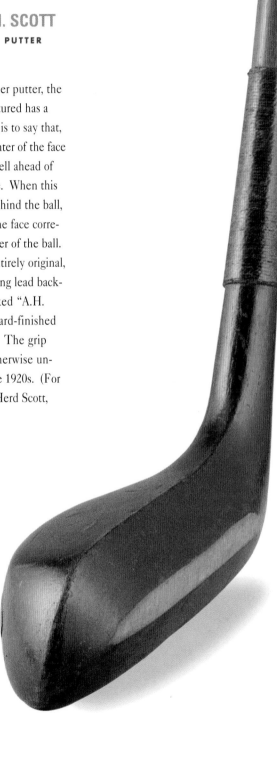

ANDREW H. SCOTT
RIDGE FACE PUTTER

To the making of a good club there goes an amount of knowledge, skill and intelligence that few players are aware of, however much they may appreciate the result. In the case of wooden clubs, the use of machinery stops at the rude, almost formless, blocks out of which the head is to be shaped, and the long square which will by-and-by be fashioned into a shaft. These lengths of hickory are sometimes supplied roughly turned, but many of the best makers will not have them so, insisting on their being reduced by hand-planing from the square. Every club so made is, therefore, a direct product of human intelligence, and its development from mere wood to the finished implement is, to a mind given that way, a process of the highest interest. There is very little about a golf club that can be done by rote. To each new head and shaft the same intelligence has to be applied afresh, for the reputation of the workman and his employer is at stake in every club turned out (W.L. Watson, *Golf* [ny], Feb. 1898: 24).

Unlike any other putter, the pristine putter pictured has a ridge face—which is to say that, lengthwise, the center of the face projects forward well ahead of the rest of the face. When this putter is placed behind the ball, the thin ridge of the face corresponds to the center of the ball.

This club is entirely original, complete with a long lead backweight. It is marked "A.H. Scott" across its hard-finished leather wrap grip. The grip helps date this otherwise unmarked club to the 1920s. (For more on Andrew Herd Scott, see page 136).

L.A. YOUNG COMPANY?
WOODEN SAND WEDGE

Between 1890 and the end of the wood shaft era, traditional woods (such as drivers, brassies, and spoons) were occasionally made with metal clubheads. However, traditional irons (such as mashies, mid irons, and niblicks) were almost never made with wooden clubheads. The incredible exception to this rule is pictured on this and the facing page—a sand wedge made from *wood* !

The club pictured is both quite similar and very different from the popular Hagen Concave sand wedge produced in 1930 (see p. 242). Like the Hagen Concave, this club is a sand wedge, with 55 degrees of loft and a 36 inch long shaft; the face is dramatically curved; and it was almost certainly made in 1930, concave faces becoming illegal in 1931. Unlike the Hagen Concave, however, this sand wedge is made from wood, not iron; its face is curved heel to toe, not top to bottom; and it was never popular. Remaining examples are extremely rare.

Marked "Beckley-Ralston \ Walter Hagen" on the top of the head, "W.H. \ B.R." on the aluminum soleplate, and "Pat. Pend." on a brass plate that covers the head behind the soleplate, the club pictured was probably made by the L.A. Young Company, the maker of "Walter Hagen Golf Equipment," shortly after their introduction of the Hagen Concave sand wedge. The author believes the wooden sand wedge to be a product of the L.A. Young Company for a few reasons.

First, the only other wooden sand wedge known to the author is simply marked "Tommy Armour" on the top of the head. Before Tommy Armour became a staff member of the Crawford, McGregor & Canby Company, L.A. Young produced a few Walter Hagen clubs that also bore Armour's name. For example, a set of wood-shafted circa 1930 Hagen irons also marked "Made for Tommy Armour" is known.

Second, the Hagen "Sandy Andy" sand wedge, produced by L.A. Young in the early 1930s, is very similar to this wooden club. The Sandy Andy does not have a concave face and is made from aluminum, but the underside of the head consists of a large, convex sole that simply rounds up to the back of the head. This is very similar to the sole on the wooden sand wedge shown. Furthermore, the Sandy Andy also has a thin ridge across the top of the head, behind the face. This ridge, as on the wooden sand wedge, gently slopes down to the back-line of the head and bears the Walter Hagen name.

Third, the wooden sand wedge has more in common with the Hagen Concave sand iron than it does with any other club.

What all of these clubs have in common is the Walter Hagen connection. It should be noted that the Beckley-Ralston name on the wooden sand wedge is not especially significant—the Beckley-Ralston company sold clubs other than those of their own make.

The wooden sand wedge pictured began the patent process, but a patent was never issued. Because of the 1931 rule against concave faces, the club's inventor had no reason to complete the patent process.

Hints on Care of Golf Clubs.

If the saying that cleanliness is next to godliness be true, many golfers, to judge from the state of their clubs, must be hardened sinners. . . .

Iron clubs should be cleaned every time after use either by the player or his caddie, and this should be done with fine emery paper, not coarse, a drop of oil on back of emery before using is helpful. Rangoon oil is one of the best for iron heads, but any good cycle oil will do . . . . Dirty irons look slovenly.

For all shafts and wooden heads when dry, a little oil is good occasionally, the best for this purpose is linseed. Care must be taken not to put it on face, scare, sole, nor touch twine, and after oiling rub with a dry cloth. . . .

Clubs, like tooth-brushes, should never be lent, but if you live near a golfing centre, keep a few spare clubs to lend (W.W., *Golf Illustrated*, 27 Nov. 1903: 172).

261

Golf has this advantage over law: You are your own judge, jury, and advocate. You write your own instructions, furnish your own witness in the person of a purchaseable caddie, assess the damage yourself, and if you want a new trial all you have to do is begin at No.1 and try it all over again.

(*Golfing*, Dec. 2, 1909: 20)

Sole Design

The sole is not the territory of wild ideas or outlandish designs. It is usually dictated by the shape of the head. For the most part, the sole is simply the bottom of the club—out of sight, out of mind.

Every club has a sole, but on most wooden clubs the only consideration given to the sole was how to protect it, how to keep it from denting and cracking as it came in contact with the ground, the ball, a rock, or whatever. Therefore, clubmakers methodically employed ram's horn or fiber across the leading edge of the sole and/or metal plates across a much larger area of the sole. Irons, of course, did not need such elements.

Soleplates have many incidental features. They come in a wide range of outlines. Sometimes the plate is on only the front half or back half of the head; sometimes it is narrow, sometimes wide; and occasionally two different pieces of metal make up the soleplate. In the world of collectibles, none of these aspects matter much because they are minor and not very interesting. After all, most woods have a ram's horn or flat soleplate of some kind.

The soles presented in this chapter were designed with the intention of affecting the golf shot, not just to protect the wood from breaking. Of course, a few clubs elsewhere in this book also have very interesting and collectible sole designs. However, those clubs, such as the Hagen Concave sand iron, the Roger Brown rake iron, and the Maxmo curved face putter, have other more prominent features.

The first patent relating to sole design, Robert Henry's British patent (No. 8261) dated May 14, 1891, covered a solid brass (or other metal) soleplate cast in one piece with the backweight. This patent, however, is more for a backweight than it is for a soleplate.

The next patent relating to sole design, Charles James Rivett-Carnac's British patent (No. 10448) dated June 19, 1891, was the first to deal only with the soleplate. This patent covered inlaying a metal plate behind, and flush against, the usual horn under the leading edge of a wood.

Neither of these patents is of much interest as far as their designs go. However, their historical relevance is important, and for that reason clubs produced directly under these patents would be collectible if found.

Following Rivett-Carnac, Willie Dunn Jr. received the next patent that dealt with the shape of the sole. Dunn produced some clubs under this patent, and an example is discussed on the next page.

Above the ball he takes from his bag a beautiful mashie niblick, his best-liked club. It is autographed by Abe Mitchell and was secured for him at great pains, in addition to the expense, by good old Angus McAngus. The man parks his feet correctly, frowns down the fairway, glances off at a distant motorcar, not hiding his annoyance, and fires when ready. The ball rises gracefully from its couch, achieves the altitude record, develops distance promisingly, but then angles insanely to the left. It plunks into the opal sea. . . . The lucid water closes above it and the opal glint is again unmarred. . . .

The man stands a moment in deep contemplation. Then once again he swings the perfect mashie niblick autographed by Abe Mitchell. He has the correct stance, he breaks the wrists perfectly, the shot is well timed, and the follow through beyond criticism. The club rises gracefully into the air, develops distance as it whirls, and it, too, sinks beneath the opal sea, autograph and all. There is a deadly glitter in the man's eyes as the deep swallows his pet (Wilson 1923, 15-16).

WILLIE DUNN, JR.
"CONVEX SOLE" BRASSIE

At first glance, it is the insert in Willie Dunn Jr.'s "Convex Sole" brassie (pictured) that draws the most attention. However, the unique feature of Dunn's club is the convex shape of the sole. Leather inserts, originally used to repair long nose woods, were a standard feature on many new clubs made after 1890.

To fit the convex shape of the sole, which it completely covers, the soleplate is cambered. When this club is placed behind the ball, the center of the brass soleplate extends below all other areas, the soleplate curving upward in all directions from its center.

Willie Dunn Jr. received a British patent (No. 22,574) dated December 28, 1891, that covered this club. After identifying Dunn as a professional, teacher, and golf club and ball maker located at "the Golf Club, Biarritz, France," Dunn's patent dealt only with the shape of the sole:

The improvement consists in the sole of the club being made convex, instead of flat as in clubs at present made.

Dunn calculated that his convex sole would effectively handle certain types of difficult lies:

By this means the ball receives the full force of the blow, and the player is enabled to drive the ball out of a hollow place in the ground without cutting up the earth, and out of dents and long grass.

In America during the late 1890s, Dunn advertised this club as able to "[help] a player out of a cuppy lie with more advantage than any other club" (*Golf* [ny], Nov. 1898: 320).

Dunn's Convex Sole brassie pictured is stamped "Willie Dunn's \ Patent \ Convex Sole"

on the crown. The patent granted for this club was the second patent ever issued that dealt primarily with the sole and the first to suggest a new shape for the sole. Dunn's Convex Sole clubs are also desirable simply because they were patented and made by Willie Dunn Jr. One of the finest players, best known personalities, and innovative club and ball makers of his day, Willie Dunn Jr. left behind a legacy for both the golf historian and the golf collector. The October 1897 issue of *Golf* (ny) (16-20) reports at length on Willie's early history as does the March 30, 1895 issue of *The Golfer* (201-202).

Born at Blackheath in 1865, Willie Jr. was the son of Willie Dunn, the prominent professional. When Willie Jr. was thirteen months old he moved with his family to Leith, Scotland, where,

"almost as soon as he could walk, our young hero learned to handle his clubs on the links." At the age of six he moved to Musselburgh with his father, who set up shop there as a clubmaker. While at Musselburgh, Willie Dunn Jr. and Willie Park Jr. became fast friends off the course as well as great rivals on it. Speaking of their relationship, Willie Park Jr. states:

We were great friends indeed, and at the same time great rivals in our golf. We were always playing together. We played each other for the few pennies that came our way, for the balls that we possessed, and for our few and most prized clubs. . . . I was never averse—I was indeed rather anxious—to stake everything that I had in the world on a game of golf. Thus, in turn, Willie Dunn and I had our joyful ups and our miserable downs, one or the other of us being

constantly in a state of bankruptcy, and the times when we were both fairly well-to-do, but neither of us opulent, being mutually unsatisfactory. We played each other day in and day out until we were about eleven or twelve years of age, and then one day there came the tidings—sorrowful for me—that Willie was wanted in London, and that he must go there forthwith (Leach 1907, 101-103).

When he was twelve years old, Willie Dunn Jr. left for Wimbledon to learn clubmaking from his older brother, Tom. In 1880 Willie and Tom moved to North Berwick where they continued in the clubmaking business, and Willie helped Tom manage the North Berwick Links.

In 1886 Dunn and Park played another match, only this time it was as young men, not children. Attesting to their level of skill, the record shows that Willie Dunn scored 5, 4, 2, 2, 3, 5, 4, 3 –28– over North Berwick's last eight holes in gaining an edge over Park, 70 to 71, in the morning round:

When the news of this brilliant play reached the town the storekeepers closed their shops and hastened to the links to witness the second round, which resulted in a win for Dunn at the thirteenth hole by six up and five to play (The Golfer, June 1898: 82).

Later the same year, Willie left North Berwick for Devon, England, where he took charge of the Westward Ho! golf course. Before leaving North Berwick, Willie received a gold watch and chain subscribed for by more than one hundred golfers as a memento of their appreciation.

In 1888 Willie went to Chingford, near London, where he became the superintendent of the club and greens at Royal Epping Forest after first laying out the course. Shortly thereafter, due to the dampness of the climate around London, his health began to suffer. Following the advice of his physician, Willie left Chingford for Biarritz, in the south of France. He worked at the golf club there for approximately five years.

In 1893 Dunn came to America. In addition to accepting a summer job as a professional instructor at Shinnecock Hills Golf Club in Southampton, New York, he laid out a number of courses in neighboring areas, such as Meadowbrook, Islip, Lakewood, Orange, East-Hampton, Oyster Bay, Rockaway, Hunting Club, and others. Finding success, Dunn continued to establish himself in America, returning to France only during the winter months.

In October of 1894, Dunn won what was billed as both the Golf Championship of the United States and the first American Open championship. This event was sponsored by the St. Andrews Golf Club and held over their Yonkers, New York, course. With match play determining the champion from among four contestants, Dunn won both his matches and received the one hundred dollar first prize and a gold medal. This victory is not recognized by the USGA because the USGA was formed after this event, on December 22, 1894. When the first USGA Open Championship was held, in 1895, Dunn finished second. He lost to Horace Rawlins by two strokes, 175 to 173, over 36 holes.

In 1896 Dunn became the first professional at Ardsley Park Country Club, Ardsley-on-Hudson, a course in New York designed by Dunn. In the winter of 1896, Dunn opened a "golf gymnasium" at 306 Fifth Avenue, New York City. Inside what is now termed the old Madison Square Gardens, Dunn gave indoor golf lessons in a room 76 feet long, 30 feet wide, and 28 feet high. Classes were limited to six persons each:

The pupils stand behind each other on a long strip of india rubber matting, with the places for the feet carefully marked in chalk. The "swing proper" is carefully taught, and for lofting, a bunker "seven feet high" is constructed, while for putting there is provided "a large putting green, covered with green baize, undulating in places, with a regulation hole in the centre (Golf, 22 Jan. 1897: 345).

Dunn not only gave golf lessons in his golf gymnasium, he continued as a club and ball maker, providing a good selection of both for his customers, while also offering to lay out courses in any part of the country.

Moving from one business to the next, in early 1898, after laying out a course in Dayton, Ohio, Dunn was hired by "the Dayton Last Works of Dayton, Ohio, a very large concern, to make golf clubs" (The Golfer, 9 Mar. 1898: 183). Dunn worked in a supervisory capacity with the Crawford, McGregor & Canby Company, formerly the Dayton Last Works. This relationship did not last long. In March of 1900, an advertisement for Dunn's clubs states, "Crawford, McGregor & Canby clubs are no longer made under his supervision" (Golf [ny]: 192).

Also in 1900, Dunn was credited with originating the indoor golf school when he reopened "his own school in Forty-Second Street for the fifth consecutive season" (Golf [ny], Dec. 1900: 442).

During the summer of 1901, while working as a club professional, Willie encountered hazardous duty:

Willie Dunn, the well known player, who is professional at the Innes Arden Club, near New York, met with a bad accident last week, being struck with a cleek in the hands of a member. Dunn was stunned, an ugly wound being inflicted, but his numerous English friends will be glad to learn that he is progressing well towards recovery (Golf Illustrated, 2 Aug. 1901: 84).

The August 5, 1909 issue of Golfing states "Dunn spent over ten years in America." It also reported that:

Willie Dunn, of North Berwick, has been appointed to succeed Arthur Butchart as professional to the Bramshot Club, Fleet, Hants (4).

Dunn apparently never took this job because Tom Ball succeeded Butchart at Bramshot in 1909 (Jackson 1994, 114). Dunn returned to England permanently in 1940 and "died . . . in London in his 88th year" (Golfing, Mar. 1953: 5).

During his life, Dunn created some wonderfully imaginative and creative clubs. His Rotary putter, Unexcelled wood, Indestructible wood, and pyralin putter (made by The Kempshall Mfg. Co.) are highly collectible and pictured elsewhere in this book.

In addition to producing a duplex metalwood in the early 1900s, Dunn (residing in California at the time) received a U.S. patent (No. 1,541,126) dated June 9, 1925, that covered a metalwood with a concave sole and a convex crown, both intended to raise the center of gravity within the clubhead. On January 5, 1926, Dunn received a U.S. patent (No. 1,568,888) that covered a hollow metalwood designed to hold a liquid that would supposedly shift towards the ball at impact. The amount of liquid inside the club could be increased or decreased through a threaded plug in the head. Loaded with "quick silver," this metalwood, called the "Willie Dunn Magician," could be purchased with matching "Pot Hollow Irons" (Fraser's 1931, 424). The author has handled two Willie Dunn Magician metalwoods and two matching irons. None of these clubs, all of which had metal shafts, had a plug of any type, and liquid could not be detected in the head.

Dunn also produced some interesting golf balls. His "Stars and Stripes" gutty ball actually had stars and stripes impressed into its surface. This ball was covered under a U.S. patent (No. 27,441) dated July 27, 1897—the first U.S. patent ever awarded for a golf ball!

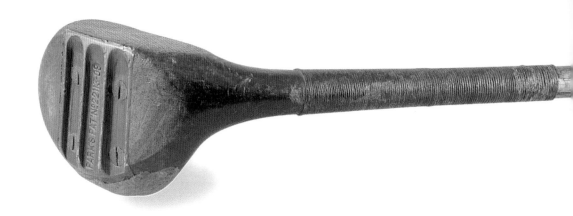

WILLIE PARK, JR.
"PIKUP," GROOVED SOLE

In the midst of his greenmaking duties Park has found time to invent and patent a new wooden club. It is called the "Pikup," and . . . is designed for playing bad-lying balls either on wet or hard ground. . . . The "Pikup" has simply a brass plate about an inch and a quarter long let into the sole. The plate has three deep grooves cut into it . . . . to minimise friction with the ground and permit of the passage of loose or wet soil, which, in the ordinary club, sticks either to the face or sole of the club. The "Pikup" is beautifully made and balanced . . . (Golf Illustrated, 31 Dec. 1909: 26).

Willie Park Jr. received a British patent (No. 22,113) dated September 28, 1909, that covered his Pikup club, shown above. According to his patent, the objective of the corrugated brass soleplate was "the reduction of friction between the bottom surface of the club head and the ground during the stroke," so the golfer could hit the ball farther and reduce his or her prospects of injury:

It will be understood that the reduction of the contact surface at the bottom of the club will enable the [player] to drive the ball a longer distance . . . and will minimize the jar communicated to the arm of the player, and prevent to a considerable extent what is commonly known by players as "golfers elbow."

The splice neck club pictured above is marked "W. Park's Pikup \ Rd. 552861" on the crown. "Park's Pat' No 22113 – 09" is stamped in the corrugated brass soleplate recessed into the head. The number "552861" is a British design registration number that dates towards the end of 1909. Pikup drivers, brassies, and spoons were made with either a socket or splice neck.

R. FORGAN & SON
"FRIKSHUNLESS," GROOVED SOLE

The unique brass soleplate on the splice neck wood pictured below might appear to be an after-market addition to the club because the plate is not recessed into the sole. However, the writing on the head identifies the plate as an original part of the club.

The top of the head is stamped "Frikshunless \ R. Forgan \ St. Andrews." The "King's crown" mark used by Forgan between 1902 and 1910 is also present. In very small letters, the brass sole is marked "Patent Applied For" in the bottom of one of the long grooves.

"Patent Applied For" and "Frikshunless" indicate that this club bears an unusual characteristic—a feature designed to reduce the club's friction with the ground. Obviously the raised, grooved soleplate, which has a much smaller "footprint" than the bottom of the head, is the feature.

Although the patent application for the Frikshunless soleplate lapsed, Ben Sayers Jr. received a British patent (No. 244,925) dated January 7, 1925, that covered a wooden club with a "Gruvsol"—a recessed soleplate having a number of small, parallel grooves extending across its entire length, to "direct the club head in a straight line . . . over the turf." Prior to receiving this patent, Sayer's produced a "Gruvsol" (grooved sole) putter.

The Sayers Gruvsol putter and the Frikshunless wood are good entry level collectibles. Gruvesol putters are found with regularity; Frikshunless woods are not.

GILBERT LEGH
WEIGHTED SOLE

The Honorable Gilbert Legh of King's Lynn, in the county of Norfolk, England, received a British patent (No. 27,874) dated November 30, 1910, that dealt with soleplates.

As pictured above, Legh's brass soleplate is more than just a soleplate—it is a head weight. According to Legh's patent, the only purpose of the traditional soleplate was to keep the bottom of the club:

from wearing away by the constant friction with the ground when in use, the weight of such metal soles . . . being small and not distributed in any definite way.

Therefore, his invention would ensure that:

the center of mass of the club head will be as nearly as possible in line with the shaft.

In order to position most of the clubhead weight in line with the shaft, Legh's patent proposes either inlaying a heavy metal bar in the bottom of the head, in line with the shaft, or covering the entire sole with a special metal plate. The putter shown above employs the latter idea with more engineering than meets the eye. In order to position most of the soleplate's weight in line with the shaft, the front portion of the plate is thinner than the rest of it:

The thickness of the plate along the front edge must be so small that when the ball is struck fairly the contact between club and ball is confined to the wooden face of the club head.

Legh's putter pictured is marked "Legh's Patent \ No. 27874/1910" across the sole-plate. Note the numbering. It is stamped twice or double stamped. On a club with unusual *structural* features, a double stamp is of little significance. When considering smooth face irons such as those made by John Gray, Robert White, or their contemporaries, however,

the stamp (cleekmark) takes on more importance. On such irons, the stamp is the primary feature. Therefore, a double stamped iron is not as desirable as an iron with a clean stamp. If the double stamp is prominent and unsightly, it is less desirable than a single faint stamp or a stamp that has lost a few letters.

Remember, when considering the name stamp on a club, the critical element is the unmistakable identification of the club. A club should be judged primarily on what it is and its condition, not on how deep its letters are. It should be noted, however, that the quality of the name stamp is much more of a factor when evaluating the more common clubs.

Another aspect of Legh's putter is the shape of its head. The untrained eye might classify this club as a long nose with a brass soleplate. However, true long nose clubs were only made during the long nose era. If a club was made exactly like a long nose but after such clubs went out of fashion, it is termed a "long nose style" club. After 1890, a number of clubs made from wood and even aluminum were produced with long nose style heads. A basic long nose style club does not have the same collectible value as a true long nose.

Some putters, such as this Legh putter, were made with long heads but without the shape of a long nose. These putters are loosely termed "long head mallets."

JAMES DALGLEISH
RIDGE SOLE BRASSIE

On November 29, 1899, James Dalgleish, a British citizen residing in Chicopee Falls, Massachusetts, applied for a U.S. patent (No. 645,944) to cover the golf club pictured. Issued on March 27, 1900, Dalgleish's patent provides the sole of a brassie with a rounded ridge extending "rearwardly from the striking-face of the club." In addition to covering the ridge with a brass plate, Dalgleish weights the ridge with a cylindrical lead weight that, beginning "in the rear side of the head," extends well into the head. The ridged sole allowed his brassie to effectively strike a ball in a grassy or cupped lie. The weight in the ridge added power to the club:

It will be seen that the ridge . . . makes it possible to hit the ball a full fair blow, even though the ball be resting on rough ground, whereby the player can with greater certainty make a long straight drive. The position of the weight in line with the striking-surface formed by the rearward end of the ridge adds to the force of the impact of the club at the striking-point against the ball.

The brassie pictured is marked "J. Dalgleish \ The Spalding \ Patent Applied For" on the top of the head.

James Dalgleish, a golf club and ball maker originally from Gailes, just a few miles up the coast from Troon, Scotland, was a respected clubmaker prior to leaving for America:

James Dalgleish, the professional of the Glasgow Golf Club at Gailes, has decided to go to America, and sets out early next month, his destination, in the first instance, being New York, in connection with which, it is well known, there are a large number of golf clubs. Dalgleish will be an acquisition to the ranks of the professionals there, for he is a steady, reliable man, a first-rate clubmaker, and though not in the first rank as a golfer, he plays a good round, while having a thorough knowledge of the game, both theoretical and practical. He is a good coach. He learned his trade and his golf with A. Forgan, Glasgow, and prior to his connection with Gailes was connected with Alexandra Park. There seems to be a good opening in the United States for such men as Dalgleish, and with his knowledge of all that pertains to the game of golf, he cannot fail to get an opportunity for the exercise of his talents (Golfing, 11 Mar. 1896: 8).

Once in America, Dalgleish apparently became connected with Spalding. Not only is his club pictured here marked "Spalding," his patent lists his address as Chicopee Falls, Massachusetts, which is just up the street from Chicopee, the headquarters of A.G. Spalding & Bros.

By 1909, Dalgleish was working at a golf club in Kansas City, Missouri:

James Dalgleish, a Scotch golfer who is instructor and clubmaker to a golf club in Kansas City, Missouri, came over from America the other day, to be present at the golden wedding celebrations of his parents, Mr. and Mrs. Wm. Dalgleish, Earlston, N.B., who were formerly in the service of the Duke of Rosburghe (Golfing, 30 Dec. 1909: 4).

WILLIAM GIBSON & CO.

RIDGE SOLE IRON

Reminiscent of James Dalgleish's ridge sole brassie, the Gibson iron pictured has a strikingly unusual face, the middle of which extends down farther than the heel and toe.

The back of this blade is marked "A. Matthews \ Rhyl" inside an oval, and "Reg No 386911 \ Hand Forged \ Niblick" along with Gibson's "star" trademark. The head of this club was forged by William Gibson; Matthews shafted and/or sold the club. The registration number "386911" dates to the early part of 1902.

William Gibson had a reputation for being among the best at his trade:

A more painstaking cleek-maker never lived than Willie Gibson, and it would do a man who upholds drop forged work a considerable amount of good to spend an hour at Gibson's and see an iron head go through its whole stage of manufacture (Golfing, 15 Mar. 1900: 16).

After apprenticing to James Anderson of Anstruther, Scotland, Gibson began working on his own in 1890 as a cleek maker in Edinburgh. Before becoming William Gibson & Company, Gibson worked as a partner in the firm of "Stirling and Gibson," which began operating in 1897:

The recent death of Mr. Stirling (late of the firm of Stirling and Gibson) has caused a change in the title of the cleek-making business, where Willie Gibson can generally be found by the visitor to Morningside, Edinburgh. At the forge in Jordan Lane work is conducted now by Wm. Gibson and Co. (Golfing, 15 Mar. 1900: 16).

After Stirling's death, Gibson needed more room for his expanding business, so he moved his company to new quarters in Kinghorn, Fife, Scotland. This move was completed by May of 1903 (*Golfing*, 21 May, 1903: 28). A few years later, Gibson, known primarily as a cleekmaker, apparently began making wooden clubs as well.

In addition to Gibson's cleekmark, the back of the iron shown also bears the mark of Alfred Matthews. Matthews was the professional at Rhyl from at least 1902 through 1917. A good golfer, "[Matthews] is also a skilled craftsman, and makes a very complete line of first-class clubs" (*Golfing*, 23 July 1908: 24). Matthews advertised, "[Making] clubs to pattern a specialty. Best material and workmanship" (*Golf Monthly*, May 1914: 238).

Unfortunately, the design registration number on this iron does not identify a British registered design for a golf club. However, Robert Simpson, the famous clubmaker, received a British patent (No. 11,264) dated May 14, 1913, that covered a similar iron. Although Simpson's club is not designed exactly the same as the one pictured here, both clubs appear to share the same purpose. According to Simpson's patent:

The object being to so design a club that the weight will be concentrated . . . at the striking centre and that the bottom or sole will be rounded away at the heel and the toe in order that the turf cannot be cut by these parts of the club.

By such a design the ball can be more readily moved from a hole or rut and in striking the ball a less frictional surface is presented because of the rounded parts thus preventing "slicing" or "pulling."

As illustrated in Simpson's patent, the sole of his club is all on one level and not divided into two levels as is Gibson's. Simpson's iron simply rounds away the sharp leading edge under the heel and the toe as well as the corresponding edges on the back of the blade.

RICHARD CRANKSHAW
"DUNLEWY," ANGLE SOLE

Richard Louis Crankshaw, of Dunlewy, Gweedore, Ireland, received a British patent (No. 253,394) dated September 25, 1925, that covered the wood pictured above. Crankshaw's wood appears to be designed for playing a ball in a cupped lie or nestled down in grass, but that is not the stated purpose of his club.

In his patent, Crankshaw states that the standard golf club, particularly a driver, is difficult for the ordinary player to strike on its center because:

there is no indication or mark to enable the player to sight the ball accurately with the centre of the driving face.

Therefore, the object of Crankshaw's club was to help the golfer accurately identify the center of the face when addressing the ball. By designing what he termed a "V" sole and corresponding soleplate, "the apex of which is on the vertical centre line of the driving face," Crankshaw theorized that the golfer could:

sight a ball correctly by aligning the apex of the V with the vertical centre line of the ball.

The club above is stamped " 'Dunlewy' \ Patent 253394" on the top of the head. The Dunlewy was patented in the United States (No. 1,619,566) on March 1, 1927.

Related to the Dunlewy, the Loftum wood has an angled sole similar to the Dunlewy's, but it has an ordinary face. Like Dunlewy woods, Loftum woods occasionally turn up.

B.H.H. COCKBURN
"THE BOMBE," RIDGE SOLE

Designed to help the golfer play a ball either resting in a small depression or nestled down in grass, Cockburn's "The Bombe" provides another type of ridged sole. As shown below, the ridge extends only halfway across the sole.

The central portion of the face on The Bombe extends down much farther than the heel and toe portion. This is similar to the Dalgleish ridge sole (p. 268).

The top of the club shown below is marked "B.H.H. Cockburn \ Le Touquet" inside an oval with " 'The Bombe' " stamped directly below it. In 1907 Cockburn became the professional at Le Touquet Golf Club, located in France, and remained there until 1914, when he accepted the professional's position at Frinton on Sea, in England. He worked there until 1921 (Jackson 1994, 18).

A club similar to The Bombe is the "Confidus Spoon." Originally marketed in England by Cann & Taylor and endorsed by J.H. Taylor, the Confidus was also offered by the Burke Golf Company, of Newark, Ohio, in their 1917 catalog.

Hints to Beginners . . . . If you cannot play golf with a golf club, you had better leave golf alone (Golf, 30 Aug. 1895: 484).

WILLIAM BALLINGALL
FLANGE SOLE
IRON & PUTTER

William Ballingall's British patent (No. 925) dated January 16, 1894, was the first patent granted for a flange on either an iron or a putter. According to his patent, by having a flange that extends approximately half an inch behind a "rolled" or bevelled leading edge, his clubs would "slide easily over the turf without tending to cut it up."

Ballingall's flange sole irons, originally made by Simpson of Carnoustie, were marketed as "Ballingall's Patent Cleeks, Irons, and Mashies" (*Golf*, 23 Mar. 1894: 32). In 1894, a brief review described the flange on Ballingall's clubs:

The plate [flange]extends the entire length of the back of the blade, is semicircular in shape, and at its greatest width is about half an inch broad (*Golf*, 9 Mar. : 407).

Although half an inch does not sound like much, it at least doubled the size of the sole on an ordinary iron, which was usually no more than one-fourth of an inch thick and often closer to three-eights.

Ballingall's flanged iron pictured at the bottom of this page is stamped "R. Forgan & Son \ St. Andrews" on the back of the blade. The King's crown mark, also stamped on the back of the blade, identifies this club as being made just after 1902 (see p. 69). The putter pictured directly below is unmarked, but, because it appears to date to circa 1900, it was most likely made by Robert Simpson:

To the Editor of "Golf."
Sir,—Could you tell me where I can get a "Ballingall's Patent Putter"? I have made inquiries, but without success.
I am, Sir, etc., J.S. Morris
(*Golf*, 24 Mar. 1899: 53)

To the Editor of "Golf."
Sir,—In reply to J.S. Morris, he can get all kinds of Ballingall's patent iron clubs from R. Simpson, clubmaker, Carnoustie, N.B., who is sole agent for same.
I am, Sir, etc., W. Trickett
(*Golf*, 31 Mar. 1899: 76).

Flanged irons were also produced under Francis Brewster's British patent (No. 24,832) dated November 14, 1903, (see p. 206) and Louis Rose's British patent (No. 20,698) dated September 13, 1913.

Rose's flange, also designed to keep the club from digging too deeply into the turf, is flat and quite broad. According to the patent, the flange could vary in breadth, but was not to break the following R&A rule:

"That the length of the head from the back of the heel to the toe shall be greater than the breadth from face to back of head."

An example of Rose's flanged iron sold at auction in 1989. Compared to Ballingall's iron, Rose's club has a much larger flange, a stronger visual presence, and is both more rare and more collectible.

In 1894 Reginald Brougham devised a flanged putter not covered under any patent (see p. 281).

A relatively large number of irons produced after the turn of the century have soles that include the beginnings of a flange. In actuality, these irons are better described as having a thick sole —a sole that does not affect the collectibility of the club. Such thick sole irons are not as exaggerated as Ballingall's patent irons with their much larger flange. Few Ballingall flanged irons/putters remain today.

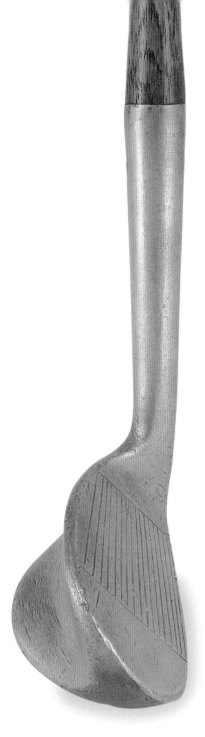

GEORGE WORTHINGTON
FLANGE SOLE IRONS

On June 8, 1925, George C. Worthington, of Elyria, Ohio, applied for a U.S. patent to cover the irons pictured. A patent (No. 1,617,090) was issued on February 8, 1927. According to his patent, Worthington believed beginning golfers have a tendency to hit many of their shots "fat":

There is a tendency on the part of most beginners in the game of golf to swing a club slightly high or too low when making an "iron" shot. In the latter case, the sole of the club head will strike the ground considerably to the rear of the ball and will result in digging into the sod, thereby not only being destructive to the course, but also dubbing the shot and causing the player to lose confidence in his game.

To overcome the tendency to "dig in," Worthington designed his irons with a large and slightly cambered sole that, when contacting the ground, would "tend to 'lift' the club head out of the sod."

As described in Worthington's patent, the iron pictured above has a lead plug set in the center of the sole, to help weight and balance the head. The iron below uses a small amount of brass, running down through the back of the head. In spite of the large flanges, which appear to provide plenty of head weight, the added weights were needed because Worthington called for making his irons from *aluminum* (which is lighter than iron) in order to keep the overall weight of his flanged iron manageable.

Aluminum was occasionally used to make putters and metal-woods as far back as the 1890s. However, the early aluminum clubs designed to function *in effect* as irons, made by such makers as William Mills, were still shaped like woods. Producing aluminum irons shaped like irons was un-heard of before Worthington.

The December 4, 1896 issue of *Golf* contains a letter to the editor requesting "aluminium cleek wanted" (231). One week later, two responses were printed. The first, from T. Dunn and Son, stated they could build one, but it would "need to be a great deal thicker" than the standard cleek because aluminum is so light. The other response, from W.G. Jamieson, stated that Messrs. Bowen and Co. could possibly construct one if a model was pro-vided, but also observed that an aluminum iron was not practical:

Aluminum is too light for cleeks and mashies. To get the right weight they become too clumsy in size (Golf, 11 Dec. 1896: 249).

Although Worthington's sole appears to be specifically designed for use in sand, Worthington's patent does not mention such a possibility. This is not surprising. The flanged irons previously patented were also less lofted and designed to keep the clubhead from digging into turf.

Worthington's club pictured below, matching his patent illus-tration of a mid-iron, is unmarked; the other club, which appears to be a mashie niblick, is marked "Pat. Apd. For" straight up the heel side of the face.

A. TOOLEY & SONS
"POWERFUL" MASHIE, UPSIDE-DOWN BLADE

Hoping to cash in on the vast golf market that developed in the late nineteenth and early twentieth centuries, clubmakers tried any plausible idea when designing golf clubs. If an idea had not been tried, that was reason enough to try it. All the inventor then had to do was think of a sales angle—some way to justify his idea to the marketplace. This task was perhaps the most inventive work of all. But who knew? Maybe the idea would catch on, even though most did not. A case in point is Tooley's "Powerful mashie."

Entirely unlike the flanged clubs previously discussed, the Tooley & Sons Powerful mashie has as thin a sole as possible. Furthermore, the blade gets *thicker* as it progresses up to its top-line. The Powerful mashie pictured, covered under a British design registration number (No. 701,352) issued to Arthur Tooley on October 22, 1923, is stamped "Rustless \ Warranted Hand Forged \ A. Tooley & Sons 40 Fetterland London E. S4 \ Powerful Mashie \ Patent Applied For \ Reg No. 701352" along with "Grip" inside a circle and Tooley's "Forest Brand" "tree" trademark. Although applied for, a patent for this club was not issued.

According to a Tooley & Sons advertisement, " 'Powerful' Irons" were produced as cleeks, irons, mashies, mashie niblicks, niblicks, and jiggers. Powerful Irons were designed (as almost any golf club advertisement is expected to state) to help the golfer hit the ball farther. But according to Tooley's ad, these clubs do not stop at that. They will also hit straighter, keep the ball from ever skying, cheat the wind, and render woods unnecessary:

A club designed to ensure greater length and accuracy from the tee or through the green. An iron club to fulfill the duties of the wooden club and easier to handle. These clubs, made with the weight at the top of the blade instead of the sole, the reverse of ordinary clubs, force the player to strike with the heaviest part, thus ensuring greater length. Furthermore, the sole of the blade being the lighter and thinner part, is below the centre of the ball when struck, and consequently there is little or no danger of "skying." The trajectory of the ball struck with this "Powerful" club is low, therefore wind has little effect on its flight. It is a wind cheater.

The advantages are accentuated when we come to mashies and mashie niblicks. A full shot with an ordinary mashie is a three-quarter shot with this 'Powerful' mashie. No bunker, bush or rut is too ugly for the 'Powerful' niblick; the weight is in the right place, it is behind the club as it strikes the obstruction and gets to the ball and forces it out. Try a 'Powerful' club and see your handicap come down (Fraser's 1924, 255).

Powerful Irons were not well received. Golfers saw them for what they were: highly impractical.

The face on a "Stoddart" putter, an upside-down blade putter produced by W.E. Stoddart, is very thin at the sole and much thicker at the top of the blade. The primary difference between Stoddart's putter and Tooley's iron is that only the area of the blade directly behind the face of Stoddart's putter gets dramatically thicker as it rises up from the sole. At the top of the blade, the heel and toe are only slightly thicker than the sole. By locating the weight atop the blade, Stoddart's putter would supposedly impart topspin to the ball.

There is no doubt that, within the limits of their craft, there are many workmen ... who are true artists, experiencing a just pride in the thoroughness and beauty of their work, and showing a proper jealousy of their reputation.

(W.L. Watson; *Golf* [ny], Feb. 1898: 24)

Clubhead Materials

Including Combination Heads & Face Materials

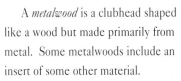

In June of 1876, Thomas Johnston received the first patent ever issued for a golf club. His British patent covered long nose woods made from vulcanite (see p. 82). Although Johnston was the first to make clubheads entirely from nontraditional material, he was certainly not the last.

This chapter presents many of the various materials used to make clubheads. Rather than recount the materials commonly used (the iron used in iron heads and types of wood used in wood heads), this chapter focuses on materials that broke from tradition.

Antique irons, because they were always made from metal, were not made from a wide variety of materials. Even the irons that employed inserts, like the Cran, Ayrton, and leather faced Nicoll, maintained the basic metal head. The concept of making an iron out of something other than metal was not explored until 1935, when Allan Lard became the first person to receive a patent for an iron-shaped club made entirely out of nonmetal material. His U.S. patent (No. 1,988,043) dated January 15, 1935, covered a metal-shafted iron-shaped head made from "moulded mutilated fabric such as canvas, bakelite, . . . texto-lite, or formica." The club's design included only a small metal plate across the sole.

Iron clubheads had one significant problem: they tended to rust. In order to solve this problem, clubmakers began to experiment with various types of metals and metal alloys. Clubs made from some of these alloys, such as monel metal, stainless steel, and an alloy Crawford, McGregor & Canby advertised in 1913 as "Em-an-Em Metal," do not appear much different from the traditional iron heads, and as a group they are not rare. However, non-rusting iron heads made from brass, bronze, or gunmetal, not to forget a British copper-plated iron produced by J. Melling in 1902, are quite visual and appealing. Such irons produced prior to 1910 are rare and collectible.

Unlike irons, woods and putters were made, albeit briefly in many instances, from a variety of alternative clubhead materials. They were constructed from such elements as iron, aluminum, brass, bronze, gunmetal, horn, paper fiber, hornite, vulcanite, condensite, leather, celluloid, ebony, pyralin, gutta percha, etc.

These different materials, as discussed within this chapter, also relate to metalwoods, combination heads, and face materials.

A *metalwood* is a clubhead shaped like a wood but made primarily from metal. Some metalwoods include an insert of some other material.

A *combination head* is a clubhead made from two or more different materials that not only are separate and *visible* somewhere on the head (except the face) but also relate to the structural aspects of the head. Excluded from qualifying a club as having a combination head are any expected or normal materials, such as brass or lead backweights, lead sole weights, or soleplates. Also excluded is any material used over a very small area, such as might be used for alignment guides or to affix material inside the head.

Face material refers to any material exposed on the face that is not visible anywhere across the entire top of the head beyond the depth of a normal insert. It includes unusual inserts, materials that cover the entire face, and spring-face clubs. Face material does not include leather inserts used to repair clubs (as found on many long nose clubs).

The next chapter, which continues the discussion of materials started in this chapter, also discusses *multipiece heads*. Not often seen, multipiece heads are clubheads made from two or more pieces of *the same* or very similar material.

In 1885, nine years after Johnston received the first patent for a golf club, James Davidson received a patent for lawn tennis handles. This patent, however, mentions the idea of applying similar handles to golf clubs (see p. 239). The third patent that applied to golf clubs was Walter Herbert Cook's British patent (No. 363) dated January 8, 1889. Cook's patent primarily targets rackets and cricket bats, but it does mention the possibility of molding the "ends of golf clubs" along with shinty and hockey clubs, croquet mallets and handles, bagatelle cues and rests, and fishing rods . . . out of "pulped paper stock."

Willie Park's lofter received the fourth patent for a golf club (see p. 239). The fifth patent, which, incidentally, was the third patent for a unique clubhead material, was Robert Brand's British patent (No. 9,015) dated June 11, 1890. This patent calls for making wood shape heads from "celluloid or xylonite" (see p. 300).

Following Brand's patent, the next patent to cover constructing a clubhead from nontraditional material was issued in 1891 to William Currie Jr. His patent, the first to cover a metalwood, is discussed on the following page.

WILLIAM CURRIE, JR.
BRASS METALWOOD

During the early 1980s, golfers thought wooden clubs were undergoing a revolutionary change. At the time, woods made from metal were taking the market by storm, primarily the result of the Taylor Made Golf Company's metalwoods introduced in 1979. Prior to this, most golfers had never heard of a legitimate driver or fairway wood made of metal. Metalwoods were seen only as the cheap, ugly clubs you rented at a driving-range if you were unlucky. To golfers in the 1970s, the concept of a stylish and well-made metalwood seemed like a space age idea. However, it was not futuristic at all—such metalwoods date back to the 1890s.

The first patent for a metalwood, a British patent (No. 5741) dated April 3, 1891, was issued to William Currie Jr., an india rubber manufacturer (W. Currie & Co., Caledonian Rubber Works) in Edinburgh, Scotland. According to his patent, Currie wanted to construct a brass clubhead filled with elastic material exposed on the face:

The head is made of [metal], preferably brass, hollowed or chambered out into one or more compartments into which is placed and secured a filling of elastic composition. The filling that I prefer to use is a compound of one or more of the following substances, namely: india-rubber, balata or gutta-percha or mixture of them, may be vulcanized in the manner well known to manufacturers of these materials. I would, however, remark that the materials may be used in an un-vulcanized state if desired. I prefer, when making up the filling composition to add one or more such substances as ground or granulated cork, sawdust, wood pulp, rags, asbestos, or the like . . . .

The filling composition may be fixed in the metal head by cement or by forming projections or spikes on the interior surfaces of the head, round which the composition would be run, or yet again by forming grooves in or upon such interior surfaces.

Currie specified a socket neck joint for his metalwood:

I propose to use the method which is at present used by all golf club makers for fixing on cleek and iron heads namely by means of a socket which forms part of the head.

Currie's ideas came together in the club pictured. The brass head is filled with a mixture of gutta percha. Two screws extend into the head from the sole in order to provide projections on the interior of the head. The neck joint is a perfect example of an iron hosel, complete with nicking and a pin located in the proper position.

The clubhead shown here, the only known example, matches the clubhead illustrated in Currie's patent, complete with a protruding gutta percha face. The shaft is stamped "R. Forgan & Son \ St. Andrews," as they probably shafted this head. The only metalwood produced prior to Currie's, a single example made as an experiment, was reportedly made in 1887:

*Some eight years ago the first metal-headed driver was made, at the suggestion of a customer, by Messrs. Anderson, of Edinburgh, durability being the primary intention. This head was made of sheet iron, and the difficulty and expense of production were quite sufficient to prevent any repetition of the experiment. Some years after this, another Edinburgh maker [Currie] tried gunmetal for the same purpose, with doubtful success; and this was followed by the use of a white metal alloy of aluminium, this last idea being patented by Mr. Brougham (*Golf*, 27 Dec. 1895: 339).*

The gutta percha used in the face of Currie's metalwood is the same basic material used during Currie's day to make golf balls. In 1898 gutta percha was described as follows:

All gutta-percha comes from the Straits Settlements, Cochin China, Cambodia, etc., and it arrives here [the U.K.] in a very adulterated condition. As it comes from the tree the gum is of a cream colour, but it is largely mixed with resin; white bark, gravel, and other impurities are added by the natives to give it weight.

It reaches the manufacturers in a dry state, and the first process is to cleanse it of these impurities. By the time the pure gum is arrived at, the gutta-percha becomes black, owing to oxidation. According to the thoroughness of this cleansing process is the quality of the guttapercha [sic]. After being well mixed by the use of masticators, it is made into long sticks, and the balls are moulded from these. The best balls are made from the pure gum, without any admixture whatever, but less pure qualities are used for cheaper purposes.

A ball is at its best six months after being made and painted, and may be said to deteriorate from that point. . . . Of course the best guttapercha will keep in condition the longest time, but even the best becomes hard and brittle in time from exposure to air (Golfing and Cycling Illustrated, 10 Feb. 1898: 11).

Gutta percha could not only become black, as mentioned above, it could be made red by using additives. Golf ball makers in the early 1890s offered both red and black gutta percha balls. In the advertising section of the October 9, 1891 issue of *Golf*, Peter Paxton announces "Red and Black Gutta kept in Stock." Usually, though, when gutta percha was used as an insert, it was black. One advantage in using red gutta percha, however, was that the clubmaker did not have to wait months for the insert to cure before sending a club out the door:

The question is often asked and debated, which is best—black or red golf balls to play with? And, while some golfers have a preference for the red as being more durable, still the majority of players hold by the black, soft and easily destroyed in shape as it often is by hard hitting. There is not the least doubt that this evil is caused by the want of seasoning or hardening of the gutta, after the manufacture. The heating of the gutta percha in warm water and consequent immersion in cold water after the moulding process, are the means of a certain absorption of moisture, which however carefully it may have been "cupped" or moulded, is only to be erad-icated or cured by two to three months drying in a fixed temperature, neither too high nor too low. The red gutta ball, on the other hand, by having an admixture of foreign substances is less porous, and so less liable to take moisture into its com-position in the manufacturing process; and though not capable of flying quite so far—by reason of its composition—is, for a new ball more to be depended upon in keeping the shape, and not hacking. When a golfer can rely on getting a thoroughly well seasoned black "gutta" to play with, it is by far the better ball, as regards its keeping shape and styling properties (The Golfer, 25 Aug. 1894: 12).

Following Currie's patent, six more patents were granted for metal-woods filled with gutta percha (among other materials) at the face. A brief list of these patents follows:

James McHardy and Frank Bryan's British patent (No. 18,555) dated October 4, 1893, provides a steel or "steel equivalent" shell, open at the face, wherein gutta percha or wood is affixed; a splice neck attaches the head to the shaft.

Ralph H.C. Nevile's British patent (No. 22,157) dated November 20, 1893, describes an aluminum or alloy socket head wood. A recess in the back of the head may be filled with wood, cork, iron, etc. The face is preferably solid, but provisions in the patent allow an insert of leather or gutta percha to be attached to the face or set in a recess in the face if desired.

Malcolm Drummond's British patent (No. 5,368) dated March 14, 1894, provides for a metal head formed as a shell enclosed on all sides except the face—wood, gutta percha, celluloid, etc. to be inserted therein (see p. 278).

Thomas A. Vesey's British patent (No. 5,783) dated March 20, 1894, describes a hollow metal head, preferably steel, open at the front and filled with gutta percha, vulcanite, or other plastic-type material. This patent also mentions the possibility of using a regular wood shaft or a shaft having a metal core covered by wood or another substance such as india rubber (see p. 279).

Frank B. Felton's U.S. patent (No. 723,258) dated March 24, 1903, provides a rubber shell filled with gutta percha inside a metal head and a gutta percha striking-face.

Charles T. Thompson and Frank P. Mitchell's British patent (No. 27, 509) dated January 25, 1906, and their U.S. patent (No. 838,284) dated December 11, 1906, describe a hollow aluminum head filled with resilient material such as gutta percha, rubber, or rubber mixed with feathers. Circular openings across the face, crown, sole, and back of their metal clubhead were to be filled with interior material (see p. 290).

Of these six additional patents for metalwoods possibly filled with gutta percha, the author knows of three that were produced: Drummond's, Vesey's, and Thompson/Mitchell's. Metalwoods with gutta percha faces, however, are extremely difficult to locate.

A few final comments about William Currie Jr.:

In 1877 Currie received a British patent, (No. 4,838) dated Decem-ber 20, that covered making either golf balls or the cores of golf balls from india-rubber blended with ground cork, ground leather, or vegetable fibers. The surface of Currie's ball was to be textured by lining the ball mold with canvas. Currie's was the first patent to cover *only* a golf ball. Two prior patents that discussed making golf balls—H. Nicholson's June 18, 1860, British patent (No. 1,478) and D. Stewart's August 31, 1876, British patent (No. 3,428)—also applied to making balls for other sports such as cricket, rounders, and tennis.

The same day that Currie applied for his metalwood patent (No. 5,741) he also applied for a patent to cover a combination wood head. This patent (No. 5,731) calls for "a vulcanite, celluloid, or wood head made hollow or with a portion of the face cut away . . . and replaced by an elastic composition" such as india rubber, gutta percha, or balata. The portion cut away could be located between the face and the back of the head and the resilient material placed therein would be visible at the top and bottom of the head. Currie also mentions the possibility of applying a metal faceplate to the front of the resilient material. No examples are known.

MALCOLM DRUMMOND
"GUTTAPULT" METALWOODS

The Guttapult woods pictured were covered under Malcolm Drummond's British patent (No. 5368) dated March 14, 1894. At the time, Drummond, from Crawley in the county of Sussex, England, lived near Jack Rowe, the professional at Royal Ashdown Forest in Forest Row, Sussex, England, from 1892 until 1947 (see p. 491).

Three Guttapult metalwoods are known to the author: the two pictured and one that sold at the January 1991 Phillips golf auction in Chester, England. The driver selling at auction was marked "Guttapult \ "J Rowe \ Forest Row" and "9" on its head; the driver pictured here, above left, is unmarked. Both drivers, virtually identical, are characterized not only by a metal (aluminum) head and a gutta percha face but also by three screws: one in the sole, one in the underside of the toe, and one in the leading side of the neck (the tip of this screw

is visible on the following side of the neck). The spoon pictured above right is marked "4" on the top of its head and has two large openings in the sole, two in the back of the head, and one on the underside of the toe. Gutta percha fills these openings, and a screw is used only in the neck.

According to Drummond's patent, the screw in the neck helped fasten the shaft to the head while the screw in the center of the sole and in the underside of the toe helped affix a wood block inside the head, behind the gutta percha face:

The head of the club is hollow and open only at the face, the metal being continuous above, below, and at the sides excepting only the front, the metal thus forming a casing enclosing the cavity.... Into the said cavity is driven and fixed by screws or pins, a core of wood... having the grain of the wood running across the head in a direction at right angles with the surface of the face. The said cavity may be

wholly filled with wood or the wood may be partly cut away and the space thus left be filled with gutta-percha celluloid or like material extending to and forming the face. The gutta-percha is fixed to the wood by being forced into the holes bored in the wood in a slanting direction ... or as with any other like material by screws or pegs.

Drummond's patent also contains a provision for including an adjustable weight in the back of the head:

[This invention has] also if preferred the advantage by means of the moveable and adjustable weight at the back of the club of allowing the balance of the club to be altered at will by moving the said weight either forwards or backwards [towards the toe or the heel].

It is not known if Drummond produced a club with a movable weight, but it is doubtful.

THOMAS A. VESEY
STEEL (IRON?) METALWOOD & ALUMINUM METALWOOD

Thomas Agmondisham Vesey, Rector of Marske, Richmond, in the County of York, England, received a British patent (No. 5,783) dated March 20, 1894, that covered the metalwoods pictured. According to Vesey's patent, one of his clubs could do the work of both a driver and a brassey.

In constructing his club, Vesey called for filling a "preferably" steel metalwood, left open at the face, with gutta percha:

The club consists of a light, preferably steel shell, made in the same shape as the head of any ordinary wooden driver, but slightly smaller and open on the front side . . . . In place of being made of steel, it can however be made of brass, iron or other suitable metal. The hollow in this shell is filled with melted or soft plastic gutta percha, vulcanite or other similar tough hard material. The gutta percha if used should be boiled in water, not dry melted, and run in the case of liquid, or firmly pressed and tamped in the case of plastic material, into the shell.

The gutta percha exposed at the face could be repaired if it began to wear:

The gutta percha can be repaired if necessary in a few minutes, by steaming it with steam of a kettle; this is better than heating it before a fire or with a red hot poker, as the latter is apt to overheat the surface and cause the evolution of gas, thus destroying the quality of the gutta percha. From time to time, as the gutta percha wears, it can be softened in this way, and a little liquid or the softened gutta percha added.

The three Vesey clubs known to the author have wood shafts, but Vesey's patent includes some unusual shaft ideas:

The shaft is either of wood or of steel core surrounded by wood or equivalent material. It can however, be of steel covered with india rubber or similar hard tough material, plastic when hot or on being formed, but such as will not soften with the heat of the hands.

The advantages stated for Vesey's club were its superior driving power, greater durability owing to the strength of the case or shell, and the lasting yet repairable qualities of the gutta percha facing.

The club above right, the only metalwood made from steel (iron?) known to the author, is marked "Vesey's Patent" in tiny letters along the top of the head next to the face. "G. Newby" is stamped on its lemonwood shaft. In addition to being visible across the face, the gutta percha inside this clubhead is visible in three large circular holes on the sole and three large oval holes across the back of the head. These holes served two purposes. They helped fasten the gutta percha in place and reduced the weight of the steel shell.

The aluminum metalwood above is marked "Vesey's Patent" in a circle on the crown. On both clubs, a screw in the back of the neck fastens the shaft in place.

REGINALD BROUGHAM
METALWOOD

Ralph Nevile's British patent (No. 22,157) dated November 20, 1893, was the first to specify aluminum as the material of choice when constructing a metalwood clubhead. The next patent to do so was Thomas Yeoman's British patent (No. 2,248) dated February 1, 1894. (This patent also allows for dovetailing a "plate of hard wood" into the face.) The clubs covered under Nevile's and Yeoman's patents were either produced in very limited numbers or not at all. The Honorable Reginald Thomas Dudley Brougham's British patent (No. 2,416) dated February 3, 1894, was the third patent to list aluminum as a clubhead material (Drummond and Vessey called for hollow *metal* heads). However, it was the first to be produced and receive significant market exposure.

The December 27, 1895 issue of *Golf* includes an article that recounts the different metalwoods made by the end of 1895. The article lists Anderson's single example made in 1887, then Currie's gunmetal model made a few years later, and then Reginald Brougham's clubhead made from a "white-metal alloy of aluminum." Brougham's clubhead, the article continues, was modified in design by Ramsbottom of Manchester and then by Braddell of Belfast. No mention is made of a club by Nevile or Yeoman, and no examples of their clubs are known today.

Brougham's club pictured here is marked "R. Brougham's Patent, Clubs Are Trumps" and "Trade Mark Registered" around the outline of a shamrock on its crown.

Brougham's patent calls for making a wood-shaped head from "aluminum or an alloy of the same, say 85% of aluminum and 15% of brass," with "an opening at the face to receive a block of wood or other material." Two screws fasten the wood block in place, one through a slot on the sole and the other through the back of the head. The provisional specification for Brougham's patent calls for screwing the shaft into the hosel.

Brougham advertised durability as the chief virtue of his club:

Combines the advantages of a wooden with the durability of an iron club. . . . Can be used in the wettest weather without damage! Drives a longer ball than any other club. Will outlast a dozen wooden drivers or brasseys! . . . You can't break it! (Golf, 13 Apr. 1894: 87).

The durability of Brougham's club was provided by the aluminum framework of the head. The wood block, which supplied the positive characteristics of the traditional wood head, *could* become damaged, especially given the hardness of the gutty ball. However, if that happened, the block could easily be replaced. The golfer simply needed to remove two screws and slide the block out of the head. Brougham's advertising points out this feature by noting that the "only wearing part [can be] replaced in a moment," leaving the club ever the same as to lie, weight, and balance (*Golf*, 8 June 1894: 276).

Brougham's driver received a lengthy review which reads in part:

In his patent driver the Hon. Reginald Brougham has designed a club which will rank, if we mistake not, in importance with the introduction of the bulger over the long, straight, narrow-faced clubs of earlier days. Mr. Brougham's idea has been simply to utilize metal for the driver-head in place of wood; and the manner in which the idea has been practically embodied is ingenious, artistic, effective, and ridiculously simple when one sees it. Other inventors have striven to construct an indestructible driver-head, but those we have seen in vulcanite, celluloid, and other composite material have, in practice, been rejected after a short trial (Golf, 23 Mar. 1894: 18).

This review also notes that Brougham's metalwood could be made in various lies depending on the bore given to the neck. Consequently, a golfer could purchase a Brougham club suited to his or her needs and never have to worry about replacing it due to a damaged head:

All golfers have experienced the chagrin when, after breaking a favourite driver, the new head, though ostensibly made to pattern, is wrong either in the lie or the balance. Regrets of this kind are for ever dispelled with the aluminum head . . . . One other advantage the club has though it may be . . . a minor one— there is no danger of fracture from shifting lead at the back of the club.

Selling at 10 shillings 6 pence per club, the Brougham metalwood was expensive. The usual price for a wooden club at the time was between 5 and 7 shillings. Few Brougham metalwoods remain today.

ROBERT RAMSBOTTOM
METALWOOD

Brougham followed the introduction of his aluminum driver by offering an aluminum head brassie:

The patent aluminium club-head invented by Mr. Reginald Brougham, with its small block of wood as driving face, is now pretty well known among golfers . . . . Mr. Brougham has now carried his idea a little further, and has brought out a brassey modelled on the same lines . . . . The brassey is similar in construction to the driver, except that the face of the club is a little deeper, and is "grassed," so to speak . . . . The face is composed of a new material, which is at once hard and proof against the injurious effects of wet weather. This material is vulcanized fibre (Golf, 20 July 1894: 458).

Later in 1894 Brougham also developed a brass putter with a flange:

The Hon. Reginald Brougham . . . has designed and patented a new form of metal putter. In shape it corresponds to the now familiar gun-metal blade, with this difference, that it has a sole plate projecting an inch behind. This sole plate is raised on two narrow metal ridges, which serve as a guide to the steadiness of the stroke, and a means of allowing the putter head to glide smoothly along the turf in striking the ball. . . . Mr. Brougham claims it will save four to five strokes a round (Golf, 5 Oct. 1894: 62).

In late 1894 a unique metalwood was produced by an enterprising dealer in golf goods: Robert Ramsbottom of "The Sportsman's Depot" on Market Street in Manchester, England:

Mr. R. Ramsbottom . . . has brought out a new aluminium driver. It has a short socket at the neck, through which the shaft passes to the sole, a few inches of whipping being added at the junction of the shaft to the socket . . . . The face is of some hard indestructible material, "let in" like a piece of leather in a wooden club, though, if necessary through wear and tear, the face can easily be replaced at the desire of the player (Golf, 14 Dec. 1894: 245).

Ramsbottom's metalwood also includes the same basic claw-like hosel used on his Crescent iron and covered under his British patent (No. 14,799) dated August 2, 1894 (see p. 155).

Originally, the top of the neck on the Ramsbottom wood pictured was bound with whipping. The visual interest of the claw hosel, however, makes it quite acceptable to display this club without whipping.

A comparative review between the Brougham and Ramsbottom metalwoods reads:

The chief difference between these two forms of the aluminium club seems to be that Brougham's Patent possesses the better shape and model of head, so far as general appearance is concerned; but, on the other hand, Ramsbottom's method of joining head and shaft gives greater strength at this point; and further, the hornite face extends from top to bottom of the head, whereas Brougham's wooden block is hounded above and below by the metal shell, which is apt to make ugly marks on the ball if half-topped or taken heavy. This latter consideration, should, of course, be no disadvantage theoretically, but, taken in conjunction with the shallowness of the head, and the highly practical nature of golfing error, it is a somewhat serious drawback. In driving-power there seems but little to choose. Hornite appears to be an excellent material for facing a club, and produces much "sweetness" of impact. Brougham's blocks, on the other hand, can be made of any wood preferred by the user, and, if necessary, faced with leather, this advantage, again being lessened by a weakness due to the looseness consequent on the alternate expansion and shrinkage of the wood in wet and dry weather (Golf, 27 Dec. 1895: 339).

The club pictured is marked "R. Ramsbottom" directly on the top of the insert and "Patented" low on the face of the insert. Ramsbottom offered his metalwood as "a club for a lifetime—the improved aluminium driver, with patent dovetailed hornite face" (Golf, 7 June 1895: 241).

Ramsbottom did not receive a patent for his metalwood, but he apparently considered the idea in November of 1894, when he applied for a golf club patent (No. 22,150) that never came to be.

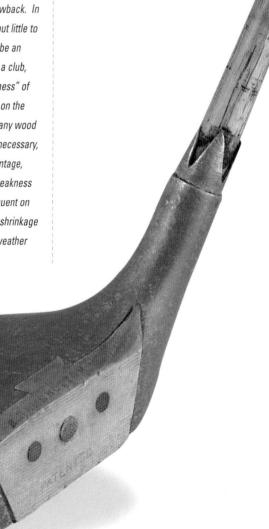

CHARLES PLAYFAIR
"BRADDELL" METALWOOD

Playfair's metalwood, which followed on the heels of Ramsbottom's metalwood, was produced under a British patent (No. 23,391) dated December 3, 1894, and granted to "Charles Playfair trading as Joseph Braddell & Son, 21 Castle place, Belfast, [Ireland]." A marvelous example of Playfair's club, usually referred to as a "Braddell metalwood," is pictured. The top of the head is marked "Braddell \ 1734 \ Patent." "Braddell" is stamped on the shaft.

According to Playfair's patent, his aluminum clubhead includes a "false face of hardened leather." The leather insert is genuine, but it is attached to a large *wood block* inside the head, directly behind the insert.

When looking at the Braddell shown, note the number of small nails driven through the leather insert. According to the patent, these nails are driven into a wood block "placed in a recess formed in the metallic head." The wood block served two primary purposes. It allowed the leather to be fixed in place, and, at impact, it provided the metal head with the feel of a wooden head—in theory at least.

Shortly after its introduction, the Braddell metalwood was described in *Golf:*

Following on the lines adopted by Mr. Brougham and Mr. Ramsbottom, in the construction of their aluminium clubs, Messrs Braddell and Son . . . have brought out another club of the same form . . . . The head is aluminium, with a chamber into which is fitted a

T-piece of hard wood. On the top of this is fitted a hard leather face for striking the ball, and this face is flush with the metal as in an ordinary wooden head (10 May 1895: 151).

In the world of metalwoods, the Braddell caught hold. Over 3,800 were produced by 1900, and they were made as drivers or brasseys with either a "bulger" or "straight face" (*Golf,* 2 Feb. 1900: 112). "The celebrated 'BAP' " model was also offered. These early metalwoods were available in either an "ordinary finish" or a "special finish" with either "deep or shallow faces." Even though more than 3,800 were produced, only a small percentage have survived to this day.

The club shown has the special polished finish. The ordinary finish has a flat, non-reflective appearance. The special finish clubs included a cork grip, which the club pictured has. Special finish clubs sold for 12 shillings

6 pence while the ordinary model sold for 10 shillings 6 pence.

Playfair's metalwoods were appreciated not only for their variety but also for their durability:

One of the first of the aluminium clubs to attract attention, Braddell's patent is probably one of the best and certainly one of the most popular. To those players who cannot keep a fragile wooden driver for long, and to all golfers in wet weather, we strongly commend these aluminium goods. Though apparently more expensive, their indestructibility renders them far cheaper in the end. They are made in all shapes and weights and are very highly spoken of by those who have persevered in the use of them. Wisden and Co., of Cranbourne Street, are the London agents . . . (*Golf Illustrated,* 23 Feb. 1900: 178).

The Braddell was well received as far as early metalwoods go, but only a small percentage of golfers at the time found aluminum head woods appealing:

So far as durability is concerned, it seems probable that aluminium-headed clubs cannot be beaten, as this material, if judiciously alloyed, is very tough, and not at all very liable to become brittle. The average golfer, however, with the traditions of the game before his eyes, will naturally turn from a metal-headed play club (as he would from a brassy, were the metal anywhere but where it is – i.e. out of sight) to the alternative forms of longevity in clubs (*Golf,* 27 Dec. 1895: 339).

Aluminum head clubs, produced primarily by William Mills, did not gain substantial circulation until the early 1900s.

WILLIAM MILLS
METALWOODS

William Mills of Sunderland, England, was the most prolific designer and manufacturer of early aluminum head golf clubs. He created The Standard Golf Company (William Mills, Limited), a division of The Atlas Works, to produce his clubs, commonly referred to as "Mills" clubs. While his metalwoods were eventually accepted by many golfers, his aluminum head putters were popular with the masses.

William Mills began experimenting with the construction of aluminum clubheads as early as 1892 (*Golfing*, 22 May 1902:19). He eventually received five British patents and two U.S. patents that covered metalwoods. His first patent, which followed Charles Playfair's, is a British patent (No. 13,545) dated July 15, 1895. According to this patent, the metallic head is formed:

in a series of compartments separated from each other by metallic strengthening ribs or divisions, each compartment being filled up or rendered solid.

Therefore, three open chambers, tapering towards the rear, run from the face to the back of the head. The interior walls forming the chambers were "roughened or slightly serrated . . . to prevent any removal of the wood when once driven home."

The "wood" referred to is three wood blocks placed in the chambers. These blocks "unite together to form a continuous wooden striking face." Any wood protruding out of the back of the head was to be "sawn off flush with the head."

Furthermore, each block of wood was to be "well coated with paint or equivalent solution before being driven home in order to preserve it from damp."

Shown above are two Mills metalwoods with wood face inserts. The club on the left is marked "Mills Patent \ 7. 3 \ W. Mills Sunderland" in a small oval on the head. Although the shaft in this club was covered under Mills's second British patent, the head was covered under his first. The club on the right is a Mills metalwood produced years later as one model among many in the Standard Golf Company's 1909 catalog.

A description of the Mills metalwood published shortly after its introduction describes in detail the early Mills club pictured:

The shell of aluminium in Mr. Mills' club is entirely hollow, at the back as well as at the striking surface; but two ribs of the metal running transversely across the head cut the interior hollow into three compartments, which from being broad at the face taper gradually into a wedge at the back. Into those three compartments are fitted corresponding pieces of well-seasoned beech, and when the blocks of wood are thoroughly pressed home a conspicuously compact and solid driving club head is secured. . . . A notable feature of Mr. Mills club is the method in which the weight and lie of the club are registered, so as to admit of easy and certain reduplication without variation. Where the maker's name figures on the club-head will be found, for example, these letters, "R. m. 7 3." This signifies that "R" means the registered shape of the head, "m." medium lie, and "7 3" means seven ounces and three drachms; so that once a player obtains a club which suits him exactly as to lie and weight, the figures on the head always constitute a guide towards the reproduction of another club which shall be scientifically exact (Golf, 25 Dec. 1896: 278).

This account continues by stating the perceived advantages of a Mills metalwood:

1. The head is practically indestructible, thus saving the annoyance of continually having to buy new drivers, which are so apt to put players off their play.

2. Combines all the advantages of a wood head with the durability of metal - in fact, it is simply a wood head bound round with metal.

3. It can be produced in perfect duplicate, not like wood heads, which are usually a matter of guesswork as to weight, balance, &c. Each individual head is stamped with its particular shape, lie, and weight.

4. The wood being end on, and bound round with metal, will not wear away, peel, or split off, as in the case of wood heads where the grain runs lengthways.

5. The head, owing to its peculiar construction, is perfectly solid. The heads are perfectly balanced, and must remain so, owing to the solidity of construction.

Mr. Mills might also have added that there is no danger of the balance of a club-head being disorganized by the lead shifting at the back.

Mills also received a U.S. patent (572,436) dated December 1, 1896, that covered his early metalwood.

The second patent granted to William Mills was a British patent (No. 1,078) dated January 16, 1896. This patent seeks a better way of attaching the metal head to a shaft. Instead of inserting the end of the shaft into a socket, Mills spliced the shaft to a small piece of wood extending up from the socket, and secured it "by lashing or otherwise in the usual way" (glue and whipping). The wood extending up from the neck was to "be cut or altered to the required 'lie' or angle or line of the shaft proper." In this manner "any professional club maker can cut or adjust the piece with regard to its shaft."

The pristine Mills wood shown below and to the left on the previous page has the splice shaft with whipping applied as illustrated in the 1896 patent. The wood blocks extending through the head are visible at the back of the head.

The club pictured above right on the previous page is marked "Standard Golf Company \ Mills \ 161627 \ Patent \ Sunderland England" on top of the head and "The Mills \ WD Model \ Medium Lie \ 7 ozs 0 drs" on the sole. The oval shaft stamp reads, "Shafted by Standard Golf Co. Sunderland." The 1909 Standard Golf Company catalog lists the "WD Model" as having a "wood face." Obviously modeled after Mills's first metalwood, the wood in this later model does not extend all the way through the head. The wood block set into the face is one piece, although in the example pictured it has cracked directly down the lines of two metal ribs inside the head.

Following their introduction, Mills metalwoods languished because the golfing public was not comfortable with them:

The bright head is, to some, a drawback to its speedy adoption by many who appreciate its perfect balance and scientific construction (Golfing, 6 Jan. 1897: 5).

In 1900, after Harold Hilton used a Mills aluminum putter while winning the British Amateur, the Standard Golf Company decided to "give serious attention" to the production of aluminum golf clubs (Standard Golf 1909, 4). Shortly thereafter, Mills clubs came into prominence.

The success of many amateur players using Mills aluminum clubs in the 1901 British Amateur, along with Hilton's success in defending his title, did not go unnoticed—nor did the rejection of Mills clubs by many professional golfers:

The success attained in the Amateur Championship by the wielders of Mills' aluminium clubs has caused a great stir, and bids fair to create something like a revolution in the club-making art. Mr. Hilton and others have shown that the Aluminium Baffy can do all and more than any iron club of the ordinary makes, and they avow that it is easier to play with.

The professionals at the Mid-Surrey Tournament had a good deal to say of the new-comer, and it is significant that more than one was using a Mills' putter, and doing excellent work with it. But the pros. naturally look upon the success of aluminium pretty much as Allan Robertson regarded the advent of gutta-percha. If aluminium clubs are to take the place of steel, the professionals will lose the profit which they have on the sale of steel clubs—a very serious matter for them.

The best thing the pros. can do with the aluminium clubs is to do what Old Tom and other wise men of old did with the gutta-percha balls when they first came in. Let them give them a fair trial, and if they are satisfied on their merits, stock them and sell them (Golf Illustrated, 17 May 1901: 132).

With his growing success, Mills began to design additional models:

[Mills] sought to reproduce, in aluminium, with such improvements as were obvious, the old baffies and spoons which were used before the days of cleeks, irons, and mashies" (Golf Illustrated, 28 June 1901: 275).

The Mills clubs modeled after the older long nose woods were designed to replace irons. The caption under the picture of a long nose style "BSD 2" Mills spoon included with the article just quoted, reads, "This club

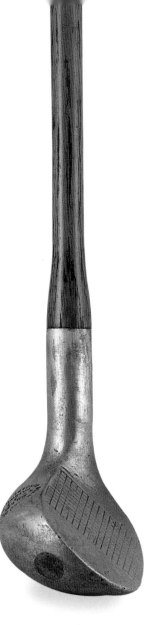

takes the place of an iron." The article also reports that these long nose style aluminum spoons could be supplied in any required lie, weight, or loft:

so that players can choose or order a club to suit themselves instead of being compelled, as is often the case with other clubs, to adapt themselves to the club.

The club pictured right, a Mills long nose style spoon, is stamped "Standard Golf Co \ Mills \ A 3637 \ Patent 20915/00" on the crown with "1 \ The Mills \ Cleek \ BSD1 Model \ Standard Lie \ 8 ozs 4 drs" stamped on the sole. The shaft is stamped "Shafted \ Standard Golf Co. \ Sunderland."

This club was produced under William Mills's British patent (No. 20,915) dated November 20, 1900, the first patent granted for a completely homogeneous metal head wood. Prior to this, metalwoods included at least an insert of some other material.

Inasmuch as Mills designed his long nose style metalwoods to play shots normally assigned to an iron, he also made various matching clubs in order to provide matched sets. In fact, the BSD, BS, MSD, and MS models were each offered as "Long, Mid, Baffy, and Bulger Spoons" in order to "play all the strokes that can be played with irons" (Standard Golf 1909, 11).

The BSD models have long heads with deep faces, the BS models have long heads with shallow faces, the MSD models have short heads with deep faces, and the MS models have short heads with shallow faces. The metalwoods produced within each model relate to iron clubs as follows: "1" is a "Long Spoon equivalent to Cleeks," "1 1/2" is a "Medium Long Spoon equivalent to Driving Irons," "2" is a "Mid-Spoon equivalent to Irons," "2 1/2" is a "Short Spoon equivalent to Medium Lofters," and "3" is a "Baffy equivalent to a Pitching Mashie." In addition, a MSD 3 1/2 and 4 were offered as "Special Spoons" (Standard Golf 1909, 12-17).

In addition to making metalwoods that replaced irons, Mills also made aluminum drivers and brassies. Such models as the DA, DB, BA, BB, WD, WB, BGS, and others were produced. In addition to the various clubs used to advance the golf ball to the green, Mills marketed a wide variety of putters (see p. 310).

Most Mills clubs were produced in large numbers and embody few distinguishing features. Therefore, when collecting Mills clubs, the most unusual ones in either shape or construction command the most interest. This principle also applies to the various lofts of these clubs: the greater the loft, the more interest it generates. In general, when clubs departed from traditional shapes and styles, fewer of them were made.

Pictured left is a Mills NK niblick. It is marked "The Mills \ NK Model \ Lie \ 8 ozs 14 drs" on the sole and "Standard Golf Co. \ Mills 32339 Patent \ Sunderland" atop the head.

The Mills NK niblick is described in the 1909 Standard Golf Company catalog as follows:

The shape of this club is an entirely new creation. Will take balls out of "sand bunkers" or "bad lies" with wonderful ease, and has the same advantage over the iron Niblick as the spoons have over the irons (20).

The Mills NK niblick, with its odd head shape and considerable loft, is a popular collectible.

William Mills received three more patents following his November 20, 1900, patent.

His British patent (No. 7,279) dated April 9, 1901, covered aluminum clubheads made with recesses in the back or on the side to hold wood blocks. Mills produced clubs of this type in large numbers.

His British patent (No. 13,531) dated June 9, 1909, covered aluminum clubheads with inserts and soleplates of hard metal. It is not known if this club was produced.

His U.S. design patent (No. 43,885) dated April 22, 1913, covered a two-level aluminum putter head, the back half of the mallet head being lower than the front half. This putter, produced in large quantities, has an elementary design.

Occasionally Mills clubs are found stamped "B.G.I." Before they went out of business, the Bridgeport Gun Implement Company, of Bridgeport, Connecticut, was the sole agent for Mills clubs in America.

For more Mills clubs, see pages 310 and 416.

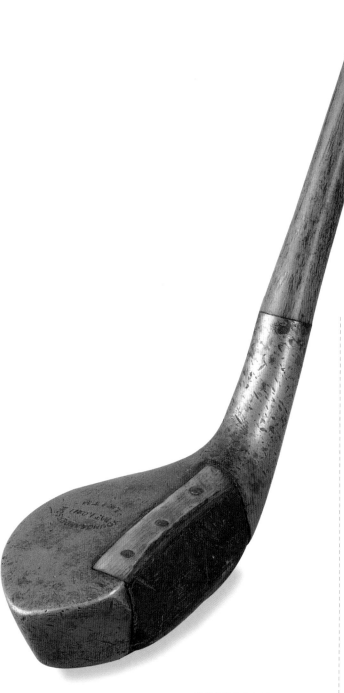

GEORGE YOUNG
GUNMETAL METALWOOD

George Young, of Leith, Scotland, received the next metalwood patent to follow the one issued to William Mills in 1895. Young's British patent (No. 10,211) dated May 13, 1896, covered a metal head driver and putter. The Young driver pictured, the only one known to the author, is stamped "Young & Anderson \ Pat. 1,0211 [sic] \ Leith" on the top of the head.

According to his patent, the "preferably gun metal" head was to be "made hollow and contain a block of wood" to serve as the striking face:

The advantage is that as the driving face gets worn the club can be made the same as new by simply inserting a new block of wood.

Changing the wood block is accomplished by sliding the block out of the head after unscrewing two screws (which extend into the block) in the back of the head.

The front of Young's clubhead includes strips of horn fastened to both the top and bottom of the wood block. According to his patent, above and below the insert:

a strip of horn or the like [is] inserted so as to prevent the metal [from] coming into actual contact with the ball.

Contemporary with Young, J.&A. Simpson of Edinburgh briefly produced a wooden head that included a wood face insert affixed in similar fashion:

Messrs Simpson take a piece of specially seasoned and selected wood, and so secure it by horn above and below, that it can neither come out nor split (*The Golfer*, 25 Mar. 1896: 208).

Young's metalwood is an outstanding collectible for several reasons, not the least of which is its gunmetal head. Only two other brass-colored metalwoods produced prior to 1925 are known to the author. The first is Currie's 1891 brass metalwood, discussed on page 276. The second example, which the author has not seen, is reportedly marked "J. Smith" and made from brass and lead.

On April 2, 1896, just before Young applied for his patent, W.M. Bryson applied for a metalwood patent which he later abandoned. Bryson, however, produced his club (apparently in extremely small numbers) as indicated by a brief mention in the December 2, 1896 issue of *The Golfer*. This account identifies Bryson as an Edinburgh golfer and describes his aluminum driver as containing:

. . . a strong steel spring, lying the whole length behind the face of the club. This spring is slightly arched, and in the centre of the club-face, where the ball is struck, it rests upon, and receives propulsive force from, a strong spiral spring going back in the interior of the head towards the lead. Another feature of the club is a thin slip of leather on the face, behind which the spring rests (443).

EDWARD SLADE
SPRING-FACE METALWOOD

Edward Slade, of Newton, Massachusetts, received the first U.S. patent that covered a metal-wood. Dated July 28, 1896, his U.S. patent (No. 564,655) describes the aluminum alloy used to construct the head, the wooden block set in the face, and the elastic material placed behind the wooden block:

The head may be of any suitable metal, but I prefer to make it of aluminum, and I have found that the following formula gives the best results: copper, two percent.; zinc, three per cent.; aluminum, ninety-five per cent. On the front edge of the head a recess is formed, which may be of any desired size and shape. . . . In the recess I insert a piece of rubber or other suitable elastic material, made of a shape to fit it. In front of this is placed the face made of any suitable material, though I prefer to make it of dogwood, box-wood, or fibre.

A recessed screw in the back of the head attaches to both the wood block and the elastic piece behind it. This design allowed for replacing the wood block if it became damaged. The block, the elastic piece, and the screw were designed primarily to function as a spring-face:

When the club meets the ball, the shock of concussion forces the move-able face against the elastic block and moves the screw a short distance in the hole. The elastic block instantly rebounds and drives the face against the ball with great force, causing it to fly to a great distance. As the screw is free to move it allows the face a certain amount of play. If the club strikes by accident a hard immovable substance, such as a stone, the face will be allowed sufficient motion to prevent injury thereby.

Slade's spring-face metalwood is pictured. The space around the wood block allowed for its spring-face movement. The block itself displays a small amount of movement when pressed.

But what golfer is there who has not heard some brother enthusiast declare that he has been "trying to break this old driver-head for years, and now, thank goodness! it has gone at last? . . . What then would be the feelings aroused by one of these patent indestructibles after years of impatient longing for their demise? (Golf, 27 Dec. 1895: 338).

William Garlick and Arthur James Jackson received a British patent (No. 12,743) dated June 22, 1901, that covered the clubs pictured. Their patent, relating to putters, putting cleeks, and lofters, includes a number of distinct concepts. Among their ideas are the following:

We connect the handle socket to the back of the club head so as to leave a free and wholly unbroken contact face so that the liability to "heel" the ball is avoided. To play the ball with greater accuracy . . . we so form the club head that the load is brought directly behind the striking point on the face of the club.

The wholly unbroken face on each of the clubs pictured is created by positioning the face well ahead of the hosel.

Garlick and Jackson's patent also specifies that their clubs should be made from an unusual aluminum alloy strengthened with a steel liner or core:

Under the remaining part of our invention we construct the golf club heads and sockets of aluminium with an addition of 4 per cent of copper or thereabouts.

By a series of experiments we have found that this alloy of aluminium provides an elastic contact surface equal to wood without its liability to quickly wear away.

In practice however, when using aluminium the socket is apt to break away from the head or become ruptured . . .

To obviate this we provide the socket and head with a liner of tough sheet metal such as steel . . . .

The three matching aluminum clubs pictured—a cleek, mashie, and niblick—are each stamped "The 'Timperley' \ G&J \ Patent No 12743" on the top of the head. Each sole is marked as follows: the club on the left is stamped "Cleek 7 3/4 oz," the club in the center is stamped "Mashie 9 oz," and the club on the right is stamped "Niblick 9 1/4 oz." Given their marks and corresponding shaft lengths, these clubs were obviously designed to function as irons. The cleek is also stamped "Baby" and "Mitchell \ Manchester" on the top of the head; the shaft of the niblick bears the "Mitchell \ Manchester" stamp.

A Timperley putter was also produced. An example selling at the July 1996 Phillips auction in Chester, England, looked nothing like the two center-shafted putters illustrated in Garlick and Jackson's patent. Instead, it looked like a Schenectady putter and was undoubtably produced after the Schenectady (p. 193).

Because the three clubs shown are an early and rare *set* of metalwoods, they are quite collectible. Their unusual head shapes add to their collectibility.

Garlick was from Ashton-on-Mersey; Jackson was from Bramhall. Both of these towns are located in greater Manchester, England, as is the town of Timperley.

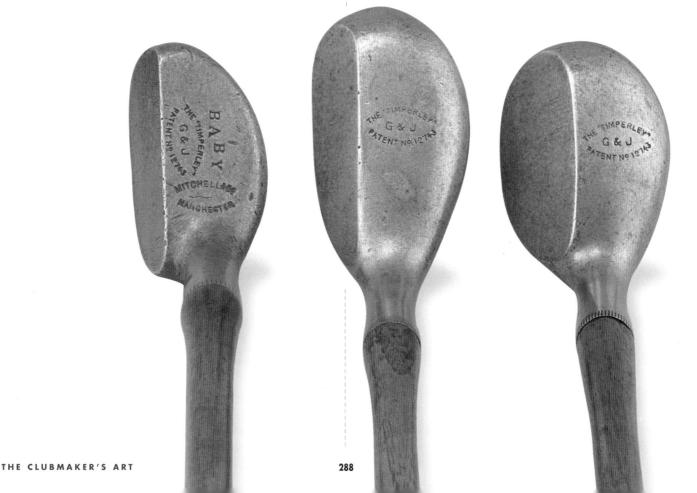

HENRY VEHSLAGE
"DAISY" METALWOOD

The Aluminum Golf Head Co., of Newark, N.J., is making a new driver head, called the Vehslage patent driver. It is made of aluminum, forming a shell with an open face filled with wood, the end grain being out for the striking face. In theory one can secure greater distance with a wooden club by using the end grain for the striking surface instead of the side grain as used in the ordinary wooden clubs. The club is practically indestructible and not affected by weather. It is well balanced, nicely finished, and should prove popular. The company also makes solid aluminum heads for every style of club in different lofts, lies and various weights (Golfers Magazine, Apr. 1904: 250).

Henry De Long Vehslage of Irvington, New Jersey, received a U.S. patent (No. 684,532) dated October 15, 1901, that covered the club pictured. As stated in his patent, Vehslage wanted to build a low cost clubhead out of aluminum and wood that would "enable the ball to be driven to the extreme distance possible." To this end, Vehslage calls for constructing a metal head driver with a wood block, visible across the face, set into the head. Two inner side walls and a flat inner wall located across the back of the head brace the wood block:

This position is desirable, since there will be no tendency for the block to be forced to one side and splinter or rupture, but will give direct resistance in the line of the stroke.

The wood block is inserted in the head with the end grain exposed across the face. In addition to allowing the ball to be struck "with full force with little cushioning effect," running the grain in this direction also "render[s] the block more dense." Vehslage notes that if the side grain were positioned across the face, the pressure on the wood fibers from fitting the block into the opening "would tend to bulge them apart and make the block more elastic and less effective."

Before the wood block was installed, its back side was bored with holes and filled with lead, to obtain the desired swing weight. After the block was installed, it was fixed in place by three screws extending up from

the sole: two screws under the leading edge and a third screw under the middle of the head. By removing the screws, a clubmaker could replace a damaged wood block.

The Vehslage patent driver pictured is marked "Patrick Bros. \ Daisy" on the crown and "Pat. October 15. 01." in very small letters across the toe portion of the sole. Spalding also sold the Vehslage patent driver as demonstrated by the one known example marked "Spalding." Overall, the author knows of only three Vehslage patent drivers.

As can be seen, this particular Vehslage metalwood saw some action in its day. The surface of the head is nicked in places, and a piece of aluminum has broken off the top of the neck. Early aluminum clubs often show such wear and tear. Nevertheless, this particular club is still a very good example, especially considering its rarity. The wood insert

is solid and tight, the shaft is original, and the head is still attractive and playable.

The Vehslage patent driver was the second metalwood actually made in America even though two U.S. patents were granted for metalwoods before Vehslage received his. The first patent was issued to Edward Slade, of Newton, Massachusetts. His U.S. patent (No 564,655) dated July 28, 1896, covered the first aluminum metalwood produced in America (see p. 287).

The second U.S. patent for a metalwood (No. 572,436) was granted to William Mills on December 1, 1896. Mills, a British citizen making metalwoods in Sunderland, England, obtained this patent in order to gain U.S. protection for the first metalwood he patented and produced in Great Britain.

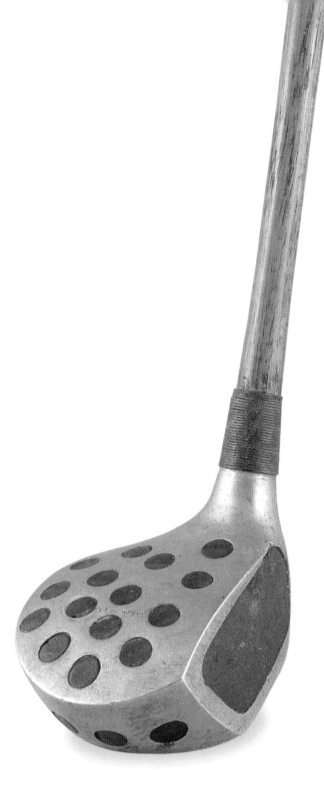

CHARLES THOMPSON & FRANK MITCHELL

METALWOOD

If you want to increase the distance of your drive and brassey shots, why not try The New Gutta Club. A hollow aluminum shell, into which gutta percha is forced and secured by holes through the shell. Gutta percha is much more resilient than wood and is not affected by dampness. If your dealer does not keep these clubs, send me three dollars and I will deliver one for you to try, and if after ten days' trial you do not find it satisfactory, return the club and I will send back the money.... Frank P. Mitchell, 1312 Filbert Street, Philadelphia (Golf [ny], June 1906: 64).

On January 25, 1906, Charles T. Thompson, of Philadelphia, Pennsylvania, and Frank P. Mitchell, of Laurel Springs, New Jersey, applied for a U.S. patent to cover the stunning driver pictured on this page and advertised above. According to their patent (No. 838,284) issued on December 11, 1906, the purpose of their invention was to produce:

an improved golf club by which the construction is simplified, the resiliency of the driving-face increased, the elastic force of the blow strengthened, and the durability of the club improved.

As produced, Thompson and Mitchell's clubhead consists of a metal shell—a "casting . . . of aluminium or other light metal" open at the face and back with circular holes across its crown and sole—filled with resilient material:

Within the hollow shell thus constructed there is inserted a mass of plastic material. This may consist of gutta-percha or of hard or vulcanized rubber or of rubber mingled with feathers . . . or other similar material. This material is rendered plastic by heating . . . and while in its plastic condition is run or molded into the hollow casting, sufficient pressure being applied to cause the material to enter the apertures as well as to completely fill the head. The material is then closely trimmed to the outer surface of the casting both to form a front and back face and wherever it protrudes through the apertures.

The Thompson and Mitchell club pictured, the only one known to the author, is marked "Pat. Ap'd. For" on the top of the head. There are fifteen holes on the crown and nine holes on the sole. The back of the head has four holes like those on the rest of the head and one larger opening centered behind the face. All the holes and openings, including the face, are filled with gutta percha from the inside of the head.

On December 3, 1906, Thompson and Mitchell applied for a patent (No. 27,509) to cover their club in Great Britain. Their application was granted on May 16, 1907.

For more on metalwoods with gutta percha faces, see William Currie's metalwood on page 276.

JAMES A. McMAHON
METALWOOD

UNKNOWN MAKER
METALWOOD

On March 11, 1922, James Alexander McMahon, of Hamilton, Ontario, Canada, applied for a U.S. patent to cover the black metalwood pictured. According to his patent (No. 1,485,685) granted on March 4, 1924, the object of his invention was:

to devise a metal construction for the heads of clubs such as drivers, which have formerly been made of wood, whereby a club of superior appearance and greater durability is produced, and a further object is to so construct the metal head, that a very exact balancing of the club may be readily attainable.

To accomplish his objectives, McMahon included three wooden inserts and a metal weight in his metal clubhead:

My invention consists of a golf club having a cast metal head suitably cored for lightness and adapted to receive the shaft, said head provided with inwardly extending orifices in the driving face thereof into which are secured hardwood inserts, and provision being made for placing a balancing weight within the central portion of the head behind the wooden inserts.

McMahon's metalwood pictured is marked "J.A. McMahon's \ U.D.S. \ Patented 1923" on the top of the head and "Made in Hamilton, Canada" on the sole. The shaft is stamped "M. Hunter \ Calgary." The "U.D.S." mark stands for "Union Drawn Steel." Another McMahon metalwood known to the author is marked "Union Drawn Steel \ Beaver Falls, Pa." The reference to steel is particularly interesting since McMahon's patent calls for constructing the head from an aluminum alloy.

This club has its original black painted finish. Although no other metalwood makers painted their clubs black, William Mills gave some of his early aluminum clubs a darkened finish in order to reduce the glare of ordinary aluminum.

The filing of the pin on the hosel suggests this club has been reshafted. However, the matching shaft stamp and the old whipping indicate that the shaft is

original. This club might have been sold disassembled, or the pin was possibly added later to tighten the neck joint. The patent does not call for pinning the shaft like an iron. Instead, it calls for sinking a screw through the back of the neck and into the lower end of the shaft.

Three cylindrical hardwood inserts are set into the face. Three nails extending up through the sole help fasten these wood inserts in place—one nail per insert.

In addition to being wider, the middle plug, which extends into the center of the head, is approximately twice as long as the two wooden inserts that border it. A disc-shaped weight is located directly behind the middle insert, in the end of the recess. According to the patent, this positions the weight adjacent to the clubhead's center of gravity.

The area behind the head's interior framework is hollow. Only one brace inside the back of the head helps support this framework. The brace connects the back of the head with the

center of the framework directly behind the middle insert.

McMahon did not invent the idea of three cylindrical wooden inserts. In 1896 William Frier tried this idea in a conventional wooden head. On November 8, 1910, Charles Jacobus received a patent for a triple insert (p. 328).

Pictured above left is a distinguished metalwood marked "Patent App For \ Moline, Ill" in a circle on the sole. A word inside the circle is too faint to read. Unlike any other metalwood, this driver, measuring 44 3/4 inches in length, is characterized by a large red fiber insert set in the face and a short hosel. Two screws in the sole and one in the back of the head fix the insert in position. A screw in the back of the hosel holds the head on the shaft. This club, the only such club known to the author, probably dates to the early 1900s.

ALFRED A. GUERNE
METALWOOD

Alfred A. Guerne, of Kalamazoo, Michigan, received a U.S. patent (No. 1,562,956) dated November 24, 1925, that covered the club pictured—a metalwood with a porcelain insert. According to Guerne's patent, an "impact block" of porcelain fills a chamber, open at the face, in this hollow metal head. The chamber extends approximately halfway back into the head.

The porcelain block, having "side grooves and end grooves," was set in rubber before being placed into the head:

The block [is] inserted and then the rubber vulcanized with the block in position, thus permanently securing the block in the chamber with its curved faces in direct engagement with the walls of the chamber. Its sides and ends however are held in spaced relation to the walls by the vulcanized rubber or other suitable plastic material which is substantially nonelastic.

The vulcanized rubber is visible on the face as the red outline around the insert.

Another unique feature of Guerne's club is the way the weight inside the head, directly in line with the face, was installed. A threaded rod, screwed into a hole in the center of the back side of the insert chamber's rear wall, extends back into the hollow behind the insert chamber. Circular weights were placed on this rod and held in position against the back of the insert chamber's rear wall by a nut. The rod, the weights, and the nut were installed through a threaded opening in the back of the head. The rear wall of the head was "closed by a closure plug threaded into the opening."

The club pictured is marked "Guerne Clubs \ Kalamazoo, Mich. \ Pat. Pend." on the sole. Guerne's patent was applied for on March 23, 1925. The shaft is split cane—six lengthwise pieces of bamboo— surrounding a circular core of hickory.

The porcelain insert in Guerne's club is a prime feature. No other clubs with porcelain inserts, nor patents (from the wood shaft era) that mention porcelain inserts, are known to the author. A few patents included the idea of *glass* inserts and even glass heads. It is not known if any clubs were produced from any of these patents. Nevertheless, the following information is provided for reference.

The first patent to discuss glass inserts was Oscar Heeren's British patent (No. 172) dated January 3, 1903, which was also granted as a U.S. patent (No. 734,065) on July 21, 1903.

His patent covered a face insert made from a block of glass, quartz, flint, or the like.

Moses Swift's British patent (No. 4,949) dated March 3, 1903, and his U.S. patent (No. 722,927) dated March 17, 1903, provide for a metal, stone, or glass face insert that would also cover a small part of the sole's leading edge.

Tom Heffernan's British patent (No. 11,850) dated May 18, 1912, and his U.S. patent (No. 1,088,571) dated February 24, 1914, covered glass face inserts (dovetailed into the head) backed by leather or other elastic material, to allow for movement of the glass. Heffernan's patent also provides for running one or more holes through the head, front to back, to reduce wind resistance.

John Southerst and Frederick Metcalf's British patent (No. 16,800) dated July 4, 1908, covered a putter head made entirely

of flint or glass with a metal socket in the center of the head.

Herbert Challis and Samuel Williamson received a U.S. patent (No. 1,454,267) dated May 8, 1923, that covered a glass mallet head putter with a metal hosel.

Before anyone received a patent covering glass clubheads, C.W.M. Greenhill applied for a British patent to cover a driver made with a head of:

clay or stoneware, moulded to the proper shape and dried and burnt in any of the ways employed in the manufacture of bricks, tiles and other stoneware goods (Golfing, 4 Oct 1895: 13).

Applied for on May 17, 1895, Greenhill's patent (No. 9,745) was not issued, and no such clubs are known.

In the early 1920s Alfred Guerne produced a mechanical putter. The hosel could shift to change the lie of the head, which allowed for adjustable faces of aluminum, brass, or steel.

JOHN HODGKIN?
COMBINATION WOOD

In 1893 Joseph Roberts of Wimbledon, England, introduced "Roberts' Combination Driver," a club with a wood and metal clubhead:

This club has a metal neck like a cleek or an iron, and there is a metal crescent-shaped band running round the back of the wood from heel to toe . . . . The driver shaft is fixed into the metal neck in the ordinary way, and there is a nodule of very hard beech wood fixed in the claw, as it were, of the head (Golf, 9 June 1893: 228).

Roberts's club received a lukewarm review (the balance of his club was considered suspect), but its name aptly describes all other clubs made in similar fashion. When the exposed portion of a clubhead, excluding backweights, inserts, and soleplates, is made up from two *completely different* materials, usually wood and metal, such clubs are loosely referred to as combination clubs or as having combination heads (see p. 275).

John Hodgkin, a chemical manufacturer based in Richmond, Surrey, England, received the first patent (No. 820) that covered a combination club. Dated January 13, 1893, Hodgkin's British patent calls for constructing his club from a block of wood placed between an open frame made of iron:

This invention . . . . consists of holding a block of suitable percussive material in a metal loop, binder or open frame of suitable design. I prefer to use a wooden block set in the frame . . . , and I prefer to use a steel frame or holder into the aperture of which the block is fitted. . . . The holder is provided with a socket to receive the shaft, as in ordinary golfing irons.

As illustrated in his patent, Hodgkin's club has an iron hosel formed integrally with two metal strips that extend out to the toe on both the top and bottom of the head. These strips are thin, no wider than the hosel itself. Screws extending all the way through the entire head, top to bottom, were used to fasten the wood block to the metal frame. Hodgkin's patent, however, notes:

The shape of the frame and block may be varied according to the special purpose for which any such club may be required.

The reshafted, unmarked club shown here, with a leather face held in place by eleven nails, is slightly different from the one illustrated in Hodgkin's patent. This club does, however, possess the basic characteristics of Hodgkin's club. A metal frame made from iron, completely open on all sides except for the socket, is filled with a solid wood block. Six screws or rivets extending all the way through the entire head, top to bottom, fasten the block to the frame. The neck consists of an ordinary iron socket.

Following Hodgkin, Joseph Roberts (mentioned earlier) designed the next combination head. His clubheads were produced by "Wilson, South Street, St. Andrews [William Wilson, 193 South Street]" (*Golf*, 28 July 1893: 342). In addition to designing a combination driver, Roberts also developed a corresponding putter.

James McHardy, a self-described "scientific expert," and Frank Bryan, a London athletic outfitter, received the second patent to cover a combination wood. According to their British patent (No. 18,555) dated October 4, 1893, the entire bottom of the club, from the top of the splice neck to the tip of the sole, was a steel shell. A second steel shell could be used to cover the top of the head, or a completely enclosed shell open at the face could be made. Wood or gutta percha was to fill the head.

Tom Hood, an Edinburgh clubmaker, produced a combination putter sometime during the 1890s. It had a long wooden mallet head attached to a swan neck iron hosel and integral iron sole. Complete with "Tom Hood" stamped in script on the top of its head, an example of Hood's putter sold at Christie's 1995 golf auction held at Pebble Beach, California.

Prior to the 1899 introduction of Dunn's "Indestructible" wood (see p. 295), the only other patent for a combination club was granted to Charles Ashford. His club is described on the next page.

Charles Ashford received a British patent (No. 21,383) dated November 10, 1893, that covered a wood-style clubhead made from both wood and metal with a metal neck. Although Ashford's patent shows many design variations for the combination head, both of the Ashford patent clubs known to the author have a full metal sole integral with a metal hosel. Ashford used iron for his metal, not aluminum, and called his club the "Skibbie." The Skibbie pictured, produced by W.&G. Ashford (of Birmingham, England), is marked "W.&G. Ashford \ 'Pat Skibbie' " in an oval around a fox head trademark on both the crown and the sole.

Improved durability and power were among the perceived benefits of the Skibbie:

The "Skibbie" is a new club . . . with which we make acquaintance for the first time. It is an ordinary bulger or driver head, but the fastening to the shaft is by means of an iron socket like an iron, and there is a sole plate. It is useful not only off the tee, but through the green where lies are bad or heavy, and as the inventors say, "it combines the durability of an iron with the driving power of a wooden club." Another advantage is that when once a player is suited both as to lie and balance, the club remains the same indefinitely, for, with the exception of the face, the club is practically indestructible (Golf, 2 Nov. 1894: 138).

The first U.S. patent for a combination club was granted to George Mattern, who assigned it to the Crawford, McGregor & Canby Company. Dated May 12, 1903, this patent (No. 727,819) shows the hosel, sole, and face form a metal casing. A strip of elastic material is placed between the face and the block of wood fastened behind it.

Elzie Harness's U.S. patent (No. 1,552,297) dated September 1, 1925, covered a wood very similar to Willie Dunn's "Indestructible" (p. 295). Harness placed a solid wood block (visible across the top of the head) in an aluminum frame. However, Harness specified screwing a metal plate to the wood face.

It is not known if either Mattern or Harness ever produced their clubs.

WILLIE DUNN, JR.
"INDESTRUCTIBLE"
COMBINATION WOOD

The nearly unused Willie Dunn "Indestructible" combination wood pictured is stamped "Willie Dunn's \ Pat App. For \ Indestructable" on the top of the head. Although it was applied for, a patent for this club was never granted—not unusual for a Dunn club. Between 1892 and 1902, "Dunn" applied for at least eight patents that were never issued. Most likely, either Willie or his nephew, John Duncan Dunn, applied for these patents only to abandon their applications after determining that the proposed inventions did not have a promising future.

Dunn advertised his "Indestructible" driver in 1899. It was reviewed shortly after its introduction:

The new indestructible driver invented by Willie Dunn is creating considerable interest. It is not a "freak," but a very sensible club, particularly for inexperienced players, or those who are located at inconvenient distances from repair shops. The head is composed of an aluminum case, which takes the place of the metal on a brassey, and the lead of a driver. Into the case is snugly fitted a block of seasoned wood giving 2 1/2 inches of solid driving material behind the ball. Previous inventions of this character left an almost impossible cavity in which to accurately fit the wood, with the result that there was

sometimes a space between the wood and metal, which of course necessitated loss of power. Those who have used the new club tell me it is a most serviceable weapon and drives a very long ball (Golf [ny], June 1899: 385-386).

As implied in this review, a damaged wood block could be replaced after removing the five screws around the perimeter of the sole.

In 1899 Dunn advertised four advantages for his club: First, the short cleek socket provided the desired spring close to the head. Second, there was no horn or lead which could work loose. Third, elasticity was gained by removing the lead and leaving 2 1/2 inches of solid wood behind the striking face. Fourth, the grain of the wood ran directly with the blow (*Golf* [ny], June: 324).

After Dunn produced his "Indestructible" club, Martin McDaid, operator of the "Golf Works" in Edinburgh, made a similar club:

Martin McDaid has been amusing himself and edifying golfers with a cross between a driver, a brassie, and a metal idea of his own. A description would advise that the head thereof is partially enclosed in a metal casing so that the player enjoys the advantages of the brassie combined with the joys of a capital wet weather club. He has not "pushed" the sale of this

choice specialty, but he avers that where it goes it pushes itself (Golfing, 22 Mar. 1900: 14).

R.B. Wilson, of St. Andrews, produced a similar combination head as well:

[Wilson's driver] is composed of an aluminium case, with wooden (persimmon, beach or dogwood) head inserted; riveted like a cleek and screwed on the sole like a brassie; the wood only showing on the top and at the face. The shaft goes through to the sole after the fashion of Scott of Elie's drivers. It can be used either as a driver or a brassie, and it is claimed for this combination of aluminium and wood that it has more spring than the head wholly composed of the former, and is more durable than the ordinary wooden driver-head (Golf Illustrated, 10 Jan. 1902: 27).

WAVERLEY HORTON
"WONDER CLUB"
COMBINATION WOODS

Waverly [sic] Horton's New Golf Club: The much talked about and latest invented, and improved golf clubs, are Horton's new wonder clubs. A combination of all the best features of golf clubs, making them 100% golf clubs. Twenty-six years in the business as a clubmaker.... These clubs were invented and are made by Waverly Horton, the well-known golf club maker.... Driver, Brassie, and Spoon, with the weight distributed to all sides of the head, back of the face, regardless of where the ball is hit on the face, the proper amount of weight is behind it ... where it should be. There is no one-sided weight in the construction of this head. The head is indestructible, the neck, sole, toe and top being of metal, forming a hollow casing in which a striking block is placed (Golfers Magazine, June 1919: 41).

When the advertisement just cited was originally printed in *Golfers Magazine*, it included a picture of the metal frame driver shown above left. This club was covered under Waverly Horton's U.S. patent (No. 1,361,258) applied for on March 21, 1919, and granted on December 7, 1920. Horton produced two other similar combination clubs, which are also pictured above.

The club above right is a 41 3/4-inch spoon marked "Waverley Horton \ Wonder Club \ Pat'd December 7, 1920" on the top of the head. In addition to having a wood block inside an aluminum frame, the head has a large brass backweight.

The club in the center, a 43-inch driver, bears the same marks as the spoon except that the writing is located on the top of the aluminum at the back of the head.

Shortly after Horton began selling his Wonder Club, it received the following review:

The "Wonder Club," Waverley Horton's latest contribution to the game, is being well received. He claims his new club embodies features which enable the player to get a farther and truer carry.

The striking block is contained in an aluminum casing, with the weight evenly distributed so that no matter where the face of the club strikes the ball, the proper amount of weight is behind it. The Horton Golf Company, 6952 Wellington Ave., Chicago, are distributors (Golfers Magazine, Aug. 1919: 42).

Horton's Wonder Club, although marketed by a small company—"Horton Golf Company, Not Incorporated"—was available for a few years and offered a few options. An advertisement in

the April 1923 issue of *Golfers Magazine* offered Horton's Wonder Club (the model shown above right) with a shaft of either steel or hickory, the former costing $10 and the latter $6.50 (10). A Wonder Club with a solid fiber striking block cost $15. For $25 the solid striking block included an ivory insert. But best of all, a Wonder Club with a solid ivory striking block that covered the *entire face* was offered at the incredible cost of $45! The author has never seen a Wonder Club produced under either of the last two options.

RALPH G. TYLER

"BALL TO BALL" &
ANOTHER COMBINATION
WOOD

On April 3, 1923, Ralph G. Tyler, of Bradford, Pennsylvania, applied for a U.S. patent (No. 1,574,213) to cover a combination club wherein the neck, sole, and back of the clubhead were made from aluminum. Tyler produced this club and called it the Tyler Rear Impact Driver (*Golfers Magazine*, Apr. 1923: 53).

In his patent, finally granted on February 23, 1926, Tyler states the purpose of this club:

My object is to provide a club head of such construction that besides affording balance calculated to facilitate true poising by the player, there is no tendency of the head to twist or shudder at the moment of its striking or hitting contact with the ball.

Tyler's patent also specifies that his Rear Impact Driver could be weighted with "a slug of steel

or iron suitably threaded and screwed through a threaded bore therefor in the sole."

The "Ball to Ball" driver, pictured above left, is a direct descendant of the Tyler Rear Impact Driver. However, before Tyler received the patent that covered his Ball to Ball club, he applied for and received another U.S. patent.

Tyler's U.S. patent (No. 1,535,270) applied for on November 1, 1924, and received on April 28, 1925, covered the club above right. This club has an aluminum sole integral with the aluminum neck and a "web," or brace, that extends out from the neck in line with the shaft. While the design of this club is certainly attractive to the eye, the design of the web includes some resourceful engineering that is not visible.

This patent (No. 1,535,270) refers to the aluminum extension from the hosel through the head as "the web or weighted piece." However, it also served as a brace. It is solid top to bottom, but is flat only on the side abutting the wood block used to strike the ball. Three screws in this web and two screws in the sole fasten this forward block in place.

The back of the aluminum web is deeply recessed behind the toe and heel. This design locates most of the web's weight directly behind the ball. The block of wood fixed to the back of the head, via three screws from the sole, extends into the recessed areas.

A primary purpose of Tyler's second combination wood is stated in his patent:

It is obvious that with the weight distributed as above described and with the shaft in longitudinal axial alignment with the said weight piece, there is produced a balance which is of such effect that in the hitting of the ball there is no vibratory or torsional tendency. A hammer like blow is accomplished and a true and dependable impulse is imparted to the ball. With the absence of tendency of the shaft to chuck, tremble, or shiver, the enjoyment and skill of the player in making his strokes are greatly increased.

The club pictured above left is stamped "R.G. Tyler \ Ball To Ball" on the crown. As previously mentioned, this club is similar to Tyler's Rear Impact Driver except that the Ball To Ball wood has a solid metal core running from the soleplate straight up through the head and a thick circular plug of wood set into the face. Tyler's Ball to Ball wood was covered in Tyler's final patent, a U.S. patent (No. 1,595,589) dated August 10, 1926.

Referred to in his last patent as an "impact element," the round "end grain" wood plug set into the face extends into the head where it abuts the solid metal core running up through the head (visible at the top of the head). The core itself is recessed to receive the end of the impact element. Tyler believed that by such an arrangement:

... the impulse imparted to the ball is more positive than when said impulse is imparted through the face block. [Furthermore] the golf club as an entity is not only steadied, but the full value of the weighted body portion as a means to give distance to the ball is matured and realized.

A machine screw that runs from the aluminum frame at the back of the head into the metal core was supposed to transfer the shock of impact to the rear of the head. According to Tyler, this way "the impact is in the rear, but the weight is not."

According to an advertisement, the manner in which Tyler's Ball to Ball club was weighted and balanced made it most effective:

The Tyler Ball to Ball Club. Guaranteed the straightest and longest driving club in the world. Your money refunded if you don't find it so. Made in driver, brassie, and spoon. Its principle is the reverse of the ordinary wooden club—in that its weight piece is longitudinally off the shaft, the impact is transmitted to the rear, and the head has an actual balance which means that any one half of it equals the other half in weight. Write for Circular R.G. Tyler, Muncie, Indiana. Hand made to your specifications and shipped on receipt of $7.50 (Golfers Magazine, Oct. 1923: 50).

With the exception of his "Rear Impact Driver," Tyler designed all his combination woods and putters to have their weight centered on a line extending straight out from the shaft. Tyler was trying to mimic the way an iron is weighted so that his woods would play as easily as irons.

WILLIE PARK, JR.
COMPRESSED WOOD

Willie Park Jr.'s compressed wood shown above appears to be nothing more than a transitional splice-neck driver. However, its method of construction was quite unconventional.

The July 21, 1893 issue of *Golf* provides the first reference to Park's compressed wood:

Willie Park has brought out a new head, which he calls "compressed wood," a material we do not understand (325).

Published shortly thereafter, a review of Park's compressed wood describes the unique characteristics and qualities claimed for this club. The review points out that Park was not the first to produce a club from compressed wood (though he was the first to *patent* the idea):

Willie Park is again to the front with something new.... There is nothing revolutionary in the look of the patent.... The improvement consists in the wood forming the head being compressed, and being so moulded that the grain curves round the neck, and runs up the "scare," as the junction between the head and shaft is technically termed. This, however, is an improvement which we recorded as having been carried out by John and Gourlay Dunn in January last. The beech heads were steamed, and the grain was made to run round the neck, as in Park's club. The result claimed is greater durability, and, in fact, that the club is practically unbreakable.

The compression of the wood makes it much more solid, and at the same time does not destroy, but rather seems to improve its elasticity. The "feel" of the club is all that can be desired; the ball goes away very sweetly, with a good firm click that is pleasant to hear, and betokens substantiality. It is a noteworthy feature that the face does not get hammered in, nor does it break with repeated strokes. . . . Another feature of the patent is that every head can be made of the same degree of hardness (Golf, 11 Aug. 1893: 372).

More than a year after the review was published, Park finally applied for a British patent to cover his compressed wood. He received a patent (No. 21,424) dated November 7, 1894.

According to his patent, Park sought to construct better clubs by bending the wood head to shape:

I use a piece of wood (preferably hickory) which is bent from the straight form . . . to a curved shape . . . . The wood is compressed either before of after being bent so as to give it additional solidity and strength. The head is cut or shaped out of the bent piece . . . .

The wood was bent so that the grain would run straight across the head and straight up the neck. Park, using steam and pressure to bend and compress the wood, believed his club would be extremely durable:

I endeavoured to manufacture a club-head which, while able to stand more strain than a beech head, would yet not be inferior in driving power, and for some time past I have been making club-heads of wood compressed and otherwise treated to make it more enduring. In this club the wood forming the head is bent so that the grain runs down the neck and along the head, making it practically unbreakable; and, in fact, I guarantee that with ordinary tear and wear such heads are indestructible (1896, 32).

Park's patent does not describe his process for either steaming and bending wood or for compressing it. Steaming and bending a piece of wood is basically self-explanatory, but compressing wood is a bit more involved.

John Hyatt of Newark, New Jersey, patented a method for producing compressed wooden articles. His U.S. patent (No. 987,368 issued March 21, 1911) mentions golf clubs and refers to the structural aspects of the compression process. He reports that in the past:

in the compressing operation . . . the wooden article is subjected to pressure substantially in one direction only and this pressure may take place either lengthwise of the grain of the wood or laterally of the grain, according to the article produced.

Hyatt's patent proposes compressing wood both "laterally and longitudinally":

This lateral pressure should be sufficient to considerably reduce the lateral dimensions of the block, say, from five to ten per cent . . . . After the block has been subjected to the lateral compression referred to and its lateral dimensions thus reduced as stated, the block is subjected to a very heavy pressure lengthwise of the grain or fibers of the block. This pressure can best be applied while the block is

still within the control of the agencies employed for producing the lateral pressure and should be sufficient to reduce the lengthwise dimension of the block from twenty to forty per cent., according to the character of wood employed or the article to be produced.

Like Park, Hyatt believed that compressing wood made it more durable:

The effect produced by these heavy pressures applied in the manner described to a wooden block is to greatly condense the fibers of the block and to increase the hardness and toughness as well as the elasticity of the wood as compared with these characteristics of the same wood in its natural or uncompressed condition.

Hyatt, however, also acknowledged the unstable nature of compressed wood:

Care should be taken that the blocks and the articles fashioned therefrom are protected from undue moisture, as if either the blocks or the articles are permitted to absorb large quantities of moisture they will re-expand and lose their shape and the qualities due to the treatment which has been given them. The articles may be protected either by subjecting them to paraffin baths, or, in many cases, by varnishing them with shellac.

While Hyatt's patent does not describe the exact specifics of Park's compressed wood, it does give a clear idea of what was involved.

Even though a patent for compressed woods was issued to Willie Park, it did not stop other makers from producing similar clubs:

Paxton warrants oak heads for six months, and, along with Park, McEwan, and others, offers "unbreakable drivers," made of what is called compressed wood (Golf, 7 June 1895: 241).

J.&D. Clark, clubmakers in Musselburgh, even solicited compressed wood:

Wanted — compressed hickory blocks for golf club heads of highest quality. Send sample and lowest price for cash on delivery for gross lots (The Golfer, 2 Feb. 1898: 90).

Park also warranted his compressed clubheads against breaking, as acknowledged by a golfer who owned one:

Another first-class club I recently bought is one of Park's compressed-wood drivers. The heads are light but extremely hard, and Park undertakes, with much confidence, to replace them if broken within three months from date of purchase (Golf Illustrated, 20 Oct. 1899: 53).

The driver pictured on the facing page is stamped "W. Park's Compressed Patent" in an oval on the top of the head. The shaft is stamped "W. Park" below the grip. Although Park's patent calls for using hickory for the head, this head is made from a heavily grained wood that appears to be oak (see p. 492). In addition to the transitional head model on the previous page, Park's compressed woods were also made with bulger heads.

ROBERT BRAND
"CELLULOID" DRIVER, CELLULOID HEAD

Those who have been unlucky enough to acquire a faulty style, which in too many instances leads to prolific club smashing, will be a good deal interested to learn something about the Celluloid, invented and patented by Mr. Brand, of the North British Rubber Company. I have had the opportunity of testing one of them, and I am bound to say the Celluloid appears to embody all the elements of success. Its principal virtue is that no golfer need have the slightest fear of breaking the head. . . . As a driver it deserves nothing but praise, and in the hands of a strong player it is capable of performing wonders in long driving. At present the Celluloid is rather more expensive than wooden rivals. . . (Golf, 3 July 1891: 270).

In spite of the glowing review, Robert Brand's Celluloid drivers did not fare well—they were prone to falling apart. Brand's British patent (No. 9,015) dated June 11, 1890, calls for splicing his celluloid clubheads to their shafts, but this was apparently easier said than done:

I want to draw your attention to a new head which has been patented by Mr. Brand . . . . The heads are made of celluloid, but failed on account of their not being able to be made to stick to the shaft of the club. A great improvement has now been made on them. The security of their fixture to the shaft has been achieved. The colour of the head is very much improved, and the driving power is certainly as good as of any head made of wood (Golf, 18 Dec. 1891: 222).

Charles Brand's "improved" club, which used a socket neck instead of a splice neck, was also poorly received. Possessing a stubborn faith in celluloid, Brand invented a celluloid golf ball, white throughout, for use with his wood. Brand surmised that golfers using his club and ball together would help the sales of both:

For some time we have not heard much about the celluloid ball, which Mr. Brand . . . was some time ago supposed to have brought to perfection. It seems that, while with irons the ball was playable enough, yet its unyielding nature was too much for wood, and we heard of several golfers who lost their (club) heads in trying to drive with the celluloid. Mr. Brand, after considerable toil, has now, however, got a celluloid clubhead manufactured which he thinks will overcome the defect, and having got the ball softened a little in composition, he intends the club and the ball to go together and to be suc-

cessful. . . . The head is one block, and the shaft is neatly dovetailed into it. Whatever future is in store for the celluloid club and ball there can be no doubt that Brand's patent celluloid facings . . . are becoming more and more popular (Golf, 24 Feb. 1893: 380).

Unfortunately for Brand, golfers did not accept either his ball or his club.

The Brand Celluloid driver pictured is made without a horn on the sole or a lead backweight. The top of the creamy white celluloid head is stamped "Brands Patent" in a small circle. In 1891 celluloid was defined as follows:

The substance known as celluloid consists usually of dissolved paper, although cotton or other vegetable fibres may be used. In its manufacture, tissue paper is treated with nitric and sulphuric acids, the product is then washed and camphor added. The mass is then ground. Colouring matter is now added, and the mass is made into a paste with alcohol, it is then pressed and broken between rolls (Golf, 23 Jan. 1891: 299).

The dovetailed socket neck on Brand's club was influenced by Robert Anderson's socket neck woods covered under his British patent dated March 3, 1891 (see p. 134). The Brand club pictured also bears a marvelous mechanical grip (p. 405).

A celluloid-headed club is very strongly to be recommended to a man against whom you are going to play a match for money (Golf, 14 Nov. 1890: 137).

CHARLES J. JACOBS
GUTTA PERCHA HEAD

Born in 1867, Charles John Jacobs, "well-known for his club-making, his regular customers including many first-class players," was more than just a golf professional:

There are few men who can claim, as Jacobs does, to have acted the roles of coach-builder, soldier, musician, inventor, caricaturist, rifle-shot, and golf-player, greenkeeper, teacher, and club-maker (Golfing, 27 Jan. 1907: 38).

Charles Jacobs received a British patent (No. 12,019) dated June 21, 1894, that covered clubheads molded from gutta percha. His clubheads, described as being unaffected by wet weather, were made in London by "The India Rubber, Gutta Percha, and Telegraph Works Co., Ltd.," the same company that made the popular Silvertown gutta percha golf balls:

The Silvertown Gutta-Percha Company are sending out a new clubhead, which, like the aluminum head, marks an important fresh departure in the material out of which club-heads may be manufactured. The new clubhead is made of the best gutta-percha, and is the invention of Mr. Jacobs, the club-master of the Royal Isle of Wight Golf Club, Bembridge. It is in form of the now familiar bulger, and possesses the special recommendation, like the aluminum head, of being both indestructible and able to resist the deteriorating influences of the heaviest rain or wettest grass. The gutta-percha head is made with a short socket, which has a hole bored through the neck out to the sole, like the Anderson and Brougham clubs. It can, however, be made with the ordinary "scare" of the clubs now in use .... The weight is imparted to the head by a hollow chamber in the sole, which is fitted with

a brass plate. As this plate can be readily removed by the player, the weight can be increased or diminished, according as his fancy dictates. The gutta head drives as long a ball as the best seasoned beech. On heavy, wet greens, at this season of the year, it is just the club to use, for wet has no prejudicial effect upon it whatever; and in this respect it ought to be a source of economy to the great bulk of players everywhere. In order to prevent the ball from slipping off a smooth surface, the makers have very wisely roughened the face with cross-markings, so as to impart the necessary grip to the ball when it is being struck. In all respects it is an admirable clubhead, and marks a noteworthy advance in improving the materials of the game (Golf, 9 Nov. 1894: 156).

A few months after its introduction, the Jacobs gutta percha club was redesigned:

We have received from the Silvertown Gutta Percha and Telegraph Company a new form of Jacob's [sic] Golf-club head .... The new form of head follows the ordinary lines of the wooden head. The pierced socket is abolished, and so is the loaded chamber for weight-giving purposes on the sole. Instead, we have a roughened "scare" to permit of the shaft being glued to the neck of the club, and the weight is imbedded, like the fly in amber, immovably somewhere in the center of the head (Golf, 12 Apr. 1895: 71).

Because the neck joint in the Jacobs patent driver was such a problem, the Silvertown Company not only changed it from a socket to a splice neck but also included special glue with each club sold:

A special feature introduced by the company in connection with Jacob's [sic] patent head is that they supply all club heads with a sufficient quantity of special compound to be used in fixing the head to the shaft in place of the ordinary glue. The club is meeting with a satisfactory sale . . . (Golf, 28 June 1895: 317).

Still not satisfied, Jacobs, in tandem with John F.C. Hamilton, received a British patent (No. 4,933) dated March 4, 1896, that covered a tongue and groove splice neck for use with his gutta percha clubhead.

Although Jacobs patent clubs supposedly met "with a satisfactory sale," few have survived to this day, and those that have are often in poor condition. However, the Jacobs gutta percha driver pictured, marked "Jacobs Patent" on the crown, is in superb original condition.

Jacobs's clubhead was not the first ever made from gutta percha. Gutta percha clubheads were briefly tried in 1848:

For about a year, golf balls, and also heads of clubs, have been constructed of gutta percha (Roger 1849, 79).

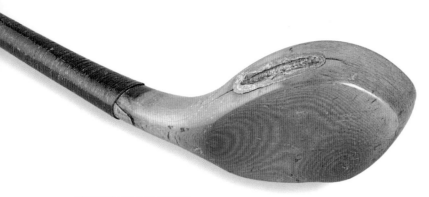

ROBERT MUNRO
FIBER HEAD

Robert Munro . . . was born in 1871, at Arbroath . . . . He served the first years of his apprenticeship as a practical club maker with D. Lowe, of Blundellsands, and later with famous Robert Simpson, of Carnoustie. He was Simpson's first apprentice, and remained seven years with him, leaving eventually to take up the position of foreman in the late Tom Dunn's workshop at Tooting Bec. Next he went as professional to the Mid-Surrey Club, and was about seven years in that berth (Golfing, 2 April 1908: 6).

Munro was the professional at Royal Mid Surrey until 1899, when, after working briefly at Ashford Manor, he became the professional at Chislehurst. In 1902 he left Chislehurst for Royal Wimbledon, where he worked until 1908 (see also Jackson 1994, 68).

Pictured is a mid to late 1890s laminated head driver marked "R. Munro" and "A.E.R.," the initials of a former owner, on its crown. The intriguing aspect of this clubhead is the material from which it is made. The small hairline stress marks occurring along the lamination lines in the back of the head/neck, the thin layering visible across the crown, and the lack of a horn slip in the sole suggests that this head was constructed from "hornite"— vulcanized fiber processed to approximate the durability of horn. However, there are other construction methods and materials worth reviewing that may relate to this Munro club.

The first laminated or multi-layer club was patented by David Grindlay Robertson, a clubmaker from Edinburgh, Scotland. His British patent (No. 7,573) dated April 16, 1895, shows wood-shaped heads made from vertical strips of leather glued together and compressed in a mold. Robertson obtained a second British patent, (No. 11,250) dated June 8, 1895, that also dealt with laminated leather wood-shaped heads. This patent, however, calls for horizontal lamination. Robertson's club reportedly appeared quite natural despite its unique construction:

Robertson, of the firm of Robertson & Anderson, Golf Club Makers, 11 Tarvis Street, Edinburgh, has patented a club-head which is made entirely of leather and can be used with or without horn or brass . . . . In appearance the new patented club is, when finished, not readily distinguishable from the present manufacture. Close examination reveals that the leather is in layers, . . . and by great pressure and through the undergoing of the patent process, the material is practically solid (The Golfer, 5 July 1895: 6).

Robert Simpson's British patent (No. 21,475) dated November 8, 1894, calls for a clubhead made from hornite (shown on the facing page). Even though Simpson's club looks slightly different from Munro's club, the basic elements are the same. Fiber can be made from various materials and can appear slightly different.

The stress marks across the back of the Munro head resemble those sometimes found across the top of a hornite insert in a Ramsbottom metalwood. The layering in the Munro resembles that of paper fiber. Constructing clubheads from paper fiber was considered even before Munro, Ramsbottom, or Simpson produced their clubs. Walter Cook's British patent (No. 363) dated January 8, 1889, which dealt primarily with tennis rackets, cricket bats, etc., included the possibility of making clubheads from "pulped paper stock."

ROBERT SIMPSON
"PAPER MACHÉ" DRIVER, HORNITE HEAD

Bob [Simpson] was born at Earlsferry in 1862 . . . . From 1878 to 1882 he was apprenticed to George Forrester, the Earlsferry golf clubmaker . . . . Shortly afterwards . . . [Simpson] migrated to the Mecca of Golf, and became associated with the Messrs Forgan—clubmaking, of course, claiming a good deal of his attention. . . . When the position of club and ball maker to the Dalhousie Club became vacant [the Dalhousie Club played on the links at Carnoustie], Simpson applied for the position, and, although only twenty years of age, his credentials were of such a high character that he was appointed out of a leet of thirty-five (The Golfer, 24 Mar. 1897: 231).

Robert Simpson was a fine golfer. A consistent competitor in the British Open, Simpson's best finishes were a tie for fourth in 1885 and a tie for sixth in 1893. Simpson was best known, however, as an outstanding clubmaker:

Bob has been close in his attention to business, and his name perhaps will be handed down to posterity more for his clubmaking abilities than to any great achievement on the links. Unquestionably he is in the first rank of clubmakers. . . . For many years Simpson had charge of the green at Carnoustie; but, on account of the exacting claims of an ever-increasing business, he had to resign the office of curator of the links (The Golfer, 24 Mar. 1897: 232).

The club pictured, marked "Patent \ R. Simpson \ Reg. No. 21,475" on the crown, is the first club patented by Simpson. Undistinguished in appearance, this clubhead is unusual in its construction and material. It looks like varnished wood only because it was originally *painted* to do so! In order to produce a stronger and more durable clubhead, Simpson's British patent (No. 21,475) dated November 8, 1894, specifies making clubheads from hornite:

The head . . . is fashioned of "hornite," that is to say hard vulcanized fibre, a known composition, which, as its name implies, imitates horn. . . . It may or may not, as desired, be provided with brass sole plates and painted to as nearly as possible imitate varnished wood.

In his patent, Simpson states that each head is made as follows:

It is first sawn out of a sheet of the material . . . after which it is soaked in boiling water for about twenty minutes in order that it may become flexible. It is then placed in a press somewhat similar to a letter copying press . . . and bent the desired amount. [To keep the head from cracking] I introduce a thin steel plate between the head and the movable plate, and then press and bend the two into shape. The head is left in the press for about twenty minutes in order that it may partly set, after which it is removed to the appliance and kept there for about a week until it is thoroughly dry. The appliance consists of a wooden plank into which are driven a number of wooden pegs so arranged that the heads may be kept from getting out of shape . . . . [This appliance was designed to keep the angle between the head and neck constant. Otherwise, the angle had a tendency to flatten out.] When the heads are thoroughly dry they are finished in a manner similar to wooden ones—except that they do not have the "horn" in the striking edge as a facing or protection . . . .

After Simpson began producing his club, it received a positive review:

Mr. Robert Simpson, of Carnoustie, has invented a club which ought to be classed among the good things. It is a patent unbreakable head; it resembles wood so closely in the reed and in sawing, filing, and polishing, that every one could not tell that it is not wood. It is not affected by wet, and although it is harder than most woods, yet it possesses sufficient elasticity to drive well. . . (Golf, 23 Aug. 1895: 470).

A little over a year later, *The Golfer*, reporting on the growing popularity of Simpson's club, revealed that the head was made from *paper* fiber:

The paper composition club patented by Mr. Robert Simpson, Carnoustie, a year or two ago has gradually forced its way into favour with large numbers of players. Its indestructible nature is its leading recommendation, and in the exceptionally damp weather we lately experienced the Simpson club was one which could be taken round the course when other favourites had perforce to be left behind (The Golfer, 4 Nov. 1896: 364).

Simpson's club was also referred to as "his *papier maché* club" (*The Golfer*, 24 Mar. 1897: 232). Simpson was not the only maker of fiber clubheads. See the Forganite club on the following page.

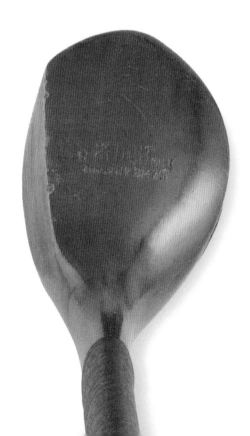

R. FORGAN & SON
"FORGANITE" WOOD

Metalwoods were devised to be durable and waterproof, but most golfers disliked them. Therefore, a few clubmakers produced wooden heads designed to be impervious to moisture. The "Forganite" wood pictured, stamped "R. Forgan, St. Andrews \ Forganite" on the top of the head, is one such club.

Forganite clubs were made without a horn on the sole and were publicized as being practically indestructible. Dating to 1924, they were designed to resist heat, cold, and moisture. The heads are made of wood impregnated under heavy pressure with a sealant. This process increased the weight of the wood so much that lead weights were not needed in these heads. To understand how Forganite clubs were waterproofed, it is helpful to examine a very similar club, Forgan's "Weber Patent."

Dr. C.O. Weber, a chemist living near Manchester, received a British patent (No. 6377) dated March 24, 1899, that covered a waterproof wooden clubhead. According to the patent record brief, Weber's club was waterproofed as follows:

To preserve the heads of golf clubs, such as drivers and brasseys, from the effect of moisture, concussion, & c. [sic], the moisture is expelled and the pores of the wood are filled in with a water-repellent substance. For this purpose, the heads are immersed, in vacuo, if desired, in a bath of hydrocarbon such as paraffin wax, ceresine, or ozokerite, or in a bath of beeswax, carnauba wax, or any solid fatty acid, sulphuretted fatty oils, or a mixture of these ingredients. When sulphuretted fatty oils are employed, the heads after treatment are placed in a stove.

Forgan apparently made a few clubs under an earlier patent granted to Weber. In 1898 Forgan reportedly "acquired a patent"

and by a process "known by the name of Weber" produced water-repelling clubs (*Golf*, 10 June: 248). As winter approached, Forgan's Weber patent clubs received a positive recommendation:

This is the season for making a trial of the Weber Patent Waterproof head. R. Forgan & Son, St. Andrews, who make the clubs, have already sold nearly 500 of this make—the clubs are numbered progressively,—and one of the first clubs turned out has been in use for nine months, in all weathers, and is as good as ever. By the Weber process, beech heads are made impervious to wet, and thus the expense and annoyance of having to get club heads faced with leather or wood is obviated (*Golfer's Magazine*, Nov. 1898: 388).

Forgan's "Weber" clubs are easily identified. According to an ad for Weber's Patent Waterproof Golf Club Head, "every head is stamped 'Weber's Patent Waterproof' in the form of a triangle" (*Golf Illustrated*, 21 Dec. 1900: 261).

There are a few other all-weather clubs. Carruthers's Sylviac, Dickson's Wood-Fibre, Paxton's Oak, and Jacobs' Gutta Percha, among others, are described in the December 27, 1895 issue of *Golf* as being examples of "durable woods" (339).

Robert Simpson's Indestructible driver was described as being "impervious to wet" (*Golfing*, 29 Jan. 1896: 14).

Fred Saunders of Handsworth, Birmingham, England, developed a wet-weather driver:

Saunders has devised a club with a special wet-resisting force . . . . The material used is American fibre, which has the appearance of hard leather,

but is absolutely impervious to wet (*Golf Illustrated*, 10 Nov. 1899: 127).

The February 1899 issue of *Golfer's Magazine* reports "George Forrester, Earlsferry . . . has a patent fibre-head club which stands all weather" (529).

J.H. Taylor made dogwood clubheads that were described as exceedingly tough and able to withstand wet weather. One writer called dogwood "a better wood for club heads than any that has yet been tried" (*Golf Illustrated*, 8 Feb. 1901: 123).

The J.W. Golf Syndicate advertised:

The "J.W." Fibre Driver. Increased drive. Indestructible. No facing required. No horn or fibre bits necessary. Perfect balance, feel and appearance (*Golf Illustrated*, 21 June 1912: 38).

In the 1920s, Kroydon produced "Kroydonite" woods. Similar to Forganite woods, Kroydonite woods were made as follows:

Seasoned persimmon-wood heads are placed in a retort, and every atom of air and moisture is drawn out by vacuum. Then a new chemical known as Kroydonite is forced into every pore and fibre of the wood. When dry, these heads are waterproof. Their parts will not work loose, and they are so flinty-hard, so dense, that they are by far the hardest hitting wood clubs ever made (*Golf Illustrated*, Sep. 1925 : 37).

Willie Macfarlane used Kroydonite woods in the 1925 U.S. Open when he defeated Bobby Jones after *two* 18-hole play-offs.

Forganite clubs are found with regularity and, in clean original condition, make nice collectibles.

G. CHARLES
VULCANITE-COVERED HEAD

UNKNOWN MAKER
"EXCELITE,"
VULCANITE-COVERED HEAD

The Ealing Professional, G. Charles, is another product of the Leven nursery, which has given us some of the brightest ornaments of the professional ranks. Charles was born 24 years ago, and, like most Leven boys, took up the game in very early infancy. He must have developed his golf with unusual rapidity, for, at the age of 14 he won a competition for boys, completing the first nine holes in the low score of 34, and finishing eleven strokes ahead of his nearest opponent. After this, he was admitted to membership of the Leven Thistle Club, and when only 16 years old, he played from the plus 2 mark.

He served his apprenticeship with Alex. Patrick, from whom he went to Montrose, under James Winton. His first position in England was as assistant to Tom Winton at Totteridge, and subsequently he also acted as assistant at the Acton and West Middlesex

clubs. He has been engaged as professional to the Ealing Club for the last two years, and holds the record for the course with a score of 69 (*Golfing*, 21 March 1907: 12).

The Charles driver shown above left consists of a wood head completely enclosed inside two different materials. The face is covered with a piece of white celluloid, and black vulcanite covers the rest of the head. "G. Charles\Ealing G. C." is stamped on the crown. Vulcanite and celluloid were used to waterproof this head and increase its durability.

The idea of encasing a wood head was tried in 1895 by Robert Anderson, of Edinburgh. He covered wood heads in leather!

This firm has lately modified their driver-heads by encasing them in specially prepared leather, a very great advantage in diminishing wear and tear (*Golf*, 27 Dec. 1895: 338).

The author has never seen one of Anderson's leather-covered clubheads. The extreme scarcity of Charles's vulcanite-covered club suggests that it was never accepted by the market.

Also pictured is another very rare club—an "Excelite" driver. This club, marked "Excelite \ Regd \ Covered," is similar to Charles's vulcanite covered club. The clubhead consists of a wood head completely encased in black vulcanite. The covering is apparently vulcanized into place, as the horn and its pegs are identifiable under the vulcanite.

HARDMAN & WRIGHT

"HARDRIGHT" DRIVERS
CONDENSITE HEADS,
THREADED SOCKET

Now for a good long ride and on to the green in one. You can do it with a Hardright Driver or Brassie Head— the club with 10% more "go" that gives you 10% more distance.

You get that extra 20 yards that you can't get with a wooden head. Hardright heads are made of "Condensite" a gum composition (no rubber) that's as tough as iron and as resilient as ivory. That's why they drive the ball farther—they're so much more resilient (Golf Illustrated, July 1917: 2).

Pictured are two different Hardright drivers, with Condensite heads, originally offered by Hardman & Wright, later renamed "The Hardright Company" of Belleville, New Jersey. According to The Hardright Company, Condensite was invented by a chemist who worked for Thomas Edison, the great American scientist:

Condensite [is] the latest invention of Mr. J.W. Aylsworth, who is now and for twenty-five years has been chief chemist to Mr. Thos. A. Edison (Golf Magazine, Sep. 1914: 87).

A Hardright Company advertisement defines Condensite as:

a black hardened gum of peculiar properties, which maintains a brilliant polish, is absolutely non-absorbent, and will not chip or crack (The American Golfer, June 1916: 153).

Condensite clubheads were advertised as being "far better than a wooden club with ivory facing."

Hardright woods were offered in two different forms. Golfers could either spend $5.50 and order the club complete or, if they wanted a more custom fit, they could order the head for $3.50 and have their professional fit it with a screw-in shaft.

The driver pictured near left, with the long brass neck and brass horn, was sold with the shaft affixed by the Hardright Company. "Hardright" is marked lengthwise on the neck. The other driver, with the short aluminum neck and an aluminum horn, was sold as a head only. "Hardright \ Driver" is stamped across its neck. The shaft was fitted by a professional and screwed into place. (This particular shaft can also unscrew from the head, see page 153.)

Hardright drivers and brassies were offered in 1914 and for approximately the next five years. They were available only by mail order, with discounts given to professionals. The fact that few Hardright clubs remain and that they were sporadically advertised for five years suggests that these clubs sold in consistent but small numbers.

Despite being advertised as extremely durable, Hardright clubs are sometimes found in rough condition. They *could* crack, chip, and loose their rich original luster. The two examples shown are in superb condition. (For more on Hardright clubs, see page 153.)

FREDERICK SCHAVOIR
"SCHAVOLITE" WOODS, MOLDED HEADS

The first time you tee off with a Schavolite, you experience a thrill of amazement. Yet there is a simple, though scientific explanation for the tremendous extra distance these remarkable clubs give you. They are molded, under ten thousand pounds of pressure, of a fibrous composition that contains a proportion of rubber. . . .

Schavolite clubs are absolutely impervious to moisture and to the action of the weather. They will not warp, chip or break—the face will not dent in. They are lifetime clubs with a two-year warranty. . . .

*Get more satisfaction out of your golf. Driver, Brassie, and Spoon set retails for $37.50; Putter, $10. Also sold singly (*Golf Illustrated *[ny], Sept. 1928: np).*

On November 23, 1927, Frederick H. Schavoir, of Stamford, Connecticut, applied for a U.S. patent (No. 1,867,103) to cover the clubs described in the above advertisement and pictured above in the middle row. According to his patent, issued on July 12, 1932, these clubs were made with vulcanized rubber heads:

In carrying out the process which constitutes an embodiment of this invention, the following ingredients may be employed in about the proportions which are specified: 32 parts rubber, 50 parts ground hard rubber dust, and 18 parts sulphur, together with a small amount of a known accelerator such as diphenol-guanadine. . . . These materials are mixed together in a dry state in a regular rubber working machine until the "dough" has been thoroughly conditioned. Then a suitable amount of the same is placed in a properly shaped mold of the two-part type . . . . The mold is then placed in a suitable heated press and subjected to vulcanizing heat for a period of approximately 30 minutes. The mass at the end of this first heating stage has imparted to it the desired shape but is still in a pliable condition. It is now removed from the mold and subjected to open heat at about 280° F. for a period of about three hours . . . . [Afterwards] the surface of the head is . . . ground to remove all projections and then polished on a cotton wheel in the usual manner.

Schavoir's patent also states that his clubhead would include a metal liner/sleeve inside the neck, the liner extending down the neck and then angling into the body of the head. The metal liner would bolster the strength of the head and facilitate the use of steel shafts.

After filing his first patent application, Schavoir applied for and received another patent, (No. 1,641,062) applied for on August 15, 1928, and issued on January 12, 1932. This patent, identified as a continuation of his first application, includes the idea of creating a gas-filled (air or ammonia) cavity in the center of the head to make the head more resilient. It also calls for extending the metal neck liner down to the sole as well as branching it off into the head.

The wood-shafted rubber head driver shown center front, marked "Speedway Links \ Washington D.C." around a picture of the dome on the United States Capitol Building, was apparently produced before the steel shaft clubs shown above took shape. This club does not use a soleplate. It has an unusual fabric-backed, wrapped rubber grip.

The steel-shafted rubber head brassie and driver pictured in the second row were produced under both of Schavoir's 1932 patents. These clubs have the metal liner in the head, visible around the tip of the shaft on the sole, and the triangular soleplate illustrated in the patent. Note the mold line readily visible on both these clubs and the wood shaft club pictured.

The matching set of three clubs in the back row has, as marked on each aluminum sole-plate, a "Head Moulded of Textolite \ By General Electric Co.\ Exclusively For \ Schavolite Golf Corp. \ L.I. City, N.Y." The top of each head is marked "Schavolite" and "Textolite" underneath a circular General Electric "GE" logo. Introduced in 1931, these clubs were made by molding the head, which reportedly used fabric in its composition, directly onto the shaft. Costing only six dollars a club, they were much cheaper than previous Schavolite clubs. Judging from the many remaining examples, Textolite clubs were surprisingly popular. Rextolite clubs, produced in the U.K. by John Douglas Sons & Company, were modeled after the Textolite clubs.

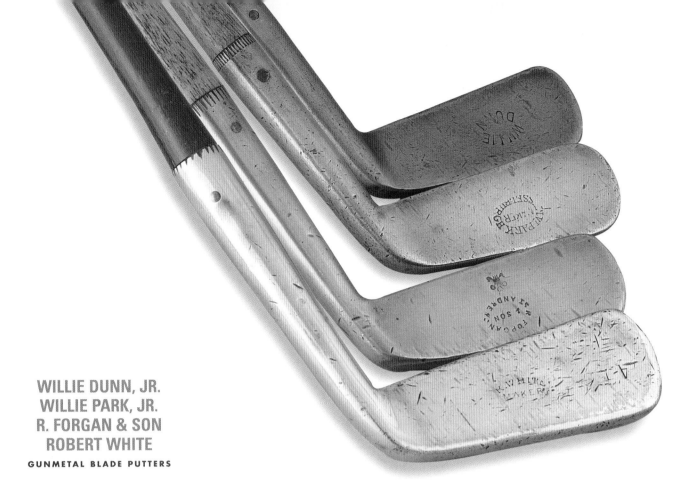

WILLIE DUNN, JR.
WILLIE PARK, JR.
R. FORGAN & SON
ROBERT WHITE
GUNMETAL BLADE PUTTERS

The four gunmetal blade putters pictured represent the work of four famous clubmakers; however, many clubmakers produced blade putters from gunmetal (a type of bronze similar to brass in appearance) as well as brass. Gunmetal putters became popular during the 1890s. Prior to the 1890s, metal putters were seldom used:

Some Golfers affect an iron green putter, fashioned much in the same manner as any of the iron clubs, but having the face, as in the case of a wooden tool, perfectly upright and without a curve. We most decidedly counsel against their use; they are most dangerous inventions to play with, being liable to catch in the grass or soft soil, and have no counter-balancing merit (Farnie 1857, 37).

In 1919 Horace Hutchinson recalled acquiring an iron putter some forty years earlier and thinking it was, at the time, a strange club:

In the old Iron Hut at Westward Ho! on days when the rain kept us in and the time hung heavy, we used to solace its tedium by bringing out our clubs from their lockers and trying to do a deal with each other, whether by exchange or by sale and purchase, and during one of these barterings an utterly unknown weapon was brought out. . . . The strange weapon . . . was though we hardly knew then how to name it, an iron putter. It was inches deep in rust. . . . I gave for it, in exchange, an old and much mended spoon, and it was that iron putter which I have used for forty years since (Hutchinson 1919, 38-39).

With a comment that reflects more on the rarity of early iron putters than the facts behind their creation, Hutchinson continued to discuss his iron putter:

That was the first iron putter ever seen in the West, and I believe it to have been the virtual parent of every iron putter that ever has been seen since.

Iron putters actually date back to the feather ball era. Royal Musselburgh Golf Club has a circa 1800 iron putter made by "the ringmaker" (see p. 105). Royal Blackheath Golf Club still has the iron putter depicted in the portrait of Henry Callender that was first published as a mezzotint in 1812. The Los Angeles Country Club has a circa 1800 iron putter with a 5 3/4-inch hosel. Despite such early efforts, metal blade putters did not gain general acceptance until the early 1890s:

Putters may be constructed of either material; but the metal putter seems to be gradually superseding its wooden rival (Norris 1892, 604).

By 1897, metal putters were in the majority:

The substitution of metal for wood in the putter, is no longer the vexed question that it was half-a-dozen years since. At that date the dogmatic old golfer, in decrying the improvement tendency, would point triumphantly to the wooden putters of the profession, as an unanswerable argument in favour of his contention so far as this club was concerned. Now, however, the professional putts indifferently with either variety, and though the fact that the majority of putters now made are of metal proves nothing conclusively as to the relative merits of the two materials used, it yet goes far to show that metal seems preferable to wood for holing out. A wooden putter, moreover, can only be used satisfactorily on a perfectly smooth green, whereas the metal one suffices equally well for sea-side or inland links.

Many players prefer the metal putter on account of the right angle which the whole head, front and back, makes with the line of putt, whilst others object to it as liable to catch the eye, this tendency being especially noticeable in the horrible brazen variety, with its garish and generally toy-shoppy aspect. Another objection to the metal putter is that it is liable to catch the ground in coming forward, but this danger may easily be minimised by rounding off the sole (Golf, 9 July 1897: 351).

In 1903 John Low identified three basic types of putters:

Putters may be divided into three classes, viz—1. The putter (vulgarly called the 'wooden putter'). 2. The putting cleek. 3. The iron putter. The last named is a straight-faced, rather heavy weapon, sometimes ... made of gun-metal. It has existed in some shape or form from early times, but except as a gift to an enemy is not to be recommended. We are left, therefore, with the putter and the cleek to choose from, and an examination of their rival claims will, I think, show that a golfer should make himself master of both weapons (Low 1903, 119).

The putting cleek differs from an iron putter "only in that its face is slightly laid back" (Hutchinson 1902, 68).

As implied by Low, gunmetal putters had their critics:

There is something particularly loathsome about a gun-metal putter. It is hard to say what it is, but I have never seen one yet that was at all a possible weapon. They are usually without balance and the shaft is set absolutely at right angles to the head, and they are invariably seen in the hands of beginners and duffers. One would never be wrong in giving odds to a man who used a gun-metal putter. I have never heard what special advantage there is in gun-metal—if it is gun-metal these clubs are made of—but it is very soft and has not the clear click of steel (Golf Illustrated, 22 Apr. 1904: 64).

Today gunmetal blade putters from the 1890s are found with consistency. The most desirable examples are those made by the more famous makers such as those who made the clubs pictured on the previous page. McEwan putters as well as those made by Willie Wilson or Tom Morris are also very desirable. Condition is of paramount importance when collecting gunmetal or brass putters, as they are so common and usually show significant wear.

From the late 1890s through the end of the wood shaft era, blade putters were the standard. They numbered in the millions, but most were made from iron.

One final comment. The difference between greenheart and hickory shafts can be seen in the picture on the facing page. The putter at the bottom of the picture was made by Robert White and has a greenheart shaft, distinguished by its dark reddish-brown color and its fine grain. The other shafts are hickory.

Gunmetal *blade* putters were produced in quantity by many makers, but gunmetal *mallet* putters were not. The mallet putter shown above, introduced in 1904 by Alex Anderson of Anstruther, features an iron face set into a gunmetal head. Promoted as being adapted for use with rubber-cored balls, this putter, marked "Zozo" on the top of the head, is a good entry level collectible. Examples in *nice* original condition, however, are seldom seen.

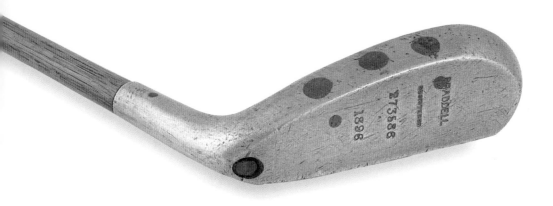

CHARLES PLAYFAIR

"J. BRADDELL"
ALUMINUM PUTTER

WILLIAM MILLS

"KL MODEL"
ALUMINUM PUTTER

Clubmakers first began making aluminum metalwoods during the middle 1890s. But aluminum putters, which followed the introduction of aluminum metalwoods, were the most popular aluminum golf clubs.

Because William Mills was the most prolific maker of aluminum golf clubs, collectors often credit him with being the first to produce and sell aluminum putters, most likely in 1899. However, the long nose style putter pictured above and near right presents evidence to the contrary.

The bottom of this putter is stamped "Braddell \ Registered \ 273586 \ 1896." Charles Playfair, doing business as Joseph Braddell & Son, a sporting goods manufacturer, followed the introduction of his metalwood in 1895 with a British design registration (No. 273,586) that covered this putter on March 27, 1896. This was three years before William Mills began offering aluminum putters. Chances are, because

Playfair /Braddell was located in Belfast, Ireland, this putter went unnoticed at its introduction and died out shortly thereafter. Mills putters, on the other hand, became well known shortly after their introduction. The press gave widespread coverage to the fact that Harold Hilton used a Mills aluminum putter when he won the 1900 British Amateur and 1900 Irish Open.

This stylish Braddell putter measures 5 inches long, 3/4 of an inch in face depth, and 1 3/8 inches wide.

Seven good resolutions for the New Century :—

Be up.

Keep your temper.

Don't Swagger.

Put back the turf.

Don't Press.

Read the Rules.

Buy an Aluminium putter

(*Golf Illustrated*, 4 Jan. 1901: 2).

A review in the October 5, 1900 issue of *Golf Illustrated* states that William Mills modeled his first aluminum putter after a Hugh Philp putter:

The Mills Aluminum Putter . . . is an attempt, and in our opinion an entirely successful attempt, to reproduce the creation of the immortal Philp. . . . The head, we believe, is an exact copy of a perfect specimen of one of three old putters of which that past-master of putting, Mr. John L. Low, is the happy possessor, the only difference being that it is not composed of wood and that its face is cross-hatched to give the club a better grip of the ball (12).

After observing that Harold Hilton used a Mills putter "with such conspicuous success in the Amateur and Irish Championships," this review describes the qualities of the new Mills putter:

The advantages of this old pattern of putter are not sentimental. In the first place, its long face makes it easier to lay the putter at the true angle to the line of the putt. The length of the face makes it easier to see, and consequently to lay, the right angle, than with a shorter faced club. In the second place, the longer face makes any slight inaccuracy in hitting the ball off the true spot, of less importance than in the case of a shorter-faced club. . . .

Two months later the Mills aluminum putter received more praise:

Mention of putting reminds us of a new putter on the market, which has been received with great favour, and Mr. Hilton speaks of it in unmeasured tones of praise. This is the Mills aluminium putter. It is claimed for it that it combines all the advantages of the old wooden putter together with those of the metal putter which is in common use today. The old wooden putter was, of course, liable to be damaged by wet, and when particularly hard and dry was apt to give a slight bounce to the ball when used to deliver the stroke. On the other hand, the aluminium putter is impervious to wet, and although giving a clean shot, does not appear to bounce the ball at all. Mr. J.E. Laidlay, who is looked upon as the champion putter, is using one of these putters and speaks highly of it . . . .

During the Amateur and Open Championship and at the Irish meeting a putter used by Mr. Hilton attracted considerable attention. . . . The "Mills'" putter, for so the patent is designated, has became quite popular with other players besides the Amateur Champion, and has evidently, unlike most Golf patents, come to stay. . . (*Golf Illustrated*, 9 Nov. 1900: 123).

Mills putters quickly became *very* popular:

I hear that the Mills' Aluminum Putter has created something like a rebellion in many golf clubs, as it has been found that those players who have been fortunate enough to possess themselves of the new club have been winning all their matches and "scooping" all the prizes! The fortunate owners of these putters estimate that their games have been improved from four to eight strokes per round, and I understand that an all-round revision of club handicaps has been instituted (*Golf Illustrated*, 21 Dec. 1900: 244).

William Mills and his Standard Golf Company (a branch of his aluminum casting firm "The Atlas Works" in Sunderland, England) went on to produce more aluminum putters than any other aluminum clubmaker during the wood shaft era. Mills produced two basic types of putters—long nose style and mallet heads—which came in various weights and lies.

The long nose style putters were the first models Mills produced. Eventually, during the early 1900s, they were marketed together with his mallet head putters, which quickly became the more popular of the two styles. Mills continued to offer mallet putters well into the 1920s, long after the long nose style putters went out of production.

The putter pictured to the right on the facing page is stamped "The Mills \ KL model \ Upright Lie \ 10 ozs 4 drs" on the sole. The top of the head is marked "Standard Golf Co. \ Mills \ 155996 \ Patent \ Sunderland." The number "155996" is not a patent number; it is a production serial number. Serial numbers were given to all clubs produced by the Standard Golf Company. Unfortunately, no records remain to identify the actual beginning and ending numbers, any breaks in the numerical sequence, or the relationship between particular numbers and various models. However, the author has seen an early Mills putter with a three digit serial number and believes the serial numbers began with "1" and continued upward in unbroken order.

With a five-inch head, the "KL Model" has the longest head of any Mills putter. The "KL" designation acknowledges Hugh Kirkaldy and

John Low for their role in helping Mills produce his initial aluminum putter. According to John Low:

At Mr. Hilton's request, I had a putter made for him which was supposed to be a copy of the somewhat out-of-date tool which I used . . . . Mr. Hilton's putter did not turn out quite to his mind; still it was good enough to suggest to him that a club of the same shape might be made of metal which would have the advantages of the wooden putter without its disadvantages. We consulted together, and by the aid of Mr. Mills have become the parents of a club which, for a patent club, is, I think, likely to be useful to golfers (*Golf Illustrated*, 2 Nov. 1900: 99).

According to Harold Hilton, the initial Mills aluminum putter, designed "in imitation of the famous Philp wooden putters," was made for him in 1899 (*Golf* [ny], Apr. 1909: 213-214).

John Low stated that the long nose putter which served as "a model for subsequent clubs [including] the original of the K model as used by Mr. Mills" was given to him by Hugh Kirkaldy "not long before his death" (Low 1903, 128). Kirkaldy, a former British Open Champion, died in 1897, when he was only thirty-two years old.

Other long nose style Mills putters are the Y, L, Z, SS, K, and X model. The X model is described in the 1909 Standard Golf Company catalog as "an exact copy of the putter used by Mr. H.H. Hilton at the Championship, 1901" (8).

One of the earliest advertisements for Mills putters, printed in 1900, states that they were available either as clubheads or as finished clubs. The manufacturer was listed as "The Standard Golf Company, Atlas Works, Bonners Field, Sunderland" (*Golf Illustrated*, 28 Sept.: 282).

Mills aluminum putters were quickly accepted by golfers at every level:

The Mills Aluminium Putter is becoming a great favourite on our courses, and a majority of the constant and scratch players carry one. It is certainly the best Golf invention since the advent of the mashie . . . (*Golf Illustrated*, Jan. 11, 1901: 42).

When Mr. Mills introduced his aluminium putter a year or two ago I ventured to predict a huge success for it. That prediction has been abundantly justified, for this aluminium putter enjoys today an enormous popularity amongst golfers of all classes (*Golf Illustrated*, May 13, 1904: 121).

A very large number of the professionals were following the example of "the great quartette," and playing with the "Braid-Mills" aluminum putter. This famous putter, which is manufactured by the Standard Golf Co., of Sunderland, is becoming increasingly popular, and well deserves its success (*Golfing*, 27 June 1907: 36).

The Braid-Mills, an ordinary-looking mallet head putter, was very popular and produced for many years. To collectors today, Mills long nose style putters are much more desirable than the commonly available Mills mallet head putters. The KL putter is found only occasionally and, having the longest head of any Mills putter, is the most desirable of all Mills long nose style putters.

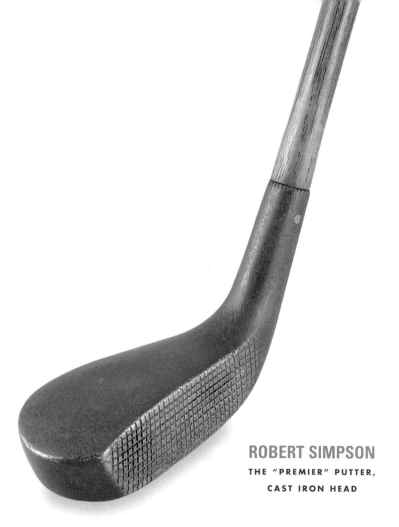

ROBERT SIMPSON
THE "PREMIER" PUTTER, CAST IRON HEAD

The long nose style clubhead of Robert Simpson's "Premier" putter (pictured) is made from cast steel. This is highly unusual because aluminum was the material of choice when clubmakers produced long nose style putter heads from metal.

Premier putters are usually stamped "R. Simpson \ Maker \ Carnoustie" only on the shaft, as is the example pictured. However, an example stamped "Simpson" and "Premier" on the head sold at auction in July of 1995. On the center of the Premier's sole, the outline of a circular plug made from the same material as the head is visible. A plug was used because the head is hollow. A solid iron head of this shape would be extremely heavy.

Simpson and his Premier putter, introduced in 1903, came highly recommended:

The traditions of Hugh Philp, whose clubs combined balance with excellence and beauty of workmanship, are still kept alive by the best makers, and none is more keenly

imbued with those traditions than Bob Simpson, the head of the famous family of golfers. Bob has just put two clubs on the market which will challenge comparison with any golf clubs that have ever been made, alike from their playing qualities and their finish. The first is the Premier Putter, a weapon in shape and design like the creations of the immortal Philp, but made of an alloy of malleable cast iron, cast steel, brass, etc. The weight and balance of the club are alike admirable, and its finish is perfect (Golf Illustrated, 3 Apr. 1903: 15).

(The second club alluded to above is Simpson's ball faced iron, see page 443.)

Simpson advertised his Premier putter as follows:

The "Premier" Putter, Reg. 27219. Finest malleable cast steel, enamelled & electro plated, practically indestructible" (Golf Illustrated, 10 Apr. 1903: 48).

This advertisement includes the patent number assigned to Simpson at the time of his application in 1902. Simpson, however, abandoned his application.

In addition to being a fine clubmaker, Simpson was a well-respected individual and a key person in placing the links at Carnoustie (the Dalhousie Golf Club) on the golfing map:

It all stemmed from the fortunate choice . . . the Club Council made the day it decided to bring Robert Simpson to Carnoustie. For this quite apart from all other considerations, the town owes a tremendous debt to the men who made the decision.

Their new clubmaker soon proved his worth. He established his workshop as a hive of industry, at one time employing as many as thirty clubmakers, every one of them a scratch or low handicapped player. Simpson-made clubs were in demand all over the golfing world, and both Robert and Archie were called on to lay out new courses in Scotland. Robert was eventually elected to Carnoustie Town Council, and became a member of the Magistrate's Bench (Chapman 1968, 18).

The rarity of Simpson's Premier putter indicates that it was produced for only a short period of time.

RALPH G. TYLER
COMBINATION PUTTER

Ralph Tyler's U.S. patent (No. 1,535,270) applied for on November 1, 1924, and issued on April 28, 1925, covered the center-shafted putter pictured above, as well as related drivers and fairway woods. As shown, Tyler's putter has an aluminum sole integral with the aluminum "web" or frame extending out from an aluminum neck. This club looks intriguing, and it possesses some resourceful engineering that is not visible.

Just below the top of the head, the back of the aluminum frame is deeply recessed behind the toe and heel. Consequently, most of the web's weight is located directly in line behind the ball. The block of wood fixed to the back of the head, via three screws from the sole, is formed to fit into the recessed portions on the back of this brace.

According to his patent, the balance of Tyler's combination woods and putters would improve the golfer's play:

It is obvious that with the weight distributed as above described and with the shaft in longitudinal axial alignment with the said weight piece, there is produced a balance which is of such effect that in the hitting of the ball there is no vibratory or torsional tendency.... With the absence of tendency of the shaft to chuck, tremble, or shiver, the enjoyment and skill of the player in making his strokes are greatly increased.

Tyler received three additional patents that covered other combination clubs (see page 297).

JOHN HENRY TURNER
COMBINATION PUTTER

John Turner's patent putter pictured below, one of two Turner putters auctioned together in 1992, is marked "Patent Applied For" on the metal frame which is visible across the sole and the top of the head. The shaft is stamped "Specially Selected." The companion putter reads "Turner's Patent Ap No. 17088" on the sole, as does a Turner patent brassey known to the author. A patent for Turner's combination clubs was applied for but not issued.

The metal hosel on Turner's patent putter is integral with a metal frame running through the center of the head, heel to toe. Two wood blocks attached to the frame form the front and the back of the head. These blocks are held in place by four large screws in the face, two at the heel and two at the toe. The screws extend straight back through the face, the frame, and into the back of the head.

A nice touch of class on Turner's patent putter is the small ram's horn, held in place with three wooden dowels, on the sole. Turner's putter does not have the full metal sole usually found on combination clubs.

Turner combination clubs date to the early 1920s and were made by Sherlock, Ray & Turner, a clubmaking firm located in Abingdon, England. The fine quality of construction and excellent workmanship add to the appeal of Turner's clubs.

WILLIE DUNN, JR.
PYRALIN HEAD

While living in Manhattan, in the city and state of New York, Willie Dunn Jr. applied for and received a U.S. patent (No. 745,044) dated November 24, 1903, that covered the Pyralin putters shown above and below. According to this patent, these clubheads are made from "Pyralin or xylonite" to "materially increase the driving power of the club." The sides of each head are:

parallel and substantially at right angles to the face for a short distance, so as to aid in fixing the direction of the shot.

Dunn believed the elasticity of Pyralin, a type of vulcanized rubber (see p. 415), would cushion the shock while adding power to the golfers shots:

The head, though resilient, because of its elasticity, thereby yielding upon impact against the golf ball and correspondingly lessening the jar upon the shaft, nevertheless resumes its normal shape with such extraordinary promptness that the energy momentarily stored up by the blow within the head, is almost instantly imparted

to the ball, so that the latter receives the full benefit of the momentum of the head.

Dunn's Pyralin putters are center-shafted in order to reduce "the leverage around the shaft to a minimum, thus lessening 'slicing' and 'pulling', and greatly improving direction."

Dunn assigned his patent to The Arlington Company, of Arlington, New Jersey. To obtain patent protection for his club in Great Britain, Dunn applied for and received a British patent (No. 5080) dated March 1, 1904.

The black Pyralin putter shown is marked "Kempshall Mfg Co. \ Arlington, NJ" on the crown. The white Pyralin putter, which is even rarer than the elusive black model, is unmarked. Because patent clubs were occasionally left unmarked, the lack of a stamp does not usually trouble a knowledgeable collector. Collectors are more concerned with what a club *is* than whether or not it was stamped. A club's design, rarity, condition, and quality of workmanship are of greatest impor-

tance. The rarest items, those which were tried only briefly, were often left unmarked.

Dunn's patent does not call for a faceplate on his putter, but the Kempshall Manufacturing Company produced Pyralin putters both with and without brass face-plates. Both examples shown have the brass face-plate, which is cross-scored. (For more on the Kempshall Mfg. Co. see page 415.)

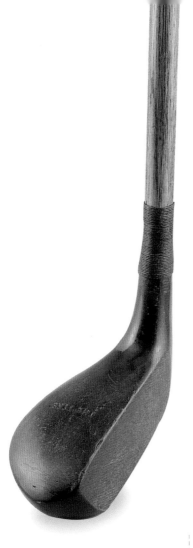

THOMAS W. WARD

"THE TYKE,"
BUFFALO(?) HORN HEAD

"The Tyke" is the name of a solid horn golf club head which we have lately examined. Like vulcanite and gutta percha heads, it is not only practically indestructible but it is particularly useful in wet weather, though, of course, it is equally suitable for play in fine weather. Herd, who has tried the club in play, says that it drives splendidly, giving him long shots off the tee. The club is sent out by the Tyke Golf Club Company, of Sheffield, and the price is 7s. 6d. (Golf, 1 July 1898: 312).

Tyke clubs were patented by Thomas William Ward, an iron merchant from Sheffield, England. His British patent (No. 12,265) dated May 18, 1897, calls for making a durable golf club that would not wear rapidly along the leading edge:

I effect this by employing specially prepared horn such as buffalo horn, the solid portion of which has a specific gravity about equal to the loaded hickory . . . . The preparation of the horn consists in subjecting it to heat so that the tine or pointed end of the horn can be twisted or turned to the requisite angle or curve to fit the stick of the club.

Tyke clubs were advertised as being durable:

The Solid "Horn" Golf Club Heads . . . . Almost unbreakable, still retaining the elasticity of wood. Drives splendidly in all kinds of weather (Golf, 24 June 1898: 300).

The putter pictured above is stamped "The 'Tyke' "atop the head. Tyke clubs, made as drivers, brassies, and putters, are scarce.

UNKNOWN MAKER

IMITATION
TORTOISE-SHELL HEAD

The very rare and unmarked gem"-style putter head shown below has an iron core covered with imitation tortoise shell made from celluloid. Imitation tortoise shell was occasionally used in the handles of mirrors and brushes, etc., during the 1890s and early 1900s. A small crack in the tortoise shell around the neck of this club shows evidence of repair.

R. FORGAN & SON
EBONY HEAD PUTTER

A 1902 R. Forgan & Son advertisement listing many different clubs offered "Solid Ebony Headed Putters" (*Golf Illustrated*, 3 Jan.: 19). Today these putters are hardly ever seen; but when they are, they are easily recognized by two traits. First, the entire head is jet-black. Because the wood itself is naturally black, even the scoring lines are black. Second, the sole does not have the traditional horn slip along the leading edge.

Ebony putter heads were made from the wood of a tropical tree:

Ebony . . . [is] a hard, heavy, durable, dark wood from tropical trees of the African and Asian genus Diospyros (Random House 1991, 422).

In addition to ebony, a most beautiful and dramatic wood, clubmakers also made clubheads from other types of wood. The following is a brief review, originally published in 1905, of some of the different varieties tried:

Thus it is that of the various popular woods beech has almost fallen into disuse, as being too soft for the new [rubber core] balls, although really good elastic beech was unrivalled with the gutta ball, and persimmon (Diospyros virginiana) and dogwood (Cornus florida), both natives of North America, are generally employed, the latter being undoubtedly superior, although it is customary in the trade to push persimmon in preference. . . .

. . . Of home-grown [U.K.] woods, beech as has been said is . . . too soft. Holly is good, but scarce; both pear and apple are really fine, close grained, and altogether suitable woods, but their value as food producers renders their being felled in prime condition commercially difficult, if not impossible. Hornbeam has merits of its own, but is rather given to develop serious cracks or shakes in seasoning, and yew has the same peculiarity. . . . Yew makes excellent heads, if sound, but is commercially unobtainable. Oak has been tried and found wanting, having little elasticity, and being inclined to split. The evergreen oak (Quercus ilex) is a hard, heavy, and very handsome wood, extremely difficult to season, owing to splitting, and is not available in large quantities. Its behaviour in the shape of club-heads is now on trial. Boxwood is too heavy and costly (Golf Illustrated, 27 Jan.: 94).

The nearly unused ebony head putter shown is marked "R. Forgan" on the top of the head and "W. Anderson" on the shaft. Anderson was the Forgan employee who either made or used this club, or both. He was also a fine golfer who once worked as a professional:

Mr. Low, in the Athletic News, writing of W. Anderson, the talented golfer, who is in the service of Mr. Forgan, remarks:

He is a clubmaker, working in the employment of Messrs. Forgan, but he does not play for money prizes, nor does he teach on the links or perform any of the functions of the ordinary professional golfer. He is, moreover, a member of the St. Andrews Golf Club, and holder of the Royal and Ancient medal, yet he is not eligible to compete for the Amateur Championship or similar trophies, of course, in his case, he labours under the disadvantage of having been at one time an out-and-out professional, and as such, by the law of the amateur meeting, can never regain his status (Golfing, 15 Aug. 1901: 5).

Forgan did not mark this ebony head with either the Prince of Wales plume or the King's crown because this club was made after Prince Edward became King Edward VII in January of 1901 and before Forgan & Son began marking their clubs with the King's crown in early 1902, following their appointment as Golf Club Makers to His Majesty King Edward VII (see p. 69). The author has seen a Forgan ebony putter that *is* marked with the Prince of Wales plume.

WALTER HAGEN
STERLING SILVER PUTTER

Hagen Sterling Silver Putter. Autographed by the great golfer, a unique gift for any golf fan—male or female. Not a toy or a miniature—a full size club made for actual play. In fact, it already has a fine tournament record behind it.

It is the exact replica of the putter used by Walter Hagen in four open championships. Head and cap of sterling silver, shaft of selected wood. Suitable gift inscription can be engraved on back of club....

It costs only $35.00 and it's a gift that any golfer will prize as a delightful personal possession....

Originated and made only by Lambert Brothers Jewelers. Third Ave., cor. 58th St., New York" (Golf Illustrated, Dec. 1925: 37).

Complete with a sterling silver grip end-cap, the Hagen Sterling Putter shown here beside two circa 1924 sterling silver tethered tees (also produced by Lambert Brothers) is marked "Sterling" on the hosel, "Lambert Bros \ Jewelers \ New York" on the sole, and "Walter Hagen \ Putter \ Golf Party of W.D. Martin, Jr. \ Oakland Golf Club \ Aug-26-1930 \ Kickers Handicap \ Won By \ R.D. Scott" on the back of the blade. Given all the writing on this head, it is interesting to note that the marks on other Hagen sterling putters are not always in the same location. Such variety is to be expected because each sterling silver putter head was made and marked by hand. Some of the hickory shafts in Hagen Sterling Putters have a traditional finish, and some have a black finish which complements the silver head.

This putter was presented as a prize to R.D. Scott. The minimal "bag wear" on the club-head suggests that Scott seldom used this club. Because Hagen Sterling Putters were made for play, they were often used; and because sterling silver not only shows dents and dings but also collects them with great ease, Hagen silver putters are often heavily worn. The less wear on a sterling putter head, the better it is as a collectible.

Sterling silver golf clubs date back to the 1700s, although most examples were not made to be used. Rather, full size clubs—woods, irons, and putters—made either in part (just the head or head and grip) or entirely (shaft and all) from sterling silver were constructed as trophies to honor the winners of various annual competitions held at a number of British golf clubs. These sterling silver presentation clubs usually remained in perpetuity with the particular golf club that held the event. Some of the more famous sterling clubs are identified in the next two columns.

Three sterling silver long nose woods belong to the Honourable Company of Edinburgh Golfers, in Gullane, Scotland. Dating 1744, 1811, and 1879, these silver clubs were presented to the Honourable Company by the town of Edinburgh. According to the March 7, 1744 minutes of the Council Records of the City of Edinburgh, a silver club was:

to be annually plaid [played] for on the Links of Leith at such time and upon such conditions as the Magistrates and Council should think proper (Kerr 1896, 43).

In London, Royal Blackheath Golf Club also has three silver clubs, the oldest engraved "1766." The Royal and Ancient Golf Club of St. Andrews has three long nose silver clubs.

The silver clubs belonging to the Honourable Company, Royal Blackheath, and the R&A have silver golf balls affixed to their shafts. Every year, a silver golf ball, made by electroplating an actual ball, was engraved with the year and name of the captain and then fastened to the shaft. Originally a golf competition was held to determine the captain, but this practice was eventually phased out as the captain's responsibilities grew.

The Killermont Golf Club in Glasgow, Scotland, has a long nose silver club dated 1789. The USGA museum, in Far Hills, New Jersey, has a fabulous sterling silver cleek originally played for by the "Edinburgh Cleek Golf Club" between 1888 and World War I. This engraved cleek, displayed in its original case, has a *telescoping* sterling silver shaft.

Like these magnificent early silver clubs, other sterling clubs dating from the late 1800s and early 1900s still exist, mostly held by private golf clubs in the U.K.

In 1924 Black, Starr & Frost, jewelers in New York City, advertised a sterling silver blade putter similar to the Hagen Sterling Putter. It sold for forty dollars and did not have a sterling silver grip end-cap (*Golf Illustrated* [ny], Sep. 1924: 38).

Ninety strokes, be it known, is a wonderfully small number to go round the course of eighteen holes in.

(*Once a Week*, 12 Dec. 1863: 696)

More Materials

In presenting the various unusual materials clubmakers used in constructing clubheads, the preceding chapter dealt with face materials and combination clubs. This chapter continues that discussion and introduces *integral soles* and *multipiece heads*. Integral soles are soleplates constructed as part of a faceplate or backweight. Multipiece heads are clubheads made from more than one piece of the same material, not counting inserts, backweights, shafts, or appendage pieces. The material can be slightly different—for example, brass combined with steel, or persimmon with beech—but the material must be all metal or all wood. When determining whether or not a clubhead is a multipiece head, the collector ignores any inlaid material and any substance located completely inside the head. Only the actual framework of the head—the actual structure—is considered. A multipiece head will always consist of two or more pieces that are visible across its surface.

Although this chapter discusses various face materials, it does not discuss traditional leather inserts commonly found in woods, except for the following observations.

In his 1896 book *The Game of Golf*, Willie Park discusses the origin of leather face inserts and their accepted use in clubmaking during his day:

Many players like their clubs to have leather faces, and I am rather in favour of this. Leather faces were originally devised for repairing clubs that had become damaged by tear and wear, but they are now frequently put into quite new heads. A leather face put into a new club helps to make it last better, and when put into a damaged club will often save the head from breaking, and permit of its being used for a considerable time longer. This in a favourite club is no small matter, and whenever signs of tear and wear begin to show, it is as well to get the repair made at once (32).

The leather usually installed in a clubface could become somewhat "pulpy" in wet weather (Travis 1901, 112). Therefore, exotic (and collectible) leather inserts, in addition to other insert materials, were tried. A well-tanned rhinoceros hide insert was used in Willie Park's "Noceros" driver:

The Noceros driver.... The insert in this case is not leather or wood, but rhinoceros hide, a really superior substitute for leather (Golfing, 12 Oct. 1899: 12).

The leather used is very difficult to procure, and is harder than wood, and impossible to chip. It takes from four to seven years to tan (Golfing, 17 Aug. 1899: 3).

The insert in Park's Noceros driver extends deep into the head, is visible across the top of the head, and covers the entire face except for a small area at the heel.

Just before Park offered his Noceros driver, Feltham & Company, of London, England, briefly offered their "Rhinos" woods. These clubs were promoted as having an indestructible face (rhinoceros leather?):

A new golf club for the new year. With indestructible face. Drivers and Bulgers 6s. each.

It cannot split or chip, as most artificial properties do when applied to the face of clubs.

It is unaffected by weather, and does not get slippery on the face, thus giving great command in direction.

Its toughness, coupled with just the amount of elasticity required, ensures it being the most lasting and longest driving club yet produced (Golf, 14 Jan. 1898: 331).

Percy Barrow's British patent (No. 8,789) dated April 26, 1899, suggests that other exotic leathers were tried in golf clubs. Barrow's patent describes making golf club inserts from:

a piece of thick hide such as hippopotamus, rhinoceros, walrus, or elephant hide, suitably tanned to preserve its elasticity and thickness.

As illustrated in his patent, Barrow's insert, extending almost halfway into the head, is visible on the top of the head and across the face from the heel to the tip of the toe.

The Rhinos and Noceros drivers were both short-lived.

A new cleek has recently come into the market. It is the patent of Mr. George Nicoll, of Leven, and consists of a leather face on the centre portion of the blade of the cleek which strikes the ball. The socket is also a little shorter than the ordinary club, resembling to some extent Forrester's or Carruther's clubs, though the shaft does not come through as in the last-mentioned club. The blade is also thickened at the back to add to the driving power, and the blade generally is short and compact. When the weather and the green are dry the leather face undoubtedly gives a better grip to the ball, and prevents the skidding which is so noticeable in playing with a smooth-faced iron club. For putting it is also very serviceable. Peter Paxton is the sole agent for the club south of the Tweed. It is undoubtedly a useful improvement, and is meeting with widespread recognition among Southern golfers (Golf, 8 Dec. 1893: 198).

George Nicoll was a Scottish cleekmaker who began making clubs in 1881. The back of the cleek pictured is marked "G. Nicoll \ Leven \ Pat. No 15425 \ Warranted Hand Forged." Although marked with a patent number, Nicoll's leather face iron was never patented.

Nicoll received the patent number marked on this club when he filed a provisional patent appliction on August 14, 1893. A patent, however, was not issued. Even without a

patent, Nicoll continued to make his leather face cleeks, marking them with the patent number assigned to his application. (For information on the patent process see page 130.)

Nicoll's club appealed to a small niche in the market and gained a few advocates:

With reference to Nicoll's patent leather-faced cleek, Mr. J. Osborne, Goodwood, Chichester, writes to Mr. Peter Paxton: – "I have tried the leather-faced patent cleek you sent me, and I certainly think it an excellent driving cleek. It drives a long, low ball with very little effort" (Golf, Jan. 19, 1894: 296).

After introducing his club in 1893, Nicoll continued making this unusual iron into the early 1900s. A 1903 Lillywhite advertisement offered "Nicoll's patent leather-faced cleek" (*Golf Illustrated*, 25 Sep.: 253). At that time, J. Lillywhite, Frowd & Company were the sole agents for Nicoll's leather face clubs.

In addition to leather inserts, Nicoll also offered gutta percha inserts in his iron:

[Nicoll's] cleek is also faced with gutta-percha, which acts in the same way, and by some is preferred to leather (Golfing, 18 Apr. 1901: 28).

Instead of a leather face, the iron pictured has the elusive gutta percha face.

George Nicoll was not the only clubmaker to produce leather or gutta percha face irons. W.&G. Braid, golf club and ball makers, Baltimore Country Club, Baltimore, Maryland, advertised "Braid's Gutta Inlaid Cleek" as follows:

The surface of the gutta being less slippery than iron or steel prevents "pulling" or "slicing." As wet weather has no effect on the gutta it is preferable to a wooden or leather faced club. Drives a very long ball. Price $2.50. (Golf [ny], Sep. 1898: 187).

The author has never seen a W.&G. Braid inlaid cleek. (William and George Braid were brothers. They made clubs together in the U.S. only briefly.)

Sotheby's golf auction held at Chester, England, on July 15, 1991, offered a Willie Park iron which the sale catalog described as "circa 1895, with rectangular insert in centre of blade (wood or leather)." When viewed, this insert appeared to be leather.

William Ayrton received a British patent (No. 11,350) dated May 18, 1898, that covered inlaying the entire face of an oval-shaped iron head, preferably made from phosphor bronze,

with gutta percha. Only one example has ever sold at auction.

Robert Condie also produced a few irons inlaid with a rectangular insert of gutta percha.

The "Coaxer" putter came with a thin leather insert covering the entire middle section of the face between the heel and toe:

Remarkable putter for short putts. . . . The ordinary-shaped metal head is used, the greater part of the face being milled out to the depth of about 1/20th of an inch, and its place taken by a piece of rubber-tanned leather— (sheepskin) leather tanned by a new and special process. . . .

With the Coaxer putter the player can hit the ball much more boldly than he can with any existing putter (Golf Illustrated, 17 Dec. 1909: 314).

Today, the Nicoll leather-faced cleek, the first iron made with a face insert, is found in only a few collections.

JAMES CRAN

"THE CRAN PATENT
BRASSIE CLEEK,"
WOOD FACE IRON

In 1992 the United States Golf Association reapproved an old and tried concept when they ruled that iron heads with face inserts were legal for play. Irons with inserts were first introduced in the 1890s, and the most famous example was Spalding's "Cran" cleek.

The Cran cleek was covered under a U.S. design patent (No. 27,190) granted on June 8, 1897, to "James Cran, of Chicopee Falls, Massachusetts, assignor to the A.G. Spalding & Bros., of New York, N.Y." The tenth golf club patent granted in the United States, Cran's design covered an iron face inlaid with wood. Two screws, the heads of which are visible on the back of the blade, hold the wood in place.

The Cran iron is a popular golf collectible for two reasons. First, it is a visually interesting club with wonderful aesthetics. Second, inlaying an iron face with wood was a dramatic break from tradition. Rarity, it will be noticed, is not a primary reason.

Spalding's catalogs reveal the large number of Crans produced. Originally advertised in their 1898 catalog as "The 'Cran' Patent Brassie Cleek," the Cran cleek was still offered in Spalding's 1918 catalog with the remark:

This club we have had on the market now for over 15 years and its popularity is still on the increase (11).

Spalding last offered the Cran in their 1919 catalog. Spalding was one of the largest golf club manufacturers in the early twentieth century, and they offered the Cran for many years, so it comes as no surprise that many remain.

The "Spalding 'Cran' Patent Brassie Cleek" pictured is one of the first ever made. Marked "The Spalding \ Cran," this cleek is also stamped "Pat Applied For," which means it was made between April 21, 1897, when James Cran applied for his patent, and June 8, 1897, when he received his patent.

This early Cran iron has a smooth wood face; those made in later years are scored with fine lines. A Cran cleek with an altered, repaired, or replaced insert is a weak example.

The wood insert supposedly gave the Cran iron the feel of a wooden club when striking the ball. According to Spalding's 1898 catalog:

The face of this cleek is hollowed out and filled with wood, and a ball goes as "sweet" off the cleek face as it does off a driver. It is unquestionably the longest driving cleek made.

During the final years of the Cran iron's popularity, Spalding's catalogs also offered a "steel face, driving Cran cleek, Cran style" iron. This steel face "Cran style" iron was Spalding's spring-face iron, first offered in their 1903 catalog as "Spalding's Hollow Steel Faced Golf Club." Spalding marked their spring-face and Cran irons with the same patent date (see page 338).

Following James Cran's lead, Ben Sayers Jr. produced a:

very canny-looking 'cleek' with a wooden face, which Sayers claims is much easier to play with than an iron cleek" (*Golf Ill.*, 30 Oct. 1908: 110).

James Cran's other U.S. patent, (No. 645,942) dated March 27, 1900, covered a movable weight inside a cavity running lengthwise across the back of an iron head. As designed, a setscrew extending through the weight tightens against the bottom of the cavity. The movable weight allowed for adjusting the balance of the iron heel to toe. It is not known if Cran's movable weight club was ever produced.

JOHN HENRY TURNER

THE "PEGGY" IRON, MIRALITE FACE

The "Peggy" Iron, patent miralite and wood face, drives like a wooden club, made in cleeks, irons, and mid irons . . . only from J. Turner, Denham, Bucks (Golfing, 11 Apr. 1912: 25).

Pictured is John Turner's "Peggy" iron, devised in 1909. The back of the blade is marked "J. Turner \ Bucks \ Denham \ Pat 15364 \ 1909 \ Patent Miralite Face \ 3 \ Hand Forged \ Special," along with the "diamond" trademark of W.M. Winton & Company, of London and Montrose.

Even though a patent number is marked on this club, a patent was not issued. Turner probably abandoned his application because his club was poorly received. To a collector, however, such a response increases the desirability of a club, especially when coupled with a radical departure from traditional construction and materials.

The construction of Turner's insert is quite involved. The miralite insert, also visible across the top and bottom of the blade, is keyed into the head (the back of the insert is wider than the front). Within this insert are twenty-eight wooden pegs: four columns of five pegs and two columns of four pegs. These wooden plugs might simply be glued in place, but they also might be threaded and screwed into position. A plug of what appears to be iron is located in the upper heel portion as well as

the lower toe portion of the insert. These metal plugs act as rivets, to help hold the miralite insert in place.

Such an elaborate insert system is unknown in any other iron. The only similar iron the author has seen, also designed by Turner though made by William Gibson, had four rows of ten wooden plugs set in an otherwise ordinary face (no miralite insert).

The purpose of Turner's unorthodox insert appears to be twofold. First, by using a miralite insert, the head would be more heel and toe weighted. Second, the use of wooden pegs was a step toward providing an iron with the feel of a wood.

Born in 1880, John Henry Turner was a respected British professional:

John Turner, (Denham) who will shortly be taking up his new appointment as professional to the Filford Heath Club, is a native of Oxford. He was assistant to Sherlock at Oxford for two years. He afterwards became professional to the Flackwell Heath Club, where he stayed for six years. He holds the record for this course with a score of 67. For the past three years Turner has been professional to

the Denham Club. . . . He is a particularly clever club-maker, and has invented several patent clubs. Turner, who is of a quiet unassuming nature, is extremely popular with members and his fellow professionals (Golf Illustrated, 26 Dec. 1913: 33).

Turner applied for and received four minor patents. To the collector, the ideas embodied in these patents and the visual characteristics of the clubs constructed under these patents are of minimal interest. His last three patents were issued at the end of the wood shaft era. The four patents are as follows:

His first patent, a British patent (No. 21,422) dated September 27, 1906, covered drilling a few holes into a wooden head in order to weight it in such a way as to reduce hooks and slices.

His next patent, a British patent (No. 310,209) dated May 19, 1928, showed small, colored alignment plugs on the top of a putter.

His third patent, a British patent (No. 352,462) dated April 8, 1930, described a metal sleeve on the shaft in the grip area; the sleeve to be wrapped with rubber, fabric, adhesive tape, etc.

Turner's final patent, a British patent (No. 353,661)

dated July 4, 1930, covered the use of a nut and bolt to affix the clubhead to a metal shaft.

Turner's Peggy iron, however, has good collectibility. Turner also devised and produced a combination club (see p. 313).

In 1924, Leonard Maurice Edward Dent applied for a British patent to cover an iron similar to the Peggy iron. Dent's iron, as designed, uses a thin aluminum face plate that is dovetailed and riveted into the head. Wood dowels were not called for. Dent's patent (No. 243,435) was accepted on December 26, 1925.

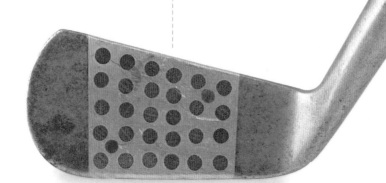

LEWIS ANDERSON
"CORK CENTER" PUTTER

During the final sixty years of the wood shaft era, a few club and ball makers tried using cork as a component in constructing clubs and balls. In making balls, cork was mixed with gutta percha to make solid balls and used without any additives as core material. In constructing clubs, cork was almost always used to make grips. The primary exception to this practice is found in Spalding's "Cork Center" putter, pictured. Cork fills its brass head, forms the face, and remains exposed flush across the back of the head. Despite being advertised from approximately 1915 through 1920, Spalding's "Cork Center" putter was perceived as just another gimmick club and, therefore, was not popular.

The example shown is marked with Spalding's "Accurate" cleekmark along with "Spalding \ Gold Medal" inside an oval on the top of the head. In addition, the crown is also stamped "Putter \ Pat. Applied For." and "C P", the initials of a former owner. The shaft is stamped "A.G. Spalding & Bros. \ Gold Medal."

On January 26, 1914, Lewis Anderson applied for a British patent (No. 2,003) to cover a putter with a cork face. Granted on December 10, 1914, Anderson's patent reads in part as follows:

At the present time many varieties of putter are in use and generally they have a practically non-resilient striking face. Such putters are apt to be so used as to give the ball too solid a blow, and, with a non-resilient face, are not sufficiently sensitive for short putts. From a rigid striking surface, the ball is apt to be half hit and to lose its direction.

According to my invention I provide putters with a face of very resilient material which preferably covers substantially the whole of the striking face.

I use a layer of cork or very resilient rubber, and such is let into the striking face and suitably dovetailed thereto.

Anderson's patent goes on to note that:

the strip of cork or resilient rubber may stand out beyond the line of the metal at the front of the putter or may be level therewith.

Although Anderson's patent begins by describing the evils of using a putter with a non-resilient face, it eventually presents the benefits of cork:

With the provision of a very resilient face of cork or rubber I anticipate greater control in directing the ball when putting, as well as a cushioning effect when the ball is struck.

The author believes Spalding employed Anderson's patent in producing their Cork Center putter. The date of the patent fits, as does the intent and use of cork in Spalding's putter head.

The small differences between Anderson's patent illustrations and Spalding's putter (Anderson's patent illustrates a thick muscle-back head inlaid with cork) were simple modifications referred to in Anderson's patent:

It is obvious that my improvements are applicable to various types of putters and that slight modifications may be necessary . . . .

The author once saw a Spalding Cork Center putter offered at a gathering of golf collectors. The cork, however, had long since been removed and a wood block inserted in its place. A club with such a serious alteration is nothing more than a distant shadow of what it originally was; it should be valued in corresponding fashion.

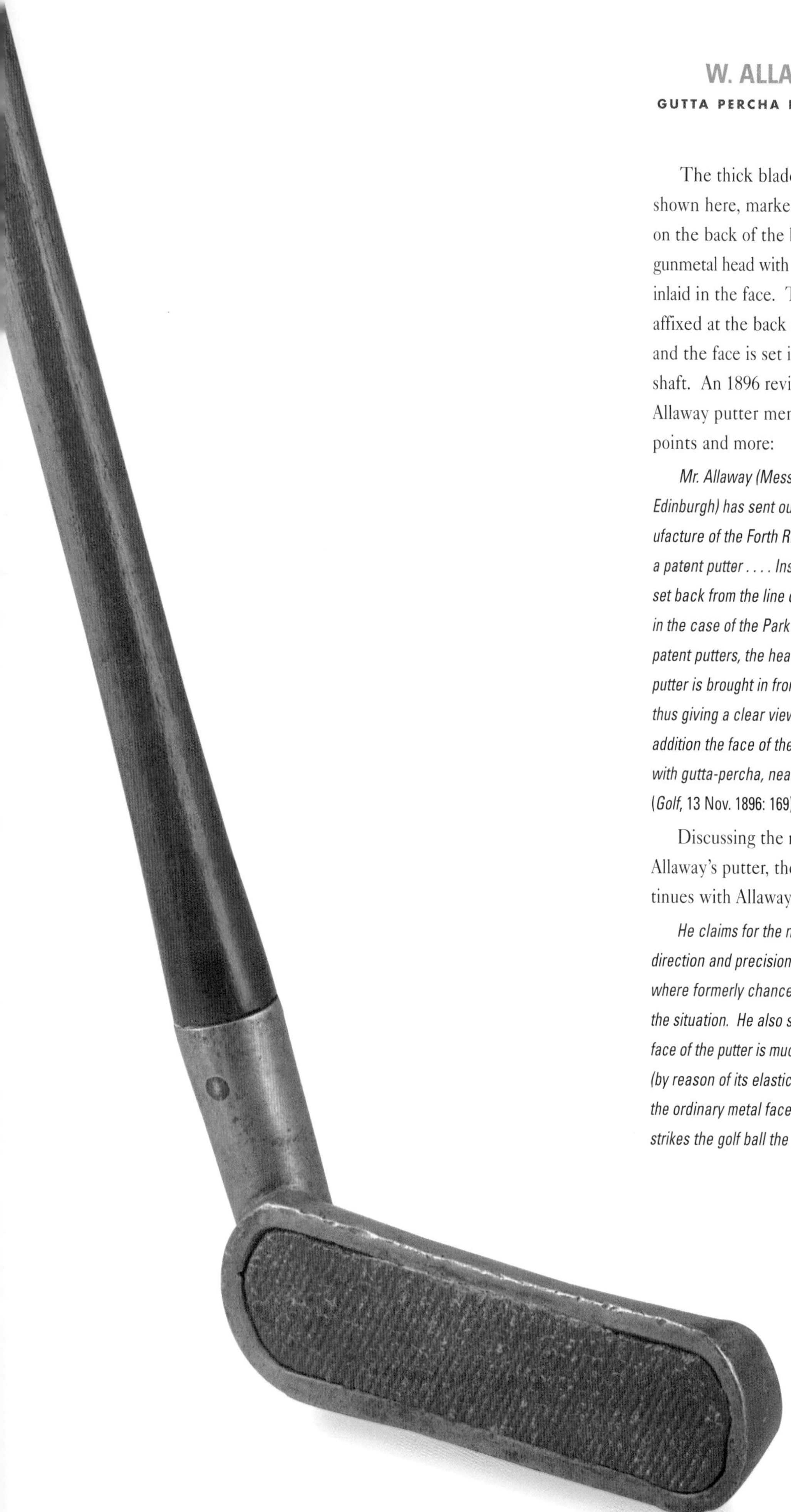

W. ALLAWAY
GUTTA PERCHA FACE PUTTER

The thick blade putter shown here, marked "Allaway" on the back of the blade, has a gunmetal head with gutta percha inlaid in the face. The hosel is affixed at the back of the heel, and the face is set in front of the shaft. An 1896 review of the Allaway putter mentions these points and more:

Mr. Allaway (Messrs A.&D. Padon, Edinburgh) has sent out from the manufacture of the Forth Rubber Company a patent putter . . . . Instead of being set back from the line of the shaft, as in the case of the Park and similar patent putters, the head of the Allaway putter is brought in front of the shaft, thus giving a clear view of the ball. In addition the face of the putter is laid with gutta-percha, neatly grooved (Golf, 13 Nov. 1896: 169).

Discussing the merits of Allaway's putter, the review continues with Allaway's claims:

He claims for the new putter that direction and precision are secured where formerly chance was ruler of the situation. He also says that the face of the putter is much more yielding (by reason of its elastic nature) than the ordinary metal face. When it strikes the golf ball the gutta-percha is contracted during the moment of impact, immediately afterwards expanding to its natural size, and adding to the force of the stroke the energy which it develops in expansion; consequently the ball has a greater recoil, and it rebounds more readily off the face of the putter. As the tendency of the stroke is upwards, it will travel through the air in a slight curve and stop very shortly after touching the ground, so that, if the force of the stroke be proportional to the length which the ball is required to travel, then the ball will always fall exactly where wanted, and the uncertain roll which the ball makes (when playing with the metal-faced putters) after touching the ground will be avoided, and a great drawback to attaining perfection in the game will be removed.

"W. Allaway" applied for a patent in September of 1896 to cover "an improved golf club." Allaway, however, let his application lapse. Two other Allaway putters are known to the author. One sold at the Phillips 1988 January golf auction held in Chester, England, and the other is displayed in the British Golf Museum in St. Andrews, Scotland.

JOHN KNOX
WOOD FACE PUTTER

The brass mallet putter pictured above, marked "John Knox \ Belfast" atop its head, is constructed from a brass shell filled with a block of wood that is visible across the face. Three screws across the sole fasten this wood block, made from two pieces of wood glued together, in place.

Walter Sinclair Traill, of Blanford, Dorset, England, received a British patent (No. 4,631) dated March 10, 1900, that covered a putter similar to the one pictured. According to Traill's patent, his putter head was to be constructed:

of a suitable metal and of partially hollow construction, such head being in a form generally known as fish backed having an open front.

"Fish backed" refers to a distinct hump, which becomes thicker towards its middle like a fish, across the back of the blade.

Traill's patent continues:

Within the hollow portion of the said head I insert a core, formed of hornbeam, beech, or other tough and resilient wood, gutta percha, or hard leather, such core closely conforming to the shape of the recess . . . .

Screws are employed for the purpose of holding the core within the recess of the club. The surface of the said core is made flush with the rim of the shell-like head and constitutes the striking face.

Traill believed his design would create a more efficient putter:

This invention . . . is designed with the object of providing . . . a putter, which shall be capable of effecting a better and longer and more accurate putt, with less exertion to the user than heretofore, the essential features of the said golf club being the improved striking surface by means of which greater resiliency and propelling power is obtained than using equal force . . . with the metal putters . . . .

Knox's putter could easily have been produced under Traill's patent; however, there are a few differences. First, the screws holding the wood in Knox's head are in the sole. Traill's patent illustrates them in the back of the head. Second, Knox's head is clearly a mallet head while Traill's illustration shows a club best described as a thick muscle-back putter.

UNKNOWN MAKER
WOOD VENEER FACE PUTTER

Given a quick glance, the unmarked club pictured below appears to be a Spalding Cran cleek. It is not. Closer inspection reveals a number of interesting differences.

The club pictured is a putter, not an iron as are all Crans. It has an oval insert inlaid into the entire face, but the insert is not made from solid wood. Instead, as revealed by a chip off the lower portion of the face, this insert consists of lead covered with a wood veneer.

This interesting club appears to be reshafted—the hosel pin has been replaced and some type of filler bridges a gap where the top edge of the hosel meets the shaft. Since no other example is known, however, this club is an excellent item. It will serve a collection well until a better one is found, *if* that should ever happen. The reshaft has nothing to do with the aspects that give this club its collectibility. Therefore, collectors will not be as critical of this club as they might be of a more common item.

A putter related to the one pictured was covered by John Youds in his British patent (No. 212) dated January 3, 1908. Youds developed an aluminum mallet head putter filled with lead at the face. Youds originally produced and marketed his club, which he marked "J. Youds, Maker, Chislehurst." The Youds putter was then sold by A.G. Spalding & Bros. from approximately 1912 through 1918. The Spalding examples included Youds's name along with their own. Small circles were usually stamped in the lead to call attention to the different face material. When Youds putters are found today, the lead face often goes unnoticed; the color of the lead blends in with the surrounding dark aluminum.

Placing lead in the face of a putter was supposed to do more than move the center of gravity closer to the ball. It was thought that lead, being a soft metal, would afford the golfer greater "feel." However, because lead *is* such a soft metal, easily dented and marked up, the putter pictured included a wood veneer over its lead face.

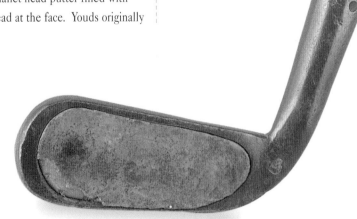

THE REMSON COMPANY
RUBBER CENTER PUTTER

Try this putter 15 days FREE!

We believe you can cut down your game from 3 to 6 strokes with the Remson Putter. We want you to try this putter 15 days at our expense, and if not satisfied, send it back and we will pay charges both ways.

The hard rubber center of the Remson Putter gives it the "touch" of a billiard cue; true direction, precise distance, and a forward-rolling motion on the ball.

Made of non-rusting phosphor bronze, in right-handed straight putters; upright, medium, or flat lie; $6.00. Gooseneck patterns $6.50. Left-handed patterns, medium lie only, same prices. Special models subject to correspondence.

The Remson Co., Erie, PA. (Golfers Magazine, Feb. 1922: 4).

The Remson's putter pictured above is marked "Trademark \ Remson \ Erie Pa \ Pat. Appld For" on the sole. The unique profile of the blade and the circular insert of hard rubber are visible as shown, but the styling given to the back of the blade is not. The back of the head behind the insert is the thickest part of the blade due to the deep cavity holding the insert. The bottom of the blade has the beginnings of a flange.

Just as the hard rubber insert and its circular shape give this club a nice degree of collectibility, so does the unique profile of the blade. A few other putters, such as the "Triumph" and the "Verden," sport a similar though less radical profile. The face of David Anderson's "Triumph" putter is shallow at both the toe and heel, but increases as it approaches the center of the blade where it comes to a point above the sweet-spot. On the "Verden," an aluminum mallet putter, both the face and the crown round gently up then back down, heel to toe.

ARTHUR MONK
BRASS INSERT

The splice neck putter pictured below is marked "Arthur H. Monk" and "F.C.S." across the top of its head. Arthur Harold Monk was born at Guildford, England, in 1894. From 1913 to 1920, Monk was the professional at Royal Winchester Golf Club. However, between 1914 and 1918 he also served in the military, taking part in World War I. From 1921 into the 1930s, Monk worked as the professional at Felixstowe Ferry Golf Club (Jackson 1994, 66).

Monk's putter has a nice head shape, but the use of the unusually large brass insert is what sets his club apart from all others. Monk's insert is fixed in place by five screws—two screws on each end of the face and one in the middle—and is visible across the sole and crown.

Monk's putter is termed a "long head" mallet putter for three reasons: First, this club is not a long nose because it was not made during the long nose era. Second, it is not built in "long nose style." Other than having a long head, this putter is not shaped anything like a long nose. Third, the head is too long to simply term it a mallet. Ordinary mallet heads do not possess the same look found in a long head putter.

JOHN ROBERTSON, JR.
FIBER FACE

John Robertson Jr.'s distinctively shaped driving putter, complete with a full fiber face affixed by six wood dowels, centrally located lead backweight, and greenheart shaft, is pictured. Marked "Robertson" in a semicircle on the top of the head and "Stilton" in a straight line underneath Robertson, Robertson's club was one of the first wooden clubs to include an insert made from material other than leather.

Robertson's clubs originally came with a smooth white celluloid face:

Mr. John A. Robertson, Junr. of Stilton, Peterborough, has sent a driver containing two improvements. One is a slip of thin celluloid along the face of the club, thereby doing away with the horn on the sole, and the other is the manner in which the lead is let in behind. Instead of the lead being all along the back of the club it is concentrated in small space immediately behind the point of impact. Of the celluloid face it may be said that the general effect is to drive a long ball with a low flight, and with a click very much resembling a cleek shot. The designer of this club, however, who is, we believe, an old Fifeshire golfer, must guard against making the heads of the clubs too heavy. The club we received is much too heavy in the head to be satisfactory. The celluloid should either be a trifle thinner, and roughened on the surface to give grip to the ball, or the weight of the lead should be greatly curtailed. . . . The club ought to be particularly serviceable in wet, windy weather (Golf, 19 Aug. 1892: 376).

Less than a month after publishing the above review, *Golf* published a letter to the editor wherein the author, "H.M.B.," writes about his use and appreciation of Robertson's club (*Golf*, 9 Sep. 1892: 428-429). Mr. B. had tried golfing with a celluloid ball, a "Brand's patent pneumatic"; however, the hardness of the ball was damaging his wooden clubs. (Mr. B. even lent the ball to a friend who returned it a week later with a note, " 'The first drive went away very well indeed; so did the head of my driver after it.' ") After relating a few other difficulties, Mr. B. then tells of his satisfaction upon trying Robertson's celluloid face club on both celluloid and gutty balls:

I tried a "Robertson" at Gullane last week, and drove several long balls, but I found I could drive gutta percha a few yards further. I got several local players to test it, but they would only give it a negative commendation, "It's no' a bad club," and, unfortunately, one hard hitter, endeavoring to eclipse us all, caught the heel of the club heavily, producing the old, fatal result of celluloid vrs. wood!

Mr. B. concludes his letter by suggesting how to improve the club:

With regard the "Robertson" club, I should prefer it with a face slightly spooned, as celluloid does not give at all, and a putter-faced driver requires a high tee, and is of no use through the green.

Robertson made some changes and produced the club pictured:

We have received from Mr. J.A. Robertson, Stilton, . . . a driver with a face which appears to be celluloid, but which we are assured is not. Some time ago we took occasion to notice a club sent out by the maker with a celluloid face. . . . The suggestion which we made at that time as to roughening the face and lightening the head considerably has been adopted. Another improvement is that the present material, which has the appearance of celluloid, is stained brown, like a piece of leather, with the result that the face and the wood harmonise in colour, and the eye is not distracted by the white strip of celluloid (Golf, 16 June 1893: 246-247).

The face material on Robertson's second model was not identified other than to note that it was not celluloid, but it looks like vulcanized fiber. By 1897 fiber was widely used by clubmakers, especially in America:

How few professionals in these days use horn in facing the soles of clubs. Vulcanized fibre, red, black or grey has almost entirely superceded it in this country. It is much cheaper and appears to be quite as serviceable (Golf [ny], Sep. 1897: 51).

Robertson's wood is a uniquely styled transitional head. The long, graceful head is flat along its entire leading side, even up the neck. The lead backweight, visible only as a small oval in the back of the head, extends deep into the head where it becomes wider directly behind the ball. The sole does not employ a horn or soleplate of any kind.

The newest things this year turned out by the house of Spalding are the Jacobus patent clubs. These have three pieces of wood inserted in the face, which are so placed that the ball is hit with the grain of the wood. The theory of this club is that it gives the hardest possible striking surface and hence gives the greatest possible distance (Golf [ny], May 1913: 311).

Shown here is a near mint Jacobus patent wood marked "Spalding Gold Medal \ J." inside an oval on the top of the head. The sole is marked "Pat'd December 7, 1909 \ Pat'd November 8, 1910."

Charles Jacobus, of Springfield, Massachusetts, received a U.S. patent (No. 974,888—assigned to A.G. Spalding & Bros.) dated November 8, 1910, that covered the club pictured. Hoping to improve the driving power and durability of drivers and brassies, Jacobus devised an insert that, according to his patent, used three thick wooden dowels glued into the head with their grain "substantially parallel with the direction of the stroke, or at right angles to the grain of the head itself." The longer side inserts were installed prior to drilling out the cavity for the shorter and wider middle insert—so the inner end of the middle insert would rest "against [the] shoulders formed on the other two parts." In this fashion:

the central plug is supported in part by the side plugs and in part by the material of the head itself secur[ing] a more effective distribution of the forces due to a blow upon the striking face to the interior of the head.

Spalding's 1914 Spring and Summer catalog tells a little about Jacobus and his "triple circular insert":

Mr. Charles Jacobus, the well known roque and croquet expert for over thirty years, and maker of fine mallets, has carried his inventions into golfdom. The well-known facts that the grain of the wood of a mallet should lie in the direction of the force of the stroke, and that the arch is supreme for strength and endurance, are in his invention perfectly exemplified. He commands at once the endorsement of every expert and has solved a problem upon which inventive minds have long been engaged (5).

According to Spalding's 1917 Spring and Summer catalog, the wooden inserts were made from mahogany:

An exceedingly hard driving surface [is] obtained by inserting specially prepared mahogany segments so that the impact is imparted to the ball by the end of the grain of the wood (18).

The idea of installing three wooden inserts in the face of a *wooden* head did not originate with Jacobus. William Frier tried such an insert back in 1896:

A new form of golf club has been patented by Mr. William Frier, clubmaker, Braid Hills, Edinburgh, the face of which is pierced in three places, into which are inserted pieces of hard wood secured with wooden pins driven through the centre. The middle piece of wood is specially hard, and is placed where the club should strike the ball. For a driver who can use his weapon with reasonable accuracy the club should enable him to send a longer ball than he can with the ordinary weapon (The Golfer, 3 June 1896: 408).

Frier applied for a patent to cover this club in March of 1896, but he later abandoned his application.

Jacobus patent woods were produced from 1913 through 1923. During this long production run, Jacobus clubs were reasonably popular. Consequently, they are seen with some frequency today. (For a similar triple insert, see McMahon's metalwood, p. 291.)

Jacobus triple insert woods usually include a backweight patented by Frederick Rigden, as does the club pictured. On December 7, 1909, Frederick Rigden, of Chicopee, Massachusetts, received a U.S. patent (No. 942,353—assigned to A.G. Spalding & Bros.) that covered a brass backweight centered behind the ball "both in a vertical plane and in a horizontal [plane]."

Rigden's backweight was the first brass backweight to be patented. Nevertheless, by itself, Rigden's backweight has minimal collectibility. It is not very unusual and was used for many years in vast quantities of Spalding woods.

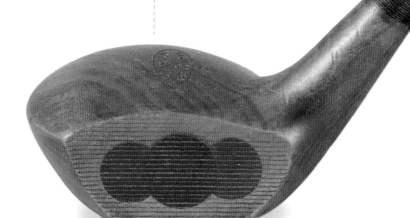

JAMES BRADBEER
STEEL-FACED "PEGGY"
DRIVER

Bradbeer's Steel-Faced Clubs. Designed to make the rubber-cored ball fly and fly well, James Bradbeer has constructed drivers and brassies quite on an original principle. Bradbeer claims that they drive a rubber-cored ball 10 yards further than an ordinary club will. They can be had with either an aluminium or horn face (Golfing, 3 Dec. 1903: 28).

A little-used example of Bradbeer's steel "peg-faced wood" marked "Jas. Bradbeer \ Patent No. 4705" on the top of the head is pictured. Bradbeer applied for a British patent (No. 4705) on February 25, 1904, but he later abandoned his application.

Appearing to be nothing more than a bunch of screws driven into the face, Bradbeer's "insert" provides more than meets the eye:

The maker's own claims are as a follows:

"The steel face consists simply of screws driven into the face, but around each screw and behind it is a little rubber thread, woven round and driven in with the screw. This rubber thread allows the screw to give a little, thus the face of the club is less likely to split or the screws to come loose.

The face is a hard face to hit with; and with the combination of the steel, rubber and wood, the desired amount of spring is apparent, which is necessary for negotiating rubber-cored balls.

"A very hard face causes a rubber-cored ball to collapse too much, which results in a high drive and comparatively straight drop, but with Bradbeer's clubs the ball runs well after touching the ground" (Golfing, 3 Dec. 1903: 28, 30).

Bradbeer's Steel-Faced clubs were originally produced with only eleven screws in the face (rows of four, three, and four). In early 1905, Bradbeer changed to fifteen screws as seen in the driver pictured. A year later, the construction of Bradbeer's club was described as follows:

Twelve or fifteen holes, about one inch in depth, are drilled in the face of the club, in three parallel rows one above the other, and almost touching each other. These holes are then filled with the best elastic rubber, and into them are screwed ordinary 5-8th inch steel screws, flush to the face of the club, thus forming a solid face, comprised of steel, wood and rubber (Golfing, 15 Mar. 1906: 18).

James Bradbeer was born at Berrow, England, in 1879. He first worked as a professional at Ivythorn Golf Club (in Glastonbury) from 1897 to 1900. He was the professional at Finchley from 1900 until he moved to Porters Park, at Radlett, England, in 1905. He remained at Porters Park until at least 1933, but his time there was interrupted (from 1915 to 1919) by his military service during World War I (Jackson 1994, 10). A brief mention of Bradbeer contained in the May 1914 issue of *Golf Monthly* lists his "Patent Steel-Faced 'Peggy' Faced Clubs" as his specialty (237).

Walter George Toogood received a patent for a club distantly related to Bradbeer's Peggy driver. Instead of calling for a number of screws in the face, Toogood's British patent (No. 7,287) dated April 2, 1908, calls for screwing a single large bolt into the center of the face, the head of the bolt to serve as a striking insert. No examples of Toogood's club are known.

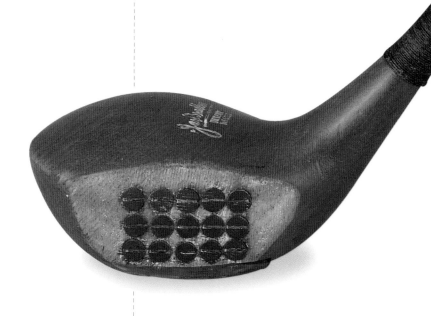

PHILLIP SAMSON
"SAMSON FACING,"
WOVEN FABRIC INSERT

One of the most striking features of the [1911] Open Championship, just concluded at Sandwich, was the great interest aroused by the newly-invented Samson facing. Harry Vardon, Arnaud Massy, first and second respectively, and Alec Herd, who tied for third place, used this new face in their drivers and brassies, and there is little doubt that both in regard to direction and length it was of material help to them in the gaining of premier honours. [Vardon, Massy, and Herd] confirm the opinion that it grips the ball well, and most decidedly adds to the length and accuracy of a drive; and declare that it is without exception the best face that has yet been invented.... A company has been formed in connection with this invention, ... the Samson Golf Syndicate (Golfing, 6 July 1911: 6).

Phillip Edward Samson received a British patent (No. 11,744) dated May 15, 1911, that covered the club pictured. According to this patent, Samson's club would drive the ball farther and reduce the "slicing" and " 'pulling' caused by the ball slipping on the face, more noticeable in wet weather."

To accomplish this goal, Samson's initial provisional specification for his patent proposes making an insert from "ferodo fibre," a composition "sold for the linings of motor car brakes and other purposes by the Herbert Frood Co., Ltd."

Two days later Samson filed another provisional specification in order to alter his original patent application "as regards the fibrous textile material" used in facing his club. His second application proposes using "a similarly made material containing asbestos as the sole or principal fibrous element, woven or plaited . . . and treated or impregnated" as described in his original patent application.

Even after filing his second provisional specification, Samson had not settled on his insert material. His complete specification filed on December 13, 1911, was different still. Having had time to experiment, he specifies constructing his insert as follows:

I have found that such fabric solidly woven from cotton strands to a thickness of approximately a quarter of an inch gives satisfactory results. Other materials for example wool, linen, rhea, jute, hemp, hair, or asbestos may be used. Plaited, braided, knitted, or woven strands or strands otherwise closely intertwining may be employed.

I prefer to impregnate the fabric with the binding material after it is woven or otherwise formed and to use a binding substance which is of the nature of the non vitreous enamels used in enamelling metals and which enamel is dried off by stoving the fabric at a high temperature.

The fabric was impregnated to make it waterproof and durable and to provide it with enough elasticity to give length to the drive. In spite of the waterproofing treatment, Samson's club was still perceived as doing better in dry than in wet weather, and this hurt sales. (See *Golf Ill.*, 22 Sep. 1911: 11.)

The Samson driver pictured is marked "Samson Facing \ Special \ London" inside an oval on the crown along with "Glorious" directly underneath the oval.

Applied for on April 8, 1912, a U.S. patent (No. 1,094,599) for Samson's insert was granted on April 28, 1914. Samson clubs were briefly produced in America by the Crawford, McGregor & Canby Company, of Dayton, Ohio. Their 1913 catalog offers:

"J. MacGregor" Samson Face Drivers and Brassies . . . Model 27-H "The Samson." Favorite club of Harold H. Hilton [Hilton used a Samson face club in winning the 1911 U.S. Amateur].

In the manufacture of our J. MacGregor Samson Drivers and Brassies, we use only the genuine imported facing, each piece stamped "Samson Facing" fitted into the face of our "Famous" model 27-H Drivers and Brassies. . . . An "ideal" facing in an "ideal" club (Crawford 1913, 7).

According to Samson's patents, "the edges of the recess may be overhung, and the facing is shaped to fit such recesses." This provision refers to retrofitting a solid wood face with a Samson insert. The Samson Golf Syndicate used this marketing angle and advertised, "Get your professional to fit it at once" (*Golf Illustrated*, 7 July 1911: 58).

Jack White invented a similar insert:

It consists of gut, of the sort used in the manufacture of tennis rackets, and is compressed and converted into pieces of the required size by a special process. The idea came to White . . . while he was playing lawn tennis. Happening to have a golf ball in his pocket, he "served" it, and lo! it went about 150 yards. With the help of one skilled in chemistry he set to work to produce the facing which, according to plenty of golfers, puts yet another 20 yards on their shots (Golf Illustrated, 1 Dec. 1911: 169).

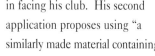

A.G. SPALDING & BROS.
HILLERICH & BRADSBY
IVORY INSERTS

The first patent to cover an ivory face insert, a British patent (No. 18,788) dated August 22, 1906, was granted to Frank Fernesley Figgis of Belfast, Ireland. With the objective of improving "the driving qualities" of drivers and brassies, Figgis proposed screwing a "cylinder of ivory" into the center of the clubface. This cylinder was to have a diameter measuring slightly less than the depth of the face, and its outer end was to fit flush with the face.

The next patent for an ivory insert, a British patent (No. 14,736) dated June 23, 1909, was granted to Vincent Booth Hubbell of New York City. His patent calls for gluing a much wider ivory cylinder in the center of the face. The insert as designed would fit across the face, but would extend well above and below the face. Hubbell specified sanding the top and bottom of the insert to make these areas flush with the top and bottom of the head (see the wood on the left on the following page.)

Following on the heels of these two patents, the use of ivory as an insert material steadily increased, hitting its peak in the 1920s and early 1930s. Ivory was promoted as being able to add distance to the golfer's drive, but it also made clubs more attractive. In addition to using ivory inserts, some club-makers inlaid ivory in the back of the head, across the crown, and/or in grip end caps. Because such clubs looked *so* attractive, their beauty enticed many golfers into becoming proud owners.

The use of ivory crossed over into the steel shaft era. In fact, most of the clubs made with ivory inserts or backweights are steel shaft "fancy face" woods produced between the mid-1920s and mid-1930s.

A commentary about ivory inserts, printed in *The American Golfer*, reflects a concept still true today:

Now that so many players have begun to use a driver with a piece of ivory set in the face, the question naturally arises what is the advantage of it. Ask any player who uses one and he will immediately tell you he can get considerably more distance with it than with the wooden driver. Yet is this a fact? Undoubtedly when the ball is hit with the center of the ivory face the result will be a long ball, but isn't it true that when we happen to get hold of one in the center of the ivory that we attribute the corking good drive to the ivory instead of to the fact that the ball has been hit in the middle of the club? We think it is; but it is a difference of opinion which makes people like different clubs (The American Golfer, Mar. 1913: 448).

Pictured above left is a Spalding Model 4 driver, marked "Spalding \ 4" on the crown, offered between 1909 and 1912. Unlike this club, the vast majority of Spalding's Model 4 woods do not have ivory inserts. Rather, their faces, like those on most woods produced during the wood shaft era, were solid wood. According to Spalding's 1912 catalog and those that followed for the next few years, a golfer could "special order" an "Ivory Face" for an additional charge of $2.50. This was a large premium as the entire Model 4 club itself cost only $2.50. Spalding did not offer a stock club with an ivory insert until 1915, when the "Rigden club with ivory face" was offered in their catalog—for $6.00.

Pictured above right is a Hillerich & Bradsby Company "Par-X-L" driver. The ivory insert in this club is set in a metal faceplate that is integral with the soleplate. The crown of this club is marked "Par-X-L \ ALB" above "Hillerich & Bradsby Co. Louisville, KY" inside an oval. "B" is stamped on the sole. The shaft, which has a cork grip, is stamped "Made by Hillerich & Bradsby Co. Louisville, Ky \ Kork Grip Pat. \ September 15, 1914."

H&B's integral face and soleplate was covered under John A. Hillerich's U.S. patent (No. 1,509,429) dated September 23, 1924.

There is also a metal back-weight on the club pictured. It appears to be made from the same type of metal used in the face\soleplate.

CRAWFORD, McGREGOR & CANBY COMPANY

"J. MACGREGOR IVORY FACE" DRIVER; "J. MACGREGOR MODEL 4" DRIVER, FIBRE LOCK IVORY FACE

Pictured above left is the "Ivory Face" driver produced by the Crawford, McGregor & Canby Company. In shape, outline, dimension, and material, this insert is the same insert covered in Hubbell's 1909 patent mentioned on the previous page. As produced by Crawford, McGregor & Canby, however, the Hubbell insert uses five fiber dowels.

An advertisement in the October 1916 issue of *Golfers Magazine* presents four "special faced" clubs—the "Ivory Face," "Steel Face," "Bull Dog," and "Six Spot"—with the notice that "golfers are finding out that a plain faced driver hasn't the necessary push to get maximum distance" (91). The Six Spot model also used ivory, but instead of one large circular insert, five smaller circular ivory inserts form a semicircle above one slightly larger circular ivory insert.

Crawford, McGregor & Canby first sold woods with ivory inserts in 1912. Their 1913 catalog advertised these woods as the " 'J. MacGregor' Genuine Ivory Face Drivers and Brassies." They used the Hubbell insert, but included two fiber dowels advertised as "fibre lock pins." The 1913 catalog description for these clubs reads in part:

Used by Charles (Chick) Evans and many other prominent golfers. The J. MacGregor Ivory Face Clubs have made a big hit the past year. They are perfect in balance and conform to all the laws of motion required in a classy club. The Ivory is inserted in a circular form. The perfect joint being reinforced by our improved fibre lock pins. The Ivory face lengthens the drives of the moderate hitter (6).

The J. MacGregor Ivory Face driver pictured is marked "Alex H. Jolly \ Ridgemoor C. C. \ Chicago" inside an oval on the crown. Jolly retailed this club and possibly shafted it as well:

Alex Jolly, one of the family of "Inimitable Jolliers," . . . has been signed as instructor and greenkeeper for 1911 at the Ridgemoor Golf Club, near Chicago. He succeeds his brother, David Jolly, who it is understood, will prosecute his dental studies temporarily suspended when the young man came from St. Andrews, Scotland . . . . "Jack" Jolly is the third brother of this trio (American Golfer, 11 Feb. 1911: 811).

Pictured above right is a "J. MacGregor Model 4" driver with a "Fibre Lock Ivory Face" as advertised in Crawford, McGregor & Canby's 1917 golf catalog. Besides noting that this club came with a "Russia Calf Grip" and "second growth hickory shaft," the catalog states that the Model 4 driver includes:

Another new design in which the ivory insert, an inch in diameter and 7/8 inch in depth, is encased in a cylindrical fibre wall, securely fastened to the pin-locked fibre face.

This double wall, allowing for all possible expansion and contraction affords the best protection to the ivory of any club of this character that has yet been put on the market. A "distance face" club that combines great distance driving with extreme durability (10).

On July 5, 1921, George Mattern of Dayton, Ohio, received a U.S. patent (No. 1,383,654) that covered this insert. Mattern's patent, applied for on August 12, 1919, and assigned to Crawford, McGregor & Canby, also covered MacGregor's "Six Spot" insert.

The J. MacGregor Model 4 driver pictured is stamped "Geo Meeker \ Select." Meeker retailed and/or shafted this club.

Note: Crawford, McGregor & Canby sold "MacGregor" golf goods, and the company itself was often referred to as "MacGregor." The spelling change (Mc to Mac) was employed by the company in order to form "a stronger identification with the Scottish tradition in the game" (Wishon 1985, 23-2).

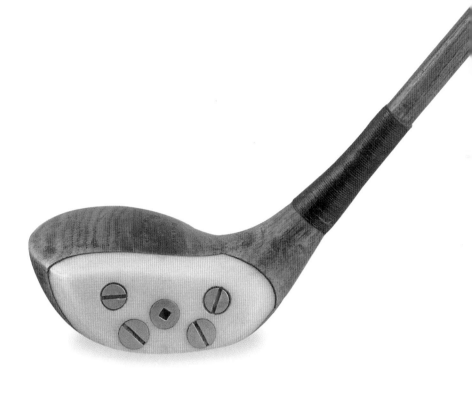

ST. ANDREW GOLF CO.
**IVORY FACE WOODS,
IVORY BACKWEIGHTS**

CRAWFORD, McGREGOR
& CANBY COMPANY
**"CHIEFTAIN"
FANCY FACE WOODS**

Pictured above is a matching pair of woods made by the St. Andrew Golf Company, of Dunfermline and Glasgow. These clubs are unique in that the entire face of each club is made from a solid piece of thick ivory, as are the backweights.

The industrial strength screws used in both the face and backweight draw attention to the fact that ivory is not the most durable of materials. Ivory, in fact, was susceptible to chipping and cracking. Spalding's 1919 Fall and Winter catalog offered their Autograph woods with an ivory insert (special order only), but added this disclaimer: "Real Ivory Face (not guaranteed against checking or cracking)" (42).

Evolving from the use of genuine ivory, white fiber and white plastics were eventually used in club construction. These alternative materials were cheaper and usually more durable than ivory. Consequently, more woods were made using ivory *substitutes* than were made using *genuine* ivory.

Of related interest, the Crawford, McGregor & Canby Company produced a brass putter with a circular "ivora" insert set into the center of the face. The top of this insert was cut flush with the top of the blade, so a golfer addressing the ball could see the blade's sweet-spot. In the August 1915 issue of *Golfers' Magazine*, the "Ivora Putter" was advertised as giving "smooth action to the ball" as well as being "a 'deadly' club" (81). Ivora putters are found with some consistency.

Of superb construction, the Chieftain embodies the best efforts of MacGregor Golfer-Workmen in design, workmanship, and finish. Streamline type with scruloc inserts in the face, ivory inlay across the top, solid ivory back and brass keystone sole plate. The ivory inserts of the faceplate are white in the Driver, while the center one on the Brassie is green Yardsmore inlay and the corresponding insert on the Spoon is red inlay.

The color code is observed in the center dot of the ivory inlay on the club top and the two dots on the ivory back weight thus making instant identification possible from any viewpoint (Crawford 1928, 4).

The Chieftain was once the top of the line MacGregor wood. In 1927 and 1928, Chieftains sold for $20 a club; in 1929, the price jumped to $25 each. During this period, other MacGregor fancy face woods (advertised as "Special Face Clubs") were offered for either $12 or $15 each; plain face MacGregor woods (no insert) were $5.00 to $8.50 each. In the 1932 MacGregor catalog, the last catalog to offer the Chieftains, their price dropped to $18.00 each and the "Harmonized Master 30" model, at $22.50 per club, replaced the Chieftain as the most expensive MacGregor wood (see page 524).

The 1928 MacGregor catalog offered Chieftains with either Bristol steel shafts or hickory shafts. At that time, most MacGregor clubs were offered and sold with steel shafts. In 1929 a redesigned Chieftain with two primary changes was offered. First, Chieftains would be constructed only with steel shafts. Second, the brass keystone soleplate offered in 1928 was dropped in favor of aluminum soleplates.

According to the 1929 MacGregor catalog, Chieftains had "select Russia calf grips with sheepskin trimming, conforming to the color code, and bell tops." "Conforming" sheepskin trimming refers to the colored trim at the bottom of the grip. The trim matched the color (either black, green, or red) of the dot in the ivory insert on the top of the head; the color of this dot (actually a scruloc insert) identified the club as either a driver, brassie, or spoon. "Bell tops" refers to grips with slightly thicker butt ends. Today, Chieftain woods, with their extensive use of ivory, rich colors, and overall beautiful appearance, are popular collectibles. Because there are far fewer wood shaft than steel shaft examples and because they have *wood* shafts, the wood shaft Chieftains are more valuable than steel shaft examples. Furthermore, because a matched set of wood shaft Chieftains is difficult to find, a matched set is worth considerably more than three single Chieftains assembled to make a set.

The left-handed matched set of wood shaft Chieftains pictured below has been refinished. The original finish was dark mahogany. A set with a clean original finish would be best, but a stained and oiled finish is very presentable.

Each of the clubs pictured is marked "MacGregor Chieftain" on the crown. "Driver"-"Brassie"-"Spoon" is marked on the respective soleplate of each club; "Reg. U.S. Pat. Off. \ Patented \ October 21-19 - November 14-22 \ Mar 27-23 - April 24-23" is marked on each soleplate. These dates acknowledge the following four patents.

On October 21, 1919, a U.S. patent (No. 1,319,233) was granted to George W. Mattern, who assigned it to the Crawford, McGregor & Canby Company. It covered extending the backweight to the top and bottom of the head. The ivory backweight on each Chieftain is visible across a large portion of the top and underside of the head.

On November 14, 1922, a U.S. patent (No. 1,435,318) was granted to George Mattern, assignor to Crawford, McGregor & Canby. It covered screw-threaded inserts or plugs that screwed into the head. MacGregor used these inserts and referred to them as "scruloc" inserts:

Scruloc—A threaded face insert used in all MacGregor special face clubs. The method of threading and applying these inserts is responsible for the fact that we have never heard of a single one coming loose (Crawford 1929, 5).

All the small circular ivory inserts in each Chieftain as well as the colored "Yardsmore inlays" are threaded and screwed into a threaded socket. Yardsmore inlays are made from material once known under the registered trademark of "galalith." According to Walter Byrd So Relle's U.S. patent [No. 1,449,559] dated March 27, 1923, galalith was a casein product made from goat's milk! This patent was also issued (to the Yardsmore Golf Club Manufacturing Company, of Delaware, the assignees of So Relle) as a British patent (No. 203, 317) dated August 17, 1923.

On March 27, 1923, a U.S. patent (No. 1,450,091) was granted to Allan Lard, assignor to the Metallic Shaft Company, of Wilmington, Delaware. It covered a number of different aspects concerning the construction of steel shafts. Crawford, McGregor & Canby produced Chieftains with both wood and steel shafts, so including this patent number on all Chieftain soleplates simply covered an option.

On April 24, 1923, a U.S. patent (No. 1,452,695) was granted to George Mattern, assignor to Crawford, McGregor & Canby. It covered placing a trapezoidal soleplate, recessed into the sole, flush against the bottom front of the backweight. This design supposedly helped rearward impact shocks to be "laterally transmitted to the clubhead." MacGregor called this soleplate their "Keystone" soleplate.

Some MacGregor Chieftains use a soleplate marked with one additional patent date: "March 3, 1926." This date acknowledges John R. Gammeter's U.S. patent (No. 1,528,017) that covered streamlining the shape of a wood head. On the Chieftain, the top and bottom of the head slope towards each other, in almost mirror fashion, across the back of the head. This positions the back line of the head midway between the crown and the sole. The "Streamline Design" is referred to in both the 1928 and 1929 MacGregor catalogs.

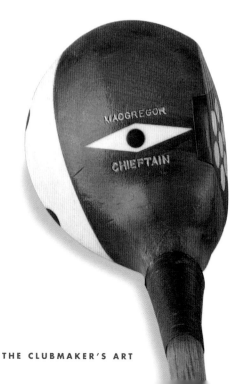
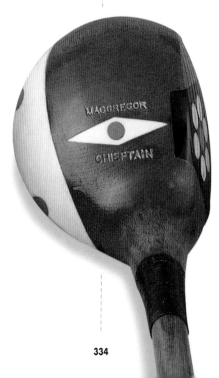

A.G. SPALDING & BROS.
"KRO FACE" FANCY FACE WOOD SET

In 1927, Spalding began using the "Kro face," an insert marked with a crow in flight. Spalding used this fancy face insert for many years, but only between 1927 and 1929 did Spalding offer Kro face woods with a choice of *either* steel or wood shafts. Beginning in 1930, Kro face woods were available only with steel shafts. The ratio of remaining steel shaft to wood shaft Kro face woods that date 1927-1929 indicates that the wood shaft examples were not nearly as popular as the steel shaft examples. This is understandable. By 1927 steel shafts, already USGA approved for two years, were well on their way to dominating the game.

According to Spalding's 1927 Spring and Summer catalog, the "Kro-Flite Registered Wood Clubs" pictured here, complete with a Kro face on each club, were offered as sets "perfectly matched right from the very beginning of their manufacture." A driver and brassie cost $30 and a matching spoon was an additional $15. The catalog describes the virtues of these matched woods as follows:

The important feature of these clubs is not the fact that the club, when broken, can be duplicated, but that unless a driver and brassie are perfectly matched from the very beginning of their manufacture, it is practically impossible to select two regular clubs from stock that are directly related to each other.

As Registered Wood Clubs are made up, two rough turned heads of exactly the same weight and type of wood are selected. They are weighted exactly the same. Two shafts of exactly the same weight in the same size and of exactly the same texture are selected. Every assembling and working operation is carefully checked as to size, the result being that when the clubs are finished each club is an exact duplicate of each other club of a pair.

A complete record is kept of all stages of the manufacture so that in the event of a breakage it is only necessary to know the Registered number to start through another wood block exactly the same wood as the first, weighted the same, assembled to a shaft of exactly the same weight and texture as the first, and so exactly duplicate the original (34).

Besides offering "registered" matched sets of Kro-Flite woods with Kro faces, Spalding's 1927 catalog also offered unmatched Kro-Flite Kro face drivers and brassies ($25 a pair and spoons for $12.50). Models 965, 1015, and 54D were manufactured as matched sets; models K965, K1015, and K54D were manufactured as individual clubs. The 965 did not have a backweight; the 1015 had a full backweight visible at the top of the head; and the 54D had a backweight extending halfway up the back of the head.

In 1928 Spalding no longer offered unmatched clubs from the "K" series. Instead, they offered the models 1000 and 1015 as registered matched clubs. In 1927 the Kro-Flite model 1000 had a solid wood face. In 1928 a Kro face was added to the model 1000, as it replaced the model 965. Like the model 965, it did not have a backweight. In 1929 Spalding again offered the model 1000 and 1015, both with the " 'Kro' face."

The clubs pictured above are marked "A.G. Spalding & Bros." on the crown of each head, "Reg No. 28,757" on each soleplate, and "1015" in the wood above the soleplate. The registration number appears to be a sequence number. As with almost all sequence numbers on antique golf clubs, it is not known if the sequence was exclusive for one particular model of wood or if it included various models. Furthermore, the beginning and ending of the sequence are unknown. The woods pictured date from 1929. Their soleplates are curved and their backweights run straight across the back of the head. In 1928 the backweights rounded into the top of the head. Both 1928 and 1929 Kro face woods have "curved" soleplates, that is the sides of the soleplate curve inward. The soleplates used in 1927 have straight sides.

WILLIAM ROSS
SPRING-FACE IRON

Golfers who desire a long ball, and that means every man who handles a club, should turn their attention to the Ross patent spring-faced club. A cleek of this patent is an effective substitute for a brassey. The head is of a specially-prepared bronze [aluminum bronze], and has a spoon-like cavity on the face. This cavity is covered with a strong, tempered steel plate, which forms the striking surface. The ball, when struck, has a spring action added to the force of the impact, and travels a long distance. The club is now in actual use, and has proved thoroughly effective. It is a nicely-finished club, and is non-corrosive. Messrs. Wm. Ross & Sons, 27 Thistle street, Glasgow, make and supply the clubs (Golfer's Magazine July 1898: 195).

William Ross's spring-face cleek, complete with three large circular bronze "rivets" that hold the steel face in place, is pictured. "Ross Patent" is stamped in a small circle on the back of the

bronze head. Although the above review dates from 1898, Ross's spring-face iron goes back a few years earlier.

William Ross, a self-described engineering draftsman from Nottingham, England, received a British patent (No. 3,822) dated February 21, 1893, that covered his spring-face iron. In describing his iron, Ross's patent states:

A cavity is formed in the face of the wood or metal club or implement and over this cavity is fixed a thin plate of steel . . . which forms the striking face or surface. . . . The cavity formed behind the plate allows the elasticity of the latter (plate) free action, thus forming a spring which is brought into action on the impact in striking the ball. The object being to increase the distance to which the ball may be driven, by adding the spring action to the force of the stroke.

Despite being patented in 1893, Ross's club was not marketed for a few more years. It was early in 1896 when *Golf* reviewed Ross's spring-face club under the heading "A New Cleek":

A New Cleek.—We have received a new form of cleek from Messrs. William Ross & Sons, Brassfounders, Oxford Street, Glasgow. It has a short socket, is broad in the sole, mussel-backed, and appears to be hollow in the interior, with a thin, strong steel slip, slightly roughened, as the striking surface of the blade. This thin steel slip acts as a kind of spring in propelling the ball, while the broad sole and increased weight behind impart great driving power. Some years ago we saw the cleek in its experimental stage in the hands of Tom Dunn, who drove very long shots with it; and this was the experience of some other good players who tried it at the time. We have tried this cleek now sent to us, and find it to be very satisfactory

both off the tee and through the green. The finish of the club is also all that can be wished for (21 Feb. 1896: 496).

A few months after this review, a small advertisement for Ross's patent spring-face golf clubs listed them as made with a "crucible mild steel" head and available in the following models: cleeks and driving cleeks, driving, medium, and lofting irons (*Golf*, 3 Apr. 1896: 88).

Ross spring-face clubs were not well received. Therefore, few remain. However, this club is collectible for more reasons than its spring-face. Not only is the attractive combination of metals used to construct the head very significant, so is this club's place in history as the first spring-face iron to be patented.

GEORGE WALKER
SPRING-FACE PUTTER

George Walker, an instructor of horology from Coventry, England, discussed the principle of "spring" between the club and the ball in his British patent (No. 1,554) dated January 23, 1895. He begins this discussion as follows:

Firstly, motion is imparted to the ball by its being made to suddenly take up that of the moving club-head when it comes into contact with the ball.

Secondly, motion is also imparted to the ball by the reaction between the face of the club and the ball, due to the elasticity of the materials composing them, coupled with the inertia of the club-head and ball, which allows of their surfaces being compressed when the club strikes the ball. On this reaction, in a great measure, depends the direction and length of carry of the ball.

When a solid iron club-head is used to strike the ball, the reaction between the club-head and the ball is practically due to the compression of the ball alone. With a wooden club-head the reaction is due, not only to the compression of the surface of the ball, but also, to that of the head of the club. *For this reason a wooden headed club will "drive" or carry the ball farther than a solid iron one; but the elasticity of the face is liable to become exhausted by prolonged use. Faces of wooden headed clubs are rapidly destroyed by play in wet weather, and the heads are liable to break. Consequently a metal head is superior to a wooden one in so far that its face is practically indestructible.*

Walker then states the purpose of his patent:

The object of my invention is to combine the elasticity of the wooden face with the durability of the metal one.

To accomplish this, Walker's patent proposes no fewer than five different ways of incorporating a spring-face in a metal head club. Walker states:

I do not confine myself to these methods of carrying out my invention, which consists in the application of a metallic spring face to the head of a golf club of any kind, whether a "driver," a "putter" or otherwise.

Matching the illustration in his patent, Walker's rectangular putter with a piece of spring steel fastened to the face is pictured here. "Patent" is stamped on the back of the head along with a word too faint to read. The only other Walker spring-face putter known to the author was sold at the Sporting Antiquities 1996 golf auction, held in Andover, Massachusetts.

"Who," asks Mr. Horace Hutchinson, "shall advise a man in the choice of a wife or a driver?" I bow before the implied rebuke. Far be it from me to rush in where ex-Amateur Champions fear to tread (Holm Greene, *Golfing,* 15 July 1909: 8).

A.G. SPALDING & BROS.
SPRING-FACE PUTTER

A.G. Spalding & Brothers have put a new cleek upon the market specially intended for use with the lively ball. The club is made on the principle of the Cran cleek, which, as is well known, has a wooden face set in the steel. In this case the highly tempered steel face, about a sixteenth of an inch thick, is riveted on the face of an iron club. And the head of this club being hollow, there is decidedly more spring from the face, particularly in using the rubber-cored ball. Golfers who have tried the new club say that it adds decidedly to the length of the full shots in playing through the green, and should largely supersede the brassey, especially in playing out of rough ground and from indifferent lies. In appearance it resembles the ordinary cleek, and is well made and balanced (Golf [ny], May 1902: 339).

The above review (originally published in America) states that Spalding's spring-faced iron head is hollow, but a review published in Great Britain states that it is filled with gutta percha:

Spalding's Steel "Spring Faced" Cleek. This cleek is one of the most powerful driving cleeks we have ever tried; indeed, with a rubber-cored ball, it appears to drive the ball as far as a wooden club will, and with hardly any effort. The principle of the club is a spoon-shaped cavity of steel filled with gutta-percha, on which is fixed a face of fine steel. These clubs are beautifully balanced, and have all the high finish associated with this firm's manufacture (Golf Illustrated, 3 Oct. 1902: 20).

Were Spalding's Spring-Faced irons filled with gutta percha or not? Spalding's 1903 U.S. catalog describes their spring-face clubs at length but does not mention filling the head with gutta percha. Nor was any mention of gutta percha made in Spalding's American catalogs between 1904 and 1919, even though these catalogs continued to offer spring-face clubs. In Great Britain, however, Spalding's advertisements

for their "Steel 'Spring Faced' Golf Clubs" described them in bold print as "Hollow steel head, filled with gutta percha, and with corrugated steel face" (*Golf Illustrated* 19 Dec. 1902: 238 and 3 Apr. 1903: 24). Apparently the spring-face iron Spalding sold in America was different from the one sold in Great Britain, at least in the beginning.

During the first few years of production, as offered in their U.S. catalogs, Spalding's spring-face irons were available as cleeks, lofting mashies, mid irons, and putters. Spalding's 1903 catalog states that their spring-face clubs provide *incredible* distance:

We know that the [spring-face] cleek, tried fairly, should improve your shots at least fifty yards, and we can make this statement safely because the assertion has been repeated to us so often by those who are using the club now.

Spalding also claimed that the stopping ability of their spring-face mid iron was well above normal:

They claim for this club that it will drive as far as a cleek, and the ball is landed dead, an obvious advantage when the player is approaching the green from a distance (Golf Illustrated, 15 Jan. 1904: 46).

Spalding's spring-face iron is one of the relatively few patent clubs that stayed in production for many years. First introduced in 1902, it was last offered in Spalding's 1919 Fall & Winter catalog. A number of spring-face irons remain, but spring-face *putters* like the one pictured are the rarest of Spalding's spring-face clubs. This is probably because few golfers were trying to obtain extra distance with their putter, nor would they care for an overly lively ball when putting.

The Spalding spring-face putter pictured on the prior page, marked "A.G. Spalding & Bros" on the shaft, has the usual six rivets located around the edge of the corrugated steel face. The rivets midway across the top and bottom of the face are the easiest to see in this picture.

In 1917, Spalding's golf catalog lists their spring-face iron as a "Steel face, driving Cran Cleek, Cran Style" under the Cran Cleek listing. Listing the spring-face as a type of Cran Cleek might seem strange, but Spalding always provided the date of June 8, 1897—the same date as James Cran's U.S. design patent for his "Cran" Cleek—as the patent date of the spring-face club. Both the Cran iron and the spring-face iron start with an empty cavity in the head. The Cran fills it with wood; the spring-face covers it with metal. Apparently, Spalding felt that the similarities between the two clubs allowed them to be categorized together.

Spalding's spring-face irons include a short drilled-through hosel modeled after the hosel developed by Thomas Carruthers. In his British patent (No. 19, 684) dated December 3, 1890, Thomas Carruthers, a self-described dairyman from Edinburgh, Scotland, explains his invention:

This invention which relates to a new or improved socket for metal golf playing clubs consists in shortening the length of the iron socket . . . and running the end of the wooden shaft right through the socket and out at the heel of the socket so that the socket is open at both ends, the object . . . being that the weight is taken from the part of the club where it is not required so as to make the centre of gravity or balance not at the heel as is the case with irons at present in use, but . . . immediately behind the ball.

. . . Owing to the socket being open at both ends a better fitting shaft is obtained. The shaft has also a better grasp of the head which gives the player a greater command of the implement. Also the increased length of the shaft gives it greater leverage, and brings the "spring" into the proper place.

J.G. McPherson provides the initial review of the Carruthers Cleek printed in the February 27, 1891 issue of *Golf*:

The socket, which is the patent part, is two inches shorter than that of the ordinary cleek, and the shaft is a little longer than my regular driving cleek. That the shaft may be firmly attached, it is made to pass right down to the heel, where the socket has an opening. After being well driven in, the projecting part is cut off and filed flush with the iron. One of the defects in the old style is the uncertainty that the shaft exactly fits the socket, for the shaft-maker did not know the cleek-maker's work. Here, however, the shaft-maker drives the shaft right through, making all perfectly tight.

Besides, when the socket is short and thin and tubular, the weight of the cleek-head is less in the heel and more in the blade. If an unshafted cleek of the old make be balanced, you will find that it will rest when leaning over a stick which passes through between the socket and the blade. But in this case the metal is so adjusted that the cleek-head balances on a stick, right under where the ball should be struck, in the centre of the blade. In striking the ball with the patent cleek, therefore, the greatest certainty is available, the centre of gravity of the head being on the same spot as in the case of a wooden driver by the adjusting of the lead. In the old cleek the centre of gravity of the head—on the line of balancing—is at the heel, whereas here it is just behind the best striking-place of the ball. In this way greater power and more certain direction are secured. For there need be no heeling—a capital exception in the game (378).

Another commentary concerning the new Carruthers Cleek is found on the same page as McPherson's review. This commentary was written by Gregor McGregor and relates his own appreciation for the club:

Still another tribute to the popularity of the Royal Game is announced in the invention of the patent socket for iron clubs by Mr. T. Carruthers, Edinburgh . . . . Without in any way derogating from the credit due to previous inventors, I am free to say that I have not come across any invention so meritorious in my own judgment as this one. . . .

For years back I have been in the habit of selecting my cleek-heads, and altering them myself to suit my fancy. There is great pleasure to be derived from operations of this sort by golfers. My first point was to secure superabundance of metal to stand reduction. My second was to select the shortest neck, and I preferred also a short blade, and this involved thickness of blade which I regarded as of first rate importance. Having laid aside after careful weighting a few heads that fulfilled these conditions, I then introduced my pencil into the socket and selected the one which had the tube reaching down furthest towards the sole, or in other words that had the longest hollow in the neck.

. . . The cleek being now firmly shafted, I filed down the shell of the socket till it was little more than sufficient to hold the wooden shaft, in order to concentrate the weight as near as possible at the point of contact between the blade and ball. Every golfer knows that for effective driving this is of the greatest importance. . . . .

Now all the advantages I was seeking and obtaining on a modest scale are secured by Mr. Carruthers most happily and in abundance.

In the patent two inches are taken off the socket. The tube is carried down the neck and out at the sole. The metal thus taken from the socket is transferred to the blade, and the result is two inches longer of the wooden shaft, and, the weight being equal, the centre of gravity is transferred from the angle in the old to near the centre of the blade in the new. The sole is a good deal broader, and minimizes the agricultural proclivities of this most effective weapon, and the strength is fully kept up, there being as much wood in the new as in the old socket.

The Carruthers Patent Socket was one of the few patent clubs to be well received:

Mr. Carruthers has done a great trade with his patent clubs, and up to the present has sold over 35,000 driving cleeks. There is always a demand for them, and only the other day he received a large order from New York (Golfing, 16 Mar. 1899: 8).

Not only did Spalding produce irons with a Carruthers-type socket, so did other various makers, even into modern times.

A final note about Thomas Carruthers:

It is not only as a golf club and cleek maker that Tom Carruthers is known in the world of sport. In the sixties and early seventies he was undoubtedly the best all-round athlete in Scotland, and close on forty years ago won a Sheffield handicap. On the flat, over the hurdles, or in the long and high jumps, he was well-nigh invincible. . . .

At the age of 32, however, Tom had perforce to abandon athletics, owing to a broken leg, a mishap he sustained while competing in the long jump at Dumbarton. He then turned his attention to the golf club trade—his business address now being 5, Gillespie Place, Edinburgh—in which he has been very successful. His patent socket for iron clubs is distinct from all others, and stands out by itself on account of its perfect balance; it is the longest driving cleek in the world (Golfing, 16 Mar. 1899: 8).

Mr. R.B. Wilson, club-maker, St. Andrews, sails for America on the 28th, inst. to again take up his summer duties as greenkeeper to the Hartford Club, Connecticut. Mr. Wilson is taking with him a large number of his recent invention . . . . It takes the shape of either a cleek, iron, or mashie, and is for use especially with rubber-cored balls, and may be described thus: In the face of the iron club is a groove about an eighth of an inch deep, over or across this groove is a wrought-iron plate, securely riveted at each end, and in the vacant space between is compactly filled with leather specially compressed: this gives great elasticity to the club, as it were, to which the rubber-cored ball responds in a marked manner (Golf Illustrated, 20 Feb. 1903: 143).

Wilson's spring-face mashie described above is pictured right. The edge of the spring steel plate is visible across the top of the blade and down the face, next to the hosel. The compressed piece of leather behind the steel plate is visible across the top of the blade. The steel plate is fastened to the head by two rivets at the toe and two at the heel. These rivets blend in quite well with the face, but are somewhat more evident on the back of the head. The back of the head is marked "A.H. Scott" in script along with "A.H. Scott \ Elie \ Earlsferry" and the Prince of Wales "plume"

mark earlier associated with Robert Forgan clubs. After R. Forgan & Son became club maker to King Edward VII in 1902, Andrew Herd Scott became the clubmaker to the new Prince of Wales.

R.B. Wilson's spring-face iron pictured was not made by Scott, only sold by him. According to Henderson and Stirk, A.H. Scott made woods and not irons, so Alex Anderson of Anstruther (initially at least) "made the iron clubs for A.H. Scott of Elie" (1979, 189). Scott was not known as a cleekmaker, but this did not stop him from developing ideas about iron clubs. A review in the February 28, 1896 issue of *The Golfer* tells of the "Invincible" cleek Scott devised and marketed:

I would like, and so would all green keepers, to see Scott of Earlsferry's "Invincible" cleek adopted by golfers. The feature is the rounded bottom edge, and this innovation does away to a considerable extent with the cutting of the turf, and, what to golfers will probably be of more importance, saves hacking the ball. It is worrying to find a cherished new ball badly damaged at the first hole perhaps through an awkward cleek-shot, and the rounded edge is a safe preventative (131).

Wilson's spring-face iron was short-lived. Spring-face clubs sounded useful in theory, but practical experience proved otherwise. Consider the words of Lieutenant C.K. Hutchinson originally printed in 1906:

For instance, if the eleventh hole at St. Andrews has to be negotiated with an adverse wind, what an advantage it is to be able to force the ball up to the hole with that powerful push shot, that Mr. Edward Blackwell, Mr. R. Maxwell, Andrew Kirkaldy, and other fine exponents employ so successfully. Attempts have been made to emulate these shots by means of mechanical contrivances, such as the spring-faced cleek or iron. But experience teaches that these clubs are apt to be treacherous, and their use not infrequently results in dire disaster, and subsequent vexation of spirit. One of the best foursome

partners that I have ever had the pleasure of playing with, possesses one of these clubs, and although I have seen him play extraordinary shots with the weapon, its appearance at a critical juncture fills me with uneasiness, which is not allayed until I see the ball well on its way towards the hole (Golf Illustrated, 6 July: 30).

A Wilson spring-face iron, marked "The Haskell Cleek" on the back of the head, is in the USGA's collection of antique clubs kept in their museum, in Far Hills, New Jersey.

WILLIAM MULES
SPRING-FACE WOOD

W. Mules, the professional to the Glamorganshire Club, has patented a driver and brassie with a steel face. The idea is that a roughened steel plate, very carefully tempered, is let into the face of the club, behind which is a backing or cushion of resilient material. Mules claims tremendous driving qualities from his invention, and this has been completely endorsed by many Welsh players who have tried it (Golfing, 28 Feb. 1901: 24).

The William Mules spring-face wood pictured is marked "W. Mules \ Penarth" inside an oval on the crown and "Reg'd No. 20069" in small letters in the center of the face. Dating to November 7, 1900, Mules's British patent (No. 20,069) states that his wood was designed:

to increase the elasticity of the part of the club which comes in contact with the ball [and] increase the hold or grip obtained by the club on the ball and so diminish the tendency to side slip.

To accomplish this, Mules affixed a steel plate over a pad of resilient material set into the head. The steel plate is "roughened over a greater part of its surface" and when screwed to the face compresses the pad of resilient material "whereby a certain proportion of the elasticity inherent in the pad . . . is communicated to the metal plate."

As described in his patent, the compressed pad, "preferably [made from] hard gutta percha," is designed to control the trajectory of a shot. A pad of uniform thickness allows a well-struck shot to fly with a normal trajectory. A pad thicker at the top provides a higher trajectory. A pad thicker at the sole provides a lower trajectory.

Originally made by William Mules and his assistants, Mules steel-faced woods found a niche in the market shortly after their introduction. By mid-1903, the firm of Cann & Taylor was appointed the sole maker of Mules patent drivers and brassies, which they built using a rubber pad behind each faceplate. Mules also received a U.S. patent (No. 708,575) dated September 9, 1902, that covered his club.

The earliest patent to mention the possibility of building a metal face spring-face wood is William Currie Jr.'s British patent (No. 5,731) dated April 3, 1891:

This invention consists essentially of a vulcanite, celluloid, or wooden head made hollow or with a portion cut away at the playing side or face or intermediate portion of the head and replaced by an elastic composition or cushion with or without a vulcanite, celluloid, wooden, or metal face.

Even though Currie obtained the first patent that described producing a spring-face wood, it was someone else who first produced one. W.M. Bryson, a golfer from Edinburgh, developed an aluminum head spring-face wood in 1896:

His improvement takes the form of the insertion of a strong steel spring lying the whole length behind the face of the club. This spring is slightly arched, and in the centre of the club-face . . . it rests upon, and receives propulsive force from, a strong spiral spring going back in the interior of the head towards the lead. [There] is a thin strip of leather on the face, behind which the spring rests (The Golfer, 2 Dec. 1896: 443).

Following Mules's patent, three of the more interesting patents for spring-face woods not covered elsewhere in this book were granted to Christian Gray, Charles Clark, and Richard Beamer.

Gray's British patent (No. 18,134) dated August 18, 1902, covered a wood inlaid with vulcanite wrapped with rubber cord. After being wrapped around the vulcanite, the rubber cord is covered with gutta percha and placed in the head behind the face.

Charles Clark's British patent (No. 27,143) and U.S. patent (No. 777,400) both dated December 13, 1904, covered a metalwood head formed in outline only. Top to bottom, the body of the head is completely open (when viewed from above, it resembles the letter "D"). This design supposedly allowed the metal face to flex. Two such clubs are known.

Richard F. Beamer's U.S. patent (No. 1,359,220) dated November 16, 1920, calls for setting a metal plate in the face of a wood. The area directly behind the plate is hollowed out so the plate might "vibrate in its natural period."

In 1909, Henry Williams wrote a letter to the editor of *Golfing* that described a spring-face wood Williams made by installing a one-eighth inch thick brass faceplate backed with rubber three-sixteenths of an inch thick. In response, Willie Dunn sent the editor a letter to announce that he was currently marketing such a "driver with face of brass and rubber," but Dunn's clubhead was apparently made from aluminum (6 May 1909: 38).

UNKNOWN MAKER
WOOD FACE PUTTER

The July 28, 1893 issue of *Golf* reports on two wood face iron putters. Joseph Roberts of Wimbledon, England, produced a putter described as follows:

There is a thin slice of wood for the face, and a band of metal behind to give weight. . . . The grip is also a good one, the wood below the leather being square (342).

The originality of Roberts's putter was called into question by the description of the second putter:

We have doubt, however, about the novelty of the principle as applied to putters, for months ago we noticed a putter by Mr. Norman Foster, hon [sic] secretary of the Royal Wimbledon Club, which corresponds almost exactly with the club of Mr. Roberts, except the neck of Mr. Foster's club is not metal, but the ordinary wooden form of club neck.

The putter pictured above appears different from either of the two just mentioned. Notice the way the metal at the bottom of the neck slopes back towards the golfer, the way the metal bends and runs behind an extraordinarily (3/4 inch) thick block of wood serving as the face, and the extreme degree of offset that still remains. Such design features make for a wonderful collectible. This club, the only one known, was probably made in the mid-1890s.

Note: There is whipping on the base of the shaft because the shaft, which might have been damaged or replaced when this club was in use, is not quite as thick as the hosel. Three screws located across the back of the head hold the wood block in place.

WILLIAM GIBSON
"WOODFACED PUTTER"

Gibson's Woodfaced Putter pictured below is of the Smith-neck anti-shank variety. The back of this blade is stamped "Lockwood Brown's Ld \ 42 Jermyn St. S.W." inside an oval along with "Woodfaced Putter \ Warranted Hand Forged" and William Gibson's "star" trademark. The shaft, which is round except for the square length under the grip, is marked "Lockwood Brown & Co Ltd. \ 42 Jermyn St. \ London S.W." The wood face is held in place by four screws, one in each corner. Each screw tip is visible on the face. A small mention is made of the Woodfaced Putter, as offered by Lillywhite's, in the August 13, 1909 issue of *Golf Illustrated* (208).

Sotheby's auctioned a somewhat similar putter at their July 1990 golf sale. Made by James Gourlay, this blade putter had a wood insert in the center of the face.

In New York during 1901, Slazenger imported and sold an aluminum putter "fashioned in exact imitation of an old Philp model." The face reportedly had a "piece of beech let in, in order to grip the ball firmly" (*Golf* [ny], Mar. 1901: 230). The Slazenger example known to the author does have a shapely Philp-style head, but it is smaller than a Philp putter, and the wood block is in the back of the head.

CRAWFORD, McGREGOR & CANBY COMPANY
STEEL FACE DRIVER

The MacGregor driver pictured right, like the next four woods presented, has a metal face—metal is fixed across the entire face, not just inserted into a portion of it. Metal faces in the early 1900s supposedly provided woods with greater durability while allowing the relatively new rubber core ball to reach its distance potential. Not only is the entire face of this driver covered with steel; the neck is also covered—for added protection. The shaft reads "Made by \ The Crawford, McGregor & Canby Co. \ Dayton, Ohio."

This wood has been refinished, and a layer of varnish remains on the metal. It would have been better if the original finish had been left alone. The rust (and varnish) on the metal can be cleaned off, but leaving it "as is" for now is fine. Given too much restoration, the club will lose its charm.

A.G. SPALDING & BROS.
STEEL FACE BRASSIE

The "Spalding Medal Model 16" wood pictured below, marked "Spalding \ Medal \ 16" on the crown, has an original steel face. In 1920 and 1921, Spalding offered their "Spalding Medal Model 16" wood, along with a few other models, as a standard wood with a solid wood face. However, Spalding allowed golfers to special order these models with a special face. According to Spalding's catalog dated January 5, 1920:

Popular Medal clubs are furnished with plain face. For those who desire special faces we will supply special orders at extra charges . . . (43).

Ivory, fiber, and steel inserts, as well as the Jacobus triple insert, were available for an additional charge.

This Medal 16 also has what appears to be a hardened leather or gutta percha filling located directly behind the steel insert. This backing tapers inward as it approaches the bottom of the face.

A.G. SPALDING & BROS.
BRASS FACE DRIVER

CHARLES EARNSHAW
"XLNT" BRASS FACE DRIVER

The driver pictured above left, stamped "Spalding" on the top of the head, dates from somewhere between 1906 and 1912, since that is when Spalding clubs were marked in the lettering style used on this club. This Spalding driver was originally made as pictured, with the thick piece of brass fixed across its face. Note the proper amount of face progression (the distance the face extends ahead of the shaft) provided by the brass piece. Remove this piece and the remaining wood head will not have the appropriate proportions of the traditional outline. The horn on the sole is directly behind the brass face. (For a gunmetal face driver, see page 439)

Charles Earnshaw of the Dyke Golf Club, Dyke (near Brighton), England, received a British patent (No. 267,755) dated May 20, 1926, that covered the club, marked "Earnshaw's \ XLNT \ Patent No. 267755," pictured above right. With the stated purpose of providing "a wooden golf club which is suitable for use with modern golf balls," Earnshaw's patent covered attaching a brass plate across the entire face of a wood. The back of this plate and the face of the wood are flat, so they fit flush together. The brass plate is beveled across its face in order to provide a fair amount of what the patent terms "curve known as bulge."

Now that four metal face woods have been presented, the Cuirass driver on the next page provides a more detailed understanding of metal face woods, their purpose, and where they fit in the evolution of the golf club.

A certain club that grows old in our company is naturally a part of our existence. We describe it as the "Bread-winner," and treat it accordingly. The death of a relative would not affect us to the extent that the loss of the "Bread-winner" would, for relatives increase as a general rule, whereas the "Bread-winner," once destroyed, is irretrievably lost to us, and life is so short that no time remains for another to take a like place in our affections (Fulford 1919, 78-79).

LONDON GOLF COMPANY
"CUIRASS,"
INTEGRAL METAL FACE/SOLE

One of the latest and best of new clubs is the "Cuirass" driver, made by the London Golf Company Ltd., 13, Copthall Avenue, E.C. It is a well recognized fact that the new rubber balls fly relatively further from metal than they do from wood, as compared with gutty balls. Why this should be so is not quite clear, but the fact remains, and the makers of the "Cuirass" driver have accordingly fitted a ribbed face of finely tempered and elastic steel to the ordinary driver. The steel covering also turns over on to the sole of the club and takes the place of the horn, the whole "Cuirass" being one piece of metal. With this club we find that a rubber-cored ball can be driven quite as far as from a wooden one, and with a lower trajectory and consequently greater run. These clubs are beautifully balanced and finished, and as the "Cuirass" renders the club practically indestructible, they are well worth the 10s. 6d. charged for them. On wet days and on wet courses the advantages of the "Cuirass" are obvious (Golf Illustrated, 27 Nov. 1903: 171).

The Cuirass driver shown has a metal face integral with a metal horn. In tiny letters, this club is marked "London Golf Company" across the top of the steel insert, "Copthall Avenue" across the bottom of the insert (though "Copthall" is worn), "Patent" on the steel horn, and "London Golf Co. \ Cuirass" inside a circular logo next to "D.G.S." on the crown.

In 1905 steel face woods, and the Cuirass in particular, were reviewed by an advocate of such clubs. However, the reviewer duly notes that such clubs were not popular and remained unknown to many players:

Everyone who has used a well-made, steel-faced driving club must agree that a rubber-cored ball flies off it more sweetly and with greater velocity than off anything else he may have tried, and, given the highest initial velocity, the lower trajectory and greater length follow as matters of course upon a truly-hit blow. Parenthetically, it may be mentioned that the calculated impact on the ball of a full drive is about three tons. Various forms of steel-plated clubs are procurable, but they have not been pushed with any special ardour, and numbers of players are still ignorant of their advantages. For simplicity and strength of construction the best form in which the idea has as yet been presented is that adopted in the clubs advertised under the name Cuirass, in which the thin and very hard steel plate covers the entire striking surface of the club, and also extends beneath in place of horn; the fastening, by means of four long, thin screws to the wooden head, being so contrived under compression as to create tension, which binds the steel plate to the wood without any possi-bility of it becoming loose. These plates are of No. 18 B.W.G. fine steel, and are so light that they do not affect the balance of the club in the smallest. Apart from its power in driving, this pattern has very obvious advantages in withstanding severe treatment in rough places, the steel edge cutting through awkward lies like a cleek does (Golf Illustrated, 27 Jan. 1905: 94).

To demonstrate its durability, the Cuirass driver was tested during cold and frosty weather. It was determined that the club could endure not only cold temperatures but also frozen ground!

During the recent spell of cold and frosty weather the "Cuirass" steel-faced wooden clubs . . . were tested under conditions that were exceptionally severe. In every case the clubs gave entire satisfaction, and many of those who saw them in use for the first time have placed orders. It is beyond question that these clubs are admirably suited for bad weather and frozen courses . . . (Golf Illustrated, 9 Dec. 1904: 206).

For the golfer who wanted to retrofit his or her existing driver or brassie with a metal plate similar to that of the Cuirass, Lindsay G. Ross, the professional and clubmaker at Streetley, Sutton Coldfield, produced and sold "Ross's Patent Angle Plate" (Golfing, 15 Oct. 1903: 28).

GILBERT LEGH

INTEGRAL FACE/SOLE/HOSEL, SPRING-FACE PUTTER, BRASSEY, & CLEEK

Major The Honorable Gilbert Legh, of The Dove House, Thornham, King's Lynn, in the County of Norfolk, was, among other things, an inventor of golf clubs. Between 1906 and 1915, Legh received six different patents in the U.K., two of which were also granted in the U.S. His first three British patents, which covered his more creative and visual clubs, are discussed here.

The putter shown at the top and bottom of this page was produced under Legh's first British patent, No. 5,994 dated March 12, 1906. According to this patent, Legh was trying to improve the balance of a golf club:

This invention . . . has for its object to throw the centre of the mass of the club head forward as far as possible towards the driving face, and this is effected by providing the club head with a heavy iron or steel face plate formed integrally with a well defined sole . . . which may be extended upward to form a socket for the reception of the shaft.

Legh further specifies thinning the soleplate towards the rear "so as to throw the center of mass well forward."

Legh's patent also deals with the design of a spring-face golf club. It calls for positioning the metal face clear of the hosel and placing a hollowed out wooden block behind the faceplate in order to "give a resilience to the face plate on impact with the ball." Legh allowed for filling the hollowed portion of the block with india-rubber or other resilient material, if so desired. In addition to putters, Legh produced irons under this patent.

The putter shown is marked "F. Whiting \ Leghs Patent \ No. 5994" on the crown. Fred Whiting, born in Worcester, England, in 1874, learned club-making as an apprentice to David Brown at Malvern. Whiting was the professional at West Cornwall from 1901 to 1911 and at Royal St. Georges from 1911

to 1947 (Jackson 1994, 101). He was a meticulous clubmaker:

Whiting's clubs all look as though they are individually thought out (Golfing, 6 Nov. 1902: 22).

On August 20, 1907, Legh received a U.S. patent (No. 863,728) that duplicated his British patent No. 5,994.

The Honorable Gilbert Legh's second British patent, No. 2,309 dated February 1, 1908, modifies the design of the metal and wood golf club covered in his first patent. According to his 1908 patent, cutting away the rearward bulging portion of the head at the back of the sole will:

bring the center of mass of this turned up portion as close up as possible to the line of the shaft.

To help shift the weight of the head forward, the heavy steel sole integral with the steel face is "turned up over the rear of the face of the club head" (the back of the head).

Like his first patent, Legh's 1908 patent calls for hollowing out the block of wood directly behind the face:

Usually also the club head would be hollowed out in the centre of its face to form a cavity in rear of the steel face plate, which cavity may be filled with india-rubber or other resilient material or partly with such material and partly with additional metal weighting.

A club covered under Legh's February 1908 patent is shown above and on the right. The top of the head is marked "Leghs Patent \ No. 5994." This club is marked with Legh's 1906 patent number because Legh's 1908 patent identifies itself as a modification of his 1906 patent. The sole is marked "No. 3 \ Leghs Patent" along with "2309/08" in faint lettering. The shaft is stamped "F. Whiting \ West Cornwall C.C., Lelant."

In Legh's third British patent, No. 12,051 dated May 14, 1910, he calls for making a much shorter metal hosel integral with the metal face/sole and allows for the possibility of fastening the shaft between two metal tangs in Simplex fashion

(see p. 158). According to this patent, the short hosel will "take full advantage of the flexibility of the shaft." While he retained the principle of an integral metal soleplate, faceplate, and hosel, Legh also allowed for the possibility of extending the metal from the soleplate onto the back of the wood block and not the face.

The club pictured below was covered under Legh's May 14, 1910 patent and marked "Legh 5994" on the sole, between two screws holding the wood block in place. This club is marked "5994," which refers to Legh's first patent, because Legh's third (1910) British patent identifies itself as a modification of his first. The head on this club is even thinner, front to back, than his 1908 patent wood, but this might not necessarily be the case with other clubs produced

under Legh's 1910 patent. To begin with, Legh's 1910 patent identifies itself as relating to drivers, brassies, cleeks, and mashies. Furthermore, this patent provides great leeway in clubhead design. (Creative freedom was sought by many inventors in order to modify the clubs covered by their patents). Its 41-inch shaft and minimal face loft indicate that the club pictured below is a driving club. (For more on Gilbert Legh, see page 267.)

ROBERT SIMPSON

"THE MATCHLESS,"
INTEGRAL METAL FACE/SOLE,
DRIVER & SIMILAR PUTTER

GEORGE WEAGER &
ROY WHITE

"THE DINT," INTEGRAL
METAL FACE/SOLE

Robert Simpson's driver shown below has a steel sole integral with a faceplate that borders a fiber insert. The crown is marked "R. Simpson \ The Matchless"; the sole is marked "R. Simpson, Carnoustie \ The Matchless."

Robert Simpson's putter shown directly above has a full brass soleplate that extends onto the face and borders what is either a fiber or a gutta percha insert held in place by a few nails. The crown is stamped "R. Simpson \ Special"; the shaft is marked "R. Simpson, Carnoustie."

The May 1914 issue of *Golf Monthly* lists Simpson's "Perfect Balance," "Matchless," and Medalist" drivers and brassies as his specialties (239). A Robert Simpson & Son catalog, circa 1920s, describes the "Matchless" driver and brassie as follows:

The "Matchless" Drivers and Brassies have a combined brass sole plate and face with fibre centre inserted, dispensing entirely with the horn, and protecting both the heel and point of the club. These clubs are most admirably suitable for hard ground or inland course, and are practically indestructible (5).

The driver pictured directly above is stamped "A.G. Spalding & Bros" on the crown and "Driver \ Silver \ The Dint \ Pat. No. 1458564/23" on the sole. The number on the sole identifies the June 12, 1923, U.S. patent that duplicated the October 9, 1913, British patent (No. 22,777) granted to George Weager and Roy White, both professional golfers from Kent, England.

In their patent, Weager and White designed a soleplate integral with a faceplate made from lightweight metal. Furthermore, they called for forming a "thick rib" across the inside of

the faceplate. This rib, which fits into a recess along the leading edge of the wood, was designed to strengthen the leading edge:

The sharp strengthened edge of the head enables the same to cut through grass very readily.

The "Dint," a nice entry level collectible, was produced in quantity both in the U.S. and the U.K. Dint woods and putters were produced in Great Britain by the " 'Dint' Patent Golf Club Co., Malvern Link."

RALPH G. TYLER
"THE TYLER PUTTER,"
INTEGRAL METAL FACE/SOLE

As a hammer is to a nail this putter is to a golf ball (Ralph G. Tyler).

Patented in the United States, Tyler's putter is a continuation of ideas devised by earlier inventors of similar clubs. Tyler, however, brought a few new wrinkles to the construction and desired qualities of his putter.

Applied for on March 22, 1922, Tyler's U.S. patent (No. 1,517,476) issued December 2, 1924, states its objective as:

to provide a putter having such form and structure and in which the shaft is so positioned and secured, that while the putter is rugged and durable, the implement as an entirety is of such gravity and central balance that all tendency of the putter to swerve or oscillate when making contact with the ball, is eliminated, and a crisp, hammer-like impact at the ball is assured.

An undated broadside describes Tyler's putter, in part, as follows:

The head of the Tyler Putter, neat and graceful in appearance, consists of but two pieces of material, one of highly polished yellow brass, the other of well seasoned persimmon wood. . . . The Tyler putter when placed on two supports, as for instance your two forefingers, will turn face up showing a true and equal balance. It is this perfect balancing feature, differing materially from any other putter, that causes an uncanny accuracy of stroke (Tyler).

The same advertisement then lists the primary features of his club. A few of the more interesting ones are as follows:

1. It is a center shafted putter which is center balanced, that is, balanced at that point—not the middle—where the shaft connects with the sole, and the only center balance putter ever offered to golfers. Thus its swing is positively accurate as the face automatically remains at a right angle to the line of play during the stroke.

2. The sole and face is one piece of brass thus insuring firmness of impact.

3. The weight of the club is in the brass sole which is distributed over the entire bottom thus equalizing momentum. This uniform distribution of weight together with the even balance greatly eliminates any possibility of the club turning in the player's hands regardless of where on the face the ball is hit.

4. The shaft is connected by socket and screw directly to the sole, which is the weight substance of the club, thus producing absolute solidarity. As a hammer is to a nail this putter is to a golf ball.

5. It is designed so as to impart a forward rolling to the ball, thus increasing trueness of run.

An advertisement in the May 1922 issue of *Golfers Magazine* indicates that Tyler produced his putter shortly after applying for his patent (55). Tyler went on to produce and patent other combination woods (see page 297).

I left school at 12 years old. . . . I left the school on the Friday and I started work on the Monday. The club maker had to serve four years apprenticeship. It was hard work in those days. The heads had to be cut out of blocks of persimmon and the shafts had to be rounded by hand from square lengths of hickory (James Forrester, upon his retirement from half a century in the clubmaking business, *East Fife Observer*, 5 Oct. 1950).

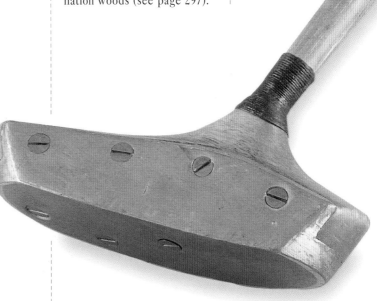

GEORGE BREWS

INTEGRAL
SOLEPLATE/BACKWEIGHT

In his British patent
(No. 13,939) dated June 18, 1906,
George Brews, a professional golfer
and golf club maker from The
Box, Minchinhampton, sought a
better way of concentrating weight
behind the face. According to his
patent, his invention would:

*so form and dispose of the weight
that it acts along a line parallel to the
striking face of the club being practically
equally distributed along a portion of
such line approximately corresponding
to the entire length of the striking face.*

In order to "get a perfectly
balanced club," Brews, in his
patent, calls for attaching a solid
brass soleplate integral with a
brass backweight to a wood head,
as pictured.

The club shown is stamped
"Spalding Model" on the crown.
Brews, however, also made and
marked his own putters.

Although this club looks
nice—no nicks or dents, rich col-
or, gold lettering, brass backweight—this club is actually
heavily reworked and therefore
a very weak example. When
this club last changed ownership,
it was in horrible condition.
Refinished earlier in a grotesque

*Golf was invented by a Scotchman.
It is too fast for the Germans, too slow
for the Irish; the French despise it; the
Spaniards think it is a drink instead of
a game, the Americans affect it, and
the English are born with a sixth golf
sense (Golfing, 2 Dec. 1909: 20).*

red oil base stain, the head
needed to be refinished again in
a less obnoxious but similar color
in order to blend with the old
stain. When this club was first
refinished, the letters in the
wood portion of the head were
re-etched and filled with gold
paint. Although re-etching was
once an acceptable practice when
restoring steel-shafted classic
clubs, it is now considered extremely detrimental to an antique
club. With the increasing
number of fake and replica clubs
encroaching upon the world of
antique clubs, the more original
a club is, the better. Note the
deep and widely spaced scoring
lines. They are not original;
they are part of the initial restoration work which, in this case,
only defaced the club.

Because of its heavily reworked
condition, this putter would not
be of much interest to a discrim-
inating collector. However,
including such a reworked club
in this book helps make an
important point against over-
restoration.

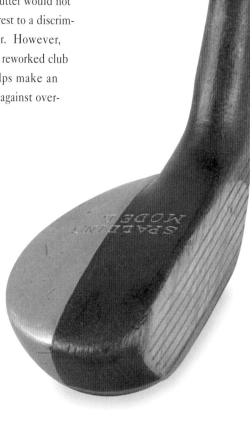

WILLIAM E. BUSSEY & JOSEPH S. PINDER

"STEEL SOCKET," MULTIPIECE HEAD

William Eaton Bussey, a manufacturer residing in London, and Joseph Samuel Pinder, an artisan also of London, received a British patent (No. 16,953) dated Oct. 23, 1890, that covered a clubhead made from two pieces of metal. In addition, this patent, the seventh ever granted for a golf club, also covers grips (see p. 528) and a fork splice wood joint (see p. 136).

Bussey and Pinder developed what they believed was a better way to attach the shaft to the head, whether the head was made of wood or iron. According to their patent, their iron clubs are constructed from two separate parts—the blade and the hosel—made from "steel, solid drawn or seamless." The hosel is made as a hollow tube. An approximately 3/8 inch high extension (boss) atop a very short "neck portion" of the blade fits inside the lower end of the hosel. Once joined, the head and hosel are brazed together. The shaft is then placed into the regular hollow portion of the hosel where it is "secured therein by means of cement, glue, or otherwise."

At first glance, these "steel socket" irons appear to be constructed the same as other traditional irons. On close inspection, however, a very fine seam around the hosel, just above the blade, can usually be located. Some of Bussey and Pinder's putters, such as the one pictured above, have gunmetal blades and iron hosels. These examples are easy to recognize, their two-piece construction made obvious by the use of two different metals. Because they are so attractive, the Bussey putters made from gunmetal and steel are considered more desirable, in terms of collectibility, than the Bussey irons and putters made from two pieces of steel. The rarest of Bussey's steel socket clubs is their *iron* made with a steel hosel and gunmetal blade. The USGA's museum has one of these clubs, marked "Newmetal" on the back of its blade.

The Bussey and Pinder iron shown below is marked "Bussey & Co. \ London \ Thistle \ Patent Steel Socket" on the back of the blade and "George G. Bussey & Son \ Patent Perfection Mashie" on the sewn grip. The putter shown above is marked "Bussey & Co. \ London \ Patent Steel Socket" on the back of the blade along with the "GGB" trademark with an arrow running through it.

As opposed to combination heads (heads made from two unrelated materials), the metal clubs covered under Bussey and Pinder's 1890 patent have multipiece heads (heads made from more than one piece of the *same* or similar material, not counting inserts, backweights, shafts, or appendages [see p. 275]).

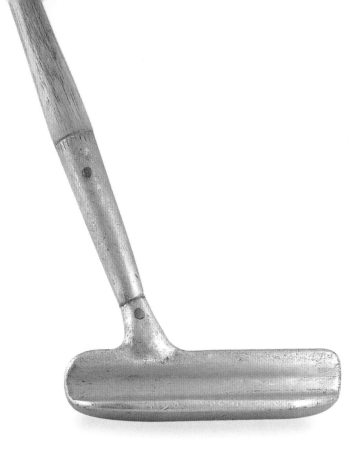

HUGH WILLIAMSON
MULTIPIECE HEAD

Hugh Williamson, of Bournemouth, England, received both a British patent (No. 216,725) dated July 17, 1923, and a U.S. patent (No. 1,543,636) dated June 23, 1925, to cover the idea of constructing an iron head from two separate pieces, the blade and the hosel. There are three notable differences between Williamson's patent and Bussey's patent (see previous page). According to Williamson's patent, a threaded extension (boss) at the base of the hosel *screws* into the very short neck portion of the blade; the blade is also *pinned* to the hosel; and the hosel is made from *lightweight* metal, such as aluminum, and the blade from steel.

According to his patent, Williamson was trying to change the balance of a golf club. He wanted to lighten the hosel in order to put more weight into the blade. The unmarked Williamson putter pictured above, the only Williamson club known to the author, includes a small flange.

Williamson also allowed for force fitting an "unthreaded" hosel into the blade, though both the threaded and unthreaded hosels were to be pinned to the head as pictured.

UNKNOWN MAKER
MULTIPIECE HEAD

The multipiece putter pictured below has an aluminum head and an iron hosel. This clubhead was probably made from two materials because the inventor, wanting to produce an aluminum putter head, knew aluminum hosels were prone to cracking or breaking around their top.

The iron hosel extends through the head and is visible across the sole. Inside the head, the base of the hosel has an irregular shape. Because the shape is not round, it locks the head to the hosel and prevents the head from turning. Also, the head is pinned to the hosel to keep the head from coming off.

Where a professional is concerned, a club engagement . . . is entered upon for a fixed weekly wage, and with the understanding that he shall be allowed to take part in various competitions. That arrangement may sound very well to the uninitiated, but the actual position, I regret to say, is this: That unless a professional player combines the manufacture of golfing requisites with his art, he finds it quite impossible to make any great profit out of the game; indeed he may make very little (Taylor 1902, 58-59).

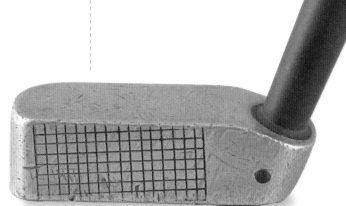

WILLIE DUNN, JR.
"UNEXCELLED,"
MULTIPIECE HEAD

In 1908 *Golfing* published what may have been a review of Willie Dunn's "Unexcelled" driver:

Willie Dunn, the famous professional, who returned to this country last year after a sojourn of some year's duration in the United States, has invented a new socketless driver, the head of which is made of compressed horn. No lead or bone is required in its construction, and Dunn claims that it will drive a ball further than will clubs of the ordinary pattern (2 Apr. : 26).

The Unexcelled driver pictured, stamped "Willie Dunn's Unexcelled \ Pat. App. For." on the crown, appears to contain the elements of the club discussed in the above review. It is a driver; it does not have a socket (meaning neck); it is made of some material other than wood; and it uses no lead or bone (or soleplate of any kind). However, the review does not mention the most incredible aspect of the Unexcelled: The top and bottom of the head are constructed from *two* separate pieces, and the pieces do not touch each other!

Despite being marked "Pat App. For," this club was not patented, so no patent record exists. Furthermore, the author was unable to locate any ads or other written references that identify the Unexcelled.

What is known about Dunn's club is what is visible.

The head is made from two pieces of something besides wood—"compressed horn," if the 1908 review was for this club. These pieces, which constitute the upper and lower half of the head, are fastened together by four dowels also made from the same material. The screwdriver slots on the top of the dowels indicate that the dowels, whose ends are visible on the top and bottom of the head, are threaded and screwed into place.

There is a uniform, narrow gap between the two pieces of the head. When the club is held at the correct angle, the viewer can see daylight through the clubhead. Why this clubhead included such a gap is a mystery. It was obviously done on purpose and appears to be the reason for constructing the head from two halves. This clubhead appears to be made of fiber and was probably constructed in the early 1900s.

A few makers were experimenting with fiber clubheads at that time. One such club was:

G. Forrester's fibre golf clubhead, called the 'Simpson.' It is specially designed for hot weather, and to

stand hard usage in all weathers" (*Golfing*, 26 Jan. 1899).

Another such club was:

The 'J.W.' Fibre Driver. Increased drive. Indestructible. No facing required. . . . No horn or fibre bits necessary (Golf Illustrated, 21 June 1912: 38; see p. 357).

The total ineffectiveness of the Unexcelled driver, its radical construction, and the fact that the one shown is the only one currently known, indicate that few were made. For more on Willie Dunn Jr., a creative innovator in the world of early American golf and a craftsman par excellence, see page 264.

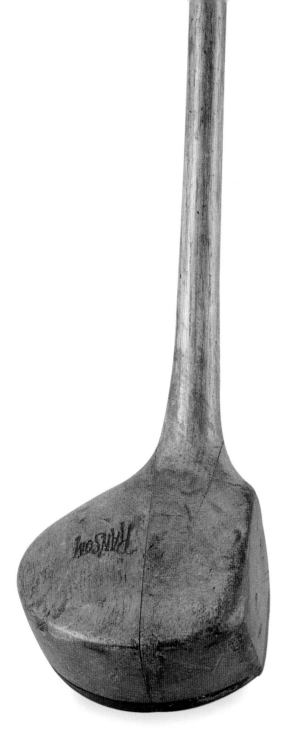

WILLIAM RANSOM

MULTIPIECE HEAD, ONE-PIECE NECK

William Ransom's driver (pictured) is not only a one-piece wood, which is to say this club does not have a neck joint, it also has a multipiece head. The shaft is formed integrally with the center section of the head, completely dividing the front of the head from the back and extending all the way out to the nose.

William McClenahan Ransom of Warren, Rhode Island, initially patented this driver in the United States. Applied for on January 23, 1901, his U.S. patent (No. 690,996) was granted on January 14, 1902. In his patent, Ransom states that in order to obtain the best results with drivers and brassies:

[the] shaft should be made with a suitable handle and very small at the neck. [The shaft] should be constructed of a . . . quality material, which must be light, tough, and whippy, so that it may be wielded quickly and with great force, while the head should be constructed of a material which is tough, hard, and heavy and capable of withstanding the impact received when it comes in contact with the ball, and the whole should be most carefully and accurately balanced by a weight placed in the head. This weight should be so placed that it should come in a direct line with the impact and as near the face of the club as practicable.

After identifying the qualities of an ideal driver, Ransom explains why other clubs fall short:

A like result cannot be obtained with a driver made with a spliced shaft, as the neck cannot be made so small and still retain the elasticity and strength where it is most essential, while the expensive construction of the one-piece driver keeps it from coming into general use.

Ransom next discusses how to construct his club and how constructing it his way will fulfill the stated goals for the ideal driver and brassie:

In my construction it will be seen that the shaft may be sawed into the desired form out of a board of suitable material for a shaft, with a portion of it extending out at the usual angle from the shaft into the head, to which the face and back of the head of a different kind of wood or material are secured by glue and screws, rivets, or other suitable fastenings.

. . . Constructing the club in this way insures the strongest possible connection between the shaft and head and admits of making the rest of the head of other wood than that which is found best for the shaft or handle, which requires a springy resilient wood, like second-growth hickory or ash, while a heavier close-grained hard wood, like second-growth hickory, boxwood, lignum-vitae, &c., is desirable for the blocks. It also makes it easy to use the face and back blocks made of vulcanized fiber or some similar composition which may be molded to the exact form . . . .

Another feature of Ransom's club is the way it is weighted. Although the lead backweight appears very small, the head contains a large amount of lead. A large cavity within the inner portion of the head (inside the middle piece and into the forward section) holds a large amount of lead directly behind and in line with the point of impact.

In addition to the U.S. patent, Ransom received a British patent (No. 3,065) dated February 6, 1902, that covered the club shown. Ransom's one-piece neck and radical multipiece head make this club, the only one known to the author, an outstanding collectible.

Prior to McClenahan's patent, Warren Briggs of Bridgeport, Connecticut, received two patents that covered a multipiece wood head. In his two U.S. patents, (No.'s 556,042 and 556,043) both dated March 10, 1896, Briggs presents the possibility of constructing heads from sections of wood in order to locate the end grain across the face. (See page 138 for a club produced under one of these two patents.)

WILLIAM BURKE
"ENDGRAIN"
MULTIPIECE HEAD

You get distance, more durability, no shock of impact, and better feel by using the Burke Patent Endgrain Head. The body of the head is selected persimmon, the grain of which runs at right angles to the striking face, the neck is straight grained, second growth hickory, inserted with a screw and glue joint. . . . Goften Mfg. Co., Newark, Ohio (The Golfers Magazine, April 1914: 65).

Pictured are two examples of William Burke's "Endgrain" clubs, complete with heads made from two separate pieces of wood. Burke, of Newark, Ohio, received both a U.S. patent (No. 1,089,900) dated March 10, 1914, and a British patent (No. 22,616) dated October 7, 1913, that covered his two-piece clubheads. As stated in his U.S. patent, applied for on August 18, 1913, Burke designed his clubheads with the following objectives:

To reduce liability of splitting or cracking of the head from impacts due to use, and practically to eliminate danger of fracturing of the neck. A further object is to provide a practical end grain golf head.

To accomplish these objectives, Burke constructed the body and neck from separate pieces of wood in order to position the grain of each piece in a certain way when the head is assembled. Consequently, the clubs produced under Burke's patent have three basic features—end grain across the face, neck grain running with the shaft, and a unique head/neck assembly:

The feature . . . first named resides in disposing the grain of the head at right angles to its striking face, whereby the impact from the

balls is transmitted to the head in the same manner as the blows received by a mallet or maul in use. By this disposition of the grain of the head, splitting and cracking are practically eliminated, and a larger proportion of the force of the stroke is transmitted to the ball, thereby securing greater distance in the stroke, and finally absorption of the shock of the impact with the ball . . . .

The feature . . . second named resides in having the grain of the neck extending parallel with the longitudinal axis of the shaft, so that the neck is caused to present resistance to fracture or splitting with equal force throughout its entire length, and in assembling the neck with its grain perpendicular to the grain of the head.

The feature . . . third named resides in providing the head with a counter bored mortise, and in forming the terminal of the neck with a tenon shaped to fit the mortise and to be secured therein by glue . . . .

To demonstrate the third feature, Burke's patent illustrations depict the neck piece extending down into the head. The head is bored out to the sole in order to correspond with and accept the neck piece. The portion of the neck piece that fits into the head has two different diameters. The upper portion (which fits halfway down into the head) is almost as wide as the exposed part of the neck. The lower portion (which extends to the sole) is much smaller and can be seen on the sole, where it looks like the tip of a shaft in a drilled-through socket.

Produced in the U.S., the putter pictured above left is marked "Burke \ Endgrain" on the crown. The driving putter pictured above right is marked "Brevet \ Driver \ Pat 785,212" on its crown and "Burke Patent 785212 End-grain" in the lead backweight. The number "785,212" is the British design registration number assigned to this club.

The Brevet Driver is an unusual driving putter that appears better suited to putting than driving. However, the 36-inch shaft (which was slightly longer than standard for a putter), the deep face, and the much heavier than standard head provided a very short driver for any golfer who wanted to try one. (*Everything* was tried at some point!)

The Burke Golf Company, of Newark, Ohio, produced two other models of Endgrain clubs. The wood heads on these models position their endgrain across the face, but the necks are integral with the rest of the head. One model is shaped like the examples pictured above (but without the deep face). The other model, the "Burke Endgrain Hammer Head" putter, is styled like the Schenectady putter and is usually found with a thin strip of fiber inlaid across the head to indicate the direction of the grain. Neither of these models approaches the two-piece heads in terms of collector interest. (Burke also made two-piece Endgrain woods.)

The idea of using end grain in the face of a golf club was mentioned as early as 1891. Discussing a club designed by Andrew Morison and produced by Willie Fernie, the September 11, 1891 issue of *Golf* reports that Morison's clubface will not break apart because of:

the insertion into the face of the club of a block of hard wood, the grain of which runs perpendicular to the face of the club, or towards the back of the club. It is evident that no amount of impact on the face of the club will lead to paring off with this protection (432).

Morison received a British patent (No. 12,207) dated July 18, 1891, that covered this club (see p. 146).

If anybody sees a club maker with a real St. Andrew's dialect roaming around loose in New York, please notify Nichol Thomson, the Birmingham, Ala., professional, and receive reward. "Nick" recently sent to Scotland for a club maker to help him out, and the steamship authorities report that the man arrived safely in New York. Since then he hasn't been heard from (Golf [ny], May 1907: 272).

HARRY IVORY JORDAN
"LAMINO" MULTILAYER HEADS AND SHAFTS

Harry Jordan's clubs are made from laminated heads *and* laminated shafts. Shown above, the lamination is visible across the face of the putter and the top of the driver head. However, the lamination in each shaft is difficult to discern. (The reason for this is explained later.)

The driver pictured is marked "U.S. Pat. 1457528 Lamino Perfect Shaft June 5, 1923" on a shaft label. The exceptionally large head of the putter pictured is marked "Lamino" in small block letters across its top near two small ivory alignment dots. Both of these clubs were produced under two patents granted to Harry Jordan of Auburn, Maine. One patent specifies shafts made from laminated wood; the other patent specifies heads made from laminated wood. Jordan's patent for the laminated wood head, a U.S. patent (No. 1,567,323)

applied for on October 19, 1921, and granted on December 29, 1925, states that the objective of his invention was:

to construct a head of fabricated or laminated wood so formed and arranged as to give a very hard and non-elastic playing surface.

After noting that good hickory heads were becoming very scarce due to the increasing demand for golf clubs, the patent continues:

Thus, a cheap fabricated material which will do the work as well or better than hickory is of considerable value.

The patent's references to hickory clubheads (hickory was seldom used to make clubheads) creates doubt as to just how knowledgeable Jordan was as a golfer or a clubmaker. At any rate, to fulfill his objectives, Jordan's patent calls for producing clubheads from fabricated or laminated wood identified as plywood:

In making up the club head, the plies are made of veneer strips of maple or any other strong hard wood suitable for the purpose.... The surface of each ply is then coated with a special water-proof glue and the whole body is then subjected to a very high pressure at right angles to the plies. This pressure amounts to 1500 to 2000 lbs. per square inch and the result is a very hard compact wood, the fibres of which are crossed and locked together so that no portion of the wood can be detached.

In this clubhead, the direction of the grain alternates with each layer of wood. The grain in half the layers runs at a right angle to the striking face while the grain in the other half runs parallel to the striking face. Layering the wood this way produced a more durable clubhead, and it also supposedly helped the golfer hit the ball straighter:

This arrangement on the playing face produces a corrugated surface which tends to remain corrugated since the strips having the end of the grain in the face will wear longer than the other strips where the wear comes on the side of the grain and will project farther than the other strip. Such a corrugated surface tends to get a better holding effect on the ball and prevents slicing and hooking.

Jordan's patent for a wood shaft, a U.S. patent (No. 1,457,52) applied for on November 25, 1921, and granted on June 5, 1923, covered "wooden shafts for golf clubs made up of a plurality of sections glued together." Believing that the supply of old growth hickory shafts did not meet the demand, Jordan states his intentions as:

to produce a fabricated wood which may be cheaply manufactured and which will approach in quality if not excel, the old growth hickory now so much sought for golf clubs.

It is difficult to see the lengthwise strips of wood that make up the shaft because the grain does not alternate from one strip to the next. In his patent, Jordan calls for pressing the plies together with the grain in all the strips running in the same direction. Jordan acknowledges that alternating the grain in each strip would help the shaft resist warping and reduce torsion, but he also contends that alternating the grain would "diminish the strength and the resiliency of the shaft." Jordan specifies fabricating the shaft from hickory.

Jordan states that the stiffness of the laminated shaft is directly affected by how the shaft is installed—which way the grain runs in relation to the plane of the swing:

When the plies are in the same plane as the swing of the club, the shaft is stiffer than when they are at right angles with the plane of the swing. When the layers are at right angles to the swing of the shaft the latter is in its most flexible position. In various positions between these two, different degrees of stiffness and different resistances to torsion may be brought out in my improved shaft.

Jordan received two British patents identical to his U.S. patents. His British patent (No. 207,478) dated November 29, 1923, covered the laminated shaft, and his British patent (No. 251,902) dated May 13, 1926, covered the laminated head.

The idea of layering a clubhead was originally proposed in Gustav A. Ruemmler's U.S. patent (No. 513,733) applied for on February 10, 1893, and granted on January 30, 1894. Ruemmler's patent calls for constructing a one-piece wood (no neck joint) with layers of wood affixed above and below a continuous extension of the shaft into the area of the head. The layers fill out and strengthen the head.

Ruemmler's club was covered under a British patent (No. 1,959) applied for on January 30, 1894. This British patent was issued to Samuel Walkey Gillett, a patent agent, who received it as a communication from Walter Edwin Hodgman. At the time, Hodgman had a one-third interest in Ruemmler's patent.

In 1895 David G. Robertson received two British patents that covered a clubhead formed from layers of *leather* cemented together (see p. 302).

JOHN WOOD, JR.
"J.W." FIBRE PUTTER, TWO-PIECE HEAD

The vulcanized fibre drivers, made by the J.W. Golf Syndicate, 122, Golden Lane, London, E.C., have had a great success, and the firm are now manufacturing brassies and putters of the same material with equally satisfactory results. The advantages claimed for these clubs are indestructibility, no facing or horn required, while their feel and appearance leave nothing to be desired. In regard to the weight and balance of these clubs, the head is made in two sections, which are joined by means of a double dovetail; a hole is bored through the back portion of the club, and molten lead poured in to bring to the desired weight. This method, together with two fibre pins or dowels, form an unbreakable joint and give a perfect balance, the weight following the line of the shaft (Golf Illustrated, Feb. 7, 1913: 176).

"J.W." two-piece fibre clubheads were covered under John Wood Jr.'s British patent (No. 9,847) applied for on April 25, 1912 and accepted on April 24, 1913. The top of the J.W. fiber putter shown above is marked "Fibre Putter / Patent" underneath "J.W." inside an oval and a triangle. The owner's initials, "SA", are also stamped on the crown:

In speaking of the new fibre "J.W." clubs, . . . Messrs. Mosses and Mitchell supply the fibre from which the head is made, but the club is the invention and manufacture of Mr. Wood, whose initials are those of the "J.W." in the name of the new clubs (Golfing, 27 June 1912: 44).

In early 1913, the J.W. Golf Syndicate appointed James Halley as "their sole selling agent" (Golf Monthly, May 1913: 234). Despite the initial success attributed to the J.W. clubs, very few remain.

"Caddie, sir? Caddie?"
"Yes, but I want a boy who can count. I'm playing for the medal today. Can you add up, my boy?"
"Yessir."   "What's five and seven and four, then?" "Twelve, sir."
"Come along; you'll do."

Mechanical Clubs

During the wood shaft era, few rules governed the implements of the game. Therefore, a *wide* variety of clubs that are now illegal were once legal for regulation play. Of these clubs, the mechanical ones—clubs with one or more moving or readily adjustable parts—are among the most ingenious and fascinating.

The first mechanical club ever patented, a putter with a tilting shaft that attached to the back of the head, was covered under George Twist's British patent (No. 7,243) dated April 27, 1891. Twist's "T" putter was produced and promoted, but golfers largely ignored it (see p. 376). Nevertheless, Twist's putter introduced the idea of a mechanical club, and the new world of possibilities it promised, to a rapidly expanding marketplace.

Following George Twist, other inventors devised everything from clubs with adjustable heads, weights, and alignment aids to clubs with springs, rollers, interchangeable heads, and revolving grips. Despite their creative nature, however, mechanical clubs were not effective. Those that offered convenience came at the expense of performance, and those that offered improved performance were actually, in most instances, counterproductive. Mechanically, these clubs usually functioned as designed, but, due to their added components, they were lacking in the critical elements of balance, feel, and consistency. In some cases, the club was awkward in shape, making good performance nearly impossible. Consequently, most mechanical clubs were shunned by the marketplace, or they received limited distribution. Only the Urquhart adjustable iron was somewhat well-received and marketed for a lengthy period of time (see following page).

The lack of marketing success encountered by mechanical clubs was no different from that of most other patent clubs:

Within the past few years the market has been deluged with patent clubs, each professing to be the epitome of mechanical exactness, but scarcely one of them has made the least impression on the golfing world. The scrap heap, not the golfer's bag, has been the market they have found (*Golf Illustrated*, 3 Nov. 1905: 112).

Although they were seen as nothing more than gimmickry, mechanical clubs were ingenious, fascinating, intricate, and visually interesting—the stuff of great collectibles! An important consideration when acquiring any mechanical or adjustable club is whether the club is in working order. A rusted tight or broken mechanism lowers the collectibility of a club. Every adjustable and mechanical club presented in this book is in normal working condition.

The pictures in this chapter are highly informative, but they do not compare to actually manipulating each club. To put the adjustable mechanisms into motion is to see these clubs come alive.

ROBERT L. URQUHART
ADJUSTABLE IRONS

Mr. Robert L. Urquhart, a member of the Honourable Company of Edinburgh Golfers, has been engaged for some time in perfecting a patent adjustable golf club, which was briefly noticed in these columns on September 15th. Mr. Urquhart's test and experiments with the club have extended over three years, . . . and it is only now, after severe trials with the club in actual play by some well-known Scottish professionals scoring rounds, that he feels himself justified in placing it on the market. We have examined and tested the club, and this is our report of its merits.

The club is simply a cleek, somewhat broader in the face than the ordinary blade, and a little longer in the shaft. The object is to make this single club take the place of a whole set, or to reduce the number of iron clubs which are usually carried in the player's bag. The blade of the club is movable. It is fixed by means of a spring into the iron socket at the end of the wooden shaft, this socket being a kind of cog-wheel arrangement which hinders the head from moving or becoming loose. The face of the club can be turned to any angle of loft desired by the player. Thus, off the tee, the blade would be straight like a driving cleek. By pressing a small button at the socket the spring holding the blade is released, and by turning the blade back one or two niches in the cog-wheel arrangement and the

button released, the club is ready for an iron shot. Placed a little further back, the blade is converted into a lofting iron—and a lofting iron, remember, which shall suit any kind of lie. On the putting-green the club may be instantly converted into a straight-faced putting cleek. If a player desires it, therefore, either on the score of economy or scarcity of caddies, he has only to carry this adjustable club, or this club with a driver for the tee shots, and he is as well equipped for the round as a player with eight clubs and the aid of a caddie. . . .

The club is not only ingeniously contrived, but it is as effective as it is ingenious. The advantages claimed by the inventor are: (1) that the player can play all through the green with one club only; (2) that the head of the club can be instantly adjusted to any angle to suit the lie of the ball and the stroke to be played; (3) that the club can be used as a right or a left hand club; (4) that the weight of the club and the length being always the same,

guarantee greater steadiness and accuracy of play; (5) that the club will do for unplayable balls lying close up to bunkers, walls, or fences; (6) that it is especially suited for ladies and for boys beginning to learn golf; and (7) economy to golfers (Golf, 26 Jan. 1894:307).

Receiving four British patents, Robert Lish Urquhart sought the perfect adjustable iron. Two of his adjustable clubs are shown above. The example on the left is the standard Urquhart iron—the model Urquhart produced the most of, and the model most often seen. This club was probably produced in 1897 and for a few years thereafter. The Urquhart adjustable pictured on the right is described in Urquhart's British patent (No. 20,642) dated November 1, 1895. Only five remaining examples produced under his 1895 patent are known to the author.

The standard Urquhart iron pictured is marked "Urquharts Patent \ No 2436" on the back of the hosel. The Urquhart trademark of a "U" inside a circle is stamped on the back of the toe along with "No 2436," which is believed to be a production sequence number. "Mitchell \ Manchester," the retail outlet that sold this club, is stamped on the shaft. This iron contains the word "Urquhart" and crisscross scoring lines inside an oval on the face. Straight scoring lines are above and below the oval. Pressing down on the lever outside the hosel disengages the mechanism. The blade can then be pulled away from the hosel, adjusted to the desired loft, and placed back into the serrated base.

The back of the 1895 Urquhart iron is marked

"Urquhart's Patent" inside the outline of a ribbon and "1071." The smooth face blade on the 1895 example is thin and broad. The blade on the standard model has a much lower profile with a distinct hump running across the back of the blade.

Robert Lish Urquhart was the first person to patent an adjustable loft iron. However, his British patent (No. 8,176) dated April 30, 1892, preceded Bussey and Pinder's British patent (No. 8,864) for an adjustable loft iron by only ten days (see next page). As designed, the head covered in Urquhart's 1892 patent adjusted by simply pulling the spring loaded blade away from the serrated base at the end of the hosel.

Urquhart applied for his second British patent, (No. 9,419) dated May 11, 1893, with his brother from Glasgow, David Inglis Urquhart. In this patent the Urquharts, exploring many ideas, discussed and illustrated nine different styles or "modifications" of an adjustable iron.

Robert's third British patent, (No. 20,642) dated November 1, 1895, covered another mechanism. To operate this one, push in the lever on the hosel, pull out the spring-loaded blade a short distance, rotate the blade to the desired loft, and fit it back in place. A "circle of grooves or teeth" located around the tail piece of the blade fit into corresponding grooves within the "internal recess." The earliest of the remaining Urquhart irons were covered by this patent.

In January of 1897, Robert and David Urquhart applied for another British patent (No. 689) to cover an adjustable iron. This application was abandoned. The author suspects, however, that the standard Urquhart adjustable iron took shape in this application because the design of the standard Urquhart is not found in any of Urquhart's earlier patents. Furthermore, it was immediately after applying for this patent that Urquhart finally turned his sights to the retail market.

In early 1897, Robert and David created a new company to produce and market their adjustable irons. In an effort to obtain funding, they registered their company and went about the business of selling stock:

The Urquhart Golf Syndicate, Limited, is a new company which has been promoted to acquire and work the patent adjustable club-head, brought out some time ago by Mr. R.L. Urquhart.... The capital is £20,000, divided into 20,000 shares of £1 each, of which 11,500 are offered for subscription. The purchase price is £3,500 in cash and 8,500 fully-paid shares. The shares available for working capital are 8,000. It is also intended to carry on the business of club and ball making, as well as of other sporting requisites... (Golf, 30 Apr. 1897: 145).

The same issue of *Golf* includes a full-page advertisement promoting the sale of stock in the Urquhart Golf Syndicate. In addition to providing a prospectus, the advertisement states that the club has been tried and praised by some famous golfers:

The club heads have been thoroughly tested, after two or three years' careful trials, and testimonials as to their efficiency have been received from many of the best golfers, both amateurs and professionals, such as Mr. P.L. Anderson, the Amateur Golf Champion, Tom Morris, J.H. Taylor, W. Fernie, Andrew Kirkaldy, Charles Hunter, Jack Duncan, and many others (163).

This ad also notes that the second and third place finishers in both the 1894 and 1895 British Opens included an Urquhart adjustable club in their playing set:

The patent adjustable club was used by Andrew Kirkaldy and Douglas Rolland (along with their other clubs) in the 1894 Championship, and by D. Herd and Andrew Kirkaldy, who were second and third respectively in 1894 and 1895.

On October 17, 1902, and in conjunction with his wife, Edith Mary Urquhart, Robert Urquhart applied for his last British patent (No. 22,590) that covered an adjustable iron. In this patent he kept the same basic mechanism found in the standard Urquhart adjustable while incorporating a dovetailed insert of ram's horn, gutta percha, leather, or "other suitable springy material" across the greater portion of the face. The author has seen only one club produced under this patent. It had a ram's horn face.

Urquhart also received two U.S. patents. His U.S. patent (No. 569,438) dated October 13, 1896, duplicated his 1895 British patent; his U.S. patent (No. 776,368) dated November 29, 1904, duplicated his 1902 British patent.

In addition to all the patents they received for adjustable head clubs, Robert and David Urquhart, either separately or together, applied for five other British patents not already mentioned which they later abandoned: No. 27,197 dated Nov. 20, 1897; No. 10,776 dated May 11, 1898; No. 18,575 dated Oct. 18, 1900; No. 12,975 dated June 5, 1906; and No. 20,474 dated Sept. 14, 1907.

A patent clearly based on Urquhart's 1902 British patent was granted to John and James Law, of Gilmore Works, in Edinburgh. The Laws's British patent (No. 9,433) dated April 27, 1903, was the result of their attempt to capitalize on Urquhart's efforts! However, the Laws met resistance from Robert Urquhart:

A case of much interest to golf inventors and inventors generally (says the Scotsman) was decided by Sheriff Henderson, himself a golfer of no mean ability, in the Edinburgh Sheriff Court last week. Mr. R.L. Urquhart, ... who has spent much time and money in perfecting his invention of the adjustable golf heads, which he has patented, laid before Messr's J. and J.S. Law, Gilmore Place, his views as to the improvements on his golf club-head, with the object of having some further improvements made by that firm. The work was done, and when the new club was tried some defects were found, and then it was taken back to the Messrs. Law, along with some notes of the desired improvements.

Subsequently, however, a dispute arose as to which party could really claim the perfected tool. As between the two parties, the Sheriff was strongly in favour of Mr. Urquhart, awarded him £30 damages, and ordered re-delivery to him of the club head (Golfing, 3 Mar. 1904: 24).

The standard Urquhart adjustable iron became the most widely produced wood shaft adjustable club. Consequently, they are the most available and best known to collectors today. However, the standard Urquhart pictured on the previous page has an added feature: It came from the Harry B. Wood collection. Harry Wood was the author of "Golfing Curios and the Like," the landmark book on collecting golf memorabilia published in 1910 (see p. 106).

WILLIAM E. BUSSEY &
JOSEPH S. PINDER
ADJUSTABLE IRON

With reference to Mr. Urquhart's "Patent Adjustable Golf Club" referred to in last week's issue, Messrs. George G. Bussey and Co. write, calling attention to the fact that Mr. Urquhart's club appears to be very similar to the patent "Interchangeable" club which Messrs. Bussey brought out some time ago. This club (Bussey's) is described as follows:—"The blade and socket are separate pieces, the former being united with the latter by an extended pin passing through a hole at the foot of socket or shaft, and secured by a nut. By this means not only can different heads be used on one shaft, but they can be set at any angle." We have seen neither of the clubs in dispute, and therefore cannot give an opinion as to whether the one club clashes with the other (Golf, 22 Sep. 1893: 22).

Ten days after Robert Urquhart applied for a British patent to cover an adjustable loft iron, William Eaton Bussey and Joseph Samuel Pinder also applied for such a patent. However, in their patent, (No. 8,864) dated April 10, 1892, Bussey and Pinder present two additional concepts

beyond that of adjusting the loft of the blade. First, they consider using an interchangeable head:

Thus one head may be used as a putting iron, or adapted to the other forms herein before mentioned by simply altering the angle of the head, as required. Or several forms of heads may be used, interchangeable, to the same handle and socket; the advantage of this interchangeable arrangement being that one shaft can be used for any kind of metal head, thus avoiding the necessity of carrying a number of clubs.

Bussey and Pinder formed their head in the simplest of ways: a threaded extension from the blade fits through an opening in the base of the hosel and an adjustable nut is attached to the end of the extension. The patent describes the arrangement as follows:

We form the metallic head in two parts; one part consisting of a socket which is fixed to the handle in the usual manner. An eye is formed at the end of the socket to receive a stem

formed at the end of the head. This stem is made sufficiently long to project through the eye of the socket, the projecting end being screw-threaded to receive the nut, whereby the head is secured to the end of the socket.

This mechanism is uncomplicated, but the golfer needed to carry a wrench of some type in order to tighten and loosen the nut. To eliminate such an inconvenience, most of the adjustable loft irons introduced after Bussey and Pinder's operate without tools.

The second additional concept found in Bussey and Pinder's patent is the idea of incorporating metal into a golf shaft. This patent was the first ever to present this idea. Bussey and Pinder allowed for the possibility of running a wire up the center of the shaft in the area near the head:

Our improvements in handles consists in passing a wire longitudinally through same, in a central or other position, where spring and strength are most required; whereby additional strength and elasticity are secured.

For a more complete discussion on metal and shafts, see pages 497-500.

The Bussey and Pinder iron pictured is simply stamped "Patent" on the back of its head. The lack of additional marks is not surprising because this club was crafted when irons bore little, if any, "advertising." Few of these irons were produced. Currently, this iron is the only such club known to the author.

George Francis Pittar, of Wimbledon, England, received a British patent (No. 28,312) dated December 8, 1913, that covered an adjustable iron with a mechanism similar to Bussey and Pinder's (a nut on the end of the blade stem, etc.). The basic difference is that Pittar's club, as designed, allows for adjusting the *lie* of the head as well as the loft. It is not known if Pittar's club was ever produced.

HARRY CUSHING, JR.
ADJUSTABLE IRON

A club that can be used for every purpose from the tee to the hole is the invention of Mr. H.C. Cushing, Jr., of the Country Club of Westchester. The idea in itself is an old one, but Mr. Cushing's principle of adjustment is simple, strong, and easily manipulated. By means of a thumbscrew the lie of the club can be instantly changed to any one of three positions. The advantages of a "one-club" outfit, in the absence of caddies, are obvious (Golf [ny], August 1900: 144).

On November 20, 1899, Harry C. Cushing Jr., living in the borough of Manhattan in New York City, applied for a U.S. patent (No. 651,920) that covered the smooth face adjustable iron pictured. He assigned his patent, granted on June 19, 1900, to the Adjustable Golf Club Company located in New Jersey.

According to Cushing's patent, he wanted to provide:

[a club] capable of effective operation in any ordinary lie on the fair green or putting green. . . . In other words, capable of effective use as a cleek, mashie, lofter, or putter.

Therefore, Cushing designed a:

golf club having an adjustable head, the inclination of which can be varied to form a good effective club of any desired type.

The Cushing adjustable iron pictured shows the back of the blade, marked "Adjustable Golf Club Co. \ 6 Walls St. NY \ Pat. 6-19-1900." The added thickness given to the toe counterbalances the added weight of the mechanism at the hosel.

Cushing's clubhead is easy to adjust. Simply loosen what the patent refers to as the "nut having a finger-piece" and pull the blade away from the three slots on the side of the hosel. Once the blade is loose, reposition the small extension at the top of the blade into one of the other slots—thereby changing the loft of the head. To hold everything in place, tighten the nut back down.

Designed with a nice bit of foresight, the "finger-piece" (the part sticking up underneath the back of the hosel) returns to the same vertical position when the blade is tightened. According to the patent, this keeps the finger piece "entirely out of the way."

The Adjustable Golf Club Company was a short-lived operation. Nevertheless, they produced at least one advertisement for their adjustable iron with its list price of three dollars:

Why carry a bagful of clubs when you have them all in a single club? Perfect in balance, finish, and adjustment. Every club warranted best drop-steel forgings. For one-club matches no one can beat you. You can change from a cleek to a mid-iron, mashie, lofter, or putter in an instant (Golf [ny], Aug. 1900: 79).

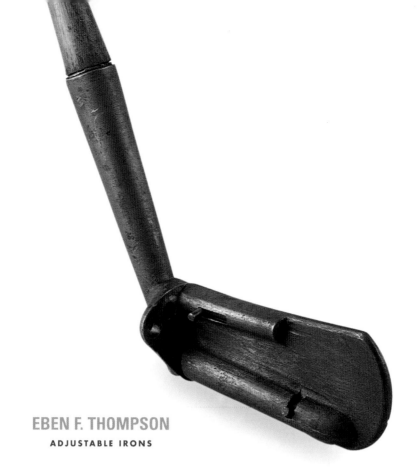

EBEN F. THOMPSON
ADJUSTABLE IRONS

Two different adjustable irons created by Eben Thompson of Worcester, Massachusetts, are pictured on this page. Made from gunmetal, both irons adjust to three different lofts even though their mechanisms are quite different.

Thompson received a U.S. patent (No. 670,522) dated March 26, 1901, that covered the iron pictured below. In his patent, Thompson describes adjustable irons:

To avoid the expense of purchasing a considerable number of different golf-sticks and to avoid the labor of carrying the same around the course, it has heretofore been proposed to provide adjustable golf-sticks which may be adjusted to set their striking-faces at different angles to the handles. These adjustable golf-sticks have not, however, come into general use, and it has heretofore been impossible to secure an equal degree of rigidity between the handle and an adjustable head or blade as can be secured when these parts are formed integrally.

To create a strong bond between the blade of the "golf-stick" and the hosel, Thompson designed a mechanism that provides a high "degree of rigidity." According to his patent:

The clamping mechanism . . . for securing these parts together comprises a screw extending loosely through the shank and which is threaded into the adjustable blade and is also threaded through a clamping-nut.

The steel head of this screw is visible to the left of the hosel in the lower picture. This screw extends into the bullet-shaped housing on the back of the blade. The "clamping-nut" fits on the screw and is visible between the head of the screw and the back of the hosel. Integral with this nut is an "actuating-lever" that extends well up the hosel, as pictured.

The patent continues:

The screw . . . has different screw-threads—that is to say, the portion of the screw fitting into the adjustable blade is provided with screw-threads of one pitch or coarseness, while the screw-threads fitting into the clamping-nut have a different pitch or coarseness. The clamping-nut is preferably provided with an actuating-lever having a projection which snaps into a recess at the back of the shank.

Two sets of threads on the screw allowed the golfer to tighten the blade to the hosel, no matter what loft was selected, as tight as he or she wanted while returning the lever to its upright position:

By means of this construction I have provided a clamping device which may be set so that by turning the lever to its upright position any desired degree of pressure may be exerted between the shank-piece and blade of the golf-stick. For example, suppose that when the blade is set to the desired angle it is found that the parts are not clamped together tightly enough to secure the desired rigidity. If this should be the case, the clamping-lever is first turned from its locked position and the screw is advanced or turned. When this has been done, the difference in pitch between the threaded sections and of the screw will draw the parts together, so that when the clamping-lever is again turned to its clamped or locked position it will exert a greater degree of pressure, and by thus varying the adjustment any desired degree of pressure may be secured and the parts may be clamped together as firmly or rigidly as desired, while at the same time the use of a clamping device of this construction will fully compensate for any looseness arising from long-continued use.

Both of Thompson's clubs are adjustable to three different lofts, but usable as *four* different clubs. On Thompson's 1901 patent iron, the heel end of the blade fits into any one of three vertical slots cut into a plate at the hosel. Unscrewing the clamping-lever loosens the blade from the hosel, so the blade can be set in the desired position. The forward slot provides a cleek or putter, the middle slot provides a mashie, and the rear slot provides a niblick. The clamping-lever fastens everything back down as previously described.

The Thompson adjustable iron pictured at the top of the previous page was not patented. It also adjusts to three different positions, but uses an entirely different mechanism. Two thin tubes run lengthwise across the back of the blade. A long rod inside the bottom tube is fastened to the bottom of the hosel. This rod does not move; rather, it allows the blade to pivot, so the blade can adjust backward or forward to achieve the desired loft. A small rod extending out of a small vertical slot across the lower tube not only regulates how far the blade can rotate around the long rod inside the tube but also keeps the blade from sliding off the long rod.

The tube running across the upper portion of the blade houses a spring loaded rod, one end of which fits into one of three holes located in the plate at the hosel. Pulling the small metal "finger hold" extending out of the slot on this tube (pulling it straight away from the hosel) slides the rod out of whichever hole it is in. The blade can then be adjusted to the desired loft and the spring-loaded rod reset into the corresponding hole.

Neither of these clubs is marked on its head. Only the spring-loaded adjustable has "McEwan" marked on the shaft. No fewer than four McEwans, all born in Musselburgh to the Peter McEwans of the famous McEwan family of clubmakers, were working as golf professionals when Thompson produced this iron. Douglas, born in 1869, worked at Musselburgh 1895-1899, Ilkley 1900-1903, Worthington 1905-1909, Leasowe 1909-1919, and Woolton 1919-1920. William, born in 1872, worked at Royal Epping Forest Golf Club (Chingford) 1890-1893 and Formby 1896-1930. Peter, born in 1873, worked at Southport 1895-1919 and Huddersfield 1919-1942. David, born in 1875, worked at Formby 1893-1898 and (Royal) Birkdale from 1899 to at least 1933 (Jackson 1994, 62). This McEwan stamp identifies one of these McEwan brothers, but which one is not known. David's excellent reputation as a clubmaker was shared by his brothers:

[David McEwan] received his education as a club-maker in his father's shop. He obtained his first appointment in 1893 when he went as playing professional to Formby Club. . . . In 1899 he was appointed professional to the Birkdale Club and there he has been ever since. . . . He has an excellent reputation as a club-maker. His specialty is copying clubs, in which branch of his work he does a large trade, and is looked upon as an expert (Golfing, 30 May, 1907: 20).

The complex construction of Thompson's adjustable irons, the poor way they sit when addressing a ball, the lack of any identification marks on the heads, and the lack of a written reference to either club beyond Thompson's 1901 patent, are all aspects that make it doubtful that more of these will be found anytime soon. Currently, this pair of adjustable irons are the only ones of their kind known. They might also be the only such clubs ever made. The fact that both of these clubs were located in the same estate suggests that they were the only ones made—samples produced and then abandoned when the idea of marketing the clubs was dropped.

A little craze sprang up once for securing autographs, and I can recall one championship where I must have signed as many programmes or books as I played shots . . . . This is not exactly a hobby which I have not any wish to encourage, for the professional golfer is not always as expert with the fountain pen as he is with his cleek, and I can remember many worried pros. standing, with book in hand, laboriously tracing out their names (Harold Hilton, Golfing, 29 Dec. 1910: 16).

UNKNOWN MAKER
ADJUSTABLE IRON

The blade on the engaging adjustable iron pictured has a profile similar to a light bulb (though probably not designed with a light bulb in mind) and can rotate 360 degrees. The blade looks and performs the same way for either left- or right-handed golfers. The shape of the thin blade, however, makes it difficult to hit the ball solidly—especially because of the minimal sole area that has contact with the ground.

The loft of this iron is adjusted by turning the square metal extension at the back of the hosel; this will loosen the blade from the hosel. A hole running side to side through the square metal extension allows for inserting a special tool, probably a thin metal rod of some type, in order to obtain greater leverage when tightening or loosening the blade. Of course a wrench could be used, though it, too, would be inconvenient for a golfer to carry around.

The small grooves cut in the base of the hosel mesh with grooves cut in the end of the blade. By having many small grooves, the blade can adjust to more lofts than can most adjustable irons, which have larger grooves. The number of lofts available on an adjustable loft iron has no particular influence on its collectibility.

The bull's-eye circles on the face are a nice feature. They add to the flavor and artistic design of this outstanding collectible.

The impractical head shape, the type of mechanism employed, and the overall nature of the head, are all indications that this club dates to the early 1900s. The author has seen three other adjustable clubs that use this mechanism. Instead of the bull's-eye circles in the face, however, two of these clubs have widely spaced scoring lines and a more traditional blade shape.

Tom Morris was playing with an old gentleman, Captain Broughton. The hole seemed utterly lost, Tom's ball lying in a whin, and the captain called out, "You may give up!" "No, no, captain; I may hole it." "I bet you £50 to a shilling you don't." "Done with you, captain," was the reply. He played and holed his ball, the chances being at the least a thousand to one against such a feat. Nothing was said at the moment, but next morning the good old skipper, not a wealthy man by any means, walked into Tom's cottage, and tendered the £50. Tom replied, 'Na, na, captain, we were joking. I canna' tak' the money," and would not do so. Tom would only be making some 15s. a week at this time (Golfing, 17 Nov. 1898).

When it comes to slick designs, this circa 1910 adjustable iron has one. The shape of the blade is unlike that of any other, and the adjusting mechanism is located in the back of the head where it functions with the flick of a lever: Pulling up on the lever loosens the blade, which can then be rotated to the desired loft; pressing the lever back down locks the blade in place.

Notice the holes drilled in the hosel. Such "Maxwell" hosels, as they are called, had two purposes. First, the weight removed from the hosel could be added to the blade, usually by making the sole thicker. Second, by force fitting the wood shaft into the hosel, the shaft would expand into the holes and form a tight bond with the head.

Maxwell hosels were covered under the British design registration (No. 549,492) issued to Ben Sayers, of Royal Wimbledon Golf Club, on September 18, 1909. Sayers's design registration describes his club as having slots, instead of holes, spiraling around the hosel:

A golf club, the novelty lying in the pair of tapering spiral slots out in the shaft socket.

Maxwell irons, advertised as "the novelty of 1910" (*Golf Illustrated*, 29 Apr. 1910: 119), are usually marked "Maxwell":

*Ben Sayers, Jun., asks us to call attention to the fact that his "Maxwell" Irons are now to be made by Messrs. Wm. Gibson & Co., Ltd., of Kinghorn, whose "Star" will appear together with the trade mark "Maxwell" on each club (*Golfing*, 2 Feb. 1911: 17).*

Many otherwise ordinary irons were produced with Maxwell hosels. After a few years, Maxwell hosels fell out of favor. If the wood exposed in the hosel became wet, the shafts were liable to rot, though efforts were occasionally made to prevent such deterioration:

*The professional who shafted the iron for me was inclined to "sniff" at these holes, and suggested that wet would get in and rot the shaft. So it would, no doubt, if the end of the shaft were left (as it was by him) unprotected; but a drop of varnish in each hole would keep the wood watertight. I have waterproofed my own shaft by putting a little ball of "S.F." puncture-putty into each hole and ramming it home with the end of a match. The cycling golfer will be familiar with this useful roadside-puncture-repairer . . . (*Golf Illustrated*, 27 May 1910: 204).*

The adjustable iron pictured is unmarked—a sign that the maker was not concerned about advertising his club for repeat business nor about producing it in quantity. The example pictured is the only one known. A related club was patented by Lee L. Turney, of Milwaukee, Wisconsin. Turney's U.S. patent (No. 1,568,485) dated January 5, 1926, covered an adjustable loft iron that used an actuating lever recessed into the top of the blade. No examples are known.

CARLYLE BUCHAN
ADJUSTABLE IRON

Carlyle Buchan, a potter from Portobello (near Edinburgh), Scotland, received a British patent (No. 23,578) dated November 1, 1901, that covered the unmarked and reshafted gunmetal clubhead pictured. Buchan's patent calls for producing a club usable as "a cleek, iron, mashie or putter." To make his club adjustable, a threaded stem on the heel end of the blade projects through the hosel where a "nut with a thumb portion" fits on the end of the stem. In order to vary the angle of the blade:

the nut is slackened sufficiently to allow the two sets of engaging teeth to be disengaged [so] the blade [can be] set to any required angle, the nut being then tightened up again.

The advantage of his invention:

is the blade can never get slack because the nut and screw will take up any wear and tear that there may be.

Two features illustrated in Buchan's patent are different from the club actually produced. First, the club pictured above employs a wing nut that has two projections, whereas the "thumb portion" on the nut illustrated in Buchan's patent has one projection. Second, the interlocking teeth shown in the patent are smaller than those in the iron shown above. The patent even refers to the possibility of having thirty-two teeth around the joint. These differences, however, are more cosmetic than structural. The adjustable club pictured matches the actual claims made in Buchan's patent.

The differences between many clubs as represented in their patents and as actually produced was often the result of a very natural process—practicality taking its undeniable precedence over theory. As long as the club still met the patent's claims listed individually at the end of the patent, minor cosmetic changes did not void the club's patent protection. Unsure of the best way to achieve their claims, patentees often included variations of their inventions in their patent. Furthermore, the patentee did not know how well one form of his invention would sell compared to an alternative form.

William Elliot, of Port Glasgow, Scotland, received a British patent (No. 214,466) dated April 24, 1924, that covered an adjustable iron similar to Buchan's, complete with the option of using a wing nut on the end of a stem extending through the hosel. In his patent, Elliot acknowledges Buchan's patent and points out that their clubs share a similar outward appearance. However Elliot's mechanism uses a small metal extension, on the heel of the blade, that interlocks with any one of six slots inside the hosel. When engaged with a slot, this small metal extension would not be visible. It is not known whether Elliot's club was produced.

J.C. LAMB
ADJUSTABLE IRON

J.C. Lamb produced an adjustable iron that, although simple to operate (loosening the circular nut behind the hosel loosens the blade), required no small effort to construct. There are four basic parts to Lamb's clubhead, three of which are visible below—the blade, hosel, and serrated nut. The fourth piece is a beautifully machined piece of steel welded onto the end of the blade adjacent to the hosel. It has gear-like interlocking teeth and a threaded stem. Four spot-welds affix the fourth piece to the drop forged head; two welds are ahead of the blade and two welds are behind the blade.

The back of the blade shown is stamped "Lamb. Loanhead \ Patent Applied For \ Rustless \ Warranted Hand Forged," and the shaft is stamped "J.C. Lamb." Loanhead is a small town on the perimeter of Edinburgh, Scotland, but, using a play on words in the context of an adjustable iron, Loanhead could also mean "lone head"— only one head is needed. The patent application lapsed for unknown reasons.

Lamb's clubhead is made from two basic materials. The head is made from rustless steel and the hosel is made from the same rustable iron found in most golf irons. Consequently, the color differs between the blade and the hosel.

Like most adjustable irons, Lamb's club did not lend itself to playing good golf. Specifically, Lamb's iron does not sit well on the ground, and the blade is too flat across the sole, heel to toe. The latter negative feature is accentuated by the long blade of Lamb's iron. Furthermore, the base of the hosel is too low to the ground. This lengthens the sole even further. When striking the ball, this club could easily turn in the golfer's hands if the exact lie of the head, a lie that allows no room for deviation, was not maintained at impact. For this reason, the blades on most other adjustable loft irons extend below the base of the hosel.

Lamb's club is easy to operate, but the easiest adjustable loft iron to operate was covered under Percy Cooper Whittaker's British patent (No. 28,749) dated June 12, 1914. Whittaker's adjustable iron has a simple spring-loaded mechanism: just pull the blade away from the hosel (which pulls the stem of the blade out of a spring-loaded receptacle in the side of the hosel), rotate the blade to the desired loft, and the spring then draws the blade back into place. Serrations in the neck and blade mesh together and, in conjunction with the spring, hold the blade in position. The author has seen one example of Whittaker's club and two examples of Lamb's adjustable club. Lamb's club was probably made around 1910.

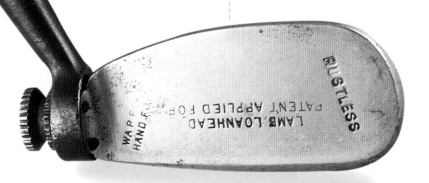

CHARLES N. CURRY
"ALL-ONE" CLUB, ADJUSTABLE IRONS

Mr. Curry, a Chicago man, has patented a new golf club, the "All-One" club, which is an adjustable iron club arrangement that can be made into a cleek, midiron, mashie, niblick or putter. The inventor has started a small factory and will soon place his club on the market (Golfers Magazine, Feb. 1914: 189).

On April 25, 1913, Charles N. Curry of Chicago, Illinois, applied for a U.S. patent to cover an adjustable head golf club. A patent (No. 1,083,434) was granted on January 6, 1914. While retaining fifty-one percent of his patent, Curry assigned twenty-five percent to Latimer Goodrich and twenty-four percent to Charles "Chick" Evans Jr., both from Chicago.

Four U.S. patents covering variations on Curry's adjustable iron followed Curry's original patent: No. 1,206,104 dated No-vember 28, 1916; No. 1,206,105 dated November 28, 1916; No. 1,250,301 dated December 18, 1917; and No. 1,258,212 dated March 5, 1918. The first three of these patents were granted to Alonzo G. Goodrich, also from Chicago, and the last was granted to Latimer Goodrich.

Both adjustable irons pictured bear the 1914 patent date despite being patented in two different years by two different patentees. The iron pictured above right is the club Curry patented. It is marked "Goodrich Sales Co. \ 76 W. Monroe St. \ Chicago, U.S.A. \ All One Trade Mark \ Pat'd January 6, 1914." The only one known to the author, this club is the initial model produced by the Goo-drich Sales Company.

The iron pictured above left was covered under Latimer Goodrich's 1918 patent, which described itself as an improve-ment on Curry's 1914 patent. Along with the Goodrich trademark, this club is marked "Goodrich Sales Co. Chicago \ All-One \ Pat'd Jan 6.–14" inside a circle on the back of the blade. This second example, offered by the Goodrich Sales Company for only a few years, is the standard production model. Yet, even these are seldom seen— only two or three change hands every year.

The mechanism in Curry's adjustable iron (above right) is located in the hosel. The small metal finger-hold extending out of a curved slot in the hosel con-nects to a spring-loaded rod (termed a "plunger" in the patent) inside the hosel. On the club shown, there is supposed to be a small metal "shield" that fits tightly around the finger hold, but it is missing. It cov-ered the slot in the hosel and kept dirt out of the mechanism. Pulling up on the finger hold lifts the plunger out of a hole in the top of the blade, so the blade can be adjusted to another loft. The top of the blade, which has three holes, rotates either back-ward or forward underneath the lip on the front of the hosel.

The standard Goodrich adjustable (above left) operates on the same basic principle, but the spring-loaded plunger inside the hosel is operated by rotating a ring in the neck, just above the blade. This action draws the rod up and out of whichever hole it is in. Rotating the ring in reverse lowers the rod into the newly selected hole.

The Goodrich Company marketed their club using the promotional angle of "familiarity brings consistency":

Familiarity means certainty. Good golf requires muscular familiarity with the club plus mental certainty—confidence. Every good teacher starts the novice with one club—usually the mid-iron—and says "stick to it till you are sure of it." Familiarity makes certainty. Even today you have one club you play best because you play it most. Familiarity again. You would be a better golfer if that club could be your only club. The "All-One" club makes this possible. . . . "More clubs more difficulties." That's what Chick Evans wrote in a recent article . . . . Familiarity will make it easy, easy to stop slicing and pulling, easy to control the ball at all times (American Golfer, July 1916: 231).

The standard Goodrich adjustable iron was produced for only a few years. Today, it ranks third in number of known wood-shafted adjustable irons—the standard Urquhart is the most common, followed by the Novakclub. Apart from these three, other adjustable irons are hardly ever seen.

The slots in the hosel on the standard Goodrich iron were designed to function like the holes in a Maxwell hosel (see p. 367). On May 14, 1918, George W. Mattern received a U.S. patent (No. 1,266,529) that covered such slotted hosels. Mattern assigned this patent to the Crawford, McGregor & Canby Company, which eventually produced many clubs with hosel slots.

William F. Breitenbaugh, of Philadelphia, Pennsylvania, received a U.S. patent (No. 1,137,457) dated April 27, 1915, that covered the adjustable iron pictured below. The premise for his adjustable club, as given in the patent, was related to versatility as well as cold weather!

It frequently happens that in cold weather, a golfer may be desirous of playing around a course with but a single iron club, as a cleek or mid-iron, since when the ground is frozen, injury to the wooden clubs is liable to result, but in playing with a single club, as is well-known, lies may be encountered, from which it is difficult with the use of a single club to extricate the ball unless the club can be adjusted to such conditions. It is also essential and desirable for a golfer to provide himself with a left-handed club which can be readily and instantly manipulated so as to be employed as a left-handed club, in order to extricate the golf ball from lies which may be inaccessible to the right handed club.

Breitenbaugh's adjustable club operates on the previously tried basics of a nut on a threaded blade stem that extends through the hosel. However, unlike the other adjustables that use a nut on a blade stem, the Breitenbaugh has a forked hosel, and the milled nut is located between the two prongs. To operate the blade you rotate the nut. Rotating the nut in one direction moves the blade away from the hosel so it can be adjusted to the desired loft; rotating the nut in the opposite direction draws the blade tight to the hosel and locks it in place.

The back of this Breitenbaugh head is also scored and designed to strike the ball. Consequently, both right- and left-handed golfers could use *either side* of the blade, could use the blade either right-side-up or upside-down. An ingenious concept, this allowed any golfer to select from two different blade shapes depending on the type of sole desired—either rounded or straight.

The club pictured below, offered in the Burke Golf Company's 1917 catalog, is marked "Breitenbaugh's \ Master Golf Club \ Pat'd Apr 29, 1915" on the reverse side of the blade amidst scoring lines identical to those on the face.

The Breitenbaugh adjustable iron is a unique, ingenious, and fascinating golf club. The way the hosel angles down at the mechanism, the fork in the neck, the attractively milled adjusting nut, the dual design of the blade, and the adjustable blade make for a very attractive collectible club. The fact that few Breitenbaugh clubs are seen today indicates that most golfers simply stayed out of the cold and away from frozen ground!

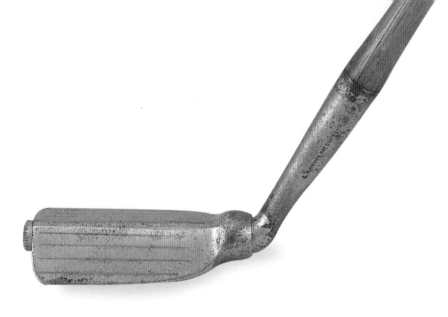

LOUIS H. VORIES
"EMERGENCY" CLUB, ADJUSTABLE IRON

Mr. L.H. Vories, of the National Biscuit Co., is not only a practical and ardent golfer, but one who has given much thought to the game and its clubs. He is in favor of using caddies in some more productive employment during the present crisis [World War I], and with this object in view has patented a universal iron club which certainly seems to be far in advance of some others that have from time to time made their appearance in the golfer's kit. Mechanically the new club is very simple, and consequently strong, and balances perfectly. In practice it fulfills the various duties of a straight faced putter, driving mashie, mid-iron, mashie, mashie-niblick, and niblick, and can be also adjusted to do away with terrors of the stymie–for Mr. Vories at least. The club can be instantly adjusted in all its phases for either right or left-hand, and for this reason has been suitably christened the "Emergency" club (Golf Illustrated, June 1918: 36).

The Vories adjustable iron pictured is marked "L.H. Vories Pat. December 28, 1915" along the leading side of the hosel. The head has *three* different striking surfaces, but only two were normally used (which two depending on whether the golfer was right- or left-handed). In the picture below, the wide striking face is positioned for a right-handed golfer. A narrow face is pictured above.

The blade works as follows: The head revolves around a long rod, integral with the hosel, that extends horizontally through the head. To adjust the head, begin by turning the screw at the toe. Next, pull the head away from the hosel until the base of the hosel and the heel of the head separate; then adjust the head to the desired angle. Push the head back in until the geared end of the head meshes with the base of the hosel. Finish by tightening the screw at the toe.

While living in New York City, Louis Vories received a U.S. patent (No. 1,165,559) dated December 28, 1915, that covered his adjustable club. As designed in this patent, the back of the blade is rounded and consequently not usable. Therefore, Vories applied for and received a second patent—a U.S. patent (No. 1,219,417) dated March 13, 1917. This second patent, also issued as a British patent (No. 111,937) dated January 11, 1917, kept the same mechanism covered by his first patent but added two new faces on the back of the head. The club pictured bears the 1915 date of the first patent, but was produced under the second patent. The author is not aware of any clubs produced as shown in Vories's first patent.

An advertisement for the "Vories Emergency Golf Club" describes its versatility:

It is adjustable to eleven different angles for either Right or Left handed player with two striking faces for each way of playing. With wide striking face you have two angles for putting, a Cleek, Mid-Iron, Mashie and Niblick, either right- or left-handed.

With narrow striking face you have two angles for putting, an approaching Cleek, Jigger and for Stymie-shot.

Try a round with your Driver and this one Iron.

Have wide face flat on ground for Stymie (Golf Illustrated [ny], June 1918: 37).

Vories sold only clubheads (for $5.50), not assembled clubs. The buyer was responsible for shafting the head.

ALPHONSUS GAVIN
"NOVAKCLUB,"
ADJUSTABLE IRON

Leave it to a Catholic priest to design the most refined adjustable iron made during the wood shaft era!

A Catholic priest, Father Gavin, has the parish at Goldfield, Nevada. He was the leader among the scant few who laid out a golf course in the sands of the desert near town, and he became the most consistent devotee to the game. There were no caddies at Goldfield, and on hot days Father Gavin sorely felt the burden of his golf bag. "Why not an adjustable club to do away with the several I have to carry?" was his thought. He worked on the problem and designed a club. Bringing it to San Francisco, golf mechanics improved and perfected it, with the result that absolute success is claimed for it. Joe Novak, professional of the Berkeley Country Club and the present State Open champion, played his home course with a driver and the All-In-One iron, and turned in a 72 on his first attempt. Shortly afterwards he played four rounds with the same two clubs, and averaged 71, his best round being 69. That was enough for Joe. He immediately connected himself with the new venture, and it was decided to use his name on the invention. It will henceforth be known as the "Novak Club." The iron is simple to adjust—merely a twist of the shaft with one hand and a setting of the blade at the desired angle with the other, and then a twist back of the shaft to lock it in its new position. It is so constructed that every stroke tends to tighten it rather than loosen it (Golf Illustrated [ny], May 1926: 50).

Gavin's Novakclub is well thought out. The mechanism is discreetly located in the hosel and adds little extra weight. The blade has a normal profile (compared to other clubs of its day)

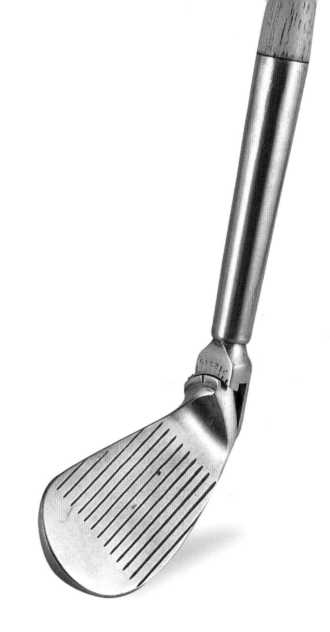

and provides a playable head no matter which loft is selected.

The unused Novakclub pictured is marked "Novakclub \ 60 Federal St. \ San Francisco \ Trade Mark Reg. \ Patent Pending" on the back of the blade.

The clubhead has three basic sections: the hosel, the blade, and the mechanism. The mechanism consists of two pieces: A base piece that extends down out of the hosel and attaches to the heel of the blade; and a lock pin, the bottom of which is serrated, that runs down through the center of the base piece and interlocks with the top of the blade. As pictured, the base piece is marked "P-1-2-3-4-5" to indicate the loft selections. Holding the blade in one hand and turning the shaft/hosel clockwise with the other hand loosens the lock pin inside the mechanism and unlocks the blade so it can be adjusted. Rotating the shaft a few revolutions in the opposite direction tightens the blade to the hosel.

Gavin filed for a U.S. patent (No. 1,703,581) to cover his adjustable loft iron on February 26, 1926. His objective was to devise an adjustable club "which will not differ greatly in appearance from the ordinary non-adjustable golf club" and to manufacture "such clubs in weights not greater than that of standard clubs." He assigned this patent, finally granted on February 26, 1929, to "Novak Club Inc."

The Novakclub went to market shortly after Gavin filed for his patent. A full page advertisement in the June 1926 issue of *Golfers Magazine* reports that the Novakclub was available from the "All In One Adjustable

Golf Club Corp.," in San Francisco, California.

Early Novakclubs had wood shafts. After a short time, however, Novakclubs were sold with metal shafts. The "New Novak Adjustable Putter" and a "Novakclub that unscrews to fit your suitcase" were also early metal shaft examples (*Golfers Magazine*, Oct. 1927: 44).

Using no fewer than four different blade shapes, Novakclubs were produced primarily with full-length steel shafts. Such examples do not approach the collectibility of the wood shaft model, nor does the steel shaft model that unscrews in the center of the shaft.

Four more patents assigned to "Novak Club, Inc." followed Gavin's. Joseph A. Novak and Franklin C. Fisher applied for

two: a U.S. patent (No. 1,697,998) applied for on April 15, 1926, and issued on January 8, 1929; and a U.S. patent (No. 1,702,916) applied for on December 27, 1926, and issued on February 19, 1929. These patents refined the adjusting mechanism. Joe Novak received a U.S. patent (No. 1,665,791) applied for on January 26, 1927, and issued on April 10, 1928. This patent covered metal grip collars used to affix the ends of a leather grip. The Allinone Adjustable Golf Club Corporation received a British patent (No. 267,737) dated April 29, 1926, that duplicated the January 8, 1929, U.S. patent (No. 1,697,998).

Sherman L. Boles, also from San Francisco, received the only other patent that relates to the Novakclub. His U.S. patent

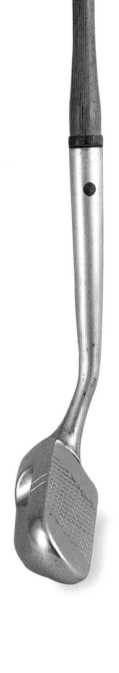

(No. 1,676,518) applied for on July 7, 1926, and issued on July 10, 1928, describes an adjustable iron very similar to the Novak-club—same basic mechanism, same basic head shape. However, he makes no mention of "Novak Club, Corp." or "The All In One Adjustable Golf Club Corp." His patent allows for interchanging heads in addition to adjusting the loft.

When Gavin's patent was finally granted in 1929, Joe Novak was a prominent professional at the Bel-Air Country Club in Los Angeles, California:

Although Joe Novak is still a young man, he is a veteran in the golf field. He started playing golf . . . in Butte, Montana, and began teaching the game at the age of sixteen at the Helena Country Club. . . . He moved to California, shortly before the World War, where he was connected with the California Country Club of San Francisco. . . . In 1925 he won the California Professional Championship. Novak was the first golf instructor to broadcast golf instruction (Golfers Magazine, 29 Aug. 1929: 22).

The adjustable club pictured on this page, usable either left- or right-handed, brings together a number of creative features. Specifically, it has a unique head shape, a novel mechanism, a longer than standard hosel, a leather washer located between the top of the hosel and the bottom of the shaft, and a solid wood grip.

The central area across the back of the head is twice as thick as the area above and below it. With this design, it did not matter if the club was used left- or right-handed—the weight would still be concentrated across (and behind) the middle of the face.

To operate the mechanism, a tool (either some type of Allen wrench or a screwdriver) is needed to loosen a screw in the back of the blade. Once the screw is loose, the blade can be rotated to the desired position. When the screw is tightened, a gear-type mechanism inside the heel of the head locks the blade in place.

This hosel is longer than most. This stylish feature dates to the 1920s (see page 184). The leather washer at the top of the hosel acts as a buffer, isolating the wood shaft from the metal neck. Over time, and as a result of

continued use, shafts sometimes cracked where they contacted the top of a rigid metal hosel. This problem occured primarily with cane shafts, so cane shafts usually had wood ferrules that extended into the hosel. The shaft in the club pictured is solid wood, but it is very slender—hence the leather washer.

This club has a wood grip, with circular rings cut around it, that is integral with the shaft (see p. 528).

The club pictured is most likely the product of William Spiker. Spiker applied for a U.S. patent (No. 1,983,196) on August 13, 1931, to cover an adjustable iron "applicable to the short approach shot club, or chipper." Spiker's club, as described in his patent, and the club pictured share not only the same purpose but also a very similar head profile. Spiker's patent, however, presents a slightly different mechanism (a circular nut is between the hosel and the blade) and illustrates the alignment line as running across the length of the blade.

The refined chrome finish and the year of Spiker's patent date this club after 1931.

DETROIT ADJUSTABLE GOLF CLUB COMPANY
METAL SHAFT ADJUSTABLE WOOD

Only a few adjustable loft woods were made during the hickory shaft era, and all of them date after 1920 and use only steel shafts. Five different adjustable loft woods dating prior to 1930 are presented here: four which the author has seen (all having metal shafts) and one known only as described in a patent.

The earliest patent for an adjustable loft wood was issued to Edwin C. Allen of Chicago, Illinois. His U.S. patent (No. 1,486,823) applied for on November 6, 1922, and granted on March 11, 1924, related "particularly to . . . putters although not restricted to this class." Allen advertised his club as an adjustable putter that could also play as either a mid-iron or a jigger (*Golfers Magazine*, Apr. 1923: 8). However, one Allen adjustable seen by the author functioned as both a wood and a putter.

The head on Allen's wood consists of a rectangular wood block placed lengthwise in a metal frame that borders the top and ends of the wood block. The shaft extends out of the exact center of this metal frame, directly over the top of the wood block. The ends of the metal frame extend down and attach to the ends of a steel rod running lengthwise through the middle of the wood block. A small amount of clearance between the metal frame and the wood block allows the block to rotate inside the frame, so three of the block's four sides can function as a striking face, each with its own unique loft. A lever operating the mechanism is located outside the frame at one end of the wood block. The shaft pivots back and forth above the head to accommodate both left- and right-handed golfers.

The next patent for an adjustable loft wood, a U.S. patent (No. 1,665,523) dated April 10, 1928, was issued to Edward C. Boyce of New York City. In his patent, Boyce notes that the decreased cost and light weight of adjustable clubs provide advantages over complete sets of clubs. But he also states that adjustable irons are not viable:

Adjustable iron clubs as heretofore proposed are scarcely feasible, as expert players generally concede that the iron clubs . . . should be progressively heavier as the loft decreases, and should be provided with progressively shortened shafts as the weight decreases. However, there is no inherent objection to a universal club designed to replace the three wood clubs . . . because it is generally agreed that any given golf player's driver and brassie should be identical in all respects except loft.

Optimistic about the feasibility of adjustable woods, Boyce patented a traditional-looking wood head with a face that could tilt back and forth. As illustrated in his patent, Boyce's club looks very similar to the Detroit adjustable pictured here. Boyce did not specify his clubhead material, but did call for making the adjustable face from aluminum. Instead of having a mechanism that operates at the top of the head like the Detroit Adjustable shown here, Boyce's clubface as designed adjusts at the back of the head. A rod, which projects out of a slot in the back of the head, connects to the back of the face. Raise the rod up and the face tilts forward; pull the rod down and the face tilts back.

The face of the aluminum Detroit Adjustable club pictured is tilted by turning a dial on the crown of the head. This dial, marked "Detroit Adjustable Golf Club Co. \ Detroit Michigan," has four settings: "Driver, Brassie, Spoon, H.F. Spoon."

The steel shaft in this Detroit Adjustable bears a "True-Temper Design No. 73,777" decal. This decal identifies Robert Cowdery's U.S. design patent dated November 8, 1927. Cowdery's patent dealt with shaft "step-downs."

The Duo-Set Golf Company, also from Detroit, also produced an adjustable loft wood. This metal shaft wood was originally paired with an adjustable loft metal shaft iron and sold as "ten clubs in two" (*The American Golfer*, Apr. 1928: 3). The Duo-Set wood, advertised as having a "first-quality persimmon polished aluminum head; genuine Bakelite face," changed its loft by replacing its face! Pulling a lever on the back of the head releases the entire face. The face comes completely off the body of the head, so another Bakelite face with a different loft can be installed. In addition to the fact that both clubs were made in Detroit, the Detroit Adjustable and the Duo-Set wood share other similarities. The Detroit Adjustable wood and the Duo-set wood both have four lofts; the Detroit Adjustable includes an "H.F. Spoon" face and the Duo-Set includes a "special 25° Hyflite Spoon" face.

The final adjustable loft wood mentioned here consists of a four-sided block of red plastic material that revolves horizontally underneath a small circular piece of flat metal, positioned horizontal to the ground, on the end of a metal hosel. Each side of the block, which is wider across its bottom than across its top, provides a face with a different loft. This club was offered in the May 1994 Sporting Antiquities auction, held in Andover, Massachusetts.

GEORGE F. TWIST
"TWIST'S PATENT 'T' PUTTER," ADJUSTABLE PUTTER

The "T" Putter. This is a new club designed . . . to minimise the difficulties and uncertainties of the golfer when he reaches the putting-green, and his ball is within holing distance of the haven of rest. It has been designed and patented by Mr. G.F. Twist, of Keresley, near Coventry . . . . When one sees the club for the first time all one's conservative golfing impulses seethe up in rebellious turmoil and cry out for the blood of the unoffending patentee! It is so unlike the time-honoured cleek or wooden putter.

The "T" putter is a metal blade of about four inches in length, perfectly straight in the face, and a little over a quarter of an inch in thickness throughout. It is fastened to the shaft in the center of the blade by means of a screw and a nut, for the slackening or tightening of which there is a key. . . . The advantages claimed for the putter are these:— (1) The shaft, being attached to the center of the putter head, tends to guide the eye when striking the ball. (2) The point of impact being in the center of the club diminishes the chance of a putt being heeled or toed, and, consequently, greater accuracy is obtained, especially in playing short putts. (3) The putter is capable of ready adjustment for a tall or short player, either right or left-handed. (4) The putter can be immediately altered to suit a particular lie of a ball in a hazard, or, if necessary, can be at once converted into a left-handed club or vice versa. (5) The putter is well adapted for playing running-up shots (Golf, 10 July 1891: 286).

The putter pictured, marked "T. Putter \ Patent Pending" on the blade back, is the first *adjustable* golf club ever patented. Designed by George Francis Twist, the putter was covered under a British patent (No. 7,243) dated April 27, 1891.

"Twist's Patent 'T' Putter," reminiscent of an upside down "T" when the hosel is positioned perpendicular to the blade, consists of a thin blade with a bolt in the center of the blade's back. The bolt extends through the hosel, and a nut placed on the end of the bolt fastens the blade in place. Loosening the nut loosens the blade. The blade can then be adjusted to the desired lie.

According to Twist's patent, his putter was "capable of adjustment for use by persons of varying heights, and for both left- and right-handed players." Furthermore, his putter was more than just a putter. It was credited with an ability:

for getting out of a difficulty in a "gorse whin" or other hazard, and said tool or club is admirably adapted for playing a running up shot.

Twist's putter was advertised briefly following its introduction, but the only other example known to the author is displayed in the Royal and Ancient clubhouse in St. Andrews. A putter similar to Twist's was covered under Alphonso Anthony Verel's British patent (No. 1,230) dated January 17, 1907. The top of Verel's blade as designed is distinctly rounded and a spring is used in the mechanism. It is not known if any examples were made.

ANDREW P. OLSON
ADJUSTABLE PUTTER

On September 7, 1920, Andrew P. Olson, of Chicago, Illinois, received a U.S. patent (No. 1,352,020) that covered the adjustable putter pictured. According to his patent, the purpose of Olson's invention was:

to provide a club of such character which may be used by either right-handed or left-handed players without disassembling the parts, and which may also be adjusted without disassemblage by any player to change the usual relation between the shaft and head in which such player would normally use the club to accommodate any changed position or stance which he may wish to take.

In other words, Olson's club adjusts by simply tilting the *shaft* to the new position desired—no loosening or tightening of anything.

Like the Sprague putter (see p. 383), Olson's hosel/shaft can rotate to literally any usable position either left-handed, right-handed, croquet style, or shuffleboard style. Olson's patent describes the adjustable feature of his club as follows:

By soleing the club on the ground and applying sufficient pressure on the shaft to overcome the resistance of the joint the player may shift the shaft more or less either transversely of the head or longitudinally toward or from the face to accommodate the club to any usual stance or position which the player may desire to take or be compelled to take by the hazards of the course. And of course, after the play from such unusual position is completed, the player may in the same way restore the shaft to its original position.

The mechanism is centrally located in the top of the head and works as follows: A ball integral with the end of the hosel is located in a socket. The solid end of a spring loaded rod inside the head is shaped to fit against the side of the ball. The spring-loaded rod enables this club to adjust:

The pressure releasing holding devise [the spring-loaded rod] retains the shaft in any position on the head against the usual stress of play, but allows the shaft to be instantly adjusted without disassembling any parts.

Words and pictures cannot describe the fascination of actually shifting this shaft into *any* position and watching it stay firmly in place with no further adjustment. Ironically, this "automatic locking mechanism" is probably the very reason why this is the only Olson adjustable club known. Not only was it illegal for USGA play when built, but who would trust it?

The example on this page is marked "Patent Apld For" on the back of the head. Olson's patent was applied for on April 23, 1919.

EDWARD M. FITZJOHN & ELMER A. STANTON
ADJUSTABLE PUTTER

Edward M. Fitzjohn, a British subject residing in Oneida, New York, and Elmer A. Stanton, a U.S. citizen also living in Oneida, received a U.S. patent (No. 1,250,296) that covered a *nonadjustable* putter with a head similar to the one on the adjustable putter pictured (see p. 178). Fitzjohn and Stanton's patent, applied for on May 11, 1915, and issued on December 18, 1917, describes the main objective of their clubhead design as:

> . . . to establish such relation between the head and the handle that when the club is held in striking position, the head will automatically balance or adjust itself into proper position for striking the ball squarely, as distinguished from those clubs in which the shank or socket of the handle is attached to one end of the head . . . .
>
> In other words, we have sought to bring the striking surface of the head as nearly as possible in the center of gravity of the club as a whole when suspended from the extreme upper end of the handle.

Using the design objectives of the club in his patent, Fitzjohn went one step further with the club shown and made the head adjustable. By running a bolt through the back of the hosel and into the head, Fitzjohn created a putter that could be adjusted to any lie and used either right-handed, left-handed, or croquet style.

The clubhead pictured is marked "Ed Fitzjohn." Its shape, in conjunction with the location of the hosel, places most of its weight in line with the center of the face.

The author knows of four adjustable Fitzjohn putters.

JAMES H. BOYE
MULTIFACE, DUAL FACE ADJUSTABLE PUTTER/CHIPPER

James H. Boye's U.S. patent (No. 1,437,463) dated December 5, 1922, relates to woods as well as to:

clubs employed for making short approaches to the putting greens and getting the ball out of bunkers lying close to the putting greens.

Marked "Boye Patent \ 1437463" on the sole, Boye's club is pictured on this page. It has an adjustable hosel that tilts back and forth, heel to toe. This allows the clubhead to be used right-handed, left-handed, or croquet style. To operate the mechanism, simply push the hosel to the desired position. Nothing needs to be loosened or tightened.

The adjustability of Boye's club makes it very collectible, but Boye's patent does not describe his club as being adjustable. Instead, the design of what looks like the back of the head is actually a unique dual face (a face with two different lofts) and is the patented feature.

On Boye's club, the flat side of the head is used for putting and the uneven (dual face) side is used for chipping. The Boye club as pictured below right shows its chipper face with two lofts—one positive and one negative. According to Boye's patent:

the standard inclination of the striking face . . . extend[s] only about three-fourths of the full height of the face of the club. Above the face is an upwardly and forwardly inclined face extending from the upper end of the face to the top of the club.

In other words, the lower portion of this face has a routine degree of loft while the upper-most portion, curling forward, is inversely lofted.

Boye's dual face was designed to remove all backspin imparted to the ball at impact, at least in theory:

The main object of the present invention is to provide an improvement in the character of the striking face of such clubs, by which, without impairing the lofting function of the club, the back spin may be prevented or checked, so that greater distance of flight may be obtained with a given stroke, and the ball when it strikes the ground will not stick but will bound and roll forwardly.

. . . In a properly played stroke, the ball will be first struck at a point below its central horizontal plane by the lower surface, which will cause the ball to rise and at the same time impart a backward spin thereto causing the ball to roll upwardly on the face of the club. In doing so, the surface of the ball at a point well above the horizontal plane of its center strikes the upper forwardly inclined surface of the face of the club. This instantly checks the back spin, and as the club is carried through, causes the ball to sail forwardly practically without any spin and as it strikes the ground to bound and roll forwardly.

Boye's patent also states that his dual face will not impart backspin to mis-hit shots.

Boye's club is a multiface club, "multiface" denoting that more than one side of the head was designed to strike the ball. In other words, on a multiface club the head has two, three, or four sides designed specifically as striking faces. Clubs with two faces on opposite sides of the head are also referred to as duplex clubs.

Note: This Boye clubhead is not cracked, but some examples are. The metal used to construct these heads (which are hollow) was not very durable, especially when put to the task of hitting a golf ball. Cracks are often found across the sole and up into either face. Because Boye clubs are scarce, those with minor clubhead cracks are duly accepted; but when actual pieces are missing, interest in the club drops substantially.

EDWIN C. ALLEN

**MULTIFACE, DUAL FACE
ADJUSTABLE
PUTTER/CHIPPER**

Edwin Allen's adjustable club, pictured above, is very similar to the Boye club just discussed. Allen's hosel pivots back and forth, heel to toe, in order to make the club usable either right-handed, left-handed, or croquet style; furthermore, Allen's clubhead provides both a putting face and a chipping dual face. Differing from Boye's club, Allen's club has a gunmetal hosel that rotates to lock the head in position, and its dual face does not use negative loft (the lower half of the face is lofted while the upper portion is perpendicular to the ground).

The back of the head, used if a lofted shot was needed, is shown. The front of the head has a flat, line-scored face used for putting. This club, incorrectly marked "Pat Feb 11, 1924" on the lofted face (no U.S. patents were issued on this date), was produced under Edwin C. Allen's U.S. patent (No. 1,486,823) issued *March* 11, 1924. Allen's patent covered the adjustable hosel on this putter as well as a rotating head which this putter does not have (see also p. 375). The writing on the sole is faint and unreadable. Only a small number of Allen adjustable putter/chippers remain.

WALFRED LINDGREN

**MULTIFACE ADJUSTABLE
PUTTER/CHIPPER**

Let a Center Shaft Putter be your Guide to the Hole. Lindgren's Adjustable Putter will give you results that are surprising to your game. The advantage of this club is that you have a perfect balanced Pendulum Swing Putter. Two clubs in one, straight face Putter No. 1; No. 2 face more lofted for approach Putt. Shaft is set by simply shifting from ground for either right or left hand player any lie or angle to fit player's particular form (Golfers Magazine, August 1927).

Walfred Lindgren's U.S. patent (No. 1,599,336) dated September 7, 1926, covered the adjustable club pictured below. The hosel tilts back and forth, allowing both the line-scored lofted face and the cross-scored straight face to be used either right-handed, left-handed, or croquet style. When the hosel is adjusted, a strip of spring steel inside the head, behind the removable face, applies pressure to the base of the hosel and holds the hosel in place.

Produced by F.B. Lindgren & Company (which became Lindgren Brothers) of Chicago, Illinois, Lindgren's adjustable club was occasionally advertised between 1925 and 1928. Nevertheless, it was not popular, and few remain.

"The New Patent Duncan Twin Putter," an adjustable club similar to Lindgren's, was tried years earlier in Great Britain. It, too, had a pivoting hosel above the center of a duplex head. One face was straight "for use on the green"; the other was lofted "for running up and short approach shots" (*Golf Illustrated*, 13 Aug. 1909: 208).

RALPH N. LONGSWORTH

MULTIFACE ADJUSTABLE PUTTER

Above illustrates a truly center shafted, perfectly balanced putter. It is so constructed as to allow you to adjust the head to any desired lie (for either right or left-hand players) and lock it. This is done by simply turning the shaft ferrule, which threads in, and spreads a split brass cylinder, rotatively contained in center of aluminum head. Parts accurately machined and highly finished. Less skill is required with it, for an accurate putt, than any club built. Think this over and order one, postpaid $6.50. We manufacture full line of clubs, shafts, heads and grips. I.R. Longsworth Co., Somerset, Ky. (*Golfers Magazine*, July 1927: 52).

Few Longsworth adjustable putters remain. Apparently, hardly anybody thought much of this club after "thinking it over." Of course, being produced by an obscure maker and marketed in a minimal way did not help its market acceptance either.

On September 20, 1927, Ralph Longsworth, of Somerset, Kentucky, received a U.S. patent (No. 1,643,250) that covered the club pictured above. His patent describes an adjustable putter with two different faces: one face is slightly lofted and the other is not. The adjusting mechanism, located inside the center of the head, allows the shaft to tilt back and forth heel to toe. Depending on the shot, or whether the grass was long or short, the player could use either the lofted or the vertical face either left- or right-handed.

To adjust the head, hold the head in one hand while rotating the hosel with the other. This loosens the hosel. Reposition the head to the desired angle and lock in place by turning the hosel in the opposite direction.

The putter pictured is marked "10 \ Made By \ R. Longsworth \ Somerset K" on the sole. "Patent Pending" is stamped on

the top of the head. The slotted end of the brass cylinder, which provides the tilting mechanism inside the head, is visible on one side of the clubhead. It is flush with the face, so the face can be used to strike the ball. The opposite face, the more lofted of the two, is line scored.

A nice (but easily overlooked) feature of this club is the square nut that is cast integrally with the base of the brass hosel. This nut allows the golfer to use a wrench to loosen the mechanism, if it becomes too tight to loosen by hand.

Longsworth's putter is a multiface club, "multiface" denoting that more than one side of the head was designed to strike the ball. Traditional blade putters are not included in this definition because the back of the blade was not specifically designed to be used as a striking face.

A multiface club is different from "The Multiface Putter" patented in 1906 by Wilfrid Short. Short received a British patent (No. 23,691) dated October 25, 1906, that covered a putter made with interchangeable face inserts. According to an advertisement for Short's "Multiface Putter," four interchangeable facings— steel, aluminum, fibre, and wood—made:

it possible for the player to adapt his putter to his temperament of the day, or to the green on which he is playing (*Golf Illustrated*, 5 Mar. 1908: 11).

The Multiface Putter was offered by the "Gravitator Golf Ball Co., London." The "Gravitator" golf ball was also Short's invention.

BALTIMORE PUTTER CO.

"TRIANGULAR PUTTER,"
MULTIFACE ADJUSTABLE PUTTER

Ready! The New Triangular Adjustable Putter. Thousands of golfers have been waiting for this adjustable putter. Made of aluminum, with best hickory shaft and leather grip. Six putters in one—3 lofts may be obtained for right and 3 for left-hand players. There are many clubs used on the fairway and only one putter. Naturally, if you have three to choose from you will gain confidence and save many strokes on the green (Golfers Magazine, Mar. 1923: 56).

In 1923, this putter could be ordered for eight dollars, delivered anywhere, and returned within ten days for a full refund if the buyer was not satisfied. Offered by the Baltimore Putter Company, of Baltimore, Maryland, the Triangular Adjustable

Putter has three different faces, each with a different loft. According to the advertising terminology, the "straight" face has straight scoring lines, the "medium" loft face has vertical and horizontal scoring lines, and the "acute" loft face has diagonal crisscross scoring lines.

The Triangular Adjustable Putter shown above left is adjusted for left-handed use. By holding the shaft in one hand and pulling the head straight down, directly away from the circular end of the hosel, the head comes loose via a spring mechanism inside the head. After the head is rotated to the desired location, the spring pulls the head back into a locked position. In the picture above right, the head has

been adjusted for right-handed use. Notice that a sight line is provided for all faces, both left- and right-handed.

Judging from the handful of Triangular Adjustable Putters known, they met with very little acceptance notwithstanding their generous return option and claim of "becoming an immediate success." In spite of all its adjustable features, this putter was ineffective.

In 1907 Reginald Marriott and Allen Ransome patented a multiface triangular putter similar to the Triangular Adjustable Putter. Marriott and Ransome's putter, however, has a fixed head (see p. 422).

WILLIAM W. DAVIS
"SPRAGUE"
MULTIFACE ADJUSTABLE
PUTTER

The following is a brief description by Wm. W. Davis concerning a recent invention of his:

"The putter invented by me is a rectangular block of aluminum having four scored or gnarled faces, each of which may be used as a striking surface. This head is provided with a shaft which is secured to the head by a flexible ball and socket joint, so that the head may be set at any angle to the shaft, and so that any of the four faces may be used. One of the longer faces is upright, like the face of an ordinary putter, the other longer face is lofted to be used for running-up strokes over rough grass. The advantages claimed are several, of which the following are the chief:

"It may be used by a right or left handed player, or, as some few prefer, forward and backward between the feet.

"Its rectangular shape suggests continually to the eye the right angle, which is the base of all putting strokes.

"The ball may be struck off the exact center of gravity, irrespective of the position of the shaft.

"Every one seems to recognize that putting is largely a matter of nerve or sentiment. Whatever, therefore, gives one the 'feel' of security and accuracy is a good putter for him" (*Golfers Magazine*, Nov. 1904: 204).

Pictured is a pristine example of William Whiting Davis's adjustable putter as produced and sold by G.S. Sprague & Company. To adjust the shaft, the locking ball joint mechanism in the center of the head has to be unscrewed. This is done by holding the head firmly in one hand while turning the hosel with the other hand.

After the ball joint becomes loose, the shaft will swivel in any direction. Once repositioned, the shaft is locked in place by holding the head and turning the hosel in the opposite direction.

The putter pictured is marked "G.S. Sprague & Co. \ Boston \ Pat. Jan 12, 1904" inside an oval on the top of its rectangular head. According to his U.S. patent (No. 749,174) dated January 12, 1904, William Davis made his putter head rectangular in order to remedy the difficulty of lining up a head having "curved or unusual projections." Davis, of Christ Church Rectory, East Orange, New Jersey, also received a British patent (No. 4,895) dated February 27, 1904, that covered his putter.

The Bridgeport Gun Implement Company offered Davis's "Sprague" putter in their 1904 Golf and Tennis catalog. Such examples were marked "B.G.I. Co. \ Agents \ G.S. Sprague \ Patent." Most of the known Sprague putters were sold through B.G.I. These examples have only two faces because the narrow ends of each head gently curve under to the sole.

Both models, the B.G.I. or the G.S. Sprague & Co., are fine collectibles. The latter has four faces and is harder to find (the example pictured is the only G.S. Sprague & Co. model known to the author). If a Sprague putter, or any adjustable for that matter, has a frozen or broken mechanism, it has a *serious* defect.

HEFFRON BARNES
ADJUSTABLE PUTTER

Barnes Adjustable Putter can be adjusted to 50 different "lies" or angles in a second. Find your perfect, comfortable stance, then lock. The head remains rigid and will not become loose in play. Degree markings enable you to know exact degree of angle you need.

The Barnes Adjustable Putter is a specimen of expert workmanship. Has the "feel" of your pet club. The accurate distribution of weight gives it a pendulum swing regardless of the "lie" you use. Face accurately adjusted to make ball hug the green. Patent adjustable lock is in the heel of the club, and will not be noticed unless attention is called to it.

No need to buy several putters trying to find one for your stance. Buy one and adjust it.

The Barnes Adjustable Putter is a beautiful club. Head is made of non-corrosive alloy, shaft of hickory, finished in golden oak with calf skin grip. Made in different lengths and weights. . . . Barnes Adjustable Putter Co., Yorkville, N.Y. (Golfers Magazine, April 1922: 50).

The Barnes putter pictured is marked "Barnes Adjustable Putter \ Model B \ Patent Pending" on the back of the blade. The shaft decal reads "Made in Yorkville, N.Y., U.S.A."

Differing from the adjustable putters previously discussed, the hosel on the Barnes putter is located at the end of the blade, not in the center of the head. Consequently, a Barnes putter can only be used right-handed—though it can be adjusted in such a way that a golfer lying flat on the ground could still sole the clubhead behind the ball! As seen in the upper picture, the neck is marked from 0 to 90 degrees where it adjusts.

Adjusting the head requires a special key, originally sold with the club, designed to fit the square opening in the neck bolt. (There are actually two "bolts" in the neck. The bolt visible at the front of the blade is, according to the patent, "a solid screw bolt." It screws into the "hollow screw bolt" visible at the back of the blade.) Once loosened by turning the bolt in the back of the neck, the neck can be adjusted to a new angle.

The "non-corrosive alloy" referred to in the advertisement is little more than pot metal. Such material is brittle and easily broken. In the lower picture, notice the small piece missing off the rearward extension of the hosel on the back of the neck. Barnes putters did not sell well, and few have survived. Even fewer are, like this one, in working condition.

Heffron Barnes, of New York Mills, New York, protected his putter with both a British patent (No. 241,091) dated March 9, 1925, and a U.S. patent (No. 1,550,665) applied for on May 7, 1923, and issued on August 25, 1925. Barnes also received a U.S. patent (No. 1,535,707) dated May 28, 1925, that covered a similar adjustable putter. It is not known if this putter was produced.

SIR RALPH PAYNE GALLWEY

"ROLLER GOLF CLUB,"
ROLLER HEAD

The Roller Golf Club. For putting, running up, approaching, and playing through the green.

Cannot cut or even mark the ball. Striking the ground does not check the swing, or follow through. No heel or toe as usually defined, hence pulling and slicing prevented.

Right or left handed. The best general club ever designed, as nearly all shots can be played with it.

Scores of 73-75 have been done with this club alone. Invaluable for a stroll round the green on a Sunday;

Very suitable for ladies, moderate players and beginners, and particularly deadly for anyone to carry for putting and long running shots.

Can be obtained from all well-known dealers in golf clubs, or direct from the inventor—Sir Ralph Payne Gallwey (Golf Illustrated, 13 Dec. 1907: 234).

Produced early in the twentieth century, Sir Ralph's Roller club, pictured, has a revolving cylinder clubhead. Built with a ball-bearing mechanism inside the head, the roller revolves when it comes in contact with the ground. Surprisingly, this club was not sold simply as a putter. Instead, it was offered as a multipurpose club, usable "through the green," that could play "nearly all shots"!

Like his club, Sir Ralph Payne Gallwey was an interesting character. Using a 200-year-old Turkish bow and an arrow, he once played an 18 hole match against a professional golfer using ordinary clubs. The match, played during the summer of 1906 across Gallwey's home

course in Richmond, England, was close, but Gallwey lost to William Hunter, 73 to 71 (*The World of Golf*, 12 July 1906: 299). Sir Ralph's archery golf did not catch on, but it brought him additional fame:

Sir Ralph Payne-Gallwey is known to most golfers as the inventor of the roller-head putter, which was tried with some success at Ganton a couple of years ago, and also perhaps as an exponent of the bow and arrow versus club and ball form of golf (Golfing, 25 Mar. 1909: 10).

Sir Ralph also experimented with golf balls and how far they traveled under various conditions and when made from different

materials. He eventually produced a golf ball called the "P.G.," and in a most generous spirit:

Sir Ralph Payne Gallwey hand[ed] over the profits from the sale of the ball to a charity (Golf Illustrated, 11 Nov. 1910: 145).

Sir Ralph was not the only person to attach his name to a rolling head club. Morgan George Lloyd, of Tenby, in the County of Pembrokeshire, England, received a British patent (No. 8,897) dated April 27,

1905, that covered a rolling head putter similar to the one pictured. In Lloyd's patent, the roller, held in place by a large nut at the end of the head, is made from either wood or metal. A variation allows for placing grooves lengthwise in the surface of the roller. Lloyd's putter, as illustrated in his patent, is definitely similar to the Roller Club. It is not known whether Sir Ralph had anything to do with Lloyd's patent; however, Sir Ralph did apply for his own patent. British patent indexes confirm that "Pat. 15144 \ 1907," as marked on the hosel of most Roller putters, was applied

for by Sir Ralph. A patent was not issued, so no record remains.

In addition to the short, non-tapering hosel of the example pictured, roller clubs were also made with slightly longer, tapering hosels (the hosel becoming smaller as it approaches the head). The long hosel version is believed to be the "improved pattern" of Gallwey's Roller Golf Club advertised in the May 29, 1908 issue of *Golf Illustrated* (204).

Putters with stationary cylinder-shaped heads were also produced (see p. 247-250).

Although Sir Ralph Payne Gallwey developed the roller head putter, he was not the first to employ a roller in a putter head. The credit for that goes to James Montgomery and his roller sole putter as made by H.J. Gray & Sons.

James Colin Montgomery, of Southsea, Hampshire, England, received a British patent (No. 5,902) dated March 21, 1894, that covered his roller putter. According to his patent:

The roller may be arranged . . . more or less within the sole of the club, suitable bearings being formed integrally with the sole of the club for supporting the roller which is furnished with a pin or spindle at one end, while a screw, plain at the upper part, may be passed through the second bearing and screwed into the other side of the roller.

Montgomery's putter received a glowing review:

We have received from Messrs. H.J. Gray & Sons, golf-club makers, Cambridge, a patent roller putter. The idea embodied in this new patent is a particularly ingenious one, and ought to commend itself to a large number of golfers. It is an ordinary gun-metal putting cleek, the sole of the club being a metal roller. The utility of the roller is obvious. It hinders a player from foozling his putt by striking the ball the least bit heavily on the turf behind, thus causing the ball either to run off the line, or not to run the distance of the hole. By means of the roller the putter cannot catch the turf and thus cause a foozle. The club follows through after the ball, no matter how heavily the stroke might hit the ground. The roller thus obviates all such contrivances as broadening or rounding the sole of the club, and is infinitely more effective in allowing the player to putt fair and true in all kinds of lies on the putting green. It needs, of course, a good deal of practice to play with a new club, as the tendency is to get the balls a little too strong at first, owing to the smoothness with which the club glides over the turf in making the stroke. But that is a point in play which is remedied by half-an-hour's practice. The balls are always hit true, and they run clean and straight on the line. We have no hesitation in recommending the new putter (Golf, 22 June, 1894: 330).

The example pictured below is marked "Montgomeries Patent \ No 5902" in a circle on the back of the blade along with "Gray & Sons \ Cambridge" also in a circle. H.J. Gray & Sons were well-known makers of sporting implements by the early 1890s:

Messrs. H.J. Gray and Sons, Cambridge, the well-known makers of athletic implements, have for some time been paying serious attention to the making of Golf-clubs and balls, and this department has been added to their business. . . . First rate Golf-club makers from Scotland have been engaged, and Golf-clubs are being turned out which for shape and excellence of workmanship cannot be surpassed (Golf, 28 Oct. 1892: 105).

"An ex champion racquet player of England," H.J. Gray employed ten workmen by 1894 (Golf, 6 Apr.: 54-55).

An interesting incident in the life of James Montgomery occurred while he was the secretary of the Mid-Surrey Golf Club. In 1895 Montgomery was charged with having maliciously published a libel concerning one Alice Maud Ludgater. Montgomery had released Miss Ludgater from her employment at the Mid-Surrey Golf Club for questionable activities and reported these activities in a letter to Miss Ludgater's mother. This letter provided the basis for Miss Ludgater's claim of "published libel." In his letter, Montgomery wrote:

I regret to have to tell you that we have been obliged to discharge your daughter Alice, owing to it that she has been in the habit of going to the rooms, in Richmond, of a certain member of this club. She also went along with our other waitress to places of amusement in London, on two occasions with two of our members, who the last time treated them to a dinner at the Holborn Restaurant, and plied them with champagne and other wines. Of course, such conduct could not be tolerated, and both have been discharged (Golf, 20 Sep. 1895: 24).

One week later, the charge against Montgomery was dropped because "the magistrates were of opinion that the letter was not written maliciously" (Golf, 27 Sep. 1895: 52).

Unfortunately for Montgomery, his putter did not remain available much longer than did Miss Ludgater at the Mid-Surrey Golf Club.

THOMAS H. B. BLACK
DOUBLE ROLLER SOLE

HARRY L. SUTTON
TRIPLE ROLLER SOLE

The inventors are very busy just now. The very latest is a wooden club with a ball-bearing attachment in the sole which is intended to prevent sclaffing. A couple of steel rollers are fitted so that if the ground is touched before the ball the head still "goes through" and the shot is a success. It is attached to drivers and brassies, and also to putters. We are getting near perfection now! (Golf [ny], June 1903: 415)

Thomas Hutcheson Bonthron Black's wooden putter pictured above, complete with two cylindrical brass rollers and a splice neck, is marked "Black's \ No. 11463 \ Patent" inside an oval on the crown. The shaft is stamped "J.&A. Dickson \ Maker \ Edinburgh."

Black also produced a brassie with two ball-shaped rollers. According to a brief article titled "Clubs on Castors":

Messrs. J. and A. Dickson . . . Edinburgh, have forwarded to us a brassie and a putter . . . . In the sole of

each club is cut a space in which are inserted two small easy sliding metal rollers. In the case of the brassie they are ball shaped and in the putter cylindrical. The idea is to prevent the fatal consequences attendant on a duffed or sclaffed shot. Certainly the rollers do appear to carry the club through with little diminution of force if the ground be hit too far behind the ball, and in the case of the putter considerably facilitate operations both in addressing and striking the ball. The clubs are beautifully balanced and finished (Golf, 14 Aug. 1903: 132).

Black received a British patent (No. 11,463) dated May 20, 1902, that covered his roller sole designs. Black believed his rollers would:

prevent the stroke of the club being spoiled by the head or sole of the club coming into contact with the ground or turf before reaching the ball, such a stroke being commonly known as "duffing."

This was not Black's first patent. He had already received a British patent (No. 13,423) dated August 26, 1890, that covered an oval grip. According to this patent, regular round grips would frequently move or turn in the "left or upper hand and consequently the club [would] not strike the ball fairly or true." Black believed that by making the upper portion of the grip oval, it would fit:

into the hand exactly in every way and so materially preventing the club from moving or turning in the left or upper hand.

The head of Black's roller sole putter is shaped along the lines of a long nose club, but it is more transitional in size. Black's clubs are very difficult to locate and eminently collectible.

The aluminum head putter shown above, with three rollers on the sole, was produced by Harry L. Sutton, the professional at Sutton Coldfield in Streetley,

England, between 1925 and the early 1930s (Jackson 1994, 91). In addition to the three aluminum rollers, this putter has a bulger face (see page 258).

Sutton's club dates well after Black's. Although this mechanical Sutton putter is not marked, one of the other two mechanical examples known to the author is marked "Prov. Pat 27,230" across the face. This is a provisional British patent number assigned after 1916, when a patent for this putter was applied for. The patent was never issued.

Sutton's roller sole putter could also be used without the rollers, which were removable (see p. 258).

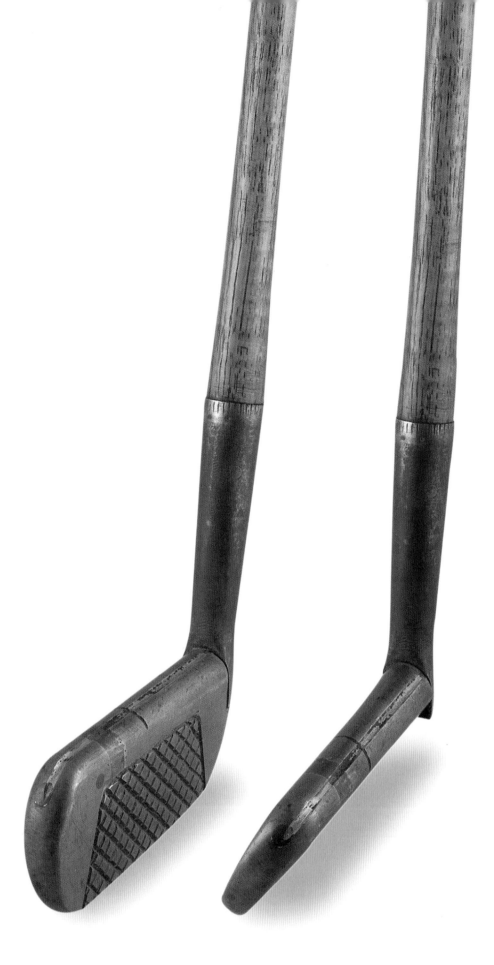

UNKNOWN MAKER
HINGED BLADE PUTTER

Designed to help the golfer with a penchant for stubbing his or her putts (as were the roller putters just presented), the putter pictured has a spring-loaded, hinged blade that gives way should the sole strike directly into the ground. The spring inside the blade works in conjunction with a steel rod, also inside the top of the blade. The steel rod, on which the blade hinges, extends from the back of the hosel to the tip of the blade's toe. The spring-loaded blade is calibrated with considerable tension, so the blade will move only if the sole strikes the ground with significant force. Impact with the ball will not move the blade because the ball contacts the upper portion of the blade, and this does not provide the necessary leverage.

In addition to a hosel made from iron, this unmarked, unique putter, the only one known to the author, has a gunmetal blade with a distinctive cross-scored face and concave back. Everything about this club is well-engineered and well-made; the hinged blade is still in perfect working order.

Golfer's wife.—"Have you been a good girl to-day, Edith?"

Golfer's daughter.—"Yes, Mummy, I have—with a handicap."

G. W.—"What do you mean by that ?"

G. D.—"Well, Daddy says that a handicap means pretending you've done better than you have" (Golf, 6 Oct. 1893:54).

W. CLAUDE JOHNSON
REMOVABLE HEAD, ADJUSTABLE WEIGHT WOOD

One of the latest improvements, and also one of the best, in wooden golf clubs we have seen is that of Mr. Claude Johnson. Not only does the improvement consist in the form of the head, but in the manner of its construction. . . . Mr. Johnson . . . has invented simple rotary cutting machinery, by which he can turn out heads expeditiously and absolutely uniform in point of size, shape and weight. . . . The club-head is a little broader than the ordinary straight-faced club or bulger. It has a brass sole, and no lead is let in at the back of the club. The weight capacity is obtained by grooving a small chamber in the centre of the head, where the name of the club-maker is usually stamped. In this chamber are inserted five or six pieces of metal about the size of a shilling, and then a thin brass plate is screwed down over the aperture. If the club is too heavy, the chamber is opened, and one or two of the metal discs taken out, their places being taken by cork discs of similar size. The club has no neck, as golfers understand the meaning of the word. There is a thin piece of tubing screwed into the head at the angle desired by the player, and this piece of tubing projects about an inch above the surface of the head. In this, the club shaft is firmly fixed . . . . The brassies and drivers are made slightly convex on the sole, which is an advantage in picking a ball up through the green,

not obtainable as a rule by the flat sole. Each club is numbered, so that a player when he wants a new head has only to send the number to the maker, and he receives a new head in all respects similar to the old one. The advantages which Mr. Johnson claims from his club are these: —"It is of the simplest form of construction, and entirely made by special machinery. Every club (of the same description) is of exactly the same form and interchangeable. A club-head or a shaft can be renewed without skilled labour. The wood forming the head can be selected, both as regards hardness and direction of the grain, without reference to its suitability or capacity for forming the neck and splice for the usual shaft attachment. The weight of the club-head can be altered at pleasure without skilled labour. It offers less resistance to the air than any of the usual forms. The sole of this club, by reason of its convexity, will cause much less retardation to the swing of the club should the ground be taken in making the stroke. There is no joint to become unglued, nor is there any whipping to become loose. The brassies will pick up a ball from a cupped or grassy lie better than any other wooden club" (Golf, 11 Aug. 1893: 371).

The Claude Johnson brassie pictured, complete with a thin greenheart shaft, was produced by Angus Teen & Company. The convex brass plate covering

the sole is marked "A. Teen & Co. Golf Club & Ball Manufacturers \ 18 Eastcombe Ter \ Blackheath \ London S.E. \ Sole Makers." The circular brass disc on the crown is marked "Claude Johnson's Patent \ No. 983 Pattern D." The mark "983 Pattern D" is the production number of this club. If the golfer broke the head and wanted a duplicate, he or she needed only to refer to the production number:

A very useful element in the manufacture of these clubs is the numbering of the heads. A player, whether lady or gentleman, who finds a head which suits perfectly, and wishes it replaced, has only to send the number to the maker, who supplies the exact duplicate as to weight and lie (Golf, 29 Sep. 1893: 40).

Johnson's clubs were made with other variables beyond weight and lie. According to an advertisement for Johnson's club:

In ordering it should be stated:— 1. If a driver, brassy, or spoon. 2. If a flat face, bulger, or 1/2 bulger (Golf, 8 June 1894: 276).

Perhaps the most noticeable feature of Johnson's club, other than its overall design, is the brass disc located atop the center of the head. Remove the three screws in the disc and the disc comes off. Weight can then be added to or removed from a chamber underneath the disc. Weight could be in the form of flat metal disks, "gun shots," or a coil of lead wire.

Walter Claude Johnson received a British patent (No. 8,954) dated May 4, 1893, that covered this club. In addition to mentioning some of the features listed in the review on the facing page, Johnson's patent states that the prominent brass cap would:

direct the eye of the golfer to that portion of the club head which is opposite the center of the face . . . and thus assists him in striking [the ball] correctly.

Johnson's patent also provides for making putters like his woods. The putters Johnson produced, however, included an adjustable shaft:

Messrs. Teen and Co. are also the sole makers of "The Symmetrical Golf Putter," another invention due to the fertility of Mr. Claude Johnson. The head, which is of wood, resembles in shape the drivers and brassies patented by the same inventor . . . . The putter has also a ballast chamber, exactly in the centre of the head, containing the lead weights, which can be adjusted to the liking of the player. The shaft is attached to the head by a pair of metal links, which permit angular adjustment. By slacking these links with a spanner (which is provided for the purpose) the golfer can place the shaft in any possible position with regard to the head. Not only does the attachment device allow the angle of the shaft to be varied with regard to the sole of the club, but it permits the line of the shaft to be adjusted so as to tend more or less forward, or further from, that point of the club face which gives impact to the ball. . . . A prominent bar or web in the line of the stoke aids the golfer in a similar manner to impel the ball in the correct line. When the desired adjustments have been made, the two nuts are tightened with the spanner (Golf, 19 Jan. 1894: 295).

One of the most interesting features in Johnson's patent is one of the easiest to miss when examining Johnson's club. The shaft is *detachable:*

To make a good strong joint, a ferrule for receiving the shaft may be secured in such bore hole by keying or screwing and be then pinned in such a way as will prevent it from twisting or becoming loose, such fixing being effected in so simple a manner that a new head or shaft may be fitted without requiring skilled labour, and as easily as if the club head was entirely formed of metal.

The "simple manner" used to hold the shaft in place is a small screw located at the base of the brass ferrule. Clever as they might be, both the ferrule and the method for attaching the shaft attracted criticism:

It seems to us, however, that the weak point of the club in its present form will be found to be the ferrule forming the socket for the shaft. It is too small to withstand the constant hard strain, and there will be a liability for the shafts to break too readily at the junction of the metal (Golf, 11 Aug. 1893: 371).

Apparently Johnson's club had other problems inasmuch as it underwent major remodelling:

Messrs. A. Teen & Co., . . . have sent a sample of Mr. Johnson's Patent Golf Clubs, in which recent improvements have been made. Mr. Johnson has in this form of club adopted the ordinary bulger shape, but the ballast chamber, which gives weight to the club-head, is transferred from the top of the head to the sole. This is undoubtedly an improvement from the point of view of the appearance of the club-head . . . . The use of lead at the back being done away with, a player may either increase or lighten the weight in a few minutes, by unscrewing the ballast chamber in the sole (Golf, 31 Aug. 1894: 577).

Two months after the above comments were first published, an advertisement for "Claude Johnson's Improved Patent" listed additional changes in Johnson's club:

The brass ferrule has been done away with. The ballast is now inserted in the sole. The club head is deeper, and gives greater driving power (Golf, 2 Nov. 1894: 152).

Unfortunately, the promise of greater driving power was not enough to keep Johnson's club from falling quickly by the wayside.

Today only a few of Johnson's woods remain. Two are displayed at the British Golf Museum in St. Andrews, Scotland, while five or six are privately owned in the U.S.

The picture at left shows the classy design of Johnson's convex brass soleplate. Not all of Johnson's clubs had brass soleplates:

With reference to aluminium soleplates for club-heads mentioned in last weeks issue, Messrs. A. Teen and Co. inform us that they used such soles on their "Claude Johnson" clubs two years ago, and they believe them to be quite as good as brass (Golf, 29 Nov. 1895: 261).

JAMES H. STIRLING
ADJUSTABLE WEIGHT WOOD

Patented by James Hamilton Stirling, of London, England, the driver pictured has two chambers, one in the sole and the other in the handle. These chambers allowed the golfer to adjust the overall weight and balance of this club in a matter of seconds. To change the weight in the sole, the golfer had only to unscrew the threaded cap and then either add or remove weighted washers. According to Stirling's British patent (No. 194,823) dated December 23, 1921, the clubhead's weight chamber is comprised of:

a threaded stem integrally formed with a threaded plug or cap, a weight or weights adapted to be positioned on the stem, one or more threaded nuts adapted to engage the weight or weights and hold the same in position, a sleeve surrounding the said weighted stem, and threaded to receive the said plug or cap, and a base portion of the

said sleeve being secured in the cavity by means of a screw or lugs or both.

The weights could be made from "lead, brass, iron, or other suitable or preferred metal or material" and could be either threaded or loose on the rod holding them in place. Three lead washers atop four brass washers were used to weight the clubhead pictured.

As shown in the lower picture, Stirling's driver also includes a weight chamber in the end of the handle. The wood walls of this chamber are threaded down their entire three-inch length, and a threaded brass cap/plug is used to contain any weights placed inside.

Six other pre-1930 patents mentioned an adjustable weight port in the grip. Edward Meldal's British patent (No. 154,792) dated April 28, 1920, called for installing weight discs in a handle fitted with a threaded cap similar to Stirling's. Henry Taylor's British patent (No. 174,550) dated

June 14, 1921, covered using a screw-cap to access spring-loaded weights inside the end of the handle, but this patent was more concerned with cues and rackets than it was golf clubs. Sydney Jacob and James Field's British patent (No. 218,423) dated April 26, 1923, described a rod with unusually thick threads and corresponding weights that screwed into the end of the handle. Walter Mason's British patent (No. 250,815) dated August 27, 1925, offered a metal ferrule with a threaded cap that, after being installed on the end of any existing grip, could hold weight discs. Mason's invention avoided drilling out the shaft. Benjamin Lantz's February 7, 1928 U.S. patent (No. 1,658,447) provides for a cap that the golfer could unscrew in order to add or remove small lead weights inside a shallow chamber in the end of the grip. Lantz believed that counterweighting the grip would insure a better "follow through" of the club. Finally, Allen Heeter's U.S. patent (No. 1,673,361) dated June 12, 1928, covered a golf shaft that had openings at both ends which

could be filled with lead and then closed with fiber plugs.

According to Walter Mason's patent, counterbalancing a golf club at the grip end was important because:

It not infrequently happens that removal of weight from the head of the club in order to improve the balance will make the whole club too light. It is sometimes desirable therefore to add weight to the top of the shaft.

Today, golf clubs are seldom counterbalanced, but when they are, it is usually because the clubhead is too heavy (counterbalancing lightens the swingweight). The great Jack Nicklaus used a counterbalanced three-wood during much of his career.

Horace L. Kent of Brooklyn, New York, received a U.S. patent (No. 1,213,382) dated January 23, 1917, that covered an adjustable weight wood similar to Sterling's. A removable "ballast cylinder" in the sole of Kent's wood, called "The Monitor" and marketed by Harry C. Lee, is divided into one large and three small sections, so the lead can be located more or less towards the toe or heel.

In order to change the weight of a Daniel patent putter, simply unscrew the brass cap on the end of its hollow head and either add or remove weight. Screw the cap back into place, and the club is ready to use.

Percy Gordon Eckersley Daniel, of Clevedon, in the county of Somerset, England, protected his invention with both a British patent (No. 17,579) dated December 5, 1912, and a U.S. patent (No. 1,167,387) applied for on November 1, 1913, and issued on January 11, 1916. Daniel's patents relate to woods and putters; both were produced. The author knows of one wood and two putters. On the wood, the weight port is centered in the back of the head; on the putter, it is located in the end of the toe.

The Daniel duplex putter pictured is marked "P.G.E. Daniel \ Pat. Adjustable \ Balance \ Clevedon Somerset" inside an oval on the top of the head and "Patent \ No. 17,579" on the brass cap that screws into the end of the toe. Unscrewing the cap requires a special tool with two properly spaced lugs, such as a golfer's spike wrench.

Daniel's British patent states that his invention, which applied to golf clubs in which the weight or balance or both could be varied to suit the user, has as its objective:

to provide improved accommodation for a weight or weights so as to avoid any chance of the weight or weights shifting or shaking about when in use. . . . The principal feature of the invention lies therefore in providing means for bringing pressure to bear upon the sides of a weight or weights

when in position in a suitable socket member, as well as mere end pressure, so as to avoid any chance of the weight or weights shaking about under severe jars or shocks.

The patent calls for filling a hollow cavity in the clubhead with either a brass cylinder or a number of metal discs designed to fit the cavity. And it suggests different ways to keep the weights immobile. One idea was to see:

that a number of slits are formed in the wall of the socket and further that the screw-threaded portions of the socket and cap are tapered slightly. Hence when the cap is screwed home upon the socket, the wall of the latter where it is slotted will be compressed slightly, to grip the weight which is being employed and prevent its shaking about.

Another method provides guides inside the cavity and metal weights that correspond to the guides.

The club as produced, however, used a number of heavy and light discs of the same diameter. By using weighted and dummy discs, both the weight *and* the balance of the club could be adjusted:

In this case the small weights preferably consist of discs of metal of a size to fit snugly the aperture in the socket. Obviously to alter the weight of the club head or the like either some discs are added or taken away. In order to avoid any chance of the discs rattling about, dummy discs of some relatively light but firm material such as aluminium, wood, or ebonite may be employed to take the place of those weights which have been removed. By providing dummy discs as just stated the actual weights may be concentrated in any desired position in the hole so that the balance of the

head may be varied. For instance some dummy discs may first be inserted and then the real weights inserted behind, thus tending to bring the centre of gravity of the head further back, and vice versa.

Daniel's patent also includes the option of installing a weight port "in the handle shaft of the club" so that "a marked difference in the balance of the club may be effected." It is not known if Daniel ever produced this option, but the idea of counterweighting the grip end of a club has been around even longer than Daniel's club (see p. 534).

ROBERT W. ELLINGHAM
ADJUSTABLE WEIGHT PUTTER

UNKNOWN MAKER
**"STRATE-PUT" ADJUSTABLE
WEIGHT PUTTER**

On December 9, 1924, Robert W. Ellingham, of Springfield, Massachusetts, received a U.S. patent (No. 1,518,316) that covered the putter pictured above. Ellingham's putter includes a weight port located midway across the back of its Schenectady-style head. A threaded rod, centered on the inside of a threaded cap that closes the weight port, holds any weights installed inside the head. According to Ellingham's patent, the weights were to be made from "Babbitt metal which is heavy and sufficiently hard to properly retain the shape of the screw threads."

The Ellingham putter shown is marked "Ellingham \ Spfld, Mass" on the sole. A coin slot on the cap facilitates the cap's insertion and removal.

Pictured below is a duplex putter marked "Strate-Put \ Pat. App For" on the top of its rectangular head. The Strate-Put does not concentrate its weight behind its sweet-spot, but it functions the same as Ellingham's club. A threaded screw-cap is used to access a chamber in the head where weight can be added or removed.

The Strate-Put's threaded plug is loosened or tightened using the edge of a coin. This is exactly as specified by Edward Meldal in his British patent (No. 154,792) dated April 28, 1920, which covered an adjustable weight putter. However, the walls inside the Strate-Put's chamber are threaded exactly as specified by James Govan in his U.S. patent (No. 1,133,129) dated March 23, 1915, which also covered an adjustable

weight putter. Govan specified using threaded weights that screwed in place, but the Strate-Put shown uses an unthreaded lead rod that might be original to this club (the threads inside the chamber have chewed up the weight). Because the Strate-Put does not match any patent illustrations and is similar to at least two different patents, its creator is not identified here.

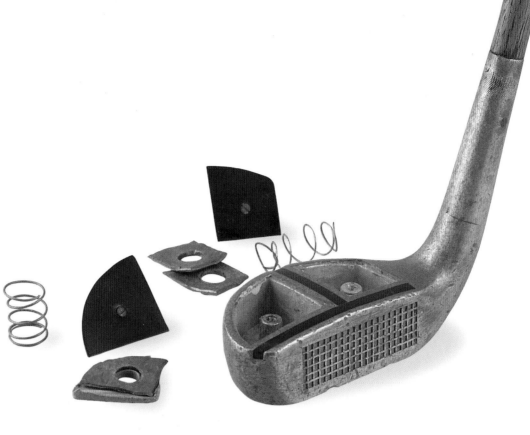

ALBERT McDOUGAL

"T SQUARE" PUTTER, ALIGNMENT AID & ADJUSTABLE WEIGHT

A well lined putt is half won. The McDougal Putter makes you do what in nine cases out of ten a player cannot do with the ordinary style of putter. It makes a player line his putt right. It makes him putt right. It shows him if he is playing his stroke along the line to the cup. It will improve your game by five strokes (The American Golfer, Sep. 1916: 419).

On January 21, 1919, Albert McDougal of New York City received a U.S. patent (No. 1,291,967) that covered the putter advertised above. According to McDougal's patent, applied for on August 30, 1915, the objective of his invention was to help golfers accurately line up their putts. Therefore, the crown of McDougal's putter includes a "true line parallel to the face of the club head intersecting a line parallel to the hole." These lines are made from:

hard rubber strips inset in the upper portion of the head by a dovetail construction or by forming dovetail recesses and correspondingly con-

necting the strips of hard rubber and insetting said strips in the grooves so that their upper surfaces will be flush with the upper surface of the head.

The putter pictured, marked "The McDougal \ Putter \ Patent No. 1291967 \ Thistle Putter Co. NYC \ Upright" on the sole, includes two such alignment lines. Every McDougal putter has alignment lines, but not all McDougal putters are the same. The example pictured, McDougal's improved model, also includes two chambers in which the weight and balance of the club can be altered.

An advertisement for "The New Improved McDougal Putter," found in the May 1926 issue of *Golfers Magazine*, announces that a new weight feature has been added to the initial McDougal "T Square" putter (65). The advertisement's illustration shows the improved McDougal putter taken apart, similar to the above picture, so a prospective customer could visualize how easy it was to adjust the putter's balance and weight. Simply put, there are two cavities on the top of the head. Lead weights fit

around a post located in the center of each cavity. To keep the weights from moving, a spring is placed between the weights and the black, hard rubber pieces that screw into the top of each post and cover the cavities.

McDougal's initial putter is a nice entry level collectible, but the improved version is much more interesting and more sought after.

McDougal's patent allows for using red, white, or blue alignment strips. It is not known if McDougal's club was ever produced using such colors.

An adjustable weight putter related to McDougal's was patented by Marcus MacDonald, of London. His British patent (No. 197,815) dated April 19, 1922, covered a putter with a sliding cover atop a hollow rectangular head that contains interchangeable weights. An example of MacDonald's putter is known.

THOMAS TODRICK
"SLOG-EM 2 IRON,"
REMOVABLE IRON HEAD

Clubs with detachable clubheads that can be quickly installed or removed without using any special tools were devised no later than 1890. Alfred Donald Stuart, a contractor's agent from Manchester, England, received a British patent (No. 17,211) dated October 28, 1890, that discusses different ways to readily connect or disconnect a shaft from an iron head:

The connection between the head and its shaft may be made by means of a screw, bayonet joint, shank and socket with spring catch or any equivalent coupling which will hold.

The idea of detachable clubheads usually took intellectual shape for one of two reasons: either to facilitate the quick and easy repair of a broken shaft or to allow the use of various iron heads on a single shaft. The first type of detachable head is referred to as a "removable head"; the second type, found on a shaft designed for use with many heads, is called an "interchangeable head."

Between the U.S. and the U.K., there are no fewer than six pre-1930 patents that describe a removable head on a wood shaft. At least two clubs were produced from these patents: Thomas Todrick's club, shown on this page, and Claude Johnson's wood shown on page 389.

Todrick's 1928 patent was the only patent that dealt simply with a removable iron head on a wood shaft. His club pictured above and below is marked "The Slog-em 2 Iron" on the back of the blade, along with Hendry and Bishop's "bishop's mitre" trademark and "Archie Compston \ Autograph \ Pat. Applied For," etc. "Patent applied for" refers to Thomas Todrick's British patent (No. 320,273) dated November 27, 1928. Despite being patented at the end of the hickory shaft era, this club is a fine collectible because of its interesting, inventive, and unique mechanical features.

According to Todrick's patent, his club concentrates the weight in the head and strengthens the shaft:

The principle object of the present invention is to construct a golf club in such a manner that the weight is concentrated as far as possible near the striking surface of the club. A further object . . . is the elimination of the usual pin which passes through the shaft and by which the latter is held in the socket, it being obvious that this pin weakens the shaft.

Todrick designed a removable head that was threaded at the top of the hosel to correspond to a threaded collar. The hosel's thinner than normal walls and four lengthwise cuts allow the hosel to crimp down on the shaft as the collar is screwed down. These threads are lefthanded on the right-handed club pictured, so impact with either the ball or the ground will only tighten the head.

Todrick received a second British patent, (No. 332,354) dated June 11, 1929. This one covered an iron head screwed onto a metal golf shaft.

ANDREW ROBERTSON
GUNMETAL PUTTER, INTERCHANGEABLE HEAD

The "Robertson" Patent Clubs.

We are in receipt of a set of the "Robertson" patent clubs, which are evidently designed with a view to the extinction of the genus caddie and the pleasing of the pretty fancy of those who "caddie" for themselves. The entire set of clubs consists of two shafts and the usual number of heads, which are screwed on as wanted. The longer shaft has as its complements a driver, brassie, and cleek head for screwing on, and the shorter, the usual iron heads, iron, mashie, and putter; but (and here we must be Irish) the iron club-heads are all of gun metal. The shafts are fitted with protective "ferrules," and when they are fixed can be used as walking sticks. The shafts and heads are beautifully fashioned, and to certain and sundry who do not and will not patronise caddies they would be most distinctly useful and convenient. For our part, however, we do not think the caddies need worry, as even if the sale of these "Robertson" clubs exceeded the proprietors' most sanguine expectations the caddies would always find plenty of employment. . . .

We give below particulars of the prices as taken from the window card of the proprietors.

Gun metal club heads (five a full set), 5s. each; wood heads play club and spoon, 5s. each; shafts, long and short, with patent verrels [sic], fit all patent clubs, 4s. 6d. each; set of four clubs, one wood, three metal, and two shalts [sic], 29s. per set. The clubs may be had from Messrs. Robertson, 27 Main Street, Anderston, Glasgow (*Golfing*, 17 Mar. 1904: 22).

A Robertson patent club, with an interchangeable putter head (defined on the previous page), is pictured on this and the facing page. The back of the head is marked "Robertson \ App 10867"; the base of the hosel is stamped "Patent."

Andrew Mallock Robertson, a self-described medical practitioner, received a British patent (No. 10,867) dated May 13, 1903, that covered his interchangeable clubheads. Robertson clubs,

which screw together with left-handed threads, were produced only briefly. This is the only such club known to the author.

Robertson's club was not the first club with interchangeable heads. One of the earliest such clubs belonged to P.G. Tait, father of the 1896 and 1898 British Amateur champion, Freddie Tait:

Another idea which professor Tait has hit upon is a club which is, in itself, a whole pack. The professor has, however, been forestalled in this suggestion, for two years ago we saw the same principle given effect by Mr. A.D. Stuart . . . . Mr. Stuart had only one shaft, and the cleek, iron, and putting club-heads were carried like cartridges, in a belt fixed round the waist, each head screwing off and on. But not much came of the idea . . . . Professor Tait's idea is this: There is a thin, tough steel tube for the shaft, to which a steel rod like a pencil is attached, either as one piece, or with a hinge, in order to alter the lie at pleasure. The head of the club (steel, iron, wood, platinum, &c.), has a hole bored through it which fits on the

pencil rod, and it is then fixed by tightening a hexagonal screw nut by means of a little key, which the player carries in his pocket. The section of the head may be of any form, and by setting it at the proper angle on the pencil rod and keying up, you can get driver, spoon, cleek, iron, niblick, putter, mashie, &c., at will, and each of these is right or left-handed at pleasure. One spare head, at the most, and the key, are all you have to carry. Some of the faces are flat, some cylindrical, some grooved, to give the underspin; some are narrow (vertically) so as to get at the under parts of the ball; some, for use as spoons or mashies, are as smooth as possible. Professor Tait has himself played a good deal with this universal club, and it has been tried by many players at St. Andrews (*Golf*, 11 Aug. 1893: 371).

Wood shaft clubs with interchangeable heads are outstanding, but exceptionally rare, collectibles. Other pre-1925 patents that mentioned or dealt specifically with interchangeable heads are listed next.

William Bussey and Joseph Pinder's 1892 patent includes the idea of using more than one blade on their adjustable loft iron. (See page 362.)

Edward A.E. MacMunn's British patent (No. 24,711) dated December 20, 1894, covered a metal iron head that used interchangeable face blocks (via a dovetailed groove in the face) to make a lofting iron, driving iron, cleek, mashie, putter, etc. This club was produced by Messrs. Joseph Braddell & Son, of Belfast, Ireland (*The Golfer*, 12 Jan. 1895: 29).

John and James Law's British patent (No. 9,433) dated April 27, 1903, allows for interchangeable heads. As designed, their adjustable loft iron was blatantly based on an Urquhart adjustable (see p. 360).

Frederick James Brown's British patent (No. 16,896) dated August 2, 1904, and U.S. patent (No. 796,802) dated August 8, 1905, covered a golf shaft adapted to fit multiple clubheads. The heads were to be carried on a special belt when not in use.

Albert L. Emens's U.S. patent (No. 782,955) dated February 21, 1905, covered interchangeable clubheads with an attaching mechanism at the top of the hosel.

David and Kenneth Roberts's British patent (No. 3,365) dated February 9, 1914, and U.S. patent (No. 1,135,621) dated April 13, 1915, covered interchangeable and reversible clubheads. As designed, one clubhead could provide two different face angles, depending on whether the head was attached right-side-up or upside-down.

Frederick Addis's British patent (No. 151,505) dated November 24, 1919, covered a joint containing a spring at the bottom of the hosel and a double spring catch on the shaft. The catch comes out two slots on opposite sides of the hosel—to permit the use of interchangeable heads.

Henry Wilson's British patent (No. 164,970) dated June 25, 1920, covered a shaft screwed into a hosel that is threaded to accept interchangeable heads. The direction of the threads insures that striking a ball will only tighten the connection.

William Elliot's British patent (No. 214,466) dated May 1, 1923, covered an adjustable loft, interchangeable iron head. It shows a wing nut on the back of a bulb-shaped hosel (round at the bottom when viewed from the toe) through which a stem from the head passes.

The next patents date after 1925, when steel shafts became legal under USGA rules. Because patents do not always state a shaft preference, some of these clubs might allow for, or have been produced with, metal shafts.

Louis V. Barach's U.S. patent (No. 1,559,299) dated October 27, 1925, covered a shaft screwed into a metal hosel on a wood allowing the use of interchangeable heads.

Lester L. Bourke's U.S. patent (No. 1,623,523) dated April 5, 1927, covered a shaft using a bayonet-type joint on two sides of the hosel—to receive corresponding wood and iron heads.

Leon D. Brooks's U.S. patent (No. 1,650,183) dated November 22, 1927, covered an adjustable length wood shaft used with interchangeable clubheads. As designed, the outer surface atop a slit hosel is threaded so a ferrule on the shaft can screw onto the hosel and hold the head in place. The length of the shaft can be changed by adjusting the grip up or down.

Norman D. Mattison's U.S. patent (No. 1,676,270) dated July 10, 1928, covered a metal shaft practice club with interchangeable heads. As drawn, adjustable stops extend through the shaft and are accessed on the outside of the shaft. Sliding weights are inside the shaft. When the club is swung, audible clicks occur to inform the user of correct tempo.

Herbert Hartley's British patent (No. 325,677) dated January 31, 1929, describes a club with interchangeable head capability and a shaft that converted into a walking stick by means of interchangeable parts.

Steel shaft clubs with interchangeable heads vastly outnumber their wood shaft counterparts.

LIBERTY D. HOLDEN
ALIGNMENT ROD PUTTER

The mechanical aspect of the putter pictured is quite simple: screw in the alignment rod before using the club, then unscrew it when finished.

Liberty Dean Holden, of Cleveland, Ohio, received both a U.S. patent (No. 653,023) dated July 3, 1900, and a British patent (No. 10,051) dated May 31, 1900, that covered a removable rod screwed into the center of the blade back. According to his British patent, acquired by using the services of chartered patent agent Alfred J. Boult, the direction rod was:

preferably so placed that when the club is properly held in addressing the ball this rod is horizontal. [Furthermore, the] direction rod is made removable for two reasons—

first, so that it may be more conveniently carried in said bag, and, second, so that it will not be liable to become bent or broken when not in use.

The back of the putter pictured is marked "Lockner \ Warranted Hand Forged \ Putter" and "Oxford" in a clever trademark used by James Sherlock, the well-known and popular professional at Oxford University between 1895 and 1908. This putter is of the Smith neck anti-shank variety, complete with the extra weight on the toe.

Prior to Holden, Robert Ramsbottom developed another type of alignment rod:

Mr. Ramsbottom . . . [from] Manchester, is bringing out a new putter. It is of the ordinary type, but on the upper edge of the head a "pointer" or sight is fixed, set at right angles to the face. This secures perfect alignment with the hole, and when allowance has to be made for bias of the ground the extent of the allowance is plainly perceivable. It is applicable to wooden putters as well as metal, and will be a very useful adjunct to approach irons, as it is much more accurate in indicating the line of the stroke than the plain surface of an ordinary club (Golf, 9 Oct. 1896: 68).

An attachable alignment aid sold separately was also tried:

Mr. C.V. Childs of 5, Laurence Pountney Hill, E.C. is the inventor of an ingenious little arrangement which he calls the 'Inspiration' putter attachment . . . . It consists of a concave rubber disc attached to a vulcanite pointer, the whole bearing a close resemblance to the mouthpiece of a pipe. It is attached to the back of the putter by simple pressure on the suction principle, the metal being preferably slightly greased beforehand. A white line runs along the vulcanite to guide the eye, and the claim is that it is easier to keep the putter head exactly in the true line at right angles to the putt (Golf Illustrated, 29 Mar. 1901: 276).

HOWARD E. BAACK
"TRU-LINE"
ALIGNMENT ROD PUTTER

Following Liberty Holden and his removable alignment rod putter, Howard E. Baack designed a similar putter but included a place in the putter head to store the rod when not in use. As seen in the upper picture, the alignment rod screws into the end of the toe when not in use.

On February 14, 1928, Baack received a U.S. patent (No. 1,659,231) that covered the putter pictured. In his patent, applied for on April 30, 1927, Baack embellishes the obvious feature of his putter to an inordinate degree. Instead of simply saying that his putter includes a removable alignment rod that, when not in use, can fit inside the head, he resorts to the following turgid exposition:

The present invention contemplates the provision of directional finder means to enable extremely accurate manipulation of the club so as to effect bee-line directional movement of the ball which results from the correct disposition of the club face.

One object of the present invention is the provision of means to enable the more accurate manipulation of golf clubs.

Another object is to provide means which indicates the position in which a golf club is to be held prior to imparting motion to a ball.

Still another object is to provide means in association with a club head which will indicate the direction in which the ball is to be driven.

A further object is to provide direction indicator means capable of ready association and disassociation with a club head.

A still further object is to provide means movably associated with a club head to enable the selective use thereof as a direction indicator.

Still a further object is the provision of means adjustably associated with a club head to enable the use thereof as a direction indicator without effecting the weight of the club.

Other objects and advantages will appear from the following description . . . .

The club on this page is marked "Tru-Line \ Putter \ Pat App For \ Patent Eng. Co. \ Wrigley Bldg \ Chicago" on the back of the blade. Although this putter dates from the end of the wood shaft era, it nevertheless represents an ingenious, elusive, and wonderful collectible.

GEORGE A. REES

"'REES' WIZARD PUTTER," ALIGNMENT ROD

Produced only briefly, "Rees' Wizard Putter" stands as a testimony to the creativity of the golfing mind. Forget its effectiveness or its lack thereof, this club is truly ingenious!

As seen here and on the opposite page, the Rees Wizard has a telescoping alignment rod that fits inside the head when not in use. To deploy the alignment rod, simply push down the plate on the back of the bronze head and watch the spring-loaded rod automatically swing out into position. After the plate is returned to its fixed position, thereby covering the cavity which held the alignment rod, the rod can be extended to three times its collapsed length. A small spring-loaded ball bearing recessed into the head, underneath the plate, puts outward pressure on the plate to hold it in place.

On February 29, 1916, George A. Rees of Chicago, Illinois, received a U.S. patent (No. 1,173,384) that covered this putter. Marked " 'Rees' Wizard Putter \ Patents Pending" on the back of its head, the Rees Wizard Putter with a "head of bronze" was advertised as follows:

Perfect your putting by the use of Rees' Wizard Putter. The merits of the club must be apparent to you from merely looking at the illustrations. The indicator enables one to accurately place the club for the putting stroke and to strike perfectly. The result is a hole-out with one to two less strokes on the putting greens, where the majority of games are lost. Space here will not permit of describing its many advantages in making every one play better golf. Price $6.00 —if not satisfactory you can return club in good condition and money will be refunded. Manufactured and sold by Duntley Products Sales Co. Chicago, IL. (Golfers Magazine, May 1915: 75).

In his patent, applied for on October 26, 1914, Rees states that the alignment rod was designed primarily for practice:

My invention concerns itself with the provision of means which are of a disappearing nature so that it may be used during practice games and so that this instructional device may be collapsed into its disappearing position when playing regular or match games.

In addition to the pre-1930 mechanical alignment aid putters already discussed on the previous pages, others are recorded in the U.S. and British patent records presented next.

William Robertson received a British patent (No. 12,026) dated July 3, 1900, and another (No. 2,840) dated February 9, 1901, that include the option of providing either a fixed alignment aid or a pivoting alignment rod on the back of the head. Robertson received a U.S. patent (No. 697,542) dated April 15, 1902, that covered these same features. As produced, Robertson's putter has a short semicircular alignment guide, integral with the back of the head, positioned flush with the top of the blade. Robertson also received a British patent (No. 109,891) dated November 30, 1916, that, in dealing with the design of a sole-plate made thicker at the rear than at the front, includes the option of attaching an angularly adjustable alignment pointer to the crown.

James Ross Brown, of water iron fame, also included the option of using an alignment rod in two patents. His British patent (No. 14,608) dated June 29, 1904, which describes his water irons, mentions the possibility of attaching a swiveling pointer to the neck. Brown's British patent (No. 25,146) dated November 19, 1904, which describes his swan neck putter, includes the possibility of attaching a rotating pointer to the foremost part of the hosel extending out over the head, the pointer being able to rotate from vertical when not in use to horizontal when in use.

Josiah Byram Millet's British patent (No. 10,863) dated March 24, 1905, covered an alignment sight that even unskilled people could readily

attach to the backs of ordinary blade putters. This add-on item consists of a pivoting arm, which could swing out ninety degrees, inside a shallow rectangular box.

William Guy Ruggles's U.S. patent (No. 1,327,171) dated January 6, 1920, covered a mirror mounted on the top of a putter head. This oval mirror, which could be either fixed in place or adjusted via a ball and socket joint, sits at an angle so the golfer can view the target in the mirror when addressing the ball.

Edward Vassallo Hartford's U.S. patent (No. 1,331,499) dated February 24, 1920, describes, among other things, an alignment aid mounted on a putter. A pointer atop a vertical base on the top of the head can swivel out over the top of the ball. The USGA museum, in Far Hills, New Jersey, has one of these—a fine piece.

Just prior to receiving this patent, Hartford also produced at least one putter with what was termed a "sword blade"—an alignment rod that extended approximately twelve inches directly behind the head:

First there is the sword blade attached to the back of the wooden head, which is supposed to snap back out of the way by a simple pressure.

This sword back is claimed to hold the putter head squarely at right angles in the line of play when the golfer squats down and sights along the aiming rod and then tips the club back on its sole preparatory to hitting the ball. The length of [the] aiming rod is not given, but it extends out of the top of the head about a foot (Golfing, 28 May, 1918: 10).

Luther Baugh's U.S. patent (No. 1,556,062) dated October 6, 1925, covered attaching a lens to the top of the clubhead. The lens would refract inside its housing so the target could be viewed, complete with cross hairs, through another lens aimed up at the golfer. (The only thing missing appears to be the trigger . . .)

Sir James Henderson's British patent (No. 273,546) dated October 18, 1926, covered a practice device that consisted of mirrors within a clubhead. When not in use, the mirrors could be removed and replaced with compensating weights.

Currently, only Robertson and Hartford are known to have produced the alignment devices decribed in their patents. This is consistent with the exceeding rarity of any club with a mechanical alignment aid.

For *fixed* alignment aids, see pages 432-435.

There are many patent drivers, each variety aiming at the introduction of one or more advantages by the peculiarity of its construction. One point almost universally claimed by the patentees is long driving power, due to some peculiarity of balance, material, or general conformation; but endless are the means by which this end, along with the others claimed, is to be attained. There is the driver with "ballast chambers" for regulating the weight of the head; the indiarubber-cushioned face; the double-ended hammer, which if adopted, would go far to justify that opprobrious cry of "Scotch Croquet" which is such a favourite with the Philistinic anti-golfer; and doubtless the introduction of the extra long carry driver, with a dynamite cartridge in the face, is only a matter of time (Golf, 27 Dec. 1895: 338).

It was several more years before somebody designed a golf club with a dynamite cartridge in the face (see Hollingsworth patent description on page 404), but George Frederick Wilford, with his "XL" adjustable spring-face driver, sought to achieve the same explosive effect . . . without the worry of how to set the club down.

As pictured, the spring-loaded face of Wilford's driver juts out in front of the head itself. The spring behind the face winds around a threaded rod inside the head. One end of the rod screws into the back of the face;

the other, appearing as the slotted head of a large screw, is visible in a recess in the back of the head. Turning the rod changes the tension of the spring, which, in turn, can either increase or decrease the resistance given to the face; the idea being that when the face strikes the ball, the face will recoil and then spring forward, thereby adding distance to the shot. The concept behind Wilford's club sounds great in theory, but was just the opposite in practice. Nevertheless, Wilford protected his idea.

George Wilford received a British patent (No. 17,790) dated February 8, 1912, that covered his spring-loaded clubface. According to his patent, the object of his invention was to provide "improvements in the means for guiding the movable face and in the general arrangement of the parts." To this end, Wilford designed his club as follows:

The head of the club and the sliding face are made of an aluminum compound for the purpose of securing the necessary strength and lightness. The head of the club is in the form of a hollow casing provided with guides for the face to slide in, and the face is provided with a hollow extension which is fitted to slide in the head guides. The face is normally held in its most forward position by means of a spring which is arranged between the inner surfaces

of the head and the face and is mounted upon a pin [rod] which is screwed into a boss carried by the movable face.

To ensure smooth operation, the guides were designed to prevent "twisting and locking of the movable face as it moves to and fro in the head." While the guides helped the mechanism work, the club did not work in the marketplace The example pictured, marked "XL \ Patent No 17790 \ 1912" inside a circle atop the aluminum head and "Applied For" next to the circle, is the only one known.

Charles Clark's U.S. patent (No. 769,939) dated September 13, 1904, describes a wood with a round, spring-loaded disc set into the center of the face. It is not known whether Clark's club was ever produced.

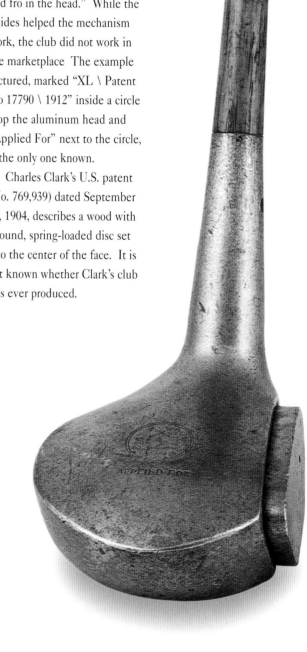

STEPHEN COLLINS & HAROLD PEARCE
SPRING-FACE DRIVER, MEASURING MECHANISM

The Honorable Stephen Ogle Henn Collins, of London, England, and Harold Vyvyan Pearce, of Seaford, East Sussex, received a British patent (No. 28,688) dated December 20, 1911, that covered the ingenious golf club pictured. Not only does this club register the force of the golfer's swing when striking a ball, it also indicates the point of impact relative to the center of the clubface.

There are four springs behind the face, which extends well out in front of the rest of the head. Attached to the back of the face are two long metal rods, one behind the toe and one behind the heel. These rods run parallel to each other, at right angles to the face, and extend straight back to the rear of the head where they are spring-loaded. To allow rearward movement for each rod, the end of each rod (the rear third of which is reduced in thickness) is actually outside a metal plate on the back of the head and bent to a 90 degree angle. Halfway back inside the head, the rods are notched or "toothed" in order to hold a sprocket between them. A shaft extends up from the center of the sprocket and attaches to the circular dial

(metal disk) visible on the top of the head. A slot in the top of the head allows for the rearward movement of the circular dial.

If the golfer strikes the ball directly in the center of the spring-loaded face, both rods inside the head are pushed back an equal distance and the circular dial on the top of the head moves back but does not rotate. However, if the golfer strikes the ball on the heel or the toe, one of the two spring-loaded rods will move back more than the other. This causes the sprocket to rotate, which in turn causes the circular dial to rotate as it moves back.

After striking the ball, the golfer can check the results of his or her swing. After moving, the circular disk is held in place by two small plungers (the tops of which are visible just in front of the circular disk) that fit into the ratchet teeth atop both parallel rods. Pulling up on each plunger returns each spring-loaded rod to its original position. This resets the circular disk.

Prior to receiving their 1911 patent, Collins and Pearce had received a British patent (No. 18,616) dated August 12, 1909. This patent was the first for a golf club with a built-in measuring

device. The club described in this patent is similar to the one shown but uses a different internal mechanism. Its spring-face rests much closer to the head, and a needle on the top of the head registers the results on a grid underneath it. The needle is attached to a rod that can rotate and move backwards in a slot in the head. This invention also received a U.S. patent (No. 1,039,491) dated September 24, 1912. The only Collins and Pearce indicating driver known to the author is the one shown.

CHARLES LEVEN
THE "LEVEN" PRACTICE DRIVER, W/MEASURING MECHANISM

Charles Leven's practice driver, covered under a British patent (No. 186,210) dated July 28, 1921, has a built-in mechanism that measures how far a golfer's *practice* swing *would have* hit a golf ball. This mechanism, located in the top of the head, operates on the principle of centrifugal force and, according to his patent, includes:

a chamber in which is mounted a slide or guide in which is movable a weight against the action of a spring.

When the club is swung, the weight inside the head moves towards the toe. The harder the club is swung, the farther the weight moves. A ratchet device then locks the weight at the most distant position it attains. A small triangular mark, visible in the top of the head, registers the weight's movement against yardage measurements printed on the mechanism's cover plate. (The cover plate is open down the center so that the triangular mark, which moves underneath it, can be seen.) Pushing a small button on the back of the head resets the mechanism and moves the triangular mark (indicator) back to zero.

The cover plate on this almost unused Leven driver is marked "The 'Leven' Practice Driver \ Patent Applied For," along with the yardage measurements "0, 75, 100, 125, 150, 175, 200, 225, 250, 275, 300."

The mechanism in this club works well. In the picture, the triangular indicator is pointing to the 200 mark, the result of the

author's inside-out swing. Leven Practice Drivers are sometimes found with broken or frozen mechanisms. Because Leven drivers are not seen very often, even those with broken mechanisms are collectible. Working examples are naturally valued well above nonworking examples.

Leven's original British patent also describes an alternative mechanism for measuring the effectiveness of a golfer's practice swing. This mechanism, which also operated on centrifugal force, was located in the shaft. The author has never seen such a club, but *has* seen a Leven patent iron with the measuring mechanism inside the hosel. This iron, a mashie produced by Hendry and Bishop, is marked " 'Leven' Pat. No. 186,210." To indicate yardage, a slot on the side of the hosel is marked from 30 to 120 in increments of ten.

To further protect the ideas covered under his British patent, Leven received two U.S. patents. His patent (No. 1,471,794) dated October 23, 1923, covered the shaft mechanism, and his patent (No. 1,492,039) dated April 29, 1924, covered the head mechanism.

In the realm of clubs with measuring devices, a few others were patented. It is not known whether either of the following clubs was ever produced.

Frank Searle's British patent (No. 233,529) dated May 24, 1924, covered a club with a marker (pencil, chalk, or similar) that was recessed into the crown and emerged at the sole. When

swung over a piece of linoleum, Searle's club would leave a mark indicating the direction of the swing and whether the head passed over the spot where the ball would have been.

A U.S. patent (No. 976,176) dated November 22, 1910, covered a club that, should one ever be located, would qualify as my teenage son's favorite. This

patent, granted to Merrill W. Hollingsworth of Santa Barbara, California, covered a club with an *audible* indicating mechanism. If the ball struck a disc in the center of the face, the disc would trigger the explosion of a replaceable cartridge located inside the back of the head! A bad hit produced no explosion. Hey, what kid wouldn't love such a club!

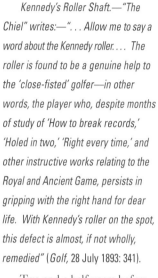

Kennedy's Roller Shaft.—"The Chiel" writes:—". . . Allow me to say a word about the Kennedy roller. . . . The roller is found to be a genuine help to the 'close-fisted' golfer—in other words, the player who, despite months of study of 'How to break records,' 'Holed in two,' 'Right every time,' and other instructive works relating to the Royal and Ancient Game, persists in gripping with the right hand for dear life. With Kennedy's roller on the spot, this defect is almost, if not wholly, remedied" (Golf, 28 July 1893: 341).

Two and a half years before printing the above review of Kennedy's Roller Shaft, *Golf* briefly mentioned a revolving grip:

Then there is a club with a revolving grip for the right hand—a heroic remedy which may meet cases which the ordinary golfing doctors have pronounced hopeless (14 Nov. 1890:137)

This mention, when originally published in 1890, followed a description of Brand's celluloid clubhead printed on the same page, and apparently with good reason. The revolving grip pictured near left, in perfect working condition, is found on a Robert Brand celluloid head driver. The revolving cylinder appears to be made out of celluloid, which is not surprising given the celluloid head (see p. 300).

Gilbert Lewis, an engineer living near Manchester, England, patented a revolving grip similar to the one shown in the middle. Dated January 31, 1896, Lewis's British patent (No. 2235) covered a grip with a revolving sleeve of aluminum covered with whipping. This sleeve, located between "two fixed washers" on the lower half of the grip, allowed a slight sliding action up and down the shaft. The upper half of the grip was to be "covered with leather, slightly flattened where the fingers grip, the fastening being curved to suit the fingers" (*Golf Illustrated*, 12 Jan. 1900: 37). The grip pictured does not have an aluminum sleeve covered with whipping nor leather wrapped around the upper half of the grip. It does have, however, a metal cylinder between two fixed washers and a slight sliding action to the cylinder. The upper portion, which was made from a wood block, is slightly flattened and curved to suit the fingers. This grip is on a splice neck driver stamped "Hutchison" on the crown. A steel tube, over which the metal cylinder revolves, extends down through the center of the handle.

Three years after patenting his grip, Lewis admitted that it was counterproductive:

After some trial with this apparatus, I am convinced it would not be found of any advantage to an old golfer . . . . I have given to the sleeve a slight sliding action as well as the twisting. The result is an uncertainty of grip which confuses rather than aids the player (*Golf Illustrated*, 12 Jan. 1900: 37).

Aside from the two roller grips pictured, the only other such grip known to the author is found on a 1920s driver marked "Reflex \ Manufacturing Co. \ Cin'ti, O" (Cincinnati, Ohio). The Reflex roller grip, pictured far left, was made with twenty revolving plastic washers on the lower half.

STERLING W. DAWSON
ADJUSTABLE GRIP PUTTER

In the 1907 British Amateur, Harold Hilton, then a two-time British Open and Amateur champion, used a very unorthodox style of putting:

Hilton adopted a new style in putting. He placed his left hand in his pocket, grasped the putter low down with the right hand, and putted single-handed. It was ungraceful but effective (Golfing, 6 June 1907: 20).

Twenty years after Hilton tried putting with just his right hand, Sterling W. Dawson patented a putter that provides another way to give the right hand more control. Furthermore, as specified in Dawson's U.S. patent (No. 1,618,640) dated February 22, 1927, the grip on this putter can shift up or down!

Dawson's grip (pictured above) is designed with three basic parts: a wood shaft, an aluminum tube covering the grip end of the shaft, and a hard rubber or celluloid sleeve covering most of the aluminum tube.

The wood shaft has two flat spots, each measuring 3 1/2 inches long, centered underneath the front and back of the grip.

The aluminum tube covers the entire grip end of the shaft except for the two flat spots, which are left exposed. The aluminum tube is 3 1/2 inches longer than the celluloid sleeve.

The celluloid sleeve has a 3 1/2 inch range of movement up or down the aluminum tube and two small openings, one on the front and one on the back. No matter what its position, the sleeve always exposes a portion of the shaft's flat spots. To prevent the sleeve from revolving, a small "pin" on the inside of the sleeve extends into a lengthwise slot in the aluminum tube.

The adjustable length of Dawson's grip allowed the golfer to move the sleeve:

up or down to expose various portions of the flat spots, as determined by the length of putt about to be made.

Dawson also designed his grip to be held in a unique manner of his own devising. To hold Dawson's adjustable grip properly (assuming one is right-handed), place it snugly between the index and middle finger of the left hand. A portion of the middle finger fits into the opening along the back of the sleeve and against a flat spot on the shaft. The tip of the thumb, which is on the same side of the shaft as the index finger, fits into the sleeve's top opening and against the other flat spot. The index finger wraps over the tip of the thumb. The rest of the fingers then wrap around the grip. In this fashion the back of the left hand aims directly at the target, the palm of the hand wraps around the grip, and the wrist and arm run parallel to the length of the shaft. The right hand grips the club in normal fashion below the left hand. Gripping the club this way supposedly allowed the left hand to stay aligned to the hole while giving the right hand control of the stroke.

Dawson, believing in his grip method, notes in his patent:

I have found that when the shaft of a putter is gripped by a player in the manner just mentioned, excellent results can be secured, as is attested by the fact that some of the leading professional and amateur golfers have adopted this manner of gripping in their putting.

Dawson's movable grip, marked "Pat. February 22 - 1927," is shown above. A brass putter head, marked "Dawson Golf Co. \ Chicago" on the sole, is attached to the other end of the shaft (not shown).

Located in England, the Wilkinson Sword Company produced a grip distantly related to Dawson's. Wilkinson's "Sword Grip" driver provided a flat oval grip for the left hand to grasp along with a depression for the left thumb (*Golf Illustrated*, 25 Feb. 1910: 192).

FREDERICK H. FORD
FITTING CLUB, ADJUSTABLE GRIP

The primary object of my invention is to provide means for enabling a golf player or dealer in golf clubs to quickly and accurately determine which of a series of golf clubs will best suit the requirements of the player due to his height, length of arms and characteristic posture.

More specifically stated, my object is to provide an adjustable golf club to be used for testing purposes and which is made variable in length, (preferably length of shaft), and provided with an index suitably calibrated with reference to standard clubs of differing lengths, whereby, when the test club has been properly adjusted in accordance with the requirements of an individual player, the club best adapted for such player's requirements will be indicated by said index (Frederick H. Ford, U.S. Patent No. 1,943,066).

Frederick H. Ford's "fitting club," with its adjustable handle, is pictured. The grip itself can move up or down, thereby varying the length of the shaft. According to Ford's patent, this adjustable grip enabled:

. . . a player to hold the club head in proper position, or swing it naturally into such position, readjusting its length, as often as may be necessary until assured that the club is of the proper length to suit his requirements. The index will then indicate to him, his dealer, or to an instructor, the length of the golf club which he should select.

The exterior of Ford's adjustable grip consists of a metal tube with a setscrew. Underneath the tube, the shaft is flat on two opposing sides. One side has index marks, and the other has a metal strip fastened to it. The setscrew, flat on its end, extends through the tubular grip and fastens against the metal strip. Loosening the screw allows the grip to be repositioned; tightening the screw locks the grip in place.

The length of the club shown is adjustable between 39 3/4 inches and 44 3/8 inches. The index marks consist of the letters "A," "B," "C," and "D" spaced at one-inch intervals and the numbers "1," "2," and "3" spaced at quarter-inch intervals between each letter.

Ford's patent also covered the idea of adjusting the neck in order to vary the lie of the club, so that golfers could experiment with what they might want. It is not known whether a wood shaft club with an adjustable lie feature was ever produced.

The club pictured, marked "Pat Applied For" across the measuring marks under the grip and "Shaler" on the crown (made by The Shaler Company, of Milwaukee and Waupun, Wisconsin), is the only example of Ford's club known to the author. Because Ford, of Waupun, Wisconsin, applied for his patent on May 29, 1930, this club was made between that time and January 9, 1934, when his patent was granted. In spite of its coming at the end of the wood shaft era, this club is one of the more interesting wood shaft clubs created.

407

The true art is not
the execution of difficult
shots, but the power to
leave oneself easy shots.

(*Golf Illustrated*, 3 June 1910: 221)

Multipurpose Clubs

This chapter examines nonadjustable clubs that were usable in more than one way. Such multipurpose clubs usually have two or more faces designed to strike the ball.

In general, clubs with more than one face are termed multiface clubs. Clubs that have two opposing faces (the faces are on opposite sides of the head) are specifically referred to as duplex clubs and were often usable both left- and right-handed, but not always.

The first person to patent a multipurpose club was Sir Walter Dalrymple. His British patent (No. 16,148) dated September 9, 1892, covered a duplex club with a hammer-type head that was made in three different models (see p. 412).

Charles Reginald Blathwayt was the next person to patent a multipurpose club. His British patent (No. 9,522) dated May 15, 1894, covered a duplex iron that could be used both left- and right-handed. In his patent, Blathwayt designed a triangular-shaped head, the sole and both faces making up the three sides. He included the option of squaring off the toe, so his iron could, if desired, have a third face and be used to play a ball out of a wheel rut or similar situation. He also included the option of integrating wood blocks into the head, so the head could have one or more wooden striking faces. The author has seen an unmarked 1890s duplex iron similar to the one outlined in Blathwayt's patent. One face of this duplex iron was designed for putting, the other face was lofted for chipping. A wedge of wood was

inserted into the sole and filled the area between the two blades. The wood was held in place by a few rivets running through the lower portion of the blade.

Following Dalrymple and Blathwayt, other inventors received patents for multipurpose clubs during the wood shaft era. Most of these clubs are discussed in this chapter. However, two particularly novel clubs not mentioned herein were patented by Charles W. Dayton of Manhattan, New York, and John H. Dwight of Des Moines, Iowa.

Dayton's club, presented in a U.S. patent (No. 1,436,579) dated November 21, 1922, was a multiface backwards putter (see p. 215). As illustrated in Dayton's patent, this putter provides a face on both the front and back of a mallet head along with a comparatively small face on the end of the head, at the base of the hosel. Dayton's putter was usable left-handed, right-handed, or croquet style. Dwight's club, presented in a U.S. patent (No. 1,441,492) dated January 9, 1923, was a rocker sole approach iron with a second blade perpendicularly attached to a squared off toe. This second blade, which was centered on the toe and slightly wider than a golf ball, allowed Dwight's approach iron to also be used as a putter. It is not known if either club, Dayton's or Dwight's, was ever produced.

Needless to say, not all multipurpose clubs were patented. In fact, the oldest "unique" golf club known is a duplex wood that was never patented. This club is presented on the next two pages.

UNKNOWN MAKER
DUPLEX WOOD

The oldest known golf club created with a unique design and nontraditional function is pictured on this and the following page. Although this club might loosely be referred to as a "patent club," it was made *long* before 1876, when the first patent for a golf club was issued.

This duplex club is one of approximately sixty clubs once collected by Harry B. Wood, a prominent figure in the world of collectible golf clubs (see p. 106). Using his collection of clubs, balls, and other golf-related artifacts, Wood authored the first book on golf collectibles, *Golfing Curios and the Like*, first published in 1910. Articles about Wood and his clubs were published in various periodicals of his day. A picture of Harry B. Wood's collection of clubs, including the duplex wood pictured here, is found in the June 1914 issue of *Golf Illustrated and Outdoor America* (23).

The club pictured was designed for either right- or left-handed use. The tag Wood attached to the shaft, a portion of which is visible at the top of the picture, contains his brief comment about the club:

Combination Club - Driver, Brassie and Putter --- Specially made for an ambidextrous player. About 1885.

The tag is quite faded because this club was displayed for many years directly underneath an electric light in the top of Wood's display case.

Wood's commentary is helpful, but his "about 1885" estimation is highly inaccurate. Harry Wood collected many wonderful golf clubs, yet, as one might expect from such an early golf club collector, he made some glaring mistakes when dating them. For example, Wood states that the Anderson crescent head iron included in his collection was "patented by Anderson, Edinburgh about 1870" (Wood 1910, plate VII). In reality, it was patented on May 28, 1892, and introduced to the public in April of 1893 (*Golf*, 7 Apr. 1893: 58). (Anderson's iron is discussed in detail on page 188.)

Besides being unmarked, this duplex club has too many early and otherwise unique characteristics to name 1885 as the year it was made. For example:

This club has an ash shaft, and the shaft is obviously hand split—one can feel its "sides" when turning it in a closed hand. Both the ash shaft and the evidence of hand construction are normally found in clubs dating from the early 1800s or before.

A socket joint unlike any other was used to connect the head to the shaft. As can be seen above, the tip of the shaft was split and then wedged with a separate piece of wood, to prevent the head from coming off the shaft. Furthermore, a ridge integrally crafted around the shaft directly above the head kept the head from working its way up the shaft. When the socket joint was introduced and patented in 1891 by Robert Anderson, the tip of the shaft was tapered and simply glued in place, and the top of the neck was bound with whipping. Also, this club is center-shafted, with the tip of the shaft visible underneath the toe.

The grip is made from two hard-finished pieces of leather sewn together. (The hand stitches are clearly visible in the picture at the bottom of the opposite page.) In the mid to late 1800s, leather was neither so precious nor rare that two pieces would be sewn together to make a grip. Furthermore, throughout the 1800s sueded sheepskin grips were the standard.

The grip does not have an underlisting. Instead, the wood shaft is larger underneath the grip and the leather is attached directly to the wood. This can be seen in the picture by comparing the thickness of the butt end of the shaft with the area where the grip begins. Clubs from the 1800s always have an underlisting, usually made from wool, wrapped around the shaft underneath the grip.

The end of the shaft is cut square, a characteristic associated with many clubs made *before* 1800. Clubmakers during the 1800s bevelled the edge around the butt end of the shaft.

Thin steel bands are fastened around the face. The only other golf club with metal bands around its face is the circa 1890 Alexander wood presented on the following page. Alexander's metal bands are *much* different from those on Wood's duplex club.

Top to bottom, this club is distinct from all other clubs created in the 1880s or later. Furthermore, the characteristics of this club are not the product of an untrained hobbyist. The skilled craftsmanship that produce these early traits clearly date this club to the early 1800s, if not earlier.

The idea of a club being both left- and right-handed is understandable given the immovable obstacles golfers may encounter. However, duplex clubs were also designed for driving. In 1908 William Butler, when reminiscing on "old-time" golf, recalled:

a two-faced driving putter for driving against the wind, which just skimmed the ball off the ground, the lead being in the sole (Golfing, 6 Aug.: 32).

The idea of making a duplex club for an ambidextrous player is unusual but not unknown. In mentioning Frank Johnston's new dual face putter, the May 2, 1901 issue of *Golfing* notes:

Ambidextrous golfers, whose number is not legion, may like to possess themselves of a specimen (26).

An ambidextrous golfer from Australia was briefly mentioned in the January 17, 1902 issue of *Golf Illustrated*:

One of our suburban clubs, says the Sydney Mail, is proud to claim a player who is unique so far as I have heard or seen. He is a well-known professional man, and ambidextrous.

So he has two separate sets of clubs—right and left—each in a separate bag and with a separate caddie to carry them, and he calls on his right or left caddie just as he feels inclined, or as the lie suggests (43).

Given the exquisite uniqueness of Wood's duplex club, its drawbacks are so minor they are almost nonexistent. The 42-inch ash shaft has a small crack, indicated by the whipping applied to the shaft. Also, one of the steel face bands is loose in one spot. Neither of these imperfections is a problem. They are minor in nature, provide evidence of the club's age and purpose, and, because there are no other clubs like this one, are easily accepted.

Harry Wood's duplex club could easily be considered one of the premier collectible clubs known. It dates well back into the feather ball era, is beautifully crafted, is the earliest specialty club of any type, and is the only such club.

SIR WALTER DALRYMPLE
THE "HAMMER" DUPLEX CLUBS

R. FORGAN & SON
DUPLEX CLUB

Andrew Kirkaldy And The "Hammer" Club. —It was not to be expected that professional golfers would take kindly to Sir Walter Dalrymple's new club. The feeling seems pretty general that the latest patent will not be adopted by first, or even second-rate golfers, although, doubtless, many will be disposed to give the new venture a trial, for the novelty, if for nothing else. Sir Walter was a prominent figure at Muirfield last week, hammer club in hand, industriously engaged in singing its merits. Rebuffs might naturally be expected, but probably the severest came from Andrew Kirkaldy, the well known St. Andrews professional. Scene— Front of the Club-house, Friday, 5:30 p.m., (immediately after close of play). Sir Walter approaches a group of St. Andrews professionals who look considerably down-hearted.

"Bad day for the professionals," says Sir Walter to Kirkaldy. "Better luck next time, sir," quoth Andrew. "By the way," says Sir Walter in his blandest tones, "seen my new club?" holding out the hammer. "Ca' that a club?" sneered Kirkaldy, "I'd siner play wi' a tea-spin!" Kirkaldy turns on his heel in disgust and Sir Walter retires amid a general titter.–Haddingtonshire Courier (Golf, 7 Oct. 1892: 52).

Shown above, left and center, are two of Sir Walter Hamilton Dalrymple's "hammer" clubs. The Baronet of North Berwick, Dalrymple received a British patent (No. 16,148) dated September 9, 1892, that covered his "double faced hammer headed club." Dalrymple felt that the hammer shape of his clubhead would give wood:

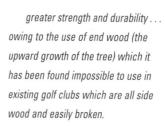

greater strength and durability . . . owing to the use of end wood (the upward growth of the tree) which it has been found impossible to use in existing golf clubs which are all side wood and easily broken.

Dalrymple's patent describes three different models of his duplex club. Each model was designed to function as two different clubs. His first model (above center) provides a driver and a brassey. This model was to be made of:

wood with a sheathing of brass secured by screws so that a brass sole is presented to the ground whichever face of the club is used.

His second model (not shown on this page) consists of an iron and a "bleek." Dalrymple refers to a "bleek" twice. He either meant "cleek" or used

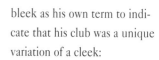

bleek as his own term to indicate that his club was a unique variation of a cleek:

In this case [the iron/bleek] the two faces and the sole may be formed as one brass casting; the central part being wood.

His third model (above left) consists of a mashie and a putter:

In this case the whole of the head may be cast in brass with the exception of the part marked "e" [illustrated as a circle in both sides of the head] which may be of wood or other light material.

According to Dalrymple, passing the shaft through the center of the head at right angles and fitting it "in the same way as the handle of any ordinary hammer or mallet" would help his club play better:

By passing the shaft at right angles through the centre of the head . . . the point of impact is in line with the shaft thereby securing accuracy of aim and greater driving power also it is also impossible for the club to turn in the hands of the player. By the said formation of the head a universal lie is obtained or in other words the angle of the sob [sic; sole] or base suits every one be they short or tall.

Dalrymple's hammer club was short lived:

The Dalrymple "Hammer" club was the comet of last season, and has now disappeared from the firmament (a few copies remaining in Hutchison's may be picked up by collectors of curiosities) (Golf, 27 Jan. 1893: 315).

Today, Dalrymple clubs are difficult to locate and eminently collectible. The driver/brassie pictured (facing page), faintly marked Dalrymple's Patent \ J. Hutchison, North Berwick" on the top of the head is one of only two offered at auction. Approximately ten mashie/putters are known.

The aluminum club pictured on this page (right) and on the facing page (above right) is one of only two such genuine aluminum hammer-head clubs currently known. It is marked "Pat Applied For" on both sides of the head and "R. Forgan & Son \

St. Andrews" on the shaft. Despite being constructed differently from those discussed in Dalrymple's patent (the aluminum head is slightly bigger and the shaft is flared next to the head), this aluminum duplex club might be a Dalrymple club.

In August of 1892, Sir Walter Dalrymple applied for a British patent (No. 14,966) to cover "The amble-faced or hammer-headed golf club" (*Golf*, 16 Sep. 1892: 6). This application was abandoned. One month later, however, he applied for the patent (No. 16,148) that covered the hammer-head clubs previously discussed. Possibly the aluminum club pictured was his first effort. If so, this hammer-head club would be the earliest golf club ever made from aluminum. The first patent to mention the use of aluminum in constructing a clubhead, Ralph Nevile's British patent (No. 22,157) dated November 20, 1893, was applied for more than a year *after* Dalrymple first applied for a patent to cover a hammer-head club.

Two aluminum hammer-head clubs are known; both are stamped "R. Forgan & Son" on the shaft. This is in contrast to the clubs Dalrymple produced under his patent (No. 16,148).

These clubs, when they are found marked on either the head or shaft, bear the name of James Hutchison of North Berwick. It should be noted that Bennett Lang was the craftsman that Dalrymple actually employed to make his clubs:

Lang remained in Perth until 1892, when . . . [he accepted] an engagement in Ireland with the County Down Club at Newcastle, where he acted as professional during the summer season. He next sojourned to North Berwick, where he was employed by Sir W. Dalrymple in making various types of clubs which the Baronet patented. According to the agreement the work was done in the establishment of Jamie Hutchison (Baxter 1899, 35).

Because of the Forgan shaft stamp and the use of aluminum, the aluminum clubhead pictured was probably modeled after Dalrymple's and was assembled by either Forgan or one of his wholesale customers. Still, the similarities in style between these clubs, the fact that both of the known aluminum hammer-head clubs are marked "Pat. Applied For," and the fact that Dalrymple's first patent application was for a

hammer-headed club cannot be entirely dismissed.

The shafts extend through the heads of both the aluminum and brass duplex clubs. In order to spread the tip of the shaft and thereby tighten it to the head, a small brass wedge is driven into the tip of the Dalrymple shaft and a screw is screwed into the tip of the aluminum head shaft.

On November 2, 1894, Dalrymple filed a patent application (which he later abandoned) for a British patent (No. 21,036) to cover a unique spring-face club:

Sir Walter Hamilton Dalrymple . . . has invented an improvement on the golf club . . . . From what we hear regarding the nature of the patent club it seems that a piece of indiarubber or something of the kind is inserted in the face of the club at the point of impact of the ball when fairly struck and the spring of the indiarubber, which is raised like the side of a marble, gives the additional "go" to the ball. Mr. Macfie and Mr. A. Stuart have both tried the spring-face idea without much success. It remains to be seen whether . . . the true secret has now been discovered (Golf, 9 Nov. 1894: 160).

G. ALEXANDER
DUPLEX WOOD

Duplex woods were made in two different styles. One style allows one face to be used right-handed and the other face left-handed. The other style allows the golfer to use either of the striking faces when playing from one side of the ball, e.g. right-handed. Harry Wood's duplex club presented on pages 410-411 is usable either right- or left-handed. The Alexander wood pictured here, like the Dalrymple clubs just discussed, is usable only right-handed.

Alexander's duplex wood is modeled after a jeu de mail club. Jeu de mail was a French game, somewhat similar to golf, that "went out of fashion in the early eighteenth century" (Henderson 1979, 3). In Garden Smith's article "Jeu de Mail, Golf In The Making," he refers to a translation of *Academie des Jeux* published in 1739. *Academie des Jeux* contains a chapter on jeu de mail rules and instructions. After noting that jeu de mail was, indeed, somewhat similar to golf, Smith remarks that:

In Holland it developed or degenerated into Het Kolven, in England into Pell Mell and Croquet (Golf Illustrated, 22 Nov. 1907: 164-165).

Besides borrowing from jeu de mail, a few clubmakers during the 1890s borrowed from other games, such as shinty, billiards, cricket, and especially croquet, when experimenting with new club designs.

The club pictured, complete with a wide iron band around each end of the head, is marked "G. Alexander" on both sides of its head. Some collectors have attributed this club to George Alexander "the prominent British actor working in London during the 1890s" because he was a keen golfer whose name matched the club's, but it is more logical to attribute this club to one of two other "G. Alexanders" who were actually involved in the golf business. The Alexander who most likely made this club is referred to in J.H. Taylor's article "In My Early Days" published in 1950. In this article, Taylor, reminiscing about his youth at Westward Ho!, recalls a big professional tournament held to commemorate thirty years of golf on the links at Westward Ho! He notes that the top professionals:

were all Scotsmen, mostly attached to clubs in England, such as Peter Paxton, Douglas Rolland, Jack Burns, David Brown, George Alexander, and James Kay (Golf Illustrated, 19 Jan. 1950: 2047).

Taylor's article also includes a photo, captioned "A great photo of the early stars in 1889," taken at the time of this tournament. G. Alexander is identified along with Old Tom Morris, Charlie Gibson, Robert Simpson, John Allan, J.H. Taylor, Peter Paxton, David Brown, Ben Sayers, and others. Because this Alexander duplex club dates circa 1890, it seems likely that Taylor's G. Alexander—a Scottish professional who once worked at a club in England—made this club. This G. Alexander is believed to be the same George Alexander who worked as a professional at Douglas Park from at least 1902 until 1907 and at Cowglen from 1907 to 1909 (Jackson 1994, 1).

The other Alexander who might have made this club is the H.G. Alexander (who could even be the same Alexander just referred to) mentioned in the February 12, 1892 issue of *Golf*:

Mr. H.G. Alexander, of Fordwich, Kent, has sent two putters of his own design and manufacture to be reported on. One of the putters is the ordinary wooden putter with a smooth metal face. . . . The other putter is what may be described as a "convexo-plane cleek." The club has a convex, bulger-like surface towards the ball (342).

Similar to the jeu de mail clubs of old, the white grip on this club is bound at the top and bottom with a piece of red leather.

No matter who made this club, its rarity, intriguing style, and dubious abilities work together to create a handsome collectible of great merit.

WILLIE DUNN, JR.
DUPLEX PYRALIN WOOD

The Kempshall Mfg. Co., Arlington, N.J., ... has gotten out a new club, made with the Pyralin head, which is the double-faced club. It is intended to be used for either right or left-handed players or for a left-handed shot where a right-handed player is in trouble (or vice versa), and can not make a shot without playing back, as may be the case if the ball lodges against a fence or some other obstruction. . . . It should prove a desirable addition to the caddy-bag to have for emergencies, which are liable to happen to any golfer (Golfers Magazine, April 1904: 250).

The club pictured was produced under Willie Dunn Jr's. U.S. patent (No. 745,004) dated November 24, 1903, which covered making golf clubs out of Pyralin, a type of vulcanized rubber. Dunn assigned this patent to the Kempshall Manufacturing Company, which also produced a Pyralin driver and putter (see page 314).

In 1904, Dunn's Pyralin "rubber-headed" clubs were described as follows:

The idea of using a rubber compound for driver heads is not new, but hitherto the experiments along that line have not been successful. Either the vulcanization would be carried too far, depriving the club of driving power, or the degree of elasticity would not be properly proportioned to that of the ball. Willie Dunn, the well-known professional, has been working on the problem for some time, and appears to have solved it. His rubber-headed club drives a very long ball, and works equally well with gutta-percha and rubber-cored balls. The head is beautifully proportioned, impervious to wet and virtually indestructible. It would seem as though the new club were especially adapted to the needs of players who really prefer using the solid ball, but who cannot afford to give distance on every tee to their opponents of the rubber-cored tribe. The club will be on the market shortly (Golf [ny], April: 282).

Prior to making Pyralin clubs, the Kempshall Manufacturing Company produced "Kempshall's Patent Drivers and Brassies"— woods with a thin Pyralin insert. Kempshall also offered individual Pyralin face inserts as well as Pyralin golf ball paint (*Golf Illustrated*, 15 Aug. 1902: 139). The Pyralin inserts, designed for installation in existing woods, were "composed of three layers of celluloid, with two layers of a composition sandwiched in between" (*Golfing*, 31 July 1902). Many of these inserts were marked "Kempshall Mfg. Co. \ Pyralin Club Face \ Pat. May 6, 1902" in the center.

In 1906 Kempshall advertised "The Latest Thing In Golf - Kempshall Rubber Cored Golf Clubs." These clubs consist of a wood head with two "rubber cores" directly behind and abutting a vulcanized fiber face. According to an advertisement for Kempshall Rubber Cored Golf Clubs, which includes an illustration wherein the cores appear to be round, the rubber cores gave the golfer added distance:

By inserting hand made rubber cores in the head of the driver or brassie, and confining them with hard vulcanized fibre faces, put on under great pressure, a club of wonderful resilience is obtained. The action of the rubber cores in the clubs is similar, in every way, to the action of the core in the ball. After the most careful tests, it has been shown that by the use of these clubs a much greater distance can be attained, quite 20 to 30 yards further than with the ordinary driver and brassie (Golfing, 21 June 1906: 36).

Kempshall's Rubber Cored clubs are marked "Rubber Cored" inside an oval manufacturer's stamp on the top of the head.

The insert, which covers the entire face of the club, is held in place by five screws.

The first rubber core wood was produced and advertised by Spalding in 1903:

Spalding Rubber-Cored Clubs. (Dunn's Patent, May 5, 1903). Gutta percha head, with elastic wound under tension three-eights of an inch behind the face and parallel with it (Golfing, 17 Sep. 1903: iv).

"Dunn's Patent" referrs to John D. Dunn's U.S. patent No. 726,885.

WILLIAM MILLS
"DUPLEX" METALWOOD

The inventive genius of W. Mills has again asserted itself, this time in the shape of a two-faced club, which can be used both for right-handed and left-handed shots. . . .

Most golfers at some time or another get a ball in such a position that a right-handed shot is an impossibility; the only remedy for the difficulty being a stand for a left-handed shot. The adaptability of this new club is therefore at once apparent. . . . A right-handed golfer can play a left-handed shot, and a left-handed golfer can play a right-handed shot with the same satisfaction. It has been modestly suggested that the new Mills inspiration is practically "two clubs in one," but we would go farther and suggest that it is several clubs in one (Golfing, 29 Oct. 1903: 28).

Another 1903 commentary on the Mills Duplex metalwood provides a different perspective and describes the merits of the new duplex club as having little to do with its ability to be used either right- or left-handed. It reads:

The vogue of aluminum golf clubs has been steadily increasing ever since their scientific construction was first undertaken some five years ago by Mr. W. Mills, of the Atlas Works, Bonner's Field, Sunderland. Mr. Mills' first success was with the Aluminum Putter, a club that became instantaneously popular, and is now to be seen in nearly every player's bag. The graduated sets of aluminium spoons which followed have also received the widest approval, and players are finding every day that they obtain greater accuracy, on account of their perfect balance, with them than with the irons and mashies. A matter that has greatly assisted the popularity of aluminium clubs, especially those for full shots, is the advent of the rubber-cored ball.

The old gutties hardly flew as far from aluminium as they did from wood, but the new balls carry and travel from the aluminium clubs quite as far as from wooden clubs.

The accompanying illustration [a Mills Duplex wood is pictured] shows at a glance the nature and construction of Mr. Mills latest invention. Many players carry a left-handed club in their set for use in emergencies where it is not possible to stand for a right-handed shot, and the first and most obvious merit of this new club is that it can be used either way, being thus practically two clubs in one.

But this, although a most useful attribute, is the least of the merits of the new club. The great advantage it possesses over any other club we have yet seen is the absolute perfection of its balance. As will be seen, the weight of the head, unlike any other make of club, is equally divided on each side of the shaft, and it is not possible, without handling the club, to form any idea of the comfortable feel it has in the hands and the feeling of confidence which it engenders. Its symmetrical shape helps this, and the hitting surface is clearly visible to the player. The club drives a ball with a great loft on it as far as a cleek, and the ball falls singularly dead off it. It is in approaching, however, at all distances, that the merits of the club are most conspicuous. Many players who are able to raise the ball with an iron or mashie have never been able to master the essential art of keeping straight. For such this variety will be a god-send. It may be that it is the narrow sole of these iron clubs and the way they lie to the shaft that renders the taking of aim and the keeping of it with them so difficult. But these difficulties do not appear to exist with the new club. It lies flat to the ball, and does not require to be held up to it at the

required angle like an iron club; and, as has been said, its balance is perfect. We have even found it useful for the very short approaches and for the shots usually played with a putter–long putts from the edge of the green. It keeps the ball very straight, and the ball can be pitched with great accuracy and with very little run on it.

Altogether, we predict a great success for the new club. We have not seen any which is so well adapted for its purpose or which gives such uniform and satisfactory results (Golf Illustrated, 16 Oct. : 47).

Mills was somewhat successful in marketing his duplex clubs, as he continued to produce them for a few more years.

The Standard Golf Company's 1909 catalog describes four different Mills duplex clubs: "No. 1" was a "cleek," "No. 1 1/2" was a "driving iron," "No. 2" was an "iron," and "No. 2 1/2" was a "medium lofter" (Standard Golf 1909, 21). It is interesting to note that this catalog implied these clubs were new models by stating, "Although so recently introduced, these clubs are becoming the most popular of all recent golf inventions" (21). Perhaps they were discontinued for a time and then reintroduced. If so, this would explain the comments found in the April 2, 1909 issue of Golf Illustrated.

After referring to the difficulties of playing the ball from the golfer's opposite side when such a shot was the only one possible, this review continues:

All these disadvantages are neutralised by the introduction of that ingenious club known as the "Duplex," made by the Standard Golf Co. of Sunderland (better known as Mills clubs). The "Duplex" is the latest of the famous Mills clubs . . . (47).

The Mills duplex club pictured on the previous page is marked "Standard Golf Co. \ Mills \ 47969 \ Patent \ Sunderland" on the crown and "Rd. No 413464 \ The Mills \ R&L 2 1/2 Model \ Standard Lie \ 9 ozs 1 drs" on the sole. "Shafted by \ Standard Golf Co. \ Sunderland" is stamped on the shaft. The registration number "413464" dates to mid-1903. The number on the crown, "47696," is a production number and has nothing to do with the model or any patent.

Willie Dunn Jr. also applied for a patent, which he later abandoned, to cover an aluminum duplex head club. Three of his aluminum duplex clubs, which appear to date to the early 1900s, are known. The faces on Dunn's duplex clubs are smooth, and Dunn's name is marked on the head.

The vast majority of all remaining antique duplex woods are of the Mills variety. Nevertheless, Mills Duplex metalwoods are far from common and are very collectible. (For more Mills clubs, see page 283.)

Not many players carry a left-handed club in their bag, but there are times when its value cannot be over-estimated. One such occasion that came under my notice was when J.H. Taylor, the English crack, was playing at Myopia. His ball was lying quite close to the fence and a right-handed stroke was virtually impossible. Taylor, equipped for the occasion, took his left-handed iron, and playing out with an exceedingly good shot saved the hole. Ben Sayers is another well-known professional who has used a left-handed club to great advantage on many occasions. It may be remembered that to preach the necessity of being ambidextrous was the lifelong hobby of Charles Reade, the famous novelist. It may be assumed that he had not devoted his talents to the subject of golf. If he had, he would have realized that it would be the work of two lifetimes to play golf both ways.

However, I did really know one ambidextrous golfer. He could play equally well either way, and usually carried two or three left-handed clubs in his bag. What preferences he had was for right-handed play. I remember my astonishment when, after watching him play a hole or two in the usual way, I saw him play an iron shot from an open course left-handed. He told me afterwards that he did not like the stance for the shot right-handed (Golf [ny], April 1909: 208).

Although the clubhead shown on the right still has its original finish, the second name stamped atop the head is unreadable. The head is marked "Patented \ Grant \ —" with mostly indiscernible paint-filled Gothic lettering. Because no other such clubs are known, the indiscernible word after "Grant" (be it a name or a location) can not be checked. Therefore, the author simply refers to this club as "Grant's" duplex wood.

As pictured, the bottom portion of the shaft is wrapped with whipping. Such additional whipping usually means that the shaft was cracked in the line of duty. Given a choice between this club with its heavily whipped shaft and another example with a perfect shaft, a collector obviously would want the perfect example. However, if he or she collects unusual clubs and does not know of another Grant's duplex wood, the whipping on the shaft becomes less significant, especially considering the good original condition of the head.

GEORGE REITENOUR
"RITZ" DUPLEX WOOD

Unlike a double-faced person, a double-face club is eminently safe and usable (Golfing, 24 September 1908: 24).

The "safe and usable" double-face wood pictured was patented in the United States on August 12, 1924, by George W. Reitenour of Union City, Indiana. The objective of his invention was to:

provide a double faced symmetrical club suitable for either right or left handed use, furnishing parallel lines for the eye of the user as an aid in properly stroking the ball, and weighting the club symmetrically, so that it will have no tendency to swing out of proper alignment, whichever face is used, so that the metal will act as a rivet, and so that the momentum of all the metal will be applied directly to the ball, whichever face is used.

To help accomplish his objectives, both faces are identical:

in shape, equal in extent, equally inclined to the verticle [sic], and parallel in horizontal section. In this way two parallel lines are furnished for the eye of the user that will aid in keeping the face of the club at the desired angle to the direction of its movement when it strikes the ball.

Both faces are recessed and filled with lead. However, the lead itself is all one piece, connected through holes bored in the center of the head between the faces:

In forming the club, there is bored in each face a shallow cavity . . . . The centers of these cavities are connected by boring holes through the head. Then one face is placed on a suitable smooth support, so that the cavities in that face are closed on the bottom by the support. Then suitable molten metal, which melts at a comparatively low temperature, is poured into the upper cavity, runs down through holes, and fills the lower cavity, and, when it hardens, forms one integral piece of metal constituting plates and connecting pins. In this way the plates and pins form in effect rivets.

The Reitenour duplex wood seen here is marked "Ritz" in the narrow lead alignment line across the top of the head. "Made by Geo W. Reitenour \ Walnut St. \ Union City, Ind. \ Patent Applied For" is stamped on the shaft. Unlike ordinary shaft marks created by stamping a steel die into the wood, this shaft is marked with an ink stamp on the surface of the wood. The patent for this club was applied for on May 8, 1922.

Even though this club is the most recent of the duplex woods discussed, it is still one of the best collectibles from within their ranks. The Reitenour duplex wood pictured is one of only two known. Do not expect to see many more.

ALEXANDER S. GAIR
"MIDGET MARVEL"
DUPLEX IRON/PUTTER

A new putter, which seems to combine the virtues of several iron clubs in one, is the 'Midget Marvel' sold at 6s. 6d. by Mr. Alexander S. Gair, of 18, Broughton Street, Edinburgh. It is a short, thick bladed club, the blade being only 2 1/2 inches in length, with a base of about one inch, and it is claimed to possess all the following good points:—It combines the advantages of a wooden putter, is perfectly balanced and absolutely true, is the best club for all distances (from 1 to 100 yards), is especially useful for playing approach shots against the wind, or for playing out of a cupped lie through the green, and can be used as a right or left handed club. Such a very adaptable weapon is surely worthy of a trial by every player (Golfing, 30 July 1908: 24).

According to the drawings that accompanied the above review when originally published, the Midget Marvel came in three styles: a left-handed cleek with a right-handed putter blade; a right-handed cleek with a left-handed putter blade; and an iron having the same loft both left- and right-handed.

Shown on this page is the left-handed cleek with the right-handed putter blade. Marked "Warranted Hand Forged \ Midget \ Gair's \ Marvel \ Patent Appld For" on the sole, this club was made by William Gibson. His "star" trademark is stamped on the sole. Gibson also produced a "Bi-Fron" iron identical to Gair's Midget Marvel.

Fixed blade duplex irons are difficult to collect because few were produced. The following related information is presented for the persistent collector who

might come across one of these rarieties.

Charles Reginald Blathwayt received the first patent that covered a duplex iron, a British patent (No. 9,522) dated May 15, 1894. Blathwayt designed a triangular shaped head, the sole and both faces making up the three sides. He included the option of squaring off the toe so his iron could, if desired, have a third face and be used to play a ball out of a wheel rut or other similar situation. He also included the option of integrating a wood block into the head, so the head could have one or more wooden striking faces.

William Nicol received a British patent (No. 13,307) dated June 13, 1904, that covered a duplex iron usable as both an approach club and a putter. Nicol included the option of making his club usable croquet style. (Nicol's club is discussed further on page 427.)

John Radel received a U.S. patent (No. 1,685,826) dated October 2, 1928, that covered a duplex iron with a hollow sole. In cross-section, Radel's club-head looks like an inverted "V." Radel's patent also allows for filling in the area between the blades and for making the sole solid, but the one example seen by the author was shaped like an inverted "V" in cross-section.

George Forrester produced one of the earliest known duplex irons. His club is similar to the club described in Radel's patent even though it was produced more than thirty years before Radel's patent was issued:

Mr. Forrester has also brought out a new double-faced cleek to suit either a left-handed or a right-handed player. The sole is broad, and the space between the two blades is hollow. The balance of the club is in no way destroyed. We have often recommended the carrying by right-handed player of a left-hand club in important matches, in case of difficult shots against a paling or a wall; but with this powerful driving cleek of Mr. Forrester in the bag, the carrying of an extra club is thereby obviated (Golf, 16 Oct. 1896: 92).

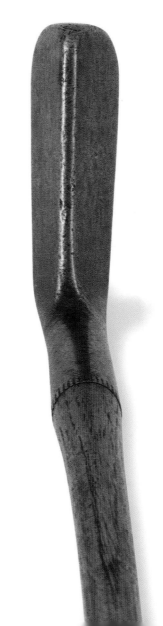

RALPH G. TYLER
"TYLER NIBLICK"

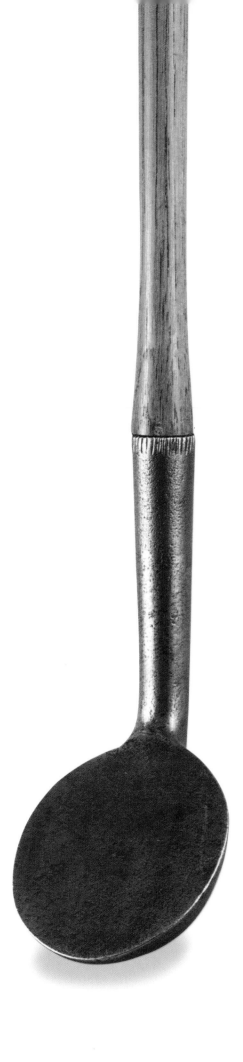

*Here is something entirely new—
the most useful club you can put in
your bag. Listen—the same club can
be used right or left handed. About
the only time you use a niblick is when
you are in trouble and about half of
the time—it seems more—a right hand
player needs a left hand club to play
away from an obstacle, while a left
hand player needs a right hand club.
The Tyler Niblick solves the problem;
play it right or left handed—out of trap,
away from stones, fences, or trees,
out of cuppy lies. Great to get out of
long grass with—goes through with
least resistance. You will like the
Tyler Niblick; you ought to have one*
(Burke 1917, 19).

Ralph Tyler, known for his
combination woods (see page
297), received a U.S. patent (No.
1,139,738) dated May 18, 1915,
that covered the circular iron
pictured here. Tyler calculated
that this iron, designed for both
left- and right-handed use, could
effectively play shots that other
clubs could not. Specifically, according to his patent, his iron
would be useful when playing a
ball from soft ground, sand, tall
grass, a small hollow, a long narrow
hollow, beneath an overhanging
rock, beneath the lower board of
a fence, behind the lip of a
bunker, in a rut, or in any other
difficult place.

Tyler was not the first person
to use a circular or oval blade
centrally located underneath the
hosel. Edward Rawlins received

a British patent (No. 23,018)
dated November 5, 1905, that
covered a putter having a perfectly round head located in
just such a position. According
to his patent, his putter was of
such a shape so:

*the player . . . cannot lose his
nerve and executive skill by hesitating
which particular part of the putter to
use, but such player would be provided
with one circular definite driving surface,
consequently the skill of the player
would be immediately directed to
striking the ball.*

Rawlins's circular "solid
forged steel putters" were advertised only briefly. Prior to Rawlins,
Robert Condie forged at least
one circular head putter. An
example marked with Condie's
"rose" trademark on the head
and "Hutchison" on the shaft
sold at the Phillips July 1994 golf
auction, in Glasgow, Scotland.
Prior to Condie, a mid to late
19th century cleekmaker produced an unmarked iron similar
to Tyler's Niblick, but the cleekmaker's blade was not angled to
the hosel like Tyler's. This 19th
century iron was offered at
Christie's July 1992 golf auction,
in Glasgow, Scotland.

Offered in Burke's 1917
catalog, Tyler's club met with
almost no acceptance. The only
other example known to the
author is in the USGA museum
in Far Hills, New Jersey.

UNKNOWN MAKER
DUAL FACE PUTTER

The duplex putter pictured directly above possesses many interesting features. Rectangular in shape, made from wood, and built with a unique metal face on each end of its head, this club is made for right-handed, left-handed, or croquet style use.

Each metal face includes a brace that extends across and well into the body of the head. Because these metal braces extend so far into the head, they are offset from each other. Therefore, the four nails affixing the brace of the left-handed face enter the top of the head while the four nails affixing the brace of the right-handed face enter the bottom of the head.

Each face is also nailed in place. As seen above, the right hand face contains three nails: one in each upper corner of the insert and the third at the bottom of the face.

Because the hickory shaft extends straight up out of the center of the head, this putter can be used croquet style. Because the sole is cambered towards one side and from one end to the other, the head can also be used either right- or left-handed.

Consistent with the absence of a maker's mark on the head, the unrefined design and wonderful hand-crafted nature of this club date it to the 1890s, if not a little earlier.

UNKNOWN MAKER
MULTIPIECE HEAD, DUAL FACE PUTTER

Although the basic nature of the club pictured directly above—a rectangular, center-shafted wooden head with two faces on opposite ends of the head—is similar to the previous club, it is also substantially different. On this club, one face has more loft than the other; the head is designed only for croquet style use; the thick shaft is made from greenheart; and no facings were employed. However, the primary difference is that this head is made from two separate pieces of wood. A seam between these two pieces is clearly visible across all four sides of the head.

The reason this head is made from two pieces of wood is not known, but it might relate to attaching the shaft inside the head or to any added weight inside the head. The two-piece head might also have been intended to reduce shock or improve the feel of the head. Only one other club known to the author has a similar two piece head: The "Unexcelled" driver made by Willie Dunn Jr. (p. 353).

The club shown above also sports an 1890s india rubber grip similar to Cole's Holdfast grip (see p. 529).

REGINALD MARRIOTT & ALLEN RANSOME

THE "PENDULUM" THREE FACE, CROQUET-STYLE PUTTER

There have, from time to time, been brought out new forms of fancy putters, which have had a short popularity, and players who have tried them have reverted to the ordinary putter, which they have found more reliable and generally useful. In view of our experience of former fancy putters we should not have thought it worth while to trouble our readers with a notice of this latest form of putter, but that it certainly possesses extraordinary advantages, especially for the average player, the general verdict of those who have tried it seems fairly to establish.

The Pendulum Putter, as will be seen from our illustration, is a triangular block of metal about an inch thick, with an ordinary putter stick fixed vertically in its centre. The three sides of the putter heads are each shaped with a different angle, one of which is at right angles to the lower face, while the other two are sloped upwards at more or less acute angles, one having considerably more slope than the other. The vertical side is generally used on the green, but for long putts, or when the ball has to pass over rough ground, the inclined faces should be used, as by so doing it can be slightly lofted over any inequalities on the outskirts of the green.

When using the Pendulum Putter the player places himself directly behind the ball and holds it as shown in our illustration [the illustration shows the hands are a distance apart: the golfer's left hand, with the hand turned so the thumb is highest on the grip, grasps the top of the grip while the golfer's right hand, with the thumb running down the shaft, is positioned low on the grip], and when properly placed his position is such that a straight line drawn from the centre of the hole to the centre of his body would pass through the centre of his ball. Having carefully placed himself in position, a pendulum movement is given with the right hand, while the left lightly grasps the upper part of the stick, the center of movement being situated about the centre of the left hand. The player delivers the stroke with his eye on the ball, and the result is that the ball invariably goes straight to the hole, and a very little practice will enable the players to calculate the amount of force necessary to insure a successful putt.

The advantages claimed for the Pendulum Putter are as follows: — Better line of sight, better centreing of sight, better judging of strength, absolute guarantee against pulling or slicing the ball.

The wholesale agents for the Pendulum Putter are Messrs. A.G. Spalding and Bros. . . ." (Golf Illustrated, 18 Oct. 1907: 80).

The Pendulum Putter, pictured, was patented in Great Britain by Major Reginald Adams Marriott of the Governors House at Her Majesty's Prison in Chelmsford; and Allen Ransome, engineer of Stanley Works, in Newark-on-Trent. Their patent (No. 10,497) was dated May 6, 1907.

The Pendulum Putter shown is marked "Marriott & Ransome's Patent" on the top of the head. Spalding advertised this putter in Great Britain as "The 'Lincoln' Pendulum Putter" (*Golfing*, 17 Oct. 1907: 9).

Marriott and Ransome's Pendulum Putter was unpopular and short-lived. Consequently, few examples remain. Today, the Pendulum Putter is an outstanding collectible and makes a nice companion piece when displayed with the Baltimore Putter Company's adjustable triangular head putter (see page 382).

EDWARD L. SAMUEL
THE "CERT" FOUR FACE, CROQUET-STYLE PUTTER

D.M. PATRICK
THE "TYKE" FOUR FACE, CROQUET-STYLE PUTTER

The "Cert" Golf Putter. The latest and most accurate putter introduced. The chief advantages of this club are its simplicity and reliability in the hands of an ordinary player, enabling him to practically make every stroke a success and amply justifying the title selected for the club (Golf Illustrated, 1 June 1906: 202).

The club pictured above is marked "The Cert \ Patent Applied For \ F.H. Ayres \ London" on the head and "F.H. Ayres" on the shaft. Ayres manufactured, advertised, and sold this club.

The Cert was patented in Great Britain by Sir Edward Levien Samuel, Baronet, from Hyde Park, in London. As specified in his patent (No. 8,336) dated April 6, 1906, two of the four faces—one long side and one short side—have the same loft while the other two faces are vertical. All four of the faces are "roughened, chequered, or indented to increase the effective hold or grip on the ball":

By these means I am enabled to produce a golf club such as a putter in which a hammer-blow can be given with a clean swing and accurate delivery and force.

The putter pictured right, complete with a brass soleplate covering the entire sole, is marked "D.M. Patrick" on the shaft and "Tyke" on the rectangular wooden head. This "Tyke" putter should not be confused with the "Tyke" solid horn clubs on page 315; nor should D.M. Patrick be confused with Alex Patrick:

Alex. Patrick of Leven, Fife, claims to be the second oldest firm in the trade, and the name is a good one and is a guarantee for good workmanship. The other firm of the same name, D.M. Patrick, has its place of business at Lundin Links, at the eastward end of the Leven links; and the Patrick wooden putting cleek, which has been patented, is likely to take the fancy of many golfers. D.M. Patrick was formerly at Wimbledon (Golfer's Magazine, May 1898: 100).

The Patrick wooden putting cleek mentioned is actually "Foster's" patent putting cleek. It has a thin (one inch deep) wood head "to secure the advantages of the narrow head and straight back" of a blade putter with the benefits of a wood face (*Golfing*, 19 Apr. 1900: 14). Mr. Foster's patent application did not result in a patent.

RONALD C. EVANS
CROQUET-STYLE
STYMIE PUTTER

BURKE GOLF COMPANY
"SAV-A-SHOT MODEL 22,"
CROQUET-STYLE
PUTTER/CHIPPER

In match play prior to 1952, a "stymie" occurred whenever player A's ball was directly in the path between player B's ball and the hole. Player B, the furthest from the hole, had to negotiate player A's ball and could not ask player A to remove his ball unless it was within six inches of player B's ball. Stymies usually occurred on the putting-green. Players negotiating a stymie could try to go around or over their opponent's ball. If the player tried to go over the ball, he or she usually used a lofted iron to do so. But in the continuing effort to answer the golfer's every dilemma, a few clubs were designed specifically to handle the stymie.

Ronald Calcott Evans received a British patent (No. 22, 400) dated Oct. 22, 1908, that covered the center-shafted stymie putter

pictured directly above. According to his patent, his golf club was:

designed with a view of combining the advantages and uses of a "putter" on the one part, and a "stymie" or lifting club on the other.

Therefore, this clubhead has two striking faces—a straight face for putting and a very lofted face for playing stymie shots. The stymie face was to provide a "very acute angle to the horizontal, preferably 35°."

This particular club was made by the British Golf Company and is marked "British Golf Co. Ltd. \ Makers \ London" in a small oval on the sole. Formed in 1904, the British Golf Company was a "wholesale and export only" firm that supplied golf requisites including their own machine-made clubs (*Golfing*, 16, June 1904: 42 and *Golf Illustrated*, 15 Dec. 1905: 248).

Another putter designed to handle the occasional stymie is mentioned in the July 9, 1897 issue of *Golf*:

Another putter seems more ingenious than necessary. This wooden one, in which the removal of a part of the face (made loose for that purpose) leaves a gap, sloping gently from back to front, which may be utilised for lofting obstinate stimies, should the owner's bag contain neither a mashie nor lofting iron (351).

The stymie was completely eliminated from the game by 1952:

In one form or another this rule remained until in 1952, after much argument extending over many years, it vanished from the game (Cousins 1959, 163). [The USGA abolished the stymie in 1950, the R&A did so two years later.]

Although the Burke croquet-style putter pictured directly above is similar to the Evans stymie putter in basic design—two faces are on opposite sides of a croquet-style head—the lofted face on the Burke is more for chip shots than stymies.

The Burke croquet-style club allowed the golfer to use the same stroke when either putting or chipping. The only problem, from a marketing standpoint, was that few golfers used the croquet style as their normal method of putting or chipping.

The Burke putter/chipper pictured directly above is marked "Burke \ Sav-A-Shot \ Model \ 22" across its sole. Unlike the Evans putter, the Burke Sav-A-Shot Model 22 locates the striking faces on the long sides of the head.

The MARQUIS
De CHASSELOUP-LOUBAT
"CHANTILLY/GASSIAT"
DUAL FACE PUTTER

The Chantilly Putter. Last week I had an opportunity of both inspecting and trying the new Chantilly wooden putter used by Gassiat and Sherlock in the French Championship. It certainly is a weird—not to say uncouth looking—instrument. The head is very large and nearly square in formation, the face of the club shallow, and the lead is let into the sole of the club. I played one or two shots with it, and the ball fairly jumped off the club. It certainly drives the ball, if this can be considered an advantage in a putter. The top of the shaft is not round, but flat-sided, and there is an extra thickness at the top for the use of the left

*hand. It is not a putter which altogether lends itself to the interlocking grip, and that is perhaps the reason why it suited Sherlock, who holds his hands apart when putting (*Golf Illustrated*, 31 Oct. 1913: 134.)*

The club shown above was originally referred to as the "Chantilly Putter," after Chantilly, France, the home of its inventor, the Marquis de Chasseloup-Loubat. The Chantilly putter, however rapidly became known as the Gassiat putter:

[The] putter is . . . known as the Model L.C.L. Jean Gassiat putter, Registered No. 627732. It was invented by

*the Marquis de Chasseloup-Loubat of Chantilly, France . . . . The nose and face line of the Putter are perfectly at right angles, which does assist the player to decide his line of putt. . . . The sole makers are W. M. Winton & Co. Ltd. (*Golf Monthly*, Jan. 1914: 880)*

Born in 1883, Jean Gassiat was a talented French golf professional who worked at Golf de Chantilly, in Chantilly, France. He won the French Open in 1912, defeating Vardon by a stroke, and was the French Native Professional Champion in 1912, 1919, 1927, and 1929.

Because of its squared off nose, a Gassiat putter could also be used croquet style, but, because of the R&A ruling in 1910 against center-shafted and croquet-style putters, it could not be used croquet style during sanctioned play.

The principles behind the design of the Marquis's putter actually belong to John H. Brown, a law clerk from Edinburgh. Brown received a British patent (No. 2,930) dated February 5, 1898, that covered a mallet putter very similar to the Gassiat. According to his patent, Brown not only provided for the nose of his putter to be "cut off square and made flush vertically so as to form a putting face" used croquet style, he also designed his club for traditional use. Brown's putter differs from the Gassiat by including both a left and a right hand face in addition to the face on the end of the head. Brown's patent illustration shows three circular lead weights located across the underside of the clubhead in a direct line with the shaft. Gassiat putters have

similar lead weights located in the sole, though often set slightly behind the line of the shaft. A brass soleplate usually covers the front half of the sole, heel to toe.

Gassiat putters are found with regularity, as they were produced for many years. Slazenger's 1928 U.S. catalog, complete with an illustration of a Gassiat putter, offers:

Imported Jean Gassiat Putters, used by many of the world's best putters. Specially selected Hickory shaft with real pigskin grip. $5.25.

Even the Walter Hagen Golf Company, founded in 1925, sold Gassiat putters.

The Gassiat putter pictured on this page is marked "J. Gassiat \ Special \ Chantilly" on the top of the head. The marks are difficult to see in the photograph because the letters were never paint filled. Not all Gassiat putters are marked "Gassiat." Many are marked with the name of another professional or that of a location or golf course. Some Gassiat putters bear the British design registration number "627,732." This number, issued to W.M. Winton & Company, London, on October 26, 1913, covered the Gassiat putter. Most Gassiat putters also include the "pistol grip" on the end of their shaft. This grip is referred to in the *Golf Illustrated* review that begins this page, the top of the shaft being described as "not round, but flat sided." The putter pictured has a rocker sole, not ordinarily found on Gassiat putters, that is mirrored by the top of the head.

JOHN K. GARNER
"GARNER" PUTTER,
TRIPLE FACE, BILLIARD STYLE

The "Garner" putter, whatever its other special features may be, certainly possesses an appearance unique in the evolution of that particular variety of club which is used exclusively for holing out purposes. . . . The "Garner" putter has yet to be proven. The designer makes certain claims for it, after watching carefully various players use it, and its effect upon their play combined with his own conviction as to its efficiency. He says: "The following are what I consider the chief merits of the club: (1) *A most perfectly balanced club; (2) The hitting direction of the club is easily seen; (3) The club is easily placed in its striking position; and (4) The weight is equally divided, as the shaft enters the centre of the head"* (*Golfing*, 2 Feb. 1905: 22).

The Garner putter was designed not only for both left- and right-handed use as pictured on the facing page, it was also designed to function like a billiard cue! As pictured on this page, the brass Garner putter is resting on the sides of its disc shaped faces. This allows the sole, which is perfectly flat, to become the active striking face. With the club in this position, the golfer could strike the ball in billiard cue fashion. Using either one or two hands when crouching or kneeling, the golfer simply drew the clubhead back and then pushed it forward into the ball, the circular disc faces acting as runners, never losing contact with the ground. Although John Garner invented this clever putter, he is not responsible for the idea of striking a golf ball "billiard style."

In 1899 a letter from Ashley MacMahon to the editor of *Golf*

Illustrated questioned the validity of using a billiard cue when golfing. It reads:

Sir,–Whilst playing a match with a friend last Saturday I was much struck by seeing a billiard cue in his bag, and was more surprised on seeing him make use of it on the putting-green, where he consistently "holed-out" putts of three and four yards; indeed, he eventually won the match by five and a-half putt. I naturally disputed his right to use this object, upon which it was decided that we should refer to your valuable weekly paper for information. I shall be much obliged if you could settle this matter for us. I eventually tried the cue myself, and I must say I could hardly miss the hole (1 Sep.: 345).

The editor responded to MacMahon's letter as follows:

There is no rule of Golf which expressly forbids the use of a billiard cue or any other implement. It may be argued, however, that a billiard cue is not a club, which is a weapon with the weight at its striking end, and there is also the difficulty that it might be hard to say when a ball was pushed and

not struck by the cue. Custom, at any rate, which is a very useful thing to go by in the absence of rule, is against the use of anything but a club . . . and custom further demands that the ball shall be struck with the head of the club and not otherwise. Although no one has been bold enough to test the matter, it is extremely probable that the use of a billiard cue would not be permitted in either of the Championships. On the whole, therefore, golfers had better stick to implements in the semblance of clubs.

MacMahon's letter and the editor's response were not the first printed mention of the possible conflict between billiard cues and golf clubs. In the 1895 U.S. Amateur held at Newport, Rhode Island, Richard Peters attempted to use a billiard cue instead of a putter:

Talking on this subject, Mr. N.O. Tallmadge says, according to the Sun, New York: "The officials in charge of the Newport tournament did not make a ruling in the match between Mr. Peters and the Rev. Dr. Rainsford regarding the use of the cue; for, after

using it once, Peters, at the request of his opponent, did not use it again" (*The Golfer*, 23 June 1897: 487).

Less than a year after the 1895 U.S. Amateur, a letter to the editor of *Golf* requested a response as to the merits and legality of using a billiard cue when putting. Without referring to an official rule or ruling, the editor's one line reply was, "It is a foul stroke to use the club in this way" (6 March 1896: 529).

In 1904 a letter to the editor of *Golf Illustrated* presented a new twist on an old problem. This time, putting with a billiard cue was not in question, but putting with the end of the shaft in billiard cue fashion was! The letter, from a golfer identified as "Digitalis," and the editor's response read as follows:

Q.—The following point has arisen here in connection with a competition medal round, in which the best score returned was made by a player using a novel method of putting of questionable legality, upon which we should be glad to have your opinion. This competitor's method on the green was to use the upper end of the shaft of his putter to strike the ball with, grasping the head of the club in the right hand and using it like a billiard cue, the left hand making "a rest" as in the latter game, the player crouching down on the ground the while. The ball was not pushed but fairly struck in a similar way to a free shot on the billiard table. Does this, in your opinion, constitute an illegal shot and consequent disqualification? If so under what rule?

P. S.—Since writing I learnt that the player makes the "rest" with the left hand by placing it on the left boot instead of on the ground. It has been argued that in the latter case he breaks Rule 11 by "bending" the grass near the ball with the left hand in addressing the ball, the rule only allowing this to be done with the club and the two feet. Do you consider this a material point, or would you make no distinction in allowing or disqualifying both methods?

A.—There is nothing in the rules which expressly forbids this method of putting, nor have we ever observed that it conferred any advantage. At the same time it can hardly be considered a legitimate stroke since in golf the ball is struck with the head of the club and not with the shaft, and it might be possible to convict the player under Rules 6 match play and 14 stroke play for not striking fairly at the balls, "striking fairly" being held to mean, inter alia, with the head of the club. In this case he would suffer a penalty of two strokes for each offence. We do not consider that the stroke is made any more legitimate if the player rests his hand on his boot instead of on the ground. So far as we are aware the Rules Committee [of the R&A] have given no decision on the point (30 Sep. 1904: 10).

A decision from the R&A Rules Committee was not long in coming:

Recent Decisions by the Rules of Golf Committee. . . .

Using Club Like A Billiard Cue. The competitor who returned the best score in a medal round adopted an unusual method of putting. The competitor knelt down and used the handle end of the club shaft to strike the ball in the same manner that a billiard ball is struck with a cue. Is this legal?

Answer.—This method of putting is absolutely illegal (*Golf Illustrated*, 21 Oct. 1904: 64).

The rare Garner billiard-style putter pictured on this and the previous page is marked "Patent" on one side of the hosel and "20038" on the other. "G. MacIntosh" is stamped on the shaft. On September 17, 1904, John Kenneth Garner of Manchester, England, applied for a British patent (No. 20,038) to cover this club. In designing his putter, Garner was trying to capture the best of both worlds— a traditional golf club that could also function like a billiard cue. However, when the R&A Rules Committee outlawed using a golf club "in the same manner as a billiard ball is struck with a cue" *one month* after Garner applied for his patent, the marketing future for his putter disappeared. This left Garner little incentive to complete his patent application, which he therefore abandoned.

The "Nicola" is a rare putter remotely similar to Garner's. Patented by William Nicol, a joiner from Glasgow, Scotland, this club was covered under a British patent (No. 13,307) dated June 13, 1904. The Nicola has an unusual look. Instead of using discs, this club has a roughly rectangular head shape. (The patent refers to the faces as "rhomboid" in shape.) The clubhead, produced in both aluminum and brass models, provides for a putter on one end and a lofted, heavily scored chipper on the other. It was used primarily right-handed, left-handed, or croquet style, though it could be used billiard style despite not having a flat sole.

UNKNOWN MAKER
"THE SUB-SINKSIT" ALUMINUM PUTTER, DUAL FACE

LINUS GLOVER READ
"READ BALANCED STRAIGHT LINE WOOD PUTTER," DUAL FACE

The dual face putter pictured directly above is marked "The Sub-Sinksit" inside an oval on the heel of the left-handed face. This entry level collectible, which dates somewhere around 1910, is characterized by its thick aluminum blade, deep face, and rocker sole.

The Sub-Sinksit is very similar in design to Spalding's "C.S." putter advertised in 1905. According to a C.S. putter advertisement, the premise for its design was as follows:

The location of the shaft and shape of the sole are such that even if it strikes the ground before striking the ball, any tendency to twist is practically eliminated. Insures accuracy in direction. Can be played with by either right or left-handed players (Golfing, 28 Sep.: 28).

At Last—The Right Putter. The Read Balanced Straight Line Wood Putter is the latest achievement of Mr. L.G. Read, (Consulting Engineer) and designer of the now famous Read Balanced Drivers, Brassies, and Spoons. It is sold with an absolute guarantee that you will putt straighter with it than with any other model; or the price will be refunded. It is made of wood because wood is not only more resilient than metal, but takes much better hold and gives you finer control of the ball. Its face is flat and, having no loft, it sends the ball away, rotating on a true horizontal axis— (similar to the "follow" shot in billiards)—thus causing the ball to cling to the ground and duck into the cup—instead of "rimming" it. Looking down on this putter, you see only straight lines. This enables you to instantly get the correct line to the cup. It is hand made; of the highest quality of materials, and the price is $8.00. Usual discounts to dealers and

professionals.... Glover Specialties Company, Inc. 325 John Street, Bridgeport, Conn., U.S.A. (The American Golfer, 6 Sep. 1924: 33).

The brass plate covering the sole of the putter pictured directly above is marked "Read Wood Putter \ Patent Pending \ Glover Specialties Co., Bridgeport Conn \ USA."

The thick rectangular shape of this head is very similar to that of the Kismet Putter, designed by Max Marsten and produced by the Phosphor Bronze Smelting Company of Philadelphia, Pennsylvania. It is also similar to the Jerry Travers Putter produced under a British design registration (No. 671,039).

The Kismet, advertised as "The Sensation of 1923" (*The American Golfer*, 17 May 1923: 41), is made out of aluminum and, across the sole, "Elephant Brand 'Phosphor Bronze'." The

nose of the Kismet curves under, in traditional fashion, from the top of the head to the sole.

The Travers Putter is made of wood and often has a thin, square wood grip formed integrally with the shaft. Covered under a design registration number that dates to the end of 1919, the Travers Putter is similar to the Read Wood Putter in head shape except that its nose rounds down to the sole. Of the putters just discussed, the Read Straight Line is the most difficult to locate, followed by the Travers.

The "famous Read Balanced Drivers, Brassies, and Spoons" mentioned in the introductory quote were relatively simplistic clubs. The soleplate on these clubs covered only the front half of the sole in an effort to increase the clubhead weight immediately behind the face.

WILSON-WESTERN SPORTING GOODS CO.
"AMBY DEX"
DUAL FACE PUTTER

Amby Dex. An ingenious center shafted wood head club. Made with dual faces of brass. Its peculiar construction gives it exceptional balance. Can be used either right or left handed. For men or women. Each. $7.00 (Wilson-Western 1929, 37).

First offered in Wilson's 1925 catalog, the Amby Dex is a stylish putter with character. Wilson catalogs from 1926 through 1930 offered the Amby Dex along with a similar putter called the "Sharpshooter." The Sharpshooter is made from aluminum ("Alumo metal") with a diamond-shaped brass insert inlaid through the center of the head. This brass inlay is visible on both the left and right faces.

The Amby Dex putter pictured has two brass faces and is marked "Amby Dex" on the crown. In nice original condition, this club is undeniably attractive. Both the wood shaft

and the leather wrap grip match the black cherry color of the head.

In 1923, Thomas E. Wilson & Company merged with the Western Sporting Goods Company to form the Wilson-Western Sporting Goods Company. In 1931, "Western" was dropped from the company name (Wishon 1985, 38-2).

"Yes," said the casual player, "I won my match on the last green by running down a long putt. I thought the caddie was standing at the hole so I putted for his feet. It turned out afterwards that the hole was five yards away, but the ball went in all right!"

(*Golf Illustrated*, 12 Feb. 1909: 143)

Alignment Aids

If the golfer is aligned incorrectly when striking the ball, he or she must do something "wrong" in order to hit the target. This principle—consistent accuracy requires correct alignment—has long been understood. Consequently, various antique clubs were devised to improve the golfer's aim.

Since better alignment can be claimed for any club, this chapter deals only with those antique clubs designed specifically to line up the ball with the hole or to line up the ball with the sweet-spot on the face, or both. Significant clubs designed with only minor consideration given to alignment features, such as Hutchison's Demon and Brewster's Simplex, are not included in this chapter. Because these clubs have other more prominent features, they are dealt with elsewhere in this book. Neither does this chapter discuss any mechanical clubs designed to improve alignment, though two such clubs are mentioned on this page. Mechanical alignment aids are covered in the chapter on mechanical clubs.

The first patent to cover a club designed primarily to improve the golfer's alignment was issued in 1900 to Liberty Dean Holden. His British patent (No. 10,051) dated May 31, covered a blade putter that used a removable alignment rod. Holden's putter is discussed on page 398.

Next, William Robertson received a British patent (No. 12,026) dated July 3, 1900, that covered an alignment guide rod that could be permanently affixed or hinged to the back of the blade. Robertson then received a British patent (No. 2,840) dated February 9, 1901, and a U.S. patent (No. 697,542) dated April 15, 1902, that covered a putter with an alignment guide that consisted of either a notch in the top of the blade or a vertically pivoting arm hinged to the back of the blade. No examples of Robertson's clubs are known to the author.

Arthur Howard Proctor received a British patent (No. 26,975) dated December 6, 1902, that included the possibility of installing two alignment rods on the back of the blade. The rods, if used, were to be placed close together, so the *space* between them lined up to the target. No examples of Proctor's club are known.

After 1902, a number of different patents covering a variety of alignment aids were issued. Among the more interesting patents not discussed elsewhere in this chapter are the following:

Lt. Colonel Aubrey Maurice Maude's British patent (No. 16,834) dated July 25, 1907, covered a mirror affixed to the top of the blade. The mirror was angled so the golfer could use it to sight the target. A similar patent was also issued in 1920 to William Guy Ruggles (see page 401).

Frederick C. Blanchard's U.S. patent (No. 837,030) dated Nov. 27, 1906, covered a putter with a narrow top portion that extends out over the ball as well as behind the back of the blade.

Hubert Ernest Gilford's British patent (No. 195,812) dated February 2, 1922, covered an iron with a round metal alignment rod "projecting above the upper surface of the club and extending rearwardly beyond the back of the club, but not extending down to the bottom of the club." This patent also covered a wood with a flat metal alignment strip, set on edge, inlaid into the head. In the patent, the metal strip is flush with the top of the front half of the head, is raised above the back half of the head, and extends well out behind the back of the head. The author does not know if any clubs were produced under the above patents.

Customers are rather a trying lot. There is the youth who lays down his views as to what a club ought to be, and is ready to teach the maker his trade; then there is the lady who buys a club, plays with it, and then returns and wants it exchanged. One of the most exasperating is the fidgety golfer, who is never sure as to the balance, he has lead added, and then finds that too heavy, and it takes much tinkering before he leaves off troubling. At the same time, the clubmaker can usually rise to the occasion. We have heard of a maker who sold a very nice specially made driver to a learned man. Smooth leather had been ordered for the shaft, but, after consideration, the botanical golfer decided to revert to the ordinary style of grip. He accordingly wrote the clubmaker that he wanted the club made caulis volubilis sinistrorsum. After consultation with his wife, the clubmaker replied that they had not that kind of club in stock, and that he could not honestly recommend it (Golfer's Magazine, Feb. 1899: 524).

ARTHUR HARDINGHAM
T-FRAME PUTTER

Arthur S. Hardingham's British patent (No. 25,564) dated December 8, 1905, covered the T-frame putter pictured. According to Hardingham's patent, he proposed:

to form a putter head with a rear projection or bar at right angles to the striking face and of sufficient length to form a sight line to assist the aim of the player. The socket for the shaft may be attached to or form part of the rear bar and if situated approximately midway of such bar the latter may terminate in striking faces at both ends so as to form a putter for right and left hand use, the head as a whole being of I L T or Z shape in plan.

To keep the long alignment bar from scuffing the ground during the golfer's stroke, Hardingham noted:

It is preferable to round or curve the bottom of the club head so that the club clears the ground more evenly in the act of striking within such limits of angle as the shaft is usually held and the bottom of the sighting bar may be similarly curved.

On the putter shown, the bottom of the alignment bar curves upwards as it approaches the back of the head.

Hardingham allowed for making his putter from "gun metal, iron, aluminum, or any other suitable material" and for serrating the face "in any suitable manner to provide a non-slipping surface." The club pictured, marked "Hardingham's Patent" in large letters across the side of the 4 1/2-inch long alignment bar and "Adlams Bristol" in small letters on the sole of the alignment bar, appears to be made from gunmetal. The face, which is very small, measuring only two inches wide, is scored with sixteen thin vertical lines. These lines, which are original, are faint and difficult to see.

Wood-shafted T-frame putters of any type are hardly ever seen. This is the only example of Hardingham's putter known to the author.

UNKNOWN MAKER

T-FRAME PUTTERS

Dating from the early 1900s, the putters pictured show exceptional creativity. The brass putter has a particularly artistic design. The thin blade at the front of a thick hosel, the complete absence of any material behind the blade other than the thick alignment bar, and the way the underside of the alignment bar slopes up and then back down to the ground at its end (to assist in soling the club) are all attractive features.

Both clubs were cast, not forged—one from aluminum, the other from brass or gunmetal. The brass example appears to be hollow, as it pings when tapped

on either the face of the blade or the alignment bar behind the blade. Furthermore, there is a very small opening on its sole directly underneath the base of the shaft.

Related in design, these clubs were probably created by the same person. They share the same "T" shape alignment feature. The only two known, the clubs were obtained together from the same owner, who was not a collector. Neither club has any nicking atop the hosel. Both blades are flush with the leading edge of the hosel and their faces are square at the end of the toe. The alignment line

atop each alignment bar appears to be cut in exactly the same manner, even to the way they begin with a small point. The inventor apparently had one model crafted in aluminum and another model crafted in brass in order to explore his ideas. It is likely that neither model was marketed.

The only marks on these clubs are the initials "CRW" found on the side of the brass alignment bar. (The initials are not visible in this picture.)

HOLMAC, INC.
THE "RUDDER PUTTER,"
T-FRAME

For the normal person who accepts a steady diet of three's on the green because he can't estimate cup distance for an easy two, or whose sense of direction beyond three feet is not a thing you'd come miles to see, here's a new putter that will remove a lot of strokes from his score . . . .

We call it the "Rudder" putter because it does to putting what a rudder does to a ship; it gives direction. More than this, it gives a sense of distance. You just know you're going to bring up hole high on long putts— and you do!

In the illustration you will notice the central piece running aft at right angles to the club face. This is the stationary Rudder feature. You use it for "lining up" your ball with the hole (Golfers Magazine, June 1923: 45).

The Rudder putter, with its T-frame head shape, is very similar to Arthur Hardingham's putter discussed on page 432. There are, however, two basic differences aside from dimensions. First, the 3 1/2 inch wide blade on the Rudder putter is raised off the ground by almost half an inch (note the disparity in depth between the blade and the sighting bar). The blade on Hardingham's putter is flush with the ground. Second, the entire sole of the 5 inch long "sighting bar" on the Rudder putter contacts the ground; the sole of Hardingham's putter curves up as it approaches the back end of the head.

The putter pictured is marked "Rudder Putter \ Holmac, Inc. \ New York NY \ Pat Pend." on the heel side of the sighting bar. Besides selling complete clubs, Holmac, a golf supply wholesale house, sold everything from balls to club components. According to Holmac's 1922 catalog, their domestic clubs were manufactured by the W.C. Morehead Company of Milwaukee, Wisconsin, and Holmac was the sole distributor of Morehead's clubs.

The Rudder Putter had a very limited lifespan. It was already illegal before it was offered! In 1910 and 1911 the R&A and the USGA, respectively, ruled that the measurement across the face of any club had to be longer than the measurement from the face to the back of the head (see p. 195). The author has seen four other Rudder Putters. The worn nickel plate finish on one of them revealed a brass head underneath the plating.

UNKNOWN MAKER
T-FRAME PUTTER

In addition to its extraordinary shape, the putter pictured includes a number of fascinating features. The front half of the head is made from brass while the sighting rod, threaded and screwed into the brass portion of the head, is made from iron. Measuring only three-fourths of an inch long by half an inch wide, the sole on this putter provides the smallest "footprint" of any club known. The body of the head ties into the Carruthers-style hosel halfway up its side. The leather wrap grip is oval, its flattened sides running down the top and bottom of the grip (see p. 528).

The pitted condition of this sighting rod is obviously less than desirable. This putter would be an even stronger collectible if the condition were better. But since this is the only such putter known, the pitted condition of the sighting rod is easily tolerated. The collector understands that not only might he or she never get the chance to obtain another one of these putters, there just might not *be* another one! Although this club is not in the best condition, it is still an exceedingly rare collectible with excellent character.

Two other T-frame putters are worth mentioning: the "Grout" putter and the "Crosby Direct Line" putter. The Grout putter is an ordinary blade putter with a flat piece of iron, approximately 1 1/2 inches long, set at a right angle to the blade behind the sweet-spot. During 1899, this well-made club was advertised— "Get a line on the hole"— by the J.C. Grout Company (*Golf* [ny] Vol. 4-5 1899, 305).

The Crosby putter is similar to the Grout putter except that it has a longer alignment bar. It is a nice collectible, but the Crosby does not approach the level of collectibility enjoyed by the other T-frame putters. It was produced with a metal shaft; it dates from a more recent period; and there are more known Crosby Direct Line putters than there are wood-shafted T-frame putters of all types combined. It should be noted, however, that the Crosby putter is difficult to locate and has sold for substantial sums in the past.

A putt should never, without a very satisfactory reason, be short of the flag. Remember "Never up never in" (*Golf*, 5 June 1891: 207).

ALIGNMENT AIDS

ROBERT BRODIE
"STRAIGHTSHOT" PUTTER

The entire face on Brodie's Straightshot putter consists of a circular disc, only 1 3/8 inches in diameter, placed half an inch ahead of an otherwise ordinary blade. A vertical brace formed integrally with the back of the circular disc is attached to the center of the blade.

The back of this circa early 1900s putter is marked "R. Brodie & Sons \ Anstruther \ Straightshot \ Special \ Putter \ Warranted Hand Forged." The head has been reshafted; but the rarity of this club, together with the unique design of this blade, lowers the significance of the reshaft. This club is the only such genuine example known. (Shamefully, no fewer than three fake examples made from brass, each one unmarked, found their way into the 1993 and 1994 golf auctions held in Great Britain.)

Three putters related to the Straightshot are described in three different patents: Richard F. Breamer's U.S. patent (No. 1,589,926) dated June 22, 1926; Louis Graveure's U.S. patent (No. 1,652,404) dated December 13, 1927; and George Bennie's British patent (No. 325, 744) dated September 28, 1928.

Richard Breamer, from San Francisco, California, patented a triangular mallet head putter. The shaft angled up from the center of the head, with one of the corners made into a circular face slightly smaller than the diameter of the ball. This circular face was the only face on the putter.

Breamer's patent states that "a putter, more than any other golf club, is an instrument of accuracy and precision, since it is used to roll the ball for short distances only." Therefore, a putter with a small "striking space" will compel the player to strike "the ball at substantially the point of the striking face for every stroke." This would insure uniform putting conducive to accuracy and precision.

Louis Graveure, from New York City, devised a duplex putter with a "cylindrical projection" on each side of a center-shafted blade. Each projection was slightly larger in diameter than a golf ball and approximately half an inch thick.

George Bennie, from Bute, Scotland, patented a putter with a "projecting boss" (a small knob, flat on its end) on the face. According to Bennie's patent, his putter was designed "for the final short putts of a few feet" and was referred to as "putter No. 2." Bennie also believed that a small striking face would help the golfer "hit the ball more truly."

It is not known if Breamer's, Graveure's, and Bennie's putters were ever produced.

Charles Skinner's British patent (No. 385) dated January 9, 1905, was the first patent to cover a projecting face on a golf club. Produced in both irons and putters, Skinner's "Reliable" clubs, as they are called, are similar to, but not the same as, the club pictured below. Although the projecting face often found on Skinner's clubs covers approximately the same area as the projecting face on this Lockwood and Brown putter, the face on Skinner's clubs does not project as far and it transitions smoothly to the blade without creating right angles. Also unlike Skinner's putter, the hosel, shaft, and grip on the Lockwood and Brown putter are square.

The projecting face, or "cushion" as it was called, was optional on Skinner's Reliable clubs. The consistent feature, also covered in Skinner's patent, was the sole—it angles up, away from the ground, under the heel and toe.

FRED SAUNDERS
"STRAIGHT LINE" PUTTER

The idea of a projecting face was also covered in William Christie Wilson's British patent (No. 263,225) dated September 23, 1925. As illustrated in his patent, the entire scored area of the iron face protrudes just slightly ahead of the area at the heel and the toe. The projecting area was created by leaving that part of the face in its raw, black, and rough character, as fired in the forge, while the toe and the heel were ground and polished. Wilson felt that the untouched face would provide more back-spin than would normal scoring lines. (The "Saynor/Dronfield" putter mentioned on page 451 also has a projecting face.)

The back of the Lockwood and Brown putter shown at the bottom of the facing page is marked "LB 78 Jermyn Street \ London SW" inside a circle and "Saville Rustless-Iron \ Guaranteed Hand Forged." Saville Rustless-Iron was produced by J.J. Saville & Company, Ltd. during the late 1920s and early 1930s.

Reduce Your Handicap! This is now comparatively easy if you play with a "Saunders" Straight Line Patent aluminum putter (Registered Design 672,159) which gives you a true line to the hole. . . . Write for terms: Fred. Saunders, Highgate Golf Club. London, N." (Golf Illustrated, 2 July 1920: 484).

The Saunders Straight Line putter pictured is marked "Fred Saunders \ Highgate, N." on the top of the head. The sole is marked "L2557 A Patent \ 354265 \ Reg Des No 672159 \ Straight Line Putter \ Medium Lie \ 9 ozs 13 drs." The British registered design (No. 672,159) that covered this putter was dated October 10, 1919, and issued to Frederick Saunders, a golf club maker and golf professional in London.

Saunders learned clubmaking while working for Charles Gibson:

[Saunders] graduated in the craft of clubmaking under C. Gibson. For nearly nine years Saunders was Gibson's first lieutenant, and the experience he gained of teaching and making clubs has stood him in good stead (Golfing, 8 Oct. 1903: 28).

Fred Saunders became a popular golf professional and respected clubmaker:

He came into the world in 1876, at Northam, Devonshire, a spot which can boast of being the birthplace of several prominent golfers, including J.H. and Joshua Taylor . . . . His first appointment was with C. Gibson at Westward Ho!, whence he moved on to the Handsworth club [in 1897]. While in the Midlands, he did several good things in open competitions . . . . As a club-maker, Saunders has achieved a popularity which is as great and as

well-deserved as his playing reputation. He specialises on persimmon socket-head drivers and brassies, and centre-balance irons clubs. Many of our leading players use his goods, and their verdict is unanimously favourable (Golfing, 21 June 1906: 48).

Saunders remained at Handsworth until he took the professional's job at Highgate, in 1905. He remained at Highgate, a small town on the outskirts of London, into the 1930s (Jackson 1994, 83).

In addition to being a fine clubmaker, Saunders could sing! With no patience for those who only *think* they can sing, Josh Taylor acknowledged Saunders musical talent:

Fred Saunders, the Highgate Club's professional, is the possessor of a highly trained voice, an accomplishment all the more peculiar seeing that golf professionals as a rule are not musical. I will admit that one member is supposed to equal George

Elliot . . . but I have heard him, much to my sorrow—while another frequently murders "A Jovial Monk" and makes the night hideous by retailing the sorrows of "A Bedouin Love Song," generally finishing up the evening and the audience by singing the "Bandolero." For the benefit of those who occasionally have, much against their wills, to listen to this operatic star, I may say he has lately added to his repertoire Kipling's "On the Road to Mandalay;" may he soon take that road never to return. It would be a fitting fate, especially as he further contemplates annoying people with "Asleep in the Deep." An epitaph on his tombstone of "Asleep in the Deep on the Road to Mandalay" would read well. Let him and his unfortunate audiences take warning (Golf Illustrated, 18 Mar. 1910: 261).

EDWARD BACHELLER
"SURE THING" PUTTER

UNKNOWN MAKER
"SWEETNER" PUTTER

Edward F. Bacheller, of Lynn, Massachusetts, received a U.S. design patent (No. 58,209) dated June 28, 1921, that covered the putter pictured directly above. Bacheller assigned one half of his interest in this patent to John Hammond Stewart of Lynnfield, Massachusetts.

Bacheller's putter, marked "Sure Thing \ Products Co. \ Lynn, Mass. \ Pat. Pend." on the sole, was produced after Bacheller applied for his patent on February 10, 1921, but before it was issued on June 28, 1921.

Designed to improve the golfer's alignment, Bacheller's putter also has artistic style. The lines are strong and the design is clean. The Sure Thing putter, like the Sweetner putter discussed next, is seldom seen.

The man who invented golf deserves a monument as broad as the Pyramids and as high as the Eiffel tower. It has saved more lives than the doctors; brought health and happiness to thousands. As developer of character it has no equal (Golfing, 2 Dec. 1909: 20).

This aluminum head putter includes a "T" alignment guide across the top of its head. Although not as dramatic or stylish as the true T-frame putters such as the Rudder putter, the Sweetner putter is still a good collectible in its own right.

The sole is marked "Sweetner \ Medium Lie \ Rd. No. 723341." This design registration number dates to the end of 1926.

A putter similar to the Sweetner putter was covered under Arthur Round's British patent (No. 181,185) dated April 14, 1921. Round's aluminum putter, however, included "a quarter segment of a sphere" centrally located behind the blade and on top of the flange. When viewed from above, this segment looks like the back half of a golf ball. The rearward alignment guide was centered atop this ball-like segment.

HAROLD BAILEY
"COOMBE PUTTER"

The gunmetal putter below has a large flange with an alignment bar centrally located behind the blade. The back of the blade is marked "A. Bembridge \ Coombe Wood \ Coombe Putter" and "Rd No 640753." British design registration No. 640,753, dated August 7, 1914, was issued to Harold Bailey. "A. Bembridge" was the professional at Coombe Wood from 1911 until 1920 (Jackson 1994, 7).

"The Self-Directing Putter," advertised by "C. Ralph Smith, Expert Clubmaker," is distantly related to the Coombe Putter (*Golf Illustrated*, 3 June 1904: 192). The Self-Directing Putter has a short, semicircular flange, which is only about half as wide as a golf ball, attached to the top of the blade. Centered behind the sweet-spot, the flange includes a small alignment groove.

CHARLES H. RODWELL
"THE RODWELL NEW STANDARD PUTTER"

A. TOOLEY & SONS
INTEGRAL FACE & ALIGNMENT BAR, BRASSIE

Charles Herbert Rodwell received a British patent (No. 167,956) dated July 27, 1920, and a U.S. patent (No. 1,420,946) dated June 27, 1922, that covered the aluminum mallet putter pictured above right. This particular putter is marked "The Rodwell \ New Standard Putter \ 2025" on the crown and "The Rodwell \ New Standard Putter \ U.S. Design Patent No. 22372 \ Upright Lie \ 10 ozs 4 drs" on the sole. The design patent noted on the sole of this club is separate from the U.S. (utility) patent mentioned above.

The object of Rodwell's club, according to both his British and U.S. patent, was "to guide the eye of the player or focus his attention on the line of the putter stoke." Therefore, the top of the head has a:

semi-circular raised portion, the diameter of which is formed by a straight edge on the face of the head, and in the position which corresponds with the centre of the semi-circle is a tapered notch directed at right angles to such straight edge.

Rodwell putters were sold for a number of years. They were even offered in the Burke Golf Company's 1927 catalog (30).

The brassie pictured above left, marked "A. Tooley & Sons \ 40 Fetterlane \ London \ Reg'd" on the crown, has a solid gunmetal face integral with a half inch wide gunmetal alignment bar running across the entire head. See pages 343-346 for other metal face woods.

ROBERT D. PRYDE
INTEGRAL BACKWEIGHT & ALIGNMENT BAR

WILSON-WESTERN SPORTING GOODS CO.
"WALKER CUP," INTEGRAL BACKWEIGHT & ALIGNMENT BAR

On April 24, 1923, Robert Dalgleish Pryde, of Orange, Connecticut, received a U.S. patent (No. 1,452,845) that covered the shapely backweight in the driver pictured between the matching driver and brassie. Pryde's backweight includes a central section that projects forward and terminates at a point just behind the face. As constructed, this backweight acts as an alignment aid, but that was not its primary purpose. According to Pryde's patent, his backweight offered the golfer greater driving power and accuracy:

In this structure the weight is distributed uniformly over the entire rear of the head and the club is thus well balanced in the hand and not liable to shift or lose its position while driving. The offset portion of the weight projects in the same line as the movement of the head while driving and is directly in rear of the striking face where the ball contacts therewith and very close thereto, there being only sufficient wood therebetween to insure a striking face and not weaken the head. By reason of these features great driving power is given to the club, much more than has heretofore been possible to obtain, owing to the proximity of the weight to the striking face and its uniform distribution over the rear of the golf club.

Pryde's driver pictured is marked "R.D. Pryde" on the top of the backweight and "Pat. Ap. 24, 1923 \ Hand Made" in the wood next to the backweight. "D" is stamped on the underside of the toe. Pryde received a British patent (No. 192,025) dated July 26, 1922, that covered his club in the U.K.

Also pictured are a matching pair of Walker Cup woods, produced at some point during the mid-1920s by the Wilson-Western Sporting Goods Company. They have "alumo" backweights shaped similarly to Pryde's backweight. Between 1927 and 1930, Walker Cup woods were made in a variety of styles. At least three different face inserts were used, though only one insert per year was offered. Almost all remaining Walker Cup woods have metal shafts—seamless drawn steel covered with a black "Indestructo" sheath—but Wilson's catalogs offered a hickory shaft option until 1929. The brass soleplates on both clubs are marked "Walker Cup \ Reg. 1002" in addition to their own respective titles of "Driver" and "Brassie."

MAC & MAC
POINTED BACK PUTTER

The Mac & Mac Putter gives you a dead line on the hole—instantly. The "pointed back" demands that your swing back stay on the line of the putt. Its extra weight prevents "stabbing the ball," forcing you to let the putter head do the work—giving you an uncanny control over distance.

The grip and shaft are semi-square, automatically lining up the head, square with the hole. The grip fits naturally and delicately in the fingers giving the very necessary "feel" and "confidence" which makes you sink all the "short ones" and helps you sink most of the "long ones."

It is your long hoped for putter. The more you use it, the more you will swear by it, as it will help eliminate the "off days" in your putting.

Head is composed of highly polished German silver. Workmanship and material used in grip, shaft, and finish, are of highest possible quality, making each individual putter a masterpiece of the club makers art.

Flat, medium, or upright lie, in right or left hand, (we advise medium) (Golfers Magazine, Jan. 1923: 40).

The Mac & Mac putter pictured, marked "Mac & Mac" on its shaft, possesses a number of interesting characteristics. Along with a stylish square hosel and an unusual head shape that includes a "pointed back," this putter is made with a German silver head and a square shaft. German silver is defined as "any of various alloys of copper, zinc, and nickel, usually white and used for utensils and drawing instruments; nickel silver" (Random House 1991, 560). The square shaft, as noted in the above advertisement, was to help the golfer's alignment.

Square shafts, however, were used before Mac & Mac produced them. In 1902 John W. Moore produced woods with square shafts (see p. 504). Moore claimed that a square shaft would help the golfer hit straighter shots

In addition to the Pearson slot face iron and the Dimple Faced backspin mashie (see p. 228 and 238), Mac & Mac also offered "The Mac & Mac Guaranteed Non-Slicing Drivers, Brassies, and Spoons" (*Golfers Magazine*, Dec. 1923: 33). These "non-slicing" woods simply have the backweight located towards the toe. Only a small portion of the backweight is visible on the top of the head.

Distantly related to the Mac & Mac's putter is the Suitall putter, forged by William Gibson & Co. and marketed by A. Tooley & Sons. The Suitall consists of a blade that angles down from both the toe and the hosel and then angles up to a point above the sweet-spot. Roughly speaking, the top of the blade resembles the letter "W." Furthermore, the sole is quite rounded, heel to toe, so the lie of this club would "suit all" (*Golfing*, Jan. 1925: 42).

WILLIAM GIBSON & CO.

"JONKO" PUTTER

Gibson's "Jonko" putter, pictured, is a perennial favorite among collectors. Its design is both radical and aesthetically pleasing at the same time. Its simple yet bold shape commands immediate attention and a lingering fascination.

The Jonko shown is marked "Wm Gibson & Co. Ltd \ Kinghorn \ Scotland" inside an oval on the back of the head and "Made in Scotland \ Warranted Hand Forged" on the sole. Gibson's "star" trademark is stamped on the top of the toe; "Gibson's Star A" is stamped inside an oval on the shaft.

Once one of the largest manufacturers of golf clubs in the world, William Gibson built his reputation on producing well-made clubs. He often advertised his workmanship rather than a particular club:

The Secret of Success. Gibsons do not stint money in either material or workmanship—they believe in the best of both worlds—they select the material with great care, every detail being studied, the natural result is—the perfect club (fitted with the famous "Star A" shafts) and N.B., they cost no more than the commoner kinds. Gibsons do not ask you to accept this claim, they only expect you to make comparisons and so prove it for yourselves. The "Star" on a golf head spells "Quality." Wm. Gibson & Co., Ltd. (Golf Illustrated, 9 July 1920: 522).

The Jonko was apparently made during the mid-1920s inasmuch as a few steel shaft examples, complete with a thinner hosel, are also known. The wood shaft examples, which are rarely seen, are much more sought after than their steel shaft counterparts. Steel shaft clubs from the 1920s draw only a fraction of the price commanded by similar wood shaft clubs.

John T. Shea, of Milford, Connecticut, received a U.S. patent (No. 1,319,802) dated October 28, 1919, that covered a thick blade putter similar to the Jonko. As illustrated in Milford's patent, the heel and toe portions of the blade are only about half as high as the central portion of the blade.

Golf makes a man patient and enduring. It keeps the fires of hope continually alive. It gives one respect for one's opponent, and even makes an enemy endurable. It is the cleanest, fairest sport in the world. Show me a good golf player and I will show you a clear-brained, well-balanced, generous manly fine fellow (Golfing, 2 Dec. 1909: 20).

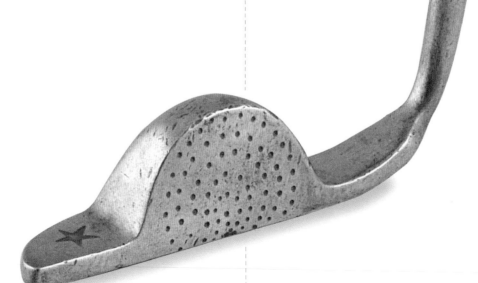

ROBERT SIMPSON
"BALL-FACE MASHIE"

The tradition of Hugh Philp, whose clubs combined balance with excellence and beauty of workmanship, are still kept alive by the best makers, and none is more keenly imbued with those traditions than Bob Simpson, the head of the famous Carnoustie family of golfers. . . .

The . . . club which we have seen is an approaching mashie of entirely novel design. Simpson says he could never see the object of having all iron heads made about double the breadth at the point [toe] to what they are at the heel, and he has gone upon the sensible principle of making the broadest and heaviest part in the centre with which the ball is struck. On the centre of this mashie accordingly Simpson has left a diced circle about the size of a golf ball whose base touches the bottom of the face and whose apex surmounts the top by about a quarter of an inch.

Behind this circle the metal is thicker, so that a larger proportionate striking surface and greater weight behind the stroke are provided than in any other club with which we are acquainted. Like the putter this mashie is beautifully balanced and its lie is perfect. Its look inspires confidence and the desire to use it. These clubs are only 7s. 6d. each, and we anticipate a large demand for them (Golf Illustrated 3 April 1903: 15).

According to Simpson's British patent (No. 19,725) dated September 14, 1903, which covered his Ball-Face iron:

The circle, in addition to affording a wider surface for striking the ball, also acts as an indicator and helps to guide the golfer in striking such ball correctly.

Simpson's Ball-Face clubs were made in three models:

cleeks, irons, and mashies. The club pictured above appears to be a mashie. It is marked "R. Simpson \ Carnoustie" inside an oval on the back of the blade along with "Reg No. 23585 \ Warranted Hand Forged."

Robert Simpson came from a family of golfers. The following biographical sketch mentions three of his six brothers:

Bob Simpson . . . is a son of Earlsferry, and is a member of a family every member of which has done something uncommon in the field of golf. Jack Simpson won the Open Championship. Archie Simpson is pointed out as the embodiment of style and grace in driving. He at one time gave promise of a high step on the ladder of fame; but his business at Balgownie engrossed his attention, and of late he has not had opportunities for much practice against his equals. Mr. David is an artisan amateur of the Willie Greig stamp. In the forefront of St. Andrews club golf for a score of years, David is as fresh and vigorous in his long game as when in his teens, and his play on the green has been

mellowed by experience in championship and interclub match.

Bob Simpson . . . has revolutionised club-making in Carnoustie. His trade relations are in many lands; but he, like a true Fifer, never forgets that home consumers have title to his services when he produces a new idea in golf. Bob . . . has a practical knowledge of the game, and had he devoted his time to the links instead of to the superintendence of the workshop, his qualifications as a golfer would have landed him high on the ladder of fame (Golf Illustrated, 31 July 1903: 91).

Because Simpson was so respected, his neighbors asked him to run for public office. When he did, he was elected:

Bob Simpson, the well-known clubmaker and professional, has been elected a Town Councillor of Carnoustie. This is a unique honour, or one should perhaps rather say a "record" for a professional golfer. The position was none of Bob's seeking, but an influential deputation of ratepayers waited upon him and pressed him to give his services to the burgh, and after due cogitation he

decided to enter municipal life. Bob Simpson's popularity is evidenced by his return without opposition (Golf Illustrated, 8 Nov. 1908: 123).

After serving two terms on the town council, Simpson "held the position of magistrate at his death on 1st May 1923" (Hackney 1988, 90).

An iron identical in outline to Simpson's Ball-Face was produced briefly by George Forrester. Titled "Forrester's Masonic Mashie," this iron is marked with the Masonic Past Master's emblem, which includes the compass and square, in the ball-sized circle on its face. The back of the blade, which is thicker behind the sweet-spot, includes other Masonic symbols. The Masonic mashie was described as a show club and an expensive luxury (Golfing, 20 Nov. 1902). Rather than stock them, the large London retail outlet of Benetfink & Company kept only one for display. Few Masonic mashies were made.

New patents in
driving-clubs are generally
ingenious absurdities.
"Englishmen buy them," said
a Scottish club-maker.

(Andrew Lang; Lang 1895, 141)

Additional Head Shapes

Like many of the clubs already presented in this book, those mentioned in this chapter are distinctive in their design and shape. However, the clubs in this chapter do not fit into any of the earlier chapters. Many of these clubs deal specifically with weight or balance in their clubhead design, but many others deal with additional features such as decreased wind resistance or a unique shape.

Given the catchall nature of this chapter and the limits of this book, a number of clubs that could be presented here are not. During the wood shaft era, many clubs were made that, in spite of bearing their own distinctive names, had only a small tweak in their design. Such clubs have been passed over in favor of the more unusual, rare, or historical clubs. However, because some of the clubs left out are still nice collectibles, a few of the more common ones will be briefly discussed at this point. The first three—the Dominie, the Brown-Vardon, and the Orion—were all made by William Gibson of Kinghorn, Scotland.

The "Dominie," first produced in 1908, is a center-shafted aluminum Schenectady-style putter with a futuristic head: the toe and the heel come to rounded but distinct points. After 1912, a Dominie putter made from iron and shaped similar to the "Brown-Vardon" putter was produced.

The "Brown-Vardon" Putter, first produced in 1912, is a small mallet head putter made from iron. The head, similar to the Harrower putter presented on page 161, has a very low profile and the face comes to a point where the toe rounds down to meet the sole. The head is usually marked "Arthur Brown" and "Harry Vardon." A brass headed version usually marked "Vardon's Putter" was also made. Other makers copied this head shape and added a few stylistic touches of their own. "The Celtic" and Spalding's "BV" model first offered in their 1914 catalog are two examples.

James Braid's "Orion" iron putter, first produced in 1913, is a blade putter with a flanged sole. The leading side of the hosel (the side that faces the target) is usually flat, as is the leading side of the shaft. Again, other makers copied the flanged blade design of this putter, but usually without the flat-sided hosel or flat-sided shaft.

Advertised in and around 1931, the "Rivers-Zamba Approach Putter" (also titled "The Scuffler") has a low profile blade, a lofted face, and a unique head shape. Each side of the head—the face, the crown, the back, and the sole—is flat. The "Semi-putter" made by Crawford, McGregor & Canby is similar to The Scuffler and dates from the same time.

The backs of many irons were designed with slight variations. These variations were usually subtle and often produced in quantity by various makers during the wood shaft era.

The first iron to sport a slightly different back was George Forrester's Concentrated Lofter. In order to concentrate the weight behind and under the ball, the back of this blade is slightly thicker behind the exact center of the face and becomes progressively more so as it approaches the sole. The overall thickness added to this blade, however, is not very substantial—the head becomes only slightly thicker. The British design registration (No. 125,240) issued to Forrester for his Concentrated Lofter dates to 1889. Forrester's Concentrated clubhead design still continues today, though more pronounced, and is referred to as a muscle-back blade.

Forrester also produced a "Centre-Balanced Cleek." This club also has a rounded back, but the weight is centered just above the sweet-spot and the thickness of the sole is normal:

The weight was rather on top than in the true center of the blade. . . . [Consequently] the ball was inclined to fly very low (Golf, 14 Nov. 1890: 136).

William Thompson received a British patent (No. 5,133) dated March 24, 1891, that covered an iron he referred to as a "Mussel Cleek." The center of the blade back is raised to a point and slants off in all four directions. By 1904 such clubs were referred to as "concentric" irons. Today, this basic design, which continued to be employed by various cleek makers during the last thirty years of the wood shaft era, is referred to as a "diamond back."

William Auchterlonie, David Auchterlonie, and Andrew William Crosthwaite received a British patent (No. 4,516) dated March 20, 1894, that covered an iron made twice as thick, top to bottom, behind the middle of the face.

In addition to the aforementioned designs, other minor variations were incorporated into the backs of both irons and blade putters. A few of the ideas employed on large numbers of clubs included beveling the heel and/or the toe on the blade back, gently rounding the blade back from heel to toe, beveling the sole, and adding a small flange at the sole. Many woods, irons, and putters were given a small nudge in the shape of their clubheads. A slightly longer head here; a somewhat deeper face there; and bevelled heels, toes, top-lines, and soles too numerous to mention.

Because modest new clubhead designs and variations during the wood shaft era did not depart very far from tradition or have their playability called into serious question, they were generally more acceptable to the average golfer than were the truly creative and "cutting edge" clubs. Therefore, the more traditional antique clubs remain in far greater numbers.

The army of inventors promises soon to rob golf of its manifold terrors, and recently the veteran Tom Morris has been applying his genius in designing a cleek specially adapted to play cupped balls. The result is a very serviceable-looking implement, and those who have been playing with it speak in high terms of Tom's idea. The straight sole of the ordinary cleek is somewhat rounded, whilst the greatest breadth of the blade is nearest the front. In general appearance it is egg-shaped, but a little elongated, the length from heel to toe being three inches. It is admirably balanced, and the rounded sole permits of the cleek being used at any angle. Besides being useful for cupped balls, it will also prove very serviceable for hanging balls. Altogether the cleek is likely to meet a felt want, and Tom is to be congratulated upon having evolved out of his own thought and experience what will prove a friend to many a golfer. The cleek has been patented (Golf, 6 Mar. 1891: 394).

Morris's smooth face "cupped ball" cleek, marked "T. Morris \ St. Andrews" inside an oval on the back of the blade along with "Patent 3059" and a small "pipe" trademark, is pictured. The shaft stamp, "R. Foulis \ Lake Forest," also ties in to Old Tom as will be seen later.

The statement that Morris's cleek "has been patented" is misleading. In February of 1891, Morris only began the process of patenting his cleek; he did not receive a patent for his club because he later abandoned his British application, assigned "No. 3,059."

Another interesting aspect of this club is the "pipe" trademark on the back of the blade. This mark was used not only by Tom Stewart, one of the finest and most respected of all cleekmakers; it was also used by Stewart's father, who was also a cleekmaker:

Mr. Thomas Stewart, Golf Cleek and Iron Maker, St. Andrews, may be said to have been born to the trade. He hailed originally from Carnoustie, where his father followed the same occupation and some forty or fifty years ago made cleek heads for George Morris–brother of the veteran Tom–who was then located there.

Mr. Stewart served his apprenticeship as a blacksmith and worked at this for some years before taking to cleek making. . . . About eleven years ago he went into the workshop of Robert White, the well-known cleek maker of St. Andrews, now in America. He worked for White for about three years, after which he began business for himself.

He has now eight men in constant employment, and his cleek and iron heads, with the pipe on the back as a trademark, are well-known to the golfing world and find favour wherever they go. The idea of a pipe as a trademark is not a new one, as it served his father before him (Golf Illustrated, 12 July 1901: 37).

According to this article, Tom Stewart went into business in 1893. Therefore, clubs that date prior to 1893 and bear the Stewart "pipe" trademark were made by Tom's father—either that or the article is a little inaccurate. Given the probability that Tom's father did not work in St. Andrews and the fact that Morris's elliptical face "cupped ball" cleek was produced in 1891, the younger Stewart must have been in business a few years before 1893. Nevertheless, notice the "pipe" mark on this club. It is smaller and has more curve than the Stewart pipe mark pictured on page 220. Perhaps the small, curved pipe mark once belonged to Tom Stewart's father. Tom Stewart died in July of 1931, handing down his business to his sons, Tom Jr. and Jack.

The "R. Foulis \ Lake Forest" shaft stamp on the club pictured is also of keen interest. Robert Foulis was born in St. Andrews in 1873. He learned his clubmaking while working, for four and one-half years, in the shop of Old Tom Morris. His father, James Foulis Sr., was the foreman in Morris's shop, where he worked for thirty-five years. In 1895 Robert came to America and helped lay out the Onwentsia Club in Lake Forest, Illinois. He later worked there as the professional and the greenkeeper during 1896 and 1897.

The "R. Foulis \ Lake Forest" shaft stamp on this club indicates this individual club was in use in 1896 or 1897. Perhaps Robert re-shafted this club or used it as one of his own; perhaps his father, while working in Morris's shop, had it reshafted and marked for him. It could even have been made in 1896 or 1897 as a special order. Origin aside, this shaft stamp touches on the unique connection between Robert Foulis and Tom Morris.

Robert was also a fine golfer, finishing tied for 15th in the 1897 U.S. Open. (His brother, James, was even better, winning the 1896 U.S. Open.) After working as the professional and greenkeeper at the Town and Country Club in Minneapolis, Minnesota, from early 1898 until 1901, Robert moved to St. Louis, Missouri, and remained there until his death in 1945. For thirty-five of those years he was affiliated with the Bellerive Golf Club.

A club somewhat similar to Tom Morris's elliptical blade iron was covered by Walter Kempton Cannon's British patent (No. 7,365) dated March 26, 1912. Cannon designed an elliptical type iron that had a pointed toe located midway up the face (the top of the blade rounds down at the toe while the bottom of the blade rounds up in mirror fashion). Cannon irons do not receive as much collector interest as the much earlier Morris elliptical face irons. Some Cannon irons, however, are quite striking. Cannon's design was "borrowed" by other makers whose copies are not always as attractive or dramatic as the originals marked "Cannon."

Continuing respect for Tom Morris adds greatly to the desirability of his elliptical face cleek, as does the fact that he produced only three patent clubs. In addition to the elliptical blade "cupped ball" iron, Morris also devised a drain pipe putter and a concave face niblick (see p. 247 and p. 241).

In addition to being a fine clubmaker, player, greenkeeper, architect, etc., Morris is to be credited with an idea that remains in use on every green today: the cup! According to a correspondent of the *Glasgow Evening Times* who once had a conversation with Morris:

While chatting with him [Old Tom] in his shop a few years ago I referred to some changes that were being made at the High Hole. "Yes," said Tom, "That hole has given me more trouble than any other hole in the course." And he added this circumstance—"It was at the High Hole that the first iron pot was used. Previously there was nothing to support the earth, and consequently complaints were numerous about inequalities and so on. So I went to an iron monger and asked him to make a pot of such and such dimensions. This pot was placed in the High Hole, and it proved such a great success that pots were used all over the course. Now they are used all over the world." Tom ended with the remark: "Whoever wants to write the history of modern golf might begin with the High Hole (Golf Illustrated, 12 June 1908: 231).

Born in 1821, Morris remained in good health for most of his life and was quite active until his death in 1908. A four-time British Open champion, Morris scored an 89 (41-48) during a match over the Old Course at St. Andrews when he was 84 years old. The same issue of *Golf* that reported Morris's score also disclosed that Morris was ready to retire from his clubmaking business:

Rumour has it that Old Tom Morris is anxious to retire from his club-making business at St. Andrews, and is disposed to turn it into a company (30 Sep. 1904: 3).

After a long life of activity in the world of golf, Tom Morris died in May of 1908:

It is with deepest regret that we record the tragic death, on Monday afternoon, of Old Tom Morris, the veteran St. Andrews golfer. The circumstances were that Tom, who was in his usual health, had gone down to the New Golf Club, of which he was a member, and, after staying in the club-room there for a time, had got up, intending, it is thought, to go to the lavatory; but, mistaking the door, he opened one immediately next to it, leading, with a long stair, to a cellar, and down this, fully eight feet, Tom fell. When found he was still alive, and was taken in an ambulance to the Cottage Hospital, but he died soon afterwards (Golf Illustrated, 29 May 1908: 187).

In eulogizing Tom Morris, T.D. Miller portrayed the love and respect that attended Old Tom in life as well as in passing:

Old Tom lived a full-rounded life; a long and remarkably healthy one, chequered no doubt like that of others, with light and shade. He stood at the very top of his profession, and goes hence beloved and lamented by all who knew him, and it is by common consent that the lines have been applied to him:–

> *"Surely never did there live on earth*
> *A man of kindlier nature."*

(Golf Illustrated, 29 May 1908: 188).

The account of Morris's funeral contained in the June 5, 1908 issue of *Golf Illustrated* leaves no doubt about his stature, not just as a golfer and a clubmaker, but as a man who transcended the competitive aspects of the game for the higher principles it embraces:

To those who had never seen him at all . . . he was but a name, a revered and respected one, no doubt, but a name, but to us, who have lived alongside of him, have seen him every day and chatted with him, he was a personal friend, and the wrench is a severe one. . . . He was revered, respected and beloved of all, and St. Andrews is immeasurably the poorer, and the attractions of the environment of her links lessened by the death of our Grand Old Man. His achievements in the golfing world were great, and will be handed down from time to time; but the great moral of his life was that, no matter in what sphere, it is character that achieves the greatest victories. Old Tom was great as a golfer, but greater still as a man (211).

Old Tom's business was kept in his family following his death:

Golfers everywhere will be interested to know that the management of the business, so long carried on here by the late Tom Morris, has now been taken over by Mr. W. Bruce Hunter, the grandson, and Mr. William Rusack, jun., grandson-in-law of the veteran golfer, so that the business for so many years associated with his name will still be retained among the descendants of Old Tom (Golf Illustrated, 4 Feb. 1910: 139).

See page 62 for more information about Morris.

UNKNOWN MAKER
RIDGE BACK IRON

The back of the left-handed iron pictured has a dramatic ridge. The design looks simple, but it is actually quite sophisticated and complex. When the clubhead is placed squarely behind the ball, the ridge runs parallel with the ground, and there is an equal amount of weight across the entire length of the blade. Making such a ridge required thoughtful planning. Because the sides of the ridge cover the entire back of the blade and the blade is higher at the toe than at the heel, the sides of the ridge must rise at increasing angles between the toe and the heel. In spite of the engineering and effort required to construct it, this ridge, which obviously weighted the head in a unique manner, was an idea that was quickly abandoned.

The hosel pin, clearly seen in the lower picture, has been replaced. A replaced pin is usually evidence of a reshafted club. In this case, however, the reshafting is tolerable for three reasons. First, the reshaft has nothing to do with the unique and collectible feature of the head. Second, this is the only such ridge back iron known. Third, reshafting a club was part of the game.

A. CRAIG
FLANGE BACK DRIVING IRON

The iron pictured right has an exceptionally large flange—extending 1 1/4 inches behind the blade—positioned halfway up the back of the blade. Given its 38-inch shaft, flat lie, and slightly lofted face, this stylish club appears to be a driving iron of sorts. The gunmetal head also has a short drill-through "Carruthers" hosel. The gunmetal head, the flange, and the hosel combine to create a visually strong club unlike any other.

"A. Craig" marked atop the flange may identify Alexander Craig, of Coventry, England. Alexander received both a British patent (No. 179,987) dated Jan 18, 1921, and U.S. patent (No. 1,429,56) dated September 19, 1922, that covered an adjustable loft iron.

However, given its late 1800s to early 1900s nature, the flange back iron pictured could have been made by a different A. Craig.

The features in this iron were not combined without thought. Because the flange adds weight to the head, a short drilled-through hosel (the tip of the shaft is visible on the sole) was used to reduce the weight of the head. The flange is located midway between the top and bottom of the blade, placing its weight closer to the center of the ball. This raised the club-head's center of balance, thereby providing the shot with a lower trajectory and, it was hoped, more distance.

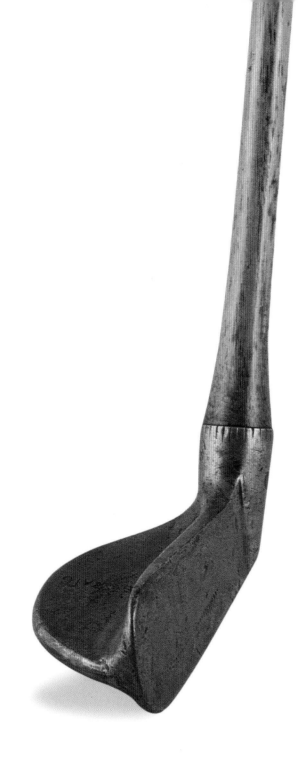

ANGUS TEEN & CO.
"BAR BALANCED CLEEK"

According to an advertisement for Messrs. Teen & Company, of 18 Eastcombe Terrace, Blackheath, their "Bar Balanced Cleek" was:

A beautifully finished cleek, only weighing half-a-pound, with tremendous driving power. Will take the place of all previous cleeks (Golf, 16 Nov. 1894: 192).

The example pictured left is marked "A Teen & Co." on the heel half of the raised bar and "BBC" (Bar Balanced Cleek) on the toe half. Angus Teen & Company, an obscure clubmaking firm, also made Claude Johnson's patent wood and Johnson's symmetrical putter (page 389.) Like Claude Johnson clubs, Bar Balanced Cleeks are quite rare.

GEORGE FORRESTER
"MASTER CLEEK"

Mr. George Forrester, Golf club-maker, Elie . . . has added to the list a new cleek which is constructed with a straight blade, but at the toe there develops a solid knob, which, according to the patentee, counter-balances the weight of the socket, and enables the player to get away a straight ball. The cleek will be known as the "Master Cleek," a similar name being given to the iron and the mashie. The idea of the patentee is to give a more solid face to the ball all along the striking surface of the blade, thereby counteracting heeled or sliced shots, which go as far and as straight as if hit true. Mr. Forrester has kindly sent us a cleek for trial and experiment. This we have done, and though from the appearance of the club we had some misgiving as to the virtues claimed for it, trial convinced us that the claim was a sound one. It was not so much the length of the shot as the straightness of the flight of the ball which surprised us; and as straightness is the essential feature of all good cleek play, we have pleasure in calling the attention of golfers to this new club, and in recommending a trial of it (Golf, 30 Aug. 1895: 483).

The Master Cleek pictured is marked "G. Forrester \ Elie \ Earlsferry" on the blade back along with "Rd No. 257927," a British design registration number dating to the middle of 1895.

George Forrester (1847-1930) was a prominent clubmaker who first made clubs in the long nose era:

The name of this famous club-maker has extended far and wide—wherever, in short, sterling club and ball are held in due repute.

Rather oddly, Mr. Forrester first began to make clubs for his own use

entirely while still serving an appren-ticeship as a mason to Mr. David Given of Elie some thirty years ago. His knowledge of the art has, in fact, been gained through pure experience and many an unsuccessful experiment. . . .

Shortly after finishing his appren-ticeship he went to the states in pursuance of his trade as a stone-cutter. He made many inquiries as to where he could enjoy a game; but golf was utterly unknown in New York, in Philadelphia, Chicago, and the Far West.

On returning home, the old love of club-making once more seized him, and he began trade as a maker for the public in 1871. He at first found it up-hill work . . . . Some, indeed, predicted that Mr. Forrester's first year in the trade would be his last . . . .

Even in trade processes he was occasionally at fault. The mere matter of staining the heads was still a jealously guarded trade secret; and the same may be said of much else. Not many years ago the golfing world was struck with indignant amazement at the thought of turning clubs with a lathe. But Mr. Forrester was alive to the value of this, and was among the very first in the country to have one at work (The Golfer, 9 Dec. 1896: 471-472).

In addition to his Master Cleek and other clubs such as his Concentrated and Centre-Balance irons (discussed on page 445), Forrester also produced a "Ball Back Patent Cleek." This iron has a raised hump centered low on the back of the blade:

The improvement consists of a protuberance on the back of the blade about a quarter the circumference of a Golf ball, and just at the portion of the club which ought to give impact to the ball. The cleek is of the ordinary pattern, with the exception of this

protuberance, which is designed to give, and does in practice give, additional carrying-power to the ball. . . . It is a particularly useful weapon where lies are heavy and soft, or where wind is apt to be disconcerting in its deflections of the flight of the ball (Golf, 9 Dec. 1892: 199).

Robert Simpson's "Perfect Balance" cleeks, irons, and mashies, patented in the U.K. on September 26, 1906, were similar to Forrester's Ball Back Cleeks. The back of a Perfect Balance iron rounds out behind the sweet-spot and gets progres-sively thicker as it approaches the sole directly below the sweet-spot. Perfect Balance irons were produced in quantity—their 1908 advertisements boast that over 10,000 were sold! These clubs reportedly reduced "divot digging," slicing, and pulling, and removed the necessity for any " 'wiggling' of the club on the ground" when addressing the ball (Golfing, 13 Dec. 1906: 38). Simpson also sold a "Perfect Balance" wood, which simply included a small brass backweight. Another backweighted iron, circa 1911, was "The Ernest Newbery Club." The blade back was moderately thicker, shaped like a half circle, behind the center of the face.

It is interesting to note that George Forrester was more than a clubmaker. He served many terms as an Elie Town Councillor, beginning at least by 1881, and he even served as the Provost (mayor) of Elie for three years, begining in 1899 (*East Fife Record*, 19 May 1899: 4; also *East Fife Observer*, 8 May 1930).

ARTHUR TOOLEY
"STRAIGHT DRIVING IRON

"Have you tried Tooley's Patent Straight Driving Clubs? They keep your ball perfectly straight; and will drive as far as any iron club. They are weighted at each end and perfectly balanced. To prevent pulling or slicing try one of these iron clubs. They speak for themselves. A. Tooley, Professional & Golf Club Maker, Honor Oak Golf Club, Honor Oak Park, S.E. (Golf Illustrated, 31 Mar. 1905: 20).

Heel and toe weighting is not of modern origin. In fact, as a *real* heel and toe weighted iron, Tooley's circa 1905 Straight Driving Iron, pictured above, surpasses anything made before or since. The club shown is marked "A. Tooley \ Honor Oak \ Reg Design 448,649." The British design registration number dates to January 1905.

A few other heel and toe weighted irons were produced during the wood shaft era, though none was as extreme in design as Tooley's iron. George Forrester's Double-Balanced Approach Mashie has a small rounded hump (thicker towards the sole) behind both the heel and the toe on the back of its blade. William Winton also produced an iron that is slightly thicker behind the heel and toe. (The weighted areas of Winton's club are subtle and do not add much weight). Another heel and toe weighted iron, this one unmarked, sold at a Phillips golf auction in Chester, England, on July 16, 1991. This club simply had two raised rectangular lumps, one behind the center of the toe and the other behind the center of the heel. Gilbert Legh's British patent (16,502) dated July 15, 1912, calls for making the back of the toe and heel slightly thicker than the rest of the blade.

A few heel and toe weighted putters were also produced. Alex Herd, the 1902 British Open Champion and four time runner-up, advertised one such putter called "Herd's Patent Putter" (*Golf*, 24 Dec. 1897: 283). It was described as follows:

Herd . . . played with a patent putter weighted at the back with two raised bars [1/2 in. wide, 1/4 in. thick] placed [1 in.] apart as if to mark the width of the face, which was meant to be opposite the ball in playing (Golf, 4 Dec. 1896: 227).

The blade on a "Par Putta" is thick behind the toe and heel while the area directly behind the middle of the face is thin. An aluminum mallet head putter marked "Saynor, Dronfield" has a rounded hump behind both the toe and heel along with a face (the central striking portion) set slightly ahead of the heel and toe.

Going beyond heel and toe weighting, Gilbert Legh's British patent (No. 29,603) dated December 23, 1913, covered a perimeter-weighted iron. It has a moderate ridge or rim that runs down the heel, across the sole, and up the toe on the back of the blade.

Cavity back irons, much like the early Ping 68 and Ping Anser irons test marketed during the 1960s, were produced in the early 1930s. They were designed by William Somerville Renwick and Robert Henry Johnson.

Renwick and Johnson received a British patent (No. 371,974) accepted on May 5, 1932, that dealt with balancing the head in order to "obtain sweetness of hitting, that is, to avoid shocks to the arms of the player when the club head strikes the ball." In addition to presenting various hosel designs, the patent notes that "in order to further lighten the heel end of the clubhead the back thereof is hollowed out as indicated." The Renwick and Johnson iron seen by the author was hollowed out from next to the hosel to just over halfway across the back of the head, as illustrated in their patent.

James B. Hunt's U.S. patent (No. 1854,548) applied for on March 27, 1927, and issued on April 19, 1932, covered a perimeter-weighted cavity back iron wherein the cavity was large, deep, and well-centered across the entire back of the head, no different from many cavity back irons produced in the 1960s and later.

WILLIAM GIBSON & CO.
DRIVING IRON-WOOD, STREAMLINE HEAD

The club pictured right is difficult to categorize: Is it an iron or a wood? The clubhead is made out of iron, but in profile it resembles a wood. Given its 40 1/2 inch length and flat lie, this club is certainly *not* a putter, despite having only two degrees of loft.

This club is marked "Wm Gibson & Co. Ltd \ Kinghorn \ Scotland" inside an oval on the top of the head along with "18652/22 \ Made in Scotland \ Warranted Hand Forged" and Gibson's star trade mark. The British provisional patent number, "18652/22," was issued in 1922. The patent application for this club did not receive a final approval—apparently another case of an idea tried and abandoned before the inventor spent any more money or effort on it.

This club has an unmistakably streamlined head. The face is very shallow and the top and bottom of the head come together in a mirror image, creating a single line around the entire back of the head. The idea of streamlining a wood head similar to this "driving iron-wood" is described in John R. Gammeter's U.S. patent (No. 1,528,017) applied for on October 10, 1921, and granted on March 5, 1925. According to Gammeter's patent, the head shape of an ordinary wood slowed down the golfer's swing:

During the playing stroke, air is carried forward in the path of travel and is packed in front of the rapidly moving parts of the club and a vacuum or partial vacuum is formed along the trailing edge thereof, retarding the progress of the club and causing it to deviate from the true line of travel.

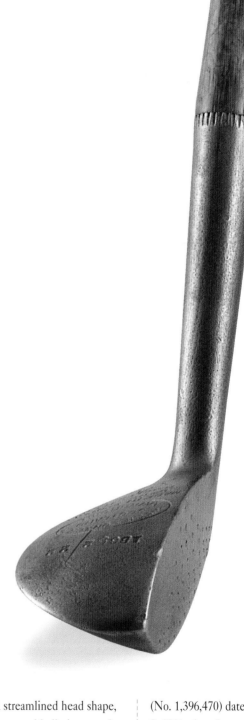

UNKNOWN MAKER
BALL BACK IRON

The iron pictured directly above concentrates nearly all of its weight directly behind the ball. The huge ball-shaped mound on the back of this exceptionally thick, *short* head makes this 39-inch driving iron the most dramatic of its type.

The absence of writing on this club, the design of the head, the bore-through hosel, and the sueded sheepskin grip date this club to the 1890s. The absence of any other identical irons suggests that this one was deemed impractical. Such heavily concentrated weight makes an iron exceptionally difficult to use.

In 1897 Spalding offered a similar, though less dramatic, "Ball Back Lofting Mashie." See page 450 for reference to similar clubs.

A streamlined head shape, however, would eliminate such problems:

During the forward stroke, the air displaced by the movement of the . . . club head will flow smoothly there-around to the trailing edge thereof, thus preventing the formation of a vacuum or partial vacuum along the trailing edge of any part of the club.

Thomas Taylor, of Chicago, Illinois, received a U.S. patent (No. 1,396,470) dated November 8, 1921, that also covered a wood head with a streamline shape similar to Gibson's iron-wood. As described and illustrated in his patent, Taylor's clubhead is made out of wood, and it appears to extend farther back than does Gibson's clubhead.

DAVID MYLES
THE "REXOR" &
THE "NIPPER"

A New Patent Golf Club. The "Rexor" is made of iron but has no resemblance to the usual type of iron club. It is an entirely new type, being an iron club with the shape of face and central balance of the Wooden Clubs.

Its central balance puts all its weight on the striking centre thus enabling it to drive a very long ball. It outdrives any other kind of through the course club, brassie included, is easy [sic] played, can be played with great accuracy and is most efficient for a long carry on to the green.

Its overhead measurement is shorter but its actual playing face is longer than that of the brassie and has slightly more loft.

For a "bad lie" where distance is required it is superior to any other club and will take a ball clean out of a lie where no other long game club could do so.

The Rexor is of perfect balance and for all round usefulness and length of ball has been exhaustively proved to be a thoroughly efficient golfing tool. It most certainly makes for lowering the score. . . .

From its inventor, patentee and manufacturer David Myles, Trades Lane, Dundee, Scotland (Golfers Magazine, Apr. 1923: 58).

The "Rexor," "Paxie," "Placer," and "Nipper" were four nearly identical clubs created by David Myles. These clubs were designed to function as

woods, complete with the face profile of a wood, but made as irons. Myles received three different British patents that covered this concept.

The basic objective of his iron club as stated in his first British patent, (No. 5,121) dated September 11, 1905, was "to improve . . . driving clubs by adapting them to suit rubber cored or pneumatic balls." (A pneumatic ball has a pressurized air chamber in its center.) In addition to the claim that his iron could drive either a rubber core or pneumatic ball greater distances, Myles also claimed his iron, due to its small head, was exceptionally playable from a heavy lie.

In designing his invention, Myles states:

I make the head of the driving clubs of metal instead of wood . . . and of a shape somewhat similar to such wooden clubs, but of smaller bulk, that is to say the length of the club is shortened very considerably, the depth of face kept the same while the weight is approximately the same as the weight of a wooden club used by the same player and for the same purpose.

Accordingly, the outline of the face on his iron is shaped like the face of a wood, and it also maintains the same approximate face area. To give his iron head the same approximate weight as a wooden club, Myles

concentrated "as much metal as possible behind the striking center" of the face. As produced, only a small amount of extra metal was used. The enlargement on the back of any Myles iron does not command much attention.

In his second British patent, (No. 18,990) dated August 6, 1906, Myles sought to improve his first patent by shifting the angle of the enlargement. According to the second patent:

while the sole of the club is parallel to the ground the enlargement at the back lies at an angle, the lower end being towards the heel and the higher end towards the toe.

Myles thought this back design would help his iron achieve the balance found in a wood. (On most woods, the back of the head is lower towards the heel and higher towards the toe).

In his final British patent, (No. 114,814) dated March 21, 1918, Myles refers to his second patent and presents a minor refinement:

I provide between the enlargement and the heel a depression, or hollow.

This depression or hollow, which was very subtle, made it possible to lengthen the blade without disturbing the weight.

The club pictured below is marked "D. Myles \ Dundee \ Scotland \ Rexor" on the blade back and "Patent \ USA \ British" inside a circle on the face. The "Auchterlonie \ St. Andrews" shaft stamp means Auchterlonie shafted and/or sold this club. The club pictured above, measuring 42 inches long, is marked "D. Myles \ Dundee \ Nipper" on the blade back. The face is also marked "Patent \ USA \ British." The shaft is original, but the neck has been repinned.

As shown by the face stamps, Myles also patented both clubs in America. Myles received a U.S. patent (No. 868,667) dated October 22, 1907, that copied his first British patent and a U.S. patent (No. 956,594) dated May 3, 1910, that copied his second British patent.

The club pictured below was produced under his second British and U.S. patents. The back of the head is weighted at an angle, and there is nothing resembling "a depression or hollow" between the heel and the enlargement. The club pictured above was produced under his first British and U.S. patents.

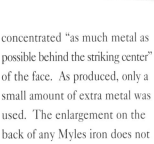

A.G. SPALDING & BROS.
"CHICOPEE PUTTER"
& "HB PUTTER"

The putter pictured below is marked "Hand Forged \ G.V. Tuck \ Wolverhampton" along with Winton's "diamond" trademark on the back of the head. Not only does this head have a distinctive profile, the sole forms a flange that extends half an inch behind the blade. The flange on the HB putter also extends back half an inch, but the flange on Tuck's putter appears smaller because its rounded corners lessen the surface area.

Tuck's putter shown is actually Winton's "The Mascot" putter, and except for having a more pointed toe, it closely resembles Cann & Taylor's "The Rex Putter." The Cann & Taylor example seen by the author was marked with a U.S. provisional patent number: "303869/08." The "/08" identifies 1908 as the year the patent was applied for. (This patent was not issued).

First offered by Spalding in their Fall and Winter golf catalog dated June 5, 1919, the Spalding Chicopee putter established a basic design that has stood the test of time. The combination of a healthy flange and a center-shafted head has been reproduced, and continues to be reproduced, by many clubmakers in an endless variety of ways. Even Spalding offered an almost identical wood-shafted remake of the Chicopee during the 1960s. The remakes are marked only "Spalding \ Chicopee" on the sole.

The original Chicopee putter pictured above left is marked "A.G. Spalding & Bros" on the sole and "Chicopee Putter" on the top of the 3/4-inch flange. It was offered in Spalding catalogs from 1919 to 1925.

Like the Chicopee putter, Spalding's "HB" or "Hollow Back" putter is a true classic. Its "Hollow Back" name reflects the fact that both the back of the blade and the top of the flange are slightly hollowed out.

First appearing in the Fall and Winter golf catalog dated June 5, 1919, the HB putter was offered along with the Chicopee putter through 1925. Spalding again offered the HB putter, complete with a hickory shaft, in 1929 and 1930. Many other putters modeled after the HB putter were produced by various clubmakers, but the most famous variations were the MacGregor "Tommy Armour" putters produced in massive numbers between 1935 and 1967.

The original HB putter pictured above right is marked "A.G. Spalding & Bros \ Putter \ HB" on the sole. The flange extends half an inch behind the blade.

During the early to mid-1930s, Spalding offered the HB putter with a steel shaft. Shortly thereafter, Spalding discontinued the HB putter and introduced the HBA putter. While keeping the HB's hollow back, the HBA putter incorporated some minor design changes. The hosel was made shorter and thinner, and it was relocated on top of the blade a short distance away from the end of the heel. The HBA putter has a thin steel shaft often referred to as a "pencil shaft."

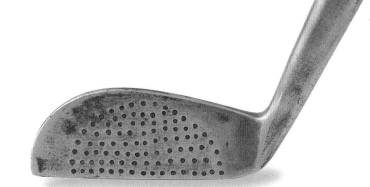

WILLIAM GIBSON & CO.
"PRINCEPS, HOLDFAST"
PUTTER

DONALD SWAN
FLANGE FACE PUTTER

The flange on the Princeps putter pictured left is behind the *top* of the blade. By locating extra weight high on the blade, this putter shared the same goal sought by Willie Dunn's Rotary putter: topspin. Unlike Dunn's Rotary putter with its negative loft, the Princeps employs a straight face. (For more on the Rotary putter, see page 254.)

The putter pictured is marked "The Princeps \ Gibson's \ Patent \ No 28443 \ Warranted Hand Forged \ Special" and "Sherardized \ Army & Navy CSL \ Holdfast \ London" on the back of the blade. A patent was never issued for this club. The five digit British patent number marked on the head was issued for a pre-1916 patent application.

A few other putters were made with extra weight located behind the top of the blade. All were intended to provide topspin.

In 1923 the Burke Golf Co., of Newark, Ohio, offered "Will's Downinone Putter." This blade putter has a slight amount of negative loft, and most of the weight behind the blade appears as a thick ridge just below the very top of the blade. The back of the blade on the Model R Putter, offered by Crawford, McGregor & Canby in 1914, is twice as thick across its upper half as it is across its lower half. Although both of these putters were designed for topspin, neither of them is as visually interesting as the putters shown on this page.

Gibson also produced a Princeps putter that differs from the one pictured. It has a square, seven-inch long hosel similar to the hosel on Albert Whiting's "His Own" putter (see p. 184).

Donald Swan, of Grosse Ile, Michigan, received a U.S. patent (No. 1,678,750) dated July 31, 1928, that covered a putter with a *deep* face and a flange that projects *forward* from the top of the blade. As pictured below, the flange on Swan's putter comes to a distinct point *above* the ball in order to help the golfer line up his or her shot. According to Swan's patent:

The pointer [forward tip of the flange] may be more accurately placed if disposed directly over one of the meshes or indentations which cover the surface of the usual golf balls–and when striking the ball the player should endeavor to have the pointer directly in line with the mark or indentation.

Made from either brass or gunmetal, the Swan putter pictured, marked "Grosse Ile Putter Co. \ Grosse Ile. Mich. \ U.S. & Foreign \ Pats. Pendg.," is the only one known to the author.

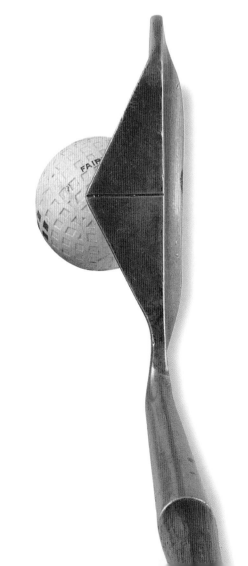

ROBERT E. F. WEMYSS
LONG NOSE STYLE PUTTER, HEAD WEIGHTS

The putter pictured was not made in the long nose era, so it is not a long nose putter. But since this putter was made in the same style as a long nose club, it is called a "long nose style" putter. This differentiation is important because values are much greater for true long nose clubs than for similarly shaped clubs made years later. The later clubs were made as either remakes or replicas, for use or for display. This circa 1908 putter, however, is a great deal more than a long nose remake. Its long nose shape was used to try a new way—a patented way—of weighting and balancing a putter.

The putter shown, marked "Patent 16,070" inside an oval on its crown, was the product of a British patent (No. 16,070) dated July 29, 1908, and issued to Robert Edward Fitzmayer Wemyss, a retired Captain in His Majesty's Regiment of Royal Artillery living in Charing Cross, a suburb of London. This patent deals with a unique way of weighting a golf club, as revealed by the seven circular lead weights in the head pictured. As shown above, four large cylindrical lead weights are in the sole and three smaller cylindrical lead weights are in the back of the head.

In his patent, Wemyss asserts that most woods are inferior to his:

In most wooden golf clubs, a weight of lead or other ponderous material is applied to the back of the club head. It is obvious that a weight so applied is mechanically bad, moreover it is unsightly—more particularly if some of it has been removed for the purpose of adjustment—and it is liable to work loose. This invention has for its object to so apply the necessary weighting material that its weight is mechanically effective and properly applied, that it is not liable to work loose, is not unsightly and is easily adjusted in amount.

Wemyss describes how to weight his clubs:

According to the invention, the weight is chiefly applied in a cavity in the club head and so positioned that the centre of mass of the whole head is as nearly as may be in the vertical plane of the shaft, as nearly as may be horizontally behind the point of impact of the ball (that is, in a horizontal plane, at right angles to the face of the club) central to the face and in a vertical plane, and usually midway in the height of the face.

The weighting material may be disposed in a single cavity in one portion, or there may be several portions in several cavities—in which case, the cavities may conveniently be cylindrical.

To accomplish his objective, the four large lead weights in the sole of the club pictured are placed "in a vertical plane of the shaft," meaning they are lined up across the sole, heel to toe, directly in line with the shaft. The three lead weights located across the back of the head are spaced apart "horizontally behind the point of impact of the ball."

This long nose style head, which is quite attractive, measures 5 7/8 inches in length, 1 inch in face depth, and 1 7/8 inches in width.

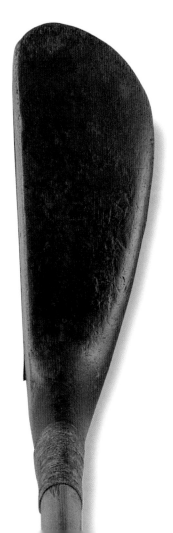

UNKNOWN MAKER
SQUARE NOSE PUTTER

This unmarked club has a number of interesting and collectible features.

As seen in the upper pictures, this club appears to be a long nose putter with its nose cut square. However, if the square nose was created *after* the club was made, altering the clubmaker's original work, it would dramatically decrease the desirability of this highly unusual club. The easiest way to determine the originality of the square nose is to examine the location of the backweight. If the backweight is towards the toe and not centered behind the face, the head was probably altered. As shown in the picture directly above, the lead backweight is perfectly centered, equidistant between the heel and toe. Clearly, this club was originally made with a square nose.

Pictured below left, the sole, which includes a ram's horn slip, is covered with a handmade soleplate of lead affixed by nails (see pages 150 and 421). Such a sole is evidence of a completely handcrafted club made by a clubmaker, neither prominent nor prolific, who nevertheless knew his craft well. This club is like a good piece of folk art. It is wonderfully creative in its own simple, unrefined way.

As seen below right, the grip and the shaft are made from a solid length of lancewood. The grip is rectangular and was left uncovered by design.

Two small cuts in the shaft, just below the grip, are six inches apart. These are "stymie" marks. Because the stymie (when player A's ball blocks the path of player B's ball) was an integral part of the game in the early days, putter shafts were occasionally marked with two cuts exactly six inches apart. Golfers used these marks to determine whether their ball was less than six inches away from their opponent's ball. If so, the player could request that the opponent's ball be lifted. (For more on stymies, see page 424.)

The healthy face depth, the fine scoring lines on the face, and the black fiber slip along the leading edge underneath the lead soleplate all suggest that this club dates to the 1890s.

Unique and completely handcrafted, this club is probably one of a kind.

ANDREW FORGAN
SHINTY-STYLE PUTTER

Andrew Forgan was a talented but obscure clubmaker. Born in 1846, he apprenticed to his brother, Robert Forgan, in the early 1860s and continued making clubs into the early 1900s. Without giving any dates, James Colville mentions that Andrew was clubmaker to the Glasgow Golf Club in Alexandra Park (1907, 55). This was during the 1890s and possibly earlier. Between 1873-1883, Andrew worked as clubmaker to the Royal Perth Golfing Society, also accepting the post of greenkeeper. (Miller 1935, 58).

The striking Andrew Forgan putter pictured is marked "A. Forgan \ Glasgow" and includes Andrew Forgan's "tree" trademark. It is believed this mark was used between 1893-1897. This club has a soft sheepskin grip and an ordinary hickory shaft. The shaft is spliced to a head modeled to some degree after a "shinty" stick. "Shinty," a field game similar to field hockey, was once popular in Scotland:

In the Highlands of Scotland, one of the most popular games, if indeed it is not the prime favourite, is that known as Shinty. Speaking generally, it may be described as corresponding to the English game of Hockey, though it ought to be played on a much larger piece of ground, and if possible with clubs specially made for that purpose (Cassell's 1896, 235).

In 1907 *The Consolidated Library* compared shinty sticks to hockey sticks:

Instead of having a long, straight blade, [shinty sticks] are curved at the lower end, so that they may be passed through a circle two inches in diameter, and they may not be more than one inch in thickness in any direction (Marden, 278).

The illustration of a shinty club that originally accompanied the above description shows the shaft as a continuation of the head—the shaft has the same width and depth as the head and is made from the same piece of wood.

Some shinty clubs were fashioned in a different way— from tree branches:

The favourite shinny [sic] stick is a tough hickory or oak branch, with a gnarled head, cut from the tree, as a rule, by the player, and trimmed to make a formidable weapon in the game or in a fight (The Golfer, 29 Apr. 1896: 319).

It is not surprising that a clubmaker such as Andrew Forgan tried using certain design features of a shinty or hockey stick. Clubmakers during the early 1890s had already borrowed from such games as jeu de mail, cricket, tennis, and croquet when trying to come up with a better club design:

"Shinty" is another early . . . game. In fact, golf is so closely associated with ball games of so many kinds, including even cricket, croquet, and tennis, that it is often difficult to decide where the one begins and the other ends (Gorham 1903, 15-16).

Made without lead in its head, Forgan's shinty-style putter is noticeably light. Light putters met with little success.

Some golfers have a craze for a light putter, and I knew a good man who lost his chance of a valuable cup through discarding his favourite putting cleek in favour of a light steel putter (Golfing, 11 May 1899: 14).

Few Forgan shinty-style putters are known.

JOHN H. DWIGHT

"DWIGHT'S DIRECTIONAL DRIVER"

There is one man who will not accept the decision of the U.S.G.A. regarding the form and make of golf clubs, but will go on playing with his own clubs. This man is Dr. J.H. Dwight, of Des Moines. Dr. Dwight has been known for a number of years because of the peculiarity of his clubs. He has had them all shapes and sizes and his "cows horn" driver has been more commented upon than any other golf club which ever appeared in Des Moines (Golfers Magazine, April 1911: 185).

Applied for on May 8, 1911, a U.S. patent (No. 1,069,359) dated May 12, 1914, was issued to John Dwight for his "cows horn" driver, advertised as "Dwight's Directional Driver" (*Golfers Magazine*, April 1911: 305). The objective of Dwight's club, pictured, was to:

drive a ball comparatively long distances and drive it in a straight line avoiding the curvature which is usually given to a ball by golf sticks of the kind ordinarily used; and further to provide a golf stick whereby the player may drive the ball in such a manner that it will be given only a slight horizontal elevation or he may drive it in such a manner as to give it a materially greater elevation, and in either instance the amount of elevation given the ball may be definitely determined by the player.

To help drive the ball straight, Dwight lined up the shaft of his wood with an imaginary line extending straight back from the center of the face, and he added a significant amount of weight to the back of the head. According to his patent:

In order therefore that the player may easily strike the ball at the point where it will drive the ball straight, I

so arrange the handle relative to the head that the center of the striking face will be in line with a longitudinal, central line through the head that is intersected by the handle. . . . By placing the handle near the front end of the head, the rear end is made heavier than the front and there will be less tendency for the handle to turn in the players hands. By placing a weight in the rear end of the head, the rear end is made materially heavier than the front end, and this tends to enable the player to more accurately hold the stick in the desired position for striking the ball.

The sole of Dwight's wood is flat directly behind the face and then angles up as it approaches the back of the head. This design supposedly allowed the golfer to choose the trajectory of his shot. The golfer could use the front sole to drive a low ball or he could lean the shaft back and use the rear "angled" sole to hit a high shot:

By having two flat surfaces at different angles, the player may plan his stroke with either face resting upon the ground so that he may accurately give to the ball the desired elevation.

To keep the head from breaking, a wood block which extends into the middle of the head was inserted into the back of the head:

The grain of [the wood block] runs substantially longitudinally of the head . . . so the two pieces of wood [the head and the wooden block] have their grains running in opposite directions. The weight is fitted around the end of the block to prevent it from splitting and is connected by a screw.

The brass backweight and accompanying screw are visible in the picture.

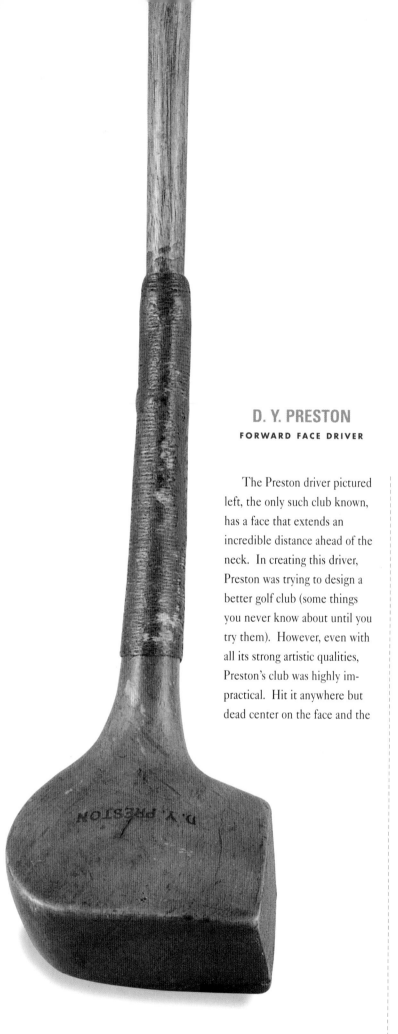

D. Y. PRESTON
FORWARD FACE DRIVER

UNKNOWN MAKER
FORWARD FACE PUTTER

The Preston driver pictured left, the only such club known, has a face that extends an incredible distance ahead of the neck. In creating this driver, Preston was trying to design a better golf club (some things you never know about until you try them). However, even with all its strong artistic qualities, Preston's club was highly impractical. Hit it anywhere but dead center on the face and the results will be quite poor if not disastrous (to say nothing about the effect of so much face progression on a well-struck shot). Yet, it is from such individual creativity and willingness to challenge tradition that an extraordinary collectible was born.

The top of the head and the shaft are both stamped "D.Y. Preston." The author has seen an ordinary wood marked by Preston that was also marked "St. Andrews."

The stylish, unmarked forward face putter pictured above is also exceedingly rare. Its long splice neck and heavy whipping date it to the 1890s. The sole is weighted with lead and includes a traditional piece of horn, installed with three wood dowels, across its leading edge. The entire clubhead, between crown and sole, is one inch thick, as is much of the neck.

UNKNOWN MAKER
"DOLPHIN" DRIVER

In 1899 [R.B. "Buff"] Wilson went to Minchinhampton and laid out the golf course there. The ground on which the course was laid out was the public common, and the commoners gave a lot of trouble by damaging the greens, removing the flags and pins, while even the hand rollers had to be locked up. So little did the local magistrates understand about golf at that time that the committee and Wilson were hauled up before them on the "heinous" charge of tearing up the common, and turning it into a golf course. The club was fined £5, and in addition was ordered to pay £5 yearly. As Wilson himself remarks, "It was the cheapest course in the country" (Golf Monthly, Oct. 1919: 35).

The Dolphin driver pictured was probably produced early in the twentieth century. The head is stamped "Dolphin \ Provl Pat." A brass soleplate covers the front half of the sole. A fiber horn slip is visible along the leading edge, between the brass soleplate and the head. A cylindrical lead weight is recessed into the back of the head.

The streamline design of this fascinating club not only reduced wind resistance, it also concentrated as much clubhead mass as possible directly behind the ball. As was true of many abandoned clubs, the Dolphin driver sounded good in theory but was impractical in reality.

A driver very similar to the Dolphin driver is in the United States Golf Association's antique club collection in the museum in Far Hills, New Jersey. The USGA's club is made with a full brass soleplate and a two-piece clubhead. The back half of the head is a separate piece of wood. The shaft is marked with the "J.H. Taylor" script stamp used by the firm of Cann & Taylor.

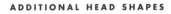

HORACE HUTCHINSON

"THE DEMON,"
SQUARE NOSE WOOD

The improvement which Mr. Hutchinson has introduced . . . is very simple, and when it has been seen the wonder is . . . why it was not thought of before. For generations, golfers have been playing with a wooden club with a rounded toe. The reason for adopting the rounded toe is, theoretically speaking, that it was desirable to concentrate the weight both of wood and metal on the centre of the head, and to minimise the dead weight of wood at the nose and the heel of the club. Mr. Hutchison's idea, however, is that the theory has been all wrong, that clubmakers have had no basis of scientific fact to go upon, and that the rounded toe in a club, like the pointed toe in a fashionable boot, is a mere whim of aesthetic fashion. Thus, he takes the wooden driver (bulger or flat-face) carries the wood right out to the nose and saws it off quite square, instead of tapering it in a semicircle. It is claimed for this improvement, that the square toe enables not only the beginner, but all kinds of players, to put the club down facing the right direction in which it is sought to drive. The square toe shows the line at once; and this is a virtue in it which not even the most captious or sceptical can deny. The breadth of the toe, with the added wood, does not derange the balance of the club, but, on the contrary, gives added driving-power to the ball. A trial was made of Mr. Hutchinson's club the other day. A crowd of jeering, irreverent golfers denounced the head for its ugliness . . . . The proof of the pudding is in the eating; so, when it was seen that the "square toe" club carried the ball with a long sustained flight with plenty of run, and true in direction, players began to handle the club and to try it, with the result that admissions were made that "there was something in it." After playing 36 holes with the club, we have no hesitation in saying that it is a particularly useful improvement in the drive, while for putters, the square toe is most serviceable in indicating the line of the putt. The difficulty we foresee, however, is that Mr. Hutchinson may have great trouble in preventing the infringement of a patent so simple and yet so obvious. Peter Paxton, of Eastbourne, is the sole maker of the club, and his name is a sufficient guarantee of the excellence and quality of the workmanship (Golf, 23 Sep. 1892: 18).

Horatio Gordon Hutchinson received a British patent (No. 14,897) dated August 18, 1892, that covered the club described in the above review. According to Hutchinson, his club offered a few unusual features:

Owing to the square shape of the head . . . it is possible to let in the lead in such a way that there shall be equal weight behind the whole extent of the "face" . . . .

. . . The "nose" is cut square, so that its line runs approximately at right angles to that part of the club which is known as the "face" . . . . The advantage of this is that when the club head is put up to the ball, preparatory to striking, the line of the squared "nose" is parallel with the line in which it is intended to send the ball—thus giving a valuable guide to the eye . . . .

. . . A further advantage of this form of club head is that greater depth of wood is thus given behind the point of impact, especially towards the "toe" or "nose" of the club, thus giving greater driving power.

The driver pictured, complete with an inlaid lead backweight, is the same as that described in Hutchinson's 1892 patent except that it was produced years later under a British design registration. The crown of this club is marked "The Demon \ Patent \ 60----," the last 4 numbers being too faint to read. Six digit British design registration numbers starting with "60" were issued in 1912. The shaft is stamped "Slazenger."

Horace Hutchinson, winner of the 1886 and 1887 British Amateur, was a highly respected player, historian, and writer in the world of golf. He wrote no fewer than eleven books on golf. Today some of his works, such as *Fifty Years of Golf* (1919), *Golf: A Complete History of the Game* (1900), and *British Golf Links* (1897), are considered classics.

JOHN L. KELLY &
PATRICK L. McARDLE

**BALL-SHAPED HEAD,
INTERCHANGEABLE FACE,
CENTER-SHAFTED
METALWOOD**

On June 17, 1913, John Kelly and Patrick McArdle, both of Chicago, Illinois, received a U.S. patent, (No. 1,064,916) applied for on June 13, 1910, that covered the ball-shaped, center-shafted club pictured:

The head is spheric in form with the center of the sphere located in line with the central axis of the shaft. A segment of the sphere is cut away in front as to form a bearing for a plate which provides the driving face of the club.... A segment of the sphere is also preferably removed at the base of the head to provide a substantially flat rest for the club when addressing the ball.

Kelly and McArdle believed the ball shape of their clubhead would be advantageous to golfers:

Our improved club ... is particularly advantageous for the reason that on account of its approximation to the shape of a sphere the center of gravity of the head lies in or near the plane containing the central axis of the shaft and the central point of the driving face, and but very little back of the prolongation of the central axis of the shaft. The club approximates perfect balance, and in its operation nearly approaches the ideal theoretical club,—that is to say, a ball at the end of a string. The removal of the lower segment of the sphere forming the head to provide the horizontal base brings the center of gravity of the head more nearly into a horizontal plane through the center of the ball and prevents "topping" the ball.

As specified in their patent, Kelly and McArdle also designed this club to be a "universal club," equally usable as a wood, iron, or putter:

In order to vary the angle of the face of the club, the face plate is attached to the head in such manner as to be removable.... A number of face plates having their outer faces at different angles ... may be applied with each club so as to provide faces which may be used in place of the various wooden and iron clubs, such as driver, brassy, mashy, cleik [sic] or mid-iron.

As designed, a stud on the back of the faceplate fits into a socket inside the head. Once the insert was placed in the face, an opening through both the stud and the socket allowed the shaft to be screwed into place and thereby fasten the insert.

The club pictured appears to have a fiber face, though it is not known if it is actually removable. What looks like whipping on the shaft is actually old black tape. Only the short hosel has a few wraps of whipping.

Kelly and McArdle's incredibly small clubhead was anything but practical. Comparison with the knitted wool practice golf ball (circa 1930) shows just how small the clubhead is. The club pictured is the only such club known; the knitted ball is consistently available.

Driving is an art, approaching is a science, and putting is an inspiration.

(*Golf Illustrated*, April 19, 1901: 46)

Oversize & Undersize

Oversize and undersize golf clubs are distinguished only by their size. They are either *much* larger or *much* smaller than ordinary golf clubs, and are easily recognized as such. Some oversize clubs were meant to be used, some were not. The same is true for undersize clubs.

Most oversize clubs have a head that is larger than normal attached to an ordinary shaft. "Giant" niblicks, for example, have a blade that is huge by today's standards. The blade on a giant niblick, the most famous of all oversize clubs, measures between 3 1/4 inches and 3 7/8 inches in face depth at its deepest point. Giant putters, however, do not have a deep blade. Instead, they have a blade that is much *longer* than normal.

A few oversize clubs have an ordinary head but a much longer than normal shaft. Even fewer clubs have both an oversize head and an oversize shaft, but such clubs were not usually built to be used.

Undersize clubs were produced in a variety of ways. A few undersize clubs were made with either a short blade or a short shaft and were designed for use by an adult golfer. The most common undersize clubs, however, are those built for junior golfers. These clubs have a small clubhead and short shaft. Some "juvenile" clubs were built for very young children. A small number of undersize clubs were made as toys or for display.

Fine craftsmanship is the most important criterion for judging oversize and undersize clubs that were not intended for use. The more closely the club resembles a standard club, complete with all the various components such as a lead backweight, horn slip, leather wrap grip, etc., the more enthusiastically it will be received by collectors.

With oversize clubs, it is generally understood "the bigger, the better." Because oversize clubs have so much visual impact and command attention without description or explanation, they are inherently popular and widely sought after. The truly small clubs do not generate the same collector interest as exceptionally large clubs, but they are worthy collectibles nevertheless. Remember, a collector should collect however and whatever he or she likes. Personal preference is what gives a collection its own character and unique charm.

No matter how you struggle to keep your heart up, there are bound to come times when golf's treatment of you produces a feeling of absolute hopelessness. It matters not that your business is prospering, that every single member of your family down to the canary is well—golf has deserted you, and the world is black, and every man's hand is against you. Some people say a complete rest from the game is good; some advise a round with the professional; but the only fitting salvation that suggests itself to you is suicide.—Manchester City News (Golfing, 8 July 1914: 31).

HENDRY & BISHOP
"CARDINAL" GIANT NIBLICK

Art and the Niblick.

"I see," says the Daily Chronicle's *correspondent, "that that well-known and high-thinking North Berwick amateur, Mr. J.R. Gairdner, is telling golfers that their best friend is their niblick, and advocating its use for all kinds of shots of the approaching variety. The average player never thinks of his niblick in connection with anything but bunkers, hedges, whins, and gorse, and it is a kind of Cinderella in his bag, treated with open contempt, while all the time it has the richest and rarest qualities for winning holes. . . . The point is that for a pitch shot, when you want the ball to pull up dead, you get a perfectly unbelievable amount of undercut on to it, and that quite in a natural way. Some golfers spend a life-time in trying to learn that most difficult and elusive of all shots, the cut mashie, while you get pretty much the same results, or better ones, without any trying at all with the niblick.*

"James Braid makes a new kind of niblick which is particularly useful for artistic work of this kind. It has a head so large that one iron mine does not make many niblicks, but it is a marvelously effective weapon, and when you are seen with one they know that you have been thinking hard, and that you are pulling aside the veil which separates the ordinary golfer from the most sacred abodes of the mysteries of the game" (Golf Illustrated, 23 Mar. 1906: 252)

Enter the Giant! One of the most popular of all golf collectibles, the giant niblick is well known and is found in many collections. Its large size is so eye-catching that even non-collectors find this club enthralling.

Identified as "a new kind of niblick" in the 1906 review above,

giant niblicks were made for many years. In 1913 William Gibson & Company advertised:

Are you without a club for heavy bunker work? Then assuredly you must have either the "Giant" Niblick or "Dreadnought" Niblick (Golf Illustrated, 5 Sep. 1913: 318).

In 1928 Wimbar, Inc. (to mention one company at random), was still offering Giant Niblicks, shafted or head only, in their wholesale catalog. The longevity of the giant niblick is demonstrated by the fairly large number of steel shaft examples known. To the collector, however, steel shaft examples are far less desirable than wood shaft examples.

Giant niblicks, also called "mammoth niblicks," "frying pan niblicks," or "Big Ben niblicks," were produced by a num-

ber of British makers such as William Gibson, Hendry & Bishop, J.P. Cochrane, Ben Sayers Jr., Jack White, Tom Stewart, William Winton, and others. Consequently, giant niblicks are not particularly rare. Their value comes from constant collector demand.

The giant niblick pictured (smaller than actual size) is marked "Special \ Hendry & Bishop \ Edinburgh \ The Giant 'Cardinal' Niblick \ Made In Scotland \ Warranted Hand Forged" along with Hendry & Bishop's "Mitre Brand" "bishop's mitre" trademark.

The Dreadnought niblick, although included with the giant niblick in Gibson's advertisement mentioned earlier, was only moderately larger than a

regular niblick. Consequently, a Dreadnought, which went by other names such as the "Junior Mammoth Niblick," does not have nearly the collector interest a giant niblick has.

A true giant niblick will measure between 3 1/4 and 3 7/8 inches in face depth at its deepest point. The closer to 3 7/8 inches (the depth of the example pictured), the more the club is usually worth; though 3 1/4-inch examples are far from inexpensive. Dreadnought and Junior niblicks usually measure between 2 1/2 and 3 inches in face depth.

Nobody knows who designed the first giant niblick, and it was not patented. The 1906 review quoted at the beginning of this account suggests that James Braid might

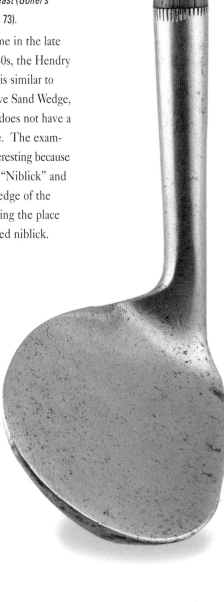

have invented the giant niblick. Maybe he did, or perhaps he was just one of the first clubmakers to make them. A William Gibson & Company advertisement published in 1914 offers "Braid's –Heavy Iron, Approaching Cleek, Giant Niblick, Orion Putter" (*Golf Illustrated*, 10 Apr.: 148). It is unknown whether Gibson was selling clubs that Braid designed or clubs like those Braid used. Braid, a five-time British Open Champion (1901, 1905, 1906, 1908, 1910), was one of the three most prominent golfers of his day. Naturally, companies were eager to sell clubs that Braid endorsed or copies of clubs he used:

James Braid . . . put his second shot into a deep trap right up against the wall. . . . It was necessary that Braid get out . . . . So in place of using his regular niblick he reached in his bag for a club that looked more like a shovel than anything else. This club had a big, round, heavy, iron head, and with it Braid struck a mighty blow at least four inches back of the ball, with the result that it popped out of the sand, just cleared the wall and lay within two feet of the hole (The American Magazine, May 1915: 19).

Average drives made with the principal clubs are as follows:
With the iron, 120 yards.
With the cleek, 140 yards.
With the brassie, 150 yards.
With the driver, 170 yards.
(Gorham 1903, 145).

The niblick pictured right has a large concave blade. It is marked "Special \ The Wedge \ Cardinal Rustless Iron \ Niblick \ Warranted Hand Forged \ Made in Scotland" on the back of the blade along with Hendry & Bishop's "Mitre Brand" "bishop's mitre" trademark. Although concave faces are routinely found on feather ball irons, they are uncommon on later irons.

A niblick could provide a delicate, well-lofted shot from a good lie, but according to Garden Grant Smith, the niblick was known for its . . . dark side:

The golfer receives in silence the only possible weapon, the niblick, and descends into the pit to battle with uncertain fate.

In all the golfer's set, no club is less cherished than this hideous engine of wrath and damnation. Like the headsman's axe, there is some-thing sinister and awful in the niblick's aspect. Its bent and crooked shaft, and its bull-dog head of steel, indented with innumerable scars, are eloquent of past disaster, and ominous of future woe. The memories that its personali-ty evokes are all hateful, whether of time, place, or association and the golfer's wrists and arms sting and jar again at the recollection of futile whacks in impenetrable jungle, and barren blows in sandy and stony places. What acres of grizzly gorse has it not laid low in pursuit of inextricable balls? What granite quarries, pebbly beaches, and stony roads does it not recall?—What impossible ditches and impracticable bunkers? How many nice new balls has not that serrated edge of steel mangled out of all resemblance to rotundity? What horrid oaths has it not heard?—of what baffled fury and hopeless despair has it not been the witness? Put it back in the bag and give us the putter!

Between the putter and the niblick there is a great gulf fixed. It is a case of Beauty and the Beast (Golfer's Magazine, May 1898: 73).

Made sometime in the late 1920s or early 1930s, the Hendry & Bishop Wedge is similar to the Hagen Concave Sand Wedge, only The Wedge does not have a flange of any type. The exam-ple pictured is interesting because it is marked both "Niblick" and "Wedge"—the wedge of the steel shaft era taking the place of the wood-shafted niblick.

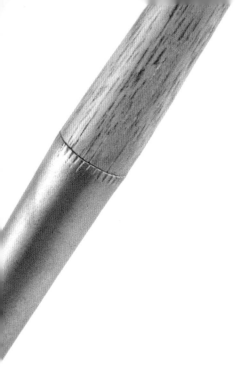

J.P. COCHRANE & CO.
SUPER-GIANT NIBLICK

Pictured (actual size) is the ultimate in giant niblicks: Cochrane's super-giant niblick.

Few collectors have handled a super-giant niblick; but, because it is so big and unlike anything else, most collectors have heard about it. Unknowing collectors often describe the super-giant niblick as having a head that measures at least 7 or 8 inches deep. In actuality, the face depth of the super-giant niblick pictured is 4 3/4 inches at its deepest point. The back of the blade itself, not including any of the hosel, measures 6 1/2 inches wide, heel to toe.

When Cochrane's super-giant niblick is seen in real life, its size impresses the viewer. When this club is held, however, its weight receives the attention—it is an *incredibly* heavy club. When this club is swung slowly, or even waggled, the shaft feels as if it would crack if swung at full speed. The weight of the club pictured is 2 pounds 1.5 ounces; its swingweight runs way off the scale.

Super-giant niblicks are truly rare items about which little is known. The author knows of only a single early reference to such a club—a picture of a super-giant niblick in the January 22, 1948 issue of *Golf Illustrated*. The picture, obviously from an earlier time, shows a man standing with an oversize giant niblick in one hand. Under the heading "An Historic Club," the caption reads:

Eustace Storey with the Secretary's Niblick, booby prize in the Society's meeting at Rye.

It is doubtful that oversize giant clubs were meant to be played, even though they are shafted and gripped to do so. Then again, it is doubtful that they were made merely as gag gifts. It is thought by some collectors that Cochrane's oversize clubs were originally made as display items or sales samples, to provide a larger-than-life demonstration of the clubmaker's craftsmanship. Cochrane's oversize giant niblicks were probably made sometime in the early 1920s.

The back of the club pictured is marked "Cochranes Ltd \ Edinburgh \Niblick \ Warranted Hand Forged \ Made in Scotland" along with Cochrane's "bowline knot" trademark. The author knows of eight such super-giants. Because these clubs are so unusual, they begged to be saved.

A wood shaft iron with a head larger than Cochrane's oversize giant niblick was made expressly for Joe Kirkwood. In addition to being a competitive professional golfer, Kirkwood, born in 1898, was the leading trick-shot artist of his day and even traveled on a world tour with Walter Hagen in 1937. Kirkwood's trick-shot niblick is on display at the Foxburg Country Club in Foxburg, Pennsylvania.

Horace Rawlins, the [U.S.] Open champion of 1895, travelled to the West in company with Willie Anderson last year. The two had matches nip-and-tuck, yet, while the matches favored Anderson, still Rawlins, in his heart, was reluctant to think that Anderson was the better player. The way that Rawlins found out that he was wrong is worth a story. At one of the hotels of California this winter, a person—one of the sort termed "fresh guys" by golfers—walked out on the lawn and, setting a beer bottle on edge and putting a Golf ball on the top, the casual offered to give Anderson fifty dollars if he could knock the ball off without a foozle. The trick was something that Anderson had never tried before. Taking a full swing, Anderson, on each trial, would send the ball flying from the bottle top for fully two hundred yards. Not once did he touch the bottle.

"Now," said Horace Rawlins, "I see by this I have been mistaken. This man is a grand golfer" (Golf Illustrated, 15 June 1900: 224). [Anderson also won the U.S. Open in 1901, '03, '04, '05.]

J.P. COCHRANE & CO.
SUPER-GIANT MASHIE

The clubs pictured above and below are much larger in real life than they appear here! The large iron actually measures 2 7/8 inches in face depth at its deepest point and 5 5/8 inches across the back of the blade. The smaller iron shown above for comparison is a normal-size mashie (R.T.J. model) produced by Tom Stewart in 1931. A companion piece to Cochrane's super-giant niblick shown directly below and on the previous two pages, Cochrane's super-giant mashie is also very rare—only six such middle irons are known. At least one of the other irons is a mashie; at least three are 4-irons.

The back of this mashie is marked "Finnigans Ltd. Manchester & Liverpool \ Mashie \ Warranted Hand Forged \ Made In Scotland" along with Cochrane's "bowline knot" trademark.

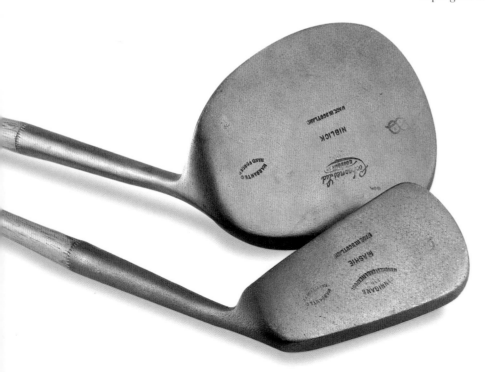

UNKNOWN MAKER
OVERSIZE WOODEN IRON

The oversize club pictured, unmarked and otherwise unknown, is classified as a "perimeter" club because it was not designed for use (see p. 537). Its massive size suggests that the club was made for some type of display, but it is anybody's guess as to why, where, when, and by whom.

This wooden iron does not have a hosel. The blade is attached to the shaft by three wooden dowels that run through the back of the shaft and into the heel of the blade (the dowels may be glued in place). This huge club measures 55 inches in overall length, 9 1/4 inches in face depth, 14 inches in width across the back of the head, and 2 1/2 inches in thickness across the sole. An Arrow golf ball (a bramble cover, rubber core ball made by the Goodyear Tire and Rubber Company in 1902) is shown for perspective.

Such clubs of unknown origins must be judged on the individuality of their character. This club does not look particularly old; it could date from the 1920s to the 1950s. The extraordinary size, unique structure, and overall character of this club give it a sense of distinction. Let the beauty be in the eye of the beholder.

WILLIAM GIBSON & CO.
SMITH NECK
ANTI-SHANK NIBLICK
FOR A ONE-ARMED GOLFER

Mr. Morris Hunt, who plays with only one arm, has recently won a medal at Nice. With the somewhat liberal handicap of 30 he finished 4 up on bogey. One-armed golfers are not by any means so rare as some people may think; indeed, there are reputed to be two or three of them about somewhere, and most of them appear to play a very fair game. Probably they do so to some extent because of that kind compensating characteristic of Nature, which is best exemplified in the case of a person losing one of his eyes or ears, the strength and adaptability of the other one almost invariably improving as the result. Still, as even two arms often seem so hopelessly inadequate to control the swing of the club in the manner desired, and the golfer so often feels that he could make excellent use of three or four,

the success of these people is very astonishing (*Golf Illustrated*, 9 Feb. 1906: 122).

One week after the above commentary was published, another commentary reported that there were more one-armed golfers than originally thought:

Ever since the recent performance of a . . . one-armed golfer was chronicled some days ago there has been coming in a steady stream of statistics concerning other one-legged and one-armed golfers until one is almost persuaded to believe that if there is not a majority of these crippled players, at least they constitute a very respectable minority. Writing from Oxford Mr. K.M. Beaumont reminds me of the case of the one-legged caddie-master at Elie who plays an excellent game, and who has won several prizes in

competitions. He is reckoned better than scratch. The case of Mr. Foster, of the Register House, Edinburgh, has already been recorded. Mr. W. Dalrymple, writing from Leven, and recalling several instances of crippled golfers, says that Mr. Ireland, late Hon. secretary of the Thistle Club, told him of a man playing golf who had actually lost an arm and a leg! (*Golf Illustrated*, 23 Feb.: 164)

Some one-armed golfers were very talented players:

A one-armed golfer, named Willie Park—not the ex-champion we need hardly say—has holed the eleventh hole on the Troon relief course in one (*Golf Illustrated*, 1 Mar. 1907: 182).

One-armed Entrant for the [Open] Championship. . . . The appearance of Yves [Botcazon], the one-armed

professional at La Boulie, at Prestwick, will be quite unique (*Golfing*, 3 June 1914: 7).

The technique of Louis Martucci, a one-armed golfer who became the professional at the South Orange Field Club in 1917, was pictured and described in an article titled "Lessons of a One-armed Golfer" (*Golf* [ny], 16 Aug. 1916: 74-77).

In 1909 *Golf Illustrated* reported, complete with pictures, the results of a match between two one-armed golfers. Both players had only their right arm and played from the "right hand" side of the ball. Serving as the reporter for this article, Harold Hilton (two time British Open Champion, four time British Amateur Champion, and once

U.S. Amateur Champion) was quite impressed with the quality of play:

To those who had never had an opportunity of watching a good one-armed player, the game between J. Scott (Silloth) and G. Haskins (Hoylake) at Hoylake last week came as a revelation. It was not so much the putts that they holed (Haskins treated the spectators to some sensational work in this respect) as the length and accuracy of their wooden club play. If one had not seen Scott drive one would wonder at the length that Haskins obtained from the tee, but his driving paled into insignificance before that of the Silloth man . . . and as he is far from a Goliath—nay! rather a fragile specimen of humanity—the distance he obtained bordered on the miraculous (9 Apr. 1909: 69).

After chronicling the strengths and weaknesses of both players (their primary weakness was their short approach shots), Hilton noted, "The game itself was almost sensationally interesting." Scott defeated Haskins by 3 and 1 over 36 holes.

Some one-armed golfers used regular length clubs while others used shorter clubs. In the coverage of the Scott/Haskins match, Hilton attributes much of Scott's greater distance to his clubs being longer than those used by Haskins. Actually, Scott used ordinary length clubs (*Golf Illustrated*, 10 Jan. 1908: 51). Haskins used shorter clubs, sacrificing distance for control.

Because the club pictured on this and the facing page was built specifically for a one-armed golfer, it represents a radical departure from the world of standard golf clubs. The head of this Smith model anti-shank iron is extremely thick and profoundly oversized (shown actual size on the facing page). The hosel measures 15/16 of an inch thick across its entire length as does the sole. The shaft is also very thick (measuring 3/4 inch at its thinnest point) and short (measuring only 29 1/2 inches in overall length). The grip is heavily textured to a degree not seen on standard clubs.

This unique club would help a one-armed golfer swing at a ball in deep rough, high grass being a common obstacle in British golf. The massive and exceptionally heavy head gave momentum to the stroke while the anti-shank neck increased the effective hitting area of the face. Both features were valuable to a one-armed golfer when swinging at the ball as hard as possible.

The grip is thick and heavily textured in order to prevent the club from slipping out of the grasp of a single hand. This club required a short shaft. If the shaft were any longer, the heavy weight of the head would be almost impossible to swing, even with two hands.

The golf spirit dies hard. . . . Thomas P. McAuliffe, formerly a caddie at Buffalo Country Club, who has lost both arms, holds his club shaft between his right shoulder and cheek and has gone round the course in 108 (Golfing, 23 May, 1918: 6).

This head is marked "Warranted Hand Forged \ Lockwood-Brown \ 42 Jermyn Street \ London S.W. \ Smith's Model \ Niblick \ Special" along with William Gibson's "star" trademark. Lockwood-Brown was the retail outlet that ordered and/or sold this club. At least one other retail firm sold clubs for one-armed golfers. Anticipating the needs of the one-armed golfers resulting from World War I:

Messrs. Haskins and Son, of Hoylake, announce . . . they have decided to make a specialty of supplying clubs for men thus maimed (Golfing, 4 Apr. 1918: 10).

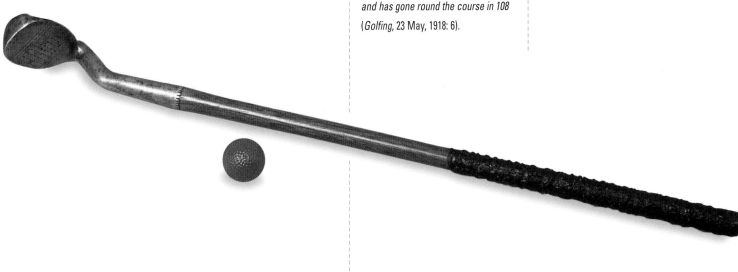

ERNEST H. SALES
WOODEN SPOON
FOR A ONE-ARMED GOLFER

Stamped "Ernest H. Sales \ Sunningdale" on its crown, the late 1920s oversize wood pictured is unlike a traditional wood in many respects. When considered together, all of the traits of this club indicate that it was made for a one-armed golfer (see p. 472).

The head is abnormally large, measuring 5 1/2 inches long, and the face is huge measuring 4 1/2 inches across and 1 3/4 inches in depth. The club measures only 35 1/2 inches in overall length. The head has twenty degrees of loft and is weighted with five lead buttons, two on the sole and three across the back of the head. (Only one of the weights is located directly behind the sweet-spot. The others are either behind the toe or the heel.) The swingweight of this club is "E-6", which is extremely heavy, and the overall weight is 16 1/2 ounces. When combined together, the short shaft, the oversized head and face, the large amount of loft, and the extra weight are features designed to help a golfer compensate for the loss of an arm.

Also pictured are two mint John Wanamaker "Radio" golf balls, one in its original wrapper and one unwrapped. The Radio ball is unquestionably the hottest golf ball ever made—or that will ever be made! It has a *radioactive* center:

> The quantity of radio-active substance which goes into one Radio Golf Ball . . . . is the secret of this Ball of Mystery—the ball that never loses life or shape. $1 each, $12 doz. John Wanamaker, New York, Sole Wholesale Distributor, U.S.A. (*Golf Illustrated* [ny], June 1918: 45).

The Radio ball was patented in the U.S. by Ellis Miller, of London, England, who assigned his patent to The Radium Golf Ball Company, Limited, New York, N.Y. According to Miller's patent (No. 1,260,788) granted on March 26, 1918, his ball has a round core formed from "radio active material and an inert filling material" that retains the radio active material in position and prevents its displacement.

The May 1918 issue of *Golf Illustrated* (ny) states that the Radio golf ball has a "Radium Center." The article includes a "radiograph [x-ray] of the material used in the core of the Radio Golf Ball" (11). According to the June 4, 1918 issue of *Golfing*, the radium center used "radium salts":

> These salts have produced wonderful results in the intensive cultivation of crops, and their use in golf balls, though not giving any mechanical aid in the matter of distance, vitalises the rubber and keeps it in perfect condition (6).

JOHN H. ADAMS
CROQUET-STYLE PUTTER

On October 12, 1897, John Howard Adams of Morristown, New Jersey, received a U.S. design patent (No. 27,732) that covered the croquet-style putter shown. In his patent, identified as being for "a new and useful Design for Golf-Clubs," Adams illustrates his club and states:

. . . the leading feature of my new design is the upwardly and rearwardly inclined face of the head of the club and the tapered rearward elongation of the head, having its bottom curved upwardly and rearwardly, and a longitudinal straight line extending along its top to which the face is transverse. The handle rises perpendicularly from the line at a point much nearer the face than the rear end of the head.

The Adam's putter shown (actual size) is the only such example known. The head measures 6 3/4 inches long and 1 1/2 inches in width and face depth. Six nails in the top of the head appear to help hold in position four circular lead weights (located in the sole) in line behind the face. The shaft has a sterling silver shaft band, engraved "H.V.R.," located just below the sheepskin grip. The shaft itself is stamped "F.H. Ayres." F.H. Ayres, Ltd., located in London and established in 1810, was self-described as being "Manufacturers of all Indoor and Outdoor Games and Sports" (*Golf Illustrated*, 18 Sept. 1900: 6) and "Manufacturers of all Requisites for Golf and all Sports and Games" (*Golfing*, 31 Jan. 1907: iv). Ayres specialized in the wholesale and export markets.

On June 12, 1906, Frederick H. Robertson received a U.S. patent (No. 823,082) for a croquet-style putter similar to Adams's. Robertson's putter, as illustrated in his patent, is not as long or narrow as Adams's putter; and it has a rounded sole, so the club could be used right- or left-handed in addition to croquet style.

CAPTAIN HAMILTON
"THE PENDULUM" PUTTER

"THE PENDULUM" PUTTER.
(From Captain Hamilton's point of view.)
Ziketty—dicketty—dock,
"The Pendulum" putts like a clock:
> *The Long game done*
> *It holes in one,*
Ziketty—dicketty—dock. –ALPHA.
(Golf, 13 Feb. 1891: 345)

Hamilton's The Pendulum putter, with its extremely large rectangular head towering well above the ball, was distinctly ineffective. When introduced, this putter was reviewed (reprinted below) and recommended only to those who suffered from vertigo, headaches, or confused vision when "stooping" to putt—and to women!

The teak wood head of Hamilton's putter, resembling a sledgehammer more than a golf club, measures 2 3/4 inches in face depth, 2 5/8 inches in face width, and 4 1/2 inches in head length across the sole. One end of the head is lofted; the other is not. One side of the sole is cambered, and the other has a sharp ninety degree angle. These features were related to the desired capabilities of this club. The club pictured (actual size) is in lovely original condition with the exception of a few dents on the edge of one side. This club is so rare, however, that such minor damage is easily tolerated. The only other known example rests in a glass case in the Royal Musselburgh clubhouse in Musselburgh, Scotland.

One side of the head is stamped "Hamilton Patent \ Rd. No. 161124." Hamilton never received a patent for his club—"161124" is a design registration number that dates to the end of 1890. The shaft is stamped "John Wisden & Co. \ 21 Cranbourn St. \ London."

A lengthy review published in the January 30, 1891 issue of *Golf* discusses many aspects of The Pendulum putter, including the observations that it was modeled after a croquet mallet and was full of drawbacks:

"The Pendulum" Putter.

This is the name of a new putter which has recently been introduced to the notice of golfers by Captain Hamilton, a member of the Royal Isle of Wight Golf Club. It is a peculiar looking implement, and is foreign to anything which golfers have hitherto seen associated with the name of putter. In truth, it is nothing more nor less than a croquet mallet modified to suit the exigencies of the game of Golf, which is played with a smaller and lighter ball than in the case of the once popular lawn sport. The head of the "Pendulum" putter is a block of teak wood, square at one end for putting on a fair level green, and sliced, or grassed at the other, for putting a hanging ball, or to retard the pace of the stroke on a sloping surface. The shaft is about the length of the ordinary iron or cleek handle, and is sunk in the centre of the block of wood forming the head, so that the weight is equally poised over the whole surface by which the blow is struck. There is no artificial weight of any kind introduced to make the head heavy, as in the case of the lead run into the wood of the ordinary putter; the whole of the weight proceeds from the large block of wood

forming the head. In order to obtain the highest results from this implement we understand it to be the theory of the inventor that the player must stand close to his ball, with his right foot, in fact, almost touching it. The weight of the body is thus placed mainly on the right leg, and by standing near, or over, the ball the player is able, so to speak, to draw an exactly straight line with his eye from the hole to the ball, and thus secure the ultimate object of all good putting–accuracy.

. . . We have recently had the opportunity of testing this putter; and it would be wrong on our part to hold out any hopes that he has devised something absolutely new or a club which is likely to revolutionise this intricate, delicate, and exasperating portion of the golfer's art. We followed his theory as to the true position to be assumed in addressing the ball; and it was found in that putting a ball ten or fifteen yards from the hole the ball certainly ran true in direction, but not more so than with the ordinary wooden putter. In attempting, however, to hole past a ball which lay a partial stimie, it was found that the "Pendulum" putter propelled the ball so true as to canon against the other ball rather too violently to be altogether fair Golf, and that it was impossible to impart that slight semi-circular spin round the other ball just sufficient to evade collision and yet catch the outside edge of the iron rim, and so hole. Thus, we found that in approaching the hole from a distance the putter answered practically all requirements, but close to the hole it was too unwieldy to manipulate with that delicacy of touch and dexterity which are the important and indispensable counterparts of accuracy. Another drawback to the use of the putter also was that it entailed on the putting-green a stiff, cramped, rigid position on the part of the player, while the blow had been struck more with the use of elbow power rather than the free use of the wrists. . . . Another defect which we noticed in the use of the "Pendulum" putter was that the upright face of the club towered an inch or two above the ball when placed against it, thus preventing so clear a perception of the outline of the ball as could be obtained by the orthodox thin-faced wooden putter. This is an important point, and it might well be worthy the consideration of Captain Hamilton whether he could not see his way to reduce the bulk of wood in his club so as to obviate this drawback.

No doubt there are many players who find it difficult to use the wooden putter and to stand either a little way from their ball, or to stoop when holing out. Stooping often causes vertigo, a headache, and a confused vision at the next tee. This, then, is the club which players liable to be so afflicted should use; and if they find on trial that the "Pendulum" putter suits them in this respect, and also enables them to hole out more easily and more accurately, then as the end justifies the means they will be right in adopting what suits them best. Lady golfers have usually a difficulty in putting satisfactorily with the common form of club, and this new putter is a weapon which they might advantageously substitute, seeing that it places them quite near their ball, allows them to have a straight view of the line to the hole, and possibly enables them to assume a general air of more grace and ease while playing. We fear, however, that golfers who have modelled their style on the models of our best professional players will not be induced by the noteworthy success of one or two adherents of the "Pendulum" to forsake the model of club which the name of Hugh Philp has endeared to them (311).

A circa 1890 mesh pattern gutta percha ball, typical of the balls in use when this club was made, is also shown.

A Woman's society in New York for political study is seriously discussing the question of having a new ground recognised for divorce, viz. golf. They allege that many business men, whose only off-days are Saturdays and Sundays, spend them entirely at their golf clubs, and are practically lost to their families. Judge Harlan, the Society's legal advisor, is reported to have stated that golf is a disease, and ought to be as valid a reason for divorce as wilful desertion (*St. Andrews Citizen*, 16 June 1900: 3).

477

A.G. SPALDING & BROS.
OVERSIZE CROQUET-STYLE PUTTER

The fascinating Spalding putter shown on the facing page is a direct descendant not simply from a croquet mallet but from a "golf-croquet" club! What was golf-croquet? Spalding's 1901 Spring and Summer catalog offers golf-croquet clubs and a description of the game:

Golf-croquet is a new game that combines the good features of both Golf and Croquet. The ball used is a small croquet ball. The mallet used is similar to a croquet mallet, only with a longer handle, like a golf club. One end of the mallet is lofted so that the first drive, which is made exactly as in the game of golf, is sent quite a distance. Vardon has driven the ball over one hundred yards. When near the wicket, of course, the approach shot, or shot through the wicket, is made with the other end. The wickets are gone through with the same as in croquet, but they are placed irregularly and at irregular distances, so that the croquet ground resembles more a miniature golf course, with wickets instead of cups.

The game was originated by Lieutenant-Commander Henry McCrea of the United States Navy, and all those who have played it are delighted with it (47).

As illustrated in Spalding's 1901 catalog, golf-croquet clubs look identical to the putter pictured except that one end of the golf-croquet clubhead is well-lofted. Spalding's golf-croquet clubs were offered in two styles identical in shape: $1.00 would buy the standard golf-croquet club; $1.25 would buy a golf-croquet club with a "beveled brass shoe on one end of [the] head to protect same." The balls used to play this game were available in red or white and were sold as "Whitewood balls."

Spalding's golf-croquet clubs were covered under Henry McCrea's U.S. patent (No. 653,483) dated July 10, 1900, and his British patent (No. 12,428) of the same date. An account, published in 1900, of McCrea's club and game reads as follows:

According to the newspapers, Washington has gone wild over a new pastime which bears the hybrid appellation of croquet-golf. It was invented by Lieutenant-Commander McCrea, and one of its great merits is that it may be played upon a much smaller area of land than even the most modest of golf-courses demands.

The paraphernalia include a set of croquet wickets and as many numbered flags. The play club is a long-handled affair that is neither a golf club, nor a croquet mallet, nor a polo stick, but a fearsome combination of all three. One end of the striking-head is used for driving and the other is bevelled so as to permit of a lofting stroke. The balls used are of wood, two and three-quarter inches in diameter, light and tough, the object being to get force and speed without great momentum, with a certainty that they will float.

The course on any field or lawn depends upon the lay of the land, the shape as well as the area being considered. The more natural obstructions there are, such as bushes, hills, and hollows, the better, as they call forth special skill in lofting and driving. The ground is made level at the starting-point and in the immediate vicinity of each wicket, but otherwise no preparation is necessary, the large size of the ball making it comparatively easy to follow and to play.

The course is marked by both wickets and flags, and the player may score by either driving his ball through the wickets or by hitting the flag-staff. The distance between the wickets varies according to the lay of the land. At the Navy Yard there is a seven-wicket course that measures nearly 1000 yards in playing distance. It has been negotiated in twenty-two strokes.

Most of the rules of golf are in force in the new game, and to play it well calls for the exercise of genuine skill and correspondence of hand and eye. Finally, since but one club is used, no caddies need be employed, and the size of the ball prevents it being lost under the ordinary conditions of play. Can it be possible that croquet-golf has a future before it? And what are we to do with our Vardon drivers now? (Golf [ny], August: 128)

The putting ability of the golf-croquet club was not lost to the creative minds at A.G. Spalding & Bros. Consequently, Spalding produced the putter shown (actual size) on the facing page. In addition to having a much shorter shaft than Spalding's golf-croquet clubs, this putter differs in *shape* from golf-croquet mallets—the mallets having one very lofted end. This seven-inch-long cylindrical putter head, marked "Spalding" on its top in two places, could be used left-handed, right-handed, or croquet style. It has a standard hickory shaft and ordinary leather wrap grip. The 33 1/2-inch overall length is within normal parameters for a wood shaft era putter. (Bobby Jones's Calamity Jane putter is the same length, as are all Spalding Calamity Jane's.)

Spalding catalogs do not mention this putter, which is not surprising. Spalding occasionally tried or test-marketed an unusual golf club. This putter was probably found to be too difficult to manipulate—too large for finesse shots.

William Mills produced an aluminum head putter similar in shape to this Spalding putter but with three differences: First, the Mills "Mallet Head Putter" was made from aluminum while the Spalding putter was made from persimmon with vulcanized fiber faces. Second, the Mills putter is shorter in head length, measuring somewhere around 4 1/2 inches. Third, a small area across the bottom of the Mills putter is flat while the Spalding head is completely circular in cross section (*Golf Illustrated*, 11 Nov. 1904: 132). The Mills putter was poorly received.

"Ringolf" was another golf spin-off. Without providing a description of either the similarities or differences between Ringolf and golf, the following brief account reports on an exhibition of Ringolf put on by two famous golfers:

J.H. Taylor and Harry Vardon gave an interesting exhibition of the new game of Ringolf in the grounds of Mr. A.W. Gamage's residence at Finchley last Monday. As a test of approaching and putting, Ringolf may be described as the best substitute for the "real thing" that has yet been invented. Playing over what one might call the approach and putting course, Taylor beat Vardon by 1 up, his score being 52 against Vardon's 53. However, when they played the cleek course, Vardon had his revenge by 5 and 4 (Golfing, 13 Aug. 1908: 6).

Tom [Morris] was singularly deficient in being short with his long putts, which reminded one of the remark of young Tommy, "that his father would be a good putter if the hole would only meet him half way" (*St. Andrews Citizen*, 27 May 1882: 4; reporting a match between Willie Park Sr. and Tom Morris Sr.).

ALEX ANDERSON
GIANT PUTTER

To the Editor of Golf Illustrated.

Sir,–I sometimes use a putter with so long a face that some of the members of a club where I play have questioned its fairness. In all other respects it conforms to St. Andrew's rules, and the only doubt is whether an exaggeration of length of face can make a club a "substantial departure" from traditional form. If it can, at what length is a limit to be set?

I am, sir, etc.,
Putter.

(*Golf Illustrated*, 7 Apr. 1911: 40)

The exact putter used by "Putter" is not known, but the one pictured above fits his description. The blade, not including the hosel, measures a full six inches straight across its center, from toe to heel.

The giant putter above, shown actual size, is marked "D.P. Watt \ Mortonhall \ Edinburgh" inside an oval on the back of the blade along with "Warranted Hand Forged \ Special" and Alex Anderson's "arrow" trademark. Anderson made this head and

Watt, the professional at Mortonhall between 1910 and 1915, sold and possibly shafted it as well (Jackson 1994, 98).

Although this long-blade putter is right-handed, David P. Watt was a talented professional who played left-handed. According to one opinion, Watt was the premier left-handed golfer of his day:

*The golfer in question was D.M. [sic] Watt, the Mortonhall professional, who recently won the Scottish Championship. I have often heard discussions as to who could be considered the finest left-handed player in the world. I have no doubt on the point now. It is David Watt, of Mortonhall, who is quite in the front rank of professional players. One feature of his game is the abnormal amount of spin he can impart to the ball when playing his mashie shots, but he is a clever player all round, and his form would suggest that left-handed golfers are not placed at so great a disadvantage as we have been inclined to believe (*Golf Illustrated*, 19 June 1914: 2).*

Sadly, Watt was killed in France during the first week of World War I, only a year after scoring a 64 at Mortonhall.

Answering "Putter's" letter, the editor of *Golf Illustrated* responded:

Common sense should be able to decide the question. Speaking broadly, we should say that when there begins to be a doubt as to which is the head of the club and which the shaft a "substantial departure" has been established.

Certainly no one would have a problem telling where the head stops and the shaft starts on this putter.

Three other wood shaft giant putters are known to the author. Two of them, both "The Frank" model putters, were made by Frank Johnson, Ltd.; the other was made by J.P. Cochrane & Company. The blade on each of these clubs is approximately 5 1/2 inches long.

ALEXANDER AITKEN
SHORT-BLADE PUTTER

A New Putter.—Among the Golf Patentees who have recently entered the lists is Mr. Alexander Aitken, the club-maker attached to the green of the Burgess Golfing Society at Barnton, Cramond Brig, near Edinburgh. Mr. Aitken's new club is an improved putter. The blade is two and a half inches long and one and a half inches deep, thick on the sole, and fairly broad and solid all through, with the face quite plane [sic]; indeed, there is nothing to distinguish the club in appearance from a truncated, broad-faced cleek or iron. On the green, however, the club is a very effective one. Its broad face entirely covers the ball, and therefore propels it forward without jerk or spin in perfectly straight line for the hole. The broad face seems to cause the ball to "bite" the inequalities of the ground on the line of putt, and thus to save it from being deflected to the same extent as the narrow-faced cleeks are prone to do. This characteristic is most notice-able when a fairly long approach putt has to be made, say, the whole width of the green. The ball goes off the club quickly, but it runs true, and if the required strength has been imparted the ball is generally pretty near the hole. All the players who have tried the club speak highly in its favour, believing that Mr. Aitken is working on the correct lines for a putter by presenting a deep, straight face behind the ball, and in allowing it to have the full benefit of impact with the striking surface of the club. We have tried the club, and can speak in this sense from actual experiment. The club, which is beautifully finished, in black leather grip and hickory or green-heart shaft, is also made in requisite weights for ladies, who, as a rule, stand more upright over their ball when putting, and to whom therefore the club ought to be particularly welcome (Golf, 13 Dec. 1895: 298).

Aitken's short-blade putter, shown actual size, is marked "A. Aitken \ Patent \ Crammond Brig" inside an oval on the back of the blade. Aitken filed for a British patent on this putter in November of 1895. His provisional application was assigned patent No. 21,170; however, he later abandoned his application.

Aitken's putter was short-lived. Nevertheless, Aitken was a golf club and ball maker of the highest reputation who took his work seriously. Believing in his talents strictly as a clubmaker, Aitken challenged Willie Park's adver-tising statement "if you want a good golf club, get a good golfer to make it":

"If you want a good club get a good club to make it;" so says Willie Park, jun., in advertising wares. "If you want a good club get a good club-maker to make it," says A. Aitken, the maker of the wonderful set presented by a hundred Irishmen to the Ex-First Lord of the Treasury [A.J. Balfour]. . . . We are inclined to settle it by putting it thus: "If you want a good club get a good golfer, who is at the same time a good club-maker, to make it." If we must decide for one we award judgement to Aitken, for though Park himself is a fine player, and a good club-maker, we could name many good players, both cham-pion and ex-champion, who could not make a good golf-club an' 'twere to save their lives (Golf, 10 Feb. 1893: 346).

In 1905 a short-blade putter similar to Aitken's was produced by W.R. Pope of Chorlton-cum-Hardy, England:

Pope's Short-Head Cleek Putter.
A very natty little club, with a face not much bigger than the ball itself. It is the ideal club for those just begin-ning to learn the game. . . . The face being so short, the player is bound to find the centre with his stroke every time, and if the correct line is taken this is the secret of all correct putting—getting the ball well away. One cannot fail to do this with one of these short-head putters (Golfing, 23 Feb. 1905: 20)

When it comes to the blade length of putters, the two blades shown on this and the previous page cover the long and short of it. Aitken's blade measures 1 11/16 inches in depth and 2 7/8 inches in width across the back, including the hosel.

A.G. SPALDING & BROS.
"TRAVIS PUTTER"

If the story of Walter J. Travis was not backed up by official records, it would not be credited. As it stands today it is the tale of the greatest individual achievement in the history of sport; the tale of an impossible accomplishment, as such things go; the record of a man who did what no one has ever done before, or will ever do again, as far as one may read the future slate. . . .

In the fall of 1896, golf and the Oakland Club picked up a recruit. This recruit was a man who had passed thirty-five, a man of medium height and medium weight, with no great physical power to back him up—and who, before thirty-five, had never played a game of golf in his life.

Apparently he was just one of many other middle-aged duffers who had taken up the game for recreation and needed exercise . . . . This is the first picture we have of Travis as a golfer—a middle-aged beginner in the fall of 1896.

Seven months later, in the spring of 1897, we get the second picture. There was a medal-play tournament

on at the Meadow Brook Club and one of the entries was a sedate, middle aged citizen who rode up on a bicycle and turned in his name at the first tee. . . . So it happened that seven months after he had first picked up a club Walter J. Travis had won his first tournament; and a week later, at Knollwood, to show there was no fluke about it, he won the qualifying medal and then proceeded to move on triumphantly through the tournament at match play. . . .

This was the start that Travis, beyond thirty-five, made. Three years later he was amateur golf champion of America. Four years beyond that he was amateur champion of Great Britain, the first . . . American who has ever achieved this honor. And nineteen years beyond his first game, in his last championship—at a time well beyond fifty—he defeated on successive days Jerome D. Travers, Oswald Kirkby, and John G. Anderson, ending a tournament career that embraced four major championships and countless minor ones, as he began it, with victory (Rice 1917, 13).

Walter Travis was more than just an outstanding amateur golfer, he was once the best. He won the U.S. Amateur in 1900, 1901, and 1903 and the British Amateur in 1904; he was runner-up in the U.S. Open in 1902. Because he used a Schenectady putter when he won the 1904 British Amateur, Walter Travis is always associated with the Schenectady putter (see p. 193). Travis, however, used many different putters during his career, even lending his name to a few modeled after the Schenectady. Over the years, both Spalding and Slazenger offered their own "Travis" model putters.

In 1907 Frank L. Slazenger advertised "The 'Travis' Putter," a wood head mallet putter with a smooth brass faceplate (*Golf* [ny], Dec.: n.p.). Stamped "The 'Travis' " on the top of the head, this putter was very similar in style to Spalding's Model T putters, described later.

The putter above, shown actual size, is marked "A.G. Spalding & Bros" on the top of the head. "Travis Putter" is stamped in the lead backweight recessed into the head. This Spalding putter is the unusual and rarely seen Travis model with a five-inch-wide face. The regular model, offered by Spalding in the 1920s, has a face only 3 1/2 inches wide (standard for a putter) and was produced in significant numbers.

In Spalding's 1904-1905 Fall and Winter sports catalog, Spalding offered two center-shafted wooden mallet putters "manufactured from models made expressly for Mr. Travis" (56). These were Spalding's "Model T Putters," "Style A" with a narrow head and "Style B" with a broad head. Both putters have a brass, cross-scored faceplate, a lead backweight, and a rounded toe and heel across the top of the head. Some of these putters are also stamped "Travis Putter."

In Spalding's 1906 catalogs, the "Style A" and "Style B" putters were changed to the "Model A" and "Model R." The Model R added a convex sole. In 1909 Spalding discontinued both Model A and Model R in favor of just one wood head mallet putter: Spalding's "Gold Medal Wood Putter." This putter remained in production well into the 1920s.

In 1920 Spalding began listing the "No. WT Putter" in their catalogs while continuing to offer the Gold Medal Wood Putter. The "WT" was described as a "Special Walter Travis Model, as approved by Mr. Travis." This putter, offered by Spalding into the mid-1920s, is the smaller head version of the putter pictured on the facing page.

In addition to playing golf and designing putters, Walter John Travis also received a U.S. patent (No. 739,458) dated September 22, 1903, that covered weighting the rear of a wooden head to prevent slicing and hooking. Weight was installed behind the toe to prevent slicing or behind the heel to prevent hooking. Spalding briefly offered "Travis Patent Drivers and Brassies" beginning in the 1904-1905 Fall and Winter catalog. These woods came in three different models, dependent on where the lead was located in the back of the head, marked either "S" for slice, "P" for Pull, or "R" for regular (for golfers who consistently hit straight). Consequently, golfers could purchase a wood designed to improve their own individual shot pattern. A look at the back of one of these wood heads reveals very little; the visible portion of the backweight is much smaller than the portion inside the head.

JOHN RANDALL
LONG HEAD PUTTER, LEAD FACE

Unlike the Travis putter on the facing page, the Randall putter (shown actual size) on this page is end-shafted, not center-shafted. However, like the Travis putter, this particular Randall putter is a rare oversize model. Its face measures 5 3/4 inches in length while the face on a standard Randall patent putter, made with either an aluminum or wood head, measures no more than 4 1/2 inches. The abnormally large heads on the Travis and Randall putters shown are what makes them such interesting collectibles, valued well above their standard counterparts.

John Randall received a British patent (No. 186,522) dated October 5, 1922, that covered this putter design but not its size. The objective of Randall's invention was to create a soft face for a putter while also providing a novel way to weight the head. To accomplish this, Randall installed two horizontal rows of lead plugs in the face of his putter. According to his patent:

The putter head . . . may be loaded by a series of plugs of lead or like soft heavy metal inserted in holes bored into the putter head through the playing face, and lying flush with the playing face.

Randall believed that a series of plugs was much better than a solid lead face, which would "soon become dented and worn, with consequent loss of accuracy in play" (see p. 325).

Randall also formed a ridge, parallel with the face, on the top of the clubhead. He promoted it as an alignment aid.

The Randall aluminum putter pictured, complete with five lead plugs in the face, is marked "X \ Registered \ No 685349 \ J Randall \ Sundridge Park \ Kent \ 10 Ozs 8 Drs. \ Up Lie" on the sole. The design registration number shows that Randall also protected the visual appearance of his putter.

Although he was an obscure clubmaker, Randall was a good one. An advertisement for John Randall's clubs reads:

Highest Honours! Golf Trade Exhibition, London, 16th June, 1920, Golf Medal and Diploma awarded to John Randall, Golf Club Manufacturer, Sundridge Park G. C., Bromley, Kent. Honours must follow if you are equipped with these clubs (Golf Illustrated, 18 Mar. 1927: 393).

R. FORGAN & SON
THE "WHEE" PUTTER

A 1935 magazine article titled "The Main Idea is to Get the Ball into the Hole" includes a picture that shows the one-handed putting style of Joshua Crane. Crane is hunched over with his left hand resting on his left knee and his right hand gripping a very short putter, a putter no longer than Forgan's Whee putter pictured here. The article says:

Both the one-handed method and the very short shaft employed by Mr. Crane are out of the ordinary. At the same time there have been numerous cases of where golfers have found that they putted very well one-handed (The American Golfer, Mar. 1935: 25).

Joshua Crane was not the first person to attract attention for using a short putter. In 1898 Douglas Bonner reportedly used a "hammer-like putter [he] carries in his coat pocket" (*The Golfer*, 26 Jan. 1898: 73).

The Whee putter measures only 14 inches in overall length and was advertised in 1924 as follows:

The "Whee" Putter, Regd. A short single handed club with perfect balance.

The "Whee" Putter is the only club by which the golfer can visualize the line of the putt without moving position; hence concentration is not disturbed.

The scientifically obtained balance—see illustration—enables the "Whee" Putter to be used as a pendulum, in this manner ensuring that most essential quality—the perfect follow through.

A flat metal core, integral with the head, continues up the length of the shaft and is visible down the front and back of the shaft. Two rivets are used to affix the hickory to the sides of the flat metal core. The metal core in the short shaft gives the club added weight which is needed on such a short club to have any chance to be effective (Golfing, May 1924: 48).

The Whee putter used to illustrate the above advertisement is identical to the one shown here.

The example shown is marked "R. Forgan & Son \ Ltd. \ St. Andrews" inside an oval on the back of the blade along with "Patent Applied For \ The Whee Putter \ Reg'd \ Warranted Hand Forged" and Forgan's "flag" trademark. The flag trademark was initially registered in the U.S. on January 1, 1922, by James Spence of St. Andrews (Kennedy 1984, 26). Forgan began using this mark after taking over Messrs. James Spence, Ltd., in early 1924. Forgan registered this mark in the U.S. in 1927.

Today, Whee putters are almost as rare as golfers who use 14-inch putters. A Dunlop Tire & Rubber Company "VRP" ball is pictured for perspective. Produced around 1910, this rubber core ball has oversize dimples.

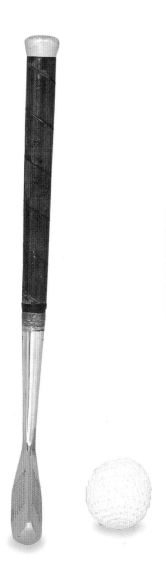

FRANK SMITH
DUPLEX "SMITHIRON"

Frank Smith of Los Angeles, California, received a U.S. design patent (No. 77,191) dated December 11, 1928, that covered the club above. As is typical for design patents, there is no written explanation, just a drawing of an "ornamental design." However, an advertisement for full-sized Smithirons notes that they have a rounded sole which:

permits the club head to slide over the turf, reduces hacking to the minimum, saves your disposition, saves precious strokes (*Golf Illustrated*, May 1932: 9).

Most Smithirons were sold in sets of full-length clubs. The twelve-inch-long duplex Smithiron shown, however, was sold as a separate club. The short shaft and duplex head allowed the golfer to use this club with one hand while crouching low to the ground, usually when the ball was in a very restricted area, such as under a tree or bush.

The example pictured, shown next to a circa late 1920s "Practo" knitted practice golf ball for perspective, is marked "Burke \ Smithiron \ Reg. 77,191" on the sole and "Burke \ Newark, Ohio" on the top of the grip cap. Burke made these short, one-hand clubs for a number of years. This example has a wood shaft under the grip, visible through the seams. Burke also produced numerous short steel shaft examples which have thinner hosels.

A full-length hickory shaft duplex Smithiron, marked "Smithiron \ Patent Pending" on the sole, is in the USGA's collection of antique clubs. The head on the USGA example is unchromed and, compared to the one shown here, thinner. Its shaft is original, not a reshaft.

INTERNATIONAL HARVESTER
OVERSIZE PUTTER

Known for making tractors, not golf clubs, International Harvester made at least one golf club—the one pictured right. In keeping with the nature of farm machinery, this putter weighs approximately forty pounds and measures 47 inches in total length!

This unusable behemoth was presented as a humorous award at a golf tournament. "SFSA Golf Tournament \ Oct 13, 41 \ Most Puttering Around \ Hot Springs VA" is cast into the back of the head as is an International Harvester "IH" trademark. This club is definitely one of a kind with its own personality. Because it was not designed for play, this putter is classified as a perimeter club (see p. 537). A circa late 1920s knitted practice golf ball, produced by the Reliable Knitting Works, Milwaukee, Wisconsin, is shown for perspective.

R. FORGAN & SON
"DREADNOUGHT" DRIVER

FRANK SLAZENGER
"DREADNAUGHT" DRIVER,
SCREW-IN SHAFT

"The Dreadnought." There is to be an epidemic of "Dreadnought" drivers. The germs are spreading from bog to bog, and, mayhap, the disease will be as evanescent as the measles of childhood. Every mother's son who has the shillings to spare, and the fancy that a few more yards are in him, given the proper vehicle for the transmission of his power, is sending to North Berwick for the fearsome instrument. And by the same token, a new era of slicing will be opened, for the heavy head of the whippy shaft is a dangerous instrument in the hands of the man whose driving at the best of times is inclined to be erratic. Mr. A.C.M. Croome describes the "Dreadnought" as a lump of wood attached to 3 1/2' of seaweed" (Golf Illustrated, 11 June 1909: 373).

In December of 1909, *The American Golfer* reported that the Dreadnought driver, "first brought out by Ben Sayers at the beginning of the season," was used by Robert Maxwell when he won the 1909 British Amateur (170). The Dreadnought was described as having a large head and flexible shaft with most of its whip located just below the grip!

In 1909 Garden G. Smith described the specifics of the Dreadnought. In part, his editorial reads:

Since the Amateur Championship, when the "Dreadnoughts" were first launched on the golfing world, it has been rather the fashion to decry the new weapons, and to class them with the freak clubs which, from time to time, attract the attention of golfers, and presently are heard of no more. . . .

In the discussion which has taken place about the alleged identity of the "Dreadnoughts". . . undue prominence has been given to the large size of the heads. Golf clubs have been made with extra large heads, in various shapes, at different periods in the history of the game . . . .

But when we come to the make of the "Dreadnought" shafts—and we mean the original "Dreadnoughts" and not the imitations of them—it has to be admitted that here there is a distinct modification of anything that has hitherto been seen in golf clubs. Supple shafts, of course, are not new; the old shafts were nearly always supple, but their suppleness was not the suppleness of the "Dreadnought." The "give" in the old shafts was located from three to four inches above the whipping, and the shaft from that point upwards thickened rapidly so that for some way below the grip it was quite rigid. But as we understand it, the true "Dreadnought" shaft is not so supple—if, indeed, it is supple at all—in its lower length, and the "give"

is transferred to the upper part of the shaft immediately below the grip, so that something in the nature of a hinge is provided and the club is transformed into a kind of sling. This, of course, is a very exaggerated way of putting it, but it serves to indicate the sort of principle which seems to underlie the idea.

. . . To get the full benefit of the slinging blow, which is the essential feature of the "Dreadnought," the swinging method of using a golf club must be employed. The greatest care must be taken that in the downward swing the club-head reaches the ball immediately after the shaft has recovered its equilibrium, for then only has it attained its greatest momentum.

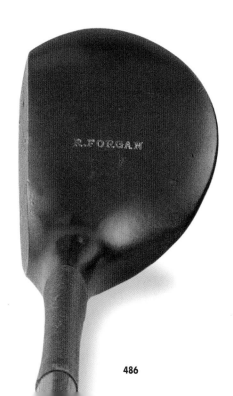

There is one weakness of limitation in the "Dreadnoughts" which should be noted. They are not adapted for playing anything but full shots, and not only full shots, but full shots from good lies. . . . The proper way to make a "Dreadnought" shaft is to thin the wood down near the grip, but the exact spot for doing this and the amount of thinning necessary are matters of extreme delicacy, depending, as they do, upon the lie of the head, its weight, and the nature of the shaft itself. We have seen many "Dreadnought" shafts that are quite useless, but a really good one has a delightful feeling of poise and balance, which at once suggests the kind of blow it is designed to deliver (Golf Illustrated, 1 Oct. 1909: 33).

The unique flex of the shaft was originally the key element in a Dreadnought driver, but such clubs are recognized by their large, round, and relatively flat heads.

Measuring 2 7/8 inches across the top of its head, front to back, the Forgan Dreadnought driver shown on the facing page is marked "R. Forgan" above the King's crown" trademark. Measuring a full three-inches across the top of its head, front to back, the Slazenger Dreadnaught driver shown on the facing page is marked "Dreadnaught \ Patent No. 682,960" and "G.H.D." on its crown. The patent number acknowledges the Frank Slazenger screw-in shaft installed in this club (see p. 152). (Note that Dreadnaught is spelled with an "a" instead of an "o" on this club.)

The Dreadnought was not the first driver to have a large, round, flat head. The "Bap" driver, tried briefly in the middle 1890s, had a head similar to that of the Dreadnought:

Scottish and English Golfers who were present at Portrush, at the big Autumn tournament held there, could not help noticing the broad-headed driver clubs sent out by John Aitken, the club-maker attached to the Royal County Club at Portrush. The appearance of the club took the fancy of some of the players, and it was played with in the competitions; and many of them found their way to Southern and Northern greens in the bags of the visitors. The club is known as "The Bap," the name given in the Scots tongue to the round breakfast roll. The head, which is made of the finest Irish beech, is three inches broad, with a face of 1 1/4 inches in depth" (Golf, 27 Dec. 1895: 341).

Prompted by the above reference to John Aitken as the originator of the Bap driver, an individual who identifies himself as "W." states in a letter to the editor that this was not the case:

Whoever made this statement is misinformed, as the "Bap" driver was invented and named by myself, in conjunction with W. Rea, the local professional at Randalstown, co. Antrim. Other club-makers have imitated this club, but, neither in wood nor in workmanship can any of these imitations come up to the "Baps" made by Rea (Golf, 17 Jan. 1896: 404).

One week later, another letter to the editor of Golf was published wherein "L." states that Tom Morris made Bap drivers before "W." or Rea ever did. According to "L.":

I see in your issue of January 17th a letter signed "W," claiming to be the first to introduce the "Bap" driver. This is a great mistake. The first "Bap" driver was brought to Portrush some two years ago, made by Morris, and I know Morris used to make them years ago. It is therefore an old club come to the front again. As for "W." saying that Rea, the local professional, was the first to make it, is entirely a mistake. When Aitken went to Portrush four years ago, Rea knew nothing about club-making, as he was a carpenter at Randalstown, and was a carpenter up till about nine months ago. Aitken gave him the information he now knows about club-making; he did not even know how to put a leather on a club (421).

The author has seen a broad-headed Bap driver made by Morris.

Because both the Bap and the Dreadnought have large, round heads, there was some confusion concerning their differences. Consequently, *Golf* printed a running commentary on the topic between August 13, 1909, and January 14, 1910. The essential differing elements were noted as follows:

The "Dreadnought" heads have perhaps as much wood in them, but the face is much more in a line with the shaft, and the bulk of the head is behind it. Then the shaft of the "Bap" was quite normal and had no trace of the suppleness just under the grip which is the essential feature of the "Dreadnought" (Golf, 13 Aug. 1909: 190).

To better illustrate the differences between a Dreadnought and a Bap driver, the September 3, 1909 issue of *Golf Illustrated* included outline drawings of both clubheads. The neck/shaft of the Dreadnought is positioned behind the face while the neck/shaft of the Bap is set back even farther—more in line with the middle of the head (262).

A direct descendant of the Dreadnought is the "Dreadnought Junior." After noting that Forgan & Sons [sic] had just started producing such a club, the December 10, 1909 issue of *Golf Illustrated* explains that the Dreadnought Junior driver kept the supple shaft of a regular Dreadnought but replaced its large head with one of regular size:

A great many players like the supple shafts of the ordinary "Dreadnoughts," but dislike the big heads, and for such, these clubs, which are called "Dreadnought Juniors," are specially designed. Like all Messrs. Forgan's productions, the "Dreadnought Juniors" represent the acme of perfection in material and skilled workmanship (285).

The September 24, 1909 issue of *Golf Illustrated* reports:

The interest in Dreadnought drivers during 1909 caused at least one maker, Charles Mayo, to resume making Bap drivers. Mayo made splendid examples of the Bap with "a perfectly normal shaft" (17).

A club called the "Scone" was mentioned in a brief interview with P.L. Forgan published in 1909. According to Forgan, the Scone predated the Bap and had a larger head than the Dreadnought:

I have had an interview with Mr. P.L. Forgan, of Messrs. R. Forgan and Son, regarding the controversy in your correspondence column on the "Bap" and the "Dreadnought." He assures me that "Baps," very broad at the heel, were first made by their firm about fifteen years ago, and an old model is now in his possession. Previous to that another large head called the "Scone" was made, the form of which more closely resembled the up-to-date "Dreadnought," it was, however, even larger (Golf Illustrated, 8 Oct. 1909: 60).

WILLIAM L. RITCHIE
JUMBO DRIVER

Measuring an incredible 2 3/8 inches in face depth, the jumbo driver pictured on this and the facing page (image on facing page is actual size) was meant to be used! To keep the weight of the head manageable, the crown slopes from the top of the face down to the back of the sole. This results in a head that is triangular in cross section, the face, sole, and crown making up the three sides. This club is marked "W.L. Ritchie \ Addington" on its crown and "W.L. Ritchie \ Special" on its shaft.

Born in 1884 at Aberdeen, Scotland, William Leggat Ritchie worked as an assistant to James Braid at Walton Heath before becoming the professional at Worplesdon (*Golf Illustrated*, 6 Jan. 1911: 48). In early 1922, Ritchie left Worplesdon to serve as the professional at Addington Club, near Croydon, where he worked until 1933. During his career, he advertised himself as a "First-class club maker and coach" (*Golf Monthly*, May 1914: 239). This jumbo driver was made during the 1920s when Ritchie was at Addington.

Prior to the creation of Ritchie's jumbo driver, Fred Whiting made deep-face drivers and Ben Sayers Jr. made jumbo drivers.

Fred Whiting, the professional at West Cornwall Club in Lelant, England, between 1901 and 1911, was an enterprising clubmaker who believed that a deep-face driver would hit a rubber-core golf ball farther than a regular face driver:

His latest specialties are drivers and brassies with deep faces, which he argues will more effectively negotiate rubber-cored balls, inasmuch as the greater expansion of the cored balls requires something on the part of the club to keep them low in flying, and consequently to give them a longer carry (*Golfing*, 5 Nov. 1903: 38).

In 1908 Ben Sayers advertised the "Jumbo" Driver:

The "Jumbo" Driver has proved to be the longest driving club ever made. Used by all the leading golfers. . . . To be had only from B. Sayers, Junr. (*Golf Illustrated*, 30 Oct.: 119).

Sayers's Jumbo drivers, well over two inches in face depth, were made with a traditional, not slanted, crown.

In 1923 a driver with a four-inch face depth was invented by Mr. H.E. Taylor:

A driver with a face four inches deep is the latest terror which has been added to golf. Mr. H.E. Taylor, who is already fabled to possess nearly a thousand clubs, is the inventor (*Golfing*, Oct. 1923: 55).

This brief mention of Taylor's club goes on to note that deep-face drivers were already in use but usually by American visitors to Great Britain who were trying to gain distance by teeing the ball extremely high. A British golfer using a jumbo driver and tees five to nine inches high is pictured and discussed in the February 1924 issue of *Golfing* (26-27). This article notes a "deeper face club becomes essential in order to allow a reasonable margin for error" when using such high tees (27).

Jumbo drivers appealed to very few golfers and are quite rare today, as is Henley's original red "Why Not" bramble cover golf ball produced in 1911 and shown on this page.

Even though the extreme face depth of the early jumbo drivers precluded their effectiveness and, consequently, their general acceptance, the idea of deeper faces and larger heads was a serious consideration to no less than Bobby Jones.

In an article written by O.B. Keeler and titled "Bobby Jones Designs a New Club," Keeler reports that Jones made a set of drawings for a pair of deep-face woods which A.G. Spalding then produced for him. Keeler notes that these were the largest clubs he had seen:

Certainly these new clubs have large heads and ample faces—the largest and amplest I have ever seen; larger, I feel sure, than the largest of the original Dreadnought designed and executed by the diminutive and original Benny Sayers some fifteen . . . years ago (*The American Golfer*, 22 Mar. 1924: 5).

Further on, Keeler notes Jones's propensity for woods with large heads:

Bobby never fell for the small-head fad. Indeed, he had his clubs made with faces deeper and deeper, until the driver he was using at Inwood, when he won the open championship, had a face nearly two inches in depth, though quite narrow at the sole.

The driver and brassie he now is using, of his own design, are of a size almost colossal. I am informed that they were even larger, as they came from the factory to the shop of Stewart Maiden, where heads and shafts were to be assembled; and that there were words—short, strong, Caledonian words—heard in that shop before the clubs were duly put together. Indeed, there was a compromise; I am told that fully an eighth of an inch was taken from the club-heads in every direction before they finally were spliced to the beautiful bamboo shafts, by the old method of a "scared" joint.

The first time I saw the clubs I told Bobby the heads really ought to be streamlined, to lessen the air resistance in the swing. . . .

The face, with only enough loft to enable the player to see the lower edge with the club grounded—practically no loft at all—is 1 9/16 inches in depth, three inches long at the top, and 1 1/2 inches long at the sole. The head measures 3 inches across the top at the widest point, front to back. The bulge is so emphatic that a line drawn across the top of the head from one extremity of the face to the other will show a protuberance of 3/8 inch at the middle of the rounded hitting surface—the most startling bulge I ever saw on a golf club.

The driver weights 13 1/2 ounces, of which 7 1/2 ounces are in the head and 6 ounces in the shaft; a radical departure from the old proportions in wood clubs, which usually had the weight of head and shaft approximately equal. This significant change was made possible by the bamboo shaft, which is lighter in proportion to its stiffness than a hickory shaft. In fact, a friend of Bobby's having one of the sample club-heads made up with a hickory shaft, found that the resultant club was so heavy that no lead could be used in the head. Very little lead is used in the head of Bobby's driver; only three-quarters of an ounce, in cylindrical form, half an inch in diameter, set directly back of the correct point of impact and extending three-quarters of an inch into the head.

The length of the club over all is 44 inches. The bamboo shaft is stiff, yet there is a bit of "feel" to it. . . .

And now to the effect of this remarkable combination, with the celebrated Jones swing. Bobby's own theory follows;

"I tee the ball about three-quarters of an inch high and try to hit it directly 'in the back.' This stroke, with a deep-faced club with practically no loft, seems to give me as long a carry as I can get with conventional clubs, and the ball has much more life and run after it takes the turf. In other words, the tendency to 'climb' by a ball hit with much backspin seems to be almost obviated. Hit in the back with this club, the ball seems rather to bore its way through the air and to retain considerable running ability on landing. I think it will be a good club for use in a hard wind. I find also that I can hit as hard as I please without the 'climbing' tendency taking length off the shot" (*The American Golfer*, 22 Mar. 1924: 5+).

The lower trajectory Jones noted was the result of two characteristics found in his clubhead: reduced loft and a higher center of gravity. These characteristics are normally found in deep-face drivers.

Keeler ends his article by commenting that Jones was probably not finished with his club testing:

But the design of the clubs, and their heroic size, will stamp this latest endeavor at least as distinctive, and Bobby's further experimentation will be watched with considerable interest (30).

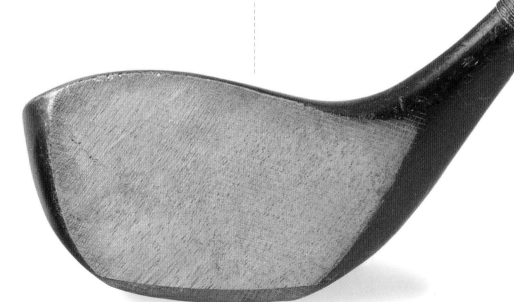

LOCKWOOD, BROWN & CO.
"THE WHITMEE CHALLENGE DRIVER"

Shown left is an enormous club marked "The Whitmee Challenge Driver" on its crown. The author does not know what the Whitmee Challenge was, but the most obvious challenge would be to swing this club and hit a ball! The approximately four-pound head at the end of the 48-inch hickory shaft makes waggling this club unbelievably difficult—your hands move, but the clubhead wants to stay put.

Lockwood & Brown's "LB 42 Jermyn Street" trademark is stenciled on the shaft just below the grip. Lockwood, Brown & Company was a London-based retail operation that sold clubs during the wood shaft era. This club was probably constructed in response to a customer's special order.

The club itself is well made in all aspects. It has a pleasing head shape, a lead weight, a ram's horn slip on the sole (affixed by two screws and one wood dowel), a nice sheepskin grip, and a cross-scored face measuring just slightly less than 4 inches deep. The head measures 6 3/4 inches from the face straight back and 8 1/2 inches from the tip of the nose straight across to the back of the neck. The shaft is exceptionally thick, measuring 3/4 of an inch in diameter at its narrowest point (just above the neck) and just under 1 1/4 inches at the end of the grip. A red "Why Not" golf ball, made in 1911 by Henley's Telegraph Works Company, is shown for perspective.

ARTHUR JOHN ROWE
OVERLENGTH DRIVER

Most drivers are approximately forty-three inches long. When a fifty-inch driver is lined up amidst a set of standard length (Spalding) woods, as is shown on the facing page, its extraordinary length becomes obvious. Marked "John Rowe" on the crown, this fifty-inch driver was made by Rowe for Harold Hilton, the four-time British amateur champion, two-time British Open champion, and once U.S. Amateur champion. Hilton, who was only 5 feet 6 inches tall, hoped the long shaft would give him extra distance off the tee. When Hilton found the club to be more than he could handle, he gave it to James Braid. In the words of Peter Marsh, a former professional at Rye Golf Club (in Rye, East Sussex, England) who also once owned this club:

The club came to me by way of my father who was assistant to James Braid at the Walton Heath Golf Club. I cannot be too precise on the dates but as I remember it Hilton, who was only about 5 feet 6 or 7, asked Rowe to make him a club longer than standard in order to get more width and therefore more length. It could not have been a success because my father was told by James Braid to thicken the grip a little and he would try it. It appears that he was playing at Ashdown Forest with Hilton and Abe Mitchell and Hilton gave him, Braid, the club to try as Braid was well over six feet in height. Braid did not like it and gave it to my father who was six feet two in height and he once told me that though it hit the ball further he had no idea where the ball was going. . . . The club was made around 1907-08 (Marsh 1994).

Walter Travis, the three-time U.S. Amateur champion and once British Amateur champion, also tried playing with a 50-inch driver. Travis's efforts were recounted in an article, titled "Mr. Travis's 50-inch Clubs," published in 1905:

The long-shafted golf club now used by Mr. Travis is the chief topic of conversation these days whenever golfers meet. Every golfer is desirous of securing the greatest possible distance consistent with accuracy on his full shots, and therefore the entire golfing world is watching the experiments of Mr. Travis. Arguments against his ability to wield the clumsy-looking long drivers and brassies without sacrificing his well-known accuracy regarding direction must give way after his recent record-breaking round of 75 at Lakewood and his low card of 78 in the qualifying round of the Garden City Tournament (Golf [ny], May: 270-272).

In addition to recounting Travis's success with his long driver, the article reports that he was also using a "long-handled cleek and mid-iron."

Going to the opposite extreme, some golfers tried short drivers in the late 1890s:

It is not an uncommon occurrence to see first-class players of the present time using a driver some two inches or so shorter than their brassey. . . . The first time I saw one of these abnormally short drivers was in the hands of J.H. Taylor, about two years ago . . . and he certainly used it with deadly precision (Golfing, 9 Feb. 1899: 13).

The brilliant sales which just now are attending Cann and Taylor's short clubs reminds me that the opposite side of the question was humorously illustrated by a golfer who preferred to drive with an extra long club. Not content was he with what the local professional turned out in the shape of length—he had a club made with a billiard cue for the shaft. This is in no way a "straight tip," and no one is advised as such to "take the cue"; but the gentleman referred to with a very long, slow swing professed himself satisfied with the result of his drives with this extraordinary implement (Golfing, 5 Jan. 1899: 14).

As mentioned earlier, Hilton's 50-inch driver was made by John "Jack" Rowe, a widely-respected professional:

Jack Rowe was a versatile man, having been an apprentice carpenter and secured an Art Teacher's certificate at Bideford School of Art. He was a first rate professional golfer and won many tournaments and important matches. . . . He never reached a leading position in national events but did creditably; he was more successful in the Home Countries and played a number of times for England in international matches. In 1922-23 he was elected Captain of the P.G.A. which was a tribute to the esteem in which he was held by his fellow professionals. . . . He was a true Club Professional . . . . He was also an excellent clubmaker and teacher (Arnell 1988, 36. See also Golf, 5 May 1899: 207).

When Rowe retired in 1947, after working at Royal Ashdown Forest for fifty-five years and one day, he became the fifth longest serving professional at one club in the history of golf.

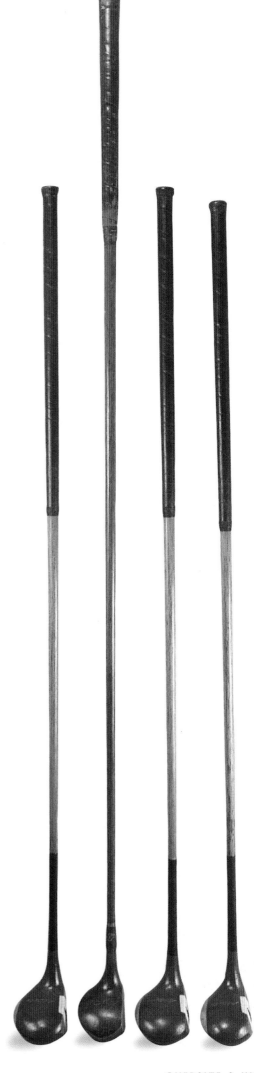

BURKE GOLF CO.
"JUNIOR" DRIVER

CANN & TAYLOR
JUVENILE DRIVER

A.G. SPALDING & BROS.
MINIATURE DRIVERS

W.H. WAY
MINIATURE DRIVER

Golf is not just for grown-ups, as these four small clubs attest. The "Burke Junior" driver shown far left measures 29 inches in total length. Burke's "Junior" clubs were intended for children eight to twelve years of age (see facing page).

The J.H. Taylor juvenile driver pictured second from the left, marked "Cann & Taylor \ J.H. Taylor" on the top of its head, measures 26 inches in total length and still has its original leather grip, which is especially nice in a juvenile club—the original grip verifying its original length. The head is made from oak, an added collectible feature in this late 1890s or early 1900s splice neck club.

A few other clubmakers also tried using oak heads. In 1895 Peter Paxton advertised "Paxton's Oak Club Heads Warranted to all Golfers for Six Months" (*Golf*, 22 Mar.: 32). The following year, J.&D. Clark offered a special line of clubs with oak heads, leather facing, and ash shafts (*The Golfer*, 2 Dec. 1896: 444). It was not long, however, before oak club-heads were abandoned:

Oak has been tried and found wanting, having little elasticity, and being inclined to split. The evergreen oak (Quercus ilex) is a hard, heavy, and very handsome wood, extremely difficult to season, owing to splitting, and is not available in large quantities (*Golf Illustrated*, 27 Jan. 1905: 94).

The circa 1897 "The Spalding" miniature transitional driver shown in the center has a splice neck and leather wrap grip. The club measures only 17 1/2 inches in length. (See the facing page for a matching iron.)

The circa 1897 "The Spalding" miniature bulger driver shown fourth from the left measures only 13 1/2 inches in length. Crafted in every detail exactly like a full-size golf club, this splice neck wood has survived the past century unscathed and remains in mint condition. It should be noted that the 1897 "The Spalding" stamp used on these two woods was reused years later on other miniature Spalding clubs, including some with steel shafts.

The circa early 1900s "W.H. Way" miniature driver shown near left, complete with a greenheart shaft and splice neck, measures only 8 3/4 inches in length. In 1898, Way advertised himself as a "Golf Club and Ball Manufacturer" located at the Country Club of Detroit, Grosse Point, Michigan (*Golf* [ny], Nov. : 318).

Miniature clubs are the smallest of clubs. They were made as toys, display pieces, or sales samples (to demonstrate a clubmaker's work).

All of the five clubs on this page are good collectibles; however, the Way driver and both "The Spalding" woods are prime collectibles for several reasons. They are exceptionally small, well-made, and realistic; they date earlier than most minature clubs; and miniature clubs are rarer than juvenile clubs.

It is especially important for juvenile and miniature clubs to have their original components. Such clubs are collectible because *everything* was made smaller.

J.B. HALLEY & CO.
JUVENILE IRON

BURKE GOLF CO.
"MIDGET" IRON

A.G. SPALDING & BROS.
MIDGET IRON

WILLIAM GIBSON & CO.
MINIATURE IRON

A.G. SPALDING & BROS.
MINIATURE IRON

Beginning on the left, the first club pictured is a mid-1920s brass mashie made by J.B. Halley & Company, of London. This 26-inch long club, marked "Mashie" on the back of the blade along with "Pyramid" underneath J. B. Halley's "pyramid" trademark, was designed for a preteen golfer.

The second iron is marked "Burke \ Midget \ Newark \ O." on the back of its tiny blade. This club measures only 19 inches in length. Burke Midgets are listed in Burke's 1917 catalog:

These are intended for children from 3 to 8 years of age. They also consist of Driver, Mid Iron, and Putter with bright colored plaid Caddy Bag, leather trimming with two miniature golf balls. $4.00 (15).

Burke's 1922 catalog describes their Midget clubs as "Toy clubs for little tots." Burke also offered Junior clubs, for children eight to twelve years old, and Juvenile clubs.

To collectors, a "juvenile club" is any small club made for a junior golfer. Burke's Juvenile clubs, however, were a specific line of junior clubs designed for youths age twelve and over. Burke offered wood-shafted Juvenile, Junior, and Midget clubs at least until 1927. Many other major clubmakers such as Wilson, Spalding, and MacGregor also offered juvenile clubs during the early 1900s.

Pictured in the middle is a circa 1910 midget size iron marked "Spalding" in block letters on the back of the head. This club measures only 18 inches long.

The fourth club is smaller still, measuring only 15 inches. The back of the blade is marked "Ella Schon \ 7-17-24 \ Mid-Iron" along with William Gibson's "star" trademark and what appears to be a "devil" cleekmark! This club was probably a keepsake given to a very young Ella Schon, born July 17, 1924. If this club was not given as a keepsake, it should have been!

Who would not rather have such a refined article of undeniable craftsmanship from their earliest days—something which speaks to the higher good in life, a memento of inexhaustible pleasure, a reflection on the joy of green grass freshly mowed to three-sixteenths of an inch—than a pair of bronze baby shoes?

The early miniature iron on the far right measures only 14 inches overall, is marked with the circa 1897 "The Spalding" stamp on the back of its brass head, and exhibits wonderful craftsmanship and realism.

Clubmakers occasionally made miniature clubs in order to showcase their talent. Charles Gibson and Ben Sayers made a set of miniature clubs measuring only 3 1/4 inches long which they presented to "Queen Mary for inclusion in the Doll's House at Windsor Castle" (Henderson & Stirk 1979, 282).

With miniature clubs, just as with oversize clubs, the quality of the workmanship and the degree to which a club is authentically crafted is of paramount importance to the collector. Juvenile clubs made for golf-related yard games are usually crudely constructed. Such clubs receive minimal or no interest. (See also the juvenile club on page 70). The gutta percha ball is pictured for perspective.

It has been said that a good shaft is a pearl beyond price and there can be but little doubt that in connection with clubs which are made of wood the shaft is the main essential toward the making of a com- pletely successful club.

(Harold Hilton; Hilton 1913, 66)

Shafts

Wood & Metal

||| ——————————————— |||

During the wood shaft era, clubmakers constructed many different types of both wood and metal shafts. To understand the rise of the metal shaft, one must first understand the background of the wood shaft.

Wood Shaft Materials: Hickory was the most common wood used to make shafts. The earliest printed reference to hickory shafts is found in the August 28, 1824 issue of *The Sporting Magazine*, which states that the shaft of a golf club "is generally of some very pliant tough wood, as hickory" (291). In 1837 an account of golf printed in *Kay's Portraits* reports that the shaft is "usually made of ash, or hickory, which is allowed to be better" (Paton, 212). The early use of hickory is corroborated by the existence of known hickory shaft clubs from even earlier periods. Also, the bulk of Hugh Philp's clubs have hickory shafts, and Philp died in 1856.

Prior to 1700, hazel, ash, elm, and a few unidentified types of wood were used to construct shafts. The use of hazel was documented during the 1600s (Johnston 1993, 136), but the use of elm was only recently discovered. In 1993 the author sent a wood sample from the shaft of a circa 1650 to 1725 juvenile iron to the Department of Forestry at the University of Massachusetts where it was scientifically examined and identified as elm. Ash, however, emerged as the primary wood used to make shafts. During the 1700s and into the 1800s, clubmakers continued to make shafts from ash while introducing lancewood, greenheart, and hickory. As hickory shafts became more popular, all other types of wood shafts were used less and less. Just prior to 1900, ash shafts made a brief and limited comeback, most notably as marked and sold by David Anderson & Sons, under the guise of being "Texa" shafts:

A remarkable fact in connection with ordinary ash is that it is palmed off on confiding golfers under the name of "texa," thereby possibly acquiring undiscoverable virtues (Golf Illustrated, 27 Jan. 1905: 94).

The production of ash, greenheart, and lancewood shafts continued on a very limited basis into the early 1900s. By the end of the 1800s, however, clubmakers were experimenting with other types of wood shafts. An advertisement by Remer, Nowell & Company, timber importers and manufacturers, in the 1893-1894 *Golfing Annual*, offers the following types of wood shafts:

Hickory, Greenheart, Lemon Wood, Lancewood, Purpleheart, Ironheart, Bullet Wood, Washaba, turned for irons, cleeks, or drivers, or in squares (*Golfing Annual* 1894, n.p.).

In spite of the variety of available woods, most of the shafts made between 1800 and the end of the wood shaft era were hickory. In 1900 it was reported that ninety-nine out of every one hundred new clubs were made with hickory shafts (*Golfing*, 19 July 1900: 18).

Another basic shaft material was bamboo. Bamboo, or cane shafts as they were also called, were usually laminated together from lengthwise pieces. Bamboo shafts were advertised in the early 1900s and tried even earlier, but they reached the height of their popularity during the 1920s (see p. 511-513).

Wood Shaft Construction Methods: Before the late 1880s, clubmakers crafted every part of a golf club one step at a time. Wood shafts, for example, were split, shaped, sanded, and finished entirely by hand. With the rise of industry during the 1890s, however, mechanization also took hold in the world of golf club manufacturing. Consequently, shafts came to be sawn and lathed by machine. To the purist at the time, there was a recognizable difference between the quality of the hand-worked "split" shaft and that of the mechanized "sawn" shaft. The sawn shaft was considered inferior because the saw did not always consider the direction of the wood grain. Sawn shafts were seen as weak, less resilient, and susceptible to warping. The split shaft, on the other hand, was "nature's own." The purist believed that by allowing the wood to split along the natural grain, the shaft would be strong, resilient, true, and durable.

Technology, however, was not to be denied. The magnitude of the change to machinery is demonstrated in the following comments by Robert Forgan:

"On one occasion when Hugh Philp had all St. Andrews to himself, he once bought a hickory log at Leith, the biggest investment he had ever made in that particular wood, and he used to sit and wonder if that log would ever go done. Now Mr. Forgan, when he goes to the wood importer, orders close on a hundred logs at a time. The firm also buys shafts cut in the square in America; they imported one lately of 40,000 from New York to Dundee. In 1856 he had only one assistant; the firm now gives employment to nearly fifty hands" (Golf, 3 Mar. 1899: 485).

Understandably, clubmakers did not fight the idea of using machines to make shafts. Machinery would certainly help increase production and possibly profits as well. Consequently, shaft lathes came into use by the early 1890s:

We have received from Mr. Charles Spinks, Leith, N.B., samples of shaped shafts for golf clubs and irons . . . . The shafts are shaped by a patented invention of Mr. Spinks, which does the work in a clean, speedy, and quiet manner, free from all shock, or jar and vibration. The invention has been the outcome of Mr. Spinks extensive trade with club makers, the best known in the kingdom having obtained the wood in the rough and finished from him. The shafts shaped by the appliances have thus been brought under the notice of the most famous makers, who all bear excellent testimony in their favour, and have given large repeat orders for them. By their use, a great deal of trouble, labour, and expense is saved. Of course, we know that strong prejudice exists in certain quarters against shafts made otherwise than by hand (Golf, 18 Sep. 1891: 4).

Machine-made shafts became the norm during the 1890s as did machine-made raw clubheads. There was no other way to meet the rapidly increasing demand for new clubs:

Club-making has been practically revolutionized, and by the introduction of gas engines, a variety of ingenious appliances, chiefly lathes and saws, have reduced it to a very mechanical process. The shafts are thinned down, and tapered at the rate of two in five minutes. The hickory square is first firmly fixed on the lathe and made to revolve with great velocity, while a ring plane is forced along the whole length, and is so compressed by the graduated pressure of the hand as to give it the necessary tapered form towards one end (St. Andrews Citizen, 22 Dec. 1900: 5).

Wood Shaft Supply: By 1913, good quality hickory was in short supply:

The big factory of the Crawford, McGregor & Canby Co., one of the largest and best known manufacturers of golf clubs in the world, was fortunate in escaping serious damage when the disastrous flood which recently swept through Dayton caused such havoc in that city. . . . There is a scarcity of good hickory in the country and as the Crawford, McGregor & Canby Co. always keep a reserve stock on hand ample for two years' supply of shafts, it is indeed fortunate that their stock of hickory was not swept away during the flood (Golfers Magazine, April 1913: 289).

Four years later, many people thought good quality hickory was a thing of the past. Douglas H. Tweedie writes about the lack of good hickory in his article "The High Cost Of The Hickory Shaft":

Hickory once grew in commercial quantities from Connecticut, New York, and southern Michigan south to Florida and west to Illinois, Missouri, Oklahoma, and eastern Texas but the original supply is now approaching exhaustion. The bulk of the supply now lies, scattered in small quantities, south of the Ohio River, and already the old cuttings are being worked, material being taken which was rejected twenty years ago.

The top shaft is made from hickory and belongs to a Willie Park Jr. brass blade putter. The next shaft is made from greenheart (note the reddish-brown color and short, dense grain) and belongs to an Robert White brass blade putter. In the middle is a lancewood shaft (the grain is very short and unnoticeable) that belongs to a Willie Park Jr. short spoon. Next is an ash shaft (note the long parallel ribbons of grain) that belongs to an early long nose wood marked "W.S." At the bottom is a cane and hickory laminated shaft (the wide, darker strips are cane) that belongs to a Spalding driver.

There are now about one million golf shafts annually consumed in the United States. To produce each one of these slender rods requires unexampled care and effort, too often resulting in bitter disappointment. Of the commercial hickory cut each year about one percent is used for golf shafts. Of the original timber cut about ten percent yields high grade sticks notwithstanding the fact that the growing tree selected for this cutting is culled out with the greatest care to insure against the quick grown, spongy wood which is the product of soil carrying excessive moisture. The best material is the three inches of sap wood adjacent to the heart. It requires about fifty years of growth to produce these three inches of perfect material (Golf Illustrated, Feb. 1917: 26).

As clear-cut as Tweedie's comments appear to be, there was a contradictory point of view that explained the large number of poor quality hickory shafts. William Burke, identifying himself as "having spent over forty years of his life in studying and handling this particular wood, twenty-one of which has been devoted to golf shaft production," responded to Tweedie's article with a counterpoint article titled "Hickory For Shafts Not Failing." Burke begins by identifying Tweedie as a:

. . . young man with no practical experience either in hickory or golf shaft making. He is a traveling salesman for a golf club manufacturing concern which is said to be preparing to market a metal golf shaft (Golf Illustrated [ny], Mar. 1917: 24).

Burke then notes that a shaft requires nearly thirty months to get "from tree to tee." Consequently, the supply of hickory shafts for any particular year was determined two to three years earlier. If the demand was greater than the available supply, that was only the result of low forecasting. Burke believed that plenty of good hickory trees were still in existence and large numbers of quality hickory shafts could still be produced. Then, after acknowledging many of the characteristics which make working with hickory difficult, Burke states that the lack of good hickory was actually due in large part to great waste in the manufacturing of hickory shafts, the result of incompetent and ignorant manufacturers:

Hundreds of thousands of poor shafts are put on the market every year, not because there is a real dearth of good hickory but because the makers are short on hickory knowledge and shaft experience, and try to cover their own shortcomings by accusing the country of hickory "exhaustion."

By 1917, the year Tweedie and Burke published their articles, metal shafts had already appeared on the market. After 1917, metal shafts continued to gain momentum because they offered club manufacturers many benefits not found in hickory. Specifically, metal shafts enjoy unlimited supply; they do not warp; they are impervious to stain, insect, or worm damage; and they have great durability. By selling metal shafts, the manufacturers did not have to inventory their shafts for two or more years, the time it took to season wood shafts. This reduction in inventory time reduced their overhead as well as their exposure to damage (fire, flooding, warping, staining, breaking, deterioration, etc.). Metal shafts could also be made to previously unknown levels of quality control and size/flex tolerances.

Metal Shafts: Metal was used to make two different types of shafts: those made entirely from metal and those made partly from metal, such as wood shafts with metal cores. Today, pre-1910 clubs made with either type of metal shaft are almost nonexistent though written references describing their designs and production remain.

The earliest description of a club with any type of metal shaft is printed in the November 14, 1890 issue of *Golf*, which reads:

Thus, there have been novelties in driving shafts—new woods, bamboos, and Malacca canes have been tried. Most have been found wanting, and the golfer has returned to his hickories. But now we have before us quite a new departure—a steel bar let down the whole centre length of shaft. It is the invention, we believe, of Mr. Adams, of Musselburgh, and though it makes the club feel heavy in the shaft, it certainly hits the ball a very shrewd blow. It is especially claimed for it that it is an assistance to those who do not hit very hard, but let the club do most of the work, and the verdict of these more deliberate drivers, to whom we have submitted it for trial, is that it helps them to put yards on their drives (136).

The "steel bar let down the center length of the shaft" and the reference to "Mr. Adams" identifies the metal core shaft briefly produced and advertised by Alexander Adams:

The Steel Core Golf Club Shaft. Patented by Alexander Adams, Royal Musselburgh Golf Club, Musselburgh. Prices: Drivers and Spoons. 7s. 6d.; Brassies, 8s.; Irons and Cleeks, 10s. 6d. ; A Special club for the Colonies.

Agents: D. M'Ewan & Son, Golf Club Makers, Musselburgh, and Chingford, Essex; Buchannan & Co., Braid Road, Edinburgh (Golfing Annual 1891, n.p.).

Receiving a poor response to his product, Adams, who never actually received a patent for his shaft, let his patent application lapse.

The next metal shaft reference printed in *Golf*, in early 1891, apparently acknowledges Adams's shaft. After mentioning the modifications made within the past few years "upon the old fashioned club," *Golf* refers to clubs constructed with:

shafts with wire cores (on the same principle as fishing rods) (16 Jan. 1891: 275).

Even though the Adams "Steel Core Golf Club Shaft" was the first of its type advertised, it was not the first to be tried. In 1895 a golfer recalled taking a lesson from Thomas Gilroy and being shown what was apparently a long nose club with a steel core shaft!

The writer well remembers early lessons generously given him at Portrush by Mr. Gilroy, and on one occasion after breaking three of his mentor's clubs going to one hole, Mr. Gilroy laughingly remarked, "I'll bring you a club after luncheon that you'll not break," and sure enough after luncheon Mr. Gilroy turned up with an old driver of McEwan's with a steel core in the shaft! (Golf, 20 Dec. 1895: 328).

The first patent to discuss using metal to construct a golf shaft is George Grant's British patent (No. 17,929) dated October 7, 1892. Although this patent sought to position the shaft "in a straight line from the hand to directly behind the point of impact of the ball," it provides the first direct reference to tubular steel shafts as well as those of solid steel:

The shafts may be made of steel, or other elastic metal, hollow or solid, or partly hollow and partly solid, or of steel or other elastic metal in combination with wood or other suitable material.

Grant saw the future of steel shafts. He believed:

The shaft so made will have greater uniformity of spring, be more lasting, and is more easily attached to, and detached from the heads.

In his patent, Grant also included the option of constructing his clubs with wood shafts (see page 190).

Reference to a metal shaft was printed in 1893. Professor Tait, of St. Andrews, had just developed a set of adjustable clubheads to fit interchangeably upon one shaft—a tubular steel shaft!

Professor Tait's idea is this: There is a thin, tough steel tube for the shaft, to which a steel rod like a pencil is attached, either as one piece, or as a hinge, in order to alter the lie at pleasure. The head of the club (steel, iron, wood, platinum, & c.), has a hole bored through it which fits on the pencil rod, and it is then fixed by tightening a hexagonal screw nut by means of a little key, which the player carries in his pocket. The section of the head may be of any form, and by setting it at the proper angle on the pencil rod and keying up, you can get driver, spoon, cleek, iron, niblick, putter, mashie, & c., at will, and each of these is right, or left-handed at pleasure. One spare head, at most, and the key, are all you have to carry. Some of the faces are flat, some cylindrical, some grooved, to give the underspin; some are narrow (vertically) so as to get at the underparts of the ball; some, for use as spoons or mashies, are as smooth as possible. Professor Tait has himself played a good deal with this universal club, and it has been tried by many players at St. Andrews (Golf, 11 Aug. 1893: 371-372).

A reference to using metal in a shaft is found in Thomas Vesey's British patent (No. 5,783) dated March 20, 1894 (see p.279). Besides filling a steel shell, "made in the same shape as the head of any ordinary wooden club," with gutta percha or vulcanite, Vesey allows for the possibility of using a steel core in his shaft:

The shaft is either of wood or of steel core surrounded by wood or equivalent tough strong material. It can however be of steel covered with india rubber or similar hard tough material, plastic when hot or on being formed, but such as will not soften with the heat of the hands.

The first patent to deal primarily with a metal shaft was Thomas Horsburgh's British patent (No. 8603) dated May 1, 1894. According to his patent:

This invention relates to the employment of a steel shaft for golf clubs for the purpose of giving them strength and elasticity.

As designed, Horsburgh's shaft screwed into the heads of either his woods or irons, his woods having a metal framework around the neck to aid in attaching the shafts. The author has seen Horsburgh's steel shaft clubs on display at Baberton Golf Club, near Edinburgh, Scotland. They appear to be thin, solid steel rods.

Another early reference to a metal shaft is found in Wilfred Lawson Bullows's British patent (No. 4,291) dated February 26, 1896. Bullows's patent covered constructing either a wood or an iron with a flat spring steel neck, but, in addition to recommending a wooden shaft for his club, Bullows also allows for using a tubular steel shaft:

I sometimes make the entire shaft of steel or other metal formed to a tubular or other suitable configuration.

In the early 1900s, steel core shafts were tried again accompanied by the application of steel ribbing around a shaft (see p. 515).

In America, Willie Dunn Jr. tried his hand at producing steel shafts:

In 1904, while in Connecticut, Dunn pioneered in another innovation. He put steel shafts into his clubs but found them too heavy (Golfing, Mar. 1953: 5).

Arthur F. Knight, who patented the Schenectady putter, received a U.S. patent (No. 976,267) dated November 22, 1910, that showed a hollow steel shaft designed to meet the patent's stated objective of producing:

a golf club in which the line of flight of the ball may more truly conform to the direction of the blow delivered by the player.

Knight's patent states:

I have finally been able to produce a club in which the necessary suppleness of shaft for a long drive and a true flight of the ball are both assured. I accomplish this by making the shaft of steel tubing preferably hardened and tempered to give as great suppleness as desired.

Complete with illustrations, Knight's patent presents three basic styles of tubular, high carbon steel shafts: tapered, step-tapered (his illustration shows three step-downs evenly spaced over the length of the shaft), or plain cylindrical tube:

With my hollow steel shaft the metal may be so distributed and the suppleness placed at such a point that a wide range of selection may easily be afforded. With the cylindrical tube the yield is put midway of the shaft length. With the stepped tube in which the tube diameter decreases at a number of determinate points, the point of greatest yielding or flexibility may be shifted by varying the position of the final step. In the straight tapered tube which is the form I personally prefer, the suppleness is near the head, as in the ordinary tapered hickory shaft, but the torsion in all is eliminated by reason of the great rigidity to torsional strain of the steel tubing and the accuracy of play is thereby greatly enhanced.

Between 1910 and 1925, no fewer than nineteen different British and American patents dealt with metal shafts. (A number of these patents are mentioned in the descriptions of the metal shaft clubs presented in this chapter.)

Between 1896 and 1925, six patents discussed shafts with metal cores, usually enclosed in bamboo or cane (see p. 515).

When steel shafts were introduced, there were no rules specifically against using them. Consequently, when steel shafts started to become viable, they caused quite a stir. By 1914, the R&A was concerned about steel shafts and their legality:

There are indications that others who are higher than the individual golfer may settle this question ["Are steel shafts legal for play?"] for him, to wit the Rules of Golf Committee. No official announcement was made upon the subject but there was a rumor very prevalent to the effect that the members of the Committee who were present at the [1914 British] amateur championship meeting had been sounded upon the subject, and that they had given an unofficial pronouncement to the effect that the steel-shafted clubs would not be permitted to gain any considerable vogue. It seemed that the Committee was doubtful as to whether, in spite of whatever merits they possessed, these shafts would really become popular, feeling that appearances and prejudices, which are fairly strong sometimes even in the newest golfers, would settle the matter. I think that since the Schenectady business the Committee has been less keen than it was before on interfering and barring. But it came to be understood at Sandwich [site of the 1914 British Amateur] that the free use of these steel shafted clubs would not be favoured by the authorities, and that, if necessary, some legislation on the subject was likely to be made, but that for the meantime the said authorities consider that such shafts are already illegal and improper in that they come under the general condemnation made in the term "any substantial departure from the traditional and accepted form and make of golf clubs" (The American Golfer, July 1914: 860-862).

The stance taken by the 1914 British Amateur championship committee—that steel shafts were illegal under existing rules—was the stance also adopted by both the R&A and the USGA. Nevertheless, the nonconforming verdict did not stop the growing acceptance of steel shafts:

The substitution of steel for wood has come to such a point that it would seem as though it was the goal towards which all were striving, and justly so, inasmuch as there has been resultant economy and satisfaction, and in many cases an added feature of safety. With the wholesale slaughter of our forests, we have had to resort to the multiple use of steel with the discovery that whereas we had no uniformity of wood or timber, we can now specify a certain kind of steel and get it (Golfer's Magazine, Nov. 1919: 40).

The September 1920 issue of Golf Monthly acknowledges the increasing dilemma of poor quality hickory shafts and the corresponding appeal of steel shafts despite their being unsanctioned for play:

The question of hickory for golf club shafts has long been a worrying problem with golf club manufacturers, but now the matter is becoming so acute that the question arises as to whether the ruling body might reconsider the matter of metallic shafts. One of the biggest firms tells me that in a case of shafts which usually contains five hundred, it is exceptional to find ten really good first class shafts. Of the remainder, not one per cent. [sic] would have been used in good class clubs a few years ago, and even in these days of hickory famine few of them are used.

The point appears to be the real scarcity of this wood . . . .

Steel shafts are forbidden, but I saw one a few days ago which I feel sure would deceive most golfers. The painting of the steel shaft to imitate wood was the work of an artist, and the weight and balance appeared to be perfect. Probably it will be necessary for the ruling body to consider the use of some other material than wood for golf club shafts before very long (54).

The "problem" of steel shafts refused to go away. Instead, by 1922, American retailers were increasing their promotion of steel shafts:

Steel shafts–debarred by the Royal and Ancient–are being pushed by many of the leading retailers in the United States. The shafts are balanced well, hang well, and they do not warp or crack like hickory (Golf Monthly, Dec. 1922: 76).

Manufacturers were running full-page magazine advertisements for steel shafts. In one such advertisement, the Horton Manufacturing Company, of Bristol, Connecticut, offered Bristol Steel Golf Shafts under the headline "The Most Interesting Development in Golf—since the rubber core ball" (Golfers Magazine, May 1922: 1). This advertisement notes that Horton was producing shafts under Arthur Knight's 1910 U.S. patent as well as additional supplementary patents. Also, Crawford, McGregor & Canby and Hillerich & Bradsby were identified as selling clubs fitted with Bristol shafts. One year later, in 1923, another Horton full-page advertisement lists Thos. E. Wilson & Company and the Burke Golf Company as retailers of Bristol Steel Shafted Clubs. Of course, the club manufacturers that offered metal shaft clubs continued to offer hickory shaft clubs.

Bravely stepping to the fore, the Western Golf Association, based in Chicago, Illinois, adopted a resolution dated May 17, 1922, that sanctioned the use of steel shafts in the Western Open, Amateur, and Junior golf tournaments. This was a very bold move, as the Western Open at that time was a major championship.

Through all this, the United States Golf Association was becoming more and more interested in the growing support for and use of metal shafts. A 1923 USGA "Implements and the Ball Committee" report describes their position at that time. After noting a few comparisons between steel shaft clubs and wood shaft clubs in driving a golf ball, the committee's decision to not approve the use of steel shaft clubs was followed by their stated desire to continue testing them, in order to give further consideration to their approval. Therefore, the Executive Committee "refused to permit the use of metal shaft clubs in the National Championships" (USGA 1923, 256-257).

The following year, the Implements and the Ball Committee reported that after further testing and receiving a great many letters concerning metal shafts:

The Committee is not unanimous in its opinion on this matter. . . . Further tests to be made and additional information to be collected (USGA 1924, 272).

At the January 10, 1925 meeting of the Executive Committee, the Implements and the Ball Committee:

recommended to the Executive Committee that the use of the steel shaft, as now manufactured, be permitted in tournaments held under the auspices of the Association, and in accordance with this recommendation the Executive Committee passed a resolution permitting such use (USGA 1925, 255).

The 1925 U.S. Open saw widespread use of metal shafts. Even Willie Macfarlane, the eventual champion, used steel shaft woods:

Steel is coming, and coming strong. [During the U.S. Open's preliminary elimination rounds], fifteen of the aspirants to the National crown sent their drives down Lido's first fairway with steel shafted woods. And twenty-five was the story the second day. In other words, forty star golfers have found in steel a suitable substitute for hickory. Now the question might arise as to what said golfers did in the qualifying rounds. Whether they passed on to Worcester [Worcester Country Club,

Worchester, Massachusetts, was the site of the Open proper]. The field there numbered ninety-two to be exact, yet a checking developed that eighteen in chase of the Walker property were swatting with steel shafts. And right here it should be mentioned that the new champion, Willie Macfarlane, used such a composition from the tees and on his brassie shots. So much for steel, which we find in the championship proper had a twenty percent call (*Golf Illustrated* [ny], July 1925: 66).

Finally, in 1929 the Royal and Ancient Rules Committee acquiesced and approved steel shafts for play. British golfers met this change with enthusiasm:

By the time steel shafts were legalised in this country [the U.K.], they had been standardised so carefully that it was almost impossible to buy a club so shafted that in feel and balance was not an obvious improvement on the stock club shafted with hickory. So steel-shafted clubs ran through our world of golf like a fire through dry stubble (*Golf Illustrated*, 1 July 1932: 3).

The change from hickory to steel shafts also brought about a change in how the game was played:

With the legalizing of steel shafts there began another flurry and flutter in the game. It was soon realized by players that the rigid steel shaft could not be made to work to the same extent as hickory with its torsion qualities. Half shots, intentional cut, slice or pull, low running shots, could not be produced however much one attempted to use the art of a Hilton or a Duncan. The soullessness of metal took the finesse out of the game—a new, more stereotyped method of hit had to be found.

The players clamoured for relief and help—the manufacturers put their heads into ice boxes for a while, and so the matched set of irons came along. The problems of play were solved by the degree of loft on the face of the club, and in case this was not at once apparent to the player a number was stamped on the sole as a guide. The player could now buy the shot. Imagination ran rife, or lack of imagination brought ruin, and the scramble of the buying of the shot forced the set up to twenty and even twenty-five clubs being carried by some players, in a quest for results which before were obtainable from five or six shafts of hickory (Harris 1953, 42-43).

Shaft Stamps: By the late 1880s, a few makers had begun stamping their name on the shafts of their clubs. This practice of marking shafts spread during the 1890s and continued throughout the wood shaft era.

When an post-1890 wood shaft club is found today, however, the original shaft is often unmarked. This could be for any number of reasons, but only three will be mentioned here. First, some makers simply did not bother to mark their shafts. Second, few makers marked all their shafts, year in and year out. Even the big companies such as Forgan, Spalding, Gibson, and MacGregor did not mark every shaft they put into a golf club. (Willie Park Jr., however, was as consistent about stamping his shafts as any maker.) Third, clubmakers routinely made clubheads which they sent to various professionals for shafting. The professional could mark the shaft if he so desired, which some did some of the time.

Consequently, the names marked on the head and the shaft are sometimes different. Shafts can include the maker's name, the seller's name, the owner's name, a patent number, a location (of the maker or the seller), or a combination of this information. Sometimes, shafts are even marked with their own model name. Unfortunately, there are no consistent rules for determining when to expect a name to be stamped on a shaft.

A shaft stamped the same as the head is a strong indication that the shaft is original. Nevertheless, it is important to remember that many prominent clubmakers and large manufacturers did significant amounts of repair work, and replacing a broken shaft was a standard operation. Consequently, it is the evidence of reshafting left at the hosel (such as a loose or poor fitting shaft, an uneven pin, fresh/unsightly file marks around the pin, or a loss of nicking) and not the lack of a shaft stamp that are the primary factors when determining whether a shaft has been replaced. In making such determinations, two additional possibilities need to be considered. First, shafts occasionally came loose from their heads—the pin on rare occasion falling entirely out of the hosel. When this happened, the shaft was sometimes taken out and reset—or the pin replaced. Such clubs only *appear* to be reshafted. Second, some clubheads were sold at the retail level as a "head only," lacking a shaft. Such clubheads sometimes appear to be reshafted because their original shafts were not installed by the initial clubmaker. (See page 27 for the effects of a reshaft on a club's collectibility.)

SHAFTS

ISAAC E. PALMER
FORKED SHAFT WOOD
AND IRON

My invention relates to an improvement in golf-clubs, and has for its object to provide a club which will be so braced as to reduce to a minimum the twisting of the head in striking the ball, which will retain its elasticity and springiness, which will present a very little wind resistance when the club is swung, and in which the line of vision will not be interfered with.

The above-named objects are carried out by providing a forked or bifurcated shaft at its lower portion, so that one arm will be connected with the head at or near its heel and the other arm a distance outwardly therefrom, the connection of the two arms with the head preferably being upon both sides of the point on the face of the head where it is intended to strike the ball (Isaac E. Palmer, U.S. Patent No. 687,539, 26 Nov. 1901).

The clubs pictured, one wood and one gunmetal iron, are probably the *only* examples of Palmer's clubs ever made. Consider: First, the wood head was drilled a few times before the shaft holes were correctly positioned (wood dowels fill the other holes). Second, on the iron, the ends of the shaft extending below the "clip sockets" were never trimmed. Third, both clubs were left ungripped, which is not surprising. Above the fork, each shaft is inordinately thick and awkward to hold on to, the result of making a forked shaft from a single piece of wood. Installing a leather wrap grip would have made the handle even thicker.

Palmer's U.S. patent (No. 687,539) dated Nov. 26, 1901, discusses and illustrates two ways to make his clubs. One way constructs the "branches or arms," as termed in the patent, from short, flat strips of spring steel; the spring steel strips attach to the shaft as well as the head. The other way, which is how the examples pictured were made, forms the branches or arms from the same piece of wood as the shaft. The ends of the forked shaft "socket" into the top of the wood head and "clip socket" into the back of the iron head using "a pair of clip-sockets on its back." On the clubs shown, the branches begin 14 1/2 inches above the wood head and 16 1/2 inches above the iron head.

"The Spalding," the only mark on either of the clubs pictured, is stamped across the top of the wood head between the arms of the shaft. After the craftsmen at Spalding made these clubs, they probably did not make any more—a "will not work" verdict being obvious.

The clubs described in Palmer's patent were completely impractical. Nevertheless, Otto Hackbarth produced a mildly popular putter that borrowed from Palmer's patent (see p. 180).

On May 11, 1900, when applying for the patent just discussed, Palmer also applied for a second U.S. patent. Similar in principle to his first, Palmer's second patent (No. 687,540) covered a flat metal brace which, as designed, could be attached to existing wood or metal clubs

then in use. The brace would extend from the base of the shaft, just above the hosel or neck, to the toe.

Two additional patents that relate to Palmer's first patent were granted. Colonel Alfred Frederick Pollock Harcourt, of Guildord, Surrey, England, received a British patent (No. 23,514) dated October 24, 1907, that covered a club advertised briefly in 1908 as "The Reliance Putter." This putter had two shafts affixed to the back of the blade, one behind the heel and one behind the toe. The shafts, which angle toward each other as they extend upward, were connected by two braces across the area of the grip.

The other patent similar to Palmer's was Frederick W. Taylor's U.S. patent (No. 792,631) dated June 20, 1901. Taylor's patent describes a croquet-style center-shafted blade putter with a shaft that branches apart towards its top, forming a "Y" shape. This design allowed the golfer to hold each branch of the shaft close to the fork in the shaft while resting the top ends of the shaft against each of his or her arms. The only example of Taylor's putter belongs to the United States Golf Association.

Designed similarly to Palmer's wood, a single 1930s wood with a forked nickel-plated shaft (the fork begins at the base of the grip) is known to the author.

The rectangular mallet head putter shown employs a flat shaft best described as a wooden slat. This shaft measures three-fourths of an inch wide and only one-fourth of an inch thick. In addition to its shaft, this club has a number of features. The distinctive rectangular head corresponds with the rectangular shape of the shaft. The full brass faceplate and three lengths of brass inlaid along the top of the head serve as alignment aids and add to the overall beauty of this club. The sole is perimeter weighted—a round lead weight is located in each corner. This putter, one of three known examples, was made by the Wilson-Western Sporting Goods Company sometime between the mid-1920s and the early 1930s. One of the additional examples is stamped "Gene Sarazen \ Joseph Crew" on its head. In 1923 Sarazen began his long affiliation with the Wilson Sporting Goods Company (formerly Thomas E. Wilson & Co.; see p. 429).

A captivating feature of this club is the shaft's exceptional flexibility when in use. The shape of the shaft combined with its position in the head creates this effect. If the narrow side faced the target, the shaft would not flex during the stroke.

To make this putter more usable, the back of the sole slopes up from the ground. This prevents the back of the head from catching on the ground during the golfer's take-away or follow-through.

The other club pictured, a brassie, employs a square shaft created in 1902 by John Moore while at Barton Court links, near Bournemouth, England:

J.W. Moore recently brought us a driver and brassie with square shafts, his own idea. . . . Moore claims that, with a club shafted and made in the square, a player gets a truer and straighter hit ball than with the usual club with the round shaft. The greater depth of wood from the corners gives (he says) a greater resistance from corner to corner, and causes a truer striking side, so that the ball is not so liable to go off at an angle as in the case of round shafted clubs (Golfing, 3 July 1902: 28).

J.W. Moore, the originator of the now famous square-shafted clubs, has informed us that the clubs are selling as well as ever [to] a very large list of purchasers (Golfing, 17 Dec. 1903: 46).

Today, even though they once were "selling as well as ever," square shaft drivers and brassies are extremely difficult to find. The square shaft driver shown, complete with a splice neck, is stamped "J.W. Moore \ Maker \ Barton on Sea \ Hants \ Milton " on the head. J.W. Moore was:

born at Blackheath in 1867. . . . He served a four years' apprenticeship under G. Brews, the Royal Blackheath professional . . . . On leaving Brews, he went as foreman club-maker to genial Peter Paxton, at Tooting Bec,

and remained in this berth for a further period of four years. . . . From Tooting Bec, Moore moved [in 1904] to Barnton Court, Hants, whence, after two years he went to Fleet, to construct the course of the North Hants Club. . . . His next appointment was with the Harwich and Dovercourt Club . . . He is now attached to the Redhill and Reigate Club.

We have already spoken of Moore's abilities as a greenkeeper. In addition, he is a fine clubmaker (Golfing, 15 Aug, 1907: 22).

Moore introduced a square shaft putter just prior to the end of 1904. Moore's putter has not been located by the author, but square shaft putters made years later are seen with some frequency.

SINCLAIR TOUSEY
RAISED RING SHAFT

BRILL
OFF-SET SHAFT

The hickory shaft pictured near right, with 22 one-quarter inch wide raised rings spaced one inch apart, was covered under three separate patents issued to New York City's Sinclair Tousey: two U.S. patents (No. 1,418,038 and 1,418,039) dated May 30, 1922, and a British patent (No. 201,983) applied for on May 1, 1922. Although the raised rings work to stiffen the shaft, that was not their stated purpose. According to all of Tousey's patents, his invention:

relates to means for eliminating the noise resulting from the rapid motion of a golf club through the air. This noise is objectionable when practising indoor golf. The noise or "swish" may be likened to that produced by a switch cutting the air at a high rate of speed. When practicing golf indoors this noise is objectionable to occupants of adjacent rooms, or others, and my invention is intended to furnish a silencer which will avoid this objection.

In designing his club to swing "silently," Tousey calculated that his shaft would eliminate the vacuum found on the following side of an ordinary shaft, thereby reducing the wind resistance of his shaft and increasing the distance his club could hit the ball:

The use of my invention also results in a more rapid movement of the club, for a given power applied thereto, as compared with clubs not having my improvement and hence other things being equal a longer drive will result from the use of my improved club in respect to that which will be given by an ordinary club.

Tousey's patent allows for the possibility of spiraling cord or wire around the shaft instead of forming integral ridges:

These ridges may be formed on the shaft or may be applied thereto in any suitable manner and of any suitable material. They may be of soft cotton cord, say one-eighth inch in diameter or may be of wire of 22 gauge and these may be laid in single or double strands.

As pictured, Tousey's shaft is part of a driver marked "A.G. Spalding & Bros." on its head. One other example of Tousey's shaft is known.

The hickory shaft putter pictured far right is marked "Brill \ Pat. Appld For" in the area of the shaft's offset, between eight and twelve inches above the clubhead. The head is marked "Brill" between two diamonds and "620" on the sole. Ordinarily, the rough shaping of the shaft where it enters the head would indicate an after-market reshaft. However, the stamped head, stamped shaft, and exceptionally upright lie of this unique club suggest that the components were made separately and assembled, albeit crudely, independently.

Golf is as welcome as an oasis in a desert, as tantalizing as a mirage, ever beckoning and alluring. It taunts and maddens; it has its favourites, as the gods have; it turns from the eager and showers its largess often in the paths of the most careless. The man who can play it regularly and not break a majority of the Ten Commandments is a Christian gentleman (Golfing, Dec. 2, 1909: 20).

ALBERT C. FOWLER
ANGLE SHAFT

In his U.S. patent (No. 959,053) applied for on August 16, 1909, and granted on May 24, 1910, Albert Covington Fowler states that his objective was to produce a shaft "which will drive the ball greater distance and at the same time straight":

In carrying out my invention I provide a club the shaft of which will be rigid during most of the forward stroke so as to prevent the shaft from bending backward and the head of the club from lagging behind the hands of the player before the ball is struck, thereby preventing slicing, but which will be springy or whippy at the moment of impact with the ball, so as to drive the ball a greater distance, whereby a straight long flight of the ball can be secured.

To accomplish his goals, Fowler designed a shaft that is oval across most of its exposed length. The oval portion is set to the golfer's right, when addressing the ball, at an angle "of about 25 degrees" from the center axis of the shaft. Furthermore, the face was to be slightly closed or "hooked."

Fowler's patent describes how his club was supposed to work:

As soon as the rearward stroke is begun, the wrists turn naturally so as to throw the head of the club backward .... In my invention it will be seen that the greatest width of the shaft is thus brought in the direction of the stroke except when the club head is near the ball, so that the greatest rigidity of the shaft is maintained during the forward stroke until just before the ball is struck. The shaft is, therefore, kept from bending backward and the club head is thus prevented from lagging behind the handle, or such bending of the shaft and lagging of the club

head is reduced to a minimum. The club head is, therefore, held up to its work. Just before the ball is struck, the wrists turn naturally forward into the position assumed when addressing the ball, and as the least width of the shaft is now only slightly inclined to the direction of the stroke, springiness or whip will then be imparted to the shaft, so that the ball will be driven a greater distance and at the same time slicing will be obviated. The slight inclination of the face in the reverse direction to a vertical plane passing through the shaft and the head of the club [i.e. a hooked face] overcomes the tendency of this club to drive a straight ball slightly to the right.

Fowler's angle shaft was made by R. Forgan & Son under Fowler's British patent (No. 10,194) dated April 6, 1910. As an added feature, Samson inserts (p. 330) were occasionally installed in Forgan's Angle Shaft woods. The driver pictured is marked "Angle Shaft \ Pat No. 10194 \ R. Forgan" on the top of the head along with the "King's crown" trademark. The shaft is stamped "Pat. No. 10194 \ R. Forgan & Son \ Selected \ St. Andrews." A personal examination of this club reveals a very distinct oval shaft, the axis of which is set at the prescribed angle. (Unfortunately, the oval nature of this shaft does not photograph well.)

There are several other non-round shafts. As mentioned on page 504, J.W. Moore's clubs were made with square shafts as were Mac & Mac's alignment aid putter, Albert Whiting's "His Own" putter, and a few others. Robert D. Randall's "True Sight" putter came with an oval shaft as did Winton's "Shiva"

putter, among others. James Braid's "The Orion" putter, made by William Gibson, usually had a shaft (and hosel) that was flat down the entire side facing the target. Various shaft shapes were used to help the golfer's alignment, to attain a particular degree of torque or flex, or to re-locate the flex either closer to or farther from the head.

George W. Mattern, assignor to the Crawford, McGregor & Canby Company, received the first patent that specifically discussed a particular shape for a golf shaft. His U.S. patent (No. 677,811) dated July 2, 1901, calls for making the shaft flat on the side opposite the target. This patent covered a "side splice," in which the splice joint for a wood is cut on the side of the neck. (The author has seen an original example of Mattern's side splice club, but the shaft did not have a flat side.)

William Laidlaw Purves received a British patent (No. 13,712) dated July 4, 1905, that covered an "elliptical" wood shaft with ridges down the front and back.

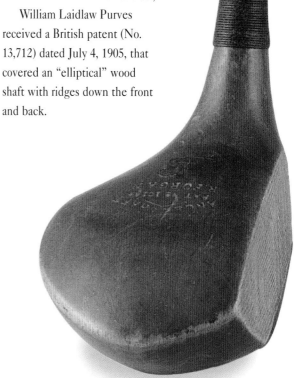

WILLIAM WARMAN & CHARLES JAMES
TEARDROP SHAFT

ARCHIE COMPSTON
"100% PUTTER,"
BENT SHAFT

The shaft pictured below has a sharp ridge running down its following side (the side opposite the target when addressing the ball). Created to act as a brace at impact, the ridge gives the shaft a streamlined "teardrop" shape in cross section. The wooden clubhead attached to the shaft is marked "A. James \ Special" on the crown. The shaft itself, marked "Rd 749294" below the grip, was covered under Charles Alexander Marshall James and William Howard Warman's British design registration (No. 749,294) dated October 10, 1929. According to their design registration, the shaft is teardrop in shape only between the head and the grip.

Teardrop wood shafts were tried and rejected, but teardrop metal shafts were once somewhat popular. John Heddon's U.S. design patent (No. 118,594) dated January 16, 1940, covered a metal teardrop shaft nearly identical in shape to the Warman and James shaft. Heddon's "Speed Swing" shaft, as it was called, was produced in large quantities exclusively by the steel golf shaft division of James Heddon's Sons, of Dowagiac, Michigan. Speed Swing shafts were made available by many large club manufacturers such as MacGregor, Wilson, Hillerich & Bradsby, Spalding, and others.

The curving back we deprecated in the case of driving-shafts we strenuously advocate in the putter (Farnie 1857, 36).

Farnie touches on a point that cannot be too strongly insisted on, with regard to the shaft of a putter, when he advocates an upward bend. We are so convinced of the truth of his view that we would go the length of saying that no putter (by this we, of course, mean what is now vulgarly called the wooden putter) can be properly shafted which has not got this upward bend. It is essential, moreover, that the bend be made in the proper place, i.e., just at the foot of the leather; a bend throughout the shaft will not answer the purpose so well. If an imaginary line be produced as a continuation of the line of the upper part of the shaft, i.e., the grip, it will now be found to run out into the middle of the club-head instead of at the heel, as in the case of the ordinary straight shaft. This will . . . aid the player to hit the ball on the centre of the club (Golf Illustrated, 28 June 1901: 265).

Throughout the hickory shaft era, many wood shaft putters were made with a shaft that curved back toward the golfer. In 1911, for example, wooden putter "replica[s] of the famous old Tom Morris shape with its long-graceful head and slightly bowed shaft" were still being made (*Golf Illustrated*, 24 Feb.: 154). Such a bowed shaft is often referred to as having a "St. Andrews bend." Frequently someone finds a putter and thinks the shaft is warped when it was actually bent on purpose. Time after time, putter shafts are found gracefully bowed directly back to the golfer—not left, right, or forward over the head.

The putter shown right, marked "Alex Patrick \ Estd 1847 \ Leven Fife \ A. Compston \ 100% Putter \ Patent No. 723,455" along with Alex Patrick's "horseshoe" trademark, was originally made with the dramatically bent shaft as pictured. The "723,455" marked on the head identifies a 1926 British design registration that covered the shape of this shaft.

Shafts with a St. Andrews bend were originally made from a straight piece of wood that was purposely curved through the use of heat and pressure. Compston's shaft was *cut* to shape from a larger piece of wood. The large, rectangular wooden grip is still covered with its original black paint. The shaft is round below the bend.

JAMES P. COCHRANE
"MARVO,"
THREE PIECE SHAFT

"Ray Marvo" Patent Three Piece Shafts. This Shaft will be the Golfing Sensation of the year. What "Ted" Ray, ex-Open Champion, says:

Dear Sirs: I have lately been using clubs fitted with your three piece "Marvo" Patent Shafts, and I must tell you, that in my opinion, they are one of the finest things in connection with golf that has been brought out.

Although being on munition work nightly limits my opportunities the more I play with them, the better I like them. They seem . . . to recover their straightness during the shot, much more rapidly than any ordinary shaft, and this gives a feeling of power to the club, giving the player the full benefit of every ounce of energy he puts into the shot. . . .

In fact, I think you have at last produced the ideal shaft, one that is light, stiff, and yet springy, and above all, will not warp after continual play (Golf Illustrated [ny], July 1917: 41).

The club pictured far left and advertised above is marked "J.P. Cochrane & Co. \ Made in Scotland" on the crown and "Ray \ The 'Marvo' Shaft \ (Regd) \ Patent 105302" on the shaft. The Marvo shaft shown, covered under James Pringle Cochrane's British patent (No. 105,302) dated August 12, 1916, is made from three lengthwise pieces of hickory laminated together. No cane is used, although Cochrane's patent allows for that possibility.

According to Cochrane's patent, because his shaft was "more or less flexible in a plane at practically right angles to the face of the head . . . whilst being extremely rigid in the opposite plane," it would hit the ball straighter and farther.

DAVID WILLIAMS & WILLIAM H. BOOTH
"WHIPPO" DRIVER

The latest invention which ought to be American, if it is not, is a new shaft containing what is described as a "sudden spring" "whereby elderly persons, ladies, and children are enabled to drive a much longer ball." Presumably youthful golfers of the male sex do not benefit by the "sudden spring," which is something to be thankful for, but what appalls me is the thought of the Ladies' Golf Union handicaps and the pars of the ladies' greens throughout the country. This will create a crisis in ladies' golf before which the rubber-ball difficulty will pale into insignificance, for the courses played on by ladies cannot be lengthened to any appreciable extent, and it is even possible that they may demand to play on the men's. So may "elderly persons and children." One can only hope that the L.G.U. will take a firmer stand in this matter than did the Royal and Ancient Club in the case of the rubber ball (Golf Illustrated, 25 November 1904: 162).

The club discussed in this tongue-in-cheek review was not made in America, it was made in Great Britain! Designed by David Williams, a coal exporter, and William Henry Booth, the golf professional at Swansea Bay Golf Club, Briton Ferry, Wales, this club is described in a British patent (No. 22,968) dated October 23, 1903, which covered a unique flexible shaft:

According to our invention we provide "sudden" spring at any convenient position in the shaft from the handle down to the head whereby the head follows through more correctly and enables elderly people, ladies, and children to drive a much longer ball.

To carry out our invention we either form the shaft of two pieces and join said pieces by a flat spring surrounded by a material such as

CARL F. MENSING
"LIMBERSHAFT," RATTAN & HICKORY COMPOUND SHAFT

rubber, or cut away at any desired position a sufficient portion of wood off the front and back sides of the shaft and fill the spaces formed with steel, gutta percha, whalebone, cane or any other kind of springy material....

The Williams and Booth driver pictured to the near left on the facing page provides the "sudden spring" by inlaying two pieces of wood, 3/8 inch wide by 6 3/4 inches long, into the leading and following sides of the shaft close to the neck. The head reads "The 'Whippo' Driver \ Sole Agents Ben Evans & Co Ld. \ Swansea \ Patent No. 22,968." (See also Williams & Booth on page 540.)

A picture, it has been said, is worth a thousand words, but neither a picture nor a thousand words will adequately describe a Limbershaft. Only when waggled does a Limbershaft reveal its exceptional flexibility. With this understood and no Limbershaft to hold on to, the reader is given both a picture and a thousand words!

The first Limbershaft patent, a U.S. patent (No. 1,662,712) dated March 13, 1928, was issued to Carl Frederick Mensing of Tarpon Springs, Florida. Mensing also received a British patent (No. 327,720) dated December 7, 1928, for the same invention. According to his patent, Mensing's shaft was:

constructed to bend easily, the degree of flexibility being such that the player using the club has a sensation rather more like that of wielding a club head tied to a piece of string than of wielding a weighted stick.

To further describe the remarkable flexibility of the shaft, Mensing states:

[If the] handle of the club is fixed whilst the shaft is bent by a loaded pull string tied to the club head.... the shaft will [bend] in an arc so as to bring the portion near the club head to a position nearly at right angles to the handle end of the shaft when the force on the pull string is not more than about 3 lbs. and not less than about 8 ozs.

Mensing considered a number of ways to make his shaft limber:

A number [of clubs] made and successfully used, have had shafts of rawhide—like an old buggy whip,—of rattan wood, and of rattan wood with a spring steel core, and it is realized that shafts may also be made of rubber, of flat or round spring steel, of coiled spring wire, and of other materials ... possessing the requisite strength and resiliency or limberness provided the limberness is not localized or limited in extend but ... is uniform or distributed from the head to the grip or even to the butt end of the shaft.

Mensing's first patent also describes constructing an indoor practice club having a "preferably rubber head" and a solid rubber shaft or a shaft reinforced with spring steel wires (no examples known). However, Mensing suggested including metal when constructing shafts for regular clubs:

For regular playing clubs, it is believed that it will be found preferably to always provide a resilient metal reinforcement of some type, as shafts made purely of rattan or rawhide, while possessing excellent driving power, are susceptible to breakage if subjected suddenly during the swing.

On June 1, 1931, Mensing applied for a second U.S. patent (No. 1,949,970) to cover his limber shaft. According to this patent, the shaft was to have a hickory core preferably surrounded by pieces of:

what is known as South American Rattan as such wood is light and possesses limberness, strength, and durability, and cooperates most efficiently with a hickory wood core in absorbing shocks of impact and in holding the face of the club in fixed relation to the core.

The shafts produced under Mensing's second U.S. patent were made from nine separate lengths of wood: eight pieces of rattan surrounding a square hickory core. The ends of these nine pieces are visible across the butt of the shaft. Such a shaft is referred to as a *compound* shaft because it is made from more than one piece of the same or similar material, such as two (or more) kinds of wood. *Composite* shafts, on the other hand, are made from two or more lengths of completely different materials, such as wood and metal.

The two clubs pictured on the previous page were produced under Mensing's U.S. patents. The driver is marked "Swingrite" on the crown and "Swingrite \ Jim Thompson Inc. Tarpon Springs, Fla. \ Brassie" on the sole. The shaft decal reads "Limber Golf Shaft \ Patent No. 1662712 \ Jim Thompson, Inc. \ Tarpon Springs, Florida \ USA." This "buggy-whip" shaft, as it is commonly referred to, is characterized by the varnish coated, braided thread which completely encases the shaft between the grip and the head. Not all Limbershaft woods, however, have this braiding.

The iron has a nine-piece Limbershaft. The back of the iron head is marked "Limbershaft \ Tarpon Springs, Florida \ Walter Hagen \ Custom Built Head \ Compact Blade \ Stainless Steel." "5 Mashie" is stamped on the sole and "U.S.A. Pat. 1652712 \ Limbershaft \ Tarpon Springs, Florida" is stamped into the shaft. The term "Limbershaft" has been in use as a registered trademark since March 23, 1931 (Kennedy 1984, 41).

On the iron shaft, the whipping near the hosel is standard. Because a thin hickory ferrule was used as a buffer between the hosel and the shaft to protect the rattan from cracking at the top of the hosel, whipping was applied to keep the top of the ferrule from splitting.

Limbershafts were also produced as steel shafts. Mid-1930s irons with brown sheathed steel shafts marked "Limbershaft," etc., are well known. By 1934, such companies as Spalding were offering "Pederson Pyratone Limbershafts" as well as chrome-plated Limbershafts in their woods and irons.

In 1934 "Genuine Limbershaft Drivers" were well promoted. For a brief period, Limbershaft clubs were offered with a generous free trial. The following is one such 1934 Limbershaft advertisement:

Never before has any club manufacturer dared make the wide-open, Free Trial offer that Limbershaft now makes you! This sensational new driver must make good—it must add 20 yards or more to your average drives—or you don't pay for the club after we've let you try it for 3 weeks free!

In the past 10 months Limbershaft has swept America. Over 70,000 of the clubs have been sold up to the time this issue of American Golfer goes to press. Now you can try Limbershaft without cost or obligation (The American Golfer, May 1934, 3).

While 70,000 Limbershafts is a large number of shafts, it is not known how many of them were made from wood. By 1934 the market interest in metal shafts had long since overtaken that in wood shafts.

According to this same advertisement, and more in keeping with metal shafts, Limbershafts were sold in three flexes:

Three degrees of limberness are offered: "A" for the 70 to 80 player, "B" for the 80 to 90, "C" for over 90 and for the woman golfer.

In his article titled "The Limbershaft–An Elixir of Youth," Bernard Darwin notes that, for all its hoopla, a Limbershaft driver served primarily to make his regular driver "jealous" and therefore play better! He suspected that most golfers who tried the club would also find it a "tonic or stimulant to their old clubs [rather] than a substitute for them" (*The American Golfer*, May 1935: 28).

The place [is] St. Andrews, Fifeshire, N.B. . . . It is here that the Scottish gentleman, in his hours of leisure, may play at the game that he loves from morn till eve, and bet his habitual half-crowns, and smoke unlimited pipes, and talk never-ending shop.

Not equally dear is it in the ears of the Scottish gentleman's spouse and daughters; and that for manifold good reasons. All that you can get them to say about it is, that the air is very bracing, &c. &c. The reason is this, the presence of a female is repugnant to the game of golf. No sooner does an unlucky woman stray on to the course than,—like the Derby dog,—she is hooted at and bellowed to, and told to go one way by one person and another by another; all which induces a most piteous state of vacillation, in the midst of which the ball whizzes past her at a pace which would inevitably prove fatal were it to hit her. It is needless to say that the unprotected female does not often repeat the mistake of straying on the pleasure-grounds of the golfer (Once a Week, 12 Dec. 1863: 694).

BAMFAR

HARDY BROTHERS
"PALAKONA"
BAMBOO COMPOUND SHAFT

CROSS ROD & TACKLE CO.
"BAMFAR"
BAMBOO COMPOUND SHAFT

ALLAN LARD
HICKORY & BAMBOO
COMPOUND SHAFT

"Palakona" built bamboo shafts will improve your game. Read these testimonials (a few out of many received) from some of our leading professionals.

Abe Mitchell writes:— "I have given the Palakona Shaft a thorough test and I find it most satisfactory. It gives one a delightful thrill as the ball leaves the club-head, for the shaft responds perfectly to the blow. I am positive that this shaft will be a great boon to all golfers."

. . . Obtainable from all professionals and stores. Sole manufacturers Hardy Bros. Ltd., Alnwick (Golf Monthly, Dec. 1934: 41).

In 1933 Hardy Brothers Ltd., the famous fishing rod makers located in Alnwick, England, established a golf factory (operated for only a few years) where they produced clubs made with their Palakona shaft. The Palakona shaft driver pictured above, second from the top, is marked " 'Palakona' (Reg)" on the top of the head and "Whpy \ 'Palakona' Regd. Trade Mark \ by Hardy Bros Ltd, \ Alnwick, England," in handwritten ink on the shaft. "Whpy" is the abbreviation for "whippy." Palakona shafts came in various flexes, medium ("Med") being the most popular. Palakona shafts are constructed from twelve lengthwise pieces of bamboo: six

inner segments and six outer. The Palakona shaft in this driver has six sides, which is not uncommon for a cane shaft, and sports a cork grip.

Marked "Bamfar \ Pat Apld For," the Bamfar shaft pictured above the Palakona shaft is rarely seen. Produced by the Cross Rod & Tackle Company, of Lynn, Massachusetts, the Bamfar shaft is hexagonal in cross section, like the Palakona. The patent referred to was probably either William Forsyth's U.S. patent (No. 1,486,572) applied for on March 21, 1921, or his U.S. patent (1,486,573) applied for on June 8, 1923. Both patents deal with six-sided bamboo shafts and were granted on March 11, 1924. Forsyth, of Swampscott, Massachusetts, assigned both patents to the Cross Rod and Tackle Company. "Bamfar" was first used as a trademark on April 1, 1921 (Kennedy 1984, 19).

Thomas Ward Goddard received the first patent to suggest using cane in a golf shaft. His British patent (No. 24, 693) dated December 24, 1895, provides for splicing cane to the sides of the shaft, but only at the grip end.

In 1898 Ben Sayers devised a shaft made from full-length pieces of cane:

An interesting patent of Sayers is a Malacca-cane-handed shaft, which can be used with any club, and for which he claims increased driving power" (Golfers Magazine, Apr. 1898: 49).

Sayers applied for a patent, but it was never issued.

The first patent to discuss constructing a golf shaft from lengthwise pieces of bamboo was a U.S. patent (No. 649,146) granted to Roberto Tice, of Albany, New York, on May 8, 1900. Although his patent refers to "constructing a golf shaft from strips of wood not unlike the

strips used in a bamboo fishing-rod" (six lengthwise pieces laminated together), Tice preferred using white ash, not bamboo. The Tice Golf Driver Company's advertisements for "The Tice Golf Driver" offered either sectional bamboo or ash shafts. A bamboo shaft driver or brassie cost five dollars; a laminated ash shaft driver or brassie was three dollars. Hexagonal in shape, Tice's shaft was advertised as:

Giving great strength, flexibility, and increased distance. . . . Especially adapted to the use of lady golfers; being light, it still retains its strength and pliability (Golf [ny], March 1901: 161).

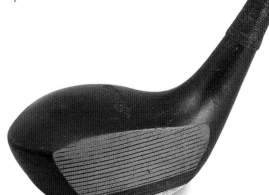

Between 1900, when Tice patented his shaft, and 1930, the U.S. and U.K. granted no fewer than thirty-two patents that dealt with constructing golf shafts from lengths of cane. Some of these patents discuss using various other materials in addition to cane. Variations in shaft shape, the number of pieces, and the manner in which the pieces were glued together were all explored.

Pictured on the bottom of the previous page is a cane shaft driver marked "A.G. Spalding & Bros" on the crown, "L 59 8W \ Pat'd Apr 24, 1923" on the sole, and "Pat'd Aug 15, 1922" on the shaft. The patent date on the shaft identifies a U.S. patent (No. 1,426,202) granted to Allan Lard and assigned to the Metallic Shaft Company, of Wilmington, Delaware. (For more on Allan Lard, see page 520.)

According to Lard's patent, the shaft pictured is made with a hickory core having "inverted V-shaped ribs," the ends of which are visible along the outer length of the shaft. The space between each rib forms a groove. Triangular lengths of bamboo are inlaid into the grooves.

The main objective of Lard's patent was to build a shaft with "greater torsional resistance than is possible with the ordinary hexagonal core of the split bamboo fishing rod construction," but the patent includes additional ideas:

A [further objective] is to provide first class shafts from cores of wood other than hickory and also to render available short lengths of hickory which would, in longer lengths be useless for golf shafts because of defects or warpage. Even soft hickory of the most inferior grades can thus be converted into first class shafts.

To accomplish these objectives, Lard's patent includes the option of making shafts by combining two shorter components: the grip and the body of the shaft. The grip portion of the shaft would be made from ash, or other suitable material, formed to receive the tapering end of the body of the shaft—the body of the shaft being constructed from seven pieces as previously specified. (On the club shown, the seven pieces of wood are visible across the butt of the shaft. Therefore, this shaft is not made from two shorter pieces.)

Lard's patent justifies moving away from solid hickory shafts by quoting a June 1, 1920 report from the U.S. Department of Agriculture which stated:

The demand for hickory handles is so great that manufacturers can no longer meet requirements' and that— "The end of hickory is in sight."

A clubmaker who is all theory labours under the disadvantage of not being able to reproduce his ideas in wood and metal; one who is all practice has no ideas to reproduce. The ideal clubmaker is he who combines theory with practice, who has clever ideas and the skill to reproduce them. It is this combination of theoretical knowledge and practical ability which has served to make C.S. Butchart's clubs so popular among golfers (Golf Illustrated, 9 Oct. 1908: 54).

Cuthbert Strachan Butchart received both a U.S. patent (No. 1,598,049) dated August 31, 1926, and a British patent (No. 264,348) dated June 7, 1926, that covered the shafts pictured on the facing page. These shafts are made with a hickory core enclosed by lengthwise strips of "hard wood such as green heart, bamboo, black palm, and the like." The hardwood strips appear to be greenheart (the dark strips) and bamboo (the light strips). According to Butchart's patent, his shaft could:

be made more slender than the ordinary shaft of a golf stick and that consequently it will be subjected to less wind resistance than a shaft of larger cross sectional dimensions.

The brassie pictured on the facing page is marked "The Butchart \ BTN \ Nicholls Co. Inc. \ Reg. U.S. Pat. Off." on the crown and "Genuine Butchart Model \ Pat 3-6-26" on the soleplate. The shaft is marked "The Butchart \ BTN \ Nicholls Co Inc." It was March 8, 1926,

when Butchart applied for the U.S. patent that covered this club. The date on the soleplate is off by two days. The iron is marked "Butchart–Nicholls Co. \ BTN \ Warranted Forged \ Special \ 11 \ Niblick \ L" on the back of the blade.

The iron has a hickory shaft adaptor which, while visible above the hosel, extends down inside the hosel. This adaptor serves two purposes. First, it encloses the base of the shaft and helps keep the shaft together. Second, the adaptor protects the base of the shaft, the cane in particular, against cracking. Bamboo was known to crack from torquing on not only the pin inside the hosel but also the top edge of the hosel.

Cuthbert S. Butchart was born in Carnoustie, Scotland, on May 19, 1876. While his father, Jack Butchart, worked as an assistant to Carnoustie's Frank Bell, Cuthbert spent many years assisting other clubmakers. After working four years for Robert Simpson of Carnoustie, two years for Robert Munro of Richmond, and two and a half years for Ben Sayers, Butchart became the professional at the Pollock Golf Club (Glasgow) in 1897. On March 26, 1899, Butchart entered the service of County Down Club, Newcastle, Ireland (*Golfing*, 27 June 1901: 14).

Once in Ireland, Butchart continued making clubs and became involved in designing courses. He then returned to London:

[In Ireland] he planned or reconstructed numbers of courses, among them the Newcastle, County Down; Bunderan, County Donegal; Antrim, Belveir Park, Belfast; Banger, Bally Kinlar and Fort William, and at the same time was clubmaker for all of them.

*In 1904 he was the professional to the Highgate Club of London and reconstructed many other courses throughout England and his fame and his clubs reached the ends of the earth (*Golfers Magazine*, Feb. 1921: 34).*

While in London, Butchart also managed his wholesale golf business, the London Golf Supply, which became Butchart's Golf Company, Ltd. After closing his business in 1907, Butchart worked as a professional at the Westhill Golf Club in Brookwood, Surrey, and Stanwell Place in Staines, Middlesex, before becoming the professional at the Berlin [Germany] Golf Club in 1911. When World War I broke out, Butchart was interned in a prison camp for the duration of the war. He was released on November 22, 1918.

After coming to America in 1921, Butchart worked at the Westchester-Biltmore Country Club, in Westchester County, New York. He reentered the clubmaking business and eventually produced a large number of bamboo shafts not only on his own but also through the Butchart-Nicholls Company, Inc. and the United Golf Products Company.

By September 1, 1926, Butchart and Gilbert Nicholls had become partners, as indicated by the registration of the Butchart-Nicholls Company "BTN" trademark on that day (Kennedy 1984, 14). Just prior to this, Gilbert Nicholls was in business for himself. An ad in the July 1926 issue of *Golfers Magazine* offered the "Gil Nicholls Combination Bamboo-Hickory Shafts for Woods and Irons" as made by the "Gil Nicholls Factory" in New York. These shafts were made from six lengthwise segments alternating between hickory and bamboo.

In December of 1926, a full-page advertisement for the BTN laminated bamboo and hickory shaft declares that, besides "possessing all the advantages of first-grade hickory shafts, they retain longer 'life' and are uniform, durable, and more dependable" (*The American Golfer*: 19). Two months later, *The American Golfer* announced the January fifteenth merger of the Butchart-Nicholls Company and the Allied-Hookless Golf Bag Company," to be known as United Golf Products, Inc." (Feb. 1927: 3). Following this merger, however, Butchart-Nicholls bamboo-hickory shafts were still advertised as being made by the Butchart-Nicholls Company (*The American Golfer*, Aug. 1928: 39).

Butchart-Nicholls bamboo-hickory shafts were produced in quantity and widely accepted. According to an advertisement in the August 1928 issue of *The American Golfer*, Johnny Farrell won the 1928 U.S. Open using Butchart-Nicholls clubs, and a number of other golfers using Butchart-Nicholls clubs placed high in tournaments that same year—Tommy Armour won the Metropolitan Open, Al Espinosa won the Mid-America Open, Billy Burke won the North & South Open, Gene Sarazen won the Miami Open, Leo Diegel tied for the Long Beach Open, and Willie Macfarlane won the Shawnee Open. At that time, Butchart-Nicholls shafts were made from "five segments of bamboo and one segment of hickory" (*The American Golfer*, Aug. 1928: 39). This shaft was patented in the U.S. (No. 1,626,477) on April 26, 1927, by Gilbert Nicholls and assigned to the Swingrite Company, Inc., of Providence, Rhode Island.

Although made for only a short time, the shafts pictured above are found occasionally and are among the most attractive shafts ever produced.

TOM MORRIS
STEEL CORE & CANE
COMPOSITE SHAFT

Dating to the early 1880s, the Tom Morris play club pictured, marked "T. Morris" on the crown, measures 5 1/2 inches in head length, 1 7/8 inches in head width, and 1 1/8 inches in face depth. This club, however, is not just another pretty long nose. It is one of the earliest clubs ever made with a cane shaft as well as one of the first clubs ever to use metal in its shaft! Both steel core shafts and cane shafts were referred to in 1890:

Thus, there have been novelties in driving shafts—new woods, bamboos, and malacca canes have been tried. Most have been found wanting, and the golfer has returned to his hickories. But now we have before us quite a new departure—a steel bar let down the whole centre length of shaft. It is the invention, we believe, of Mr. Adams, of Musselburgh, and though it makes the club feel heavy in the shaft, it certainly hits the ball a very shrewd blow. It is especially claimed for it that it is an assistance to those who do not hit very hard, but let the club do most of the work, and the verdict of these more deliberate drivers, to whom we have submitted it for trial, is that it helps them to put yards on their drives (Golf, 14 Nov. 1890: 136).

The "steel bar let down the center length of the shaft" and the reference to "Mr. Adams" identify the metal core shaft produced briefly by Alexander Adams (see the discussion of metal shafts on p. 497.)

In 1891, after mentioning the modifications made within the past few years "upon the old fashioned club," *Golf* printed a passing reference to "shafts with wire cores (on the same principle

as fishing rods)" (16 Jan. 1891: 275). This reference was probably made with the Adams shaft in mind, and the phrase "on the same principle as fishing rods" may allude to forming the body of the shaft from strips of bamboo. Even though bamboo shafts (also called "cane shafts") did not attain much popularity until the 1920s, they were tried decades earlier. In 1887 Sir Walter Simpson noted that, in addition to ordinary clubs, there were "clubs with bamboo shafts" (23). In 1900, upon the death of Robert "The Chieftain" Wilson at age 82, it was reported that Wilson, a well-known Hoylake figure, "employed bamboo in the place of the traditional hickory shaft" much earlier in his golfing life (*Golf Illustrated*, 2 Mar. 1900: 201). Gilbert Mitchell Innes, another early golfing personality, also tried cane shafts many years before his death in 1900:

[Innes] made experiments with curious kinds of wood for the shafts of his driving cleeks. Malacca canes came in for a time. But . . . he went back with pleasure to the pure split hickory (Golf Illustrated, 9 Nov. 1900: 119).

Cane shafts were usually made from lengthwise strips of cane glued together then finished to size. The number of pieces in a cane shaft varies among makers and models; however, the number of pieces used and the way they were combined are usually visible across the butt of the shaft. On the shaft of this Morris club, the butt (as shown above) reveals twelve pieces of cane—six inner and six outer—around a tubular steel

core. It is doubtful that Morris made this shaft; it was probably made by one of the two British fishing rod makers who were making steel core cane rods by 1880:

At the Great Fisheries Exhibition in London in 1883 Hardy Brothers were awarded the only Gold Medal and special 10 pound sterling prize for the "best collection" of Trout Rods, which comprised Split-bamboo with, and without, steel centres. . . . Hardys must have started to use steel centres circa 1880. . . . Fosters of Ashbourne, England, established 1833, claim to be the inventors and original makers of steel centred and steel ribbed rods. Fosters probably used steel centre(s) a year or two prior to Hardys (Hardy, 18 Sep. 1994).

According to the 1888 Hardy Brothers catalog:

These Hardened Spring-Steel Centre rods are the most powerful produced, and are practically indestructible, making splendid Salmon and Mahseer Rods. When we say that the steel is first made to a perfect taper, (by dipping in acid and withdrawing at calculated speeds to give a taper), then, tempered, so that it can be coiled up, and when released will fly perfectly straight, some idea may be formed of the immense power obtained. The heavier sizes are double built. Before the steel is built into the rod it is coated with a perfectly incorrosive substance.

. . . The steel in our rods is specially made for the work, and we have been at great expense in perfecting it. It is built in, and goes from one end of the rod to the other (Hardy, 27 Aug. 1994).

After the introduction of the steel core cane shafts, various individuals obtained patents that

included the idea of producing steel core shafts. William Bussey and Joseph Pinder, in their British patent (No. 3,864) dated May 10, 1892, considered the possibility of running a wire through the center of the shaft. Thomas Vesey's British patent (No. 5,783) dated March 20, 1894, mentions the possibility of using a shaft made with a metal core covered by wood or some other substance such as india rubber. Roberto Tice's U.S. patent (No. 649,146) dated May 8, 1900, includes the possibility of passing a metallic rod through the core of a bamboo shaft. Albert Smith's British patent (No. 4,247) dated February 28, 1901, strengthens a shaft by extending a core of spring steel "up through the neck of the shaft." John Dickie's British patent (No. 25,867) dated November 15, 1906, covered a shaft made from sections of split cane formed around a spring steel metal rod.

Francis Mitchell and the New Eccles Rubber Works received a British patent (No. 22,580) dated October 14, 1907, that covered their design for a Para rubber shaft which could include a core of cane or metal. Charles Ransom, in his British patent (No. 20,726) dated October 1, 1908, devised a wood shaft having a packed metal tube or grooved rod that extends up into the shaft from its bottom. The next patent for a metal core shaft in this chronological account was granted to Edwin Cosby and is discussed on the next page.

Steel core shafts were tried during the long nose era and by Alexander Adams in 1890. They were tried once again around the turn of the century:

The crop of spring inventions in clubs is fairly up to the average. One driver, made by a fishing-pole firm, has a steel core in its shaft (Golf [ny], May 1900: 328).

Ralph Hoagland, who is in charge of the golf department of The Fair, has secured some novelties this year, among them being a steel-cored shaft in drivers (Golfers Magazine, April 1904: 251).

The steel core cane shaft driver pictured right, marked "Hardy Brothers \ Alnwick" on the top of its head, has additional construction features. A spiraling wrap of varnished paper only nine-sixteenths of an inch wide completely encloses the shaft. Over this wrap, two thin strands of steel wire wind in opposite directions down the length of the shaft. The neck joint is whipped with thin copper wire. The grip is made from cork.

In 1901 Peter Paxton offered a driver with a shaft very similar, if not identical, to the one pictured:

The peculiarity of [Peter Paxton's new driver] is in the shaft, which is made of cane and bound with thin steel bands. Two important points are claimed for the club—extreme whippiness and a shaft that will always keep straight (Golfing, 7 Nov. 1901: 22).

The steel ribbing on the shaft pictured has darkened with age. To avoid such oxidation, Foster Brothers used rustless wire when producing similar steel-ribbed shafts:

Messrs. Foster Bros., Ashbourne, Derbyshire, have been applying to golf clubs their method of strengthening fishing-rods. The steel is applied in a network of four wires . . . . The wire is rustless, and presents a very pretty appearance. As a stiffener of a shaft that is too wobbly, or a strengthener of one that is too thin, this invention has great merit . . . . Old shafts also frequently lose their life, and the process of steel ribbing has the effect of restoring the spring and prolonging the existence of an old favourite (Golf Illustrated, 14 Mar. 1902: 212).

A shaft with Foster's steel ribbing was displayed without a clubhead at the P.G.A. World Golf Hall of Fame in Pinehurst, North Carolina, before it closed.

In response to the author's inquiry about the Hardy Brother's driver, James L. Hardy, of the Hardy Brothers family, provided an order for a single "golf club with split cane steel centre shaft & iron head" that Hardy's once received (Hardy, 27 Aug. 1994). According to this order, filled on February 8, 1907, Hardy's used doublebuilt cane, a steel core, seven feet of silk ribbon, varnish, an iron head, copper wire, six yards of Punjab wire, and cork. The workman took three hours and fifteen minutes to assemble the shaft. The completed shaft cost fourteen shillings, three pence—very expensive for a golf club in 1907.

EDWIN H. COSBY
"THE COSBY,"
STEEL, HICKORY, & BAMBOO
COMPOUND SHAFTS

The "Cosby" Split Bamboo Steel-Centre Club with the Corrugated Grip. You just have to try out this wonderful club once and you are friends for life. Carries a real wallop! . . . All hand-made and fitted with imported Scotch heads. Distance and control of direction. . . . The Lay Whip Co., Ltd. Rock Island -- Quebec (Fraser's 1925, 181).

Edwin H. Cosby's U.S. patent (No. 1,510,584) dated October 7, 1924, covered a golf shaft constructed from steel, hickory, and cane. According to his patent:

The golf club staff forming the subject matter . . . includes a core which, preferably, is made of steel, or of some other metal, the core being surrounded by a textile covering which may be in the form of a tube of braided material. About the covering is disposed a casing preferably made of hard wood [hickory], the casing being divided into two or more sections. A body made of bamboo, rattan or other like material, is disposed about the casing and is divided radially into a plurality of sections, there being preferably, more sections in the body than there are in the casing.

Along with their unique shafts, Cosby clubs (pictured left) have leather grips that are sewn closed, similar to Bussey's sewn grip, complete with a seam running down the back side. In addition, Cosby's grip has distinct "ribs":

Adjacent to the handle end of the staff, the body is supplied with longitudinal ribs. About the ribbed portion of the body is disposed a tubular grip made of leather, rubber, or other suitable material, the grip being pressed inwardly between the ribs of the body to form external ribs in the grip.

The back of the putter pictured is marked "William Gibson \ Kinghorn \ Scotland \ Cosby \ Made In Scotland \ Warranted Hand Forged \ Goose Neck Putter." The brassie shown is simply marked "Cosby."

The stylish braided string around the bottom ten or eleven inches of a Cosby shaft is standard. Braiding is also found at the top and bottom of the grip. An advertisement by the U.S. Golf Manufacturing Company, of Westfield, Massachusetts, states, "No winding to be rewound—braiding used instead on handle and neck. Looks, Lasts, Is, Better" (*The American Golfer*, Apr. 1928: 59). The U.S. Golf Manufacturing Company marketed Cosby clubs.

ROBERT MORGAN
"THE 'MORGAN' SHAFT," STEEL CORE & CANE COMPOSITE SHAFT

DAVID SPITTAL
HICKORY & STEEL COMPOSITE SHAFT

According to his British patent (No. 337,638) dated Nov. 28, 1929, Robert Morgan of West Hartford, Connecticut, believed that shafts made from steel tubing "lack the desired degree of tortional [sic] yield"; hickory shafts had the correct torsional yield but were "liable to warp, deteriorate, and fracture"; and shafts made from laminated strips of wood or bamboo had "too much tortional yield, which yield increases with use." To combine the best features of all three, Morgan patented a shaft made with a core of solid metal grooved to accept six strips of wood or bamboo.

Morgan's shaft is used in the club shown below, the grooved steel core visible in the tip of the shaft. The shaft is stamped "The 'Morgan' Shaft \ Patent Pending \ Baylis Mfg. Co. \ Hartford, Conn." The crown is stamped "Baylis," and the sole is marked "Made in New England."

David Spittal, of Chambly Basin, Quebec, Canada, received three patents—a U.S. patent (No. 1,680,817) dated August 14, 1928; another (No. 1,683,810) dated September 11, 1928; and a British patent (No. 296,225) dated November 8, 1927—that covered a shaft that was half wood and half steel. The upper half of the shaft is made from solid wood; the lower half of the shaft is made from tubular steel with a wood core, the wood from the upper half of the shaft extending down through the length of the steel portion.

Spittal believed that constructing a shaft in this fashion would combine the best qualities of both types of shafts while reducing torque. As stated in each of his three patents:

The invention has for its object to provide a club which will combine the good qualities of both the steel and

hickory shafts with attendant elimination of torsion, while maintaining the spring of the wood shaft. A further object of my invention is to re-establish the ancient club-making industry and I do this by producing a golf club having an all-wood hickory shaft sheathed with a steel shaft from the sole of the club-head for substantially half the length of the club. Both steel and wood shaft portions are rigidly anchored at the sole of the head and are united at the upper end of the steel. In this manner the steel portion of the shaft, which has heretofore been hollow, is completely filled by the hickory shaft portion, thus eliminating the vibration so common to steel shaft clubs, and therefore eliminating cracks and breakage in the head due to the vibration.

Spittal's patents also call for enclosing the joint between the steel and wood of the shaft with a "copper jacket." As produced, the entire steel portion of the shaft is coated with copper. Copper rivets were used to fasten the steel shaft to the wood underneath it:

A copper rivet locks the hickory and steel shaft portions together at the neck of the head thus effectively preventing turning between the head and wood and steel shaft portions. Another copper rivet locks the wood and steel together at the head of the steel shaft portion.

The driver pictured right is marked "Dave Spittal \ Patent" on both the head and the shaft. "Nick Gianferante," who was probably a past owner of this club, is stamped on the head three times.

EDWIN H. W. SCOTT
SQUARE STEEL SHAFT

A.G. SPALDING & BROS.
"OLYMPIC PUTTER,"
SQUARE STEEL SHAFT

A new putter has been invented by Mr. E.H.W. Scott, a prominent member of Parklangley and other clubs. It is a very elegant-looking weapon, with a square steel shaft and grip, and appears to be coming rapidly into favour (Golf Illustrated, 14 Nov. 1913: 183).

Edwin Hamilton Winkworth Scott received two British patents that covered steel shafts. His first patent, No. 30,050 dated December 31, 1912, calls for making a shaft from a uniformly tapered metal tube, the walls of which could have different thicknesses at different points in order to provide the desired resiliency. This metal shaft, applicable to putters, irons, or woods, could be screwed into the head or riveted in place. Toward the end of this patent,

Scott mentions the possibility of modifying his tubular shaft to an oval or rectangular shape. An oval metal shaft attributable to Scott is not known, but a rectangular shaft took form in Scott's next patent.

Scott's second British patent, No. 26,280 dated December 31, 1913, was a continuation of his first. It covered a "tubular" metal shaft with flat sides:

The present invention is to provide an improved construction of such shaft by making its handle not only tubular but wholly or in part of angular cross-section with the faces which meet at an angle forming a straight line lengthwise of the shaft, and parallel or approximately so with the shaft axis.

Scott thought that his rectangular metal shaft would help golfers with their alignment:

A person playing such games as golf or croquet, wherein a ball lying upon the ground has to be struck, has to hold the club, mallet, or the like, by its upper end and tends to look down the shaft to the head: in so doing the eye is unconsciously directed by the shaft and, if the shaft bear[s] one or more strongly defined straight lines, these are found to assist in directing the eye accurately.

According to Scott's second patent, the shaft attached to the head by fitting over a "tang" located on top of the neck, a rivet passing through both the shaft and tang.

As produced, Scott's shafts are square in cross-section. The

two putters illustrated both have Scott shafts. The club on the left is marked "E H Winkworth Scott \ Reg. No. 612553 \ Lillywhite Frowds \ London \ Warranted Hand Forged" on the back of the blade. Scott's 612,553 British design registration number dates to 1912. J. Lillywhite, Frowd & Company was a well-respected retail business:

The famous house of Lillywhite, Froud [sic] and Co., have gradually and substantially increased their clientele among clubmen and others in the West End of London, until at the present day their stock and resource is a bye-word among those whose business and pleasure carry them frequently to the neighbourhood of the Haymarket (Golfing, 9 Apr. 1903: 8).

The Spalding Olympic putter pictured at right on the facing page was produced under Scott's U.S. patent (No. 1,171,806) dated February 15, 1916. This patent is a composite of Scott's two British patents and allows either circular or rectangular shafts. Spalding, however, added their own wrinkle by installing Scott's shaft on a radically-shaped head. Scott's U.S. patent shows a head identical to the one on his club as produced in the U.K.

Spalding offered the " 'Olympic' Steel-Shafted Putter" in their catalogs between 1915 and 1918, and again in 1920. The 1915 Spring and Summer catalog listed the Olympic putter as:

No. 0. This putter is designed as an instrument sufficiently delicate to impart the impact to either a short or long putt on a keen green with unusual accuracy. Each, $3.50 (39).

The back of the Spalding putter shown is marked "Spalding \ Gold Medal" inside an oval, "O \ Olympic \ Reg. U.S. Pat. Off," "Hammer Brand" with Spalding's "hammer" trademark, and "Accurate" with Spalding's corresponding "arrow" cleekmark. "Putter" is stamped on the sole.

Scott's square steel shaft putter and Spalding's Olympic putter are both fine collectibles. They are the earliest steel shaft clubs that a collector has a reasonable chance of acquiring.

Winton & Co., are producing still another putter which ought to meet with a ready sale. It is named the "Shiva," and is made entirely of steel. It is a type of wry-knecked [sic] putter with a long blade, and is being made in various weights. The shaft is an oval steel tube, and the handle can be made round, square, or kept the same shape as the shaft (Golf Monthly, Mar. 1914: 144).

The Shiva putter shown left is marked "Charles Gibson \ Maker \ Westward Ho" inside an oval on the back of the blade along with Gibson's "rampant stallion" trademark and the Winton "diamond" trademark. Only one clubmaker made this club, yet it has two different cleekmarks (trademarks): the stallion belongs to Gibson, who made woods but not irons, and the diamond belongs to W.M. Winton & Company, a prolific cleekmaking firm. Because cleekmarks usually identify the maker, when a cleekmark stamped on a club belongs to a clubmaker who did *not* make the club, the mark is known as a "false cleekmark" (see Henderson & Stirk 1979, 193). Gibson's stallion, as stamped on this club, is a false cleekmark installed because Gibson *sold* this club.

Charles Gibson was born in 1860, at Musselburgh, Scotland:

Charles Gibson became interested in clubmaking at an early age and was apprenticed to Willy [sic] Dunn Senior of North Berwick. In 1888 he was appointed professional and clubmaker to the Royal North Devon Golf Club, remaining with the club until his death in 1932. A Master Clubmaker, he trained his four sons—Charles, Bill, Bob, and Jack, who became professionals and clubmakers in their own right (Davies and Brown 1989, 71).

William Winton was also a fine clubmaker, his company located in London:

A little over three years ago, in company with Mr. A.C. Clayson, [William Winton] started business and so rapid was the development that . . . it is one of the most flourishing concerns of its kind. So rapid has it developed, that the Company have taken over his brother's [James] business in Montrose (Golf Monthly, Feb. 1914: 954).

Winton also made Shiva putters with oval wood shafts; but they are much more common than the steel shaft Shiva putters, which were declared illegal only a few months after their introduction (see p. 498-499).

A wood with what appears to be a Winton oval steel shaft similar to the one pictured here, complete with an identical black finish, is in the USGA museum, Golf House. The shaft is small and round inside the socket neck, but quickly assumes a flattened oval shape just above the top of the neck. The flat sides of the shaft face 90 degrees away from the target, and the leading edge of the shaft is slightly wider than the following edge. "Arthur Hancox / Sandwell Park" is marked on the top of the head. Hancox worked at Sandwell Park, in West Bromwich, England, from 1922 until at least 1938 (Jackson 1994, 39).

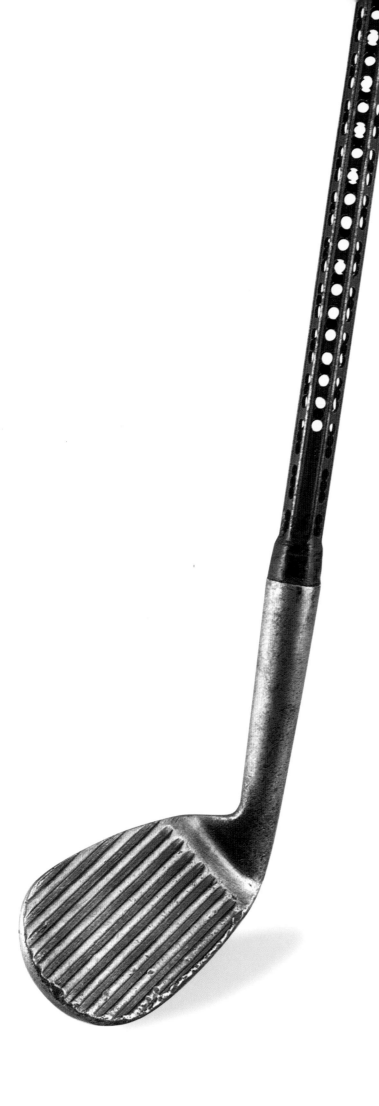

ALLAN LARD
'WHISTLER,' TWO-PIECE, PERFORATED STEEL SHAFT

The steel shaft has come into being during my active golf life. The early attempts to make a steel shaft came to my attention amongst the first because I was champion in those days. I cannot remember exactly when I saw my first steel shaft. It was a long time ago, perhaps over fifteen years. Allan Lard, that splendid old Washington golfer, had designed the first one I saw. He was always talking about it and dreaming about such a thing as early as my first visit to Pinehurst in 1911. We talked about it then and both of us agreed on the fact that a steel shaft would be straight all the time, and that fact would be a reason for success, leaving out all the others. We had both been through trouble with crooked wooden shafts. I had a mania for straight shafts and always changed the wooden ones when they became even a tiny bit off the straight line, but it was a troublesome thing to do. Nearly all hickory shafts would get varying degrees of bend after much use. And when a golfer practiced a lot he could not help having a bow in his shafts. . . .

Not long after that conversation, a year or so perhaps, Mr. Lard stopped off in Chicago with a steel shaft. It was a curious thing, with perforations. A golf club manufacturer had made a few, and I tried them out at old Edgewater. They were dreadfully stiff and lacking in "feel," but there was something very attractive about them to me. Evidently Mr. Lard did not get very far, for I did not hear much more about the steel shaft. Perhaps he tired of them (Charles 'Chick' Evans Jr., Golfers Magazine, 30 Jan. 1930: 10).

Allan Lard's perforated steel shaft was produced by Spalding for only two years, 1918 and 1919; nevertheless, Lard did not lose interest in designing shafts. Between 1915 and 1930, he received eleven patents for seven different metal shafts. (His four British patents covered some of the shafts protected under seven U.S. patents.) During the 1920s, Lard received two U.S. patents for cane shafts (see p. 512).

Allan Lard's perforated steel shaft, pictured on this page, remains as his best-known effort. This shaft is often referred to as "Lard's Whistler shaft" and is easily recognized by its six sides which include literally hundreds of holes drilled by hand to lessen the shaft's weight. When this shaft is swung, the holes create a whistling noise—hence the "Whistler" nickname. (See also the "Whistler" on page 150.)

The back of the club shown is marked "Spalding Gold Medal" inside an oval along with "Pat'd Jan 12, 1914 \ Pat'd Aug 29, 1916" and Spalding's "hammer" cleekmark. "Ded Stop Mashie Niblick \ C51 \ U.S. Pat Off." is stamped on the sole.

Dated January 12, 1915, Allan Lard's first U.S. patent (No. 1,125,029) covered a steel shaft made from four inverted "U"-shaped lengthwise ribs attached to a small, tubular steel core. The date of Lard's first patent is incorrectly marked "Jan. 12, 1914" on the perforated shaft irons Spalding produced, including the one pictured. Dated August 29, 1916, Lard's second U.S. patent (No. 1,195,994) improved the shaft covered under his first patent and included modifications Spalding used to produce Lard's perforated shaft. However, it is Allan Lard's *third*

U.S. patent (No. 1,218,091) which provides the only patent illustration that matches his perforated shaft. Surprisingly, this patent, dated March 6, 1917, deals with attaching a larger perforated handle to the perforated shaft. The basic objective of all of these patents was to construct a metal shaft with all the desirable characteristics of a wood shaft—consideration being given to weight, torsion, balance, feel, etc.

According to Lard's March 6, 1917 patent, the handle end of the perforated shaft is constructed from a separate length of metal. It is thicker than the shaft proper (the exposed portion), and has a tapered end which connects to the upper end of the shaft proper. Grip material is applied over the handle piece:

A handle thus formed and secured to a metallic shaft tends to throw the major whip and torsioning action of the club under impact lower down in the shaft than is the case where the shaft proper extends the full length of the club. The construction is also cheaper, in that the shaft proper (which is more expensive to produce than the handle) may be materially shorter than where it extends the full length of the club.

The author has examined a Whistler shaft lacking its grip, and it was, indeed, made from two lengths pinned together.

Spalding's 1918 and 1919 catalogs offer Lard's perforated shaft as "The Spalding Steel Shafted Golf Club." Spalding's 1918 Spring and Summer catalog notes that the metal shaft club had a future:

One of our important 1918 contributions to the game of golf. The

Spalding Steel Shafted Golf Club is the club of the future. It solves the problem of a successful substitute for the fast disappearing, fine second growth hickory which can no longer be had in sufficient quantities to meet the demands for perfect wood shafts.

The steel shaft will never wear out. Its torsion is just right. Its flexibility, weight and balance give to the golfer the best that is in the wood with the added advantage of steel (10).

Spalding promoted Lard's metal shafts as a substitute for the best hickory shafts, which were in short supply. Ironically, a shortage of steel interrupted the production of Lard's shaft. According to an ad for Spalding's "Steel Shaft Golf Club":

The war stopped the manufacture of our patented steel shaft–cut off our supply of steel—just about the time golfers began to recognize its merits, and our sales were daily multiplying. They had tested and found it A1. But we could make no more until the government released steel in sufficient volume to warrant quantity production. Now ready to fill all orders. The economy of the steel shaft needs no argument (Golf Illustrated [ny], May 1919: 39).

The fascinating process used to construct Lard's shaft is described in a letter from D.W. Whyte, Spalding's Brantford, Canada, factory manager, to D.M. Irwin, of Wolverine Tube, in London, Ontario, Canada. Dated January 28, 1964, Whyte's letter reads in part:

I do recall the particular shaft you refer to. A man by the name of Allan Lard apparently held this patent and I recall very well the method he used in producing this shaft in our old plant in Chicopee, Massachusetts, during the

years 1919 and 1920. Spaldings [sic] did produce a fair amount of these clubs years ago.

As far as I can recall this gentleman was a gunsmith who worked for the Springfield Armouries and used gun boring machines for boring the shaft out of a solid piece of steel, then milled the outer portion to give the hexagon effect. The small holes were drilled afterwards apparently, as you suggest, for flexibility.

In 1918 perforated shafts were available in mid-irons and mashies. In 1919 they were available in all irons. A few woods with Lard whistler shafts are also known.

The deep groove iron head on the shaft pictured is rarely found on other Lard perforated shafts. Such clubheads were mass produced for use with wood shafts between 1914 and the early 1920s (see p. 235). After July 1921, however, the R&A would not permit:

the use of corrugated, grooved, or slotted clubs . . . in match or stroke play competitions played under the rules of golf as approved by the Royal and Ancient Golf Club of St. Andrews (USGA 1922, 238).

The USGA followed suit by limiting the scoring on a club face effective January 1, 1924 (USGA 1924, 272).

A double-walled steel shaft patented by Allan Lard is shown below. Found on a Great Lakes Golf Company "Tommy Armour Open Champion" 2-iron, this double-walled shaft is tapered, top to bottom, without step-downs. An orange decal on the shaft reads "The Torsion Steel Golf Shaft \ The Horton Mfg. Co., Bristol, Conn. U.S.A. \ Allan Lard Patent Pending." This shaft is easily recognized by a seam that runs its entire length.

Lard's shaft, originally produced in the U.S. during 1928, was granted a British patent (No. 315,758) on Dec. 29, 1930. This shaft, finished with black enamel, was described as follows:

This shaft, in a traverse section, resembles a hollow, or outlined horse shoe, shaped together at the open end until the two points meet. Thus you will find it a double-walled circular tube, with its joining points open, or unsealed (Crawford 1930, 5).

HORTON MANUFACTURING CO.
"BRISTOL"
TAPERED STEEL SHAFT

ARTHUR KNIGHT W. EMMET & S. THORPE
"BRISTOL GOLD LABEL"
STEEL SHAFT

FREDERICK WALDRON
"ARDEN AERO CLUB"

Pictured above left is a steel shaft "MacGregor M-1 Bakspin Mashie" produced before steel shafts were declared legal. Backspin irons were declared illegal under USGA rules beginning January 1, 1924; therefore, this Bristol tapered steel shaft dates prior to that time. A welded seam down the back of this early tubular shaft shows evidence of the filing or grinding used to smooth the seam. The shaft's copper plate finish has darkened with time.

The copper-plated shaft shown above right is marked "The Horton Mfg. Co. \ 'Bristol' \ Steel Golf Shaft \ Pat'd November 22, 1910 \ Pat'd August 18, 1925 \ Gold Label" on a gold shaft decal. The November patent date refers to Arthur Knight's U.S. patent (No. 976,267) that covered a straight-tapered steel tube golf shaft of high carbon steel, which this shaft is. The August 18, 1925 date identifies William Emmet and Samuel T. Thorpe's U.S. patent (No. 1,550,153) used to construct Bristol Gold Label shafts, described as follows:

[The] Bristol Gold Label is a seamed, or jointed, shaft and was the first successful shaft produced after many years of costly experimenting. Imagine, if you will, a narrow strip of very thin steel about 45" long, wider at one end than at the other. This irregular shaped piece of high carbon steel is formed into a circular tube, with the edges abutting in a way to form an inseparable lock. Over this inter-meshed joint a key strip is applied and welded, producing in the end a perfect joint (Crawford 1930, 5-6).

The seam is apparent across the lower portion of this particular shaft.

Bristol also produced a "Silver Label" shaft, which:

. . . differs from the Bristol Gold Label shaft by being a continuous, or seamless, tube of cold drawn steel. That is a familiar manufacturing process, and we need not devote much space to it. . . . The Gold Label shaft is made of high carbon steel, which is very hard in comparison with low carbon steel . . . . It is a well known fact that high carbon steel cannot be cold drawn. Hence, to make a continuous tapered tube, like the Silver Label, it has to be made of lower carbon, ductile steel (Crawford 1930, 6).

The futuristic driver head installed on the end of the Bristol Gold Label shaft pictured is an "Arden Aero Club," produced during the late 1920s. The Arden Company promoted this hook-faced creature as an "Anti-slice" club with the built in ability to "Slaughter the Slice" (*Golfers Magazine*, Dec. 1927: 45).

This metalwood, which does have a hook face, is marked "Arden" in a diamond on the top of the head behind the face, and "Pat Applied For" next to the aerodynamic alignment fin. Frederick A. Waldron, of Westfield, New Jersey, received a U.S. patent (No. 1,690,388) dated November 6, 1928, that covered the Aero Club. According to his patent, the head was to be solid with most of its weight located behind the point of impact. The "wings" (thin portions of the sole) were designed to "stabilize the club" during the latter part of the swing. The fin would "improve the lateral stability of the club during the swing."

WILLIAM HARNESS
SOLID STEEL SHAFT, WOOD GRIP

William Harness of Bloomington, Illinois, patented the solid steel shaft pictured left. His U.S. patent (No. 1,677,099) dated July 10, 1928, calls for making a club from:

a solid steel rod [shaft] to the lower end of which is attached the putter head fastened preferably by shrinking on.

The example pictured is marked with the patent date on the butt of its wood grip and Harness's name on the back of its blade.

Note the unusual, solid wood grip. This grip, bored out to fit over the shaft, is riveted in place. According to the patent:

when the handle is held in the only natural position in the hands of the player, the club is always in the proper position for playing.

The Alverson Sales Co., of Bloomington, Illinois, advertised the Harness putter as having a walnut handle—"the back is rounded and the face flat, conforming to the hands in a natural, uncramped position." The blade was "made in both goose neck and straight types" (*Golfer's Magazine*, June 1928: 70).

The Beckley-Ralston Company produced many similar steel shaft putters and chippers, as advertised in the September 1927 issue of *Golfers Magazine* (2). These clubs were available with leather wrap grips, either round or square in cross-section, approximately as long as Harness's grip.

HAROLD B. BARRETT & HOWARD BARTLING
"PYRATONE SHEATH" SHAFT COVERING

The refinished set of Gene Sarazen fancy face woods pictured above was made in 1930 by the Wilson-Western Sporting Goods Company. The steel shaft in each club is covered with a "Pyratone sheath." According to a Pyratone Products Corp. advertisement:

Pyratone Sheath, weighing less than 1/2 ounce, is a live flexible tubing telescoped onto a steel shaft. This sheath replaces old finishing methods of painting, enameling, oxidizing and nickel plating. Pyratone is indestructible . . . it will not crack or wear off. It is obtainable in any color or finish (Fraser's 1931, 113).

The Pyratone sheath is a pyroxylin shaft casing patented (No. 1,600,389) in the U.S. on September 21, 1926, by Harold B. Barrett, assignor to the Pyratone Products Corp., of Chicago, Illinois. Another U.S. patent (No. 1,600,390) also dated September 21, 1926, was granted to Harold G. Barrett and Howard Bartling, assignors to the Barbarite Corp., of Chicago, Illinois. This patent related to heating, and thereby shrinking, the pyroxylin covering onto the shaft.

Pyroxylin is a nitrocellulose compound (celluloid/thermoplastic). Pyratone sheaths, used on vast quantities of early metal shaft clubs, were usually brown, yellow, or black. Besides protecting the shaft from rust, Pyratone sheaths, because they were made to look like wood, helped sell metal shafts to tradition-bound golfers accustomed to using wood shafts. Even today the unknowing often mistake Pyratone-covered shafts for wood shafts. (A magnet will quickly determine whether the shaft is wood or steel.)

When Pyratone was introduced in the U.S., a few British clubmakers tried producing clubs with celluloid covered wood shafts. Forgan's Black Magic putter, with its celluloid head, was one such club. (It also came with a coated steel shaft.)

CRAWFORD, McGREGOR & CANBY
"MASTER 30 MODEL" WOOD SET

ROBERT COWDERY
STEPDOWN STEEL SHAFT

SYLVAN JAY CROOKER
"STREAMLINER" WOODS

Offered in 1931 and 1932 at $22.50 per club, MacGregor's Master 30 Model woods, pictured, were once MacGregor's premier woods. According to a MacGregor catalog description, the shaft is a Bristol "Gold Label" steel shaft having a "black Mac-oid finish." "Mac-oid" is described as follows:

Most platings and all paints or lacquers applied to a steel shaft either chip off or wear through early in their use, resulting in a very disreputable looking shaft. After long experiments our company has arrived at a shaft finish that is not a plating and is not in the paint or lacquer class. Mac-oid, the name by which we designate it, is a variation of pyroxylin so applied by a patented process that it literally becomes an integral part of the material to which it is applied. It cannot be stripped off or removed except by whittling, grinding, or dissolving it chemically (Crawford 1930, 8).

According to MacGregor's 1932 catalog, the Model 30 head is "selected persimmon, entirely covered with black Mac-oid," with a "pearl insert across [the] top" (actually mother-of-pearl). The face is covered with "White Mac-oid . . . with 7 scruloc in- serts of same material." The "center wedge backweight" is also white Mac-oid.

Matching sets of Master 30 woods, as pictured, are difficult to locate; individual Master 30 woods are found with some con- sistency. Matching sets originally sold together are more valuable than a set of individual clubs combined years later. Combined sets usually have uneven wear patterns between the heads, shafts, or grips as well as subtle differences, such as between grip colors and overall lengths.

Each of the clubs in the near-mint set of Streamliners pictured on the facing page has a chrome-plated steel shaft with step-downs. By 1937, when these woods were patented, chrome-plated steel shafts had been in use for a number of years. MacGregor's 1930 booklet *MacGregor Sales Helps* gives a good overview of the finishes available in 1930:

Steel Shaft Finishes: These are numerous. The majority are merely variations of plating applied directly to the shaft by chemical processes. Some rust-resisting treatment is necessary, as bare steel will immediately rust. So

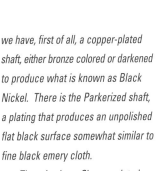

we have, first of all, a copper-plated shaft, either bronze colored or darkened to produce what is known as Black Nickel. There is the Parkerized shaft, a plating that produces an unpolished flat black surface somewhat similar to fine black emery cloth.

There is also a Chrome-plated shaft, which is very frequently used. Chrome-plating resembles the familiar nickel plating, but is much harder and more durable (Crawford 1930, 8).

Gurdon Leslie, while vice president of True Temper Corporation, where he had worked for decades, wrote about the coatings given to early steel shafts:

Chromium plating was a novelty when we first started in the golf shaft business [mid-1920s]. All of the early shafts were either copper plated and lacquered, black nickel plated and lacquered, or parkerized and black duco lacquered. Our company had one of the first chromium plating installations, but in the early 1930s the only plated shafts were those on wood clubs. Shafts for irons were finished either with a cellulose nitrate [pyroxylin] sheath or a lacquer dip. Chrome plated shafts for irons did not come into existence until the mid 1930s (Leslie 1968, 28).

Robert Cowdery, of American Fork and Hoe (which became

True Temper Corp.), was the first to patent a method for producing tubular steel shafts with step-downs, as found in his U.S. design patent (No. 73,777) dated November 8, 1927, and his U.S. patent (No. 1,670,530) dated May 22, 1928. Step-down shafts underwent further refinements and received further patents, but what came to be known as "the True Temper Stepdown shaft" failed to gain acceptance for some time. Before too many years passed, however, step-downs finally took hold and became the most common feature found in steel shafts. Although chromed steel shafts with step-downs are not collectible per se, the Streamliner heads attached to the shafts pictured are very much so!

Streamliner woods were covered under Sylvan Jay Crooker's U.S. patent (No. 2,083,189) dated June 8, 1937. Crooker's patent focuses on the aerodynamics of his radical club and is full of scientific calculations on wind

resistance, velocity, mass, force, and such things as how "the elastic coefficient of the average golf ball changes with the velocity of impact" . . .

According to an undated (circa 1937) promotional pamphlet, Streamliners were made by "MacGregor Craftsmen" and sold by "Streamliner Golf Clubs; S.J. Crooker, President; Purcellville, Virginia." This pamphlet also notes:

The NEW "Streamliner" woods will drive the golf ball from 15 to 20 yards farther than the OLD traditional woods.

The NEW "Streamliner" golf club has only one-tenth as much air resistance as the OLD style club.

The NEW "Streamliner" design locates the weight of the club head directly behind the impact center,

while the weight in the OLD head is unsymmetrical and unbalanced.

The NEW "Streamliner" design is specified by aerodynamic science, while the OLD "jest growed" like "Topsy."

If your hunting is done with a rifle, try the NEW 'Streamliner." If you hunt with a "blunder-buss" stick to the OLD (Crooker, 2-3)

Streamliners sound great in theory, but they did not work in reality (nor were they legal when built). Today they are popular collectibles, matched sets being *very* hard to find.

When your business begins to interfere with your golf it is time to think whom you will appoint as liquidator.

(*Golfing*, April 1925: 49)

Grips

Prior to the end of the wood shaft era, grips were made using a wide variety of methods, shapes, and materials. Before discussing some of the more distinctive and collectible grips, the two most common grips—hard-finished leather and sueded sheepskin—need to be understood.

A hard-finished leather grip is similar to ordinary shoe leather. The leather is smooth, without any nap to its surface; often shiny; and usually finished in black, brown, burgundy, or mahogany (see p. 501—No. 1, 2, 5, 7, & 10). Sueded sheepskin grips have a soft, napped surface, and are usually brown or somewhat orange in color (see p. 501—No. 3, 6, 9, 11, & 12). Undoubtedly some "sheepskin grips" were made from sueded cowhide, but they are included in the sheepskin category because their finish is quite similar.

Hard-finished leather and sueded sheepskin grips do not provide dependable criteria for dating a club. They were each prominent during different eras, but they also overlapped into each era. The sheepskin grip was in use during the 1700s, was the standard throughout the 1800s, and continued into the early 1900s. Hard-finished leather, which is even found on a few early feather ball clubs, eventually took hold in the 1890s and became the standard grip material following the turn of the century.

Two common variations of the leather and sheepskin grip are the gusset and the coated grip. During the 1890s and thereafter, hard-finished leather grips were occasionally installed inside out. The inside of the grip was unfinished and resembled, to a degree, sueded sheepskin. These gusset grips provided the golfer with a softer grip. A coated grip, when found today, is usually on a pre-1900 club. It consists of a sheepskin grip given a coat of wax, shellac, or varnish to protect the grip from deteriorating, or a coat of pitch to make the grip more tacky. Sometimes much of the coating is worn off; other times much remains, having a dark brown or blackish appearance. Coated grips resemble, to varying degrees, hard-finished leather grips (see p. 501—No. 4).

The earliest grips were usually made from listing (a strip of cloth, usually wool) wrapped around the handle. Listing grips date to the 1700s and earlier (see p. 33 and 43). Wool listing remained in use into the 1800s, but by then it was being covered with a sheepskin grip—hence the term "underlisting." Note that most clubs with only a listing on their handles are not from the 1700s. Clubs from the 1800s are often missing the sheepskin but still have the wool underlisting, or "rind" as it was once called.

Fabric grips were also used after 1900. These grips were usually finished to simulate leather, but close examination often reveals strands of thread.

PICTURED ABOVE: *From top to bottom, the following grip materials are shown: (1) Leather-wrapped pistol grip, on a slat shaft putter (page 504). (2) Cork grip, on a Jaques driver (page 199). (3) Corrugated, sewn buffed leather grip, on a Bussey wood (page 136). (4) Smooth, sewn buffed leather grip, on a Bussey putter (page 351). (5) Engraved wood grip, on an adjustable chipper (page 374).*

PICTURED BELOW: *From top to bottom, the following grip shapes are shown: (1) Fishing rod wood grip including brass collar at the base of the grip, on a McEwan long nose wood (page 50). (2) Square grip, on an Albert Whiting putter (page 184). (3) Detachable wood grip, on a convex blade putter (page 251). (4) Fishing rod wood grip, on a Forgan long nose wood (page 71). (5) Oval grip, on a T-Frame putter (page 435).*

W & G. ASHFORD
SEWN LEATHER GRIP & SEWN PIGSKIN GRIP

A. COLE
"HOLDFAST"
INDIA RUBBER GRIP

ARMSTRONG GOLF GRIP CORP.
"CORRECT GOLF GRIP"

The two sewn grips shown at the top of this page are installed on a smooth face lofter and similar mashie, both marked "W.&G. Ashford \ Mild Steel" around Ashford's "fox head" trademark. According to Ashford's advertisement in the November 10, 1893 issue of *Golf*, their sewn handles were "covered in pigskin, rough or smooth" (144). A few months later, W.&G. Ashford advertised "sewn leather handles covered with buffed cow hide" (*Golf*, 23 Mar. 1894: 32). The top grip is buffed cowhide. The reddish grip second from the top is smooth pigskin. Brittle to the touch, the smooth pigskin is not as thick as the brown cowhide nor is it as smooth and soft.

The Clan Golf Club Company produced a grip similar to the Ashford grip, except that "The 'Special Clan' solid leather hand grip [was] fixed by a special process without stitches" (*Golfing Annual* 1895, 514). The earliest sewn grips were patented in 1890 by William Bussey and Joseph Pinder (see page 351 and the examples on the facing page).

Pictured above, third from the top, is a circa 1890s india rubber grip installed on the croquet-style putter discussed on page 421. This grip is characterized by downward spiraling corrugations on its outer surface and a thin fabric backing underneath the india rubber. This grip is similar to Cole's Holdfast grip, reviewed in 1900 as follows:

Mr. A. Cole, the inventor of the Horse Boot, "Bogey" hole cutter, and other useful contrivances, has been devoting his talents to the all-important matter of grips. The old leather grip suffers from two great disadvantages—it wears out very quickly and gets slippery, and it is liable to ruckle and become loose. Most other grips, while they afford a good hold, are hard on the hands, and tear to pieces, while the surface gets unpleasantly wet when the hands get warm. Mr. Coles new grip, of which he has sent us a sample, appears to combine all the advantages of other grips without having any of their disadvantages. The new grip, which is called the "Holdfast," is made of corrugated india rubber, the corrugations running down the grip and not across it. The corrugated surface serves the double purpose of affording a perfectly secure grip, and it keeps the hands cool and dry, as it allows the air to circulate under the palms and fingers. Mr. Cole also claims that the grip gives more life to the club, and thinks that it adds perceptibly to the length of the drive. The new grip is unlike any other in that it has a substantial textile backing, which obviates the need of much list. The price of the grip is 2s., and looking to its obvious advantages and its greater durability, it is probably cheaper than the ordinary ones in use (Golf Illustrated, 24 Aug. 1900: 168).

Pictured above, at the bottom, is a "Correct Golf Grip" produced by the Armstrong Golf Grip Corp., of Baltimore, Maryland, and installed on a George Nicoll "Clinker Cleek" (only the "Clinker" name, not the club, is unusual). An ad for Correct Golf Grips reads, in part, as follows:

A rubber grip, non-skid, easily applied, all in one, slip on club and work is done. Every golf professional and sporting goods house is now able to equip your clubs with these popular grips. . . . Clubs may now be ordered from manufacturers, already equipped with these grips. They are made of non-skid rubber and your hands are never sore. Cyril Walker, winner of the National Open, Bobby Cruickshank, winner of the Colorado Open, and many other well known, prominent pros are enthusiastic users" (Golf Illustrated [ny], 25 Jan. 1925: 38).

The grip is marked "Trademark \ Correct Grip \ Patented" in small letters down the back of the grip.

WILLIAM LOWE
INDIA RUBBER GRIP

ARTHUR TRIMMINGS
"GRYPTA GRIP"

BRITISH INSULATED AND HELSBY CABLES, & FREDERICK COLE
"HELSBY GRIP"

Produced sometime in the 1890s, the damaged grip pictured on the near right is made from molded india rubber and installed directly over a sheepskin grip. The original grip is visible where the rubber grip has been damaged. Surprisingly, installing specialty grips without removing the original grip was a rather common practice:

Fastening above the leather a red india rubber grip . . . has the merit of both thickening the hold and being less severe on the hands (Golf, 14 July 1893: 309).

Specialty grips themselves, however, are few and far between. This india rubber grip is marked "W. Lowe \ Buxton."

According to Arthur Edwin Trimmings's British patent (No. 10,680) dated May 8, 1907, the Grypta grip, pictured in the middle, consists of both leather and rubber rings affixed to a shaft by means of "Russian fish glue or cement." The edges of the rubber rings project slightly beyond the leather rings in order to absorb vibrations and give the golfer a better hold on the club:

For those who experience a difficulty in getting a good grip . . . we would recommend a trial of the "Grypta" which has been placed on the market by the St. Andrew Golf Co. 35 and 37, Pitt Street, Glasgow. Briefly described, the "Grypta" is a built-up grip of leather and rubber, containing sufficient of the latter material to ensure a firm hold, but not

enough to fire the hand or cause blisters. As a means of preventing foozled shots caused by the club slipping in the fingers just at the moment of impact with the ball, the "Grypta" grip should prove invaluable (Golfing, 9 Apr. 1908: 24).

The Grypta grip pictured is on an iron marked "St. Andrew Golf Co. Ltd \ The Grypta Grip" etc.

British Insulated and Helsby Cables, Ltd., in tandem with Frederick Arthur Cole, an electrical engineer, received a British patent (No. 27,613) dated Nov. 28, 1910, that covered the braided rubber cord grip shown far right. According to their patent:

this invention is formed of braided rubber covered cords producing a resilient or elastic grip . . . which will reduce the liability of the handle to slip in the hands of a player and will consequently give the player more control over the club.

. . . Each of the cords used for braiding into this form is advantageously composed of a fine hemp cord or the like fibrous cord covered with vulcanised rubber or similar material.

This tubular grip . . . is slipped over the handle . . . and securely bound at the extreme end of the handle. The grip is then worked down on to the handle until it is perfectly tight, and is then bound securely . . . .

Another method is to pass the handle into a braiding machine and braid the rubbered cords direct on to the handle.

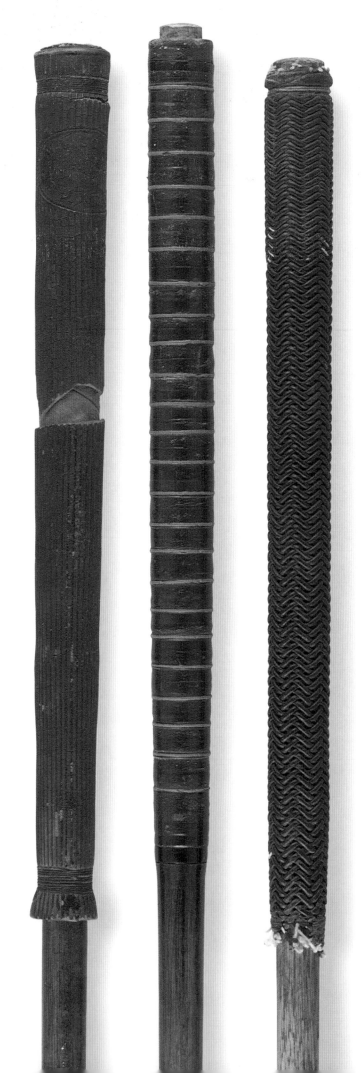

UNKNOWN MAKER
BRAIDED LEATHER GRIP

JOHN M. INGLIS
"INGLIS PERFORATED GRIP"

ERNEST WHITCOMBE
"NO. 2" GRIP

The grip shown far left is constructed from braided leather strips. While the maker of this grip is unknown, the club bearing this grip is a common mid to late 1920s iron made by Spalding and marked "Basil Smith \ 2 Iron \ Average Distance \ 170/180 \ Yards \ Hand Forged" along with Spalding's "anvil" cleekmark. This handsome grip could be the creation of Spalding, Basil Smith, or somebody else.

An Inglis perforated leather grip, installed on an otherwise ordinary circa 1901-05 Spalding Crescent mashie, is shown in the middle:

Get a grip on the game by using the Inglis Perforated Golf Club Grip. This grip absolutely prevents the club from turning or slipping in the hands, assuring accuracy rain or shine. Made from selected russet and box calf. Made only by John M. Inglis, Golf Club Manufacturer, Country Club, Montgomery, Alabama (Golf [ny], Dec. 1908: 378).

John Inglis (p. 199) was not the first to devise a perforated leather grip. In 1900, Messrs. G. Brodie Breeze, suppliers of golf club requisites and accessories, offered a perforated leather grip called the "Dormy" grip:

Many different plans have been tried with the hope of securing a satisfactory grasp of the club handle, such as wearing gloves, applying pitch, resin, wax, &c, or moistening the hands in the primitive but unpleasant manner which needs no description. . . .

The "Dormy" Grip has been designed to supply the need for a grip giving the player every confidence that his club is securely held . . . (Golfing, 6 Sept. 1900).

The three grips on the facing page and the first two shown on this page are rarely found.

On February 24, 1936, Ernest Robert Whitcombe received a British patent (applied for on August 23, 1934) that covered the spiraling black india rubber grip, with canvas backing, pictured near left. Whitcombe grips are marked "Pat. No. 443228 \ No. 2 \ E.R. Whitcombe \ Made In England \ The Avon India Rubber Company, Ltd." with either raised letters or a decal. The grip shown is on a Tom Stewart wood shaft 2-iron. In 1912 Spalding advertised a similar "spiral groove" rubber grip called the "Never Slip" grip (*American Golfer*, Oct.: back cover).

Whitcombe's No. 2 grip was somewhat popular. Today it is found fairly frequently.

MAXWELL ROBERT CAUCH-KAVANAGH
MOLDED GRIPS

The specification of a recently-patented improvement in handles for golf clubs—the patentee of which is Maxwell R. Cauch-Kavanagh, Club-House, St. Andrews—sets forth that it relates particularly to handles which require to be tightly grasped. Consists in making the handle capable of being moulded to the palm of the individual's hand. Gutta percha and cork sawdust are thoroughly mixed in given proportions and moulded into tubes of a uniform circumference of about two and a half inches, the thickness of the sides tapering from, say, three-sixteenths to one-sixteenth of an inch. The shaft is tapered to fit the taper in the gutta cover, which is then firmly jammed on the shaft. Next a wrapping of strong cotton is wound tightly round the gutta to form an envelope. The handle is now immersed in boiling water, and when the composition becomes plastic the handle is grasped by the person for whom the club is made, and the desired impression formed on it. The handle is then inserted in cold water, the wrapping removed, and the club completed (The Golfer, 22 Sep. 1897: 226).

Pictured below are two molded grips, probably modeled after Cauch-Kavanagh's grip, made from a gutta percha and cork mix. Cauch-Kavanagh's British patent (No. 20,738) dated September 19, 1896, calls for mixing the gutta percha and cork sawdust in a 4 to 1 ratio by *weight*. Such a mixture would result in a large volume of cork.

Cauch-Kavanagh's patent was the first to propose molding a grip to fit the shape of the golfer's hands. Between this patent and 1935, no fewer than eleven different patents dealt with grips custom molded to the golfer's hands. Additional patents dealt with other grip shapes such as tapered grips, oval grips, thick in the middle grips, square grips, and so on.

The grips shown are on two irons, each with different marks. One is marked "Rustless Iron \ Alex Herd's \ Own \ Hand Forged in Scotland \ Special \ Warranted" along with Winton's "diamond" trademark and "Grip" inside a circle. The other, a cleek, is marked only "A H" on the back of the blade.

Grips made from a composite of rubber and cork were tried even earlier than Cauch-Kavanagh's molded grip. In 1891, prompted by an article in *Golf* which stated that Messrs. William Currie & Company, Caledonian Rubber Works, Edinburgh, had produced a new improved solid india rubber grip (scored to imitate the spiral wrap of a leather grip), William Currie responded with a letter to *Golf's* editor in order to correct the article. Currie's grip was made from rubber and cork, not solid india rubber:

We beg to thank you for your very gratifying notice respecting our patent reliable hand grasp. In your otherwise admirably written notice you fall into one error regarding it, and as the point is an important one we shall be greatly obliged if you will be good enough to rectify in your next issue. The grasp is not made of solid rubber as you convey, but is a patented [British patent No. 10,701 dated July 10, 1890] combination of rubber and cork, a combination, we are glad to say, quite free from the disadvantages attendant to solid rubber grips. . . (27 Feb. 1891: 372).

Obviously, rubber grips were on the market by 1891. In 1892 Thornton & Son stated that they had "manufactured India-rubber grips for golf-club handles for many years" (*Golf*, 1 Apr.: 36).

JOHN MORRIS & HENRY S.H. SHAW
"CHAMPION GRIP"

Jack Morris, of Hoylake, has brought out a new grip for golf clubs which is as ingenious as it is effective. It is composed of rubber, but it is so moulded as to give what may be described as an anatomical grip of the club to both hands. The lower portion of the grip is thinner than the upper, and the right hand is separated to a very slight extent by a thin and gradual raising of the rubber at the point where the two hands grasp the club. The upper portion of the grip is a trifle thicker for the left hand, and it finishes off with a kind of rounded excrescence at the base of the palm near the little finger. The grip certainly "feels the thing" for giving security to the swing, as the hands drop naturally into the prepared spaces, imparting to the club a sensation as if the grip had been played with for years and had been moulded to the hand of a player through long use—a point of great importance in the eyes of all experienced golfers (Golf, 11 Mar. 1898: 5-6).

Pictured above are two molded Champion Grips, installed on a splice neck wood and a mashie, with "Champion Grip \ Patent \ M H Trade Mark"

impressed into their surface. These grips were patented by John "Jack" Morris, the famous professional at Hoylake, and Henry Selby Hele Shaw, a professor of engineering at University College in Liverpool. Such a team leads to speculation that Morris had the idea for this grip and Shaw knew how to go about making it. Morris and Shaw's British patent (No. 27,827) dated November 26, 1897, was the second patent to deal with molded grips (the first belonging to Cauch-Kavanagh).

According to Morris and Shaw's patent, their grip would enable "the player to obtain a firm hold of the club" while ensuring "that such hold shall be correct in regard to the relative positions of the two hands and the disposition of the fingers." Therefore, they modeled their grip after the hand position of a good player. The "projection" in the middle of the grip served "to separate the hands and prevents chafing between them, but it may in some cases be

removed." As an added feature, this grip could be removed and "more easily exchanged, if a shaft were broken, to the new shaft" (Golfing, 12 Jan. 1899: 19).

The provisional specification of their patent calls for making this grip from india-rubber, but in the final application, Morris and Shaw state that "a compound of rubber and shredded rags, moulded to shape and vulcanised, answers admirably."

Another "Champion" grip— "Sayers' Patent Champion Golf Grip"—was produced in 1895 by Ben Sayers (The Golfer, 19 July: 44). Instead of being molded, this grip came with a strip of rubber that formed a loop attached to the top end of the grip. By placing the left hand through the loop, the right-handed golfer secured his or her hold on the club. Sayers received a British patent (No. 24,473) dated December 17, 1894, for his grip.

William H. Sprague received a British patent (No. 9,816) dated April 29, 1904, that covered a

molded grip similar to Morris's Champion Grip. Called the Anatomical Grip, Sprague's grip was produced by the Anatomical Golf Grip Company, Cromer, England:

As to the three most salient points in this new grip, the prevention of pulling, slicing, and cuss words, seem to be the most enticing qualification it presents to the average golfer (Golfing, 17 Nov. 1904).

The Anatomical grip was modeled after J.H. Taylor's hand position. No less than His Majesty, the King of England was reported to have tried one of these (Golfing, 8 Dec. 1904: 20).

The Avon India Rubber Company, London, also offered a molded grip. Termed the Vardon Grip, it was described as compelling the golfer to "hold and swing the club exactly as Vardon does" (Golfing, Aug. 1924: 3).

A. TOOLEY & SONS
PEAR-SHAPED GRIP

The pear-shaped grip shown at the bottom of this page, devised by A. Tooley & Son, has a prominent ridge that runs down the *top* of the grip. Introduced in mid-1922, this grip was promoted to use on all clubs—woods, irons, and putters. Because this grip required its own shaft to provide the grip's shape, Tooley offered the grip on both new shafts and new completed clubs.

Tooley & Son advertised their grip as follows:

We have registered a new design in golf clubs, the grip portion being pear-shaped. This leaves the rest of the shaft in the same state as on ordinary clubs. The special features of this grip are:—

(1) When taking up the club one unconsciously grips the club in the correct 'V' style as taught by all leading professionals. It produces a most delightful feel with the inter-lock and finger-grip.

(2) The unique shape of the grip prevents any twisting and turning of the club on the backswing, follow-through or when striking the ball.

(3) The grip fits more comfortably into the fingers than the round grip. This grip forces the two hands to work together as one, also as there cannot possibly be any twisting or slipping of the club, it follows that a straighter and longer ball is obtained (Golfing, Sept. 1922: 45).

Tooley's grip was covered under a British registered design (No. 691,621) issued in 1922. The shaft used with the grip pictured is marked "A. Tooley & Sons \ Regd No 691621" and is installed in a W.G. Oke No. 2 putter (see p. 184).

A. HUNTLY GORDON
"HUNTLY GRIP"

Alexander Huntly Gordon, of Fontainebleau, France, received a British patent (No. 165,384) dated September 29, 1920, and a U.S. patent (No. 1,506,523) dated Aug. 26, 1924, that covered the solid wood grip pictured directly below. This rectangular grip, integral with the shaft, has a substantial groove cut down the front to accommodate the golfer's thumbs. Gordon's grip was designed to keep itself, and the club, from turning in the golfer's hands.

The Huntly grip shown is installed in an ordinary looking aluminum mallet head putter marked "Huntly" on its crown. "Patent \ 165,384 \ 1920" is stamped in the wood near the top of this grip. A healthy number of Huntly putters, collectible primarily because of their handle, remain.

The nickel-plated Doerr putter illustrated on page 255 is shafted with a Huntly shaft/grip. The Doerr putter was initially sold as a head only, and the Huntly shaft/grip was also available separately.

BURKE GOLF COMPANY
"LEDTOP PUTTER," COUNTERWEIGHT GRIP

The putter head shown atop the facing page is named and marked "Ledtop" to acknowledge the lead located inside the top end of the shaft. The back of the blade is marked "Putter \ Ledtop Balanced \ Pat. Appl'd For \ Stainless Steel" along with the flower cleekmark used by the Burke Golf Company. The grip of the Ledtop putter is pictured to show the lead in the butt of the shaft.

Ledtop putters were not the first counterweighted golf clubs:

Mr. A. Gray, of the Royal and Ancient Golf club . . . has invented . . . what he claims to be a most useful addition to a golf club, in the form of a loaded or weighted metal cartridge which can be affixed at will to the end of the handle of the club. He claims for it that it assists the power of the stroke, steadies the swing, and above all reduces materially the strain on the wrist, acting as a sort of counterpoise to the weight in the head of the club (Golf, 27 Apr. 1894: 113).

On the visit of Oxford to Combe Hill one of the chief exhibits was a putter, fitted with a handle of unusual

MURRAY

"THE MURRAY PUTTER,"
CURVED GRIP

*construction. The putter . . . which
came from [John] Cuthbert's workshop at Rye, is of far greater gross
weight than is at all usual. But when
handled it feels no heavier than a normal club. The secret is that the shaft
under the leather grip has been hollowed, and the cavity filled with lead—
the insertion is about ten inches long.
The inventor has certainly produced
an implement which inspires the han-
dler of it with a feeling that he could
hole out confidently using it* (Golf Illustrated, 9 Feb. 1912: 128).

John Wilson was the first
person to patent a counterweight
located atop the shaft. His
British patent (No. 11,118) dated
May 30, 1901, covered a lead-
filled brass cap that screwed onto
ordinary putter handles (this
item was produced). Prior to
1930, between America and Great
Britain, only two more patents
were issued for fixed counterweight designs. For information
on adjustable counterweight designs, see page 391.

Designed to provide a pendulum stroke without requiring
a croquet stance, the grip on the
club pictured curves back
toward the golfer. The shaft on
this unique club is marked "The
Murray Putter \ Pat. Apld. For."
The back of the blade is marked
"Nicolls Indicator" in a circle
and "Hand Forged in Scotland \
10 \ Putter." George Nicoll's
"hand" cleekmark from the mid
to late 1920s is also present.

Underneath the leather, the
curved grip on the Murray putter is a thicker continuation of
the wood shaft; the wood itself
is exposed at the end of the grip.
A patent to cover this grip was
applied for but not issued.

In 1911, Lawrence Claude
Edward Gray, a golf professional
located in Croydon, England,
received a British patent (No.
26,974) for an angled grip similar
to the Murray curved grip. The
upper portion of Gray's grip
angles, on a straight line, back

toward the golfer. The angle is
created either by splicing a piece
of wood in place or by bending
the top of the shaft. The entire
grip is wrapped with leather.

In 1934 Avon Pardoe, of
Toronto, Canada, received a U.S.
patent (No. 1,967,993) for a
curved grip similar to the Murray
curved grip. Pardoe observed
that since ax handles were oval,
not round, shaping and curving a
grip like the end of an ax handle
would help "insure more accurate striking of the ball, and also
a greater sense of security in
holding the grip" (*Golf Illustrated*
[ny], Mar. 1935: 37). The rubber
"Rel-Ax" grip, as it was called
when first produced, could be
added to existing clubs. In 1936
Crawford, McGregor & Canby
began offering Pardoe's grip as
the "relax" grip.

Golf is the king of outdoor sports. Skill at it is something a rich man cannot buy, nor a poor one inherit; proficiency is only gained by hard work and much prayer.

(*Golfing*, Dec. 2, 1909: 20)

Perimeter Clubs

Fitting, Training, Walking, Gardening, Practice, & Other Golf Related "Clubs"

——— ||| ——————————————— |||

Perimeter clubs, not to be confused with perimeter-weighted clubs, are "golf clubs" that relate directly to the game of golf but are not built for ordinary use on a golf course.

Everyday items, from walking sticks to weed whackers, have been produced to resemble golf clubs. Some perimeter clubs were used as fitting clubs, some were used as training devices, and still others were used in golf-related games. Other perimeter clubs were constructed as awards, built as toys, or used solely by a trick shot artist.

An example of the extremes to which inventors would go when producing a perimeter club is the diminutive club Daniel G. Lilley, of Denver, Colorado, actually patented. In his U.S. patent (No. 1,782,931) dated November 25, 1930, Lilley presents a miniature golf club that attaches to a finger:

This invention relates to improvements in miniature golf clubs and has reference to a golf club that can be attached to the index finger and used for playing golf on a miniature [tabletop] golf course.

Designed to work with the flick of the index finger, Lilley's club consisted of a clubhead; a "cup-like member" that attached to the tip of the index finger; and a short, curved hosel that connected the clubhead to the cup-like member.

Whatever their specific purpose, perimeter clubs add dimension to any golf club collection. They are a genuine part of golf's evolutionary past and reflect the passion for the game held by yesterday's golfer.

While perimeter clubs are non-playable clubs, there were other clubs designed with non-playing features. These clubs were built for ordinary use on a golf course, but their "special features" had nothing to do with club performance. For example, Charles Gibson and Henry Norris Glym Hinde designed a club, covered under a British patent (No. 28,759) dated December 12, 1913, that included a six-inch measuring stick, for measuring stymies, in the end of the grip. In like manner, Edgar J. Bloom designed a club, covered under a U.S. patent (No. 1,520,113) dated December 23, 1924, that held a pencil in the end of the grip. One of the cleverest non-playing applications is described in a patent issued to Paul A. Czichos of Washington, D.C. According to his British patent (No. 284,531) dated June 15, 1927, Czichos devised a club that would place a tee in the ground at the proper height. The golfer fits a tee into the end of the handle. (The head of the tee is held in place by four thin bow springs running lengthwise inside the handle. A threaded rod in the base of the handle can be adjusted up or down according to how much the tee should protrude.) Pushing the handle against the ground places the tee in position; the engagement of the ground with the tee is sufficient to overcome the engagement of the springs with the tee head.

The New York Times *Golf man appears to have been carried completely off his feet by the American ladies' championship. This is what he says:*

"Miss Hoyt wore almost every day a golf skirt of dark brown cloth stitched around the hem, a flannel waist, old rose in color, and heavy tan shoes. As a rule she discarded a hat and played with her sleeves rolled back above her elbows. In fact, when the sun shone at all brightly there were few of the players who retained their coats or hats. These hats, by the way, were a picturesque feature of the event. They were for the most part the now fashionable Rough Rider ones of gray or brown felt, and most of them were wound with negligée bands of vari-coloured silk plaids. The caddies carried these hats, which made dots of colour all over the course. Altogether a prettier picture than this tournament presented, with its fair and graceful young maidens, their cheeks flushed with exercise, and their light or dark hair arranged à la pompadour and lit up by the golden mellow rays of the October sun, as with long, graceful sweeps they drove the ball over the verdure-clad links, with the blue waters of the Hudson below them, and the flaming woods of Autumn around them, could not well be imagined" (Golf, 18 Nov. 1898: 211).

A.G. SPALDING & BROS.
FITTING CLUBS

The drivers pictured are "fitting clubs" designed to help golfers determine the correct length when ordering a new club to their specifications. The shaft in each club is marked in half-inch increments like a yard stick. To use this club, right-handed golfers simply position the head a comfortable distance away from their hands when addressing the ball and then check the shaft measurement behind the heel of the left hand. This measurement provides the overall length needed in a new club. If a golfer wondered what it would be like to use, say, a 46-inch shaft, the golfer could grasp a fitting club just below that point and get a genuine feel for what he or she would have to swing.

The shorter fitting club pictured is marked "A.G. Spalding & Bros." on the crown, "1" above the soleplate, and "975 \ Pat'd Apr 24, 1923" on the sole-plate. This patent date identifies George Mattern's U.S. patent (No. 1,452,695) that covered the trapezoid shape of the soleplate. Mattern's patent soleplate is inconsequential as a collectible feature. Its shape is but a subtle refinement with little interest or visual impact.

The longer fitting club pic-tured is marked "J. Martucci" \ Special" on the crown. The measuring marks on Martucci's shaft match those on the Spalding club, so it can be assumed that Spalding produced this club for Martucci.

Both clubs are flat along the upper portion of their shafts where the measuring marks are stamped into the wood. The Spalding driver is marked from 22 to 48 inches on the flat length of its shaft. The Martucci driver is marked from 24 to 50 inches. The flat side on the Spalding shaft is cut at an angle to allow the golfer to grip the shaft and position his or her thumbs in a natural fashion.

All fitting clubs are good col-lectibles, but the longer the club the better. Examples made by both British and American mak-ers range between 44 and 50 inches long. For an adjustable-length fitting club, see Ford's dri-ver on page 407.

For reference, A.G. Spalding & Bros. was founded in 1876 by the well-respected and admired Albert Goodwill Spalding and his brother, J. Walker Spalding:

Albert Goodwill Spalding . . . was born at Byron, Ill., U.S.A., 2nd September 1850, and died at Point Loma, San Diego, California, on 9th September 1915.

A.G. Spalding was one of those big men that the remote country dis-tricts of a big country seem to naturally produce. He not only stood 6 feet 2 inches in his stockings, and turned the scale at 20 stone, but he had big ideas, a big brain, and, above all, a great big heart. . . .

Although his name here is associ-ated with all that is best in golf clubs and golf balls, his heart was ever true to the game of his youth, the game he did more to popularise than any other man—Baseball.

His greatest fame as a baseball player and manager came from his association with the Chicago Cubs in 1876, only retiring as its President in 1891, when he was the most famous player in the world. . . .

It was in 1876, with his brother, Mr. J. Walter Spalding, that the great athletic goods business was founded which now employs so many thou-sands of hands, and has spread its branches right round the globe.

It was his wish to make the term "Spalding Quality" household words wherever sportsmen congregate, and he succeeded (Golf Monthly, Oct. 1915: 26).

A.G. Spalding & Bros. first offered golf equipment in 1893.

WALTER HAGEN
SWING TRAINER

The club shown below has a large and very heavy metal disk recessed into the top of the head. Attached to the center of the disk is a threaded rod that extends down, through the center of the head, to the sole. A nut screws on the rod and holds the weight in place. The nut fits flush with the sole.

The shaft has a "Walter Hagen \ Made in USA" decal applied below the grip. (Shaft decals came into prominence during the 1920s.)

Head-weighted drivers, designed for practice and not for play, are used to stretch the golfer's muscles and to help the golfer develop a full, powerful swing. This Hagen swing trainer is the earliest and only one of its type known to the author.

The original varnish has peeled off the metal plate in a few places. The neck whipping is not original.

A.G. SPALDING & BROS.
"GOLFEX,"
INDOOR SWING TRAINER

Measuring only 25 3/4 inches in length, the Spalding "Golfex" club pictured is a golf-exercise club. Its short length allowed golfers to pack this club in a suitcase, take it on a trip, and swing it for exercise—even indoors! To help this swing trainer approximate a full length club, the head is loaded with lead. The weight was installed through two holes in the face. The holes were then closed with two wooden plugs.

A hard-to-find collectible, the Golfex dates to the 1920s. A few other makers also offered such clubs. Among others seen by the author, a 28-inch-long example marked "Archie Compston" was slightly different. It was filled with lead through a small hole in the back of the head.

An unpainted Heavy Colonel ball, complete with rubber core and bramble cover, is pictured with this club. Heavy Colonel balls were made in 1914 by the St. Mungo Manufacturing Company, of Newark, New Jersey, and Glasgow, Scotland.

THOMAS L. GATKE
SPRING SHAFT,
SWING TRAINER

Thomas L. Gatke, of Chicago, Illinois, received a U.S. patent (No. 1,529,305) dated March 10, 1925, that covered the very unusual spring-shafted club, marked "Springy Shaft Co. \ Chicago" on its head, pictured here. The wood shaft in this club still bears the original black finish used to match the 3 1/4 inch long metal spring located just above the head. The spring is held in place by two long metal collars: one metal collar attaches to the head and the other attaches to the wood shaft.

According to Gatke's patent, the object of his invention was:

to promote the perfection of the player's stroke by showing errors or imperfections as they occur in the different parts thereof.

Gatke's club includes a coiled spring in the shaft, though his patent allowed for substituting either a flat piece of spring steel or a small spring hinge for the coiled spring. Gatke calculated that a spring in the shaft would help the golfer improve the tempo of his or her swing. Referring to his club, Gatke notes:

In the back or upward swing the club should begin to gain speed when the swing is about half made, or not much before that, and should gradually increase until the top of the stroke. Too much speed at the beginning of the back swing, or a jerk at any point, spoils the stroke . . . .

Gatke's patent also discusses how "the back swing should blend into the forward swing" and the problems of a "faulty follow-through." Gatke believed his spring shaft would indicate whether or not the golfer had any difficulties taking the club back, transitioning into the downswing, or following through.

Thomas Gatke was not the first person to consider incorporating the flexibility of a spring into a golf shaft. Earlier patents were granted for similar clubs intended, however, to hit the ball farther, not to train a golf swing.

Wilfred L. Bullows's British patent (No. 4,291) dated February 26, 1896, calls for making the bottom half of a hosel from a flat piece of spring steel. This patent also allows for the possibility of including a spring in the shaft.

Charles Parmele's U.S. patent (No. 695,579) dated March 18, 1902, calls for attaching a short length of "springy-metal" to the head and adjustably clamping it to the shaft. As illustrated in the patent, the springy-metal piece is thin, round, and visible for an inch or two between the head and the end of the wood shaft.

David Williams and William H. Booth's British patent (No. 22,968) dated October 23, 1903, declares that the shaft could either be inlaid with cane (p. 508) or made from two pieces of wood joined by a flat piece of spring steel surrounded by rubber. Marked "Nicholls / Special," a

Williams and Booth driver with a two-inch-long strip of spring steel located just above the neck is found in the USGA's antique club collection. A steel ferrule at each end of the steel strip connects the strip with the shaft above and below it.

Francis C. Hersey's U.S. patent (No. 826,102) dated July 17, 1906, calls for placing a section of vulcanized rubber (which could include a piece of spring steel) between the head and shaft. This "resilient section" was to be covered by "lashing." This club was advertised as the "Hersey Teledrive" (*Golf* [ny], Mar. 1908: 175).

David Wightman's British patent (No. 1,819) dated February 4, 1915, requires using a short spring to connect the shaft with the head. After adding a ferrule, the neck was to be covered with leather.

Of the five additional patents just mentioned, only two are known to have produced clubs: Hersey's and Williams & Booth's. The Gatke wood pictured is the only one known to the author.

PRO-SWING GOLF CO.

"PRO-SWING"
GOLF PRACTICE CLUB

Have you wondered why you usually play your worst game right after a golf lesson? The poor suffering pro knows. You are trying to think of too many things. With the Pro-Swing Practice Club, you have but one and only one thing to thing about—swing the club. That's all. It makes you swing correctly. It compels you to drag back the club head instead of lifting it too soon. It compels you to shift your weight correctly. It compels you to put wrist snap into the shot. It compels you to follow through.

The Pro-Swing looks like the finest of golf clubs except for one important difference. Its head is a correctly weighted ball attached to a specially designed steel spring of exactly the right tension. This spring and weight "invite" the wrists into action and gently urge your body into an easy, natural pivot. You can't sway if you want to. You can't jerk your head up. You instinctively stay down on the ball. And your arms sweep through with a wrist-snap that gives you the feel of the perfect shot perfectly played.

Even a man who has never broken a hundred will instantly see his faults corrected as he swings the Pro-Swing Practice Club. The Pro-Swing principle of balanced weight and spring induces just the right amount of pull on the arms and body to produce smooth rhythm and correctly applied power.

Regular practice with this club will groove you in the correct swing. And if you swing correctly you are bound to make lower scores.

The Pro-Swing Practice Club would be worth the cost if it were used only for strengthening the wrists. Anyone can use it. A 90-pound girl can swing it as easily—and correctly—as a 190-pound man. It can be used anywhere that you can swing a regulation size golf club: in your home, your office, on the course, or In your yard (The American Golfer, Aug. 1933: 35).

The "Pro-Swing" was publicly endorsed by Ernest Jones, "the famous teacher at the Women's National Golf and Tennis Club, Glen Head, Long Island" (*American Golfer*, Nov. 1933: 35).

The Pro-Swing practice club pictured below, marked "Copyright 1933 Pat. Applied For \ Pro Swing \ Pro Swing Golf Co. Inc. \ New York City" on a shaft decal, has a brass ball on the end of a nine-inch steel spring. Some examples have a lead ball on the end of the spring.

Pro-Swing clubs are popular collectibles and become available from time to time. In 1933, depending on when they placed their order, golfers who were so inclined could have the Pro-Swing Golf Practice Club delivered to their door for either $7.50 or $6.00. Today it will cost more . . .

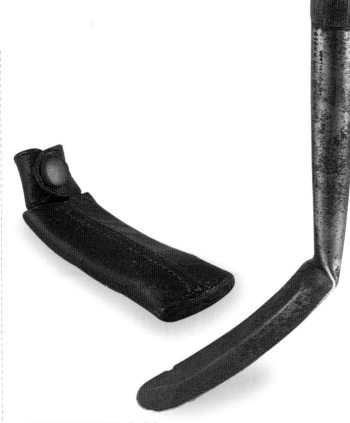

HOLTZAPFFEL & CO.

"GOLF SICKLE"

Golf Sickle. Wonderful exercise cutting grass or weeds. Swing like a golf club. Send $1.00 Postpaid. Golf Sickle Co., 4137 McRee Ave. St. Louis, MO.

Boys, make big money selling the Golf Sickle—Send $1.10 for sample and price lists (Golfers Magazine, July 1928: 52).

The golf sickle pictured above, designed as a weed cutter complete with a protective leather cover for the blade, is marked "Regd Design No. 689194 \ Holtzapffel & Co." on the hosel. The British registered design No. 689,194, which covered a weed cutter for "garden field uses," was issued on March 25, 1922, to Holtzapffel & Company, 53 Haymarket, St. James, London.

Holtzapffel's weed cutter is no ordinary weed cutter. Given the sharp double-edge blade at the end of the steel hosel, any unfortunate soul in charge of chopping off a few weeds could practice his or her swing while "hard at work." Artistically designed to approximate a golf grip, the wood along the top twelve inches of the shaft is not only ribbed but also slightly larger in diameter than the rest of the shaft.

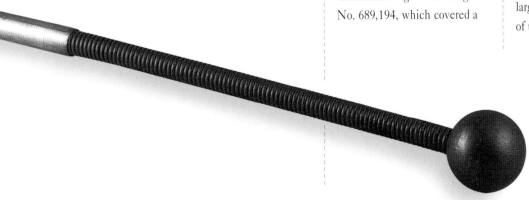

W.S. SIMPSON
LAWN, HOUSE, &
MARINE GOLF CLUBS

Lawn and House Golf . . . . is an adaptation of Golf, by which this game may be played on the Lawn (or indoors). Its great advantage lies in the use of bevelled metal discs, with a flat plateau on top and a hole in the centre of each, which are placed at any desired distance from each other on the Lawn or Floor. This does away with the necessity of cutting holes in the ground . . . . Its great resemblance to Golf in the method of playing makes it very interesting to all Golfers, or to those who wish to attain the art of playing Golf, especially for the practice of Putting. The Clubs used are of the ordinary shape and size; in fact, those who prefer it, can use their regular Golf Clubs (W.S. Simpson, 1894).

The two clubs shown here were originally sold as clubs for a game titled "The New Game Lawn and House Golf" and marketed under "Simpson's Patent." This game, manufactured sometime in the mid-1890s by B. Perkins & Son, Bermondsey, London, included:

six painted and numbered metal Discs or Holes, with flat plateau on top, four best Golf Clubs [two of each], four Colored Golf Balls, Book of Rules, &C., in a well made brass mounted box (W.S. Simpson, 1894).

These clubs were made not only for use on lawns but also for use on seagoing vessels! According to a Simpson's advertising broadside, Simpson's game

included "marine golf" and could be "adapted for decks of ships, yachts, &c., with sliders instead of balls."

Most game-type golf clubs are of little interest because they are poorly made. These Simpson clubs, however, are distinctive and well made, complete with splice necks, horn slips on the sole, sheepskin grips, and shafts that appear to be white ash.

In 1894, W.S. Simpson applied for two patents which he did not receive. His first application (No. 516) was for "apparatus to enable the game of golf to be played on lawns, carpets, and like surfaces" (*Golf*, 9 Feb. 1894).

His second application (No. 3,293) was also for "lawn, carpet, and golf" (1894 British Patent Gazette). Like many other prospective patentee's, Simpson went ahead and identified his game as patented. (See page 128 for more on the patent process.)

JOHN D. WILSON
"CROLF" DUPLEX CLUB

Wilson's duplex club, shown, was used to play "Crolf"—a hybrid of croquet and golf. A pamphlet titled *Crolf, As Good As Golf* provides a clear description of the game. Reproduced in part, it reads:

The new game, Crolf, meets the long felt want of those who do not play golf.

Crolf is the game for live societies, clubs, schools, Boy Scouts, Y.M.C.A. and Y.W.C.A. summer and winter resorts, hotels, city parks, towns and villages. Men, women and children alike enjoy the game. There are but few places where Crolf cannot be played.

The game is played practically the same as golf. The ball is knocked from a starting place into a cup (hole). Near this hole is another starting place for the second hole. The holes are a considerable distance apart. The course consists of 9 holes—the game being to take the ball thru the entire course with the fewest strokes possible.

Crolf satisfies the desire for sport and beneficial exercise. The course is shorter than a golf course [holes measuring 40 to 150 yards long were recommended]. The grounds need not be more than 5 acres. Each player uses only one ball and one club. The necessary half-days off, the extensive grounds, and the expensive outfits are not factors of this game.

Crolf gives the same opportunity for physical vigor as golf, but excessive strain is not demanded. A person with a weak body may play this game with great benefit. You can strike the ball as hard as you like. A good stroke will send it about 50 to 60 yards. You have only that distance to walk and you are ready to strike it again. Hence you have much less walking between strokes.

All you need is a set of 9 cups to sink into the ground for holes, 9 standards to mark the holes, and a club and a ball for each player. Lay your course out on a small piece of ground— three to five acres—and the game is on (National Crolf Company, 3).

The rules for playing Crolf, contained in the Crolf pamphlet, were the same as those for playing golf. Clubs were available for $6.60 each; balls were $2.50 each. "Cups and standards," designed to be left permanently in place, were also available.

The Crolf club pictured on this page has a standard hickory shaft and leather wrap grip. The head is not marked, but a few others which the author has seen are marked "Crolf" in raised

letters placed in a semicircle across the side of the head. The Crolf pamphlet also advertises a new and improved metal Crolf club having a steel shaft.

Crolf clubs were covered under a U.S. patent (No. 1,548,081) granted to John D. Wilson, of Danville, Illinois. Applied for on November 15, 1921, Wilson's patent was finally issued on August 4, 1925. According to his patent, Wilson was seeking "new and useful improvements in golf sticks" by "combining the salient features of a golf game as well as croquet." His aluminum duplex club was to be used with "a ball slightly smaller than a baseball, but of the same or similar composition."

The strange looking Crolf club is an intriguing collectible. Some collectors find it one of the most interesting clubs to evolve from golf. Other collectors might not be interested in this club because it was not made for use on a regulation golf course.

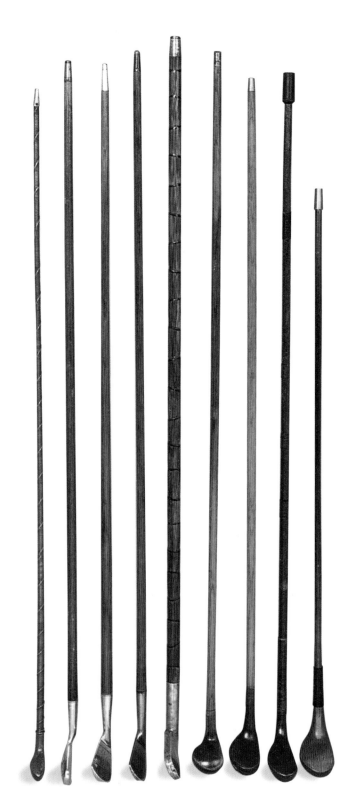

VARIOUS MAKERS
BUGGY WHIP
& WALKING STICKS

The more a walking stick looks like a golf club, the more desirable (collectible) it is. Some walking sticks are more a caricature of a golf club rather than a well-made clubhead in miniature. Such examples are of lesser interest. The golf club walking sticks and buggy whip on this page are worthy collectibles.

From left to right, the following items are pictured:

1. A flexible buggy whip marked "Pat. June 15, 1909" on the head and "Made in U.S.A." on the hosel. The shaft in this buggy whip consists of spring-steel wire wound around a thin wood core.

2. A putter walking stick marked "Gem Putter \ Rustless Iron" with "B&SA" (Brodie & Sons of Anstruther) in a triangle.

3. A line scored iron walking stick stamped "R. Forgan" with Forgan's "crown" cleekmark (see p. 69).

4. A smooth face iron walking stick marked with Robert Condie's "rose" trademark on the back of the head.

5. An iron walking stick with a hallmarked sterling silver head marked "Geschutz" (an Austrian box maker). The head has two different compartments which are gilded inside. The large compartment on the back of the blade holds cigarettes; the compartment on the back of the hosel, which includes a striking surface, holds matches. The picture below shows the compartments open.

6. A socket head wood walking stick marked "T.H.B.L." on the crown. This head has a red fiber face insert affixed by five small wood dowels, a lead back-weight, and a horn sole.

7. An unmarked socket head wood walking stick with horn sole and lead backweight. The plain appearance of this wood makes it the most common item on this page. Socket head woods are the most common walking sticks.

8. A transitional wood head walking stick marked "D. Anderson" on the crown. Complete with a splice neck, this item dates to the 1890s. (For more on David Anderson Jr. see page 90).

9. A fork splice walking stick marked "A.H. Scott \ Patent \ 21,444" inside a circle on the crown. The Prince of Wales plume, which dates this club between 1902 and 1910, is stamped on the crown. (For more on Scott's fork splice see page 136.)

Golf club walking sticks were used upside-down. The head served as the handle—like the head of a cane—and the grip end touched the ground.

F. DE COVERLY VEALE
SAMUEL E. STAFFORD
CAVITY HEAD,
UMBRELLA PUTTER

The July 3, 1891 issue of *Golf* briefly refers to a golf club walking stick produced at that time. It reads:

A golf club in miniature, suitable as a walking-cane, is now being made by Messrs. Reid and Laidlaw, whole-sale ironmongers, Edinburgh. The idea is, of course, not quite new, but the general design of this little club will, I fancy, be novel to most people. The heads are prepared as cleeks, mashies, and irons, and being fully nickel-plated, with smart greenheart shafts, the effect as a whole is distinctly attractive. Ladies will at once take them into favour, as in the large majority of cases the canes will be found quite suitable for golf as played by the fair sex, while, when tired of the game, by simply reversing the end, they are provided with a very serviceable and artistic walking-stick (Golf, 3 July 1891: 270).

The umbrella putter shown includes items patented by two different individuals: Frederick John de Coverly Veale and Samuel E. Stafford. Stafford's patent, assigned to the National Umbrella Frame Company, of Pennsylvania, covered the "connecting means" between the "umbrella ribs and stretchers." One of the metal ribs inside this umbrella is marked "National \ Pat. Dec. 20, 1904," the date of Stafford's patent. Frederick de Coverly Veale's patent covered the hollow Schenectady-style clubhead, complete with a hinged sole, that functions as the handle of this umbrella.

According to Veale's patent (No. 12,883) dated June 22, 1905, his golf clubheads:

are made in such a manner as to be able to carry a sponge, for cleaning golf balls, scoring cards, or other like objects.

His patent illustrates a sliding cover on a hollowed sole, but it states that a hinged cover is acceptable:

The cover need not necessarily be a slidable one. It might take the form of a hinged flap instead. Moreover, the cavity could be on the upper face or on any other suitable part of the head. The loss of weight consequent upon the cavity can be made up by the addition of lead or other metal suitably inserted in the head.

Even though de Coverly Veale's patent does not discuss usability, his putter head was usable—the hinges being located well below the center of the ball—but not very practical.

An example of this umbrella putter is in the United States Golf Association's collection of antique golf equipment.

For what shall it profit a man, if he gain the whole world, and lose the last hole?

(*Golf Illustrated*, 24 July 1908: 84)

Replicas & Fakes

& Other Dilemmas

He informed me that his grandfather's . . . clubs were still in the possession of his family. . . . I enquired: "Ever heard of Philp . . . ?"

"Well that's funny, sir; it's the name that's on all my grandfather's clubs—H. Philp." I tried to suppress my feelings on receiving this information, and inquired indifferently if he would like to sell them to me, giving as my reason for purchasing that, although Philp was nothing great as a clubmaker, I had a fondness for old clubs. My conscience struck me slightly, as I reflected that I was attempting to deprive an innocent creature of his family heirlooms; but it quickly passed. "Well sir," he remarked; " 'tis true that I've a doctor's bill to pay, and nothing to pay it with, but I'm sure my wife won't like the idea of parting with grandfather's old clubs.

. . . But I was firmly resolved to have them; and In the end I came away with those relics, leaving behind me eight sovereigns, and a tearful couple, who assured me that they would not be able to sleep that night, thinking of what they had done.

. . . Next day saw [me] at [my] home links, and, seeking out the professional, I requested him to pass his opinion on the clubs. . . "Well," I inquired; "are they all right?" "Well, sir," he remarked, "they . . . certainly look old and all that sort of thing, but it's the first time I ever knew that persimmon was used in Philp's time" (From "A Deal In Relics"; Golfing, 5 May, 1910: 18).

Replica clubs clearly marked as such on their heads are not a problem; however, collectors invariably come across an occasional club whose origins are suspect. Sometimes the dubious club is a fake, purposely made to take financial advantage of the unsuspecting or unknowing. In other instances, the questionable club originally sold as an honest replica, but, after changing hands a few times, it is unknowingly reoffered as genuine. In either scenario, the prospective buyer of such a club may make a large financial mistake. Good collectibles are not cheap.

Another tactic used to deceive occurs when old clubs are altered to approximate a different, more valuable club. An unusual steel shaft club can be reshafted with a wood shaft, unusual wood shaft clubs being much more valuable. A heavy-headed lofter can have its toe cut or ground "square," so it will look like an earlier and more desirable iron. A rut niblick can have its dull blade crease cut and filed, to make the crease sharp, so the club will look more like an older track iron. An ordinary iron produced after 1900 can have holes cut into its blade, so it will look like a highly desirable water iron.

Fake and counterfeit clubs, which are becoming especially troublesome today, raised their ugly heads well over a century ago. In 1902 Horace Hutchinson reported that Hugh Philp's clubs had already been blatantly forged:

There is many a club boasting Hugh Philp as its creator which that craftsman never saw— nor can we expect it would have been otherwise, since it is a matter of common report that at least two subsequent clubmakers had a "Hugh Philp" stamp with which upon the head of the club they would imprint a blatant forgery. The golfing connoisseur will inspect the time matured head of the old putter which claims Philp as its father with as cultured and microscopic a criticism as the dilettante lover of Stradivarius or the Amati will bestow upon their magic works (1902, 54).

Bennett Lang, a Scottish clubmaker born in 1849, was known to make copies of Philp clubs:

Ben had a great aptitude for hitting off a new head from an old model, and is largely employed by gentleman in the county and city who desire a worn-out club replaced by another exactly the same. At the date of our visit Lang was busy copying an old Philip [sic] baffy for a well-known Perthshire gentleman (Baxter 1899, 37).

How can you recognize an unmarked replica or a fake club? An antique dealer who once spotted a forgery about to sell at auction was asked how he could tell it was a fake. He responded, "It didn't sing to me." There is no better way to explain it. Once you know what to "listen for," real clubs will "sing." And it will be clear and unmistakable. Fraudulent clubs, void of both beauty and style, emit an air of uneasiness and discomfort. Like the person who produces them, bastard clubs are always discovered for what they are. It is only a matter of time.

In the pages that follow, the collector will find warnings, ways to detect replicas and frauds, and examples of existing fakes and replicas.

Before proceeding, however, it should be noted that a significant number of wood shaft putters were created during the steel shaft era. Crafted by such makers as Otey Crisman (Selma, Alabama) and Ted Smith (Upper Darby, Pennsylvania), these clubs were made for actual use, not display. They are clearly marked, and there is no mistaking what they are. Currently, such clubs draw little to no collector interest, collectors clearly differentiating between wood shaft clubs made during the wood shaft era and those made during the steel shaft era.

REPLICA
TROON CLUBS

Modeled after two Troon clubs, both of the woods pictured below were made as replicas during the late 1980s. The maker of these copies reproduced a number of them during the 1980s and 1990s. He always sold his clubs as replicas, but was neither consistent nor effective in marking them as replicas until recently. Many of his earlier examples were not marked, and the ones that were marked had only an initial inconspicuously stamped on either the shaft or the head. In either instance, a small bit of filing, a little stain, a coat of wax or varnish, and the inconspicuous marks will be gone with nothing appearing amiss—the unevenness of hand filing being common to both the shaft and head of authentic old clubs.

Replica clubs are not objectionable as long as the head is clearly marked in an unalterable fashion—the word "replica," the actual maker's name, or the maker's initials are all natural and appropriate solutions. Both clubs pictured are fine replicas, but unfortunately they are not well-marked as such. Consequently, as time moves on, they could be "misunderstood" and become the object of an expensive mistake.

The replica clubs pictured on this and the next page were reproduced to the exact measurements of the authentic clubs. However, as good as these copies are, they are somewhat exposed by these photographs. The replicas do not enjoy the same workmanship as the originals; their lines are not as true; and, although very representative in their own right, these clubs lack the character of the genuine items. This is to be expected; after all, they were made as replicas. Of course, the finish and the whipping are modern, though made to look old.

The upper picture on this page shows the sole of the club pictured near right. The head on this replica is 6 3/4 inches long, 2 1/4 inches wide, and 1 inch deep.

The maker of the replica clubs shown on this and the next page also produced early square toe irons, early round toe irons, and early track irons that, to the unexperienced eye, are difficult to tell apart from the real thing.

With good treatment a club will last for years. It is the rule with all first-class makers that after the selection is made the club-maker is not responsible as to what happens to the club. The customer must take it for better or worse. Of course, if there was a knot in the neck or shaft of the club where it broke soon after using it, there would be good reason for making an allowance. The chances of these defects, however, are remote, owing to the rigour of selection in material (Golf, 22 Jan. 1892: 304).

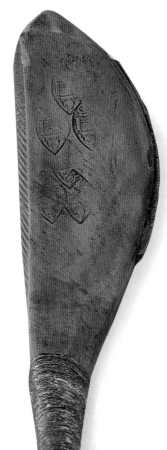

REPLICA
MID 1700S SPOON

REPLICA
"COSSAR" PUTTER

GENUINE
"DICKSON" PUTTER

The club shown below left and at the top of this page is modeled after an 18th century wood belonging to the Royal Burgess Golf Club, located on the outskirts of Edinburgh, Scotland. The original club has three small wood dowels sunk into the face and four wood dowels holding the ram's horn in place. The replica club includes these same features.

The replica head, made to the measurements of the original head, measures 6 3/8 inches long, 1 1/4 inches in face depth, and 2 1/16 inches wide.

The club shown below middle and second from the top on this page is a copy, complete with a simulated red keel finish, of the Cossar putter displayed in the James River Country Club Golf Museum, in Newport News, Virginia. Simon Cossar and his son, David, were clubmakers. Simon, born in 1766, died in 1811; David, born in 1788, died in 1816.

The replica Cossar clubhead, made by the same individual who made the other replica clubs presented on this and the facing page, measures 5 7/8 inches long, 2 1/4 inches wide, and 1 1/16 inches deep, the exact size of the original. Although the Cossar putter is exceptionally large, the genuine Dickson putter shown below right is even larger. Dickson clubs predate Cossar clubs. (Dickson, see p. 37).

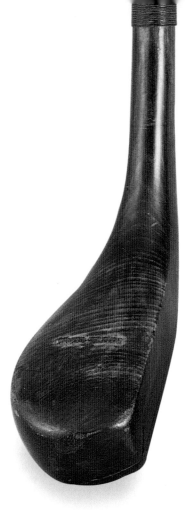

Long Nose Woods?

Pictured above are three long nose woods. The one on the left is marked "McEwan," the one in the center is marked "T. Morris," and the one on the right is unmarked. Which are replica clubs?

The McEwan club, made by Golf Classics of St. Andrews, Scotland, was advertised for sale as a replica by the "Golf Digest Gifts and Products" department in the March 1972 issue of *Golf Digest* (31). The head is 5 inches long, 1 inch deep, and 1 11/16 inches wide. The face has been stained the same color as the head in order to hide the white color of fresh cut wood.

The Tom Morris putter in the center has a red decal, located just below the grip, that not only shows a portrait of Old Tom but also lists the years he won the Open Championship. The shaft is stamped "Tom Morris \ St. Andrews \ Autograph Special." Probably made during either the 1920s or 1930s, this replica putter was merely a tourist item. Replica Tom Morris putters are still sold in St. Andrews out of the Tom Morris Golf Shop, located next to the 18th hole at the Old Course. This clubhead measures 4 3/4 inches long, 7/8 inch in face depth, and 1 5/8 inches wide. Its hickory shaft includes a nice sheepskin grip.

The unmarked play club on the right is an inaccurate and crude replica made in the early 1980s. From the white wood of the face to the basic shape of the head, everything about this club is wrong. The head is 5 inches long, 1 7/8 inches wide, and 1 inch in face depth.

All three of the clubs pictured are replicas, and there are many other replicas of long nose clubs in circulation. Some are, regrettably, marked with the name of a famous maker, such as "Wm. Park," "Wm. Dunn," and "T. Morris." Replicas have been a part of the scene at St. Andrews throughout the twentieth century. They are still being produced and are for sale in various gift and golf shops in Great Britain. A few Scottish companies are even dedicated to making replicas. A few American hobbyists have tried (and are currently trying) their hand at making replicas. Any person or business now making replica clubs should mark them as such in a clear and unmistakable way. This practice will enhance the clubmaker's reputation, not shadow it with suspicion.

The trained eye usually has little difficulty detecting replica clubs. When seen in real life, the examples shown are too small. The faces are too shallow, and the heads, with the exception of the unmarked replica, are neither as long nor as wide as the originals. The finish on these clubs is too new. Furthermore, each of these clubs lacks the shape, grace, and style found in the originals.

One-piece Woods?

Which of the clubs above are one-piece woods? The club on the far right, marked "Dunn's Patent" and also shown on page 146, certainly is.

The club second from the right, marked "Carruthers \ Sylviac \ Edinburgh" on the crown, is not. It is a socket head wood with the shaft running straight down into the head.

The club third from the right, marked "The Spalding," is the one-piece wood also shown on page 146.

The club on the far left, marked "Burke \ Grand Prize \ 849" on the crown, is not a one-piece driver. Notice that the grain of the shaft is completely different from the grain across the neck. Never mind the similar color of the head and shaft; never mind the lack of a definite line around the neck—this Burke driver is a socket neck wood with its neck tapered down in *typical* socket neck fashion. The whipping has simply been taken off the neck. The clear line between the top of the hosel and the shaft on the Carruthers wood is actually *uncommon* for a socket neck club. The line indicates that a small shoulder, used to abut the top of the neck, was built into the shaft.

"Sylviac" stamped on the Carruthers driver refers to the wood the clubhead was made from. Sylviac wood was promoted as being more durable than most woods:

Those who know the value of sylviac in club-head making may be pleased to know that the other day the good ship "Vedamore" was the bearer to these shores of 500 selected pieces of prime sylviac wood. The consignment is now being converted into sawn and bent club-heads by the well-known government contractors, Messrs. Joseph Owen and Sons, of Stanley Road, Liverpool (Golfing and Cycling, 27, Oct. 1898: 5).

An aluminium golf ball.—Recent efforts have been made to use this alloy for the purposes of golf balls; but, so far as the experiments have gone, they cannot be pronounced a success. The balls are, of course, hollow, and the first examples were made with a small hole at opposite sides. These holes considerably retarded the flight, and they emitted a weird, whistling sound in hurtling through the air. The holes have been abolished, and the latest ball we have tried in play is of the ordinary Silvertown pattern. There is no reason to complain of the weight, for aluminium is notoriously a light metal. But the ball we tried last week was flattened and indented on the side by the first blow, and every succeeding blow simply knocked the sphere into a series of angles. Besides, its flight and carry were very poor as compared with the gutta; it was difficult to get it more than a hundred or a hundred and twenty yards (Golf, 18 Dec. 1896: 267).

Water Irons?

Pictured near right is a replica water iron advertised and sold by the *Golf Digest* Gifts and Products department in 1972 as a "Water Iron 1848." Actually, it is a crude copy of a circa 1879 President iron (see p. 218). *Golf Digest* offered three additional replica clubs: two long nose woods and a "Sand Iron 1848." (The iron was actually modeled after a circa 1914 Hamsole iron [p. 223].)

These replica irons were stamped "replica" on the shaft, but more than one has been resold with "replica" unscrupulously sanded off. The example shown has a flat spot on the shaft where it once read "replica." Stain and wood burning marks were used to "age" the alteration.

The *Golf Digest* Gifts and Products advertisement for their two replica irons and two replica long nose clubs reads:

From St. Andrews, the home of Golf Classics: Handmade replicas of famous antique golf clubs. Golf Classics of St. Andrews is the only company which still practices the true art of handmaking golf clubs. These replica antique clubs are fashioned with the same patience and perfection of materials, the same design and craftsmanship as the rare originals now in priceless collections. Many golf experts say that the replicas are not discernible from the historic models (Golf Digest, Mar. 1972: 31).

This advertisement is incorrect on two points. First, these replicas were made with neither the same design nor craftsmanship of the original clubs. Second, anybody who can not tell the difference between these replicas and the real thing is not an expert.

The club pictured on the far right presents an entirely different dilemma. This club, modeled after the Roger Brown water iron (p. 226), is old but not original.

The area between each prong shows traces of the saw cuts used to create the prongs, and each prong has a different thickness. The problem is that all other similar water irons produced after 1900 (when this club was made) were drop forged. Exact dies of each head were made and a large hammer pounded these dies together, forming the hot metal inside the die to shape. Although this iron head was made that way, the prongs were not. They were cut. They could have been cut by somebody experimenting on their own, or they could have been cut by somebody who wanted a Roger Brown water iron without paying for one.

Another indication that this club was not originally designed and sold as a water iron is its weight. This club is extremely light, as would be expected after removing a substantial amount of metal from an ordinary head.

This club is clearly homemade when compared to any authentic rake iron, though the modifications may have been made during the wood shaft era. Conclusion: this club was not originally sold as a water iron and is worth only what somebody will knowingly pay for an altered club.

Sometimes clubs with aftermarket alterations or a rough finish are presented as "prototypes," a term that immediately waves a warning flag in front of an experienced collector. Such a description is usually pure hype and is used to sell a modified, unexplainable, and otherwise undesirable item. As shown by the fine craftsmanship used to construct the many one-of-a-kind clubs presented in this book, true club-makers did not lower the quality of their work when making a prototype.

In the author's opinion, a number of "not original" rake irons were offered for sale in 1994. In January a British auction house offered three fake rakes: one was modeled after the Forgan water iron shown on page 229; another was modeled after the Pearson iron shown on page 228, except it had only three slots across the face; and the third had two vertical slots through the toe and one through the heel. These clubs had many problems with their authenticity, but the most glaring was that none of the slots was symmetrical. In July two more fake rakes were auctioned. The first, marked "Fairlie A.S. [anti-shank] water iron," had a single slot cut across the blade of an anti-shank iron. The second iron had a completely open face except for two braces between the top and the bottom of the head. Not only was this club unbelievably lightweight, it was stamped "The Skeleton" at the base of the hosel in the same block letter type used on the fake Fairlie rake and a bogus "Monsoon iron" for sale at the same auction. (The "Monsoon club" had vertical grooves cut into what was once a smooth face.) Furthermore, all three of these clubs—the Fairlie rake, the Skeleton, and the Monsoon—had their unique names stamped one letter at a time. Clubmakers, almost without exception, used complete stamps in order to mark entire words or phrases on a clubhead with the single blow of a hammer. (The author has never heard of a genuine Skeleton or Monsoon iron and does not believe they exist.)

Pictured below, side by side, are two phony clubs once offered, at a serious price, to the author by an antique dealer from Southern California. Made to deceive, these clubs provide a lesson in the detection of a fake. Consider:

On the left is an aluminum head duplex club marked "Super Cleek" over one face and "Driver" over the other. The underside of the head is marked "Pat. Pend. \ W. Dalrymple." Dalrymple clubs were never marked "super" anything.

The sole, which has been artificially scuffed to approximate normal wear, has small triangular depressions struck into the head to "age" the club. The very same marks were applied to the shaft to make it look old and used.

The head is pinned through the *face*, which is unlike any other duplex club.

Dalrymple clubs do not have cross-scored faces, nor the irregular and paint-filled scoring found on this head.

The shaft was sanded and restained a darker color where it enters the head.

This head measures 2 5/16 inches in diameter, which is much larger than a genuine Dalrymple (see p. 412).

The club on the right is a super-giant niblick marked "Giant Niblick \ Special \ Pat. Pend. \ Edinburgh \ Made in Scotland \ Warranted Hand Forged." But notice how it is marked. All the letters are the same size! The letters were put on one at a time; the words are not straight and even; and all letters are from the same type, a type *identical* to that used on the Dalrymple club. Also, this club does not have a maker's mark, something all genuine giant niblicks have.

This club has a horrible head shape, void of the style and symmetry found in the real thing (see p. 469). The 4 1/16 inch face depth is not a correct size, and the 3 1/2 inch long hosel is much too short for such a big blade.

There are other "giveaways" to both of these clubs, but only one more will be mentioned. One good sniff of the giant niblick reveals that a chemical die such as "gun blue" was applied to the metal in order to age it artificially. If your nose does not work, use your eyes. The color of the metal is obviously uneven and unnatural.

The author has seen pictures of two other giant niblicks produced by the maker of the two clubs just described. Pictures of the first club were provided by another dealer who, when offered the club, suspected it was not right. It was a little different from the oversize niblick discussed here, but the head shape was not correct and also very ugly. Furthermore, it was stamped with the identical type used on the two clubs shown here—complete with uneven letters and words. Stamped "Hal Roach \ Producer \ 1927" on the head, this club came with a song-and-dance explanation that it was used by the Three Stooges in a Hal Roach movie and then bought at a Hollywood garage sale . . .

The second bogus giant niblick was stamped "Babe \ George Herman Ruth \ 60 Home Runs \ New York Yankees 1927," along with a few stars, on the back of the blade. This club consisted of a recently made blade welded onto the hosel of an old wood shaft iron, the original blade having been cut off. In an effort to hide the blade's modern origins, the entire clubhead had been "recently rusted" (easy to do). This club was offered to the New York City Sports Museum & Hall of Fame for inclusion in their December 1993 auction. When the club was recognized as fraudulent, it was pulled from the sale. The clubs were then offered for sale by a golf professional from Southern California.

FAKE
TRACK IRON

The fake track iron pictured is one of several produced in the late 1970s. These clubs were not sold as replicas; they were traded for real antiques.

There are a number of characteristics that identify this club as spurious. To begin with, the top of hosel lacks nicking. Close inspection reveals a black glue line between the top of the hosel and the shaft, and the hosel is not pinned nor was it drilled so it could be. The metal is still quite bright and, despite being aged with artificial pitting and nicks, it lacks the texture and patina of an authentic old club. The most obvious indicator that this club is a counterfeit, however, appears when one of its counterfeit siblings is placed next to it—the identical head shapes and matching finishes are glaringly obvious. Detailed inspection reveals that a few of the dents are in exactly the same places and are shaped exactly the same! The texture of the pitting is the same, and some of the highlights—the bright, smooth, rough, and grainy spots—are in exactly the same locations.

Because a number of these clubs were produced, some of them have minor differences. The author has seen one example that did have a pinned hosel, but it did not look natural. Furthermore, each of these clubs appears to have been individually aged, and their shafts are of different colors. As a final step in checking the antiquity of this club, all the individual needs to do is remove the shaft and look inside the hosel. If the hosel was drilled or cast, the club is a fake. Early irons always have an inside seam running down the length of the hosel. The seam was created when the sides of the hosel came together, one overlapping the other, while being formed by hand on a mandrel (see p. 209).

Appendices

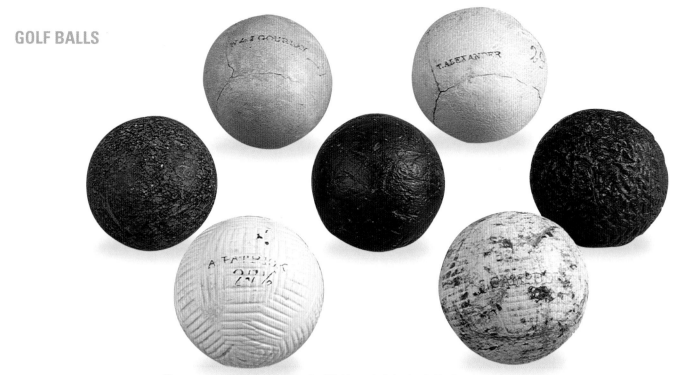

PICTURED LEFT TO RIGHT: *Top row—a "W&J Gourlay" and a "T. Alexander" feather ball. Center row—a smooth gutta percha ball, a random-marked hand-hammered gutta percha ball, and what is believed to be an experimental gutta percha ball. The surface of the experimental ball was possibly wrapped in burlap or some other fabric to create the unusual texture of the ball's surface. These gutta percha balls were left unpainted in order to allow the gutta percha to cure. Bottom row—an "Alex Patrick" and a "J. Campbell" hand-hammered gutta percha ball. Both balls are marked using the Forgan pattern.*

It is believed that the first golf balls ever used were made from wood, but no bona fide wooden golf balls from the 1600s or earlier remain:

The origin of the golf ball, like the origin of the game itself, is lost in the mists of antiquity; but there seems to be some reason for believing that the first balls were made of wood. That most painstaking of historians, Mr. Andrew Lang, has discovered a despatch of the reign of James IV. and I., in which the writer, describing the siege of a castle belonging to the Earl of Orkney, speaks of the cannon balls bursting into fragments "like golf balls" against the walls. It need not be pointed out that the leather ball stuffed with feathers . . . would not break into pieces in this fashion, however fierce the impact, but would only split open. This, indeed, was the exact fault that the users often found with them . . . (Golfing, 15 Dec. 1910: 13).

The siege of the castle belonging to the Earl of Orkney occurred in 1614 (see Johnston 1994, 66-67). However, there is clear evidence that sewn leather golf balls, possibly filled with wool if not feathers, were being made as early as 1554 (see Johnston 1994, 38). It appears that both leather golf balls and wooden balls once coexisted, the wooden balls being much less expensive and easier to provide.

Feather Ball Era.

Feather balls—made with a leather exterior and a feather-filled interior—are the oldest remaining golf balls known. Two feather balls, bearing the names of their makers, are pictured above in the top row. The "W&J [William and John] Gourlay" ball was made between 1836 and 1844, when these brothers worked together; the "T. [Thomas] Alexander" ball was made prior to 1841, when Alexander, only thirty-eight years old, died. The making of a feather ball was an art in itself:

The making of first-class feather balls was almost a science. For the benefit of the uninitiated, I shall endeavour to explain the operation.

The leather was of untanned bull's hide. Two round pieces for the ends, and a strip for the middle were cut to suit the weight wanted. These were properly shaped, after being sufficiently softened, and firmly sewed together— a small hole being of course left, through which the feathers might be afterwards inserted. But, before stuffing, it was through this little hole that the leather itself had to be turned outside in, so that the seams should be inside—an operation not without difficulty. The skin was then placed in a cup-shaped stand (the worker having the feathers in an apron in front of him), and the actual stuffing done with a crutch-handled steel rod, which the maker placed under his arm. And very hard work, I may add, it was. Thereafter the aperture was closed, and firmly sewed up: and this outside seam was the only one visible. When I say this, I of course refer to balls when new. Veterans showed the effects of service in open seams, with feathers outlooking; and on a wet day the water could be seen driven off in showers from a circle of protruding feathers, as from a spray-producer (Peter 1890, 8-9).

A few pre-1860 accounts of the making of feather balls mention boiling the feathers, the leather, or even the entire ball. These accounts are erroneous:

A London paper of 1845 says the leather, before the stuffing commenced, was previously soaked in boiling water; whilst a famous litterateur in "the fifties," who was himself an excellent golfer and a most charming writer on the game, makes a still queerer mistake, and says:— "The feathers themselves were boiled." So queer did these statements seem that we asked old Tom—the greatest living authority on the subject—and he kindly writes:— "The balls were stuffed with ordinary cocks and hens feathers, and their covering was made of bull's hide, and neither the feathers nor the leather were boiled." A saddler, again informs us that no one would ever dream of soaking leather in boiling water, but that it is occasionally steeped in lukewarm water. As to the material, it may be mentioned that pigskin was frequently used . . . (Golf Illustrated, 7 Dec. 1900: 204).

Alum was used to cure the hide. Describing how to make a feather ball, Tom Morris states:

I am not sure if many people now will know how the old featheries were made . . . . You had a little bag or pocket composed of bull's hide, which had previously been cured with alum, and then you stuffed it as full as possible with feathers. You could put about a hatful of feathers into one ball, and the stuffing of them was no easy job . . . . When that was done, you had just to sew up the opening in the side of the pocket and then your ball was made (Leach 1907, 35-36).

The use of alum was also mentioned by James Balfour when he described the process of making a feather ball:

In making [a feather ball] the leather was cut into three pieces, softened with alum and water, and sewed together by waxed thread, while a small hole was left for putting in the feathers . . . . The hole in the leather, which did not affect the flight of the ball, but slightly interfered with its putting quality, was then sewed up, and the ball received three coats of paint. A man could make only four balls in a day. They were thus scarce and expensive, and were not round, but rather oblong (1887, 16).

Feather balls were difficult and time consuming to make:

The family of Robertson, from which Allan descended, . . . were traditional manufacturers of golf balls in St. Andrews for generations. Allan himself made balls that rivalled the famous 'Gourlays' from Musselburgh, the best ball of its time. In 1840, he turned out, assisted by Tom Morris, 1021 'featheries'; in 1841 a total of 1392, and in 1844 no fewer than 2456 balls. The making of 'featheries' was an arduous and wearisome business. It was also extremely unhealthy, and many ball makers contracted lung trouble and asthma, that led to early deaths (Robertson 1967, 46).

A substantial number of feather balls were produced:

The manufacture of golf balls at St. Andrews affords employment to about ten or twelve men, constantly at work; and besides the consumption of the place, which is about three hundred dozen annually, they find means to export every year to Edinburgh, Glasgow, Aberdeen, Perth, and other places, upwards of sixty gross, or eight thousand six hundred and forty balls. A good workman makes about nine balls in a day. . . . The employment is accounted unhealthy, and many of the ball-makers have been observed to fall sacrifices to consumption; whether it be that the flue arising from the musty feathers they use being inhaled by the breath communicates a taint to the lungs, or that the mode of forcing in these feathers confines and injures the chest (Grierson 1807, 238-239).

Writing in the old "Statistical Abstract of Scotland" in 1838, the Ministers of St. Andrews give the manufacture of Golf Balls in St. Andrews as 10,000 annually, nearly one-half of which were used in the town itself. Some were sent as far as Calcutta and Madras. A good workman could turn out from fifty to sixty balls a week (Golf, 8 July 1892: 278).

Both feather balls pictured on the previous page are marked "29" in ink on their cover. The numbering of feather balls as well as gutta percha balls was a topic of considerable confusion:

Mr. H.S.C. Everard, in his book, "Golf in Theory and Practice," says, as to the weight of golf balls: "They are usually marked 26, 26 1/2, 27, 27 1/2, 28, but whether these numbers are merely arbitrary, or have some cabalistic meaning attached to them, is a question which has repeatedly agitated the mind of the inquiring golfer. The usual explanation is that they denote the weight in drachms avoirdupois; but if

a 27 ball be weighted, it will be found almost exactly to turn the scale at 1 1/2 oz.— not 27 drachms, but 24.

"Allan Robertson appears to have been conscious of this discrepancy, which he sought to explain by saying that golf balls came under apothecaries' weight . . . . But, as weighed by the man of pills and potions, the result is 10 drachms 40 grains, which leaves us more than ever in the dark. . . . A ray of light appears if we select troy weight, by which balance a 27 turns the scale at 1 oz. 7 dwt.; and as 20 dwt. equals 1 oz., we may perhaps regard the golf ball as a gem, to be estimated in pennyweights Troy, a conclusion which the enthusiast will doubtless gladly accept" (The Golfer, 3 Feb. 1897: 85).

While writing on this subject, we may allude to another singular thing in regard to golf balls, and that is the hazy notion golfers have as to the exact interpretation of the figures 27, 27 1/2, 28 stamped on balls. They denote the sizes, is the explanation accepted, and this is as much as the average man wants to know. Authorities differ, too. Willie Park, jun., for instance, and he ought to know, says that these figures represent the weight in drachms Avoirdupois; while H.C. Everard, and he ought likewise to know, has arrived at the conclusion that pennyweights Troy is what is meant. . . . We have today able golfers, men versed in the lore of the game, unable to agree on this simple little question. If we may judge the results obtained by scale, then pennyweights Troy is the explanation (The Golfer, 2 Feb. 1898: 90).

In an attempt to explain the numbers marked on gutta percha balls, "R.B.," in a letter to the editor, recalled how William Gourlay weighted the feather balls he made:

Sir,—We must go back to the days of the old feather ball to understand correctly the meaning of the weights marked on golf balls, as the marks were the same then as now. William Gourlay, of the links at Bruntsfield, Edinburgh, was about the largest and best maker of feather balls, and I have often seen him weigh them. He used no weights whatever, but simply placed the ball on one side of a pair of scales, and so many leaden pellets of shot on the other, but what size of shot I now forget (Golf, 3 Feb. 1899: 413).

Edward Blyth, a golfer during both the feather ball era as well as the gutty ball era, believed the numbers on a feather ball and the numbers on a gutta percha ball had different meanings:

Your correspondent, "T.W.G." in issue of 15th says, "there is a standard weight of Golf balls between 27 and 27 1/2 dwt., but no standard size," and that "the old feather ball varied both in size and weight according to the maker." The old feather ball was made of three pieces of leather cut with a knife. Sewn together and stuffed with feathers it was impossible to make them all to a given size, so when finished they were weighed and marked with pen and ink the number of pennyweights each weighed.

The gutta-percha ball is made in a metal mould and any quantity can be produced of exactly the same size, but the figures now used, 27 and 27 1/2, do not represent pennyweights. The weight of a 27 1/2 ball usually weighs 24 to 24 1/2 dwt., while the same ball made up runs from 21 1/2 to 22 1/2 dwt.

I played golf for many years before the introduction of guttas with feather and leather, and the weights I usually played with were 28 and 29 with the wind, 32 and 33 against it, such sizes being commonly used by other golfers . . . . From the above you will see that the weight of balls now in use is roughly 1 1/2 oz. and under, while in old times they were from 1 3/4 to 2 oz. and upwards, and while formerly there was a standard weight, now the standard is a size (Golf Illustrated, 29 Sep. 1899: 456).

Another letter writer, relating his belief on the way feather balls were sold, concluded that the numerals on golf balls—whatever they once meant—meant one thing to one maker and something else to another!

Sir,—Let me inform E.P.B. that the mark "27 1/2" on golf balls originally referred to the weight, not the size. Before the introduction of gutta percha, the finely prepared feathers, of which the balls were made, were always sold by troy weight. Thus "27 1/2" meant dwts. Latterly, however, the figures have been used to indicate size; but unfortunately, makers have not stuck to any regulation standard, one maker's "27 1/2" is different from another's; consequently, we are never quite sure of the weight and size of the ball (Golf, 3 Feb. 1899: 413).

Both weight and size were of interest to the golfer using feather balls:

We would recommend the Golfer, however, to be provided with both light and heavy balls, to play with, or against the wind. . . . A medium sized ball is, according to the ballmaker's scale, No. 28; above that number, balls are considered heavy; below light. The larger a ball is, the more easily will it be putted with; for this reason, heavy balls are preferred by those players whose chief excellence lies in the short game (Farnie 1857, 64).

Feather balls were capable of traveling long distances. Two accounts document the use of feather balls to achieve lengthy drives. These accounts, however, acknowledge the exception, not the standard.

In 1836 Samuel Messieux, "on a slightly frosty day, with a gently following wind," drove a feather ball 361 yards at St. Andrews (Browning 1955, 139). Messieux was a fine golfer famous for his strength. His drive is considered to be the longest ever made with a feather ball.

In 1786 John Gibson, at the Glasgow Golf Club, drove five feather balls for an average distance of 192 yards, slightly uphill. Another drive was 222 yards, slightly downhill. The request to measure Gibson's drives came from Matthew Orr, who was in London, and the measurement of each drive was made by two Glasgow merchants (Johnston 1993, 296). Given the distant request and the meticulous, down-to-the-inch, measurements signed by two prominent witnesses, Gibson was probably known as an exceptionally long driver. (For more on the distance achieved by both feather and gutta percha golf balls, see page 41; also Low 1905, 14-15.)

Gutta Percha Era.

By 1850 the feather ball was well on its way to obsolescence. Gutta percha, a gum derived from various Malaysian trees (see p. 277) was being used to make golf balls. The gutta percha ball was easier to make, less expensive to buy, and, as time proved, better to golf with:

St. Andrews. . . . There is a branch of manufactures almost peculiar to this place—viz. the making of golf balls from leather and feathers, which has been declining for a long time past, and appears destined ere long to be numbered with the things that were. Among the many purposes to which gutta percha is applicable, golf ball making is one in which it has attained an ascendancy, to such an extent that, we may say, the gutta percha balls have almost completely superseded the leather ones in general use. The two establishments at the links, which were wont in times past to do a thriving business in making the leather and feather balls, have since the invasion of the gutta percha, been gradually declining in prosperity, until, we believe the trade has all but come to a stand from want of demand for its productions. Popular opinion is unmistakably in favour of the gutta perchas, which have one strong recommendation in their favour, in being obtainable for a least half the price of the leather ones. Simplicity of manufacture is also in favour of the guttas, as every player may purchase the raw material and become his own maker if he likes. We believe that the superiority of the gutta percha over the leather balls for playing with is a disputed point. We suppose that the makers of the old description of balls will find it expedient to give way to the tide of public opinion in favour of the gutta percha, and turn their attention to supplying the public demand with balls of that description (Fifeshire Journal, 10 Dec. 1850: 3).

The first gutta percha ball was invented by Robert A. Paterson in 1845:

The First "Gutta."—Rev. Dr. Robert A. Paterson, the founder of the first Missionary Training College of the United States, and for many years president of the Binghampton Ladies' College, New York, is [credited] with the introduction of the "gutta" to St. Andrews golfers in 1846. In 1845 he first rolled a lot of gutta percha clippings (used in his fathers's business) into a ball, painted it, and used it on St. Andrews links, vainly trying to keep it white, and coming back each time with a cracked ball. His brother in Edinburgh improved on it, and sent several dozens to London and St. Andrews, stamped "Paterson's Composite Golf Ball." R.A. Patterson the boy, left some with Melville Fletcher, South Street, and Joseph Cook, Market Street, booksellers, and they lay ignominiously in the window and were finally dusted out. He then took them to Mr. Stewart, at the time in charge of the old "Union Golf Parlor," St. Andrews, and with the daring of an unsophisticated boy ran over to "Allan Robertson's" where "Tom Morris" and "Allan" were shoving feathers into queer looking skins, and "Allan" gave the Guttas a good examining, and then showed the whites of his great handsome eyes, but never spoke a word. "Tom Morris" rolled the white balls over and over, and handed them back all thumb marks to young Paterson. Recent correspondence between Mr. Morris and Dr. Paterson in America tells that the die was cast for the gutta ball then and there, and the grand ancient "feather fliers" had received their death blow. This was on the eve of young Paterson's going to America (Paterson 1901, 1,2; also published in St. Andrews Citizen, 25 Oct. 1895).

Robert Paterson was not alone in bringing the gutta percha ball to the world. John Paterson, Robert's brother, played a vital role. In a letter published in 1901, "D.C." recalled John Paterson and his initial involvement:

I remember the Paterson family well . . . . I knew John best. He was a man of very considerable ingenuity, and very 'handy' in many ways. I recollect of him making a mould for gutta percha golf balls, and of seeing himself and his sons moulding the balls. He sold them wholesale to dealers in the golfing trade. My own opinion is . . . that it was John and not his younger brother Robert . . . who invented the "gutta ball" (The Scotsman, 25 June).

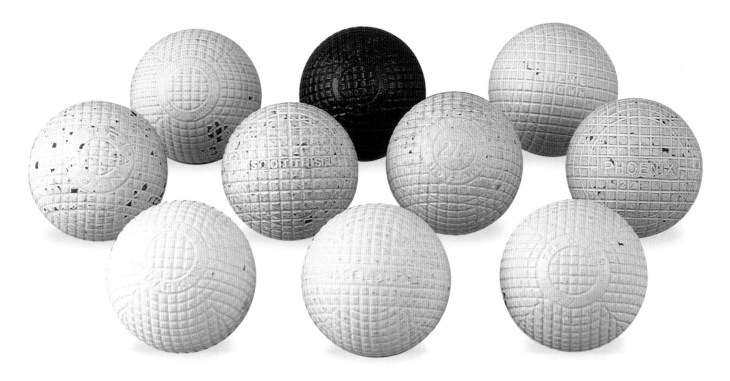

A small collection of molded gutta percha balls, circa 1890s, are pictured. Left to right, they are as follows: Top row—a B.G.I Company, an unpainted Scoto, and a Silvertown ball. Center row—a Cestrian, a Scottish, an A. Haskins of Hoylake, and a Phoenix ball. Bottom row—a Henley, a Musselburgh, and an Ocobo ball. To become durable, the better black gutta percha balls were left alone and unpainted for approximately six months (Golf [ny], Mar. 1901, 190). The Scoto pictured was left unpainted so it could become seasoned over an even longer period of time, the golfer painting it just before using it.

In actuality, Robert Paterson invented the first gutta percha ball, but John improved it (made it more durable—less susceptible to cracking) and produced the first ones ever sold.

During the initial years following their introduction, gutta percha balls were primarily made by hand. According to James P. Forgan, who, besides being Robert Forgan's brother and first apprentice (working briefly in 1856/1857), was a ballmaker by profession:

At first the gutta-percha was in the form of a sheet, which was cut up in pieces, and when softened in hot water was drawn out in the form of a ribbon and wound up into a ball and pressed with the hand on a smooth board; and then it was heated again and pressed until it was as solid as possible, and as there were no moulds at that time, the ball was rounded in the hands, and after some practice, a good ball maker could make them very round indeed. Then they were dropped into cold water to harden,

and had to be constantly moved in the water to keep them round, for if they were left still in the water, the part that was above the surface would be swelled out of shape. The golf balls were made in this manner for some years (Golf Illustrated, 27 Dec. 1907: 13).

Due to their smooth surface, early gutta percha balls had difficulties flying:

When Paterson's ball was first made, the surface was perfectly smooth, and marked only by lines, engraved by the turning-lathe, in imitation of the seams of the old leather. It did not fly well when new, but did better after being well hacked. This suggested hammering. At first this was very inartistically done, and the ball simply "bashed" here and there with the heavy hammer head. And the Rev. Dr. Forgan, in his excellent little book [1881: 41], tells us that it was actually Allan Robertson, the bitter foe of the newcomer at first, who ventured to reverse the hammer and use the sharp edge, and that a little later the lines came to be regularly crossed in

the beautifully finished diamond pattern we all remember (*The Scotsman*, 25 June 1901).

Hammering and marking the surface of a smooth gutty ball allowed it to track through the air and hold its line of flight. Robert Forgan is credited with being the first to form a regular pattern on hand-hammered balls, "and the same pattern has continued ever since" (*Golf Illustrated*, 27 Dec. 1907: 13).

Whether Forgan was the first to create a pattern for hammering balls is debatable, if not doubtful; but Forgan's pattern was adopted as the standard pattern for a hand-hammered ball. Both gutta percha balls in the bottom row pictured on page 556 are marked with Forgan's pattern.

When hand-hammering a smooth gutty ball, the maker used a hammer and a small cup, usually of wood or iron, held in a vise:

In those days the balls were hand-hammered—that is, after being moulded were indented with the

"claw" of a hammer. Jamie [Anderson] used to give occasional exhibitions of his skill at this work. The ball when undergoing the process was placed in a wooden cup and held between the fingers of the left hand for the hammering process, and he could carry it through without once having to stop to turn over the ball, a feat of which he was justly proud (Golfing, 31 Aug. 1905: 11).

Surprisingly, hand-hammering a golf ball could be done rather quickly. According to Willie Park Jr., a self-proclaimed "expert hammerer of balls":

Sixpence a dozen was the hammering fee, and each ball was given from 240 to 280 blows, according to size, which occupied me about two and a half minutes. I remember that I invented a system by which I kept my right elbow fast to my side while the forearm worked like a lever, and thus I could always depend upon the hammer coming down to precisely the same spot each time, while my left hand worked the ball (Leach 1907, 103-104).

In order to increase the speed with which a ball could be hammered, a few makers reportedly used a chisel that had more than one blade:

The hand hammered ball . . . was marked with any kind of sharp instrument. Later on a kind of chisel with either two, three, or four blades was used, which enabled the ball maker to do his work much more easily (Golf Monthly, Mar. 1914: 129).

It was not until the mid to late 1850s that ball makers in general began using molds to make golf balls. In 1857 it was published that:

Golf-balls are now made of gutta-percha; they are first cast in a mould, then hammered to give them consistency, and finally painted with several coats of white-lead (Chambers, 692).

These molds were round and smooth on their inside, so each ball still needed to be hand-hammered. The introduction of the mold, with its smooth interior, was also noted by James Forgan as he recalled returning to his brother's business in what would have been 1868-69:

After being away twelve years I came back to Robert Forgan to be his golf ball maker steady, in the interval great changes had taken place in the business. . . . The balls were now being . . . pressed in moulds which were quite round and smooth, so all the balls had still to be hand-hammered (Golf Illustrated, 27 Dec. 1907: 13).

In order to speed up production, cutting lathes were developed to cut (mesh pattern) lines into the surface of a gutty ball. These cutting lathes came into prominence during the 1870s, as is evident from the change from a hand-hammered pattern to a mesh pattern on the silver balls attached to the silver clubs at Muirfield and Royal Burgess:

The Silver clubs of the Honourable Company of Golfers, at Muirfield, to which the captains of each year affix a ball, have from 1744 up to 1865-66 the old feather ball, then for the next ten years the hand-hammered gutta, and in 1878-9 the moulded gutta first appears (Golf Illustrated, 24 Jan. 1908: 84).

[Concerning the silver balls on the first silver club at Royal Burgess] the hand-hammered gutty type first appears under the name of Kenneth Maitland in 1856, and the last of this type on the old club was that presented by William Macgregor in 1874 (Robbie 1936, appendix II: 13).

It should be noted that the Honorable Company's prolonged use of silver feather balls reflects tradition, not the continued actual use of feather balls into the mid-1860s. The "moulded gutta" balls that initially appear on Muirfield's silver club were actually machine-cut gutty balls—molded gutty balls with machine-cut lines. In general appearance machine-cut gutty balls look like later molded gutty balls—balls with molded (not hammered or cut) scoring lines. On machine-cut balls, however, the lines are sometimes askew (see p. 117).

It wasn't until the 1890s that ball makers in general began using engraved molds to install scoring lines on golf balls:

Golf ball moulds and presses . . . have been made by Messrs. John Greig and Sons, Fountain House Works, Edinburgh, for very many years—long before golf became so justly popular as it now is. The great majority of the moulds are known as plain moulds, that is to say, they have smooth internal surfaces, and when these are used in connection with a screw press, which can be had with any number of screws from one to six, and a marking or scoring machine of their new design, and capable of marking balls at the rate of thirty-six dozen or forty dozen per hour, the output is very rapid indeed. All former machines were comparatively slow pieces of mechanism—slow in their action, and consequently capable of overtaking only a limited number of balls in a given time.

To overcome this want of speed gun-metal or hard brass moulds have been introduced, with the ball markings or series of concentric rings engraved inside, thus producing balls all ready marked, and rendering the use of a marking machine unnecessary. Certainly these engraved moulds have the advantage of allowing the composition of which the ball is made sufficient time to "set," which may add to the ball's durability. But when rapid output is desired, the plain mould and Messrs. Greig's improved marking machine are unapproached as regards results in the light of speedy and cheap production. The firm supply the engraved moulds, as well as the plain ones, in all sizes (Golf, 31 March 1893: 37).

After engraved molds were introduced, smooth molds remained in use. While ball makers during the 1890s primarily produced completely molded balls, a few of them continued to make machine-cut balls as well as the old hand-hammered balls:

During the last twenty years no firm of Golf-ball makers in Scotland, has been more widely known than that of Messrs. Goudie & Co., 25, Princes Street, Edinburgh. The material which they have sent out has been uniformly good and trustworthy; and their hand-hammered balls have long been known in the North as good flyers, steady on the putting green, and capable of withstanding any amount of hard play without detriment to the shape of the ball. . . . There was a fear at one time that, with the multiplicity of ball machine moulds, the hand-hammered ball, like the feathery, would become as extinct as the Dodo; but very many first class players have long adhered to the hand-hammered ball of Messrs Goudie (Golf, 20 Jan. 1893: 295).

[Alex Patrick's] hand-hammered balls . . . have no superior, and are known the world over; but since the vast extension of the other great branch of the trade in recent years he has had less time to devote to this hand-hammering. . . . He sells all the leading makes, but finds that many of his customers have still a preference for the hand-hammered (The Golfer, 12 Aug. 1896: 126).

Hand-hammered balls, if good at all, are very good. In fact, it would be rather a travesty on the character of the ball to say otherwise; also it would be a paradox. Our correspondent has been playing with a fine specimen of a hand-hammered ball from the workshops of D.M. Patrick, of Lundin Links, Fife. It would be a difficult thing anyway to point to anything indifferent with the name of D.M. Patrick on it (Golfing, 9 Mar. 1899: 14).

During the 1890s, most golf balls were made from gutta percha and had a mesh pattern on their surface. Ballmakers and numerous inventors, however, tried different variations in both the composition and the scoring pattern of the ball. Balls made from gutta percha mixed with other materials such as cork, sawdust, india rubber, powdered horn, bone, various elastic gums, wood pulp, steel filings, ground leather, vegetable fibers, linseed oil, hemp, asbestos, and so on were either tried or patented. Balls made entirely from substances other than gutta percha, such as sawdust and glue, celluloid, paper maché, maponite, synthetic ivory, and even aluminum, were also devised. Balls were constructed with various cores, such as rubber cores, cork cores, air-filled cores, hollow metal centers, and even dried paper pulp cores. Balls were made with various surface patterns, such as diamonds, stars and stripes, spiraling grooves, and even with flat, hexagonal sides (so the ball would not roll downhill too fast . . .). The most popular alternative to the mesh pattern, however, was the bramble pattern, in which the surface of the ball was covered with a number of small bumps. According to an article about the marking of golf balls, written "By a Golf Ball Manufacturer" and printed in 1914, the bramble pattern was introduced between 1890 and 1892:

> Curiously enough the bramble pattern of twenty-two to twenty-four years ago (I am assured that these figures are correct, but cannot myself give them as definite information) . . . . was in those days called the "Agrippa," an extremely popular ball for many years (Golf Monthly, Mar. 1914: 129).

During the 1890s, as the game of golf underwent explosive growth (see p. 3-4), gutta percha balls were made by the tens of thousands:

> Slazenger and Sons have at present a stock of 5,000 dozen boxes [60,000 balls] of their "Slazenger" ball . . . . They guarantee that every ball sent out is six months old . . . . This firm has also a stock of over 7,000 dozen [84,000 balls] of the "Tru-Flite" ball ready for the season's play.

> Peter Paxton, at Eastbourne with great enterprise, set up hydraulic machinery twelve months ago for the making of balls. He has turned out 1,000 dozen of black and red gutties, and of this stock only 200 remain (Golf, 3 Mar. 1893: 394).

> Messrs. Thornton & Co., Princes Street, Edinburgh, the well known golf ball makers, have at present a very fine stock of their seasoned "Match" balls. They have 10,000 dozen (120,000) of thoroughly seasoned balls, carefully finished, and painted (Golf, 5 June 1896: 281).

By 1898, J.&D. Clark was producing the "Musselburgh" ball by the boatload:

> Once more a reference to the export of golf balls from this country to the States is rendered important by the large orders that have emanated from over the Atlantic. According to the latest advices from GOLFING Office in Glasgow we learn that the orders received last month alone by Messrs. J. and D. Clark of Musselburgh amounted to over 9,000 dozen [108,000 balls]. The orders were for one make alone, the "Musselburgh" ball (Golfing, 1 Dec. 1898: 23).

While 108,000 Musselburgh balls sold in a month is a large number, J.&D. Clark, in their heyday, sold huge numbers of balls every month, their Musselburgh ball being one of the most popular gutty balls:

> By-the-by, they [Clark] have just received an order for 5000 dozen "Musselburgh" balls . . . . Sixty thousand golf balls at one order gives the impression that there is going to be a good golfing season in '99 (Golfer's Magazine, Jan. 1899: 483).

> We are informed that [J.&D. Clark] have sold over three tons weight of their "Musselburgh" ball during the past month and that they have still orders uncompleted for over ten tons more. These facts speak volumes for the popularity and excellence of the "Musselburgh" ball (Golf, 10 March 1899: 3).

The gutta percha used to make balls was available in two main colors: red and black, black gutta percha being more durable if aged properly (see p. 277). White gutta percha—of interest because a ball made from white gutta percha would not need to be painted—was eventually devised in the mid-1890s, but was limited to the production of a few balls, primarily the Melfort, Brand, Anderson, Varsity, and Henley in the well-known Union Jack pattern. (Each of these balls was also made in black gutta percha.) Golf balls during the gutta percha era were usually painted white. However, in keeping with a tradition from the feather ball era, balls were occasionally painted red for use in frost, light snow, or daisies. One particular gutta percha ball, Robert Ramsbottom's "Yellow Aster," was painted yellow (Golf, 14 Feb. 1896: 476).

According to Willie Park Jr., gutta percha was the primary ingredient in solid "gutty" balls and in several kinds of composition balls known generically as "putty" balls:

> Of the gutty and the putty balls the former are the harder in substance, and there is no mistaking the sharp firm click emitted when struck. The putty has quite a different feel to the player, as it is heavier for its size and is softer—it has more of an indiarubber nature, in fact. A putty ball does not carry so far as a gutty, but at the end of its flight it has considerably more running power (1896, 50).

Some gutta percha balls were made and advertised as able to float, a valuable feature to golfers playing in an era that lacked rules for casual water relief (see p. 218). According to Martin McDaid, when the gutta ball was first introduced it was much heavier than it was in later years:

> The quality of the golf ball gradually improved as the manufacturers learned to cleanse and purify the gutta. One peculiarity of the gutta is that in the process of purifying it loses more in weight than it does in bulk, consequently, the later makes of solid gutta balls were much lighter, and their specific gravity was altogether different. The lighter balls brought about a transition from drams to dwts. which are the terms that are in use now. [According to McDaid, feather balls were weighted (and so marked) in drams. Because of the weight change brought to gutta percha balls, they were eventually weighted (and so marked) in dwts.] (Golf Monthly, Mar. 1914: 49).

Between 1850 and 1900, gutta percha golf balls dominated the game and proved to be one of the most important, if not *the* most important, innovations in golf:

> There is nothing, perhaps, in the whole history of golf which has given a greater impetus to the game among all classes than the substitution of gutta-percha balls for the old leather ones. The change can only be fully appreciated by those who have played golf under the old regime of those made with leather stuffed with feathers. Witness the distress of one of these balls on a wet green. It got soaked with water, and every time it was struck off came some of the paint, and ultimately— if it chanced to survive a round under such circumstances—it became so saturated with water that almost no amount of physical strength could make it fly. And then to contemplate it next morning—every seam gaping and laughing at our folly! (Golfing, 5 Jan. 1911: 5—as cited from "Robb's Golf and Golfers").

Rubber Core Era.

In 1899 Coburn Haskell and Bertram G. Work received a U.S. patent (No. 622,834) dated April 11, for a golf ball made from wound elastic thread enclosed inside a gutta percha cover. The Haskell rubber core ball, as it came to be called, initially created great controversy (especially in Great Britain) but quickly changed the game of golf for the better.

The Haskell golf ball was produced by:

The Haskell Golf Ball Co., the owner of the Haskell and Work Golf Ball patent, and the B.F. Goodrich Co., the sole licensee for the United States under the patent . . . . The Haskell Golf Ball Co. was organized early in 1901 under the laws of the state of Ohio, with Coburn Haskell as president; Bertram G. Work, vice president, and

Silas Hitchcock, treasurer (Golf Illustrated, 5 Sep. 1902: 193).

Most golfers found they could hit a Haskell ball farther than any gutta percha ball. The Haskell, however, was not without its drawbacks. The cover of the ball was susceptible to either cracking or breaking loose from the inner ball of rubber strings, and the ball itself was considered difficult to control around the hole, where extra distance was not a concern. Nevertheless, within only five years of its introduction, the rubber core ball had completely replaced the gutty ball:

The great controversy on the respective merits of the old golf ball of solid gutta-percha and the new American rubber-cored ball has ended in the complete victory of the new ball. At the most moderate estimate, not more than one in a thousand players

remain faithful to the "gutty" and the rubber-cored ball of one variety or another is the ball of the moment.

We say moment advisedly, because although the rubber-cored ball has superseded the solid ball of gutta-percha, there is not in its nature the assurance of at least partial finality which marked the advent of the "gutty." When the latter took the place of the old ball of leather stuffed with feathers, fifty years ago, several circumstances contributed to ensure for it a long lease of popularity. In the first place, it was made of an entirely new substance, and, being solid, was much more durable than the old balls. It was rounder, and kept its shape better, and was impervious to wet. It flew farther, and, last but not least, it was 1s. 6d. cheaper.

From the point of view of those who had to play with the old feather balls, which were egg-shaped, con-

stantly ripping and "moulting" their feathers, and cost 2s. 6d. each, the gutta-percha ball was an ideal ball. But the transition from the solid gutta-percha to the rubber-cored ball presents no such array of inducements. It costs 1s. more than the "gutty" ball, its outer skin is liable to crack, and it is less easily controlled, especially in the more delicate strokes.

Thus, while the gutta ball was superior in every single particular to the feather ball which it superseded, the rubber-cored has only the solitary advantage over the gutty that it flies a few yards further. The very nature of its construction seems to invite the ingenuity of inventors to remedy its defects, and the possibilities of new combinations of core and inside are, of course, endless. It is probably only a question of a very short time till a ball appears that will not only be cheaper but give even better results (Golf Illustrated, 5 Feb. 1904: 107).

One dozen Haskell rubber core balls are shown here in their original wrappers and box, complete with slipcase. These Haskells have a bramble cover pattern, the most popular pattern used with early rubber core balls. Some Haskells, however, were made with a mesh pattern. A warning to anyone who sought to reproduce the highly popular Haskell ball was included in most boxes.

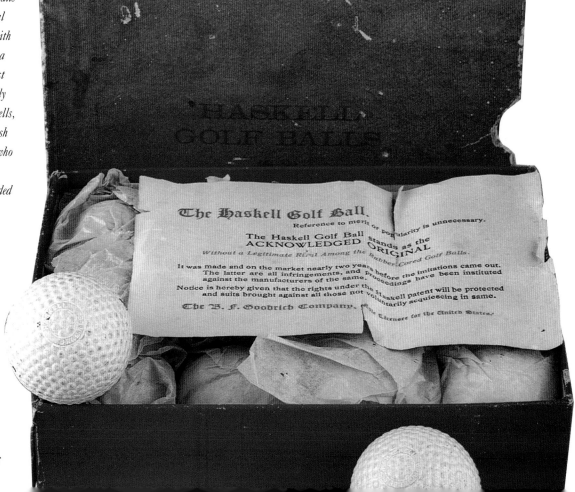

A collection of rubber core balls and one practice ball from early in the rubber core era are pictured. Left to right, they are as follows: Top row—a Silver King SW1, a MacGregor baseball pattern practice golf ball with cork center (offered in MacGregor's 1917 catalog), and a Double Dimple ball. Center row—a Farroid, a Lynx, a Super Harlequin, and a Wonderball. Bottom row—a U.S. Tiger, The Star Challenger, and a Worthington White.

In the years following its introduction, the rubber core ball was the object of continual change. Innumerable variations in both surface patterns as well as the composition of the ball were devised. While the main idea of winding vulcanized elastic under tension remained, a wide variety of centers, around which the elastic was wound, was formulated. Centers made from such mundane elements as liquid, air, glass, rubber, and steel balls; and from such exotic materials as radioactive radium salts and pieces of a bull's or bullock's penis (see W. Langstaff's U.S. patent [No. 16,488] dated July 15, 1912) were either produced or patented. Covers were devised that used such materials as paper, plastic, nickel steel, and highly nitrated nitrocellulose, among other components. Surfaces were marked with dimples, lines, bumps, discs, circles, stars, a map of the world, spiralling grooves (Henry's

rifled ball was first produced in 1898 as a solid gutty and was reintroduced in 1903 as a rubber core), and even a spider web complete with a spider, to name but a few of the patterns. In short, the rubber core ball was the springboard for endless ideas and variations in golf ball construction.

During the early 1900s, following the introduction of the Haskell, *millions* of golf balls were sold every year:

The following statistics go far to support the ever-famous dictum of the inspired Saturday Reviewer to the effect that "the ideal golfer is an idiot."... In the United States ... this year £320,000 will be spent on clubs, and 2,400,000 balls [will] be used at a cost of £1,920,000 (St. Andrews Citizen, 7 July 1900: 2).

Messrs. A.G. Spalding and Brothers state that they sold 75,000 dozen golf balls in 1901. This is roughly a million balls (Golf Illustrated, 28 Mar. 1902: 241).

It has been reckoned that at the height of the summer golfing season [in the U.K.], when the players are busy everywhere, no less than 590,000 balls are used up every week. This indeed seems to be a most reasonable estimate—less than two balls per man per week, with an enormous percentage of players out on the links four or five days a week. It was semi-officially stated in June that one firm of makers, and that not by any means the biggest, was working night and day, and turning out 400,000 balls a week (Golfing, 31 Jan. 1907: 11). [Note: the weekly estimate did not include North America or any other part of the world.]

One interesting fact which came out in the evidence was that the number of Spalding "Dimples" sold in this country during the twelve months ending July, 1913, reached the extraordinary total of 60,000 dozen [720,000 balls] (Golfing, 10 Feb. 1915: 17).

An inventor has recently made application for patents (which have been allowed) for making a substitute for rubber from skimmed milk, ... which resembles wood in texture. The inventor claims that the new material can be used for anything which is made of rubber.

The evolution of a pan of skimmed milk into Golf balls is apparently only a question of time—and a secret process. Not having the data at hand we cannot state positively just how many balls can be made from one pan of skimmed milk. Let the rubber trust beware; the humble cow may be the means of destroying one of its most profitable industries. Farmers who are ridiculing Golf may now turn their attention to raising a grade of good milch cows, selling the cream to butter makers and turning the by-product into Golf balls, thus accomplishing two ends—reducing the price of good butter and also of Golf balls (Golf Illustrated, 9 Mar. 1900: 214).

BRITISH BOARD OF TRADE DESIGN REGISTERS OF REPRESENTATIONS INDEX NUMBERS

Jan 1, 1884	to	Dec 14, 1884	1 – 18,868
Dec 15, 1884	to	Dec 20, 1885	18,869 – 39,943
Dec 21, 1885	to	Dec 20, 1886	39,954 – 63,874
Dec 21, 1886	to	Nov 16, 1887	63,875 – 87,324
Nov 16, 1887	to	Nov 16,1888	87,325 – 114,048
Nov 17, 1888	to	Nov 28, 1889	114,049 – 139,295
Nov 29, 1889	to	Oct 24, 1890	139,296 – 160,168
Nov 1, 1890	to	Jan 4, 1892	160,169 – 185,824
Jan 5, 1892	to	Dec 29, 1892	185,825 – 205,137
Dec 30, 1892	to	Dec 27, 1893	205,138 – 224,604
Dec 28, 1893	to	Jan 8, 1895	224,605 – 247,418
Jan 9, 1895	to	Nov 20, 1895	247,419 – 266,237
Nov 21, 1895	to	Nov 27, 1896	266,238 – 289,290
Nov 28, 1896	to	Dec 21, 1897	289,291 – 311,177
Dec 22, 1897	to	Nov 21, 1898	311,178 – 329,512
Nov 22, 1898	to	Feb 8, 1900	329,513 – 353,049
Feb 9, 1900	to	Dec 5, 1900	353,050 – 367,216
Dec 6, 1900	to	Dec 11, 1901	367,217 – 384,526
Dec 12, 1901	to	Dec 2, 1902	384,527 – 401,621
Dec 3, 1902	to	Feb 23, 1903	401,622 – 405,654
Feb 24, 1903	to	Jan 4, 1904	405,655 – 424,184
Jan 5, 1904	to	Jan 2, 1905	424,185 – 447,602
Jan 3, 1905	to	Jan 2, 1906	447,603 – 471,608
Jan 3, 1906	to	Feb 11, 1907	471,609 – 495,893
Feb 12, 1907	to	Dec 6, 1907	495,894 – 517,231
Dec 7, 1907	to	Dec 28, 1908	517,232 – 534,884
Dec 29, 1908	to	? (end) 1909	534,885 – 558,871
1910			558,872 – 575,438
1910 – 1911			575,439 – 591,608
1911 – 1912			591,609 – 607,976
1912 – 1913			607,977 – 624,476
1913 – 1914			624,477 – 633,122
1914			633,123 – 641,636
1914 – 1919			641,637 – 668,044
1919 – 1922			668,045 – 694,296
1922 – 1926			694,297 – 719,813
1926 – 1929			719,814 – 746,215
1929 – 1931			746,216 – 762,395
1931 – 1932			762,396 – 778,829
1932 – 1934			778,830 – 795,103
1934			795,104 – 797,999
1934 – 1936			798,000 – 813,999
1936 – 1938			814,000 – 824,444
1938			824,445 – 929,999
1938 – 1946			830,000 – 846,019
1940 – 1949			846,000 – 860,616

BRITISH PATENT NUMBERS

Before 1916, numbers repeat each year beginning with #1

Year	Number
1916	100,001
1917	102,812
1918	112,131
1919	121,611
1920	136,852
1921	155,801
1922	173,241
1923	190,732
1924	208,731
1925	226,571
1926	244,801
1927	263,501
1928	282,701
1929	302,941
1930	323,171
1931	340,201

AMERICAN PATENT NUMBERS

Year	Number
1893	488,976
1894	511,744
1895	531,619
1896	552,502
1897	574,369
1898	596,467
1899	616,871
1900	640,167
1901	664,827
1902	690,385
1903	717,521
1904	748,567
1905	778,834
1906	808,618
1907	839,799
1908	875,679
1909	908,436
1910	945,010
1911	980,178
1912	1,013,095
1913	1,049,326
1914	1,083,267
1915	1,123,212
1916	1,166,419
1917	1,210,389
1918	1,251,458
1919	1,290,027
1920	1,329,352
1921	1,364,063
1922	1,401,948
1923	1,440,362
1924	1,478,996
1925	1,521,590
1926	1,568,040
1927	1,612,790
1928	1,654,521
1929	1,696,897
1930	1,742,181
1931	1,787,424
1932	1,839,190
1933	1,892,663
1934	1,941,449
1935	1,985,878
1936	2,026,516
1937	2,066,309

U.S. Design Registration numbers are not provided, nor are U.S. Patent Application numbers or British Patent Application numbers (supplied after 1916).

"There are many varieties of golf Clubs, but those most commonly in use, and all that are really necessary for the player, are as follows: Driver, Brassy, Cleek, Mashie, Iron, Niblick, and Putter.

"All other golf clubs are either adaptations or modifications of these....

"**The Driver**—The driver is the club used from the tee if the hole be long, or if the ball lie well, whenever it is desired to play it as far as possible towards the hole. It is a wooden club with a long powerful shaft. The head should have plenty of wood in it and the face or hitting part of the head should be fairly deep. It should not be hollowed out in the middle, nor sloped back when the club head is laid on the ground.

"**The Brassy**—The head of the brassy is smaller and shorter than that of the driver, and the sole is shod with brass, to preserve the wood when the ball has to be played from stony or hard ground. The face of the brassy is often "spooned" or sloped backward, so as to raise the ball in the air, and the smaller size of the head admits of its being used when the ball lies in a "cup" or indentation of the ground, which the driver head would be too large to enter.

"**The Cleek**—The cleek is an iron-headed club with a straight and narrow face. The shaft is longer than that of other iron clubs, and it is chiefly used in playing full shots through the green, when the ball lies badly, or when a wooden club would take it too far.

"**The Iron**—The iron has a deeper blade or face than the cleek and is shorter in the shaft. Irons are made of various weights and with various degrees of pitch or loft, and are chiefly used for approaching the hole, or for lifting the ball over hazards or out of sand.

"**The Mashie**—The mashie is shorter in the head than the iron, and bears much the same relation to it that the brassy does to the driver. Like the iron, it is also made of various weights and degrees of loft, for particular strokes, and its uses are practically the same.

"**The Niblick**—The niblick is used when the ball lies badly in sand, mud, whins or other hazards, or wherever it is necessary to use great force to extricate the ball from its position. The head is round, small, and very heavy.

"**The Putter**—The putter is used chiefly after the ball has been played on to the putting-green, to play the ball into the hole. The head is made either of wood or metal. It is more upright and the shaft is much shorter than that of any other club, and should be quite stiff. There are many varieties of metal putters, no one of which can be said to be better than another. The chief points to be looked to in a putter, its appearance and make being secondary considerations, are that it should be well balanced and not too heavy" (Smith 1897, 11-16).

––––––––––

"Despite the large array of new inventions and freak importations in the matter of clubs, the leading golf sticks are as follows: Irons, drivers, brassies, putties [sic], niblicks, cleeks, putting cleeks, lofters, driving irons, and mid irons and mashies. The following is a description of the clubs:

"The *Putter* is used for playing all strokes on the putting-green. It has a short, stiff shaft, with the head nearly at right angles to [the] shaft.

"The *Cleek* is the longest driver of all the iron clubs, with the face only slightly lofted. The Driving Iron is deeper in the blade than the cleek and has more loft; it is not as long a driver as the cleek, but will pitch the ball higher.

"The *Mashie* is a compromise between the lofting iron and the niblick. It is shorter in the head than the iron, but it has less loft than the niblick, and is used for short approaches.

"The *Niblick* is used for getting a ball out of hazards, cart ruts, and other impediments. It has a small, round head, very heavy and very much lofted.

"The *Mid Iron* is the same as the lofting iron, but the blade is not pitched so much. It will drive a long, high ball.

"The *Driver* or *Play Club* is the longest driving club there is, and is used to drive from the tee or wherever the ball lies well and long distance is required.

"The *Brassie*, the same as driver, but with a brass plate on sole and generally a little more lofted; is used in playing "through the green."

"The *Brassie Niblick* is much smaller than the driver, with face well spooned back, and the sole shod with brass. It is used through the green with the object of raising the ball in the air when playing from a "cupped lie."

"The *Long*, *Short*, and *Mid Spoons* have the same head as the brassie, but are very much spooned, have long short, and medium shafts. They are almost entirely superseded by the iron club.

"Of all these clubs, however, only four are really necessary. A driver, an approach iron, a cleek, and a putter will meet all requirements. A set of six clubs would furnish a complete outfit for an expert, and might consist of a driver, a brassie, a niblick, a cleek, a mashie, and a putter" (Gorham 1903, 135-137).

––––––––––

"Quite frequently, however, good players carry one or two additional clubs as a regular part of their equipment, so as to bridge over the shades of difference existing between a brassey and a cleek, a cleek and an iron, and an iron and a mashie; thus making the playing of such hybrid strokes more easy of accomplishment [sic]. . . .

"...There is a niche between the iron and the mashie, especially when you are called upon to carry a hazard close up to the green and with some possible trouble beyond. To negotiate such a shot successfully it is necessary either to put cut on the ball if an iron is used, or to play a full mashie shot without sparing it. This is just where the jigger fits in nicely. The head is a cross between the iron and the mashie. The blade is not quite so long as the iron, is narrower, and more laid back in the face, and is weighted more towards the sole. The shot off it is principally all carry.. . .

"In addition to the several clubs mentioned, a driving-iron, or driving-mashie, or mashie-cleek, will be found very useful, especially for tee shots, or playing through the green against a strong head wind" (Travis 1901, 131-133).

American Golf. March 1900 to April 1902. New York. (Merged with "The Golfer" in 1902.) Various issues cited.

American Golfer, The. November 1908 to January 1936. New York. Various issues cited.

Arnell, Henry. 1988. *A History of Royal Ashdown Forest Golf Club.* Forest Rowe, England: Royal Ashdown Forest Golf Club.

Balfour, James. 1887. *Reminiscences of Golf on St. Andrews Links.* Edinburgh: David Douglas.

Baxter, Peter. 1899. *Golf in Perth and Perthshire: Traditional, Historical, and Modern.* Perth: Thomas Hunter.

Browning, Robert. 1955. *A History of Golf: The Royal and Ancient Game.* New York: Dutton & Company.

Burke Golf Company, The. 1917. *The Burke Golf Company: Catalogue No. 7.* Newark, Ohio: The Burke Golf Company.

- - -. 1922. *The Burke Golf Company* [Catalogue]. Newark, Ohio: The Burke Golf Company.

Cassell's Complete Book of Sports and Pastimes. 1896. London: Cassell and Company, Ltd.

[Chambers, Charles E.S.] 1887. *Golfing: A Handbook to the Royal and Ancient Game, with a list of clubs, rules etc., also golfing sketches and poems.* Edinburgh: W.&R. Chambers.

Chambers, Robert. 1862. *A Few Rambling Remarks on Golf, with the rules as laid down by the Royal and Ancient Club of St. Andrews.* Edinburgh: W. & R. Chambers.

Chambers, W.&R. 1857. *Chambers Information for the People.*

Chapman, H. J. 1968. *The Story of the Dalhousie Golf Club 1868-1968.* Carnoustie, Scotland: Privately printed.

Charlton, James and William Thomson with Roger, Katherine, and Andrew Adler. 1988. *Croquet: Its History, Strategy, Rules, and Records.* 2nd Ed. Lexington, Massachusetts: Stephen Greene Press.

[Clark, Robert]. 1875. *Golf: A Royal and Ancient Game.* 1st trade ed. Edinburgh: R.&R. Clark.

Colman, Alexis J. 1929. "The Late Willie Anderson." Rpt. in *The American Golfer.* Ed. Charles Price. New York: Random House. 1964. 131–134.

Colville, James. 1907. *The Glasgow Golf Club.* Glasgow: John Smith.

Cousins, Geoffrey. 1959. *Golfers At Law: The rules of golf, how they were evolved by pioneers, developed by events and the habits of golfers,* influenced by national and international forces, and modified by official decisions. 1st American ed. New York: Knopf. Foreword by Joseph Dey, Jr.

Crawford, McGregor & Canby Co. 1913. *General Catalogue and Retail Price List of everything required in playing the exhilarating and fascinating, royal and ancient game of Golf.* Dayton, Ohio: Crawford, McGregor & Canby

- - -. 1917. *Golf Goods General Catalogue and Price List No. 20.* Piqua, Ohio: Shaw & Marchant Studios and Magee Bros. Co.

- - -. 1928. *MacGregor Golf Goods General Catalogue & Price List No. 31.* n.p., n.p.

- - -. 1929. *MacGregor Golf Goods 100th Anniversary Edition,* Number 32. n.p., n.p.

- - -. 1930. *MacGregor Sales Helps.* Dayton, Ohio: The Crawford, McGregor & Canby Co.

[Crooker, Sylvan J.] [1937] *Newest In Golf: Streamliner.* n.p., n.p.

[Cundell, James]. 1824. *Rules of the Thistle Club: with some historical notices relative to the progress of the game of golf in Scotland.* Edinburgh: Privately Printed.

Dalrymple, W., ed. 1895. *Golfer's Guide for the United Kingdom 1895.* Edinburgh: White & Co.

Davies, E.J. and G.W. Brown. 1989. *The Royal North Devon Golf Club 1864-1989.* Westward Ho!, England: Royal North Devon Golf Club.

Dixie, P. Q. 1923. *The Royal Montreal Golf Club 1873–1923.* Montreal: Privately printed.

Doust, Dudley. 1976. "Museum Piece: A brief history of the world's most famous putter and its resurrection." *Golf Journal.* October 1976: 37–38.

East, J. Victor. 1962. "Bobby Jones and His Calamity Jane." *Golf Digest.* May: 54–58.

East Fife Observer. 1918–1959. Anstruther, Scotland. Various issues cited.

East Fife Record. 1856–1916. Anstruther, Scotland. Various issues cited.

Edgren, R. 24 Oct. 1920. "And Now Chick's Famous Putter Is Kicking Up a Fuss Among the Critics." *Seattle Post-Intelligencer.*

Evans, Webster. 1971. *Encyclopedia of Golf.* New York: St. Martins.

[Everage, L.] by An Old Golfer. 1897. *Golf on a New Principle: Iron Clubs Superseded.* Bournemouth, England: F.J. Bright & Son.

Everard, H.S.C. 1896. *Golf In Theory and Practice: Some Hints to Beginners.* London: George Bell and Sons.

[Farnie, Henry Brougham] by A Keen Hand. 1857. *The Golfer's Manual, being an historical and descriptive account of the national game of Scotland.* 2nd ed. Cupar, Scotland: John C. Orr. 1862.

Faust, W.H. [ca1930]. *This Hectic Game of Golf.* Ann Arbor, Michigan: Privately printed.

Farrar, Guy B. 1933. *The Royal Liverpool Golf Club, A History 1869–1932.* Birkenhead, England: Willmer Brothers & Co.

Fifeshire Journal. 1837–1893. Cupar, Scotland. Various issues cited.

Forgan, Robert. 1881. *The Golfer's Handbook, including History of the Game, Hints to Beginners, the Feats of Champion golfers, Lists of leading Clubs and Their Office-Bearers, etc.* 3rd. ed. Edinburgh: John Menzies [c. 1884].

- - -. 1897. *The Golfer's Manual, including History of the Game; Special Uses of the Different Clubs; Hints to Beginners; History of Golf Balls; the Feats of Champion Golfers; Golfiana; Glossary of Technical Terms; New Rules for the Game.* 6th ed. Edinburgh: John Menzies. 1973.

Fraser's International Golf Year Book. 1924. Montreal/New York: Fraser.

- - -. 1925-1926. Montreal/New York: Fraser.

- - -. 1931. Montreal/New York: Fraser.

Fraser's Magazine for Town and Country. Vol. L, July to December, 1854. London: John Parker & Son.

Fry's Magazine, March 1906. London.

Fulford, Harry. 1919. *Golf's Little Ironies.* London: Simpkin, Marshall, Hamilton, Kent & Co. Ltd.

Golf. September 1890 to June 1899. London. (Title changed to "Golf Illustrated," June 1899.) Various issues cited.

Golf. September 1897 to May 1917. New York. Cited as "Golf, (ny)." Various issues cited.

Golf Illustrated. June 1899 to Present. London. Various issues cited.

Golf Illustrated. April 1914 to 1935. New York. Cited as "Golf Illustrated, (ny)." (Title changed from "Golf Illustrated And Outdoor America," January 1923.) Various issues cited.

Golf Illustrated And Outdoor America. April 1914 to January 1923. New York. (Title changed to "Golf Illustrated," January 1923.) Various issues cited.

Golf Monthly. 1910 to present. Glasgow. Various issues cited.

Golfer, The. August 1894 to 1898. Edinburgh. (Title changed to "The Golfer's Magazine," 1898.) Various issues cited.

Golfer, The. 1894 to October 1903. New York. Cited as "The Golfer, (ny)." Various issues cited.

Golfer's Magazine. 1898 to ? Edinburgh. (Previously titled "The Golfer.") Various issues cited.

Golfers Magazine. May 1902 to September 1931. Chicago. Various issues cited.

Golfing. June 1895 to February 1897. London and Glasgow. (Title changed to "Golfing and Cycling Illustrated," February 1897.) Various issues cited.

Golfing. November 1898 to 1970. London. Various issues cited.

Golfing and Cycling Illustrated. February 1897 to November 1898. London and Glasgow. (Title changed to "Golfing," November 1898.) Various issues cited.

Golfing Annual 1888–1889. 2nd ed. London: Horace Cox. John Bauchope, ed.

- - -. 4th ed. 1890–1891. 1891. David S. Duncan, ed.

- - -. 7th ed. 1893–1894. 1894. David S. Duncan, ed.

- - -. 8th ed. 1894–1895. 1895. David S. Duncan, ed.

Gorham Manufacturing Company. 1903. *The Gorham Golf Book.* New York: Gorham.

Grierson, James. 1807. *Delineations of St. Andrews; Being a Particular Account of Every Thing Remarkable in the History and Present State of the City and Ruins, the University, and Other Interesting Objects of that Ancient Ecclesiastical Capital of Scotland.* Edinburgh: Peter Hill.

Hackney, Stewart. 1988. *Carnoustie Links: Courses and Players.* Dundee, Scotland: Ravensbay.

Hamilton, David. 1986. *Early Golf at St. Andrews.* Glasgow and Oban: The Patrick Press.

Hardy, James Leighton. August 27, 1994. Letter to the author.

- - -. September 18, 1994. Letter to the author.

Harper's Weekly, 2 Oct. 1897. New York and London.

Harris, Robert. 1953. *Sixty Years of Golf.* London: Batchworth Press.

Henderson, Ian T. and David I. Stirk. 1979. *Golf In The Making.* 1st trade ed. Crawley, England: Henderson & Stirk.

- - -. 1981. *Royal Blackheath.* Crawley, England: Henderson and Stirk.

Hilton, Harold. 1903. "Why Golf Has Improved." *Outing Magazine.* April – September: 123–126.

- - -. 1913. *Modern Golf.* New York: Outing.

[Hoyle, Edmond]. 1790. *Hoyle's Games Improved.* "The Game of Golf." Ed. Charles Jones. London: J.F.&C. Rivington/T. Payne, UK ed.

Hutchison, Horace G. 1902. *Golf: The Badminton Library,* 8th ed. rev. London: Longmans, Green.

- - -. 1919. *Fifty Years of Golf.* London: Country Life.

International Exhibition Glasgow. 1901. *Official Catalogue of the Scottish History and Archeaology Section.* Glasgow, Scotland: Chas. P. Watson.

Jackson, Alan F. 1994. *The British Professional Golfers 1887–1930. A Register.* Droitwich, England: Grant Books.

Johnston, Alastair J. 1985. *The Clapcott Papers.* Edinburgh: Privately printed.

- - -. 1993. *The Chronicles of Golf: 1457–1857.* Cleveland, Ohio: Privately Printed.

Jones, Jr., Robert Tyre. 1960. *Golf Is My Game.* Garden City, New York: Doubleday.

- - -. 1970. Letter to John W. Kolehmain, of Seattle, WA. 18 June 1970. Photocopy in the author's possession.

Kennedy, Patrick. 1984. *Golf Club Trademarks: American 1898–1930.* South Burlington Vermont: Thistle Books.

Kerr, John. 1896. *The Golf Book of East Lothian.* Edinburgh: Privately printed.

Kroyden Company, The. 1931. *General Catalogue of Kroydon Golf Clubs.* Maplewood, New Jersey: The Kroyden Company.

Lang, Andrew. 1895 "Golf, Old and New." *Harper's New Monthly Magazine.* June: 139–142.

Leach, Henry, ed. 1907. *Great Golfers in The Making: Being autobiographical accounts of the early progress of the most celebrated players, with reflections on the morals of their experience.* London: Methuen.

Leslie, Gurdon. 1968. "The Golf Shaft: From Hickory to Aluminum." Professional Golfer. Dec. 1968: 26–30.

Lewis, Peter N. 1994. "The Growth of Golf in Great Britain, 1890–1914." Golfiana 6.1: 11–14.

Linskill, W.T. 1889. *Golf.* London: George Bell.

Low, John Laing. 1903. *Concerning Golf.* London: Hodder & Stoughton.

Macdonald, Charles Blair. 1928. *Scotland's Gift, Golf: Reminiscences 1872–1927.* 1st. trade ed. New York: Scribners.

Marden, Dr. Orison Swett, ed. 1907. "Lawn Hockey." *The Consolidated Library; A Popular Illustrated Library of The Arts, History, Commerce, Sciences, Biography, Finance, Literature, Geography, Statistics, Etc.* rev. ed. Vol. 6. New York and Washington: Bureau of National Literature and Art. 277–283.

Marsh, Peter. March 15, 1995. Letter to the author.

Matthew, Sidney L. 1987. *Bobby Jones' Original Hickories.* n.p.: Privately printed.

Mathison, Thomas. 1743. *The Goff; A Heroi-Comical Poem in Three Cantos.* Edinburgh: Privately printed.

Miller, T.D. 1935. *The History of the Royal Perth Golfing Society: A Century of Golf in Scotland, with a selection of the Golfing verses by the late Neil Ferguson Balir, Esq. of Bathayock.* Perth, Scotland: Munro Press. 288–290.

Musselburgh Directory. 1848–1849. within *The Post Office Annual Directory and Calandar for 1848–1849.* 1848. Edinburgh: Ballantyne and Hughes.

National Crolf Company. [1924?] *Crolf, As Good As Golf; The New Outdoor Game.* Chicago: National Crolf Company.

Nickson, E. A. 1985. *The Lytham Century, A History of Royal Lytham and St. Annes Golf Club 1886–1986.* St. Annes-on-the-Sea, England: Privately printed.

Norris, W.E. 1892. "The Apotheosis of Golf." *The Century Illustrated Monthly Magazine.* August 1892: 602–613.

Once A Week: An Illustrated Miscellany of Literature, Art, Science, & Popular Information. Volumn IX, June to December, 1863. London: Bradbury & Evans.

Park, Willie, Jr. 1896. *The Game of Golf.* London: Longmans, Green.

- - -. 1907. *Great Golfers in the Making.* Ed. Henry Leach. London: Methuen. 99–110.

Patent Records of Great Britain. Various records cited 1876–1934.

Patent Records of the United States. Various records cited 1894–1934.

Patterson, Robert Adams. [1900]. *Discovered at last! The Inventor of the Gutta Ball.* Revised ed. n.p.: n.p.

Payton, Hugh. 1838. "The Cock o' The Green." *Kay's Portraits.* Vol. 2. 206-216.

Peter, H. Thomas. 1890. *Reminiscences of Golf and Golfers.* Edinburgh: James Thin. Clinton, Il: Chas. A. Dufner. 1985.

Random House, Inc. 1991. *Random House Webster's College Dictionary.* New York: Random House.

Rice, Grantland. 1917. "Travis the Magic Maker: The Greatest Individual Achievement in Sport." *Collier's Weekly.* 12 May 1917: 13+.

- - -. 1953. *The Bobby Jones Story: from the writings of O.B. Keeler.* Atlanta, Georgia: Tupper & Love.

Richardson, G. A. 1991. *The Hawksworth Hundred: Bradford Golf Club.* Hawksworth, Yorkshire, England: Bradford Golf Club

Robbie, J. Cameron. 1936. *The Chronicle of the Royal Burgess Golfing Society of Edinburgh, 1735–1935.* Edinburgh: Morrison & Gibb.

Robertson, James K. 1967. *St. Andrews: Home of Golf.* St. Andrews: Citizens Office.

Roger, Rev. Charles. 1849. *History of St. Andrews, With a Full Account of the Recent Improvements in the City.* 2nd ed. Edinburgh: Black & Black.

Ross, May. 1912. "Many Inventions." *The New Book of Golf.* Ed. Horace G. Hutchinson. London: Longmans, Green and Co. 340–354.

Salmond, J.B. 1956. *The Story of the R.&A.: Being the history of the first two hundred years of the Royal and Ancient Golf Club of St. Andrews.* London: Macmillan.

Sayers, Doreen. 1994. *Ben Sayers, North Berwick: 100 Years of Golf 1857–1962. Doreen Sayers Scrap Book.* North Berwick, Scotland: Stephenson Press.

Scots Magazine, The. May 1792. Edinburgh: Murray and Cochrane.

Scottish Exhibition of National History, Art, & Industry; Glasgow. 1911. *Palace of History Catalogue of Exhibits.* Vol. 2. Glasgow, Edinburgh, and London: Dalross Ltd.

Shaw, James E. 1938. *Prestwick Golf Club, A History and Some Records.* Glasgow: Jackson.

Simpson, Robert & Son. [c. 1920s.] *Illustrated Wholesale Price List.* n.p., n.p.

Simpson, Walter Grindley. 1887. *The Art of Golf.* Edinburgh: David Douglas.

Simpson, W.S. [1894.] An undated advertising Broadside in the author's possession.

Smail, David Cameron, ed. 1989. *Prestwick Golf Club; Birthplace of the Open.* Prestwick, Scotland: Prestwick Golf Club

Smith, Charles. 1909. *Aberdeen Golfers: Records and Reminiscences.* London: Privately printed.

Smith, Robert Howie. 1867. *The Golfer's Year Book for 1866.* Ayr, Scotland: Smith & Grant.

Smith, Garden Grant. 1897. *Golf.* London: Lawrence and Bullen. With a contribution by Mrs. Mackern.

Spalding, A.G. & Bros. 1898. *Official Golf Guide.* New York: American Sports Publishing Company.

- - -. 1901. *Spalding's Catalogue of Spring & Summer Sports: Season 1901.* Philadelphia, PA: J.F. Gray.

- - -. 1903. *Spalding's Athletic Library; Official Golf Guide for 1903.* Ed. Charles Cox. New York: American Sports Publishing Co.

- - -. 1904. *Spalding's Trade List of Fall and Winter Sports 1904–1905.*

- - -. 1914. Spring and Summer. A.G. Spalding Golf Catalogue.

- - -. 1917. A.G. Spalding Golf Catalogue.

- - -. 1918. Spring and Summer. A.G. Spalding Golf Catalogue.

- - -. 1919. Spalding Catalogue.

- - -. 1933. Spring and Summer. Rpt in "The History of Bobby Jones' Clubs." 1992. Sidney L. Matthew. Tallahassee, Florida: Impregnable Quadilateral Press. 107–116.

Sporting Magazine, The. August 1828.

St. Andrews Citizen. 1872–1995. St. Andrews, Scotland. Various issues cited.

Standard Golf Company, The. 1909. *The 'Mills' Patent Standard Aluminum Golf Clubs.* Burlington, Vermont: Thistle, 1987.

Taylor, John Henry. 1902. *Taylor on Golf: Impressions, Comments, and Hints.* 1st American ed. New York: D. Appleton and Co.

Travers, Jerome. 1915. "The High Cost of Golf." *The American Magazine* May: 16–19.

Travis, Walter. 1901. *Practical Golf.* New York and London: Harper & Brothers.

Trevor, George. 1930. "Enter the Sand Wedge." *The Sportsman* Oct. 1930: 63.

Tulloch, W.W. 1908. *The Life of Tom Morris, with Glimpses of St. Andrews and its Golfing Celebrities.* London: T. Werner Laurie.

Tyler, Ralph G. An undated broadside advertisement in the author's possession.

United States Golf Association. 1922. *United States Golf Association Year Book.* New York: Willis McDonald & Co.

- - -. 1923. *United States Golf Association Year Book.* New York: United States Golf Association

- - -. 1924. *United States Golf Association Year Book.* New York: United States Golf Association

- - -. 1925. *United States Golf Association Year Book.* New York: United States Golf Association

Van Dulken, Steve. July 4, 1994. Letter to the author.

Van Hengel, Stephen J.H. 1982. *Early Golf.* 1st trade ed. Bentveld, Holland: Privately printed.

Vardon, Harry. 1912. *How to Play Golf.* London: Methuen & Co.

Westwood, A. 1862. *Westwood's Parochial Directory for the Counties of Fife and Kinross, Containing the Names and Addresses of Gentry, and of Persons in Business, & c.* Cupar-Fife: A. Westwood.

- - -. 1866. *Westwood's Parochial Directory for the Counties of Fife and Kinross, Containing the Names and Addresses of Gentry, and of Persons in Business, & c.* Cupar-Fife: A. Westwood.

Whigham, H[enry] J[ames]. 1897. *How to Play Golf.* Chicago: Herbert S. Stone.

Whyte, D.W. Letter to D.M. Irwin. 28 Jan. 1964. Letter in author's possession.

Wilson, Harry Leon. 1923. *So This Is Golf!* New York: Cosmopolitan Book Corp.

Wilson-Western Sporting Goods Company. 1929. *The Gateway to Golf: A complete catalog of Wilson Golf Equipment supplemented with tips to help your game and other useful information.* New York, Chicago, San Francisco: Wilson Sporting Goods.

Wishon, Tom. 1985. *The Golf Club Identification and Price Guide.* Newark, Ohio: Ralph Maltby Enterprises.

Wright, Joseph, ed. 1905. *The English Dialect Dictionary.* 1898–1905. Vol 5 & 6. London and Oxford, England: Henry Froude.

Who's Who in Golf—Directory of Golf Clubs and Members. 1909. *Who's Who in Golf and Directory of Golf Clubs and Members.* London: Stanley.

Wood, Harry B. 1910. *Golfing Curios and The Like: with an Appendix comprising a Bibliography of Golf.* London: Sherratt & Hughes.

World of Golf, The. April 1905 to November 1906+. England. Various issues cited.

Worrell's Directory of the North Eastern Counties of Scotland 1877. [1877] n.p.

INDEX